ALSO BY GEOFFREY C. WARD

The Roosevelts: An Intimate History (with Ken Burns)

A Disposition to Be Rich: Ferdinand Ward, the Greatest Swindler of the Gilded Age

The War: An Intimate History (with Ken Burns)

Moving to Higher Ground: How Jazz Can Change Your Life (with Wynton Marsalis)

Unforgivable Blackness: The Rise and Fall of Jack Johnson

Mark Twain (with Dayton Duncan and Ken Burns)

Jazz: A History of America's Music (with Ken Burns)

Not for Ourselves Alone: The Story of Elizabeth Cady Stanton and Susan B. Anthony (with Ken Burns)

The Year of the Tiger

The West: An Illustrated History

Closest Companion: The Unknown Story of the Intimate Friendship Between Franklin Roosevelt and Margaret Suckley

Baseball: An Illustrated History (with Ken Burns)

Tiger-Wallahs: Encounters with the Men Who Tried to Save the Greatest of the Cats (with Diane Raines Ward)

American Originals: The Private Worlds of Some Singular Men and Women

The Civil War: An Illustrated History (with Ken Burns and Ric Burns)

A First-Class Temperament: The Emergence of Franklin Roosevelt

Before the Trumpet: Young Franklin Roosevelt, 1882-1905

Treasures of the World: The Maharajahs

ALSO BY KEN BURNS

The Roosevelts: An Intimate History (with Geoffrey C. Ward)

The War: An Intimate History (with Geoffrey C. Ward)

Mark Twain (with Geoffrey C. Ward and Dayton Duncan)

Jazz: A History of America's Music (with Geoffrey C. Ward)

Not for Ourselves Alone: The Story of Elizabeth Cady Stanton and Susan B. Anthony (with Geoffrey C. Ward)

Lewis & Clark (with Dayton Duncan)

The Shakers: Hands to Work, Hearts to God (with Amy S. Burns)

Baseball: An Illustrated History (with Geoffrey C. Ward)

The Civil War: An Illustrated History (with Geoffrey C. Ward and Ric Burns)

THE VIETNAM WAR

THE VIETNAM WAR

AN INTIMATE HISTORY

with an Introduction by Ken Burns and Lynn Novick

GEOFFREY C. WARD

Based on a documentary film by

Ken Burns & Lynn Novick

Picture research by Salimah El-Amin with Lucas B. Frank · *Design by* Maggie Hinders

ALFRED A. KNOPF | NEW YORK | 2017

FRONTISPIECE Lit by shafts of sunlight slanting through a triple-canopy forest, North Vietnamese troops pick their way through the Truong Son mountains on their way to war.

ENDPAPER, FRONT A GI pauses for a cigarette during a search-and-destroy operation southwest of Danang, 1967.

ENDPAPER, BACK North Vietnamese radioman at work during a battle with South Vietnamese armored troops, Quang Tri Province, 1970

THIS IS A BORZOI BOOK
PUBLISHED BY ALFRED A. KNOPF

Copyright © 2017 The Vietnam Film Project, LLC
All rights reserved.
Published in the United States by Alfred A. Knopf,
a division of Penguin Random House LLC, New York, and in Canada
by Penguin Random House Canada Limited, Toronto.
www.aaknopf.com

Knopf, Borzoi Books, and the colophon are registered trademarks
of Penguin Random House LLC

Library of Congress Cataloging-in-Publication Data
Names: Ward, Geoffrey C., author. | Burns, Ken, 1953– writer of
introduction. | Novick, Lynn, writer of introduction.
Title: The Vietnam war : an intimate history / Geoffrey C. Ward ; based on
a documentary film by Ken Burns & Lynn Novick ; with an introduction
by Ken Burns & Lynn Novick.
Description: First edition. | New York : Alfred A. Knopf, 2017. | Includes
bibliographical references and index.
Identifiers: LCCN 2017015686 | ISBN 9780307700254 (hardcover) |
ISBN 9781524733100 (eBook)
Subjects: LCSH: Vietnam War, 1961–1975.
Classification: LCC DS557.7.W368 2017 | DDC 959.704/3—dc23
LC record available at https://lccn.loc.gov/2017015686

Front-of-jacket illustration © 2017 Public Broadcasting Service
Jacket design by Carol Devine Carson

Manufactured in the United States of America
First Edition

For Dewy Ward and Robert K. Burns, Jr.,

who understood it first

Still blanketed in yellow smoke laid down to mark their position so that a U.S. airstrike would not inadvertently hit them, GIs unwind after a firefight near Hue.

OVER A wounded American and a wounded South Vietnamese soldier comfort each other aboard a medevac helicopter that has lifted them off the battlefield near An Loc, 1972.

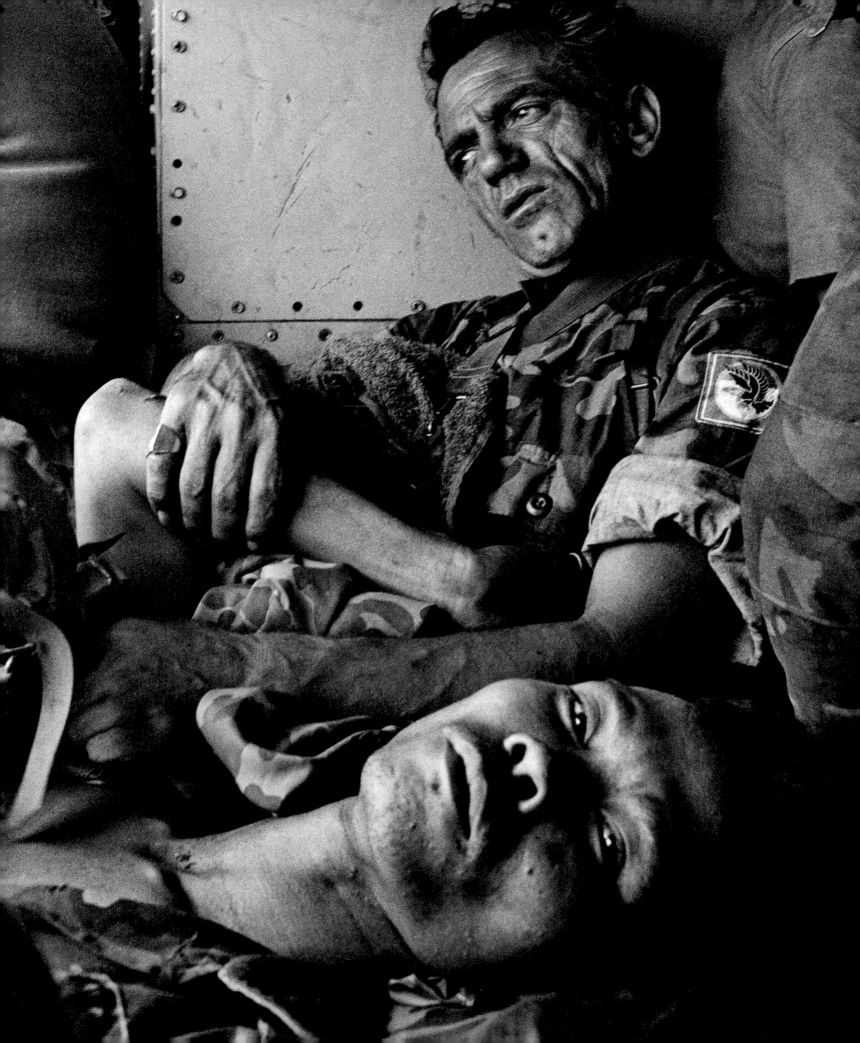

CONTENTS

Introduction   xi

CHAPTER ONE
DÉJÀ VU   1858–1961   1

PATHS TO POWER by Edward Miller   44

CHAPTER TWO
RIDING THE TIGER   1961–1963   51

KENNEDY AND WHAT MIGHT HAVE BEEN by Fredrik Logevall   90

CHAPTER THREE
THE RIVER STYX   JANUARY 1964–DECEMBER 1965   97

CHAPTER FOUR
RESOLVE   JANUARY 1966–JUNE 1967   145

CHAPTER FIVE
WHAT WE DO   JULY–DECEMBER 1967   201

CHAPTER SIX
THINGS FALL APART   JANUARY–JUNE 1968   253

CHAPTER SEVEN

THE VENEER OF CIVILIZATION   JUNE 1968–APRIL 1969   313

CHAPTER EIGHT

THE HISTORY OF THE WORLD   MAY 1969–DECEMBER 1970   383

SEEING AMERICANS AGAIN by Bao Ninh   461

CHAPTER NINE

A DISRESPECTFUL LOYALTY   JANUARY 1971–MARCH 1973   465

VIETNAM AND THE MOVEMENT by Todd Gitlin   516

CHAPTER TEN

THE WEIGHT OF MEMORY   MARCH 1973–APRIL 1975   523

DUST OF LIFE, DUST OF WAR by Viet Thanh Nguyen   566

EPILOGUE   573

Acknowledgments   589

Witnesses/Select Bibliography   591

Index   595

Illustration Credits   609

INTRODUCTION

by Ken Burns and Lynn Novick

ON APRIL 23, 1975, President Gerald R. Ford was scheduled to give the keynote address at the Tulane University convocation in New Orleans. As the president took the stage, more than 100,000 North Vietnamese troops were massing on the outskirts of Saigon, having overrun almost all of South Vietnam in just three months. Thirty years after the United States first became involved in Southeast Asia, ten years after the Marines had landed in Danang, the ill-fated country for which more than 58,000 Americans had died was on the verge of defeat. "We, of course, are saddened indeed by the [tragic] events in Indochina," the president said. He reminded the subdued crowd that 160 years earlier America had recovered from another conflict in which she had suffered "humiliation and a measure of defeat"—the War of 1812—and promised that the nation would once again "regain the sense of pride that existed before Vietnam." But, he continued to thunderous applause, "it cannot be achieved by refighting a war that is finished as far as America is concerned." The time had come, the president said, "to unify, to bind up the nation's wounds . . . and begin a great national reconciliation." Just seven days later, North Vietnamese soldiers stormed the gates of the Presidential Palace in Saigon and raised the communist flag. The Vietnam War was over.

It's been more than forty years now, and despite President Ford's optimism, we have been unable to put that war behind us. The deep wounds it inflicted on our nation, our communities, our families, and our politics have festered. As Army veteran Phil Gioia said in an interview for our documentary series, "The Vietnam War drove a stake right into the heart of America. It polarized the country as it had probably never been polarized since before the Civil War, and we've never recovered."

Nearly ten years ago, as we were completing postproduction on a seven-part series about the American experience in World War II, we resolved to turn our attention to the painful, bitter, confounding, and much misunderstood tragedy that was the war in Vietnam. It has been our privilege throughout this undertaking to collaborate with the writer, Geoffrey C. Ward, and our producer, Sarah Botstein, along with our team of editors, researchers, and coproducers. We were also ably assisted by an invaluable board of advisers, historical consultants, and veterans of the war who saved us from innumerable mistakes, but, more important, pointed us to the critical moments and astonishing contradictions that haunt any serious study of the Vietnam War.

From the start, we vowed to each other that we would avoid the limits of a binary political perspective and the shortcuts of conventional wisdom and superficial history. This was a war of *many* perspectives, a Rashomon of equally plausible "stories," of secrets, lies, and distortions at every turn. We wished to try to contain and faithfully reflect those seemingly irreconcilable outlooks.

We were interested in trying to understand the colonial experience of the French—and the way it eerily prefigured what would befall the United States in subsequent years. We wanted to find out what actually happened in the halls of power in Washington, Saigon, and Hanoi, and to get to know the leaders who made the decisions that determined the fates of millions. Through the availability of recently declassified records, ongoing scholarship, and revelatory, sometimes shocking, audio recordings, the actions and motives of Harry Truman, Dwight Eisenhower, John Kennedy, Lyndon Johnson, and Richard Nixon are laid bare, as are the complicated power struggles going on in South Vietnam during the autocratic, ruthless regime of Ngo Dinh Diem and the succession of generals who followed him. Of particular focus for us were the fascinating political dynamics in Hanoi, where the familiar figure of Ho Chi Minh fought for supremacy with other less well-known but more powerful figures.

Most important, we wanted to understand what the war was like on the battlefield and on the home front, and we wanted to find out why, as Marine veteran Karl Marlantes told us, Americans have been unable to have a civil conversation about one of the most consequential events in our history. "For years, we just did not talk about that war," he said. "You would open your mouth and you'd ask, which side was this person on? Am I going to get into a fight here? It's like living in a family with an alcoholic father . . . You know, shh, we don't talk about that."

Wars, all wars, create a kind of dissonance that obfuscates and deflects clear understanding. Vietnam is no different. To shed new light on such a complicated and unsettled time in our history, to struggle to comprehend the special dissonance that *is* the Vietnam War, we needed to look beyond the familiar stories Americans have told about the war and include as many different perspectives as our narrative could accommodate. Nearly one hundred "ordinary" people agreed to share their stories with us on camera: grunts and officers in the Army and Marines, prisoners of war, a fighter pilot and a helicopter crew chief, a Gold Star mother and the sister of a fallen soldier, a nurse, college students, reporters, protesters, military analysts, spies, and many others. To have been present as they bore witness to their experiences remains for us one of the enduring gifts of this project.

Throughout our long production, we were inspired by the architect Maya Lin, whose Vietnam Veterans Memorial was initially as controversial as the war itself, but which has become one of America's sacred places. When she unveiled her design in 1981, Lin told the press that her memorial to the Americans who died in the war would be a journey "that would make you experience death, and where you'd have to be an observer, where you could never really fully be with the dead . . . [It isn't] something that was going to say, It's all right, it's all over. Because it's not." Nothing, certainly not our film or book, can make the tragedy of the Vietnam War all right. But we can, and we must, honor the courage, heroism, and sacrifice of those who served, those who died, and those who participated in the war *against* the war. As filmmakers, we have tried to do that the only way we know how: by listening to their stories. "It's almost going to make me cry," Army veteran Vincent Okamoto told us, remembering the infantry company he led in Vietnam in 1968. "Nineteen-, twenty-year-old high school dropouts that come from the lowest socioeconomic rung of American society . . . they didn't have the escape routes that the elite and the wealthy and the privileged had . . . but to see these kids, who had the least to gain . . . they weren't going be rewarded for their service in Vietnam. And yet their infinite patience, their loyalty to each other, their courage under fire, was just phenomenal. And you would ask yourself: how does America produce young men like this?"

While Okamoto and hundreds of thousands of other Americans were fighting and dying in a brutal and bloody war overseas, hundreds of thousands of their fellow citizens were taking to the streets back home to protest that war. As the antiwar activist Bill Zimmerman recalled for us, "People who supported the war were fond of saying 'My country right or wrong . . . or better dead than red.' Those sentiments seemed insane to us. We don't want to live in a country that we're going to support whether it's right or wrong . . . so we began an era in which two groups of Americans, both thinking that they were acting patriotically, went to war with each other." A chasm opened in American society, and on both sides of the divide things were said—and things were done—that could never be unsaid, could never be undone. "When I see the war protesters . . . intellectually I certainly understand their right to the freedom of speech," Army adviser James Willbanks remembered, "but I will tell you that when I see them waving NLF flags, the enemy that I and my friends had to fight and some of my friends had to die fighting, that doesn't sit very well with me."

When Americans talk about the Vietnam War, the scholar and novelist Viet Thanh Nguyen wrote, too often we are just talking about ourselves. We were determined not to make that mistake. How could we hope to make sense of this turbulent time in our history, or to explore the humanity and the inhumanity of all sides, without hearing directly from our allies and our enemies—the Vietnamese soldiers and civilians we fought with, and against? Off and on for several years, we traveled to Texas, California, and Virginia to get to know many Vietnamese Americans who came to the United States as refugees, having suffered the unimaginable loss not just of their families, friends, and comrades, but of their country. They spoke honestly about the failings of their own government, and shared their doubts and fears about whether the Republic of South Vietnam under Nguyen Van Thieu and Nguyen Cao Ky had been worth fighting for. "Thieu [and] Ky, they were corrupt," Saigon native Phan Quang Tue remembered. "They abused their position. And they received more from Vietnam than Vietnam received from them. We paid a very high price for having leaders like Ky and Thieu. And we continue to pay the price."

To understand what the war was like for the winners, we traveled to Vietnam, traversing the length of the country, meeting and interviewing veterans and civilians. We were surprised to discover that the war remains as unsettled and painful for them as it is for us. For decades, they too have avoided speaking about what happened. The memory of the nearly incomprehensible price they paid in "blood and bone" has been too grievous. But now, as they near the end of their lives, they want their families, and the world, to know what they went through. "The war we fought," General Lo Khac Tam told us on camera, "was so horribly brutal I don't have words to describe it. I worry, how can we ever explain to the younger generation the price their parents and grandparents paid?" For Bao Ninh, a foot soldier in the North Vietnamese Army, who became a celebrated novelist after the war, the official public narrative celebrating their great, noble victory rings hollow: "People sing about victory, about liberation," he told us. "They're wrong. Who won and who lost is not a question. In war, no one wins or loses. There is only destruction. Only those who have never fought like to argue about who won and who lost."

In the winter of 2015, as we were nearing the end of the editing phase of the project, we invited Nguyen Ngoc, an eighty-five-year-old veteran of the North Vietnamese Army (now a revered scholar and teacher of literature), to travel from Danang to Walpole, New Hampshire, where we screened the fine cut of the film and asked him to share his thoughts about the war with us. After reflecting on the stories he saw onscreen, he told us that the time had come for them to be told; the people of Vietnam, he said, "are starting to rethink the war, to ask the questions. Was the war necessary to achieve justice? Was it right? What is most important now is to find some meaning, some lessons in the war for our lives."

There is no single truth in war, as this difficult story reminded us at every turn. Each of us can only see the world as we are; we are all prisoners of our own experience. We did not set out to answer every question embedded in this lamentable chapter in history. With open minds and open hearts we simply tried to listen to the brave and honest testimony of a remarkable group of men and women. If we have been able to find some meaning in this devastating calamity, it is in no small measure thanks to their generosity, humility, and humanity, for which we are profoundly grateful.

Ken Burns and Lynn Novick
Walpole, New Hampshire

AMERICA'S involvement in Vietnam began in secrecy. It ended, thirty years later, in failure, witnessed by the entire world.

It was begun in good faith by decent people out of fateful misunderstandings, American over-confidence, and cold war miscalculation.

And it was prolonged because it seemed easier to muddle through than to admit that it had been caused by tragic decisions, made by five American presidents, belonging to both political parties.

Humping the boonies: Monsoon rain lashes men of the U.S. Second Battalion, 173rd Airborne Brigade, as they ford a river near Ben Cat, September 25, 1965. They had been searching the area for twelve days without a glimpse of the elusive enemy.

Before the war was over, more than 58,000 Americans would be dead At least 250,000 South Vietnamese troops died in the conflict as well. So did over a million North Vietnamese soldiers and Viet Cong guerrillas. Two million civilians, north and south, are thought to have perished, as well as tens of thousands more in the neighboring states of Laos and Cambodia.

Wounded Marine Gunnery Sergeant Jeremiah Purdy reaches out to his dying captain during the fierce battle for Hill 484, south of the Demilitarized Zone, in 1966.

For many Vietnamese,
it was a brutal civil war;
for others, it was the
bloody climactic chapter
in a century-old struggle
for independence.

A South Vietnamese soldier flushes
a father and son suspected of
being loyal to the Viet Cong from
the rice paddy in which they had
been hiding, Mekong Delta, 1962.

For those Americans who fought in it, and for those who fought against it back home—as well as for those who merely glimpsed it on the nightly news—the Vietnam War was a decade of agony, the most divisive period since the Civil War.

Construction workers and antiwar demonstrators fight for the flag during a demonstration on Wall Street in Manhattan, 1970.

Left panel:

J C DULIN · CARE...
AROLD G GRISSOM · DELBERT E HALL · JOHN R HILL
LL W LOVE · STANLEY J MILLER Jr · GERALD E McKAY
ON · JAIME RODRIGUEZ-RIVERA · CARL D RUENGER
LAINE P SMILIE · JAMES T SWIFT Jr · GEORGE W TOM
MS · MEREDITH G ANDERSON · STEVEN R SANDLIN
C BUGMAN · CLINTON A COOK · ROBERT F FAGE Jr
AS L LUBBERS · GILBERTO PADILLA · VERNON R RILEY
E F SNIDER · RAYMOND P SUSI · JOHN D VANDIVIER
D BERNER · EDWARD J BISHOP Jr · ROBERT S BOGGS
URKE Jr · WILLARD S CANNON III · LOUIS A FAVUZZA
LES E JOHNSON · JEFFREY J KLAVES · PAUL J KOSANKE
OSE H ORTIZ · CARL E PATTEN · WILLIAM J SATTLER III
LORA W SNYDER · ROY H SNYDER · WILLIAM J STIEVE
WEBB Jr · FREDERICK E WORTMANN · BILLY RAY BAKER
HARD H DAVIS · LUTHER J DOSS Jr · ROBERT F ELSTON
ILREATH · JOHN A HERNANDEZ · DONNIE E HORTON
ARRY K KISER · KEVIN R KELEHER · GLEN L KNOBLOCK
MASSETH · WILLIAM A MEISTER · LUIS A SANTELLANO
ONNIE B ROBERTS · JON L PADGETT · JOHN L SENSING
JOHN R SMITH · DAVID W STATON · LEON A TETKOSKI
S · KEITH S ARNESON · JOHN H BARRETT · JAMES BUSH
ROBERT DOERING · LARRY R HENSHAW · JIMMY A HILL
T JARBOE · THOMAS J KAUFMAN · CHARLES H KEFER Jr
ES · CALVIN E NOLT · JACK A NOON · PAUL F ROGALSKE
RL D WOOTTEN · ROBERT ALMASY · DAVID W BARNETT
RIQUEZ CORONA · HAROLD G CRAFT · DAVID W DASH
IE RAY EATMON · CURTIS GAITHER · STEVEN J GREENLEE
RRERA · KENNETH L DEFENBAUGH · DANIEL C JOHNSON
EO J LUDVIGSEN Jr · ROBERT R NEEL · DONALD L PARKER
YAN D PRICE Jr · FRANK L RICE Jr · DALE W RICHARDSON
DAVID W SMITH · RODNEY H STONE · ANDREW J TAYLOR
ALD L VOORHEES · ROBERT M YOUNG · WILLIE BEDFORD
AWAY · ROGER G CRAIG · OSCAR A DAY · FRED DENKINS Jr
ROBERT B HANEY Jr · JOSEPH J HARPER · THOMAS G HESS
NEST R LASHER Jr · PERRY A LE CLERC · RANDALL S PHILLIPS
NNETH B THOMAS · JAMES M TREESH · GLEN R WITYCYAK
ES G ANDERSON · DEAN L BONNEAU · RONALD CHISOLM
MES F HOPKINS · GEORGE E HUSSEY · TOMMY L KEARSLEY
RY F MATTINGLY · RICHARD W PAQUETTE · DEAN L AITKE
DNEY A TAYLOR · EDDIE G TERRELL · ROBERT V THOMPSO
RY L WATKINS · DOUGLAS N WINFREY · CHARLES E AARO
Y M BEAUDETTE · NICHOLAS J BRAICO · EVERETT L BROC
CO TERONI CARVAJAL · JOHN R FEESER · ROBERT R DOW
CRAIG J FOX · RAMON L GRAYSON · DAVID C GUNDERS
LLER · JAMES M KELLER · GERALD A KULM · JACK D LEOPA
ER J MARTINEZ Jr · RICHARD S MODEN · GEORGE A MAS
HELL Jr · TSCHANN S MASHBURN · THOMAS M McDO
ND · DUANE A PETERSON · JAMES L PULLAM · ROBERT
TH · JAMES D SMITH · DENNIS A SPRENKLE · DERRICK
HARD L VAN DE WARKER · STEVEN E WASSON · JOHN
MICHAEL L ANTLE · ROGER B BAXTER · GEORGE W BE
M BYERLY · DENNIS P CALLAGHAN · DIONISIO G CA
RAVENS · DOUGLAS W DAY · ROBERT A DENTON
NETH L FOUTZ · LAWRENCE L GORDON · JOHN E
E KIER · RICHARD A HAWLEY

Right panel:

NASH FRY · FREDERICK D SNYDER · MICHAEL
MARK W BACHER · CARL B
JOHN E DARLING Jr · LARRY R GARCIA
MICHAEL HEINRICH · CARWAIN L HERRINGTO
JAMES J WILKINSON Jr · WILLIAM C A
ROBERT W COONS · LEWIS E COX · FLOYL
THOMAS W JOHNSON · LANNY G LADOUCEU
ALLEN D UDINK · BILLY RAY LUCAS · BILLY R
WILLIAM R SPEIGHT · JOHN S SPR
CRAIG M YANCEY · CURTIS BOA
ROY L CARTER · JOHN A CLAGGETT · DA
ROBERT L FOZZARD · GARY W
RANDALL C VAN HAITSMA · MICHAEL J MAN
ARTHUR G QUALLS · CRAIG RA
KENNETH S VORE · JOHN H WAALE
LEON N BOBO · DONALD G BUSSE · PA
CHARLES H EUBANK · ROBERT E GORSKE
LAWRENCE W HOYT · CHRIS A KEFFA
BRUCE J NICHOLS · JOE DO
ARTHUR PINA ADAME · CHARLES F ARMENT
ANTHONY L CLARK · JOSEPH M HARTL
MAXIMILIANO DAVILA-TORRES
WILLIAM N JENSEN Jr · ILLY · RICHA
RICHARD W M · OMAS H M
DAVID J ORTALS · LA SCO
JA · GEORGE
ALAN H GRO · SSING
LA · M WILL
STEPHE · RD T P
CECIL C SCH · N SOLD
STI · RONALD M
TH · W FOREMA
ANTONIO · AY MORRISON
NIC · GARY
MIN · GEORGE A BIR
CLAUDE · CARGILE
WFORD · R E DAVIS
MON FLO · DANNY L GO
NCE · D CLEKENS
R N M · OLIVO
ARLES D SHARPE
R STEVENSON · RODNEY W WIL
DAVID
SAM

Vietnam seemed to call everything into question: the value of honor and gallantry; the qualities of cruelty and mercy; the candor of the American government; and what it means to be a patriot.

And those who lived through it have never been able to erase its memory, have never stopped arguing about what really happened, who was to blame, why everything went so badly wrong—and whether it had all been worth it.

At the Vietnam Veterans Memorial in Washington, D.C., former Staff Sergeant Dwight Holliday finds the name of a friend, James Miremont, who died in his arms from friendly fire.

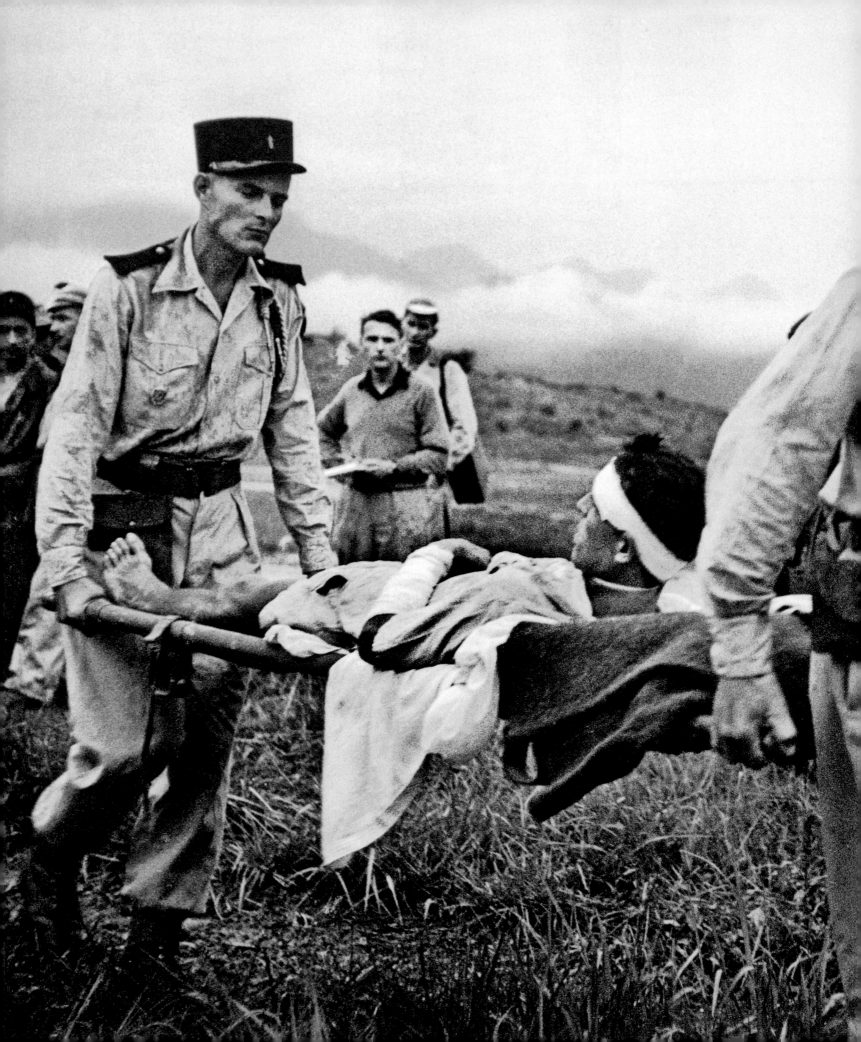

CHAPTER ONE

DÉJÀ VU

1858–1961

A wounded French soldier is evacuated from the battlefield at Dien Bien Phu, to be helicoptered to an army hospital at Hanoi in May 1954. The Vietnamese victory at Dien Bien Phu signaled the end of their war with France and indirectly ushered in a new war, with the Americans.

FOR SIX MONTHS in the winter, spring, and summer of 1919, Paris was the center of the world. The Great War had ended. The victorious Great Powers—Britain, France, Italy, and the United States—were redrawing much of the world's map, "as if they were dividing cake," one diplomat noted in his diary.

The city's streets teemed with petitioners from nearly everywhere on earth, eager to enhance their own position in the final settlement: Africans, Armenians, Bessarabians, Irishmen, Koreans, Kurds, Poles, Ukrainians, Palestinians, Zionists, and desert Arabs in flowing white robes all elbowed their way past French war widows dressed in black. The British diplomat Harold Nicolson compared the colorful scene to "a riot in a parrot house."

A good many of these supplicants asked to see President Woodrow Wilson, whose American delegation was housed in the Hotel Crillon. "About every second man . . . one meets," the journalist Ray Stannard Baker noted, "fishes out of his pocket a copy of a cablegram that he or his committee has just sent to President Wilson. It is marvelous indeed how all the world is turning to the president! The people believe he means what he says, and that he is a great man set upon securing a sound peace."

And so, on June 18, when a gaunt twenty-nine-year-old Asian man in a rented morning coat appeared at the door of the American suite and asked if he might see Wilson, it caused no particular stir. The visitor did not get an appointment—the president and his wife were out of town that day, in any case, touring the Belgian battlefields—but a secretary politely accepted a petition from him. It set forth a series of requests on behalf of the people of what we now call Vietnam, then under French control.

There is no evidence that Wilson ever saw the petition, but it was understandable that colonized peoples looked to him for help. His Fourteen Points, the wartime statement of Allied principles intended to guarantee fairness in the peace negotiations, had pledged that during "the free, open-minded and absolutely impartial adjustment of all colonial claims," the interests of the colonized should be given "equal weight" with those of the colonizers.

That was precisely what the Vietnamese petitioners wanted. As a subject people, they declared, Wilson's advocacy of self-determination had filled them "with hope . . . that an era of rights and justice [was opening] to them." They did not demand independence from France, but they did call for "a permanent delegation of native people elected to attend the French parliament" as well as freedom of speech and association and foreign

travel, technical and professional schools in every province, and equal treatment under the law.

The petitioner may have been disappointed that he'd been unable to see the American president, but his visit to the Hotel Crillon was just one of many stops he made in Paris that season. The Western world was woefully ignorant of the plight of the colonized people of Indochina, he told a friend. "We need to make a lot of noise in order to become known." He pressed his petition on other delegations to the peace talks and on members of the National Assembly, saw to it that it was published in the left-wing newspaper *L'Humanité*, persuaded a trade union to print up thousands of copies and had them handed out to Paris

OPPOSITE Ho Chi Minh in Paris, 1921. He was shy and soft-spoken, the wife of one expatriate Vietnamese living in France recalled, but she remembered being frightened by the intensity lurking in his eyes.
ABOVE "Claims of the Annamite People," a copy of the petition addressed to the American secretary of state, Robert J. Lansing, and delivered by Ho Chi Minh to the American delegation to the Paris Peace Conference in 1919

crowds—and then dispatched thousands more to Vietnam, to be distributed on the streets of Saigon, the largest city in the South.

The French Ministry of Colonies and the secret police demanded to know just who this agitator was. Three undercover agents were assigned to report on his every move. He called himself Nguyen Ai Quoc—"Nguyen the Patriot"—but his real name was Nguyen Tat Thanh. During his long, shadowy career he would assume some seventy different identities, finally settling on "Ho the Most Enlightened"—Ho Chi Minh—the name by which he remains best known (and by which he will be known in these pages).

Ho was born sometime between 1890 and 1893, ten miles west of the city of Vinh in the province of Nghe An. His father, who began life as a rice farmer, served briefly as a minor official in the colonial regime, but resented the French nonetheless. He sent his son to the finest Franco-Vietnamese schools, believing that unless young Vietnamese better understood the world of their colonial masters they could never become free of them. One of Ho's French teachers hailed him as a "very distinguished student," but in the spring of 1908, he got into trouble. When hundreds of peasants gathered in the imperial capital of Hue to protest rising agricultural taxes, forced labor, and rampant corruption, Ho volunteered to act as an interpreter when they confronted the French authorities. Things got out of hand. Colonial security forces opened fire.

Shadowed by the French secret police, Ho fled south, went into hiding for a time, and then in 1911, at the age of twenty-one, signed on as an assistant cook aboard a steamship bound from Saigon to Marseille. "The people of Vietnam," he said many years later, "including my own father, often wondered who would help them to remove the yoke of French control. Some said Japan, others Great Britain, and some said the United States. I saw that I must go abroad to see for myself. After I had figured out how they lived, I would return to help my countrymen."

He would not return for thirty years. It is impossible to know precisely where he went and what he did over much of that time. In France, he applied for a scholarship to the Colonial School that prepared civil servants to run the empire, hoping, he wrote, that the training he received might benefit his "compatriots." His application was turned down. He returned to the sea, and witnessed the impact of European colonialism in the African and Asian ports visited by the ships on which he served. He seems to have lived in London for two years, studying English and working at the Carlton Hotel as an assistant to the celebrated chef Auguste Escoffier. He also evidently visited the United States twice, working as a pastry chef at the Parker House in Boston, cooking for a wealthy Brooklyn family, and

visiting Harlem to hear Marcus Garvey denounce racism, before turning up in Paris for the peace talks.

French records suggest that Ho landed in France again, just weeks before he tried to see President Wilson. Frail looking and shabbily dressed, he seemed an unlikely revolutionary at first. He stuttered when called upon to speak in public and seemed so diffident that some Parisian radicals dismissed him as "the mute of Montmartre." But he quickly proved a prolific propagandist—"indefatigable," said one intelligence report—and increasingly scornful of older expatriate Vietnamese who urged patience in the belief that France might somehow be persuaded to reform its rule. He joined the French Socialist Party because he thought it exemplified the values of *liberté, égalité et fraternité* that had inspired the French Revolution and was bitterly disappointed when his comrades proved largely uninterested in extending the protection of those principles to the people of the French colonies. But then he discovered the writings of the mastermind of the Bolshevik revolution, Vladimir Lenin. Lenin shared the orthodox Marxist view that real revolution could only be achieved in industrial nations. But he also thought anticolonial movements had an important role to play in overthrowing global capitalism. He argued that agents should establish communist parties in colonized countries, join forces with other nationalist groups, and then, once their colonial masters had been overthrown, jettison their non-communist allies and seize power in the name of international communism.

Interviewed many years later about the impact upon him of Lenin's writings, Ho's stilted language could not disguise his initial excitement: "What emotion, enthusiasm, clear-sightedness and confidence it instilled in me! I was overjoyed to tears. Though sitting alone in my room, I shouted aloud as if addressing large crowds: 'Dear martyrs, compatriots! This is what we need, this is the path to liberation.'"

In 1920, when the radical wing of the French Socialist Party broke away to form the French Communist Party, he went with them.

Minister of Colonies Albert Sarraut, a reformer who genuinely wanted to better the lives of France's Vietnamese subjects but without granting them political autonomy, summoned Ho to his office and alternately threatened him and tried to buy him off. Those who aligned themselves with "Bolsheviks" would be crushed, he warned, but if Ho were willing to cooperate with French authorities his future could be very bright. Ho was unmoved, or so he remembered many years later. "The main thing in my life and what I need most of all is freedom for my compatriots," he said, rising from his chair. "May I go now?"

The government rescinded Ho's passport, intending to keep him in France and under continuing surveillance, but in June 1923 he managed to slip out of the country disguised as a Chi-

nese businessman, and head for Moscow. There, he underwent training at the newly established University of the Toilers of the East, and argued before the Communist International that if it wished to defeat the imperialist powers, their colonies—and the all-important raw materials they provided—would first have to be ripped from them; otherwise, he said, the Comintern would be powerless, like the man who tried to kill a snake by stepping on its tail.

He was sent to southern China, determined to put Lenin's precepts into practice among the Vietnamese students living there. In 1925, he created the Revolutionary Youth League of Vietnam, which welcomed both communist and non-communist nationalists and trained many of Vietnam's future leaders. He also drafted *The Revolution Path,* a training manual that shrewdly blended Marxist dogma with Confucian precepts and practical considerations. "Peasants believe in facts, not theories," he wrote. In 1930, he helped establish what became the Indochinese Communist Party.

He remained constantly on the move, eluding French agents and changing names and destinations. He disguised himself as a Buddhist monk and a Chinese reporter, spent two years in a British jail in Hong Kong, was presumed dead by many of his old comrades, and, when he managed to talk his way to freedom, was suspected by some in Moscow of making a deal with the enemy and sidelined.

During the 1930s, Ho remembered, his was "a voice crying in the wilderness." But through it all, one friend recalled, he remained "taut and quivering . . . with only one thought, his country, Vietnam."

ABOVE In a photograph taken by a fellow member of the French Socialist Party at its annual congress at Tours in December 1920, Ho Chi Minh seeks to persuade his fellow delegates to "act effectively in favor of the oppressed natives" of his homeland. When they did not, he left them and helped establish the French Communist Party.

TOP A French fleet attacks the Citadel of Saigon, February 17, 1859. Three years later, the city itself fell to the French, and in 1863 they laid claim to the three provinces surrounding it, the first foothold of France's empire in Indochina. Painting by Antoine Léon Morel-Fatio. **ABOVE** Annam's ostensible ruler, Emperor Khai Dinh, and the man who wielded real power, French governor-general Albert Sarraut. A relatively progressive French official who championed education and medical care for the Vietnamese, Sarraut nonetheless saw them as children who could only slowly be allowed to play a part in governing themselves.

THOSE BLUE-EYED, YELLOW-BEARDED PEOPLE

A S A NATION-STATE, Vietnam is younger than the United States. The S-shaped region we now know as Vietnam—stretching more than a thousand miles from China's southern border to the Ca Mau Peninsula in the Gulf of Thailand—was not effectively united under a single ruler until 1802. In that year, a general who called himself Gia Long emerged from thirty years of civil war and established the Nguyen dynasty.

But the roots of Vietnamese civilization stretch back much farther, to the centuries before the Christian era when Chinese chroniclers wrote of the "hundred Viets"—an assortment of non-Chinese peoples scattered across the Red River Delta in the North. ("Viet" in Chinese meant "those from beyond"—foreigners.) Off and on for a thousand years, Chinese rulers sought to conquer these groups, and Vietnamese folklore is filled with the stories of heroes and heroines who led resistance against them.

The Vietnamese may have often resented their powerful neighbor to the north, but their daily lives came to be profoundly influenced by Chinese culture—from the chopsticks they wielded to the way in which they were governed. The education and civil service systems followed strict Confucian lines; to serve the emperor, mandarins, or scholar-officials, had to pass rigorous tests in subjects that included classical Chinese history, literature, and calligraphy. Court business was conducted in Chinese by courtiers wearing Chinese dress. Even the formidable citadel the Nguyen emperors built for themselves at Hue was modeled after the imperial Forbidden City in Beijing; only the ruler and his household were allowed inside its innermost enclosure.

French mercenaries armed with up-to-date weaponry had helped Gia Long establish his empire, and he had granted trading concessions to them in exchange for their help. But neither he nor any of his successors was comfortable with their presence or with that of the European missionaries who had been at work converting Vietnamese to Roman Catholicism for more than a century.

In 1858, when the emperor had two missionaries executed, France sent a fleet to seize the port of Danang. French naval forces took Saigon the following year and then forced the emperor to cede the three surrounding provinces to them. Over the four decades that followed, French forces captured Hue and Hanoi and steadily extended their power and influence until the French colonial government could officially declare in 1900 that the "pacification of Indochina" was complete. "The great [Indochinese] possessions," wrote an early colonial administrator, "should be organized as true states . . . and made to possess all the characteristics that define states, except one: political independence."

France divided Vietnam into three parts: the French colony of Cochinchina, which encompassed the sprawling, sparsely peopled Mekong Delta in the South; and two "protectorates"—Annam, the poorest and most mountainous part of the country, just thirty miles wide at its narrowest point, and Tonkin, the densely populated Red River Delta. These protectorates were nominally overseen by a compliant descendant of the Nguyen emperors, but actually ruled—along with Laos and Cambodia—as part of the Indochinese Union by a French governor-general from his palace in Hanoi.

The French claimed they had begun to amass their Indochinese empire simply to protect the Christian faithful and professed always to be undertaking a "civilizing mission," meant to bring material and cultural benefits to an allegedly benighted people. But their initial motives were less lofty. French Indochina was meant to provide a path for penetrating the Chinese market and create a buffer against the British and Dutch, who had already carved empires of their own from India, Burma, Malaya, and Indonesia.

More important, it provided the bright prospect of fortunes to be made through exploitation of the land and its people. To that end, the French would transform much of the Vietnamese

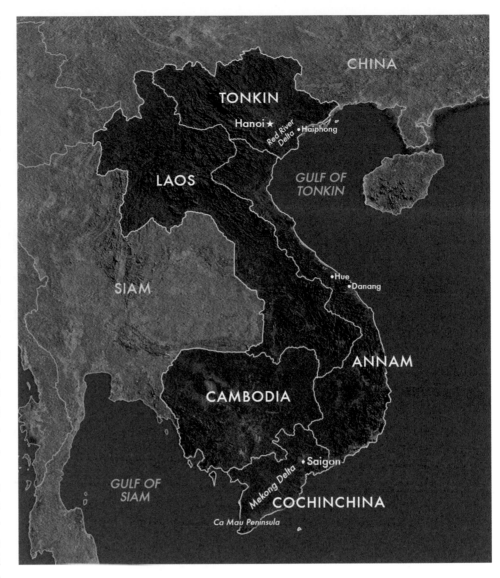

landscape. In Cochinchina, they carved out a complex network of canals that turned tens of thousands of acres of marshy wilderness into some of the most productive rice-growing country on earth. They developed modern ports at Haiphong and Danang and Saigon, too, so that Vietnamese raw material could more efficiently be shipped abroad and French-manufactured goods could more easily be unloaded. They also built a railroad to move French products north from Saigon all the way to China; one out of three of the more than 100,000 Vietnamese conscripted to lay its tracks is thought to have died along the way. The French hacked down highland forests as well, displacing tribal people who depended on them for their livelihood, and planted millions of rubber trees in their place; the miserably paid contract workers who tapped the trees were ravaged by malaria and "treated like human cattle," one colonist admitted,

ABOVE The French Indochinese Union

and "terrorized by the overseers. . . . On the rubber plantations the people had a habit of saying that children did not have a chance to know their fathers, nor dogs their masters." In the North, tens of thousands of contract laborers risked their lives beneath the earth, mining coal, tin, tungsten, and zinc for the

benefit of investors in France. They worked twelve hours a day, seven days a week, and those who tried to get away were often beaten before being forced back to work.

The French largely lived apart from their subjects on plantation estates and in neighborhoods designed and built to look as much as possible like those at home. Most did not bother to learn the language spoken by their subjects. In 1910, the year before Ho Chi Minh fled Cochinchina, a government survey found that just three French officials in the whole colony understood Vietnamese well enough to make policy decisions on their own. The French depended instead on a network of French-speaking Vietnamese willing to carry out their wishes—and all too often eager to enrich themselves in the process.

Other Vietnamese benefited by colonial rule. They became bankers, merchants, or landlords in Cochinchina, where the availability of cheap, newly opened lands created a fresh entrepreneurial frontier for those with enough capital to get started.

ABOVE French musicians entertain guests in the grand café of the Grand Hôtel de la Rotonde in Saigon, 1920s. For the French naval officer and future novelist Pierre Loti, coming ashore at Saigon provided "an unexpected sensation, that of coming home . . . the sudden rediscovery of the sound and momentum of a city, the open cafés, the women dressed in French style, the hum of cars." **OPPOSITE** A giddy French newcomer, carried ashore by Vietnamese porters, 1902. "The French usually disembarked in Indochina determined to be on the best possible terms with the Annamese," one critical colonist remembered. "It was only gradually, moving from one small misunderstanding to another, that they arrived at isolation and a separation from the Annamese world."

These privileged people created a Westernized urban world of their own; they spoke French, drank wine, and followed Paris fashions.

But for the peasants who made up 90 percent of Vietnam's population, colonial rule provided few benefits. Subject to French monopolies on salt and alcohol, sometimes dragooned to labor without pay on public works, burdened by ever-climbing taxes and saddled by debt, many stood by helplessly as lands they once had owned slipped into the hands of big landowners. By the beginning of the twentieth century, just 5 percent of the population owned 95 percent of the arable land in Cochinchina.

Resentment festered. "Our soil is fertile, our mountains and rivers [are] beautiful," the nationalist firebrand and pamphleteer Phan Boi Chau noted in 1907.

> Compared with other powers in the five continents, our country is inferior only to a few. Why, then, do we suffer French "protection"? . . . Frenchmen hold . . . the power of life and death over everyone. The life of thousands of Vietnamese people is not worth that of a French dog; the moral prestige of hundreds of our officials does not prevail over that of a French woman. Look at those men with blue eyes and yellow beards. They are not our fathers, nor are they our brothers. How can they squat here, defecating on our heads? Are the men from Vietnam not ashamed of their situation?

Three generations of Vietnamese nationalists struggled to provide answers to those questions. First, a group of Mandarins led a guerrilla war aimed at restoring the Nguyen dynasty to its former splendor—and returning themselves to positions of power. The French defeated them, but it took a dozen years. A second generation of scholar-gentry, hostile to France but increasingly open to influence from the West and impatient with the way things had been done before the French arrived, fostered nationalist movements of their own. Some championed armed resistance and called for a constitutional monarchy or a democratic republic. Others deplored violence and insisted instead that France live up to the ideals it professed to cherish and teach the Vietnamese how they might rule themselves. The French considered all opposition suspect. Some nationalists were executed. Hundreds more were imprisoned.

French officials preside over the public guillotining of a Vietnamese prisoner in Saigon, 1888. French onlookers crowd the upstairs balconies, but the grisly spectacle was intended to impress the silent Vietnamese who line the surrounding streets with the cost of defying French law.

ABOVE Vietnamese colonial troops and cooks accused of plotting to poison officers at their Hanoi garrison, 1908. Thirteen were decapitated, and four more were sentenced to life in prison. "Hanoi is currently the property of the French," a nationalist pamphlet declared after the executions, "but the traces of these heroes' blood will never be erased even for three thousand years."

None of these movements ever managed to broaden its appeal much beyond the urban middle-class world from which their leaders came. The communists were different. They set out from the first to unite Vietnam's factory workers with the peasant majority, but they were plagued by factionalism: three communist parties competed with one another before Ho brought their leaders together in Hong Kong in 1930 and united them under a single banner. Still, the French proved too strong for them, crushing peasant rebellions in Tonkin and northern Annam in 1930, and again a decade later in Cochinchina. The French strafed demonstrators, bombed villages suspected of harboring rebels, and shot unarmed civilians. Party leadership in the South was virtually eliminated.

When France meekly surrendered to Nazi Germany after just six weeks of fighting in June 1940, many Vietnamese nationalists rejoiced in the humiliation of their colonial masters. Imperial Japan, soon to ally itself with Germany and eager to move against British and Dutch colonies throughout Asia, then forced the collaborationist Vichy French to permit them to station troops in Tonkin in exchange for the right to continue day-to-day administration of the colony. Within a year, Japanese soldiers would occupy all of Vietnam.

To some Vietnamese, the collapse of the French and the coming of the Japanese had seemed to signal a welcome end to white colonial rule. But Ho Chi Minh saw things differently. To him, the Japanese were alien invaders, no more welcome than the French. France might be an "imperialist wolf," he said, but Japan was a "fascist hyena," interested only in exploiting his country, commandeering rubber for its war machine, and seizing Vietnamese crops to fill its own rice bowls. "The Japanese [have] become the real masters," he wrote. "The French [have] become kind of respectable slaves. And upon the Indo-Chinese falls the double honor of being not only slaves to the Japanese, but also slaves of the slaves—the French."

Ho identified with the Allies, sure that they would eventually defeat the Japanese and hopeful that once the war was over they would reject the now-discredited French and reward Vietnamese nationalists with the independence they'd been seeking for decades. "It was a once-in-a-thousand-years propitious situation," he told his followers, and he was determined to take advantage of it.

A MOMENT OF INNOCENCE

Like many sons of mandarins, Bui Diem, born in 1923 in Annam, was raised to resent the French. His grandfather and his father had each refused to serve at the Nguyen court because the emperors were doing Paris's bidding, and he had personally experienced the color prejudice that characterized the relationship between colonial rulers and those they ruled. Although he was well read, Westernized, and eloquent in French, he was barred as a young man from the only tennis courts in his hometown simply because he was Vietnamese.

Nonetheless, he remembered, it also sometimes seemed to him that he'd learned "everything" from the French—"their language, their culture. Studying their revolution taught me the difference between being a slave and being a free man." That lesson was brought home to him at the elite Hanoi high school he attended, by an eager young history teacher named Vo Nguyen Giap, who would one day disappear mysteriously from school. Much later, he reemerged on the battlefield to defeat first the French and then the Americans in Vietnam.

During World War II, Bui Diem attended the University of Hanoi, the sole institution of higher learning the French had seen fit to build in Indochina. When, in the spring of 1940, he and his fellow students learned that it had taken Nazi Germany just six weeks to humiliate the once-mighty French, they were swept up in nationalist feeling. There was renewed interest in resistance heroes from Vietnam's distant past. Secret societies and nationalist parties competed for young peoples' loyalty.

"Although no one knew anything concrete about these parties, what their policies were, or even the names of their leaders, we were caught in a rush of excitement," he remembered.

We felt that our country was on the verge of striking out for its freedom, and there wasn't a soul who didn't want to be a part of that. . . . Gradually, each of us joined one or another of the parties that promised to mold a reality from the desire for freedom. . . . At that time, . . . few had had any idea of the distinctions between these parties, or even a good concept of which was which. They all said they were

fighting for independence; that was enough. . . . It was not generally known, for example, that the Viet Minh was communist controlled. Ho Chi Minh was not a name anyone had yet heard of.

In the end, and only because a close friend encouraged him to do so, Diem cast his lot with one faction of the anticommunist Dai Viet, or "Greater Vietnam," Party. "Its *raison d'etre* was national freedom," he recalled, "and it had neither the time nor the inclination to look far beyond that goal. . . . It was a moment of innocence, the last one, perhaps, before the fratricidal war between communists and non-communists bore down on us."

HAIPHONG

ABOVE Bui Diem as a student at the University of Hanoi, 1940 **LEFT** Japanese troops advancing on Haiphong unopposed in September of that same year

THE DECISIVE HOUR

ON FEBRUARY 8, 1941, Ho Chi Minh, disguised as one of the local Nung people, slipped across the Chinese border into Tonkin near the remote mountain village of Pac Bo and set up headquarters with a handful of followers in a limestone cave at the side of a mountain he named for Karl Marx, which overlooked a jungle stream he named for Lenin. The surrounding thickly wooded hills were already a communist stronghold, but he made sure that if a French patrol came too close, escape back into China was only steps away. Still, for the first time in three decades, he was back home in Vietnam.

He gathered the members of the Central Committee of the Indochinese Communist Party at Pac Bo in May, and persuaded them temporarily to submerge the party within a broad patriotic front to be called the League for the Independence of Vietnam—the Viet Minh. The time had come, he said, to rally "patriots of all ages and all types, peasants, workers, merchants

ABOVE At Ho Chi Minh's jungle redoubt, Viet Minh volunteers watch an OSS weapons instructor demonstrate how to fire a U.S.-supplied rifle grenade. "To see our company . . . armed with new rifles and shining bayonets," Vo Nguyen Giap remembered, "filled us with jubilance and confidence."

and soldiers" to defeat the Japanese—as well as the French. Behind the scenes, communists would be in overall command, but nationalists of every kind would be welcome. Freedom from France would come first; party objectives like land redistribution could wait.

To build and lead a guerrilla liberation army, Ho called upon Vo Nguyen Giap, the onetime history teacher who had once instructed the children of Hanoi's elite. Giap was an early convert to communism whose lifelong hatred of the French only deepened when he learned that his wife had died after being tortured in a French prison. He had already begun to develop a distinctive theory of revolutionary warfare based on his reading of Napoleon, the Chinese general Sun Tzu, and Lawrence of Arabia. In fighting the French and the Japanese, he said, his armies would be "everywhere and nowhere."

The Viet Minh worked first to win the support of the Nung and other highland peoples living in the North, then spread their influence steadily southward from village to village across the Red River Delta. They strengthened their appeal by their efforts to alleviate the impact of the terrible famine that took between one and two million lives in the northern and north-central parts of the country during the winter of 1944–45. When neither the French nor the Japanese nor any other nationalist organization seemed capable of dealing with the crisis, the Viet Minh raided granaries, distributed rice to the hungry, and were widely hailed as saviors.

Meanwhile, the war went badly for the Japanese. By early 1945, their fleet had largely been destroyed. American forces were making one amphibious Pacific landing after another. Fearing that Indochina might be next and that their French allies would turn against them, the Japanese staged a coup on March 9. They killed some two thousand French officers and men, disarmed and interned twelve thousand more—and then, in an attempt to win Vietnamese support, declared Vietnam "independent" and allowed the puppet emperor, Bao Dai, to remain on the throne so long as he did their bidding.

In the end, the Americans never invaded Indochina. They focused instead on preparing to assault the Japanese home islands. But American agents working in southern China for the OSS—the Office of Strategic Services, wartime forerunner of the Central Intelligence Agency—sought allies behind enemy lines to gather intelligence and rescue downed American pilots. Ho Chi Minh eagerly joined forces with them, hoping that if the Viet Minh came to America's aid, then America would support Vietnam's bid for independence once the fighting ended.

A six-man OSS team parachuted into his jungle encampment, supplied Ho's men with modern arms, and marveled at how quickly they learned to handle them. Ho began to call his followers the "Viet-*American* Army."

On August 14, Japan indicated her willingness to surrender. Two days later, Ho issued "an appeal to the Vietnamese peo-ple," urging them to seize control of their country before Allied troops arrived in Indochina.

> Dear Fellow Countrymen! The decisive hour has struck for the destiny of our people. Let all of us stand up and rely on our own strength to free ourselves. Many oppressed peoples the world over are vying with each other in wresting back independence. We should not lag behind. Forward! Forward! Under the banner of the Viet Minh, let us valiantly march forward!

Popular uprisings erupted in rural districts all across the Red River Delta, some incited by the Viet Minh, some spontaneous. The Viet Minh took over Hanoi, seized Hue, forced Bao Dai to abdicate, and established a tenuous hold on Saigon, despite other nationalist factions jockeying for power in the South. The Vietnamese would remember this successful insurrection as the "August Revolution." In the years to come, its memory would inspire—and then dangerously mislead—the men who ran North Vietnam.

ABOVE Ho Chi Minh (first row, third from right) at Pac Bo with members of the OSS Deer Mission, 1945. The officer to Ho's right is the team's commander, Major Allison Thomas. The man wearing the tie is Vo Nguyen Giap.

ON THE MAP OF THE WORLD

SUNDAY, SEPTEMBER 2, 1945, the day Japan formally surrendered, was declared Vietnamese Independence Day. More than 400,000 people gathered in Hanoi's Ba Dinh Square that afternoon. Many had never visited the big city before. Ho Chi Minh had never been there, either, and when he and the members of his new cabinet stepped onto a makeshift platform, the crowd could pick him out only because he was dressed differently from his colleagues. They wore Western coats and ties. He chose the simple peasant clothing he would wear for the next twenty-four years as head of state: a battered hat, faded khaki jacket, and rubber sandals.

He began to speak, then stopped and shouted, "Countrymen, can you hear me?"

The people roared back, "Clearly!" At that moment, General Giap remembered, "Uncle [Ho] and the sea of people became one."

With OSS officers looking on, Ho began with the familiar words of Thomas Jefferson. "All men are created equal. They are endowed by their Creator with certain unalienable rights; among these are Life, Liberty, and the pursuit of Happiness." He quoted the promises contained in the French Declaration of the Rights of Man, as well, and then contrasted these high-minded ideals with the crimes committed by France against his people for more than eighty years. He declared the indepen-

ABOVE, LEFT AND RIGHT Hanoi, Sunday afternoon, September 2, 1945. A throng gathers in front of the Municipal Theater, hung with the single-starred Viet Minh flag, before making its way to Ba Dinh Square. There, while Viet Minh guards with drawn revolvers protect the podium, Ho Chi Minh declares Vietnam's independence beneath an umbrella that shields the pages of his speech from the sun's glare.

dence of the new Democratic Republic of Vietnam and then called upon the Allies to recognize the right of the Vietnamese people to full independence.

Many in the crowd wept. "I was so proud," a Viet Minh veteran remembered. "It was wonderful that our country was now officially named on the map of the world."

Ho's hope that the United States could be persuaded to support Vietnamese independence was understandable. Even before America entered the war, President Franklin Delano Roosevelt had promised a postwar world that would "respect the right of all peoples to choose the form of government under which they . . . live," and he had an almost visceral scorn for the French and for French colonialism. "Indo-China should not be given back to the French Empire," he had told his commanders. "The French [have] been there for nearly one hundred years and [have] done nothing . . . to improve the lot of the people." He was equally sure the Vietnamese were not yet ready for self-government and so hoped the United Nations would make Vietnam a trusteeship, running it for the benefit of its people while preparing them for full independence, as the United States was doing for the Philippines.

But Roosevelt had died in April, and his plans for a trusteeship had died with him. His successor, Harry Truman, had little interest in colonial questions. The Grand Alliance of the United States, Great Britain, and the Soviet Union had not survived the war it won. The Soviet Union had borne the brunt of the fighting. Some twenty-seven million Soviet citizens had died in the war, and Joseph Stalin was determined that his country would never again be vulnerable to attack from the West. Ruthless and paranoid, he refused to withdraw his armies from the eastern European countries they had overrun, insisted that states beyond those expanded borders remain within Moscow's sphere of influence, and hoped to spread that influence still further—into Iran, Turkey, and the Mediterranean.

Concern over Soviet expansion in Europe indirectly affected postwar policy toward Indochina. The U.S. State Department was sharply split. The Far East division saw that the colonial era was coming to an end and warned that American support for the restoration of French rule in Indochina would result only in "bloodshed and unrest for many years." But the European Affairs bureau disagreed. General Charles de Gaulle, president of France's provisional government, had already made it clear that restoration of the French empire was nonnegotiable; if the United States insisted on independence for her colonies, France might have no choice, he said, but to "fall into the Russian orbit." The Europeanists argued that the United States must do nothing to undercut the restoration of France's prewar empire—including Vietnam.

The Allied leaders, meeting in Potsdam, Germany, in July, weeks before Japan's surrender and Ho's declaration of Vietnamese independence, had already agreed temporarily to divide French Indochina into two separate zones for purposes of disarming the enemy and restoring law and order. Nationalist Chinese troops were to handle things north of the 16th parallel while British troops performed the same task to the south. Once that was accomplished, the future status of the region could be negotiated. The United States agreed to remain officially neutral in those talks—but would make no objection to the restoration of French rule.

COCHINCHINA IS BURNING

alist Party, allied with Chiang Kai-shek. In Hanoi, the illusion of an easy path to independence had lasted just one week.

Things had gone badly in Cochinchina, too. On Independence Day, banners hung across the streets of Saigon: "Down with French Fascism," "Give Us Liberty or Death," "Welcome to the Deliverers." Somewhere between thirty and forty thousand peasants and their families had gathered in front of the French governor-general's palace, now occupied by the Viet Minh. Some carried Japanese swords, ancient shotguns, and sharpened bamboo spears, and all hoped to hear Ho Chi Minh's words broadcast live from Hanoi. But Japanese roadblocks kept the transmitter from ever reaching Ba Dinh Square. There was no broadcast. As the disappointed crowd broke up, someone fired several shots. The Vietnamese blamed the French, killed a Catholic priest who happened to be nearby, then roamed the streets randomly beating French men and women. A rumor spread through French neighborhoods that the Viet Minh had "declared their intention to kill every white man in the city."

Two days later, the first members of an OSS team landed at Saigon. Their commander was a remarkable twenty-eight-year-old officer, Lieutenant Colonel A. Peter Dewey. He was a New York congressman's son and a Yale-educated newspaperman, an author and student of French history who had been awarded the

ABOVE A former French prisoner of war, newly released and rearmed, stands guard over Vietnamese nationalists rounded up in Saigon, September 1945. The brutality of the coup that reestablished French control of the city, one rueful Frenchwoman wrote, showed the Vietnamese "that the new France [is] even more to be feared than the old one."

ON SEPTEMBER 9, the advance guard of a 150,000-man Nationalist Chinese occupation army marched into Hanoi—weary, ragged, eager for plunder. On their way through Tonkin, they had evicted Viet Minh committees from power, and replaced them with members of the anticommunist Nation-

ABOVE Japanese soldiers guard a Saigon neighborhood against the ongoing street fighting raging in the distance, October 1945. In the confusion that followed the war's end, the shorthanded British commander felt he had no choice but to arm former enemies to keep order between mobs of angry Frenchmen and Vietnamese.

French Legion of Honor for the courage he displayed behind enemy lines in North Africa and southern France. His official mission was clear enough: he was to care for American prisoners of war, protect American property, and gather information about enemy atrocities. But he was also secretly to learn everything he could about French plans for Indochina after the war.

Saigon was in chaos. "It wasn't quite a civil war," the OSS team's translator, George Wickes, remembered, "but it was getting very close to civil war in the streets." Fluent in both French and Vietnamese, Wickes was at first delighted to find himself in Vietnam "when hardly any Americans knew where it was." But the Viet Minh seemed powerless to impose order. Snipers fired from rooftops. Mobs looted homes and shops. Terrified French civilians remained barricaded inside their homes.

Dewey tried to make sense of it all. "Right from the start he was in touch with everybody," Wickes recalled. "Not only the French but very soon he established connections with the various Vietnamese groups and sorted them out. From them he was getting a sense of which way the Vietnam independence movement was likely to go."

The British, challenged by nationalist movements in their own Asian colonies, favored the swiftest possible return of French rule in Indochina. Major General Douglas Gracey, British commander of the small contingent of Gurkha troops assigned to disarm the Japanese and reestablish order, had little time for talk of independence. He was blunt, impatient, and convinced that European rule over Asian territories was both right and inevitable; he refused even to speak to the Viet Minh. "He was inclined to restore the French," Wickes remembered. "It was not a part of his official mission, but he felt that he was simply holding the fort until the French could take over."

Gracey rearmed eight thousand Japanese soldiers and sent them out with orders to disarm every Vietnamese and to evict the Viet Minh from the governor-general's residence.

Colonel Dewey tried to broker talks between a Viet Minh spokesman and the senior French representative in the city. The talks went nowhere. The Frenchman insisted there could be no discussion of the future until French rule was restored; the Viet Minh said the French would have to promise independence before talks could begin. But Dewey's efforts infuriated General Gracey. By conferring with the Viet Minh, he said, Colonel Dewey had become a "blatant and subversive" force, undermining his authority. He declared the American persona non grata.

Dewey continued to collect intelligence as best he could. When he realized the British were watching him, he sent George Wickes, disguised as a former prisoner of war, into the streets after dark to meet with spokesmen for various Vietnamese factions and then report back.

The Viet Minh called for a general strike and mass demonstration, one organizer recalled, in hopes of attracting British and French reprisals that would "cause many casualties and attract world attention." In response, General Gracey imposed martial law, then released and armed fourteen hundred French prisoners of war. Together with a mob of angry French civilians, they stormed through the streets, clubbing any Vietnamese who got in their way. They lynched Viet Minh officials, looted shops, and raised the French flag above the city's most important buildings as a sign that France was once again in charge.

Dewey hurried to British headquarters to protest. General Gracey refused to see him—and sent orders that Dewey was to leave Saigon as soon as arrangements could be made.

At dawn the next day, a Vietnamese mob shouting "Death to Europeans" and bent on revenge stormed through a French neighborhood, butchering some 150 men, women, and children and carrying off others who were never seen again.

Dewey cabled one more report to his superiors: "Cochinchina is burning," he wrote. "The French and British are finished here and we [the United States] ought to clear out of southeast Asia."

Two days later, on September 26, Dewey and an American colleague left the villa the OSS was now occupying on the outskirts of the city and set out in a jeep for Tan Son Nhut airport, prepared to fly out to OSS headquarters in Ceylon.

"There were Vietnamese roadblocks all around the town, part of the resistance to the French and the British," Wickes recalled. "One was just down the road, and we'd passed through it many times without incident." When Dewey drove to the airport and discovered that his plane was not yet there, "he decided to come back to the villa for lunch. As he started passing through the same roadblock, a machine gun opened fire and killed him."

The Viet Minh machine gunner had evidently mistaken the American officer for a Frenchman. The first postwar American death in Vietnam was the result of a tragic misunderstanding—the first of many between the people of the United States and the people of Vietnam.

Ten days after Dewey's death, fresh French troops began arriving at Saigon to take over from the British. "We are fighting for the reestablishment of French greatness," said their commander, General Jacques-Philippe Leclerc, who had led the forces of Free France into Paris. His men quickly subdued Saigon, cleared an area ringing the city twelve miles deep, and then, as new troops arrived to swell his ranks, pushed across the Mekong Delta and up into the Central Highlands. They were harassed by guerrillas wherever they went, were able to take territory but then didn't seem able to hold on to it. "If we departed, believing a region pacified," one frustrated soldier wrote, "the Viet Minh would arrive on our heels." Combat in Vietnam would follow that pattern for the following three decades.

ABOVE Lieutenant Colonel A. Peter Dewey (top) and the monument that once marked the spot where he was killed, near Saigon's Tan Son Nhut airport. Dewey's body was never found.

A HARD LESSON

W E APPARENTLY stand quite alone," Ho told a Western reporter in Hanoi that fall. No nation, not even the Soviet Union, was willing to recognize his government. Even the French Communist Party he had helped to found refused to support Indochinese independence. "We shall have to depend on ourselves."

To keep the Nationalist Chinese occupiers of Tonkin from interfering with his government—and forestall French forces from reclaiming the region—he bribed the warlords in command with gold and opium, formally dissolved the Indochinese Communist Party (though it would continue to operate in secret), offered Nationalist rivals posts in his cabinet, and agreed to elections for a new National Assembly with guaranteed seats for the anticommunist opposition.

The delaying action did not last long. In early 1946, the Chinese and French reached an agreement: the French relinquished prewar trading rights in China, and the Chinese agreed to go home. France, already engaged in retaking the South, was now poised to retake the North, as well. Some of Ho's comrades urged him to resist. But he knew his forces were not yet up to the task of combating the French and preferred to negotiate. In the end, France and the Viet Minh reached an uneasy compromise: Paris pledged to consider Vietnam a self-administering "Free State" within a newly organized imperial framework to be known as the French Union. There was no mention of "independence." In return, Hanoi agreed to let France station fifteen thousand troops in northern Vietnam for five years. Hanoi argued that Cochinchina was an integral part of Vietnam. Paris insisted it remain a separate colony tied to France. The two sides agreed that a plebiscite would eventually settle the matter.

On May 31, Ho left for Paris, a city he knew far better than Hanoi, hoping to get the French to live up to their promises. He was greeted as if he were a head of state, spent time with old friends, visited the streets and cafés and parks he'd loved a quarter of a century earlier. But the talks went nowhere. The French definition of a Vietnamese "Free State" turned out to provide very little actual freedom, and without any warning Paris declared Cochinchina a separate "autonomous republic." Vietnam would neither be independent nor reunited.

"The French . . . wave flags for me," Ho told an American reporter, "but it is a masquerade. We will have to fight." It would be a war between the French elephant and the Vietnamese tiger, he said.

If the tiger ever stands still the elephant will crush him with his mighty tusks. But the tiger does not stand still.

He lurks in the jungle by day and emerges by night. He will leap upon the back of the elephant, tearing huge chunks from his hide, and then he will leap back into the dark jungle. And slowly the elephant will bleed to death. That will be the war of Indochina.

Ho was away for four months, long enough for General Giap to conduct a merciless purge of people he called "reactionary saboteurs"—landlords and moneylenders, members of rival nationalist parties, Trotskyites and Catholics, men and women accused of collaborating with the French or the Japanese. Hundreds, perhaps thousands, were shot, drowned, buried alive. Thousands more were sent to prison camps. Later, Giap and Ho would acknowledge that at least some of the killings had been "mistakes," but by then they had essentially destroyed all opposition to their leadership in the North. The Democratic Republic of Vietnam would be run by Ho Chi Minh, General Giap, and their inner circle.

In November 1946, a customs dispute between the French and Viet Minh in the port of Haiphong led to a day-long exchange of gunfire. Two hundred and forty Vietnamese and seven Frenchmen were dead by nightfall. A tenuous ceasefire took hold. But in Saigon, General Jean Valluy, commander of French forces in Indochina, insisted the city be punished. Accordingly a French

ABOVE This photograph of victims of the great famine that took some two million lives in northern Vietnam between 1944 and 1945 was given to an OSS officer by Ho Chi Minh himself in hopes of eliciting American sympathy and support.

WITNESS TO HISTORY

When twenty-two-year-old PFC George Wickes arrived in Saigon on September 4, 1945, just two days after Ho Chi Minh declared Vietnamese independence, he realized he would be witnessing history firsthand. "It's a most fascinating thing watching the succession of episodes," he wrote to his mother. "What will the French do? What will the Annamese do? The British? The Japs? The Chinese?"

Over the next few weeks he saw vicious street fighting, engaged in clandestine meetings with the Viet Minh under orders from Colonel A. Peter Dewey, and took part in a firefight with those who killed his commander. In November, he traveled north of Saigon in search of Dewey's body. It was never found, but

Wickes saw for himself the difficulty French troops were already having subduing Vietnamese guerrillas and wrote home about it.

The French are not quite so confident as they were at the start that this would be cleared up in a few weeks. I believe that, unless they always keep large garrisons and patrols everywhere they will not be able to keep the country submissive as it was before. . . . The Annamites' great advantage lies in the fact that he is everywhere, that he does not need to fight pitched battles . . . to be a threat and that no amount of reprisal can completely defeat him. I cannot say how it will end, but at least it will be a long time before Frenchmen can roam about the country with peace of mind.

On March 16, 1946, ten days after Ho Chi Minh reluctantly agreed to permit France to station troops in northern Vietnam, Wickes and another intelligence officer were sent to Hanoi to interview him. There,

they witnessed the arrival of General Leclerc and the advance guard of his army. "They were wildly acclaimed by hysterical French crowds," Wickes reported, while the Vietnamese watched "with singular apathy."

Ho assured his American visitors that while he was himself a communist he could not determine whether an independent Vietnam would adopt communism as its form of government. That was for the people to decide, he said, and he asked his visitors to tell Washington of his hopes that the United States would support his call for full independence.

Wickes told his mother how impressed he'd been.

When you talk to [Ho] he strikes you as quite above the ordinary run of mortals. Perhaps it is the spirit that great patriots are supposed to have. Surely he has that—long struggling has left him mild and resigned, still sustaining some small idealism and hope [that even after the March 6 agreement real independence could still be achieved]. But I think it is particularly his kindliness, his simplicity, his down-to-earthness. I think Abraham Lincoln must have been such a man, calm, sane and humble.

Seventy years later, and despite everything that happened in the intervening years, George Wickes still held to that view.

Snapshots: George Wickes, shown above on the roof of the Continental Hotel, the first OSS billet in Saigon, used his amateur camera to capture Japanese troops formally surrendering to officers of the British Indian Army and the arrival of the first French troops in Saigon on October 4, 1945.

warship shelled Haiphong, killing six thousand civilians—to "teach a hard lesson," its commander said.

In December, fighting broke out in the streets of Hanoi. Ho and Giap and their comrades fled the city and returned to their mountain strongholds along the Chinese border. "Those who have rifles will use their rifles," Ho declared in a radio address calling for the war he had tried so hard to avoid. "Those who have swords will use swords; those who have no swords will use spades, hoes, or sticks."

The London *Times* that week was prophetic: "Any colonial power which puts itself in the position of meeting terrorism with terrorism might as well wash its hands of the whole business and go home. We are about to see a French army reconquer the greater part of Indochina, only to make it impossible for any French merchant or planter to live outside barbed wire perimeters thereafter."

France poured troops into both halves of the country—Frenchmen, European mercenaries, and colonial troops from Morocco, Algeria, Tunisia, and Senegal—and enlisted Vietnamese willing to fight against the Viet Minh. Unprepared to fight in summer heat and monsoon rains, underfinanced and

ABOVE, LEFT French troops return to Hanoi, March 20, 1945. "Watching them . . . brought the taste of gall," Bui Diem remembered. "It seemed the return of Vietnam's colonial enslavement. On the sidewalks French civilian residents of Hanoi stood cheering. On the balcony each one of us was brushing away tears." RIGHT French officials escort Ho Chi Minh after he made a formal call upon the French prime minister, Georges Bidault, July 2, 1945. When a reporter remarked on the large crowds that gathered to see Ho wherever he went in France, the Vietnamese leader was not surprised. "Why, of course," he said, "everyone wants to see the Vietnamese version of Charlie Chaplin."

poorly led, these forces still managed to take and hold most of the large towns and province capitals in northern and central Vietnam and to establish some nine hundred watchtowers and blockhouses scattered across the countryside.

But the Viet Minh owned most of the rural areas in between. They mined roads, blew up bridges, ambushed French patrols that dared venture outside their strongholds, attacked French bases by night, then disappeared into the darkness. Tactics set forth by the Chinese communist revolutionary Mao Zedong were initially their guide: "The enemy advances," Mao said, "we retreat; the enemy halts, we harass; the enemy tires, we attack; the enemy retreats, we pursue."

The French often responded with brutality—razing villages, raping women, torturing and executing men suspected of aiding the Viet Minh. "We suffered losses but we also responded well and inflicted a lot of damage," one French Legionnaire reported after destroying a village. "Within a 6-kilometer radius, nothing remains: from ducks to cattle, women and children, we have purged everything."

The Viet Minh proved ruthless too. They drew up lists of persons suspected of having links to the French and then assigned "assassination committees" to eliminate them. "It is better to kill even those who might be innocent," they said, "than to let a guilty person go."

French casualties continued to mount. "There are days when we are so discouraged that we would like to give it all up," a French soldier wrote his family. "Convoys under attack, roads cut, firing in all directions every night, the indifference at home."

It eventually became clear that this was a war neither side could win without aid from elsewhere. Both sides lobbied hard to get it.

France looked to the United States for help, but American

AS FRIENDS, AS BROTHERS

Tran Ngoc Chau was one of thousands of young nationalists who volunteered to join the Viet Minh and free their country. The pampered son of a mandarin whose family had served the imperial family of Annam for centuries, he had grown up in their capital city of Hue, and spent five years studying to be a Buddhist priest before the struggle began. But he'd also served as an intelligence agent for the Viet Minh, he recalled, and when the call to revolution came, he and his two older brothers boarded a train with other volunteers and went to war.

"The French had reoccupied the South first so we had to go to the South to fight," he recalled. "Everywhere the train stopped the people came out with all kinds of food, good food that they had cooked themselves. That was my first lesson about how important it was to have the people with us. And even though at first only a few of us were communists, we heard the name of Ho Chi Minh everywhere."

There were far more volunteers than weapons at first—some twelve-man units had to share a single rifle. Chau's own gun fell apart the first time he fired it in battle. There was too little food. He was forced to walk mile after mile, week after week, without shoes. But he soon found himself part of hit-and-run raids, attacks on French outposts, ambushes of French convoys—and was learning useful lessons from every encounter. After each firefight died down, Chau and his comrades would gather to discuss what had happened and how they might do better the next time. Those who had made mistakes were required to confess them; if they failed to do so their comrades were expected to denounce them.

Most urban middle-class youths found jungle warfare too demanding and fell away, Chau recalled. He himself

suffered from malaria and was severely wounded by shrapnel. But he had a gift for leadership, was made a company commander within a year, then a battalion commander, and experienced firsthand the bitter reality of the lives led by the poor peasants who made up the majority of his fellow countrymen.

They were a revelation to him. The people among whom he'd grown up "looked down on the peasants," he remembered, "almost as if they were servants." The men with whom he served were illiterate, ill-fed, ill-informed about the world beyond their villages, and angry at the landlords for whom they and their parents had been forced to work. But they were also uncomplaining, undemanding, and willing to undergo all sorts of privation for the cause they shared. Their stoicism shamed and embarrassed him. He taught many of his men to read.

Infected wounds and recurrent malaria eventually sent Tran Ngoc Chau to the hospital for months, time he spent thinking about the struggle in which he had been engaged so deeply. He had already begun to privately question his superiors—who were now insisting that he join the Communist Party. He admired the communists' devotion to their cause, but he did not share their scorn for religion, disliked the way they punished or eliminated those who dared differ with them, and did not believe that whole classes of people—mandarins, landowners, intellectuals, businessmen—should be suppressed or annihilated, as they seemed to believe.

He also learned that other Asian colonies—India, Pakistan, and Burma—had recently won their independence without prolonged wars. And now that Bao Dai, the emperor whose forebears Chau's family had served, had returned to Vietnam as head of state, he began to

think there might be another way to win independence—a negotiated agreement between the emperor and Ho Chi Minh.

He wanted to help work toward that goal. But to do so, he would have to abandon the Viet Minh. It was not an easy decision. For five years, he later remembered, "we'd lived together as friends, as brothers," but in the end, Tran Ngoc Chau resolved to slip away from his comrades and make his way toward territory still controlled by the French.

ABOVE Tran Ngoc Chau

planners remained ambivalent about events in Indochina. The U.S. "fully recognized French sovereignty," Secretary of State George Marshall wrote, and was opposed to its being "supplanted by a philosophy emanating from and controlled by the Kremlin," but he also remained frankly baffled at the persistence of France's "outmoded colonial outlook." Why hadn't Paris been able to work more closely with the people of its colonies?

Paris argued that since Ho Chi Minh was a communist and only *pretending* to be a nationalist, it was pointless to seek a settlement with him. France hoped to win American support—and deflect Vietnamese support away from Hanoi—by installing Emperor Bao Dai as the titular head of a new "Associated State of Vietnam," ceding to him a handful of mostly meaningless powers, and then continuing to wage their war in his name. Paris hoped that this "Bao Dai solution" would help free their struggle from the taint of imperialism. (A few months later, Laos and Cambodia would also be made Associated States under local monarchs.)

Bao Dai himself, who had been Tokyo's puppet and now

CLOCKWISE FROM ABOVE LEFT The French War begins: Viet Minh troops barricade the streets of Hanoi in early December 1946, then struggle to defend their city against the French. Within a few days, French troops were in control. "If war is imposed on us," Ho Chi Minh told a French reporter before he fled Hanoi, "we will fight rather than renounce our liberties."

answered to Paris, ruefully admitted that the "solution" named for him was "just a French solution." Some in Washington saw through the smokescreen too.

But then, events overtook the United States. Back in February 1946—while Ho Chi Minh was still in Paris, arguing in vain for genuine Vietnamese independence—a junior U.S. diplomat stationed in Moscow named George F. Kennan had sent a secret telegram to his superiors in Washington. The Soviet threat was genuine, he argued, but neither open warfare nor concessions should be necessary to offset it, provided Washington pursued what he would call "a long-term, patient but firm and vigilant containment of Russian expansive tendencies."

Kennan's concept of containing Soviet power rather than attempting to roll it back would form the basis of American foreign policy for nearly half a century. To contain Moscow, Washington stationed the Sixth Fleet in the Mediterranean, provided aid to Greece and Turkey, undertook the enormous task of rebuilding western Europe, and responded to the Soviet seizure of Czechoslovakia and its blockade of Berlin by forming

UNDER TWO OPPRESSORS

"During the French War we lived under two oppressors: the Viet Minh and the French," remembered Tran Ngoc Hue—known as Harry Hue to his American friends. He was born in the imperial city of Hue in 1942, the great-great-grandson of a nineteenth-century soldier who committed suicide when Hanoi fell to the French and thereby became a nationalist hero.

In the chaos that followed the Japanese coup in 1945, eight-year-old Harry and his family fled to their ancestral village of Khe Mon, just twenty miles northeast of Hue, in a region largely controlled by the Viet Minh. There, he saw two sights he never forgot.

His father was away by then, serving as a junior officer in the embryonic Vietnamese National Army (VNA). It had been recently created by the French, ostensibly to defend their puppet emperor, Bao Dai, actually in the hope, as one Washington report put it, that "much of the stigma of colonialism can be removed

if, where necessary, yellow men will be killed by yellow men rather than by white men alone." The Viet Minh ambushed another VNA unit near the village.

The outnumbered troops surrendered. The Viet Minh dragged them into the center of the village. There, while Harry and the rest of the people watched, "they stripped them naked and buried them alive," he remembered. "They didn't want to waste a bullet on those people."

A few days later, French Legionnaires arrived, determined to punish Khe Mon even though the Viet Minh had long since disappeared. They rounded up everyone, burned a number of homes to the ground, and gang-raped one of Harry's young cousins.

"The French wanted to 'civilize' our country," Harry recalled, "and then they came and burned houses and raped and pillaged in a very evil, savage way. And on the other side, the Viet Minh claimed they were protecting the people against colonialism and then acted inhumanely.

Those images were seared into my consciousness and that's the reason that afterward I fought to protect the free South."

ABOVE Tran Ngoc Hue as a lieutenant colonel in the Army of the Republic of Vietnam, photographed at the Dong Ha firebase in 1969

the North Atlantic Treaty Organization, which pledged American protection to all of western Europe.

Until 1949, containment applied only to Europe. Then, everything seemed to change. In August, the Soviet Union exploded its own atomic bomb, ending America's monopoly on the world's most lethal weapon. A few weeks later came still more stunning news: America's Nationalist Chinese ally Chiang Kai-shek had been defeated by the forces of Mao Zedong; China, the most populous nation in Asia, was now in communist hands.

Republicans and some Democrats now accused the Truman administration of having "lost" China—as if it had somehow been America's to lose. Some charged that communists within the U.S. government itself had somehow been responsible.

In January 1950, Mao formally recognized the Viet Minh. Ho Chi Minh lost no time in asking China for the arms and equipment and military training he needed to continue his war with France. Mao agreed to help. Tens of thousands of Chinese workers hacked roads through the jungle so that Russian trucks

could carry arms and heavy weapons to the Vietnamese border. Meanwhile, in training camps within their own territory, Chinese advisers began turning General Giap's ragged army into a conventional modern fighting force. Within two years, Giap would command a well-armed regular army of 300,000 men, backed by a militia of nearly two million. Meanwhile, the Soviets recognized the Viet Minh, and also offered help.

On February 7, Washington recognized the Bao Dai regime.

International tensions continued to rise. In June, communist North Korea invaded South Korea, American troops were dispatched to repel them, and American suspicions that China and the Soviet Union were determined to conquer Asia seemed to be confirmed. "Communism was acting in Korea just as Hitler, Mussolini and the Japanese had ten, fifteen, and twenty years earlier," President Truman wrote. "I felt certain that if South Korea was allowed to fall, Communist leaders would be emboldened to override nations closer to our shores."

France encouraged the idea that Korea and Vietnam were

part of the same global conflict. "The war in Indochina is not a colonial war," one French commander claimed. "As in Korea, it is a war against Communist dictatorship."

The National Security Council now seemed to agree. It warned Truman that without U.S. help, France would be unable to defeat the Viet Minh, and once Vietnam fell, "the neighboring countries of Thailand and Burma could be expected to fall and the balance of power in Southeast Asia would be in grave hazard." An American diplomat in Saigon went further: If Vietnam were to fall, he warned Washington, "most of the colored races of the world would in time fall to the Communist sickle."

Accordingly, in July, Truman approved a $23 million aid program for the French in Vietnam—that number would rise to $100 million by year's end—and he quietly dispatched transport planes and a shipload of jeeps. Thirty-five military advisers went along to oversee their use. None of them—and no one in the American legation—spoke a word of Vietnamese.

The United States was no longer neutral. The Truman administration had firmly linked U.S. security to France's success in Indochina and turned a colonial conflict into a cold war confrontation—a proxy war. "Southeast Asia is [now] the center of the cold war," said the liberal *New Republic*. "Indo-China is the center of Southeast Asia. America is late with a program to save Indo-China. But we are on our way."

In the autumn of 1951, Massachusetts congressman John F. Kennedy undertook a trip around the world, meant to polish his foreign policy credentials for an upcoming run for the Senate. One evening he, his younger brother, Robert, and his sister Pat dined at the rooftop bar of the Hotel Majestic, overlooking Saigon. As they ate, they could see the flash of guns across the Saigon River. The next day, French commanders assured Kennedy that with more American support, French rule would soon be reestablished. But the congressman also spent two hours with Seymour Topping, a seasoned American reporter, who gave him a very different perspective: the French were losing, he said, and many Vietnamese who had once admired the Americans were beginning to despise them for backing the French. Kennedy believed the reporter. Unless the United States could persuade the Vietnamese that it was as opposed to "injustice and inequality" as it was to communism, he told his constituents when he got home, the current effort would result in "foredoomed failure."

The president's advisers did not share the young congressman's doubts, and when, in October 1952, American forces drove deep into North Korea and Chinese troops poured into North Korea to drive them back, Washington doubled, tripled, and then quadrupled its support for the French war in Indochina. By 1952, American taxpayers were paying more than one-third of the cost of France's war. When that conflict ended, the number had risen to nearly 80 percent.

NO MILITARY VICTORY IS POSSIBLE

BY 1953, the French had been fighting in Indochina for seven years. They had suffered over 100,000 deaths and failed to "pacify" the countryside. Six commanders had come and gone. Nevertheless, the seventh, General Henri Navarre, assured his countrymen upon arriving in Vietnam that year that victory was near: "Now we can see it clearly," he said, "like the light at the end of the tunnel."

Large sections of the French population had wearied of the war. Grieving for their dead and appalled by reports of French brutality, including the widespread use of napalm—gelatinized petroleum that burned foliage, homes, and human flesh—they began to call the conflict "la Sale Guerre"—the Dirty War. When returning French troops disembarked at Marseille, members of the left-wing longshoremen's union pelted them with rocks.

In July, the Korean War ended in a negotiated settlement and a still-divided peninsula. American policymakers saw it as proof that communism in Asia could be contained.

That fall, the French indicated their willingness to begin talks to end the fighting. Ho Chi Minh agreed to take part. Before the negotiators were to convene in Geneva the following May, each side sought to improve its position.

General Navarre set up a fortified base in a remote valley in northwestern Vietnam called Dien Bien Phu, where he hoped to lure the Viet Minh into a major set-piece battle. Navarre was certain that superior French firepower and the ability to call in air support would crush any attack by the Viet Minh and saw no serious threat from the jungle-covered hills that overlooked his eleven thousand men, dug in and around eight strongpoints on the valley floor. Dien Bien Phu was "like an immense stadium," one French soldier wrote home. "The stadium belongs to us; the bleachers in the mountains to the Viets." The French artillery commander was so confident of victory, he boasted that he had "more guns than I need."

General Giap saw his chance. "We decided to wipe out at all costs the whole enemy force at Dien Bien Phu," he remembered. To do it, he pulled off one of the greatest logistical feats in military history. A quarter of a million civilian porters—nearly half of them women—moved everything he needed for a siege, from sacks of rice to disassembled artillery pieces, on foot through the jungle for more than one hundred miles.

Giap surrounded the valley with fifty thousand men and two hundred big guns, dug-in and camouflaged so well they could not be spotted from the air. Thirty-one thousand more men provided support, and an additional twenty-three thousand personnel maintained supply lines back to the Chinese border.

On March 13, 1954, Viet Minh artillery on the hillsides began raining fifty shells a minute down onto the troops below. It was "like a hailstorm," one survivor recalled. "Bunker after bunker, trench after trench collapsed, burying men and weapons." The airstrip was destroyed. The besieged troops could only be reinforced and resupplied by airdrop. There was no way to lift out the wounded or the dead. The French artillery commander who had so badly underestimated the enemy blew himself up with a grenade.

The Viet Minh drew closer and closer, digging their way toward their trapped quarry. Outgunned and outnumbered, and unable to retreat, the French did their best to hold on while their desperate government appealed to Washington to intervene directly and strike the surrounding hills from the air.

President Dwight D. Eisenhower, a veteran soldier who had commanded Allied forces in Europe in World War II, was "horror-struck" by the predicament in which Navarre's troops found themselves. "They are just going to be cut to pieces," he said. He had been elected president in part because he'd promised to wage the cold war more aggressively than Truman had. And, as he explained in an April 7 press conference, he subscribed fully to what came to be known as the "domino theory."

You have a row of dominoes set up, and you knock over the first one, and what will happen to the last one is the certainty that it will go over very quickly. . . . When we come to the possible sequence of events, the loss of Indochina, of Burma, of Thailand, of the Peninsula, and Indonesia following, . . . now you are talking really about millions and millions and millions of people.

Some of Eisenhower's advisers, fearing that if the French were defeated at Dien Bien Phu they would abandon Indochina and leave the struggle against Ho Chi Minh up to the Americans, urged the president to authorize a massive nighttime bombing raid on Viet Minh positions. But Eisenhower refused open American intervention without congressional approval and support from Britain, America's closest European ally.

London refused to get involved. And, so soon after Korea, Congress was not in the mood for unilateral action. The president did secretly send American transport planes, their markings painted over and flown by civilian volunteers, to help resupply Dien Bien Phu. Two Americans died when their plane was shot down. But that was all the president was willing to do. "I am convinced," he confided to his diary, "that no military victory is possible in this theater."

Meanwhile, for the French at Dien Bien Phu, things went from bad to worse. Monsoon rains filled their trenches with three feet of mud. Wounded men drowned in the underground

TOP General Vo Nguyen Giap (left) in a still from a Soviet-made propaganda film about Dien Bien Phu **BOTTOM** During a brief lull in the shelling, a wounded French lieutenant emerges from a makeshift underground infirmary.

infirmary, where sixteen hundred helpless men eventually lay, maggots swarming over their wounds. Hidden loudspeakers ceaselessly demanded that they surrender or die.

The Viet Minh suffered, too. Mud also inundated their trenches. A single surgeon and six assistants struggled to meet the needs of fifty thousand men. Morale plunged. Political commissars harangued the wet, exhausted men, denouncing those who displayed doubt, fear, or combat fatigue for what they called "rightist tendencies." Had General Giap not been able to continually bring in fresh troops, the siege's outcome might have been different.

But on the afternoon of May 7, 1954, after fifty-five days of siege, the exhausted French forces at Dien Bien Phu finally surrendered. They had lost eight thousand men, killed, wounded, or missing. General Giap had lost three times as many, but he

ABOVE Twenty thousand men on specially reinforced bicycles carried rice and vegetables and other supplies to the Viet Minh at the front. "This method of transportation," General Giap remembered, "greatly surprised the enemy's army and completely upset his original calculations." **OPPOSITE** On the third day of shelling at Dien Bien Phu, French paratroopers run for cover. "We're done for," said one commander. "We're heading for a massacre."

had won a great victory and brought an end to what would come to be called the First Indochina War.

The next morning, representatives of the Vietnamese communists and those who opposed them, along with diplomats from nine nations, gathered in Geneva, hoping to settle the future of Indochina.

The talks, led by Great Britain and the Soviet Union, would drag on for nearly four months. Since the United States did not recognize the new communist regime in China, Secretary of State John Foster Dulles refused to speak to the chief Chinese negotiator, Zhou Enlai. The French puppet emperor Bao Dai would not parley with the Viet Minh. The Viet Minh—who now occupied four-fifths of Vietnam—demanded total French withdrawal from all of Indochina, Laos, and Cambodia, as well as Vietnam.

But now their Chinese allies refused to back them. China had lost nearly a million men in Korea, did not want to face the possibility of American troops again along its border, and was wary of Vietnamese domination of Laos and Cambodia. "I have come to Geneva to make peace," Zhou Enlai told a French delegate, "not [to] back the Viet Minh."

The Soviet Union agreed. Stalin had died, and for the moment, his successors hoped to ease tensions with the West.

Both of Ho's communist patrons pressed him to agree to a negotiated settlement, a temporary partition like the one that had finally brought the Korean War to its uneasy end. "It is possible to gain all Vietnam through peace," Zhou assured Ho. "It is possible to unite Vietnam through election when [the] time is ripe." And Ho faced other problems. The Viet Minh defeat of France had exacted a fearful cost. Its army was exhausted and depleted. If the war continued, there was no guarantee of final victory and there was always the chance that the United States still might intervene. He had no option but to give in. Once again, he would have to postpone his dream of a unified and independent Vietnam.

Vietnam was temporarily to be divided at the 17th parallel. For two years the two halves would be separated by a demilitarized zone until a plebiscite overseen by Canada, Poland, and India could be held to reunify North and South, a plebiscite everyone believed Ho Chi Minh was sure to win. In the interim, neither side was to join a military alliance or introduce fresh troops or permit foreign military bases to be established on its soil.

OPPOSITE Adding to the misery of the French troops trapped at Dien Bien Phu were day-and-night exhortations to surrender, broadcast from the surrounding hills. **ABOVE** Viet Minh march past the camera some of the ten thousand prisoners who surrendered to them at Dien Bien Phu. They include troops from French colonies in North and West Africa as well as France, Germany, and Indochina. **RIGHT** Vietnam divided

Under the provisions of the agreement, 130,000 French-led troops and their families would withdraw to the South. Simultaneously, somewhere between fifty thousand and ninety thousand southern Viet Minh regulars and their relatives would "regroup" to the North. "We promise our beloved compatriots that one bright and happy day we will return," one officer said as he packed to leave. Thousands of other Viet Minh and their sympathizers would remain in the South eager for that day, ready to vote to reunite their country and to fight for that cause if asked to do so.

Neither Washington nor a new anticommunist Vietnamese government based in Saigon signed the agreements, though they did agree to "respect" them. Even before the Geneva talks ended, American policymakers determined that Vietnam south of the 17th parallel must never come under communist rule, and sought somehow to turn the battered, demoralized region into a resilient anticommunist state.

THE BIGGEST LITTLE MAN IN ASIA

THAT TASK WOULD FALL to the man Bao Dai had appointed as his prime minister, Ngo Dinh Diem. Over the nine years that followed, Diem would routinely be denounced by his enemies as an American puppet, but those who tried to pull his strings were disappointed more often than not. From the first, he was his own man.

He was a veteran nationalist politician whose loathing for the French was matched only by his hatred for the communists who had briefly imprisoned him and buried alive his eldest brother and his nephew. A Roman Catholic in a largely Buddhist country, and a celibate bachelor who had once planned to be a priest, he was aloof, autocratic, and seemingly convinced always of the correctness of his decisions and the righteousness of his cause. He was mistrustful of anyone much beyond his own family. But he also proved to be a shrewd and ruthless political infighter, skilled at playing his rivals off against one another.

Born in Hue in 1901, the third of six sons of the high chamberlain of the imperial court, he had played many roles during his career—province chief in the French colonial government, Japanese ally, Viet Minh captive who nonetheless flirted briefly

OPPOSITE Fresh from his victory over the Binh Xuyen, President Ngo Dinh Diem paces in his Saigon palace in May 1955. "In [the] U.S. and [the] world at large," John Foster Dulles wrote, "Diem rightly or wrongly is becoming [a] symbol of Vietnamese nationalism struggling against . . . corrupt backward elements."

with joining Ho Chi Minh's government, and exile in Washington, where he lobbied for the establishment of what he called a "rallying point between the communists and the French"—a new independent government run by an anticommunist nationalist very like himself. Cardinal Francis Spellman of New York became one of his champions; so did John F. Kennedy, now a senator, and senators Mike Mansfield of Montana and Hubert Humphrey of Minnesota.

In the end, Bao Dai recalled, he chose Diem as his premier because "he was well known to the Americans, who appreciated his intransigence. In their eyes, he was the man best suited for the job and Washington would not be sparing in its support of him. . . . Yes, he was truly the right man for the situation."

Not every American official agreed. Secretary of Defense Charles Wilson and a number of senior military men had argued for immediate American withdrawal; they did not wish to become mired in another Asian conflict after Korea and thought it unlikely that the "Diem experiment" could possibly succeed. "Diem is a messiah without a message," one Saigon embassy official cabled Washington. "His only formulated policy is to ask immediate American assistance in every form."

Diem's first challenge was to manage the sudden influx of tens of thousands of refugees from the North. The Geneva Accords decreed that civilians living in either half of Vietnam who wanted to shift to the other would have just three hundred days to do so. Diem's fellow Catholics above the 17th parallel lived in fear of what the communist regime might do to them. Whole Catholic hamlets packed up to move, and the United States mobilized a flotilla of ships to carry them to safety in the South in an operation they called "Passage to Freedom." In the end, some 900,000 refugees—including more than half of all the Catholics living in the North—fled to the South and were resettled in villages of their own, a reliable source of support for Diem but a source of growing resentment among Buddhists.

Despite the influx of so many potential new supporters, Diem seemed to face insurmountable odds. No one—neither the Nguyen emperors nor the colonial French—had ever been fully in control of the Mekong Delta. The last part of the country to be settled by the Vietnamese, it was still considered a sort of frontier region, much of it virtually impenetrable—vast wetlands with thick forests along the Cambodian border—and its people lived in scattered, isolated communities.

At first, Diem's power did not extend much beyond his palace grounds. Rivals were everywhere. In addition to the Viet Minh cadre and the French colonists who wished him ill, warlords belonging to two rival religious traditions—the Cao Dai and the Hoa Hao—held large swaths of territory west of the capital. Much of Saigon itself was run by the Binh Xuyen—an eight-thousand-man criminal cartel who, with the connivance of the

CIVIL WAR

"The Vietnam War was a civil war right down to the family level," Duong Van Mai remembered. Her own family provided a vivid example. She and her eleven siblings grew up in cosseted comfort. Her father, the son and grandson of mandarins, was an important official under the colonial regime, not because of any special fondness for the French but because, when contrasted with the Viet Minh, he considered them "the lesser of two evils."

But when the French war began in 1946 and the family left Hanoi and moved to their ancestral village to escape the fighting, Mai's older sister, Thang, fled with her husband and their six-month-old son to join the Viet Minh in their mountain stronghold. Her parents, Mai remembered, were "ambivalent" about their decision, "objecting to their ideas for a social revolution but sympathizing with their struggle to recover national independence."

During the war, Mai's father served as mayor of Haiphong and governor of the surrounding Maritime Zone and helped organize training for the new Vietnamese National Army. Viet Minh assassins tried to kill him three times. But when news came of Dien Bien Phu, she remembered, her parents were "very proud that the Viet Minh had defeated the French. They felt admiration and respect on the one hand but fear on the other hand. And fear was the stronger emotion."

Mai was thirteen years old in 1954, when fear forced her and the rest of her family to flee the North and begin new lives in Saigon. "Saigon was like a foreign country to us at the time," she recalled.

Some hated us for having abandoned the Viet Minh and clung to the French; others saw us as carpetbaggers who were going to steal their jobs and their rice bowls, or who were going to drive up the price of everything and make life difficult for everyone. . . . Instead of seeing us as compatriots, many people thought of us as aliens: they called themselves "Vietnamese," while calling us "Northerners."

ABOVE Duong Van Mai, photographed in Saigon in 1960 **BELOW** Slogans on walls—some scrawled by CIA agents—urge northerners to flee communist rule. **OPPOSITE** Hundreds of Catholics crowd the dock at Haiphong, eager to board the USS *Montague* for the voyage to the South, part of the massive effort the Americans named Operation Passage to Freedom. By 1956, the diocese of Saigon had more practicing Catholics than Paris or Rome.

French, controlled prostitution, gambling, and the drug trade, as well as the police force meant to control them. And the Vietnamese National Army was commanded by General Nguyen Van Hinh, an ambitious soldier who owed his first loyalty to France and spoke openly of staging a coup to put himself in power.

Fearing the collapse of the fragile new regime, the U.S. embassy urged Diem to compromise with his rivals and create a "government of national union" in which they all could take part—and warned that aid might be cut off if he failed to go along. Instead, he resolved to pick off his enemies, one by one. First, he outmaneuvered General Hinh and sent him into exile, then began buying off warlords with U.S. funds provided by his admiring friend Colonel Edward Lansdale of the CIA.

On November 8, 1954, a "special presidential representative" arrived in Saigon from Washington with the rank of ambassador. General J. Lawton "Lightning Joe" Collins had fought on Guadalcanal, led troops in Normandy, and served as Army chief of staff during the Korean conflict. He told the press he had come to "give every possible aid to the government of Ngo Dinh Diem." But in fact, Eisenhower and Secretary of State John Foster Dulles had sent him to Vietnam to see if he thought continuing to sustain Diem was really in America's interest. Dulles himself was doubtful: he admired Diem but warned Collins that the chances of long-term success were no better than "one in ten."

Collins was a brusque, profane, by-the-book soldier with little interest in the complexities of Vietnamese politics, and quickly came to the conclusion that "Diem . . . represents our chief problem." He was too slow, too suspicious, and too stubborn ever to succeed. Collins warned Diem that America would no longer back him if he did not pursue a policy of "political means . . . without fighting" toward his enemies.

Again, Diem paid little heed. Instead, he moved against three of the armies that threatened his survival. He refused to renew the license that allowed the Binh Xuyen to reap its enormous profits from the city's wide-open vice and gambling district. And he told two of the warlords that their militias would no longer be receiving the subsidies the French had provided.

His rivals responded with an ultimatum: they wanted subsidies, cabinet posts, and permanent authority over the territories they dominated—and they wanted it all within five days. Collins tried to convince Diem and his rivals to get together. He was afraid that the Vietnamese troops he hoped to train to fight communists from North Vietnam were, instead, about to find themselves facing gangsters in the streets of their own capital.

The deadline passed. Diem rescinded Bao Dai's grant of police powers to the Binh Xuyen. The Binh Xuyen retaliated by attacking army headquarters—and shelling the palace. Scores of civilians were caught in the crossfire.

The French arranged a tenuous ceasefire. From his home on the French Riviera, Bao Dai demanded Diem's resignation. Diem ignored him. A full-scale civil war seemed only days away. Collins believed it would end in chaos—and an eventual communist takeover. He flew back to Washington, determined to persuade the president to end American support for Diem before it was too late. "[Diem's] inability to compromise, his inherent incapacity to get along with other able men, and his tendency to be suspicious of the motives of anyone who disagrees with him," Collins insisted, "make him . . . incapable of holding this government together."

Collins prevailed. On April 27, Secretary of State Dulles reluctantly cabled the American embassies in Paris and Saigon that there was to be a new South Vietnamese government; if Diem refused to support it, "the program should . . . be carried out anyway."

But just six hours later, Dulles received a telegram from Colonel Lansdale: open warfare had broken out in Saigon between Diem's army and the crime syndicate. Diem's forces had made an all-out assault on the Binh Xuyen—something General Collins had expressly told him he should not do. Troops on one side of the street battled those on the other. The fighting went on for three bloody days. Some five hundred civilians died. Twenty thousand more lost their homes. But in the end, Diem's forces prevailed. The surviving Binh Xuyen fled into the swamps south of the city, where many of those who failed to surrender were hunted down and killed. Diem's forces then went on to dismantle what remained of the Hoa Hao and Cao Dai militias.

Dulles hurriedly ordered the U.S. embassies in Paris and Saigon to burn his earlier cables: Diem had triumphed; the United States was now fully committed to him. "Whatever [the] U.S. view has been in the past," the secretary of state told America's Western allies, "today [the] U.S. must support Diem wholeheartedly."

The French, who had never trusted Diem to look out for their interests, now announced their intention to withdraw the last of their troops from South Vietnam. "That made [Diem] popular," one American remembered, "because he seemed to embody the nationalist cause in the South. Ho Chi Minh had only got the French out of the North. Diem drove the last Frenchmen from Vietnamese soil."

Flushed with victory, Diem called for a referendum between himself and Bao Dai. He left little to chance. In the old imperial capital of Hue, hundreds of suspected pro–Bao Dai voters were arrested just before election day. At the polls, government monitors kept track of who had voted for whom. The vote count was in the hands of Diem's supporters. When the votes were counted, Diem claimed to have won 98.2 percent of them. He got 200,000 more votes in Saigon alone than there were registered voters in the city.

Diem simultaneously proclaimed himself the first president of a brand-new Republic of Vietnam and announced that it would not participate in talks with the North unless it renounced "terrorism" and "totalitarian methods." The plebiscite on the question of reunification promised by the Geneva Accords would never take place. Instead, Diem believed, his republic would so swiftly outperform its northern rival and refugees would stream south in such numbers that the Hanoi regime would collapse and Vietnam would be reunified under his leadership. In the interim he saw to it that a new "representative assembly" packed with loyal supporters ratified a new constitution that invested in him as president executive powers more authoritarian than democratic. It allowed him to override any law he liked and suspend freedom of the press and assembly whenever he wished. A song dedicated to him, entitled "Adoration of President Ngo"—modeled after a song eulogizing Ho Chi Minh that was performed at public events in the North— was duly sung at schools and theaters following the national anthem.

"The president," Diem's new constitution said, "leads the nation." But he made sure that his family led it with him. All four of his surviving brothers wielded power of one kind or another: elder brother Ngo Dinh Thuc was the bishop of Vinh Long Province and later archbishop of Hue; Ngo Dinh Luyen served as Diem's ambassador to Great Britain; and Ngo Dinh Can was the warlord of central Vietnam, commanding a personal army and enriching himself by smuggling opium and siphoning off U.S. aid funds. But the most powerful—and to Americans as well as to many Vietnamese, the most sinister—brother proved to be Ngo Dinh Nhu. "If one hundred people came to Diem and called something white

and Nhu called it black," a close associate said, "Diem would believe Nhu." Nhu had helped mastermind Diem's rise to the premiership. He espoused a murky political philosophy called "personalism," supposedly a middle ground between liberal individualism and Marxist collectivism, that even its adherents

ABOVE A soldier loyal to President Diem, killed during the three-day battle with the Binh Xuyen, sprawls atop an armored vehicle in Saigon, May 8, 1955.

found hard to understand. He also ran a clandestine politi-cal party from within the president's palace that mirrored the techniques and ruthlessness of the communists, commanded his own Special Forces unit, and eventually supervised thirteen separate internal security organizations that spied on and seized enemies of the regime. His imperious wife, Tran Le Xuan—

ABOVE President Dwight Eisenhower, Ngo Dinh Diem, and Secretary of State John Foster Dulles at the White House, May 9, 1957. At a state dinner that evening, Eisenhower would toast his visitor for demonstrating "how much moral values and the concept of human dignity could count for in the minds of men." **OPPOSITE** Saigon's city hall displays the spectacularly skewed margin of Diem's referendum victory over Bao Dai, along with a portrait of the winner. While the referendum had been "a resounding success for the Diem government," the American ambassador admitted privately, "the results do not prove that Diem commands even majority support in South Vietnam."

better known as Madame Nhu—served as her bachelor brother-in-law's unofficial first lady and issued edicts of her own against contraceptives and divorce, gambling and prostitution, and beauty contests.

Under the slogan "Denunciation of the Communists," Diem set out to destroy the Viet Minh wherever its cadre and their sympathizers could be found. Tens of thousands of citizens were eventually imprisoned. Most were dedicated communists, but included among them were many people whose only crime had been having criticized Diem's regime. Hundreds were sent to Con Son Island, a former French prison two hundred miles off-shore in the South China Sea. Shackled prisoners were taken there by boat. Two paths led from the landing to the prison. One was named Ngo Dinh Diem Road, the other Ho Chi Minh Road. Those who chose the Ho Chi Minh Road were poorly fed, beaten, tortured, and chained inside so-called tiger

cages. More than twenty thousand are believed to have died there between 1954 and 1970. Survivors called it "the revolutionary university." One man remembered that the cruelty he experienced on Con Son Island had turned him into "hardened steel. My human feelings were leaving me. I was more than capable of doing the same things to my enemies that they were doing to me—no question. Without a moment's hesitation. The same and worse."

For better or worse, keeping South Vietnam from falling to the communists had become an American project. Most poli-

ticians, Democrats as well as Republicans, had come to share the current views of John F. Kennedy, just emerging onto the national stage. Now that South Vietnam was free of France, he said, it "represents the cornerstone of the Free World in Southeast Asia, the keystone to the arch, the finger in the dike. . . . If we are not the parents of little Vietnam, then surely we are the godparents . . . this is our offspring. We cannot abandon it; we cannot ignore its needs." If Vietnam fell—to chaos or poverty or communism—the United States would be "held responsible; and our prestige in Asia will sink to a new low."

When Diem made a state visit to the United States in the spring of 1957, praise for him was nearly universal. *Life* magazine hailed him as "The Tough Miracle Man of Vietnam." *Reader's Digest* saw him as the "Biggest Little Man in Asia." Thousands of New Yorkers turned out for a ticker-tape parade.

ABOVE Communist "regroupees" heading south to resume the revolutionary struggle, 1960. "They could not stand to let people in their native villages suffer under Diem's rule," one of them remembered, and "when they were finally allowed to go south they were exuberant."

And President Eisenhower himself called him "the greatest of statesmen, . . . an example for people everywhere who hate tyranny and love freedom."

To bolster Diem's regime, American civilian advisers descended on Vietnam, full of plans for reform and development, eager to turn South Vietnam into a showcase for how a beneficent America could help people help themselves.

Most important was an interdisciplinary team from Michigan State University headed by an early Diem admirer, the political scientist Wesley R. Fishel, who saw his mission as "saving" his friend's government. For seven years, he and his staff proposed American-style changes in everything from policing to public administration to the installation of traffic lights in Saigon.

Diem listened to them all, accepted almost $2 billion in aid between 1955 and 1960, and again and again went his own way. Americans urged him to make sweeping land reforms; he expropriated vast tracts of land from wealthy French and Vietnamese landlords but then failed to redistribute most of them among the landless. They suggested he encourage democracy on the local level; instead, he replaced elected village chiefs and village councils with outsiders, hand-picked by bureaucrats loyal to him. Urged to adopt principles of small-scale community development that had been adopted in India and elsewhere, he tried forcibly resettling thousands of people into new communities instead, and then required them to perform weeks of compulsory and uncompensated labor. "Coercion," he explained, "has had a vital role in most change."

Meanwhile, American advisers working for the U.S. Military Assistance and Advisory Group (MAAG) had arrived with orders to modernize, train, and equip Diem's newly named Army of the Republic of Vietnam, the ARVN. Like their predecessors, the 342 uniformed newcomers spoke no Vietnamese, and knew little about the country or its culture. Their commander was Lieutenant General Samuel "Hanging Sam" Williams, a tough-talking veteran of combat in both world wars and Korea. He understood that the immediate threat to the Diem regime came from local Viet Minh cadres, who, he said, needed to be "destroyed like vermin." But that was a "police-type task," he said, best left to two paramilitary forces: the fifty-thousand-man Self-Defense Corps, made up of small squads of local men expected to protect their own villages; and the 54,000-man Civil Guard, assigned to man scattered outposts throughout the countryside.

Williams's task was to create an up-to-date regular army, 150,000 well-trained men whose mission would be to hold the line against a full-scale conventional North Vietnamese invasion for at least a month, enough time for American forces to come to the rescue as they had done in Korea five years earlier.

A FEROCIOUS TIME

B UT NO ONE in North Vietnam was planning a conventional invasion. Hanoi's patrons, China and the Soviet Union, were steadily growing apart, and neither was willing to underwrite another war. And in any case, Ho Chi Minh and his comrades were focused on rebuilding their country. Years of fighting had taken a serious toll on North Vietnam. The French had deliberately destroyed a network of dikes. Rice production had plummeted. Railroads no longer ran. Vast areas had been abandoned by farmers who had fled to the cities for safety during the fighting.

The communists now imposed land reforms modeled on those imposed by Mao Zedong in China with a ruthlessness that left as many as fifteen thousand people dead, including not only landlords and their allies but many peasants who had fought in the ranks of the Viet Minh. Hanoi's policies were so harsh and uncompromising that one province was driven to open rebellion and had to be brought to heel.

Ho eventually apologized for "mistakes and shortcomings," as he had a decade earlier. But by the mid-1950s, more than half the families in North Vietnam had become landowners, and Ho Chi Minh—"Uncle Ho"—remained a hero to his people.

Diem's refusal to submit reunification to a vote had bitterly disappointed the North Vietnamese. Ho was still determined to reunite the country, but he felt that there was little he could do about it. He worried that if North Vietnam took direct military action, the United States would be drawn more deeply into the struggle, and so he cautioned his comrades in the South to avoid violence, to be patient and put their faith in political agitation. "Our policy," Ho explained, "is to consolidate the North and keep in mind the South."

That was cold comfort to embattled southern revolutionaries struggling to survive under the grim efficiency of Diem's increasingly harsh regime. It was "a ferocious time," one southerner remembered. "The enemy was brutally killing people," a village woman recalled. "Women lost their children and their husbands. Our leaders, our comrades observed the agreement, and did not allow any of us to break it. We didn't know what to do, we just had to accept it. I myself was very frustrated and wanted to do something."

By 1957, an estimated 90 percent of the Viet Minh cadre left behind in South Vietnam had been rounded up or eliminated; many of the rest were in hiding. They called upon the North more and more desperately for help, and some began to argue that their northern brethren were cowards.

As violence in the South intensified, other leaders began to emerge in Hanoi. Until his death, Ho Chi Minh would remain

how impressed he'd been by his eloquence and revolutionary fervor. "I had never heard anyone speak like that," he said. In the years that followed, he remembered, Le Duan seemed to embody the spirit of the southerners suffering under Diem: "The peasants in the countryside desperately wanted to rise up and Le Duan took that passion to the North."

Le Duan's passion was matched by his skill at political infighting, and he eventually rose to become general secretary of the party. As violence accelerated in the South, he and his hard-line allies steadily gained influence within the politburo until, in January 1959, the Central Committee of the Communist Party adopted a new program, remembered in Vietnam as "Resolution 15." It sanctioned armed force to "end the plight of the poor and miserable people in the South" and "defeat each wicked policy of the American imperialists and their puppets." The battle for reunification would still be fought by the South Vietnamese themselves—loyal Viet Minh as well as ordinary peasants who resented Saigon's brutal treatment of them—but Hanoi would do all it could to help them, short of waging war itself.

Bands of forty to fifty "regroupees"—armed southern Viet Minh—began slipping back across the 17th parallel into South Vietnam, following a network of jungle paths hacked through the Laotian mountains that would come to be called the Ho Chi Minh Trail. It was an arduous two-month trek. When the rice they carried ran out they subsisted on leaves and roots and birds they managed to trap. But the opportunity to strike back at the Saigon regime kept them moving. "For the liberation of our compatriots in the South," one regroupee wrote, "a situation of boiling oil and burning fire is necessary."

For most Americans, South Vietnam still seemed to be an American success story. On July 7, 1959, the fifth anniversary of Diem's coming to power, the editors of *The New York Times* wrote that "a five year miracle has been carried out. Vietnam is free and becoming stronger in defense of its freedom and ours. There is reason today to salute president Ngo Dinh Diem."

The next evening at Bien Hoa, twenty miles northeast of Saigon, six American advisers were watching a movie in their mess hall. In the darkness, guerrillas slipped silently into the compound and took up positions at the open windows. When an American snapped on the light to change reels, the guerrillas opened fire. Major Dale Buis from Pender, Nebraska, and Master Sergeant Charles Ovnand from Copperas Cove, Texas, were killed, the first Americans officially to die in the Vietnam War.

the face of the Vietnamese revolution around the world, but he was now sharing power with men who had grown impatient with his caution, men about whom Americans knew almost nothing. The most important would prove to be a single-minded one-time railroad clerk named Le Duan. He had joined the Indochinese Communist Party in 1930, survived nearly ten years of solitary confinement in a French prison, and coordinated Viet Minh and Communist Party activities in the South during the French War.

The writer Nguyen Ngoc, then a low-ranking cadre in the Viet Minh, encountered Le Duan in 1951 and later remembered

ABOVE Le Duan, photographed in 1951. Although he would be the central strategist of North Vietnam's war effort for more than a quarter of a century, he was little known or understood in Washington.

By the end of the year, some five hundred regroupees were in place in the South, more were on the way, and violence against the Diem regime was steadily accelerating. "I didn't have a gun so I made a bamboo spear for myself," one southerner recalled. "Twelve of us got together with twelve spears, and we went in to where a policeman was and we all stabbed him. And then we said that anyone who went to the funeral would be killed. No one dared go."

One hundred and fifty South Vietnamese officials were soon being murdered every month. Guerrillas began attacking ARVN patrols and isolated outposts, killing as many men as they could and seizing arms and ammunition supplied by the Americans. And for the first time, assassinations and lightning raids began to take place in central as well as southern Vietnam.

In retaliation, the Diem government enacted Law 10/59, which created mobile military tribunals empowered to stage public show trials that sent hundreds of men and women to their deaths, executed by portable guillotines ferried from one village to another. "In my village they cut off the head of a Viet Minh security guard," one man remembered, "and they invited all the people to watch. The idea was to intimidate them and crush the revolutionary movement. But all they succeeded in doing was making the revolution grow because we young people refused to be cowed. And we joined the revolution in greater numbers."

The struggle intensified. By the middle of the summer of 1960, there were running gun battles between revolutionaries and ARVN troops and mass anti-Diem demonstrations south of Saigon, with thousands of people gathered in one village or another to listen to speeches and shout slogans. Government officials and their sympathizers were forced to flee. Those who did not were sometimes beheaded with machetes in front of the crowd in order to intimidate anyone else tempted to side with Saigon. Many people, one villager recalled, felt as if they were living with two nooses around their necks, each pulling in the opposite direction.

These demonstrations and the violence that often accompanied them were remembered by the communists as "the Concerted Uprisings"—the real beginning of the mass revolt against the Diem government.

In mid-October 1960, Elbridge Durbrow, the American ambassador in Saigon, made a formal call on Independence Palace, hoping to have what he called a "frank and friendly talk" with the president. He told Diem that he feared he was "in quite serious danger," not only from the growing insurgency but also from widespread resentment of his own harsh security measures and rumors of widespread corruption and political favoritism. Durbrow suggested again that Diem welcome opposition leaders into his government and urged him to send his hugely unpopular brother and sister-in-law into exile abroad.

Diem angrily objected to everything the ambassador had to say, and promised nothing. He privately hated the reliance on the United States that made his critics call him *My-Diem*— "American Diem"—but he also understood that he could not survive without it. At the same time, he knew that if the United States was serious about maintaining South Vietnam as an anticommunist stronghold in Southeast Asia, it had no real choice except to stick with him.

On November 8, 1960, John F. Kennedy was elected president of the United States, narrowly defeating Vice President Richard Nixon. Ngo Dinh Diem was delighted. Kennedy was a fellow Catholic who had received him with special warmth during his state visit to Washington four years earlier and whose own vigorous anticommunism was beyond question. "American frontiers," Kennedy had said on the campaign trail, "are on the Rhine and the Mekong and the Tigris and the Euphrates and the Amazon. There is no place in the world that is not of concern to all of us. . . . We are responsible for the maintenance of freedom all around the world. . . . The enemy is the communist system itself—implacable, unceasing in its drive for world domination." Diem was sure that communication between Saigon and Washington was about to improve.

But three days after Kennedy's election, elite troops of the ARVN's Airborne Brigade seized parts of Saigon and began an assault on the Independence Palace itself, intent on toppling Diem and establishing a new military government. The Presidential Guard held them off while Diem stalled for thirty-six hours until loyal armored and infantry units could roll into the city and force the rebels to flee. It had been a close thing and only served to deepen the Ngo brothers' distrust of nearly everyone, now including the U.S. ambassador, whom they suspected of encouraging the coup plotters.

And more trouble was coming. On December 20, 1960, at Tan Lap, a remote jungle village near the Cambodian border, representatives of more than a dozen southern political parties and religious groups met to form a new front organization, dedicated to overthrowing Ngo Dinh Diem, ousting the Americans who supported him, and reuniting Vietnam under an ostensibly "neutral" government the communists believed they could quickly dominate. Behind the scenes, the politburo in Hanoi and the southern cadres who did its bidding would orchestrate everything. The new organization would be called the National Liberation Front—the NLF. It had an armed wing called the "People's Liberation Armed Forces," but in the eyes of its enemies in Saigon and Washington the revolutionaries were "Communist Traitors to the Vietnamese Nation"—the Viet Cong.

PATHS TO POWER

EDWARD MILLER

HO CHI MINH and Ngo Dinh Diem, the two best-known Vietnamese leaders of the Vietnam War era, have long been viewed as polar opposites. As the leader of North Vietnam during the 1950s and '60s, Ho was an icon of Third World revolution and international communism. Diem, in contrast, was a devout Catholic and anticommunist and was credited with "saving" South Vietnam from a takeover by the communist bloc. The ideological differences between the leaders were accented by their contrasting personalities and reputations. The image of Diem as an aloof mandarin stood in stark opposition to the genial "Uncle Ho" persona projected by his rival. And while popular memories of Diem are dominated mainly by the 1963 South Vietnamese army coup that resulted in his ouster and death, Ho is still remembered by many in Vietnam and elsewhere as the supreme hero of the Vietnamese revolution.

For all their differences, however, Ho and Diem also had a lot in common. Although they ended up on opposite sides of the cold war, they emerged from remarkably similar backgrounds, and their early lives and careers moved along parallel tracks. Both were born and grew up in Central Vietnam, which was the last part of Vietnam to be conquered and colonized by France. Both were members of elite families with patriotic reputations, and yet both had fathers who worked for the colonial state. As young men, Ho and Diem were deeply shaped by their interactions with French colonial leaders and institutions. Both initially tried to work as collaborators with the colonial system before eventually becoming anticolonial activists.

The most striking parallels between Ho and Diem had to do with their political ambitions. Both were activists who aspired to be state builders. Each dreamed of becoming the leader of an independent Vietnamese state and guiding his country toward its postcolonial future. Amazingly, despite the turmoil and war that wracked Indochina during the 1940s and '50s, they each found the means to realize this aspiration. As the founders of rival Vietnamese republics—Ho in 1945 and Diem in 1955—they both overcame long odds and endured considerable hardship. However, instead of ushering in an era of postcolonial peace, their remarkable political achievements laid the groundwork for a new conflict that would eventually become the Vietnam War. Ho Chi Minh and Ngo Dinh Diem took separate paths to power, but their destinies were intertwined from the outset.

THE MAKING OF "NGUYEN THE PATRIOT"

Ho Chi Minh's early life has long been shrouded in revolutionary myths, many of them crafted by official Communist Party biographers. Even the date of his birth is uncertain. We know he was born around 1890 in a rural village in Nghe An Province, one of the poorest in Vietnam. He was the son of a Confucian scholar who worked as a magistrate in the imperial bureaucracy of the Nguyen dynasty. In good Confucian fashion, Ho's father trained him to write Chinese characters and to read the books of the Chinese classical canon. When the son turned ten, his father gave him a new name: Nguyen Tat Thanh ("Nguyen the Accomplished").

Like many Vietnamese mandarins at the turn of the twentieth century, Ho's father was both a patriot and a collaborator with the French colonial state. As a loyal supporter of the Nguyen dynasty, he was dismayed by the French conquest of his country. Yet he also believed that collaboration with the French offered the best way for Vietnam to modernize and eventually regain its independence. On this point, he agreed with Phan Chu Trinh, a fellow mandarin from Central Vietnam who resigned his official post in 1904 so he could lobby the French to fulfill the "civilizing mission" they claimed to be pursuing in Indochina.

When Nguyen Tat Thanh was a teenager, his father arranged for him to attend the National Academy, a prestigious high school in the imperial capital of Hue. At the academy, Thanh learned French and studied a "Franco-Annamite" curriculum alongside the sons of court officials and the Nguyen royal family. He appeared on track to follow his father into the imperial bureaucracy.

In 1908, Central Vietnam was rocked by popular protests over taxes. Ho Chi Minh later claimed to have watched as colonial security forces killed several protestors at a demonstration. Communist Party accounts depict this episode as the moment when the young man dedicated himself to anticolonialism. But contemporary evidence suggests that Nguyen Tat Thanh did not shift so decisively away from collaboration—at least, not right away. Records show that he did not leave the National Academy until 1909. Moreover, his departure seems to have been triggered not by the protests but by a scandal involving his father, who was accused of the brutal beating of a criminal suspect.

Nguyen Tat Thanh drifted southward and eventually arrived in Saigon. In June 1911, he signed on as a cook aboard a French ocean liner headed to Marseille. In the official narrative of Ho's life, this move is represented as another deliberate step down a revolutionary path. Again, however, the available evidence points to other motives. Upon arriving in France, the young man immediately sought admission to the School of the Colonies, an institution that trained colonial subjects to serve as imperial administrators. His application stated that he "would like to become useful to France in relation to my compatriots, and would like at the same time to help them profit from the benefits of Instruction." Despite this explicit appeal to colonial ideals, his request was denied, due to his father's recent demotion.

Nguyen Tat Thanh spent the next several years crisscrossing the Atlantic and Indian Ocean basins, alternating between jobs at sea and manual labor on shore. He lived and worked in both the United States and in England. He also visited multiple colonized countries and met many Asian and African opponents of colonialism. But while he was sharpening his critique of French imperial policies, he had not yet become either an anticolonial revolutionary or a communist. Like his father, Thanh continued to admire Phan Chu Trinh and his advocacy of a reformist brand of collaboration. In 1918 or 1919, Thanh returned to Paris to live and work with Phan Chu Trinh and other Vietnamese political activists based there.

Thanh's continued interest in collaboration was revealed in his first high-profile political act: his participation in the drafting and publication of the 1919 manifesto entitled "The Claims of the Annamite People." Because Thanh signed this manifesto with the alias "Nguyen Ai Quoc" (Nguyen the Patriot), he has often been mistakenly portrayed as its sole author. And since he delivered a copy of the text to a U.S. official delegation in Paris headed by President Woodrow Wilson, the petition is sometimes depicted as a bid to win American support for Vietnamese independence.

In reality, Nguyen Ai Quoc (as Thanh would henceforth be known) coauthored the manifesto with several other Vietnamese activists, including Phan Chu Trinh. Moreover, the document was an explicit appeal for collaboration. It was addressed to the French government and made no mention of independence. Indeed, the word "Vietnam" did not appear in the text at all. Instead, the document called for the reform of the colonial system and for political freedoms for the "Annamite people." (The term "Annamite" was intended to reassure French officials, who avoided using "Vietnamese" because of its nationalist overtones.)

The main target of "Claims of the Annamite People" was Albert Sarraut, a senior colonial official and former governor-general of Indochina. Sarraut was both a republican and a socialist, as well as a strong believer in France's "civilizing mission." In April 1919, just two months before the manifesto appeared, Sarraut delivered a widely noted speech on the subject of "Franco-Annamese" collaboration. Among other things, he hinted at democratic reforms and eventual self-government for Indochina

within the French empire. In retrospect, it is evident that Sarraut's vision of collaboration was flawed and contradictory. But for many Vietnamese activists in 1919—including Quoc—it seemed to offer exciting new possibilities.

It was only after Sarraut and other French leaders failed to deliver on their reform promises that Quoc began to sour on collaboration. In 1922, following a contentious face-to-face meeting with Sarraut, Quoc published a caustic denunciation of the Frenchman's record in Indochina. Under Sarraut's governorship, Quoc wrote, his country had experienced "an increasing number of spirit and opium shops which, together with firing squads, prisons, 'democracy' and all the improved apparatus of modern civilization, are combining to make the Annamese the most advanced of the Asians and the happiest of mortals."

Quoc's shift from reform to resistance coincided with his embrace of revolutionary socialism and Marxism-Leninism. In 1920, he read *Theses on the National and Colonial Questions* by V. I. Lenin, the head of the Bolshevik Party and founding leader of the Soviet Union. While most socialist theorists downplayed the prospects for revolutions in colonial territories, Lenin hypothesized that the colonies were actually full of revolutionary possibilities. Quoc was especially inspired by Lenin's two-stage theory of anticolonial revolution, in which an initial "national liberation" revolt against European imperial rule would be followed by class struggle and the creation of a socialist system.

In late 1920, Quoc joined a group of radical socialists as a cofounder of the French Communist Party. His writings took on an increasingly Marxist-Leninist cast. In 1923, he slipped out of France and made his way to Moscow. There, he was recruited to work for the Communist International (Comintern), the Soviet agency that promoted communist revolution around the world. By late 1924, Quoc was in southern China, building a new revolutionary organization meant to operate inside Indochina. These efforts culminated in 1930 with the establishment of the Vietnamese Communist Party at a secret meeting organized by Quoc in Hong Kong.

Quoc envisioned the party as a Leninist organization, dedicated to the idea that national liberation would precede the establishment of socialism. But not all of his fellow communists agreed. In late 1930, Quoc was ousted as party leader after the Comintern line shifted to emphasize the primacy of socialism over nationalism. He spent the next several years in a kind of revolutionary limbo, eventually ending up back in the Soviet Union during Joseph Stalin's Great Terror of 1936–38, when many of his fellow Comintern operatives were jailed or killed.

In retrospect, Quoc's disillusionment with the French "civilizing mission" and his subsequent discovery of Marxism-Leninism were key turning points in his revolutionary career. Nevertheless, his journey toward resistance and revolution was far from a complete rejection of the ideals of his youth. Quoc was a dedicated communist, but he was also a nationalist who came of age at a time when patriotism and collaboration with the colonial state did not yet seem mutually incompatible, and when the meaning of revolution was still framed in Confucian terms. In this regard, he had more in common with his archrival Ngo Dinh Diem than either his admirers or his critics later cared to admit.

MAN OF FAITH

At first glance, the arc of Ngo Dinh Diem's early life and career appears radically different from that of Ho Chi Minh. Unlike Ho, who left Vietnam when he was a young man and spent thirty years abroad, Diem lived his entire youth and young adult life in his native land and did not take his first trip outside of Indochina until he was in his late forties. Diem also enjoyed substantial success as an imperial mandarin—the career that eluded Ho. And while Ho became a socialist and a communist, Diem was a devout Catholic who abhorred communism and who rejected the Marxist idea of class struggle as the driver of positive social change.

For all of their obvious differences, however, the two men had much in common. Like Ho, Diem was raised in Central Vietnam by a domineering father who was a Confucian, a patriot, and a collaborator. And while Diem succeeded for a time in forging his own career in the colonial administration, he eventually reached the same conclusion that Ho did about the French and their "civilizing mission." Most important of all, Diem shared Ho's interest in combining Vietnamese values and traditions with ideas and models from outside of Vietnam. "We are not going back to a sterile copy of the mandarin past," he once remarked. "We are going to adapt the best of our heritage to the modern situation."

Diem was the third son of Ngo Dinh Kha, a devout Catholic and prominent Nguyen dynasty official. Kha, who spent his youth studying under European missionaries at a Catholic seminary in Malaya, was an avid proponent of the "Franco-Annamite" educational system. In the 1890s, Kha helped establish the National Academy—the high school in Hue that Ho and Diem would both later attend. Around the time of Diem's birth in 1901, Kha became the grand chamberlain of the imperial court.

By outward appearances, Ngo Dinh Kha seemed a model colonial collaborator. But his collaboration was not predicated on blind faith in the French. At the royal court, Kha led a faction of reform-minded Catholics who accused France of breaking treaty-guaranteed promises to allow the Nguyen emperor to retain certain administrative powers. Colonial officials had little patience for such criticisms. In 1907, they abruptly removed the sitting emperor from the throne and sent him into exile. Kha angrily resigned in protest at this blatant disregard of Vietnamese sovereignty. In the process, he gained a reputation as an anti-French patriot. Kha's Vietnamese admirers coined a proverb to celebrate his actions: "To deport the king, you must get rid of Kha."

From childhood, Diem was shaped by the same mixture of colonial idealism, religious identity, and patriotic principle that defined his father's career. Following his graduation from the National Academy, he briefly considered becoming a priest, like his older brother Ngo Dinh Thuc. Since Diem had already sworn a vow of celibacy—a pledge he apparently kept his entire life—he seemed well suited for such a path. But his ambition and his interest in power led him to choose a career in government instead. After two years of study in Hanoi, Diem became a junior mandarin at the age of twenty. Thus began his rapid ascent through the administrative ranks. By the time he turned thirty, Diem was in charge of an entire province. In this capacity, he claimed to have crushed an uprising instigated by the local members of Ho's newly established Communist Party.

Diem's rise through the imperial bureaucracy was aided by the same group of patriotic Catholic reformers who had earlier backed his father. In 1933, the colonial government tried to mollify Diem and his allies by making him minister of the interior in the cabinet of Bao Dai, a teenager who had just been installed as emperor. By co-opting Diem, the French hoped to use his nationalist reputation to shore up the legitimacy of both the monarchy and the colonial state. But Diem refused to play along. In a move that mirrored his father's actions a quarter century earlier, he resigned after just two months on the job, citing French disrespect for the emperor's authority and their refusal to allow even small steps toward self-rule.

Diem's rejection of the French and Bao Dai strongly enhanced his stature as an uncompromising critic of the colonial state. But it also ended his career as a mandarin and left him without a clear route back to power. Diem spent the rest of the 1930s living quietly in Hue, under the watchful eye of the police. Except for occasional appearances with his older brother Thuc, who in 1938 became one of the first Vietnamese priests to be elevated to the rank of bishop, Diem kept mostly out of the public eye. Like Ho Chi Minh, Diem had definitively rejected the idea of collaboration with the colonial state on its own terms. But in the late 1930s, his chances of devising an effective alternative strategy seemed as poor as those of Ho, who was still languishing in exile in the Soviet Union. For both Ho and Diem, the opportunity to resume their political careers would come only in the following decade, with the onset of war and the arrival of new foreign actors in Indochina.

REVOLUTIONARY CONDITIONS

World War II was a time of both danger and opportunity for anticolonial activists in Southeast Asia. In 1940, Imperial Japan demanded control of key military bases across Indochina. French colonial officials were dismayed, but had no choice but to comply, given that most of metropolitan France had already been conquered by Nazi armies. Over the next five years, Indochina endured a bizarre dual occupation by French and Japanese regimes that deeply mistrusted each other.

The Japanese occupation provided Nguyen Ai Quoc the opportunity he needed to regain leadership of the Vietnamese Communist Party, now renamed the Indochinese Communist Party. Although he returned to China from the Soviet Union in 1938, Quoc did not recover effective control of the ICP until May 1941, when he crossed the border into northern Vietnam, ending three decades of exile. At a key meeting of senior party leaders held in a mountain cave, Quoc announced the creation of a new front organization: the League for Vietnamese Independence, known simply as the Viet Minh.

In keeping with the two-stage theory of revolution that Quoc had developed, the Viet Minh was an ostensibly noncommunist organization dedicated solely to the cause of national liberation. In propaganda and recruitment, the front strongly emphasized national liberation and opposition to both the French and the Japanese. Socialism and communism were hardly mentioned. The Viet Minh also organized rudimentary militia forces and established a large "liberated zone" in the Northern Highlands.

As the Viet Minh movement grew, Quoc was anxious to gain foreign backing. With the Soviet Union preoccupied with the war against Nazi Germany in Europe, he turned to the Allied powers who were actively fighting against Japan—specifically, to Nationalist China and the United States. During the war, Quoc secretly traveled back to southern China twice to meet with Chinese and American officials and to offer his cooperation. (It was during one of these trips that he first began using the alias Ho Chi Minh.) U.S. commanders eventually agreed to dispatch a small team of American operatives to the Viet Minh zone in northern Indochina to provide light weapons and training to the rebels. The American aid was insignificant from a military standpoint, but its delivery reflected Ho's intense interest in obtaining outside support.

Diem also sought foreign backing during the war years, but from a different source: Imperial Japan. For Diem, cooperation with Japan was a calculated risk. On the one hand, the country was an expansionist empire that obviously aimed to dominate all of East and Southeast Asia. On the other hand, the Japanese occupation of Indochina was relatively benign compared to the brutal military campaigns that Tokyo's forces waged in China

and elsewhere in the region. Moreover, many of the Japanese military officers and diplomats stationed in Indochina backed the cause of Vietnamese national liberation, and argued that the French regime should be replaced with a Vietnamese government under Japanese sponsorship. Several of these Japanese "idealists" lent support to Diem and protected him and his supporters from French harassment and arrest.

In the spring of 1945, it briefly appeared that Diem's Japanese gambit was going to pay off. As Allied naval forces drew closer to Indochina, Japanese leaders decided to end their marriage of convenience with the French. On the night of March 9, imperial troops detained senior French colonial officials, bringing French rule over Indochina to an abrupt end. To replace the French, Japanese commanders installed the Nguyen emperor Bao Dai as the ruler of a reconstituted "Empire of Vietnam." Bao Dai immediately asked Diem to serve as prime minister of the new government. For reasons that remain unclear, Diem turned down Bao Dai's invitation. Had he accepted, Vietnam's postcolonial era might have unfolded very differently.

As it happened, it was Ho, not Diem, who emerged as Vietnam's preeminent nationalist leader in 1945. In August, just five months after the Japanese coup against the French, World War II came to a dramatic end in the wake of the atomic bombings of Hiroshima and Nagasaki. The unexpectedly early conclusion of the war created a power vacuum in Indochina. Ho and the Viet Minh moved rapidly to fill it. Over a two-week period that became known as the August Revolution, hastily organized Viet Minh "people's committees" seized control of cities, towns, and villages across Indochina. On September 2, Ho stood before a cheering crowd of hundreds of thousands in Hanoi and proclaimed the formation of a new and independent Vietnamese state: the Democratic Republic of Vietnam.

Its creation was a historic achievement, but it was also a tenuous one. Despite its popularity, Ho's new state was exceedingly weak, in desperate need of experienced personnel, reliable communications, and funds. Since the entire membership of the Indochinese Communist Party at this time totaled only about five thousand cadres in all of Indochina, Ho could not initially count on the party to staff or administer his government. The fledgling state also lacked effective military forces and foreign allies, which deeply worried Ho, since the French had already signaled their determination to reestablish colonial rule in Indochina.

For more than a year after the August Revolution, Ho desperately sought to avoid war with France through diplomacy and negotiation. He continued his outreach to the United States, hoping that Washington would pressure Paris to reconsider its plans to restore its empire. But Ho realized that the U.S. would not provide recognition or aid in the absence of an agreement with France. So he opted for direct negotiations with Paris, in the hope that the two sides might reach a deal for gradual decolonization. In the spring of 1946, Ho went to France for several months of talks with colonial officials. It was a risky gamble that did not pay off. By the time he sailed back to Indochina that fall, both sides were preparing for war. Ho's actions came in for considerable criticism among party members, some of whom argued that war was both inevitable and preferable to any compromise with the hated French.

It was during this anxious period that Ho and Diem had their first and only face-to-face meeting. Shortly after the August Revolution, Diem was detained by Viet Minh forces in Central Vietnam. In early 1946, they brought him to see Ho, who professed admiration for Diem and offered him a cabinet position in the unity government he was trying to build. Diem was willing, but only if Ho granted him substantial powers over DRV internal security forces. Ho refused. He then ordered Diem released, over the objections of other party leaders. Asked why he allowed a dangerous rival to walk free, Ho cited the reputation of Diem's father, Ngo Dinh Kha. "The memory of such a father prevents us from laying a hand on the son," he declared. More than his comrades, perhaps, Ho understood that allies and alliances would be critical in the struggles that lay ahead.

WARRING STATES

The war that began in Indochina during 1945–46 and lasted until 1954 was a complex event defined by three main axes of conflict. First and most obviously, the war was a decolonization struggle between France and the Viet Minh, fought to settle the question of the Democratic Republic's independence. At the same time, the war was also a civil war among multiple Vietnamese groups and factions. The antagonists in this second struggle included not only communists and other supporters of the new government but also many noncommunist Vietnamese who espoused their own visions of their country's postcolonial future. Finally, the Indochina War gradually became a cold war conflict, in which three major international powers—the United States, the Soviet Union, and the People's Republic of China—played key roles. For both Diem and Ho, devising an effective strategy to address all three of these overlapping conflicts would prove a daunting task.

From the outbreak of general hostilities until around 1949, Ho Chi Minh continued to emphasize national unity and outreach to noncommunist groups and leaders. But within the party, other leaders were pushing for a different approach. Several key figures, such as General Secretary Truong Chinh, wanted more attention to the party's advocacy of socialist revolution. These leaders also favored alignment with the Soviet Union.

In October 1949, the strategic situation inside Indochina was transformed by the triumph of Mao Zedong and his Chinese Communist Party in China's long civil war. Shortly afterward, China and the Soviet Union officially recognized Ho's government and began supplying military aid and advisers to Viet Minh forces across the border in northern Vietnam. The assistance greatly improved Viet Minh battlefield capabilities and enabled them to launch their first major offensive of the war. It also afforded the Chinese advisers the chance to press their Vietnamese counterparts to demonstrate their commitment to Marxist-Leninist ideology. In 1951, the Indochinese Communist Party, which had been operating in secret, reemerged under a new and more doctrinaire-sounding name: the Vietnam Worker's Party. The party also stepped up its plans for socialist-style mass mobilization, including a military draft and a land reform campaign.

The 1949–50 period was also a turning point for Diem. Following his release by Ho in 1946, Diem spent three mostly fruitless years trying to build a coalition of noncommunist nationalists. Then, in 1949, he confronted a major new political development: the establishment of a new anticommunist Vietnamese state, known as the Associated State of Vietnam (ASVN). It was the brainchild of French colonial officials who viewed it as a way to attract noncommunist Vietnamese nationalists who might otherwise back Ho and the DRV. To bolster the new state's legitimacy in the eyes of Vietnamese conservatives, the French selected the ex-emperor Bao Dai (who had abdicated his throne during the August Revolution of 1945) to serve as chief of state.

Bao Dai's first move was to ask Diem to serve as prime minister. As before, Diem declined the former monarch's offer. Instead, he announced plans to launch an independent anticolonial political movement that would be aligned with neither the French nor the Viet Minh. Unfortunately for Diem, his call attracted little substantive support. Viet Minh leaders responded by putting his name on a list of political figures marked for assassination.

With his political fortunes ebbing, Diem embarked on a new strategy. In 1950, he departed Indochina on what would eventually become a four-year overseas exile. Diem spent much of that time in the United States, where he sought to impress American leaders with his principled opposition to both colonialism and communism. He did not win any official pledges of U.S. support during his stay in America, but he did use his Catholic connections to meet with sympathetic journalists, academics, and members of the U.S. Congress—including the newly elected Massachusetts senator John F. Kennedy. Many of these Americans would champion Diem after he became leader of South Vietnam.

In the spring of 1953, Diem crossed the Atlantic to Europe, with the goal of patching up his relationship with Bao Dai. (Despite serving as titular head of the Associated State of Vietnam, Bao Dai preferred life on the French Riviera.) This proved to be the most prescient and decisive move of Diem's career to date. While Bao Dai had not forgotten Diem's previous refusals, he recognized that the Catholic leader's reputation as an uncompromising nationalist and anticommunist would bolster the legitimacy of the ASVN. In addition, Bao Dai was impressed by Diem's younger brother Ngo Dinh Nhu, who had emerged as a leading voice in nationalist circles in Saigon. The ex-emperor also calculated that Diem would strengthen the ASVN's ties to the United States, given his connections to Americans.

Meanwhile, Ho and the Viet Minh were preparing for their biggest military gamble of the war: the siege of the French garrison in the northern mountain valley of Dien Bien Phu. To prepare for the operation, commanders pushed their forces to the breaking point, ordering hundreds of thousands of porters to transport weapons and supplies over rugged terrain. Once the siege began, Viet Minh fighters endured such hellish combat, plummeting morale, and heavy casualties that Vo Nguyen Giap, the Viet Minh commander in charge, briefly considered raising the siege. But his Chinese advisers persuaded him to continue. On May 7, 1954, the last French outpost surrendered. Ho and the Democratic Republic finally had the high-profile military success they had long sought.

But victory on the battlefield did not translate into triumph at the negotiating table for the Viet Minh. During the summer of 1954, an international conference at Geneva produced a compromise peace agreement: Vietnam was temporarily split at the 17th parallel, with Ho's DRV administering the northern half of the country and the ASVN (which Diem now headed) taking over the South. The division was supposed to last only until 1956, pending the results of all-Vietnam elections to choose a new, unified national government.

Many Communist Party members and DRV supporters were dismayed by the terms of the Geneva peace treaty. But Ho argued for accepting them. He did so in part because of pressure from his Soviet and Chinese allies, and because he expected that the Viet Minh would win the elections easily. He also feared the possibility of American military intervention against his exhausted forces if the war continued.

The promised elections were never held, due mainly to the opposition of Diem. Although he faced a bewildering array of hostile parties and factions when he took power in Saigon in mid-1954, Diem outmaneuvered all of them through a combination of intrigue, bribery, and military force. By the summer of 1955, he was strong enough to announce that South Vietnam (as the Associated State was now called) would not participate in the 1956 elections. Senior U.S. government officials, though initially skeptical about Diem and his staying power, put aside their doubts and gave him strong backing. From his capital in Hanoi, Ho protested bitterly, but to no avail. In October 1955, Diem ousted Bao Dai from power in a carefully stage-managed referendum. Three days after the vote, he announced the birth of a new state, known as the Republic of Vietnam.

Diem's creation of the Republic of Vietnam in 1955, like Ho's establishment of the Democratic Republic of Vietnam ten years earlier, was a remarkable achievement. Indeed, the two leaders and the states they founded can be thought of as the primary winners of the Indochina War. Although Ho and the Democratic Republic had paid a far higher price for its victory, Diem and the Republic of Vietnam had also emerged from the conflict with a plausible claim to lead Vietnam into the postcolonial era. In this regard, both Diem and Ho had accomplished far more by 1955 than anyone could have imagined twenty years earlier.

But even though Ho and Diem had each realized some of their most cherished ambitions, neither man was content. The era of colonial rule had ended, but the conflicts among Vietnamese appeared more sharply drawn than ever before. With Vietnam's territory now evenly divided between rival republics, the prospects for lasting peace seemed tenuous at best. In the years that lay ahead, the fates of Diem and Ho—and the states they led—would remain deeply intertwined. The consequences for them and their compatriots would prove far more destructive than either leader ever anticipated.

CHAPTER TWO

RIDING THE TIGER

1961–1963

Exhausted South Vietnamese
soldiers crowd the deck of
a U.S. Navy troop carrier,
returning to the provincial
capital of Ca Mau after four
days and nights of combat
operations in the swamps of
South Vietnam's southernmost
province, August 1962.

ANOTHER KIND OF WARFARE

ON THE EVENING of January 19, 1961—the eve of John F. Kennedy's inauguration as the thirty-fifth president of the United States—he sent his closest aides copies of a speech the Soviet premier Nikita Khrushchev had just delivered to an international communist gathering in Moscow. "Comrades, we live in a splendid time," Khrushchev had told his fellow party members. "Communism has become the invincible force of our century." Since Soviet military might was now commensurate with that of the West, he said, the "Imperialists" could no longer "unleash a world war." But "national liberation wars [will] continue as long as imperialism exists, as long as colonialism exists" and "Communists [will] fully support such just wars and march in the front rank with the peoples waging liberation struggles."

Attached to each copy of the speech was a note from the president-elect: "Read, mark, learn and inwardly digest. . . . This is our key to the Soviet Union. Our actions, our steps should be tailored to meet these kinds of problems."

The inaugural address Kennedy delivered the following morning made clear that he had already digested Khrushchev's words. "Let every nation know," he said, "whether it wishes us well or ill, that we shall pay any price, bear any burden, meet any hardship, support any friend, oppose any foe to assure the survival and the success of liberty." Then, he warned the people of the Third World of the dangers of aligning themselves with the Soviets and the Chinese.

To those new states whom we welcome to the ranks of the free, we pledge our word that one form of colonial control shall not have passed away merely to be replaced by a far more iron tyranny. We shall not always expect to find them supporting our view. But we shall always hope to find them strongly supporting their own freedom—and to remember that, in the past, those who foolishly sought power by riding the back of the tiger ended up inside.

At forty-three, Kennedy was the youngest man ever elected president. He had promised bold new leadership, and was eager to show the world that the United States had both the power and the flexibility to confront communism in every form, on every front. And he had gathered around him an extraordinary set of advisers who shared his determination, including Dean Rusk as secretary of state—Rhodes Scholar, State Department veteran, former president of the Rockefeller Foundation; National Security Advisor McGeorge Bundy—a political scientist and former dean of the faculty at Harvard, and his deputy, Walt Whitman Rostow, an economist and advocate of Third World development who had taught at Oxford, Cambridge, and MIT; and, as secretary of defense, forty-seven-year-old Robert McNamara—a liberal Republican and ardent advocate of systems analysis, who gave up his post as president of the Ford Motor Company to serve his country.

Like the young president, all of them had served during World War II. Each had absorbed what they all believed was its central lesson: ambitious dictatorships needed to be halted in their tracks before they constituted a serious danger to the peace of the world. "Like most Americans," McNamara remembered many years later, "I saw communism as monolithic. I believed the Soviets and the Chinese were cooperating in trying to extend their hegemony." To him—and to Kennedy and most of the men closest to him—it seemed clear that the "Communist movement in Vietnam was closely related to guerrilla insurgencies in Burma, Indonesia, Malaya and the Philippines. . . . We viewed these conflicts not as nationalistic movements—as they largely appear in hindsight—but as signs of a unified communist drive for hegemony in Asia."

Kennedy's men also shared his belief that in a nuclear age the United States needed to find ways to wage and win less dangerous, limited wars like the ongoing struggle in Vietnam. "This is another type of warfare," Kennedy said, "new in its intensity, ancient in its origin—war by guerrillas, subversives, insurgents, assassins, war by ambush instead of by combat; by infiltration, instead of aggression."

But for all of Kennedy's soaring rhetoric, for all the talent he gathered around him, the first months of his administration went badly: the president failed to call off a CIA-inspired invasion of Cuba that ended in disaster; he was unable to keep Khrushchev from building the Berlin Wall; and he was harshly criticized when, rather than commit U.S. forces to fight communist guerrillas in the jungles of Laos, as ex-President Eisenhower had urged him to do, he had instead agreed to enter negotiations aimed at "neutralizing" that kingdom.

"There are just so many concessions that we can make in one year and survive politically," he told a friend in the spring of 1961. "We just can't have another defeat this year in Vietnam."

During that spring and summer, Kennedy did his best to meet Ngo Dinh Diem's requests for enlarging his military.

Diem responded with somewhat graceless gratitude for the U.S. president's response to what he called the "wise and far-sighted proposals . . . which I myself have advocated for four years or more."

Kennedy sent to Saigon as his ambassador Frederick Nolting, a career diplomat who saw it as his "first commandment" to restore the Ngo brothers' trust in Washington. He also dispatched Vice President Lyndon Johnson to talk with Diem, whom Johnson publicly hailed as "the Winston Churchill of Southeast Asia." (When a newspaperman asked him off the record if he really was so admiring, the vice president answered, "Shit, Diem's the only boy we have out here.") There was talk of a "joint program of action," too, but it foundered when Washington again called for reforms Diem and Nhu were unwilling to make.

OPPOSITE John F. Kennedy delivers his inaugural address. "It was one of the most glorious of inaugurals," an aide remembered. "The Kennedy presidency began with incomparable dash." Seated to Kennedy's right are the outgoing president, Dwight Eisenhower, and Earl Warren, chief justice of the United States; to his left are incoming vice president Lyndon Johnson and outgoing vice president Richard M. Nixon.
ABOVE Defense Secretary Robert S. McNamara in his Pentagon office, 1961. Behind him is a portrait of James V. Forrestal, the first U.S. secretary of defense, appointed by President Harry Truman.

Meanwhile, the military situation steadily deteriorated. Late that summer, the journalist Theodore H. White visited Vietnam and wrote privately to the president of his concern. "The situation gets worse almost week by week," he reported. "I say this despite the optimistic bullshit now hitting the papers." The guerrillas now controlled much of the Mekong Delta, "so much so that I could find no American who would drive me outside Saigon in his car even by day without military convoy."

There is a political breakdown here of formidable proportions. . . . If we mean to win, perhaps we must do more. But what? If there is another coup against Diem by his army should we support it? If there is no natural coup and we are convinced that Diem is useless, should we incubate one? If we feel bound by honor not to pull or support a coup, shall we lay it on the line to Diem and intervene directly . . . or should we get the Hell out?

What perplexes the hell out of me is that the Commies on their side seem to be able to find people willing to die for their cause. I find it discouraging to spend a night in a Saigon nightclub full of young fellows of 20 and 25 dancing and jitterbugging . . . while twenty miles away their Communist contemporaries are terrorizing the countryside.

Three levels of communist forces were now working to destroy the Saigon regime. Most numerous were the part-time militia— farmers and their families who worked their fields by day but operated in small squads at night, defending their villages, staging small ambushes, sabotaging roads, providing supplies and intelligence for the full-time forces that came and went at will. Singling them out from the local populace, one weary American adviser would remember, was "like looking for tears in a bucket of water."

Regional Force companies served under provincial or district leadership. They were more mobile, more thoroughly schooled in class doctrine, and better armed than their part-time counterparts, and tasked with attacking government outposts and ambushing small convoys. They also sometimes aided the Main Force regulars who operated under orders from the Central Office for South Vietnam—COSVN—the communist command center hidden away in a corner of Tay Ninh Province near the Cambodian border.

In September, a thousand-man Main Force unit seized a provincial capital less than sixty miles from Saigon and held

Communist guerrillas, camouflaged with palm fronds, outflank an ARVN unit somewhere in the Mekong Delta or the Plain of Reeds.

it for six hours, during which they managed to capture a large cache of arms and ammunition, free 250 of their comrades from prison, and behead the province chief and his top aide in front of a big crowd. Since Kennedy took office, the number of armed and active communist "regulars" was thought to have risen from seven thousand to seventeen thousand. They now controlled a third of the country—and more than that after the sun went down.

Pressure grew in Washington for a greater commitment to South Vietnam. The Joint Chiefs told the president that unless he agreed to send in American troops, the country would soon go under—and with it "Laos and ultimately South Asia." Some 23,000 troops should be sent right away "to arrest and hopefully to reverse the deteriorating situation in Vietnam."

ABOVE An American gunner, weapon at the ready, escorts a helicopter filled with ARVN troops during a sweep in the Mekong Delta. Officially, advisers were only to fire when fired upon, but "when you see a man aim a gun at you and start to pull the trigger," one American asked, "what kind of damn fool would you be to let him shoot first?" RIGHT The MACV patch: The sword thrusting up through the gap in a crenellated wall—an allusion to the Great Wall of China—was meant to symbolize American military might blocking communist infiltration and aggression in Vietnam.

Kennedy put off the decision and dispatched Walt Rostow and General Maxwell Taylor, the president's military representative, to Saigon to see how they thought South Vietnam might be salvaged.

Taylor, who had commanded the 101st Airborne during World War II and the Eighth U.S. Army in Korea, was an early champion of flexible response and the soldier the president most admired. "The question was how to change a losing game and begin to win," Taylor recalled, "not how to call it off."

When Taylor and Rostow returned, they proposed that the relationship between Washington and Saigon be changed from "advice to limited partnership." In exchange for promises from Diem that he would move his regime "closer to the Vietnamese people," the United States should provide him with helicopters, light aircraft, and armored personnel carriers—APCs—along with "radical increases" in the number of military advisers working with the ARVN and other security forces. The president's emissaries also recommended that six thousand to eight thousand American troops be inserted into South Vietnam, ostensibly to provide flood relief, but actually to be available to advise ARVN combat forces—and to fight back if attacked.

Defense Secretary McNamara agreed with Taylor and Rostow that their report should be fully implemented. But Secretary of State Rusk thought such a small force was unlikely to alter the outcome in Vietnam and worried that Diem might prove in the end to be a "losing horse." Assistant Secretary of State George Ball was more blunt. "Taylor is wrong," he warned the president. "Within five years we'll have three hundred thousand men in the paddies and jungles and never find them again. That was the French experience."

Kennedy was incredulous. "George," he said, "you're just crazier than hell! This decision doesn't mean that. We're not going to have three hundred thousand men in Asia."

In the end, the president refused to send ground troops. It would be like taking a first drink, he told an aide; the effect would soon wear off and there would be demands for another and another. The war in Vietnam could only be won so long as it was *their* war, he said. If it were ever converted into a white man's war, the United States would lose, as the French had lost eight years earlier.

But Kennedy followed most of General Taylor's other recommendations. He doubled the funds for Vietnam and tripled the number of advisers. By the end of 1962, there would be more than nine thousand of them in South Vietnam, empowered not only to teach the ARVN to fight but to accompany its men into battle; by the end of the following year there would be sixteen thousand Americans working with

ASK WHAT YOU CAN DO FOR YOUR COUNTRY

John Kennedy's inaugural address was remembered both for the new president's willingness to confront America's adversaries abroad and for his faith in America's ability to improve the lives of people living in the Third World.

> To those peoples in the huts and villages of half the globe struggling to break the bonds of mass misery, we pledge our best efforts to help them help themselves, for whatever period is required—not because the communist may be doing it, not because we seek their votes, but because it is right. . . . And so my fellow Americans: Ask not what your country can do for you—ask what you can do for your country.

That call struck a chord with young men and women all over the country; by 1963, ten thousand Peace Corps volunteers were at work in forty-six countries. Vietnam was not one of them. But there were other voluntary groups in country, including International Voluntary Services (IVS), which had been seeking to improve agriculture, education, and public health in South Vietnam since the early 1950s.

Pete Hunting, a twenty-two-year-old Wesleyan graduate from Oklahoma City, joined them in July 1963. Based at Phan Rang on the south-central coast, he learned Vietnamese and taught English, and tried to live and eat and sleep as much as possible as did the people he was trying to help. Moving from strategic hamlet to strategic hamlet, he dug wells and built a school, bred rabbits and pigs, and constructed a fish pond and a smokehouse—and a windmill, which he paid for out of his own pocket. Village children called him "the Tall American" and "Mr. Big Nose."

Despite impatience with American bureaucracy and occasional close calls with the Viet Cong, he remained a resolute optimist. "There are no bombs dropping around me," he assured his parents early on. "As a matter of fact, I think most of the trouble in Vietnam is concocted in the minds of the newspaper reporters. You never see them outside a bar as far as I know. The Vietnamese are doing well, but from the sounds of things from the states, you wouldn't know it." Twenty-eight months later, in November 1965, he was still writing, "This job grows on me."

A few days later, driving on a back road, he was ambushed by a squad of Viet Cong. His jeep was riddled with bullets. He was pulled from behind the wheel and shot five times in the head—the first American civilian volunteer to be killed in Vietnam.

"Nobody could anticipate such a cruel thing would happen to such a nice man," a young Vietnamese volunteer with whom Hunting had worked wrote to his mother and father. "This is not the first time an American died on this thankless land for the service of Vietnamese people, but it is just unbearable to us." A fellow IVS volunteer who had been especially close to him wrote, too:

> Your son came to help. He felt deeply the problems of the Vietnamese people. . . . [I]deas were changed and new thoughts introduced by his long hours in and out of the classroom with the youth of this country; through his efforts clothes and food were distributed to refugees from the Viet Cong. . . . Most important of all is the greater understanding Pete gave us all of the things he felt important . . . brotherhood, service to man, and the need for peace.

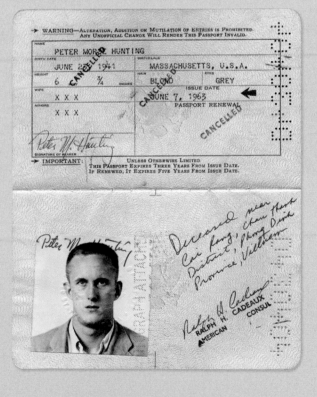

TOP LEFT Pete Hunting at work on one of several windmills he built for the farmers of Ninh Tuan Province, 1964. The irrigation system he helped develop was still in use as late as 1996. **ABOVE** Hunting's passport, marked "Deceased" by the U.S. consul

the South Vietnamese forces. Among them were Army Special Forces personnel—authorized to wear distinctive green berets as evidence of the president's special favor and expert in unconventional warfare—who were tasked with training elite South Vietnamese Rangers and turning indigenous hill peoples who occupied the central highlands into reliable anticommunist forces.

To coordinate it all, Kennedy established the Military Assistance Command, Vietnam—MACV—and placed in command General Paul Harkins, who had served under Maxwell Taylor in Korea.

Kennedy dispatched helicopters and fixed-wing aircraft, river patrol boats, tanks and armored cars and APCs. He also authorized the use of napalm; defoliants to clear foliage and deny cover to the communists along canals, rivers, roads, rail lines, and around military bases; and herbicides to destroy the crops that fed the enemy. A whole array of chemicals would be used, including one named for the color of the stripes on the fifty-five-gallon drums in which it came—"Agent Orange." The chemicals used did not "permanently sterilize the soil," an American reporter assured readers back home. "The climate and rainfall in Vietnam are such that trees and plants grow back rapidly, so that no permanent damage will be done by this operation."

The military program was given a gaudy name, Operation Beefup, but the administration did its best to hide from Congress and the American people the scale of the buildup that was taking place on the other side of the world, fearful that the public would not support the more active role American advisers had begun to play. The State Department barred the Saigon mission from providing the press with detailed information about the arrival of American personnel or equipment or to what purpose they were to be put once they were in country.

One December afternoon, Stanley Karnow, a *Time* correspondent, was having coffee with an Army press officer at the terrace café of the Hotel Majestic when an enormous American aircraft carrier came around a bend in the Saigon River and began steaming toward them, its deck crowded with forty-seven brand-new helicopters.

Karnow was astonished. "Look at that carrier!" he said.

"I don't see nothing," the Army man answered.

In February 1962, the State Department issued Cable 1006, an attempt to establish ground rules for American reporters covering the American effort. Correspondents were free to report on what Americans were doing, it said, but they should not be taken on "missions whose nature [is] such that undesirable dispatches would be highly probable." "Frivolous, thoughtless criticism" of President Diem was also to be avoided, and public affairs officers were to make it clear that "it is not . . . in our interest to have stories indicating that Americans are leading or directing combat missions."

At a White House press conference that same month, a reporter tried to find out more. "Mr. President," he asked, "a Republican National Committee publication has said that you have been less than candid with the American people as to how deeply we are involved in Vietnam. Could you throw any more light on that?"

The president chose his words carefully: "We have increased our assistance to the government, its logistics. We have not sent combat troops there. Though the training missions that we have there have been instructed if they are fired upon to . . . of course, fire back, to protect themselves. But we have not sent combat troops in the generally understood sense of the word. So that I feel that we are being as frank as we can be."

"The United States is now involved in an undeclared war in South Vietnam," James Reston of *The New York Times* wrote on February 13. "This is well-known to the Russians, the Chinese Communists, and everyone else concerned except the American people."

IT WAS A CRUSADE

I WAS A CHILD OF THE COLD WAR," the journalist Neil Sheehan remembered. "When I got off the plane in Saigon on a humid evening in April of 1962, I really believed in all the ideology of the cold war. That if we lost South Vietnam then the rest of Southeast Asia would fall to the communists. There was an international communist conspiracy. The communist nations were one solid 'Sino-Soviet Bloc.' We believed fervently in this stuff."

Sheehan was a twenty-five-year-old reporter for United Press International—UPI. Born on a dairy farm just outside Holyoke, Massachusetts, he had been a scholarship student at Mount Hermon and Harvard, and served three years in the Army in Korea and Japan before deciding to become a newspaperman. Vietnam was his first full-time overseas assignment. His only worry, he recalled, was that he would get there too late and miss out on the big story.

By the time Sheehan got to Vietnam, disaster seemed to have been averted, thanks in large part to American advisers, American training, and American weaponry. He and other reporters were sometimes allowed to ride along as the ARVN mounted helicopter assaults on enemy strongholds in the Mekong Delta and elsewhere. American pilots were at the controls. "It was a crusade and it was thrilling," Sheehan recalled. "You'd climb

aboard a helicopter with the Vietnamese soldiers who were being taken out to battle. And they'd contour-fly, they'd skim across the rice paddies about three or four feet above the paddies, and then pop up over the tree lines that lined the fields. It was absolutely thrilling. And you believed in what was happening. You had the sense that we're fighting here and some day we'll win, and this country will be a better country for our coming."

General Tran Van Tra, responsible for recruiting and training NLF troops, remembered the initial impact helicopters had on his soldiers and their supporters. "Our troops did not . . . know how to deal with such weapons. . . . The only thing . . . Liberation Army units could do was to disperse into small groups to escape, but while they fled across open fields they were frequently cut down by the enemy's armed helicopters. An atmosphere of terror and confusion began to spread from our cadre down to our soldiers." In order to evade being spotted from the air, another Viet Cong commander recalled, "every person, . . . every household, every soldier [and] guerrilla lit their fires to cook rice at 4 a.m. After finishing breakfast . . . before 5 a.m. everyone would climb into their bunkers and foxholes. . . . Later, when the enemy began using helicopters with searchlights at night, our challenges became still greater."

Things appeared to be going well for Saigon on the ground, as well. The new machine-gun-mounted M113 APCs were capable of churning across rivers and rice paddies and right through the

TOP U.S. helicopters and armored personnel carriers work together in deadly tandem, somewhere in the Mekong Delta. **ABOVE** U.S. Army Captain Gerald Kilburn (left) and a fellow adviser lead copter-borne South Vietnamese into a rice paddy in pursuit of fleeing enemy troops. "A number of our cadres and fighters became demoralized when they faced the enemy's new . . . schemes," one communist cadre remembered. "They were frightened by the enemy's weapons and heli-borne tactics."

earthen dikes that separated one field from the next. The communists had nothing with which to stop them.

"We were just overwhelming them with force, with firepower," recalled Captain James Scanlon, an adviser to the Second Armored Regiment attached to the ARVN's Seventh Division in the Mekong Delta. "The firefights would be over in a pretty short time. We were winning one after the other. And we were not meeting a heck of a lot of resistance." By early 1963, ARVN forces would be undertaking fifteen hundred to two thousand operations a month.

Meanwhile, an extraordinarily ambitious plan was under way, directed by Ngo Dinh Diem's brother Nhu, aimed at enlisting the rural population of South Vietnam in the fight against the communists—the Strategic Hamlet Program. People living in small scattered villages were to be concentrated within new hamlets, ringed by bamboo spikes and barbed wire and water-filled moats and further protected against Viet Cong incursions by blockhouses and self-defense squads. It was meant to be a "defense system in miniature," Nhu said, and within these fortified communities, an economic and social revolution was meant

to take place. The regime now reversed itself and encouraged residents to elect their own leaders; there were to be new schools and clinics, too, all meant to encourage self-sufficiency, a sense of community, and loyalty to the Saigon regime. The object was to realize "the ideals of the constitution on a local scale," Diem said. "The hamlet is a state of mind." By the end of that summer, one-third of the population of the country—more than four million people—was said to have been moved into new fortified hamlets, with some two thousand more under construction. (The plan envisioned a final total of more than eleven thousand.)

Hanoi was alarmed at the initial success of Operation Beefup and by the rapid spread of strategic hamlets that had begun to cut into communist recruitment and logistical support. Together, they caused "heavy attrition" and the loss of control of large numbers of people, according to an official report issued by COSVN. Communist commanders confessed that the revolution had virtually stalled because the "enemy pressed it by herding the people into strategic hamlets. . . . [O]ur agents were annihilated in large number. . . . Cadre encountered many difficulties. . . . The force suffered losses. . . . Pessimism spread in the ranks and among the people."

Le Duan was sufficiently concerned to instruct the leaders of the struggle in the South to avoid assaulting cities for fear of sparking further intervention by the Americans, and Ho Chi

ABOVE Communist prisoners huddle together alongside American advisers and the bodies of their dead comrades after a successful ARVN sweep, 1963.

A WORTHY CAUSE

Before Captain James Scanlon from St. Louis, Missouri, arrived in South Vietnam in early 1962, he had served three years on the border between East and West Germany and never forgot seeing the corpse of an East German, shot by border guards and left in the open to discourage others from trying to escape the communist regime. "Those of us who talked to the people who fled East Germany saw the need to stop the growth of communism," he remembered, "to stop the dominoes from being tumbled. That was a worthy cause."

Assigned as an adviser to an armored unit attached to the ARVN's Seventh Division, he was initially optimistic about the prospects of destroying the Viet Cong. "We were cleaning a lot of clocks," he remembered. But by the autumn of 1962, he noticed that his unit was being asked to undertake missions into areas where intelligence said there was no enemy.

"We called them 'walks in the sun,'" he remembered. "It was damn frustrating."

He worried, too, that some ARVN seemed careless about civilian lives. "If they got word that an outpost was being attacked," he recalled, "they'd call in artillery without any qualms whatsoever. It killed a whole lot of people that shouldn't have been killed." During Scanlon's very first firefight his APC crew spotted two tiny figures in black running from the battlefield. The machine gunner opened up at more than seven hundred yards. "Waterspouts went up right behind them," he remembered, "but they didn't get hit and when we got up there, God, it was a couple in their seventies just trying to get out. That was a shock, you know. 'Two people! Two people! Bam-bam!'"

By 1965, Scanlon would be back in the States at Fort Benning, Georgia, helping to train the First Cavalry Division, which was about to depart for Vietnam. A general asked him if he thought

sending combat units to South Vietnam was a good idea. He didn't, for two reasons: the war could bankrupt the country, he said, and Americans were simply not suited to the kind of war they'd need to fight. "I felt strongly," he remembered, "the best way to fight a fighter aircraft is with another fighter aircraft, best way to fight a tank is with a tank, so the best way to fight a guerrilla is with a guerrilla. To win, I thought, we'd need to convert our army into a guerrilla army. American fathers and mothers would have to watch their sons fight in the jungle, living off fifteen hundred calories a day, dying from malaria. We'd never do it. We take our standard of living into battle with us."

ABOVE Captain James Scanlon and his South Vietnamese counterpart, Captain Tinh, await the arrival of top brass at the Second Armored Regiment headquarters at My Tho.

Minh traveled to Beijing in search of further help. China had been equipping the fast-growing North Vietnamese army for a dozen years and had already provided Hanoi with 10,000 artillery pieces, 270,000 rifles, 2 million artillery shells, 200 million bullets, and more than a million Chinese-made uniforms. But when Ho told his Chinese hosts that American air or ground attacks on North Vietnam itself now seemed a real danger they agreed to equip 230 more battalions.

The number of NLF assaults, terrorist attacks, and incidents of sabotage fell from 550 to 350 a month; the number of NLF defectors rose. In July 1962, General Harkins told Secretary McNamara he believed that once the ARVN and Civil Guard were fully trained and engaged in hunting down the communists, the enemy's military potential could be eliminated within twelve months. McNamara ordered the Pentagon to prepare a plan for the "gradual scaling down" of U.S. assistance over the next three years. So far as most Americans knew, the United States was achieving its goal: a stable, independent, noncommunist state in South Vietnam. It was "a struggle this country cannot shirk," *The New York Times* said, and the United States seemed to be winning it.

ABOVE ARVN troops rip down a communist poster criticizing President Diem at Tam An, a communist-controlled hamlet just fifteen miles from Saigon, 1962.

AH, LES STATISTIQUES!

THE STRICTURES the State Department had tried to place on the press in Saigon only served to whet its appetite. Americans were risking their lives, reporters reasoned, therefore the American people had a right to know what they were up to. "It was terribly important that we not only win the war but that we as reporters report the truth that would help to win the war," Neil Sheehan recalled.

It didn't take him and his colleagues in Saigon long to understand that they were being allowed to glimpse only part of the picture. François Sully of *Newsweek*, Malcolm Browne and Peter Arnett of the Associated Press, and Homer Bigart and David Halberstam of *The New York Times* all quickly came to see that things looked very different from the Vietnamese countryside than they did from Saigon or Washington.

In March, for example, Sully had accompanied Operation Sunrise, a large heli-borne ARVN offensive into the Ben Cat region of Binh Duong Province, thirty-five miles north of Saigon. The mission's stated goals were lofty—to sweep the area clean of communists and kick off the Strategic Hamlet Program, meant both to disrupt the enemy and to revolutionize rural life. Sully's report was more down-to-earth.

Swooping down on a village in territory controlled by the NLF, Vietnamese soldiers ordered 205 bewildered farm families to pack up their belongings. Then the soldiers burned the villagers' huts and marched the families off to a government "strategic hamlet" in the nearby valley of Ben Tuong. Some of the peasants went voluntarily, attracted by a government payment of $20, but many had to be forced. Others fled into the jungle to join the NLF.

Homer Bigart summarized the same operation with similar candor. By taking part, the United States had "assumed moral responsibility for a harsh and drastic military measure . . . certain in the initial stages to be bitterly resented by the peasantry, whose allegiance must be won." Furthermore, by agreeing to provide more and more support for the Saigon government, Washington was "de-emphasizing the necessity for the reform of President Diem's autocratic and often capricious regime."

That kind of reporting irritated MACV and the State Department, because it suggested Americans were playing a larger role in South Vietnam than they were willing to admit. But it infuriated Diem. He controlled his own press and could not understand why the Americans couldn't control theirs. He understood that "if you bring in the American dog, you must also accept the American fleas," but stories like these were intolerable. And when Sully added insult to injury by describing Diem's brother Nhu as "a vicious political in-fighter with an unquenchable

thirst for power" and his sister-in-law as "the most detested personality in South Vietnam," Diem ordered both Sully and Bigart out of the country. When the embassy's defense of the exiled reporters struck other correspondents as tepid, it only deepened their suspicion of official sources.

Members of the press corps quickly came to understand that the Strategic Hamlet Program was not what it initially had seemed. Neil Sheehan remembered accompanying Robert McNamara to one of the first hamlets. "The Vietnamese general who commanded the area was telling McNamara what a wonderful thing this was. And some farmers were down digging a ditch around the hamlet. I looked at their faces and they were really angry"—so angry-looking that it seemed to Sheehan that if they could have, the farmers would have killed them.

Peasants resented being forced to abandon their homes, and resented still more being forced without compensation to build new and often inferior ones. One American adviser remembered overseeing the transfer of coastal fishermen and their families to a mountain hamlet sixty miles from the sea. Local officials made money selling to newcomers the barbed wire and corrugated iron roofing that was supposed to be theirs for free. Some hamlets were so hastily built that communist agents were included among those housed within them. In order to please Saigon and gain immediate access to aid funds, some province chiefs doctored their reports, claiming hamlets were fully functioning when they had barely been begun. Of the 3,353 hamlets listed as "completed" in November 1962, only 600 were actually fitted out with all the things Saigon had promised to deliver. Hamlet residents blamed Saigon when NLF fighters attacked them, or when the promised arms with which they were supposed to defend themselves failed to arrive, or when the Civil Guards were slow to answer calls for help.

On his way back to Washington after his very first visit to Vietnam—it had lasted just forty-eight hours—Secretary

McNamara assured a reporter that "every kind of quantitative measurement we have shows we're winning this war." "Quantitative measurements" were central to Robert McNamara's way of doing business. He had vowed to make America's military "cost-effective" and insisted that everything be quantified. A member of his Pentagon staff was once asked how many decisions his boss had made the previous month. "Six hundred and seventy-eight," he replied without a moment's hesitation. Someone had the job of keeping track. But decisions based on statistics were only as good as the sources that provided them. *"Ah, les statistiques!"* a South Vietnamese general was said to have told an American visitor in 1963. "Your secretary of defense loves statistics. We Vietnamese can give him all he wants. If you want them to go up, they will go up. If you want them to go down, they will go down."

General Harkins had little use for such cynicism. "I am an optimist," he had declared as soon as he reached Vietnam, "and I am not going to allow my staff to be pessimistic." Donald Gregg, a CIA official visiting Saigon, remembered Harkins telling him, "Mr. Gregg, I don't care what you hear from anybody else. I can tell you without a doubt we're going to be out of here with a military victory in six months."

Bad news was to be buried. The general insisted that the relentlessly upbeat status reports he sent to Washington be called "Headway Reports." They were filled with daily, weekly,

TOP LEFT General Paul D. Harkins, newly appointed MACV commander, inspects ARVN troops for the first time, 1962.
TOP RIGHT David Halberstam of *The New York Times*, Malcolm Browne of the Associated Press, and Neil Sheehan of United Press International—three of General Harkins's most persistent critics in the Saigon press corps. Harkins considered them irresponsible doomsayers undercutting the war effort; Halberstam thought Harkins "a man of compelling mediocrity."

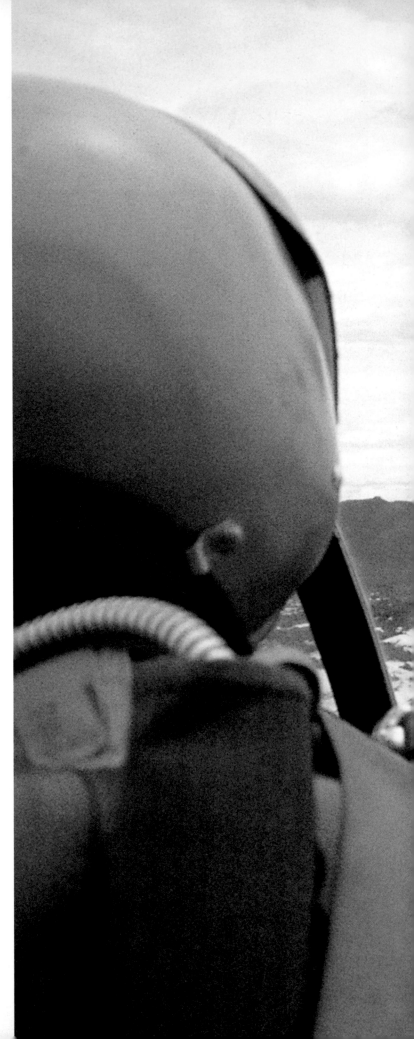

ABOVE A stolen chicken dangles from the backpack of a South Vietnamese soldier. One U.S. adviser remembered that some ARVN units, poorly paid and uncertain of their food supply, "thought nothing of stealing chickens and fruit from the villagers or trampling their rice fields even while their officers were assuring [the same villagers] of their good will." **RIGHT** American jets drop napalm on communist positions, 1963. Napalm was an effective weapon—a single 120-gallon aluminum tank could engulf in flame an area 150 feet long and 50 feet wide, and its use saved untold numbers of American and ARVN lives—but it also killed or disfigured countless Vietnamese civilians. A total of 30,357 tons of U.S. napalm bombs were dropped on Indochina between 1963 and 1973.

Strategic hamlets: **TOP** A farmer resists being forced to leave his home and move to a strategic hamlet. **ABOVE** Hamlet residents fashion a wall of sharpened bamboo, meant to ward off communist attacks. **RIGHT** Hidden hamlet defenders successfully repel an assault.

WHY WERE THEY WINNING?

A career soldier, Colonel John H. Cushman was working in the Pentagon in 1963 when he volunteered to serve in South Vietnam. He was eventually made senior adviser to the ARVN's Twenty-first Division, responsible for pacifying the four southernmost provinces, a Viet Minh refuge since the beginning of the war with France.

He was told in Saigon that strategic hamlets were "the name of the game," but quickly learned that, in his area at least, they were little more than "a typical exercise in paperwork and fake progress." He had a map drawn up in three colors. Blue denoted government-controlled areas in which officials could move about freely, village chiefs could sleep safely in their beds unmolested, and the Viet Cong were not openly collecting taxes. Areas that contained no hint of Saigon control, except when ARVN troops happened to be passing through, were red. Contested areas were yellow. When completed, the map showed that only 6 percent was blue, mostly in and around provincial capitals and district towns. Forty percent was red. All the rest was yellow.

In October, Cushman had what he called "an epiphany" when he accompanied an ARVN battalion as it visited a hamlet in a red area. "I went into a small schoolhouse [and] noticed that its books had been printed in Hanoi. I went into a village office [and saw] tax receipts and population rosters. I thought to myself, 'These people are living under a Viet Cong *government*, complete with its own tax collectors, its own village chief, district chief and province chief.' They were contesting for the same people that my government was contesting for. And they were winning. Now why were they winning? Because they had organization and ideology and doctrine."

Cushman considered newspapermen potential allies, not enemies. "We had a group of young reporters who were getting out in the countryside, talking to American advisers, trying to understand the situation," he remembered. "They were trained to look hard at things. Unfortunately, the top-level people looked on reporters as problems, whereas they really should have co-opted them and said, 'Tell us more about the problems you're finding because we're going to try to correct them.'" He remembered once having coffee with David Halberstam at an air base on the Ca Mau Peninsula, which juts out into the China Sea. It had been a Viet Minh stronghold during the French war and remained a stronghold of the Viet Cong. Halberstam had called it "the southernmost province of North Vietnam" that day, and Cushman had thought to himself, "This guy's got a good picture of things."

ABOVE Colonel John H. Cushman at the mouth of a cave that had hidden enemy soldiers, Ca Mau Province, 1963

monthly, and quarterly data on more than a hundred separate indicators—the number of troops trained and equipped, bales of barbed wire and bags of fertilizer distributed, strategic hamlets completed, communists killed, and areas allegedly cleared of the enemy—far more data than could ever be adequately analyzed.

A good many American advisers failed to share Harkins's relentless optimism. Backed by new weaponry, ARVN forces had done better after Operation Beefup, but their achievements, one senior adviser wrote, still had to be "measured against an armed force that was poorly organized, poorly trained, poorly equipped and poorly led." And as time went by, in some sectors at least, the Americans began to detect a growing reluctance to move against the enemy.

"Yesterday, I dropped a whole bunch of [ARVN] troops into a field," one American helicopter pilot reported. "Today I went back to the same field with another load and . . . that first group was still there in the field, tents up and cooking lunch. They hadn't moved a damn inch."

"Here we'd been killing quite a few and capturing a lot of weapons," James Scanlon remembered. "Then all of a sudden we're going out on operations and there was no enemy there. Why were we going where there was no enemy?" And why, American advisers began to ask, when they did find the enemy, did some ARVN officers now seem so hesitant about making contact with them? "God," Scanlon recalled. "I was told so many times, '*Dại úy*, Scanlon, *dại úy*'—very dangerous going out there. It was like we were having to *force* our help on them."

When the advisers' concerns were not taken as seriously as they thought they should have been at headquarters, some began to make their feelings known off the record to the press. "They believed, just as we did," Neil Sheehan recalled, "that we had to win this war to avoid losing Southeast Asia. One of the reasons they turned to us is because General Harkins wouldn't listen to these people. They'd hand in After-Action reports that realistically described what was happening and Harkins would just ignore them. We thought the senior officers were, like him, lying to us."

There were legitimate reasons for the apparent unwillingness of some ARVN commanders to engage the enemy. With American firepower now just a radio call away, it was safer simply to call in airstrikes and artillery and blast the enemy from a distance than to risk closing with him on the ground. Then, too, ambitious officers wanted to move as quickly as possible from the battlefield to an exalted staff job, a climb up the promotional ladder that a costly battle might fatally interrupt.

But much of the problem could be traced to the presidential palace. Americans believed the primary task of the South Vietnamese army was to save the country from communism. Ngo Dinh Diem wanted that too, but his first concern was always to keep himself in power. His anxiety was understandable. He'd survived two attempted coups by disaffected officers. A communist assassin with a machine gun had narrowly missed him. So had bombs and napalm, dropped on the presidential palace by two South Vietnamese pilots who'd hoped to start an uprising.

To guard against a repetition of such attacks he alone decided which field grade and general officers should be promoted and where they were posted. Commanders who drew too great attention to themselves were sidelined for fear they might become rivals. It was a system calculated to reward unswerving loyalty, which had the effect of discouraging initiative and aggression on the battlefield.

Behind the scenes, Harkins did press Diem to make changes. He told him again and again that "the only way to win is to attack, attack, attack," and urged him to regularize and respect the chain of command and to mount more relatively small operations instead of the massive multi-battalion noisy sweeps, favored by his generals, that rarely encountered the enemy. He also admonished him to consolidate the hundreds of isolated outposts scattered throughout the country which were often captured by the enemy—so often and so complete with their caches of modern weapons that the Americans called them "Viet Cong PXs." But in military matters, as in much else, Diem was immovable. He was winning his war, he was sure of it, and didn't want to hear of anything but "one long series of victories." Nor did he wish ever to be seen as doing the Americans' bidding.

When the largest helicopter assault to date—a day-long operation involving fifty-six aircraft—resulted only in the deaths of seventeen water buffalo, Neil Sheehan's story included the fact that the mission had been coordinated by MACV under the command of General Harkins. A military flack called to complain: "Uncle Paul doesn't want his name used. We're only here as advisers." Sheehan was livid. "Tell 'Uncle Paul' that he's in charge of the American Military Command here, that he's the man who released those helicopters, that those are American helicopters flown by American pilots, and that his name goes in my stories."

I DIDN'T WANT TO KILL ANYONE

EACH OF SOUTH VIETNAM'S forty-four provinces had its own chief. A good many were simply political allies of President Diem, interested mostly in lining their own pockets and largely ineffective in combating the communist shadow governments flourishing among their people.

Lieutenant Colonel Tran Ngoc Chau was different. A privi-

leged judge's son from Hue, he and two of his brothers had fought with the Viet Minh against the French. But he had refused to join the Communist Party, left the Viet Minh, became a major in the army fighting against them, and eventually so impressed Diem with his insider's knowledge of communist tactics that he was promoted and made chief of Kien Hoa (now Ben Tre), a province in the Mekong Delta that had been a Viet Minh bastion during the war with the French. When he arrived, only 80,000 of its 600,000 people were thought to be under Saigon's control.

Chau went to work. The trouble with the Saigonese who were trying to run the county, he believed, was that they were "Vietnamese foreigners" with no real understanding of the countryside. Rather than simply wage war on the communists, he sought to understand what drove people to support them. Against the advice of anxious subordinates, he insisted on driving through his province in order to see conditions for himself. Snipers fired at him. Three Civil Guards escorting him were killed by a land mine. He kept at it, holding twice-weekly meetings to hear farmers' grievances and then seeing what he could do to allay them. Whenever possible, he replaced political appointees from elsewhere with qualified local people. Corrupt or abusive officials were removed or arrested.

"Chau was absolutely incorruptible," Rufus Phillips, director

of rural affairs in the U.S. Operations Mission, remembered. "And people came to really understand that here's a guy who, even though he hasn't been elected, really represents us."

He trained specialized teams, tasked with gathering intelligence and providing help with digging wells and building bridges, constructing clinics and schools. Most important, he introduced an "open arms" policy, which provided NLF defectors and their families with financial help and exemption from the draft. "I didn't want to kill anyone," he remembered. "I wanted to convert them. When I located a real Viet Cong family, I tried to win them over and, through them, also to win over the family member who had left. Only after those steps failed did I order my teams to capture or kill them."

Chau served twice as province chief of Kien Hoa. During that time, the CIA estimated, some twenty thousand NLF fighters fled the province.

ABOVE Lieutenant Colonel Chau meets with the people of Kien Hoa Province. As province chief, Chau remembered, he inaugurated weekly public "open door" sessions during which people could meet him face to face. "Initially, few people came [because] they feared some kind of reprisal if they aired their grievances in such a public fashion." Soon, so many complainants came that he had to devote two days a week to them.

THE OPPOSITE OF WHAT DEMOCRACY WAS

"I can say President Diem was a patriot. I can say he was a nationalist," Phan Quang Tue recalled. "But I can never say he was a democrat. No, Diem was simply the opposite of what democracy was."

Tue and his younger brother, Tuan, learned that firsthand as the sons of a gifted sometime politician named Dr. Phan Quang Dan.

Trained as a clinician, Dan organized relief workers during the great famine of 1945, but refused to join Ho Chi Minh's government because he distrusted communism. He served as an adviser to Emperor Bao Dai, but left him when it became clear he was merely doing France's bidding and formed his own anti-colonial party in Paris. During the French war, he studied public health at Harvard and traveled widely overseas, campaigning for full Vietnamese independence.

On Dan's return to Vietnam in 1955, Diem offered him a post in his new government. He turned it down. He was already wary of Diem—whom he considered an "adventurer"—and Diem saw in him a potential rival. Security police were soon following him everywhere. When, during the very first parliamentary elections in 1959, Dan overwhelmingly defeated a government candidate for a seat in the National Assembly, Diem had his victory declared invalid. When Dan took to the radio during the failed 1960 paratroopers' coup—calling for an end to nepotism and better treatment of the peasantry—Diem had him arrested.

"That was the last time I saw my father for three years," Tue recalled. "We were left alone in our home. A mob of Diem supporters forced their way in, seized all the furniture, then set the house on fire. There was a police station right across the street but no one intervened. Diem was not able to eliminate my father physically, because he was an international figure, so he tried to destroy him and attack his integrity and his character."

Dan was thrown into a windowless six-by-four-and-a-half-foot dungeon cell below the Saigon zoo, where he was water boarded and subjected to repeated electric shocks. He was eventually made to endure a staged trial for treason and then sent to the notorious Con Son Island. "After the dungeon it was luxury," he remembered. "I was able to see the sunlight and hear sounds other than the cries of people tortured."

TOP Dr. Phan Quang Dan **LEFT** Phan Quang Tue and Phan Quang Tuan on their way to school in Saigon

AT THE BEGINNING OF THE BEGINNING

IN OCTOBER 1962, the United States and the Soviet Union came closer than they would ever come again to mutually assured destruction. The Soviets had secretly placed nuclear missiles on the island of Cuba, a little over ninety miles from the United States. The Joint Chiefs of Staff urged President Kennedy to bomb the missile sites. He resisted and instead ordered a naval quarantine to stop Soviet ships from resupplying the island. For thirteen excruciating days, the world held its breath. Finally, in exchange for a private pledge to remove American missiles from Turkey, Khrushchev agreed to remove his missiles from Cuba. Neither the United States nor the Soviet Union ever wanted so direct a confrontation again. From then on, limited wars, like the growing conflict in Vietnam, would assume still greater importance.

Just three days after the crisis eased, Senate Majority Leader Mike Mansfield arrived in Saigon, part of a fact-finding trip the president had asked him to undertake. Like Kennedy, Mansfield had been one of Diem's early champions; unlike the president, he knew a good deal of Asian history, having studied and taught it before going into politics.

He met with Diem and with American officials. They assured him things were going well. But he also spent five hours with Neil Sheehan, David Halberstam, and other reporters, who warned that while the number of enemy dead had risen, so had the number of communists; that Diem was an obstacle to progress; that the relentless optimism of official American spokesmen was misleading the American public. Afterward, when an embassy official handed Mansfield a statement at the airport congratulating the Diem government for making "progress toward victory," he refused to read it to the press.

Back home again, Mansfield reported to the president that success seemed no closer than it had been when he'd last visited Saigon, seven years earlier. "We are once again at the beginning of the beginning," he said. His old friend Diem seemed now to be faltering—"very withdrawn, very secluded . . . gradually being cut off from reality"—while power was steadily shifting into the hands of his shadowy, recalcitrant brother, Nhu. Mansfield urged that the whole question of America's interest in the region be reexamined: "We may well discover that it is in our interests to do less rather than more than we are now doing. If that is the case we would do well to concentrate on a vigorous diplomacy . . . designed to lighten our commitments without bringing about sudden and catastrophic upheavals in Southeast Asia."

The president was irritated by Mansfield's implied criticism of administration policy—and convinced that the autumn of the Cuban Missile Crisis was no time for the United States to consider changing course in Southeast Asia—but he did begin to think for the first time that the survival of the Diem regime and the survival of South Vietnam itself might not necessarily be inseparable. Mansfield's report was, U.S. Ambassador Nolting would remember, "the first nail in Diem's coffin."

A MISERABLE GODDAMN PERFORMANCE

NO AMERICAN SOLDIER in South Vietnam had stronger opinions about the way the war was being waged—or was more willing to share them with eager young reporters—than Lieutenant Colonel John Paul Vann. "We reporters admired Vann greatly," David Halberstam wrote, "not because he gave us scoops—there are no scoops in a rice paddy—but because he cared so desperately about Vietnam . . . and because whenever we were with him we had a sense that a very real war was being fought."

Vann was volatile, impatient, and paternalistic toward the Vietnamese, much as the French had been. "These people may be the world's greatest lovers," he told one reporter, "but they're not the world's greatest fighters." Still, he said, they were "good people, and they can win the war if someone shows them how."

Vann never doubted that he was that someone. He disapproved of many of the tactics the Americans were teaching the South Vietnamese. "By giving the ARVN too much gear—airplanes and helicopters—we may be helping them to pick up bad habits instead of teaching them to spend more time in the swamps than the enemy," he said. He thought the heedlessness with which artillery and airpower were being routinely called in was counterproductive. Innocent men, women, and children were being killed and wounded—and their grieving friends and family were being recruited by the communists—because ARVN officers were uneasy with ground combat. "This is a political war and it calls for discrimination in killing," he argued. "The best weapon . . . would be a knife. . . . The worst is the airplane. The next worst is artillery. Barring a knife, the best is a rifle—you know who you're killing."

As senior adviser to the ARVN's Seventh Division in the northern Mekong Delta for nine months, Vann saw firsthand the impact of palace politics on the war against the Viet Cong. The commander of the division was Colonel Huynh Van Cao, just thirty-four but a personal favorite of President Diem, whom he called "my king." Largely untested in combat when Vann joined him, he nonetheless fully expected soon to be promoted

to general and had already written a semi-autobiographical novel called *He Grows Under Fire.* Combining shrewd military advice with shameless flattery, Vann tried to see that Cao did just that. During the spring and summer of 1962, the Seventh Division outperformed its rivals, killing the enemy at night as well as during the day.

Then, during a helicopter assault on October 5, a company of elite rangers under Cao's command was ambushed. Thirteen men were killed, thirty-four more wounded. Cao was summoned to the presidential palace. If he wished to be promoted to general and given command of a corps, Diem told him, he needed to be far more prudent. Cao took the admonition to heart. Vann was cut out of military planning, and over the next ten weeks Cao mounted fourteen operations that lost just three men, all thought to have been killed by friendly fire.

On December 22, Cao received the promotion for which he'd hoped. He was now a general, commanding the Fourth Corps and responsible for the whole of the Mekong Delta. Vann cautioned General Harkins that while he had worked hard to build up "Cao's military leader image" over the past few months, the

TOP LEFT Combatants at Ap Bac: Lieutenant Colonel John Paul Vann and General Huynh Van Cao, commander of the ARVN's Seventh Division; **TOP RIGHT** Captain James Scanlon and Captain Ly Tong Ba sharing the top of an armored personnel carrier

newly appointed general had not "yet developed a real aggressive attitude on his own." There was not much either he or Harkins could do.

Vann continued to serve as senior adviser to the Seventh Division and its new commander, Colonel Bui Dinh Dam. A few days after Christmas 1962, the division got orders to capture an NLF radio transmitter broadcasting from a spot some forty miles southwest of Saigon in a hamlet called Tan Thoi, on the edge of the vast empty wetland called the Plain of Reeds. The hamlet was surrounded by rice paddies that were crisscrossed with canals. An irrigation dike with coconut and banana trees growing thickly on both embankments linked it to a neighboring hamlet called Bac. (The battle that was about to unfold there would be remembered as "Ap Bac," because the newspaperman who covered it added the prefix *Ap,* which means hamlet.)

Intelligence suggested that no more than 120 guerrillas were guarding the transmitter. ARVN officers and American advisers worked together to draw up a plan of attack. On the morning of January 2, 1963, some twelve hundred South Vietnamese troops, supported by helicopters and armored personnel carriers, were to attack the village from the south, north, and west. When the communists tried to flee through the eastern gap left open for them—as they almost always had whenever outnumbered and confronted by modern weaponry—artillery and airstrikes would annihilate them.

Planners called it Operation Duc Thang 1—Operation Victory 1. But from the first, everything seemed to go wrong. The intelligence proved faulty. There were more than 340 NLF fighters, not 120, in the area: a company of the 514th Provincial Battalion at Tan Thoi; a company of the veteran 261st Regional

Battalion at Ap Bac; and a band of local part-time guerrillas, women as well as men from both hamlets, eager to help repel the ARVN and their American advisers.

Platoon leader Le Cong Huan, a twenty-four-year-old regroupee who had arrived from the North after a five-month trek just two days earlier, was among the NLF at Ap Bac. (Like most southern revolutionaries, he fought under a *nom de guerre;* his real name was Le Cong Son.) "We knew the enemy was planning a big sweep," he remembered, "and we recognized that we needed to find a way to stand and fight. We chose this spot and brought in additional troops—one company from the province and one from the region. This was the first time we tried a joint operation. We had just two days to get ready."

Twenty-two-year-old Truong Thi Nghe, born and raised in Bac, was happy to help. She remembered the brutality with which first the French and then the Diem regime had dealt with the people of her village, had acted as a messenger for the Viet Minh while still a small girl, and was now the political officer for the local part-time guerrillas. "We did not know there was going to be a battle until the afternoon before," she remembered. "We saw our troops coming in to prepare, and their commander said they were going to fight here." At his orders, Nghe helped boil rice and wrap it in banana leaves to keep up the men's strength during the fighting. She and her comrades also helped dig shoulder-deep trenches and foxholes beneath the trees that lined the dike and overlooked the surrounding paddies. Behind the prepared positions ran a waterway connecting the two hamlets that would permit the communists to replenish their ammunition and ferry wounded men to safety by sampan.

At six thirty in the morning on January 2, John Paul Vann took off in a two-seater spotter plane so he could radio information about the fighting to Colonel Dam, the division commander, at his command post several miles away. (ARVN commanders rarely visited the battlefield, a tradition established by the French that the Americans were initially unable to change; no ARVN officer above the rank of captain would take part in the day's fighting.) Vann had been promised thirty helicopters with which to carry in three companies of infantry, but at the last moment twenty of them had been snatched away for another operation. The men would have to be brought in in stages.

Five minutes after Vann's plane left the ground, ten U.S. helicopters ferried the first ARVN rifle company to a spot just north of Tan Thoi, where it was meant to block the communists

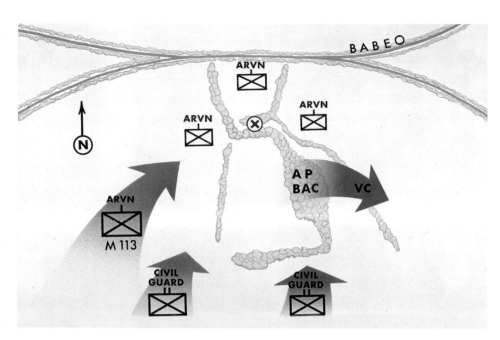

from escaping into the swamps. The men met no resistance, but would have to wait almost two and a half hours before the thick morning fog burned away and the other two companies could be brought in to join them on the northern edge of the battlefield.

Meanwhile, to the south, two ARVN Civil Guard battalions approached Ap Bac on foot. Le Cong Huan and his company were waiting for them. "We told our soldiers not to shoot until the troops were very close," he recalled. "We had a saying, 'One enemy, one bullet.'" The communist commander let the lead company of the Civil Guards get within one hundred feet before giving the order to fire. Several Guards were killed, including the company commander and his lieutenant. Survivors staggered back behind a dike and stayed huddled there all day, only occasionally exchanging fire with the hidden enemy. One of them recalled afterward that while the captain who took command of their unit had been a brave soldier, "it was clear to me that he was not going to risk his career on clearing out the Viet Cong. . . . He just did not know what to expect from his commanders."

Colonel Dam asked Colonel Vann to fly over the battlefield and pick a landing zone so that reinforcements could be helicoptered in right away. Vann swept low over the enemy positions, concealed from him by the trees, and picked an area far enough

ABOVE A map of the Battle of Ap Bac, based on one prepared afterward by Colonel Vann. "X" marks the spot where the Viet Cong radio transmitter—the initial target of the ARVN attack—was presumed to be. Communist guerrillas, dug in beneath the trees, withstood the ARVN assault from three sides and at day's end were allowed to escape to the east.

west of the fortified dike at Ap Bac to be safely beyond the effective range of communist weaponry.

But, for reasons never fully explained, when ten H-21 cargo helicopters—known to the Americans as "Flying Bananas" and to the Viet Cong as "Angle Worms" and "Flying Phoenixes"—filled with ARVN troops and escorted by five helicopter gunships, clattered in, the American pilots put down much closer than planned. "The tree line seemed to explode with machine gun fire," a pilot remembered. "It was hell." Machine gun bullets hit fourteen of the fifteen aircraft. One was damaged so badly it couldn't take off again. A second—sent to rescue the crew of the first—was immobilized. A gunship returned to pick up both downed crews, and was hit and flipped over. One of its pilots died on the spot. A fourth gunship went down nearby. A member of its crew was wounded. Before noon, a fifth helicopter would be shot down elsewhere on the battlefield.

When the communists saw that helicopters could be damaged and destroyed, they cheered. "Come on, brothers, look, we are winning!" one man shouted. He and his comrades now concentrated their fire on the ARVN troops struggling to get out of the downed helicopters. "When those poor Vietnamese came out of the choppers," an American crewman remembered, "it was like shooting ducks for the Viet Cong." Nearly half of the 102 men the helicopters had brought in were killed or wounded. The survivors took what shelter they could behind the wreckage or hunkered down in the muddy water behind the earthen dikes that divided one paddy from the next and waited for rescue.

"I didn't want to die for these rotten people using these tactics," one ARVN soldier remembered. "What did this have to do with the needs of people in my village? I was ashamed and disgusted . . . so, yes, I hid my head and fired my weapon at random."

Vann called for an airstrike. Two AD-6 Skyraider fighter bombers streaked in and hit Tan Thoi and Ap Bac with bombs and napalm. They missed the communists, concealed beneath the trees, but hit both hamlets and set them ablaze. "It was a tough situation for us," Le Cong Huan remembered, "the enemy in front of us, the fires behind." Ba Nghe agreed: "Many of the boats we had built were destroyed. We had evacuated the old people and the children, but many people stayed to support the soldiers. We had very few bunkers to go into. Many were killed. But our commander said retreat was not an option. I was a political officer and a girl, not a soldier. But when I saw how brave our soldiers were, I became a soldier too, and lost an eye."

The heat from the napalm was so intense that the ARVN soldiers, crouching in the rice paddy, found breathing painful. Some rose to cheer, nonetheless, sure that no Viet Cong could have survived the onslaught from the air; once again, American-supplied weaponry had come to their rescue. A moment later,

enemy gunfire sent them burrowing back down into the mud.

Meanwhile, Vann circled helplessly overhead, appalled and angry. He radioed Dam and persuaded him to order the Fourth Mechanized Rifle Squadron of the ARVN Second Armored Cavalry Regiment—thirteen M113 amphibious armored personnel carriers filled with troops—to race to the rescue of the men trapped in the helicopter landing zone, just a mile and a quarter to the east. He then radioed Captain James Scanlon to get the squadron to which he was attached moving.

Like Vann, Scanlon was only an adviser. His ARVN counterpart, Captain Ly Tong Ba, would have to give the order. Scanlon liked and admired him. "He was just one solid individual," he remembered. "A real tiger. He'd fought with the French, he'd fought all his life, essentially. I turned to Ba and said, 'Hey, you've got to get over there right away.' And Ba said to me, 'I'm not going. They should send the infantry.'"

Scanlon was astonished. Overhead, John Vann was apoplectic.

Vann radioed Colonel Dam again. He again agreed that Ba should move.

Ba still balked. He reminded Scanlon that he didn't "take orders from Americans," and claimed there was no way his ten-ton personnel carriers could cross the three canals between them and the wrecked helicopters in time to save anyone. Fording a high-banked canal was a slow and arduous process: branches and brush had to be cut and spread on the far side to help the first massive vehicle gain traction; once across, the first carrier had to tow the second.

It was not the terrain that made Ba hesitant; it was the needlessly complicated chain of command Diem had created. While Colonel Dam commanded the Seventh Division he was not in charge of the entire battlefield. Major Lam Quang Tho, the province chief with close ties to the Ngo family, commanded the Civil Guards stalled south of Ap Bac and the armored units in which Ba served. Colonel Dam's order therefore meant little to him. He was wary of going into battle without consulting Tho, and he couldn't raise him on the radio. If he moved without his permission and things went badly, he knew he would have to answer to Tho and, possibly, to the presidential palace itself.

Scanlon and another American adviser took two APCs and showed Ba that the crossing was possible. Trying to motivate him, they accused him of cowardice. He finally gave in and agreed to move, but it would take almost three hours for his crews to get the first pair of carriers across the three canals, long enough for the shooting in the landing zone to have died down.

As they worked, Vann radioed both ARVN commanders to get their men mobilized in the north and south to move forward and flank the Viet Cong positions. Both refused.

Meanwhile, the carriers rumbled through the paddies toward

the trapped men. "Everything was quiet," Scanlon remembered. "You could see the open expanse of rice fields. To our right, a regional Vietnamese infantry battalion had their cook fires going. They were eating lunch. And my reaction was, 'Hey it was all over.' We got right up to about a hundred yards of the downed helicopters and those people laying there, maybe even closer."

"All we have left to do now," he thought, "is to police up those chopper crews and the wounded." The first two carriers dropped their ramps. Infantry squads stepped out and took up positions in formation around them, weapons at their waists, ready to spray the tree line with automatic fire as they advanced toward it.

Always before, the spectacle of the massive APCs rumbling across the paddies toward them, firing their machine guns as they came, had been enough to make the communists scurry away. This time would be different. Beneath the trees, the company cadre moved from position to position exhorting his men, "It is better to die at one's post."

"They were prepared," Scanlon remembered, "just like we teach at the infantry school at Fort Benning. They had little white pieces of tape on the bushes indicating the span their machine guns would cover. They had done their homework." From their hideouts beneath the trees, the Viet Cong opened fire, "and boy we got raked left and right. It was like a pool table. And we were on the green and they were in the pockets shooting at us." It was quickly clear that it would be suicidal for the infantrymen to advance further in the open. They were ordered to clamber back aboard the APCs.

Two by two, eight of the carriers came under fire. Five more crossed the last canal—and stopped, their crews unwilling to face what they saw happening to the rest of their squadron.

"The APCs had always been dangerous to us," Le Cong Huan remembered. "But at Ap Bac we disabled them." A periscope allowed APC drivers to control their vehicles from within, but the heads and shoulders of the gunners, seated behind their .50-caliber machine guns, were fully exposed. Weeks earlier, Captain Ba had appealed to his ARVN superiors and to the Americans to have his APCs fitted with steel shields that would have offered the gunners at least some protection from enemy fire. They had never been installed. Eight gunners were killed. Less experienced men aboard the APCs tried to take over for them, but, as Scanlon recalled, "after the third guy came down with a bullet through the head it was darn difficult to get the fourth guy up there."

The APC in which Captain Ba and Scanlon's deputy, Captain Robert Mays, were riding tried again and again to destroy an enemy position on the right side of the enemy line from which especially damaging machine gun fire was coming. There were two men in it. They shot one man's head off. But the other kept shooting. "The carrier drove right up and fired down on him," Scanlon remembered. "At one point he threw a grenade up on

ABOVE Two of the five helicopters shot down by guerrilla gunfire at Ap Bac. The wreckage in the foreground is a UH-1 or "Huey" gunship; beyond it is what was left of an H-21 Shawnee that carried ARVN troops to the battlefield.

top of the carrier and the guys ducked inside just before it went off. I would have awarded that guy a Distinguished Service Cross. He was one brave son-of-a-gun. And he hung in to the end."

During the firefight, one of the three machine guns Le Cong Huan's men were manning jammed. When he left his foxhole to see if he could get it going again, an ARVN machine gun bullet hit him in the left leg. Guerrillas from Ap Bac helped him to a waiting sampan and poled him away from the fighting.

The battle went on. An APC armed with a flamethrower drove within range of the enemy troops, prepared to burn them from their positions—only to have the flamethrower fail to fire. "It figures," said a rescued helicopter crewman. "Everything else went wrong, so what the hell."

Ba managed to assemble eight carriers for what he hoped would be a final coordinated frontal assault, but they failed to stay in line, allowing the enemy to concentrate its fire on whichever carrier was closest at the moment.

When the first APCs came within sixty-five feet of the tree line, three guerrillas leaped down from their foxholes and hurled hand grenades. None did real damage, but the drivers were so demoralized by then that they halted, turned around, and withdrew behind the wrecked helicopters. Nothing had been accomplished.

Vann believed the battle could still be won: from his spotter plane, he called for a simultaneous assault on the enemy by all the remaining ground forces, north, south, and west. And he asked that paratroopers be dropped east of Tan Thoi to destroy the communists as they tried to escape.

General Cao denied Vann's request. "It is not prudent," he said.

Aftermath of Ap Bac: Two pictures snapped by Captain James Scanlon show: **TOP** the communist machine gunner who defied death and won American praise at the battle's height; **CENTER** the dense tree line within which the NLF fighters made their successful stand; **BOTTOM** a photograph by Reuters correspondent Nick Turner, in which fallen South Vietnamese soldiers lie alongside water-filled tracks gouged by the ARVN armored personnel carriers that tried but failed to dislodge the enemy and were forced to retreat

Vann exploded. "You're afraid to fight."

"I am the commanding general and it is my decision," Cao answered.

There would be no coordinated ground assault. Instead, just before dark three hundred paratroopers were to be dropped *west* of the villages, not east of them, a relatively harmless show of force that allowed the enemy a safe escape route and seems to have been meant simply to avoid further bloodshed. But pilot error caused many of these men to land among the enemy: fifty-two of them were hit before night fell, many shot from the sky as they hung helplessly beneath their chutes.

"The shooting finally stopped at dusk," Scanlon recalled. "But there were just one hell of a lot of guys that were . . . dead and wounded. They couldn't bring in any evacuation helicopters after dark, so all night long you, you heard the moans of the dying."

By the next morning, the enemy had melted away, carrying all but three of their dead with them to their base camp somewhere hidden in the Plain of Reeds. No one knows for certain how many of them were killed or wounded, but eighty South Vietnamese soldiers had been killed, as had three Americans. "We filled the armored personnel carriers with bodies," Scanlon said, "and stacked them up on top till we couldn't stack any more."

General Harkins never visited the battlefield, but he did fly to the ARVN command post, where David Halberstam and Peter Arnett caught up with him. What did he think of the battle? "We've got them in a trap," Harkins said, "and we're going to spring it in half an hour." Cao had evidently told him that the communists somehow still occupied their foxholes and that he was about to move against them.

At about that time, Neil Sheehan was walking through what was left of Ap Bac with Brigadier General Robert York, the only American commander who went to the battlefield to see for himself what had happened. "Well, General, what do *you* think happened?" Sheehan asked. "What the hell's it look like?" York answered. "They got away, didn't they?"

Moments later, howitzer shells rained down in and around the hamlet. "General Cao had decided to fake an attack on Bac now that the Viet Cong were gone," Sheehan remembered. "He wanted the palace to think that he was doing something to recoup . . . and instructed Major Tho to fire a barrage to soften up the enemy for 'the assault.'" Thanks to faulty map reading by the lieutenant in charge of the artillery, four of his own men were blown apart. The Viet Cong had been gone for hours.

John Paul Vann took Sheehan and David Halberstam aside and told them Ap Bac had been "a miserable goddamn perfor-

mance." "The ARVN won't listen," he said, "they make the same mistakes over and over again in the same way."

Privately, Harkins admitted to his superior, Admiral Harry D. Felt, the U.S. commander in the Pacific, that ARVN commanders had passed up an opportunity to destroy an enemy Main Force unit. But in public, he declared victory. "The ARVN forces had an objective," he said. "[We] took that objective, the VC left and their casualties were greater than those of the government forces—what more do you want?" Reporters like Sheehan and Halberstam, who had been focusing on the ARVN's shortcomings, were "doing a disservice to thousands of gallant and courageous men who are fighting so well in defense of their country." Admiral Felt backed Harkins and urged the reporters to "get on the team."

They did not. The headlines on their stories startled American newspaper readers: "VIET DEFEAT SHOCKS U.S. AIDES; U.S. ADVISERS FIND TENDENCY TO LET REDS ESCAPE; DEFEAT WORST SINCE BUILD-UP BEGAN." "We had been writing stories about all the flaws on the Saigon side—about how they wouldn't fight, about the corruption, they wouldn't obey orders, the disorganization," Sheehan recalled. "But we were doing it piecemeal. And then all of a sudden the Viet Cong, for the first time—the 'raggedy-ass little bastards,' as Harkins's people in Saigon called them—stood and fought and suddenly all the flaws on the Saigon side were illuminated like a star shell fired by artillery at night. It illuminated the battlefield. Everything came out."

ABOVE A North Vietnamese wall poster inspired by the Viet Cong victory exhorts passersby to "Emulate Ap Bac and Kill the Enemy. Destroy the Strategic Hamlets! Wipe Out Helicopters!"

The communists who had won the battle were exultant. "Every one of the cadres and soldiers were high-spirited," one volunteer remembered. "They looked happy and lively. They liked to sing and no one seemed to be homesick. They also felt very superior to the ARVN . . . and felt that they could defeat them even at ten-to-one odds."

Hanoi was exultant too. The Battle of Ap Bac was seen by Le Duan and his politburo allies as proof that even when faced with American advisers and weaponry the communists could stand and fight, inflict heavy casualties on Saigon's forces—and get away again. The memory of their victory would inspire NLF and North Vietnamese soldiers for years to come.

In Saigon, despite everything, Diem remained convinced the ARVN were winning, not losing. Ap Bac had only been a momentary setback. And he continued to resent Americans telling him how to fight his battles or run his country.

ABOVE Reuters correspondent Nick Turner helps South Vietnamese troops gather their dead after the battle.

A few weeks later, Michael V. Forrestal, a member of the senior staff of the National Security Council, wrote the president a brutally frank summary of the situation in South Vietnam as he saw it. "No one really knows how many of the 20,000 'Vietcong' killed last year were only innocent, or at least persuadable, villagers, whether the Strategic Hamlet Program is providing enough govt. services to counteract the sacrifices it requires, or how the mute mass of villagers react to the charges against Diem of dictatorship and nepotism."

On April 24, the CIA reported that Diem was about to ask that the number of American advisers be greatly reduced. "We don't have a prayer of staying in Vietnam," President Kennedy privately told a friend that evening. "These people hate us. They are going to throw our asses out of there at almost any point. But I can't give up a piece of territory like that to the communists and then get the people to reelect me."

A BUDDHIST PRIEST BECOMES A MARTYR

THAT SPRING, South Vietnam plunged into a new kind of civil strife. It had little to do with the communists. Religion and nationalism were at its heart.

On May 4, Catholics in Hue festooned the city with white-and-gold Vatican banners in celebration of the twenty-fifth anniversary of the elevation of Diem's older brother, Ngo Dinh Thuc, to the rank of bishop. In doing so, they defied a presidential edict that had forbidden such displays unless the banners were displayed beneath a larger flag of South Vietnam. Two days later, Diem's office issued a proclamation banning the flying of *all* religious flags throughout the country. He found their use "disorderly," he claimed, but his real goal was to keep them from becoming symbols of resistance to his regime.

Hue was a center of Buddhist worship and May 8 was Wesak Day, the annual celebration of the Buddha's birth, death, and enlightenment, when thousands of devotees traditionally paraded through the streets with their own multicolored banners. To many Buddhists, Diem's issuing of his decree on the eve of their important holiday seemed a calculated insult.

Tension between Catholics and Buddhists was not new. Many Buddhists identified Catholicism with France and foreignness, and saw the Ngo brothers' doctrine of "personalism" as equally alien. (Communism, too, was seen as foreign and therefore unsuited to Vietnam.) For decades, Buddhist reformers had been calling for a great revival of their faith, which, they claimed, was the essence of the Vietnamese identity. "The truth,"

CLOCKWISE, FROM ABOVE Malcolm Browne's photographs of the self-immolation of the Venerable Quang Duc. A sedan carrying four or five monks leads a Buddhist procession toward a central intersection in downtown Saigon. There, a younger monk pours gasoline over Quang Duc, who is soon sitting in the center of what Browne called "a column of flame." The martyred monk left behind a note: "Before closing my eyes to Buddha, I have the honor of presenting my words to Diem, asking him to be kind and tolerant toward his people and to enforce a policy of religious equality."

AN EXTRAORDINARY ACT

ABOVE Bill Zimmerman

"I first became aware of Vietnam because of a burning monk," Bill Zimmerman remembered. Zimmerman was a Chicagoan, a senior at the University of Chicago in June 1963, who had recently returned from spring break, working for the Student Non-violent Coordinating Committee (SNCC) in Greenwood, Mississippi.

"We had watched the civil rights movement in the South and it had set the standard for us," he recalled, "to stand up against injustice, allow yourself to be beaten up, allow yourself to be attacked by a dog or hit by a police truncheon—we had enormous respect for people who were willing to go that far. And then one day we saw on television a picture of a burning monk in Saigon. This was an extraordinary act."

Like a good many Americans, he had paid little attention to Vietnam until that moment. "No one had ever seen anything like that. I asked myself what we were doing in Vietnam and how conditions had become so intolerable that this monk and others who soon followed felt justified in burning themselves to death." Those questions continued to disturb him. Within two years, he recalled, ending the war in Vietnam became his "constant preoccupation."

---

one monk wrote, "is that Vietnamese Buddhism is a national religion." Diem had made some concessions to Buddhists—they served in his cabinet and among his top commanders—but below that level his regime blatantly favored Catholics. "My family was very Buddhist, especially my mother," Duong Van Mai recalled, "and they thought that the power and the perks that went with power usually went to the Catholics. Buddhists were shoved aside, treated like second-class citizens."

The president's brother, Thuc, now the archbishop of Hue, was a source of special Buddhist resentment; arrogant, ostentatious, and unyielding, he was keen on conversions and aggressively scornful of anyone not belonging to his flock.

And so, on Wesak Day, thousands of Buddhists defied Diem's ban, marching beneath banners that urged the people to oppose the government's "policy of injustice and cruelty." That evening, a large throng gathered around the Hue radio station, hoping to hear a monk's taped sermon that declared Buddhist aspirations "legitimate and constructive." The station's director refused to broadcast it. The crowd grew angry. Someone hauled down the flag of South Vietnam and ran up the banner of international Buddhism.

A contingent of soldiers backed by policemen tried to disperse the crowd with a fire hose. The protestors stood their ground. An ARVN major ordered his men forward. A concussion grenade exploded. The soldiers opened fire. Eight protestors were killed. Six were girls. The youngest was twelve; the oldest was twenty.

The State Department cabled the Saigon embassy: "At your discretion, suggest you urge [the government of South Vietnam to] take no repressive measures against Buddhists, offer sympathy and funeral expenses."

Diem blamed the communists for masterminding everything that had happened in Hue and thought Buddhist complaints wildly exaggerated. But when monks drew up a series of demands and laid them at the president's door—repeal of the flag ban, compensation for the victims, an end to discrimination, recognition of Buddhism as a religion rather than an "association," and the right to proselytize—Diem agreed at least to meet with them. But he refused to rescind his order and repeated his charge that communists were behind everything. Archbishop Thuc supported his brother's firm stand. "Mass movements are straw fires," he said. "They flare up quickly but they are extinguished in an instant."

The Buddhist fire had not been extinguished. Eminent monks called upon Buddhists to unite, "step onto the martyr's path and . . . defend the [eternal truth of Buddhism] in orderly, peaceful and non-violent fashion." Thousands attended memorial services for the Hue victims. Four hundred monks and nuns blocked traffic in Saigon and then underwent a forty-eight-hour fast. In Hue again, ARVN troops broke up a massive Buddhist procession with attack dogs, truncheons, and tear gas.

Diem and the Buddhist leaders continued to talk. Hoping to calm things, the president sacked two local officials and ordered the arrest of the major whose men had fired into the crowd. He also broadcast a message that admitted "errors" had been made. On June 6, a joint communiqué suggested a peace agreement was imminent.

Madame Nhu immediately undid everything her brother-in-law had accomplished. Through her own organization, the Women's Solidarity Movement, she accused the monks of lying and contesting "the legitimate precedence of the national flag," criticized the government for having been too lenient, and demanded the instant expulsion of "foreign agitators, whether they wear monk's robes or not."

Washington demanded that Diem repudiate her statement. He refused.

Now convinced that Diem had never bargained in good faith, Buddhist leaders resolved to increase their pressure.

On June 10, Malcolm Browne of the Associated Press and several other foreign newsmen received anonymous tips: "something important" was going to happen the next day at a major Saigon intersection. Browne decided to attend and brought his camera with him.

He fell in with a procession of some 350 chanting yellow-robed monks and gray-robed nuns as it moved toward the intersection. When the procession reached it, a seventy-three-year-old monk named Thich Quang Duc made his way to the center of the street and assumed the lotus posture. Two younger monks poured gasoline over him. Another handed him a packet of matches. He struck one, dropped it into his lap—and exploded in flame.

"A wail of horror rose from the monks and nuns, many of whom prostrated themselves in the direction of the flames," Browne reported.

From time to time, a light breeze pulled the flames away from Quang Duc's face. His eyes were closed, but his features were twisted in apparent pain. He remained upright, his hands folded in his lap for nearly ten minutes as the flesh burned from his head and body. The reek of gasoline smoke and burning flesh hung over the intersection like a pall.

Finally Quang Duc fell backward, his blackened legs kicking convulsively for a minute or so. Then he was still, and the flames gradually subsided.

A monk with a bullhorn repeated over and over again in English and Vietnamese: "A Buddhist priest becomes a martyr. A Buddhist priest becomes a martyr."

In Washington early the next morning, Attorney General Robert Kennedy called the White House. His brother, the president, was still in bed. The attorney general wanted to talk to him about the growing crisis at the University of Alabama,

where, at noon, Governor George Wallace was planning to defy a federal court order and block the enrollment of two African American students. As his brother spoke, the president's eye fell upon the morning newspapers on his bedside table. Malcolm Browne's photograph of the burning monk was splashed across the front pages of several of them. "Jesus Christ!" he said.

Much of the world reacted the same way. For many people, the head of the United States Information Agency in Saigon recalled, that one shocking photograph became the "symbol of the state of things in Vietnam." Fresh outbursts by Madame Nhu only made things worse: the sight of burning monks made her clap her hands, she said; if more monks wanted to barbecue themselves, she would provide the matches.

Monks assured the faithful that Quang Duc's heart had been untouched by the flames. They placed it in a glass reliquary at the Xa Loi pagoda, the Saigon headquarters of the Buddhist movement. "Lines of people came to pass by," Neil Sheehan remembered, "and I saw these women, not rich women, ordinary Vietnamese women, take off the one piece of gold they had on, their wedding ring, and drop it in a bottle to contribute to the struggle. And I thought to myself, this regime is over. It's the end."

Dean Rusk fired off a cable to the deputy chief of mission in Saigon: "If Diem does not take prompt and effective steps to re-establish Buddhist confidence in him we will have to re-examine our entire relationship with his regime. . . . He must fully and unequivocally meet Buddhist demands . . . in a public and dramatic fashion."

On June 16, Diem and Buddhist negotiators issued a joint communiqué meant to defuse the situation: the ban on religious flags would be eased, it said, and the Hue incident would be fully investigated.

It was too late. More monks set themselves alight over the next few weeks—five of them, in different cities and towns. Day after day, demonstrators took to the streets, their ranks steadily growing as students, intellectuals, disaffected Catholics, and other urban critics of the regime aligned themselves with the Buddhist cause. "People feared the Diem regime," Duong Van Mai remembered, "but perhaps more than that they hated it."

Diem hardened his position. Demonstrators were beaten, hauled away, tortured. By mid-July, the CIA reported at least three separate military plots to overthrow Diem under way in Saigon. Diem and Nhu learned of them too, and shrewdly managed to turn the generals against one another.

Meanwhile, the Kennedy administration debated whether the United States could possibly succeed in Vietnam if Diem and Nhu remained in power.

The White House announced that a new American ambassador was being sent to Saigon. Henry Cabot Lodge Jr. belonged

to an old and influential New England family. He'd been a Massachusetts senator, Dwight Eisenhower's ambassador to the United Nations, and Richard Nixon's running mate, and was a man eminent enough, the president hoped, to make Diem pay greater heed to American demands for reform. Diem professed to be unimpressed. "They can send ten Lodges," he said, "but I will not permit myself or my country to be humiliated. Not if they train their artillery on the Palace."

Eight years earlier, Diem and Nhu had taken a great risk: against Washington's express wishes, they'd gone to war against the crime syndicate that then controlled Saigon, annihilated it after three bloody days of fighting, and been rewarded for their defiance by increased American backing. The brothers now believed they could do something like that again. Diem promised outgoing American ambassador Frederick Nolting that he would take no further repressive steps against the Buddhists. "The policy of utmost reconciliation is irreversible," he assured the *New York Herald Tribune*.

Then, a few minutes after midnight on August 21 with Nolting gone and Henry Cabot Lodge's arrival still one day away—Nhu first saw to it that the phone lines of all the senior American officials in Saigon were cut and then sent hundreds of his American-trained white-helmeted Special Forces storming into pagodas in Saigon, Hue, and other cities. More than fourteen hundred monks and nuns, students and ordinary citizens, were rounded up and taken away. Martial law was imposed, public meetings were forbidden, and troops were authorized to shoot anyone found on the streets after nine o'clock.

When college students protested, Diem closed Vietnam's two universities. Scores of students were arrested, including Phan Quang Tue, the son of the imprisoned opposition figure Phan Quang Dan. "I am a Catholic," Tue remembered, "not a very good Catholic. But I was a choirboy. I didn't join that movement because of Buddhism only. I strongly believed that the government was a dictatorship. We couldn't stand it anymore. This was an opportunity to rise against it. I was interrogated and briefly tortured, beaten a little bit. It was clear to them that I was against the government. I never denied that."

High school students then poured into the streets. Diem shut down the high schools and the grammar schools, too—and arrested thousands of schoolchildren, including the sons and daughters of officials in his own government. American civilians thought to be sympathetic to the Buddhists were shadowed,

wiretapped, threatened. American reporters trying to cover the demonstrations were beaten up.

Diem's foreign minister resigned in protest, shaved his head, declared he intended to become a monk—and was arrested. Nhu's own father-in-law, the Vietnamese ambassador to the United States, resigned his post in protest at what members of his extended family were doing. Nhu warned him never to return to Vietnam; if he did, he said, he would have him hanged in public, and Madame Nhu would personally fashion her father's noose.

WE MUST BEAR A GOOD DEAL OF RESPONSIBILITY

FOR THOSE within the Kennedy administration most eager to replace Diem, the pagoda raids were the last straw. The president and his top advisers all happened to be out of town on Saturday August 24, when Roger Hilsman Jr., assistant secretary of state for Far Eastern affairs and a longtime critic of the Diem regime, took it upon himself to draft a cable to Ambassador Lodge. The U.S. government could no longer tolerate a situation in which "power lies in Nhu's hands," it said. Diem

OPPOSITE Buddhists protesting against the Diem regime clash with riot police in Saigon, July 17, 1963. More than fifty demonstrators were injured. **ABOVE** Ngo Dinh Nhu and his wife, Tran Le Xuan, better known as "Madame Nhu"

should be given a chance to rid himself of his brother-in-law and his closest allies. But if he remained "obdurate," Lodge was to tell "key military leaders" that "we must face the possibility that Diem himself cannot be preserved," and, further, that the United States stood ready to offer "direct support in any interim period of breakdown [of the] central government mechanism."

The president was vacationing at Hyannis Port, Massachusetts. Vietnam had not been uppermost in his mind that summer. He'd been horrified by the picture of the burning monk, but he'd also been preoccupied by the continuing civil rights crisis, a proposed tax cut, a trip to Europe, and winning congressional approval for a test ban treaty with the Soviets. Vietnam had been largely left to subordinates. When Assistant Secretary of State George Ball read part of the cable to him over the phone, Kennedy asked, "Can't we wait until Monday when everybody is back?" Ball thought not. It was an urgent matter. Kennedy eventually agreed to sign off on the cable, provided his senior advisers concurred. And since he had already indicated that he would do so, most of them or their deputies went along. The cable was sent.

When the president returned to the White House on Monday he found some of the officials who had not been personally consulted furious. Robert McNamara, Maxwell Taylor, Vice President Lyndon Johnson, and John McCone, the head of the CIA, all vehemently opposed replacing Diem; none of them especially admired him, but they did not believe there was any viable alternative. Former ambassador Nolting agreed; no one had "the guts, the *sang-froid,* the drive" that Diem had displayed since coming to power. Nhu was a liability, he agreed, but there should be no coup until Washington had tried harder to convince Diem that his brother and his sister-in-law had to go.

"My God, my government's coming apart," Kennedy said, but he was angry, too. He thought the way the cable had been authorized was badly handled. "This shit has got to stop!" he said. But he did not rescind it.

In Saigon, Lodge was already persuaded that regime change was necessary. One by one, he had invited the American reporters who'd been covering South Vietnam to lunch at the embassy. "We were told that we were not to question the ambassador," Neil Sheehan recalled. "The ambassador wanted to question *us.* We believed—and so did the military advisers—that if we stuck with the Diem regime we were going to lose. But if Diem was replaced by a decent military junta there was a chance we could win the war. At the end of the lunch I asked him, 'Mr. Ambassador, how do *you* see things?' He said, 'Pretty much the way you do.'"

A small group of ARVN officers had quietly contacted the new ambassador. Nhu was now largely in command of the South Vietnamese government, they said, and was thought secretly to be discussing a separate North-South agreement that would force the Americans to withdraw and lose their anticommunist foothold in Southeast Asia. They were willing to move against the Ngo brothers, provided the United States would not attempt to stop them.

"We are launched on a course from which there is no respectable turning back: the overthrow of the Diem government," Lodge cabled the White House. Therefore, he argued, "we should . . . make an all-out effort to get the Generals to move promptly" because they "doubt that we have the will power, courage and determination to see this thing through."

The president agreed, but, remembering the disaster at the Bay of Pigs, reserved the right to call things off at the last minute, and insisted on keeping his options open as long as he could. "When we go, we must go to win," he answered, "but it will be better to change our minds than fail."

Through a CIA operative, Lodge informed the plotters that Washington favored a coup but would take no active part in it. He was assured the generals would move within a week. But in the end, unsure of one another's loyalties, fearful of Nhu's power, and perhaps sensing Washington's continuing ambivalence, the generals backed off.

Two days after the coup collapsed was September 2, Labor Day, and Walter Cronkite of CBS News interviewed President Kennedy at Hyannis Port. The president used the occasion to deliver a message to President Diem. Change was necessary. The Nhus had to go.

WALTER CRONKITE: Mr. President, the only hot war we've got running at the moment is, of course, the one in Vietnam, and we've got our difficulties there, quite obviously.

JOHN KENNEDY: I don't think that unless a greater effort is made by the government to win popular support that the war can be won out there. In the final analysis, it is their war. They have to win it or lose it. We can help them, we can give them equipment, we can send our men out there as advisers, but they have to win it, the people of Vietnam.

We are prepared to continue to assist them, but I don't think the war can be won unless the people support the effort, and in my opinion, in the last two months, the government has gotten out of touch with the people.

The repressions against the Buddhists, we felt, were very unwise. Now all we can do is to make it very clear that we don't think this is the way to win. It is my hope that this will become increasingly obvious to the government, that they will take steps to bring back popular support for this very essential struggle.

CRONKITE: Do you think this government still has time to regain the support of the people?

KENNEDY: I do. With changes in policy and perhaps with personnel I think it can. If it doesn't make those changes, I would think that the chances of winning it would not be very good.

CRONKITE: Hasn't every indication from Saigon been that President Diem has no intention of changing his pattern?

KENNEDY: If he doesn't change it, of course, that's his decision. He has been there ten years and, as I say, he has carried this burden when he has been counted out on a number of occasions. Our best judgment is that he can't be successful in this basis. . . . But I don't agree with those who say we should withdraw. That would be a great mistake. That'd be a great mistake. I know people don't like Americans to be engaged in this kind of an effort. Forty-seven Americans have been killed. . . . We're in a very desperate struggle against the communist system. And I don't want Asia to pass into the control of the Chinese.

Diem and Nhu seem to have gotten at least part of the message. As concessions to Kennedy, their elder brother, Archbishop Thuc, left the country to attend a meeting at the Vatican. Madame Nhu left too, but not before denouncing American advisers as "little soldiers of fortune." Nhu himself, however, was going nowhere.

Kennedy and his advisers remained sharply divided. Some continued to argue that without fresh leadership South Vietnam could not survive. Others were equally certain that eliminating Diem and Nhu would lead only to disaster. The most basic facts seemed to be in question. At one meeting, the president asked two officials newly returned from Vietnam for their impressions. Marine Major General Victor Krulak assured him the war in the countryside was going well. "Our purpose is to *win*," he said; changing the government would only complicate that task. Joseph Mendenhall, a veteran State Department official, strongly disagreed: the war was being lost. "A pervasive atmosphere of hate and fear" gripped Saigon—hate and fear of Nhu, not the Viet Cong. The same was true in Hue and Danang. Victory was impossible so long as Nhu still wielded power.

The president shook his head. "You both went to the same country?"

The Ngo brothers had three times defied the odds and es-

caped disaster—against generals who'd hoped to topple them in 1954, against the Binh Xuyen the following year, and against coup plotters in 1960. Now they had persuaded themselves that the prospects for another triumph were bright. They had crushed the Buddhists and outmaneuvered the generals, after all. They had convinced themselves that the strategic hamlets were making revolutionary changes in the lives of the rural poor, and that they had the communists on the run. (Madame Nhu would later claim Saigon was just "two fingers from victory.") It was only a matter of time before Hanoi capitulated. In the meantime, while the Americans were always intrusive and often trying, the brothers did not believe they would dare withdraw their backing.

This time, they guessed wrong. On October 2, Lodge learned that a new coup was in the works. A large number of officers were involved, including several who would eventually play

ABOVE Ambassador Henry Cabot Lodge and President Ngo Dinh Diem meet for the first time at the Gia Long palace, September 1, 1963. Lodge saw no need for frequent meetings. "The chances of Diem's meeting our demands are virtually nil," he said.

important parts in South Vietnamese history, including Colonel Nguyen Van Thieu, who had joined Nhu's Can Lao Party and converted to Catholicism as he climbed up the military ladder; Nguyen Cao Ky, the transport wing commander of the fledgling South Vietnamese air force; General Nguyen Khanh, veteran of combat in the Central Highlands; and the ringleader, General Duong Van Minh—known as "Fatty" to his fellow officers because he was beefy and outwardly genial, and "Big Minh" to the Americans because, at six feet, he towered over most of his countrymen.

Lodge reported to Kennedy Minh's cold-eyed assessment of the current situation:

> The Viet Cong are steadily gaining in strength; have more of the population on their side than has the [Saigon government]; . . . arrests are continuing and . . . the prisons are full; . . . more and more students are going over to the Viet Cong; . . . there is graft and corruption in the administration; and . . . the "heart of the Army" is *not* in the war.

The president was again not sure what he wanted to do. He sent McNamara and General Taylor back to Saigon for yet another fact-finding trip. The war had made "great progress and continues to make progress," they reported. They still opposed a coup, but in order to gain leverage with Diem—and to reassure domestic critics already concerned that there were no limits to the American commitment—they urged Kennedy to publicize General Harkins's earlier prediction that fully trained and fully equipped South Vietnamese forces would defeat the communists by 1965, and to also let it be known that the first one thousand Americans would be withdrawn over the next three months. Kennedy followed that suggestion, but he did not oppose a coup.

Lodge told the White House that the plotters needed to know how Washington would react before they would move against Diem and Nhu. He asked for permission to reassure them.

On October 9, in an "eyes only" cable, he got it: "While we do not wish to stimulate [a] coup, we also do not wish to leave [the] impression that [the] U.S. would thwart a change of government or deny economic and military assistance to a new regime if it appeared capable of increasing [the] effectiveness of the [South Vietnamese] military effort." Lodge relayed the information to the generals.

OPPOSITE Surrounded by jeering participants in the coup, the corpse of President Ngo Dinh Diem, his hands tied behind his back, lies on the deck of the U.S. M113 armored personnel carrier in which he and his brother were murdered.

Rumors of what seemed about to happen continued to sweep Saigon and were reported so often by David Halberstam in *The New York Times* that Kennedy himself tried to persuade his publisher to have the reporter transferred out of Saigon.

On the morning of November 1, Lodge called on Diem for the last time. "Please tell President Kennedy that I am a good and frank ally," Diem said, "[and] that I take all his suggestions very seriously and wish to carry them out, but it is a question of timing."

It was too late. ARVN troops loyal to the plotters were already seizing key installations in Saigon. They surrounded the palace and demanded the president's immediate surrender. Diem and Nhu slipped out a side door and eventually found sanctuary in a church in the Chinese district of Cholon. They agreed to surrender only on the promise of safe passage out of the country. Rebel troops picked them up in an APC—and murdered them not long after they climbed inside.

In Saigon, cheering crowds pulled down statues of Diem and garlanded ARVN troops with flowers. Thousands of Diem's political prisoners were released from the fifty prisons in which they had been held, including both Dr. Phan Quang Dan—the pro-democracy politician who had endured three years of brutal treatment for supporting the 1960 coup against Diem—and his eldest son, Phan Quang Tue, who had recently been jailed for taking part in the Buddhist uprising. "Everyone was really bursting with happiness," Tue remembered. "You could feel the excitement in the air."

Duong Van Mai remembered how pleased she had been by the coup. Diem had had to go. "He was making it impossible to win the war because the people were so against him. But my father worried because we didn't know who would replace him."

"Every Vietnamese has a grin on his face today," Lodge reported. "The prospects are [now] for a shorter war," he said, "provided the Generals stay together. Certainly officers and soldiers who can pull off an operation like this should be able to do very well on the battlefield if their hearts are in it."

President Kennedy was not so sure. He was appalled that Diem and Nhu had been killed. Three days later, he dictated his own rueful account of the coup and his concerns for the future.

> Monday, November 4, 1963. Over the weekend the coup in Saigon took place. It culminated three months of conversation which divided the government here and in Saigon. . . . I feel that we [at the White House] must bear a good deal of responsibility for it, beginning with our cable of . . . August in which we suggested the coup. In my judgment that wire was badly drafted. It should never have been sent on a Saturday. I should not have given consent

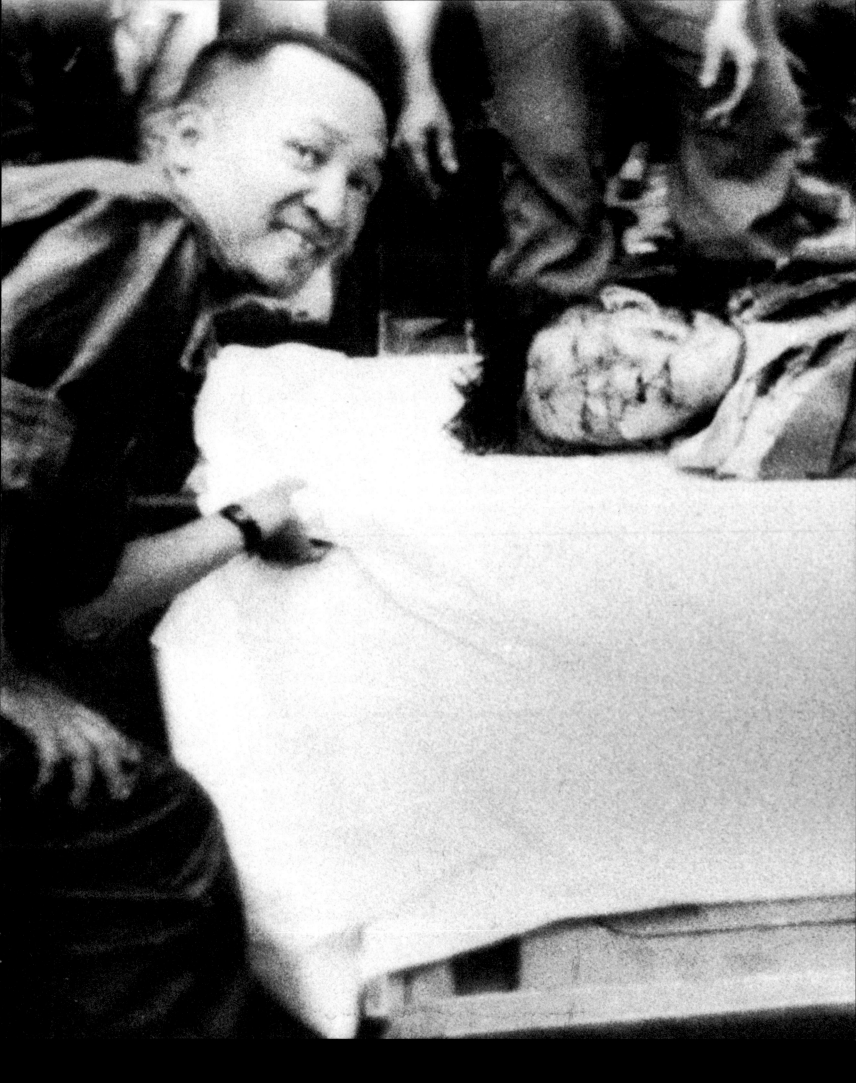

to it without a roundtable conference at which McNamara and Taylor could have presented their views. While we did redress that in later wires, that first wire encouraged Lodge along a course to which he was in any case inclined. I was shocked by the deaths of Diem and Nhu. I'd met Diem . . . many years ago. He was an extraordinary character. While he became increasingly difficult in the last months, nevertheless over a ten-year period, he'd held his country together, maintained its independence under very adverse conditions. The way he was killed made it particularly abhorrent. The question now is whether the generals can stay together and build a stable government or whether . . . public opinion in Saigon—the intellectuals, students, etc.—will turn on this government as repressive and undemocratic in the not too distant future.

Kennedy would not live to get the answer to the question he had posed. He was murdered in Dallas eighteen days later. There were now sixteen thousand American advisers in South Vietnam. Their fate and the fate of that embattled country rested with a new American president, Lyndon Baines Johnson.

OPPOSITE A jubilant South Vietnamese Marine celebrates inside the Presidential Palace grounds after the coup. **TOP** Saigon citizens turn out to cheer the ARVN troops who had toppled Diem. **ABOVE** In this rare, battered image, communist guerrillas celebrate having seized the Tan Thanh Tay strategic hamlet, some forty miles northwest of Saigon on the night of November 2, 1963—the same night Nhu and Diem were killed.

KENNEDY AND WHAT MIGHT HAVE BEEN

FREDRIK LOGEVALL

IT'S A QUESTION asked in any discussion of the American buildup in Vietnam in the first half of the 1960s: What would John F. Kennedy have done had he lived? The timing of his death in November 1963—mere days after a U.S.-backed coup against South Vietnamese leader Ngo Dinh Diem and not long before the crucial escalation decisions of late 1964–early 1965—guaranteed that the speculation would be rife, as did the fact that he died suddenly, by an assassin's bullet, leaving only scant hints about his future plans for the struggle. On top of that, there's his administration's ambiguous and complex record on Vietnam, which seemingly gives support to two opposing positions: one that a surviving Kennedy, when faced with the ultimate choice, most likely would have stood firm in the war and expanded American military involvement in more or less the same way his successor Lyndon B. Johnson did; the other that he would have avoided such a course and instead gotten the United States out, come what may.

Although historians who write about the Kennedy record in Vietnam invariably consider what might have occurred had he returned from Dallas alive, they often do so hastily and with evident reluctance. No doubt this reticence stems at least in part from the widespread belief among professional historians that such "counterfactual" or "what if" questions are superfluous to true scholarship and the equivalent of parlor games. When carefully done, however, consideration of that which never happened can enhance historical understanding of what did. For that matter, all historians, whenever they make causal judgments, are engaging in speculation, are envisioning alternative outcomes, even when these alternatives are not stated explicitly. As such, thinking about unrealized possibilities is an indispensable part of the historian's craft, conveying the variable dimensions of past situations and the presence of contingency. In the current case, it can help us better understand not merely what Kennedy might have done in Southeast Asia but what Lyndon Johnson *did* do. If it's a parlor game, it's also much more than that.

What's more, the Kennedy-in-Vietnam counterfactual is especially favorable for fruitful exploration because of the massive available documentary record for the period before and after his assassination; because of the short period of time between Kennedy's murder and the moment of truth in U.S. decisionmaking; and because of the minimal number of likely changes in other

principal variables. The following core assumptions seem reasonable: that a surviving JFK would have kept his senior advisory team (which became Johnson's) more or less intact, at least through the 1964 presidential election; that he likely would have faced Republican senator Barry Goldwater in that election as LBJ did, and would have beaten him; that, like Johnson, he would have sought to keep Vietnam on the back burner until voting day; that the situation in South Vietnam would have deteriorated at roughly the same rate as under his successor; and that, therefore, crunch time for him likely would have come at about the same time as for Johnson, as 1964 turned into 1965.

How would Kennedy have responded when the difficult decision came, when he could temporize no longer, could no longer just maintain the status quo? Here we must look in the first instance to the historical record, to what Kennedy actually said and did on Indochina during his time in public office. And what we confront immediately is a paradox: the same JFK who for a dozen years prior to his death expressed doubts about the capacity of Western military power to overcome revolutionary nationalism in the developing world, and who periodically questioned the importance of the Indochina conflict to American security, in 1961–63 oversaw a major increase in the U.S. military commitment to South Vietnam.

Already in the fall of 1951, when as a thirty-four-year-old congressman he visited Indochina during the midst of the First Indochina War, Kennedy saw through the French expressions of bravado and optimism and asked hard questions about whether France—or, by extension, any Western power—could ever thwart Ho Chi Minh's revolutionary cause. In his trip diary and in a speech to a Boston audience after his return, he lamented that the United States had attached herself to the "desperate effort" of the French to hang on to their colonial hold in Southeast Asia, an effort almost certain to fail. To act "apart from and in defiance of innately nationalistic aims spells foredoomed failure," JFK told the Boston gathering, adding that a free election would in all likelihood go to Ho and the communists.

In the spring of 1954, with the French war effort collapsing, now Senator Kennedy supported a proposed international effort to try to save the Western position in Indochina (through a concept called "United Action"), but at the same time feared where such a policy would lead the nation. "To pour money, materiel, and men into the jungles of Indochina without at least a remote prospect of victory would be dangerously futile and destructive," he declared. For that matter, would the United States ever be able to make much difference in that part of the world? "No amount of American military assistance can conquer an enemy which is everywhere and at the same time nowhere, 'an enemy of the people' which has the sympathy and covert support of the people." No satisfactory result was possible, Kennedy concluded, unless Paris accorded Indochina full and complete independence; without it, sufficient indigenous support would remain forever out of reach.

Later in the decade, as he began eyeing a White House run, Kennedy moved closer to cold war orthodoxy. He now spoke less of "nationalistic aims" and the French analogy and more of falling dominoes and the urgent need to thwart communist aggression. But the skepticism did not go away; it was always there, just beneath the surface. Sometimes he expressed it openly, as in 1957, when he went well beyond official U.S. policy in supporting Algeria in her war of independence against France. "The most powerful single force in the world today," he declared in a Senate speech on the North African crisis that summer, "is neither communism nor capitalism, neither the H-bomb nor the guided missile—it is man's eternal desire to be free and independent." Washington must respond effectively to this hunger, he went on, which meant urging French leaders to pursue negotiations leading to Algerian independence.

In early 1961 Kennedy, now president, deflected the urgings by his predecessor Dwight D. Eisenhower that he intervene militarily in Laos ("the key to the entire area of Southeast Asia," Ike insisted), where the anticommunist position had eroded significantly over the previous two years and where the North Vietnam–supported Pathet Lao now seemed on the cusp of victory. Some senior Kennedy aides likewise advocated using major military power in Laos, but he demurred, opting instead to pursue a diplomatic settlement.

That fall, JFK resisted aides' calls for committing U.S. ground forces to Vietnam to counter recent Viet Cong gains. General Maxwell Taylor, his most important military aide, remarked at a meeting among other principals on November 6 that the president was "instinctively against introduction of U.S. forces," a point noted as well by General Lyman Lemnitzer, the chairman of the Joint Chiefs of Staff, at another session a few days later. In a November 15 meeting of the National Security Council, JFK expressed a desire to keep the American commitment limited. Whereas Korea in 1950 was a case of clear aggression, he remarked, the situation in Vietnam was "more obscure and less flagrant." One could even "make a rather strong case against intervening in an area 10,000 miles away against 16,000 guerrillas with a native army of 200,000, where millions have been spent for years with no success."

The reference to Korea points to something important about Kennedy: more than most politicians of his generation, he had a sense of the vagaries of history, of its inscrutability. Increasingly as time wore on, he showed an appreciation for the limits of American power, no matter how great it might be in relative terms, and he occasionally expressed doubts about the ability of using military means to solve world problems that were at root political in nature. More clearly than many, he saw that colonialism is often in the eye of the beholder, and that for a great many Vietnamese there might not be much of a difference between the two big Western powers—first France, now the United States—coming in and telling them how to run their affairs, with guns at the ready. The French had crashed and burned, and Kennedy worried that his country could be next. "If [Vietnam] were ever converted into a white man's war," he told an aide early in his presidency, America would lose just as France had lost.

And yet. As president this same John F. Kennedy, though still harboring doubts, oversaw a major expansion of American involvement in Vietnam. Even as he steadfastly rejected the urgings to commit combat troops, he affirmed the importance of defeating the Viet Cong insurgency by upping substantially his country's contribution to the war effort. In 1962, vast quantities of the best American weapons, aircraft, and armored personnel carriers arrived in South Vietnam, along with thousands of additional U.S. military advisers. That year a full field command bearing the acronym MACV (Military Assistance Command, Vietnam) superseded MAAG (Military Assistance Advisory Group) with a three-star general, Paul D. Harkins, in command. A secret American war was under way. Ostensibly, Americans were serving purely as advisers and never engaging the Viet Cong except in self-defense; in reality, their involvement extended further—in the air and on the ground.

The reality was plain to see. "The United States is involved in a war in Vietnam," Homer Bigart, the venerable military correspondent of *The New York Times,* wrote in a front-page article in February 1962. "American troops will stay until victory." Bigart noted the "passionate and inflexible" U.S. support for South Vietnamese President Ngo Dinh Diem and speculated that Washington "seems inextricably committed to a long, inconclusive war." He quoted Attorney General Robert F. Kennedy, who on a visit to Saigon that month vowed that the administration would stand by Diem "until we win." By the end of 1962, American military advisers in Vietnam numbered over eleven thousand, and by the time of JFK's assassination in Dallas, almost sixteen thousand.

Did Kennedy become more encouraged about the war in 1962 and 1963, more confident that it could be won with the new measures? Hardly. If anything, he grew increasingly wary during his final year of life, hinting to aides in the final months that he wanted to withdraw from Vietnam following his reelection in 1964.

A few authors as well as filmmaker Oliver Stone have gone further and claimed that Kennedy did more than just talk about getting out—they argue that he had quietly commenced a full withdrawal at the time of his murder. As evidence, they cite his continual refusal to commit American ground troops to the war, despite the urgings of top advisers; the October 1963 declaration that one thousand U.S. military advisers would be withdrawn by the end of the year; the release that month of National Security action Memorandum (NSAM) 263, which they argue shows a far-reaching policy initiative to draw down America's commitment to Saigon, a policy then allegedly reversed in NSAM 273, the first such document issued under Lyndon Johnson (Stone's film *JFK* shows the two documents together, as the soundtrack plays ominous music); and Kennedy's belief, stated most notably in his September 2, 1963, television interview with Walter Cronkite, that in the end this was a war that the South Vietnamese themselves would have to win. Some also refer to private comments made by Kennedy to the effect that he was determined to get out of Vietnam, whatever the cost.

It's a seductive line of reasoning, but ultimately the evidence for this "incipient withdrawal" thesis is weak and contradictory. The way I interpret a pair of important White House meetings on October 2 and 5, 1963, for example, is that at that late hour JFK was still unsure about which way to go in Vietnam, and, moreover, that he had not given the one-thousand-man withdrawal proposal very much thought. "My only reservation about this [troop withdrawal]," he says at one point, "is that it commits to a kind of a—if the war doesn't continue to go well, it'll look like we were overly optimistic, and I don't—I'm not sure we—I'd like to know what benefit we get out [of] at this time announcing a thousand." Could this be a ruse on the president's part, as proponents of this argument claim, designed to hide his secret determination to get America out of the conflict? Possibly, but these analysts do not present persuasive evidence to that effect. As for the two NSAMs, the difference between them is slight: 263 signaled no necessary lessening of the American commitment to South Vietnam, while 273, approved by Johnson a few days after Kennedy's death, showed fundamental continuity with the earlier document, and with various other high-level missives in October and November.

Time and again in the fall months, senior officials struck a firm tone on their public pronouncements on the war. Kennedy himself, in the very same Cronkite interview in which he said the Vietnamese themselves would have to win the struggle, declared that it would be a mistake for the United States to withdraw. In subsequent weeks he continued publicly to vow steadfastness and to reject disengagement. His remarks set for delivery on November 22 at the Dallas Trade Mart, a destination he never reached, included these words: "We in this country in this generation are the watchmen on the walls of freedom. . . . Our assistance to . . . nations can be painful, risky, and costly, as is true in Southeast Asia today. But we dare not weary of the task."

The point here is not to deny the assertion by incipient-withdrawal theorists that public comments may tell us very little about private intentions and planning; it is, rather, to suggest that the constant public affirmations by JFK and his lieutenants of the Vietnam struggle's importance to U.S. security further reduced their room for maneuver. A Kennedy committed to early disengagement from the conflict would surely want as much freedom of action as possible. He would have been more cryptic in his public pronouncements and instructed aides to be likewise, and would have been less dismissive of exploring a possible negotiated settlement to the struggle.

Most of all, a president determined to quit Vietnam regardless of the state of the war would have been more reticent about endorsing a showdown between South Vietnamese leader Ngo Dinh Diem and dissident generals. From late August onward, Kennedy's moves indicate that he had resigned himself to the necessity of removing Diem (though it seems clear that he never intended for Diem to be killed). When on occasion he expressed uncertainty about a coup, it was only because of a fear that it might fail. A large question here is whether JFK understood that American complicity in the coup would increase American responsibility for subsequent developments in South Vietnam, thereby making withdrawal more difficult. The answer remains elusive, in part because neither he nor his advisers appear to have given the matter much thought. Before Diem's ouster, Kennedy seems to have believed that a change in government could actually *hasten* a U.S. withdrawal—the new leaders in Saigon would implement needed reforms, win increased public backing at the expense of the Viet Cong, and allow the United States to reduce and eventually eliminate its presence. After the coup he may have continued in this belief, but he also felt that this scenario would, even in the best of circumstances, take many months to materialize. In the short term, JFK understood, the American commitment was deeper than ever before, especially in view of the Ngos' murder. In a cable to Lodge on November 6, Kennedy acknowledged U.S. complicity in the coup and spoke of American "responsibility" to help the new government succeed.

In all likelihood, Kennedy at the time of his death was leaving his Vietnam options open, playing a waiting game. That's what successful politicians do with vexing policy problems, especially when an election looms large on the horizon. They hedge. His decisions on Vietnam since 1961 had vastly increased his nation's presence in the war, but they had usually been compromise decisions, between the extremes of an Americanized struggle and an American withdrawal, both of which he had seen as equally unpalatable. On the day before his death, Kennedy told aide Michael Forrestal, who was about to depart for a visit to Indochina, that he wanted to see him again soon, in order to plan what to do in South Vietnam. Forrestal recalled of the conversation:

> He said, "I want to start a complete and very profound review of how we got into this country, what we thought we were doing and what we now think we can do." He said, "I even want to think about whether or not we should be there." He said, because this was of course in the context of an election campaign, that he didn't think we could consider drastic changes of policy quickly. But that what he wanted to consider when I returned and when people were ready to think about this more clearly was how could some kind of a gradual shift in our presence in South Vietnam occur.

Or consider the comment from National Security Advisor McGeorge Bundy, in an oral history completed just a few months after the Dallas tragedy. "If you had poked President Kennedy very hard," Bundy commented, he would have said America was in Vietnam "because it's the best we can do and because it's certainly essential to have made a determined effort and because we mustn't be the ones who lost this war, someone else has to lose this war. But I don't think he would have said to you that *he* saw any persuasive reason to believe that this was certainly going to succeed." The implication was that Kennedy remained undecided, in large part because "he was deeply aware of the fact that this place was in fact X thousand miles away in terms both of American interest and American politics."

None of which is to deny the possibility that Kennedy had already set limits on how far he would go in defense of the Saigon regime, had already determined that large-scale war involving regular U.S. ground troops would never occur while he was in charge. It's possible that he had already decided in his own mind that he would seek some kind of fig-leaf withdrawal from the conflict following the presidential election a year hence. The Forrestal and Bundy recollections, if accurate, certainly speak to his misgivings. "We'd cross that bridge when we came to it," is how brother Robert described the administration's thinking on the prospect of a complete deterioration in South Vietnam. It is an expression that effectively summarizes Kennedy's whole approach to the war.

It would be Lyndon Johnson's fate to come to that bridge about a year after Kennedy's murder. How would a surviving Kennedy have responded in his place? A strong argument could be made that he would have swallowed his doubts and done more or less what Johnson did, pursuing large-scale escalation involving sustained aerial bombardment and the dispatch of major ground forces rather than face the prospect of defeat. The powerful effect of the Diem coup is important supporting evidence here, made more powerful by the fact that Diem and his brother Nhu were not just ousted from power but killed as well. Having helped bring the coup about, Kennedy felt an added sense of responsibility in its aftermath, not merely on moral grounds but on geopolitical ones as well—now more than ever, maintaining U.S. global credibility might demand a successful outcome in Vietnam.

It matters as well that the senior advisers advocating escalation under LBJ were the same men who counseled Kennedy. By the late autumn of 1963 Secretary of Defense Robert McNamara and other top officials had a large personal stake in the commitment they had trumpeted for so long, a vested interest in its success. Although several of these senior planners, including McNamara, were less bullish and less hawkish on the war than is often asserted by historians—McNamara was privately skeptical and staked out an aggressive posture in large part because he believed that's where LBJ wanted him to go—they had put their personal credibility on the line with their public bluster. Their stake in a winning outcome would only increase as 1964 came and went, as the war effort deteriorated, and as American young men began coming home in body bags.

Like his successor, a surviving Kennedy would have felt partisan political pressure to stay the course in Vietnam. As Democrats, he and LBJ felt susceptible to Republican charges of being "soft on communism," of failing to learn what Munich 1938 had taught about the dangers of "appeasement." Truman, too, acted partly with this concern in mind, as, indeed, did Eisenhower—his Vietnam decisions in 1953–54 cannot be understood apart from the charged domestic political atmosphere in which they were made. But the perceived power of this political imperative was even greater now, in the early 1960s, as the two presidents, feeling the vulnerability that all Democrats felt in the period, sought to avoid a repeat of the "Who lost China?" debate, this time over Vietnam.

But if a strong case can be made that a post-Dallas Kennedy probably would have pursued a course in Vietnam broadly similar to that taken by his successor, is it the best argument? I think not. Nor is it easy to see him opting for a more modest troop escalation of the type William Bundy, assistant secretary of state for Far Eastern affairs, floated in mid-1965. Under this "middle plan" the number of American combat forces would be capped at approximately 85,000, and the troops would concentrate on seizing and holding certain key "enclaves" in the South. Any decision about a larger buildup would wait until the end of the summer monsoon season, when a full-fledged assessment would be made. Few inside the administration saw this Bundy plan as sufficient to turn the tide in the war, however, which meant that the larger buildup would in all likelihood follow.

No, the better argument is that JFK most likely would *not*

have Americanized the war, but instead would have opted for some form of disengagement, presumably by way of a face-saving negotiated settlement. ("We would have fuzzed it up," Robert Kennedy said a few years later when pressed on whether his brother was really prepared to see South Vietnam go communist. "The way we did in Laos.") The components that make up this argument are not persuasive on their own; for full effect, they must be considered together and for their cumulative effect.

Consider, first, one of the points articulated above: that running through Kennedy's whole approach to the war was a fundamental ambivalence about Indochina and what should be done there. It's also true that he remained committed to the war effort at the time of his death, but this is not the contradiction it might appear to be. There are commitments and there are commitments. The Kennedy record reveals a man who sought victory in Vietnam from day one to the end, who failed to pursue a negotiated settlement, and who helped overthrow Ngo Dinh Diem, but also a man who always had deep doubts about the enterprise and deep determination to keep it from becoming a large-scale American war.

Kennedy's decision to pursue negotiations in Laos further demonstrated his disinclination to use American ground troops in Indochina. To be sure, Laos never mattered as much as Vietnam in U.S. official and public opinion, which made the decision to negotiate there comparatively easy. Likewise, it is possible, as some have argued, that the Laos decision only made Kennedy more determined to affirm American support for South Vietnam—conciliation in one place necessitated standing firm somewhere else. Still, the Laos case is further evidence of JFK's opposition to large-scale interventions in that part of the world, even when senior associates called for them.

A surviving Kennedy would have faced one significant disadvantage vis-à-vis Johnson—namely, a greater stake in the war and in seeing the administration's policy succeed. Overall, however, the greater disadvantages belonged to Johnson, and each of them served to reduce his maneuverability (real and imagined) on the war. First and most obvious, he was a new president in late November 1963, new and untested. Many in the Washington foreign policy community mistrusted him; many others questioned his qualifications. Just a few months hence, Democrats would accept or reject him at the national convention, and not long after that the general public would pass their judgment on him. Johnson believed, no doubt accurately, that adversaries at home and abroad were watching him closely, watching his responses to problems and probing for signs of weakness. Small wonder that he perceived the need not only for "continuity" in his foreign policy but also for firmness.

Kennedy, by contrast, could in no way be considered untried in the fall of 1963. He had faced an uncommon number of foreign policy crises in his tenure; to some of these he responded well, to others not, but all made him more battle tested. A little over a year before his death, Kennedy had showed strength and gained prestige in forcing Khrushchev to withdraw Soviet missiles from Cuba; regardless of whether JFK's tough stance was wise or necessary, few could question his resoluteness after that point. Then, in mid-1963, he signed the limited nuclear test ban treaty with Moscow, which he could cite as his commitment to peace. At the time of his death, therefore, he had a sizable reservoir of political credibility as a statesman, something Johnson never possessed.

Kennedy was no Vietnam expert, but he possessed a more sophisticated understanding of the dynamics of the region than his successor. As president he privately doubted the validity of a crude domino theory, whereby a defeat in Vietnam would lead in short order to the loss of all of Southeast Asia, and he perceived from early on that there was only so much the United States could accomplish in that corner of the world. He appears to have grasped, well before many of his aides and his vice president, the civil war dimension of the Vietnam struggle and the problems this might cause for American intervention.

The timing of the assassination, occurring as it did only about a year before the 1964 election, also may have served to limit Johnson's perceived freedom of maneuver. Whereas Kennedy would have faced the critical Vietnam decisions in his second (and final) term, when the domestic political implications of those decisions would be at least somewhat less pressing, Johnson faced them in what amounted to his first term—for him the eleven months between his taking office and the 1964 election were but a prelude, a kind of preliminary campaign for finally claiming the mantle of the martyred leader. The relative freedom of maneuver that might have led a second-term Kennedy to reevaluate fundamentally Vietnam policy in, say, December 1964, thus did not exist to the same degree for LBJ, or at least so he believed. Nor was it merely electoral considerations that kept Johnson focused on the domestic political costs of his Vietnam decisions; there was also his ambitious legislative agenda. Though care should be taken not to exaggerate the Great Society's role in Johnson's strategizing on Vietnam, it certainly mattered. It stands to reason that here, too, a post-Dallas Kennedy, possessing no real Great Society equivalent, would have been less constrained.

Basic personality differences between the two men may have made a difference when the critical moment came. Kennedy did not share Johnson's deep self-doubt in the role of commander in chief, or his general predilection toward self-pity. Moreover, Kennedy's worldview contained a pronounced skepticism that the Texan's lacked—when Secretary of State Dean Rusk would speak apocalyptically of the need to save "Christian civilization" by persevering in Vietnam, his words resonated with Johnson in a way they would never have done with JFK. Both presidents were intelligent men, but Kennedy possessed the more flexible and reflective mind, at least with respect to world affairs. Despite the sweeping pledge of his inaugural address to "pay any price, bear any burden," he generally chose the course of restraint in foreign policy, as in Berlin, Laos, and the Cuban Missile Crisis, and it's hard to imagine him exhibiting the obstinacy and truculence with respect to Vietnam that Johnson so frequently showed in 1965—and in the years that followed. It's hard to imagine him telling pronegotiation French and British officials that the only alternatives to present policy were to "bomb the hell out of China" or to retreat to Hawaii and California, or telling aides it was insulting to have foreign leaders "chasing over" to see him, or reading to allied officials a letter from a supportive American soldier in Vietnam to his mother, all of which LBJ did.

Kennedy did not have Johnson's tendency to personalize policy issues, or his deep dislike of dissent. He would not have seen the war as a test of his manliness to the same degree as did Johnson, for though himself imbued with a healthy dose of machismo, he was less prone to extending it to the nation, to the complex world of foreign policy. Perhaps because he had proven himself in war—Johnson had not—he never viewed attacks on foreign policy as attacks on himself to the extent LBJ did. Although politicians as a rule are notoriously averse to abandoning failed policies and altering course, these Kennedy characteristics suggest that he would have had an easier time doing so than did Johnson.

We can further assume that Kennedy's policymaking environment, comparatively open in the pre-Dallas period, would have kept that quality afterward as well, thus distinguishing it from Johnson's much more cloistered setting. This is potentially critical: a less constrained, more Kennedy-like environment, in which the chief executive encouraged a broad range of views, would have made the Johnson team more inclined after November 1964 to ask the really fundamental questions about the war, to listen to—not just to hear—the many independent voices predicting giant, perhaps insurmountable, obstacles ahead, given the chronic weaknesses south of the 17th parallel.

Ultimately, it is this bleak situation within South Vietnam in late 1964–early 1965, more than any personal attributes of Kennedy, that stands as the single most important reason to suppose he would have opted against an Americanized war in Vietnam. It's easy today to forget the despair that this condition generated in a broad cross-section of informed observers, American as well as foreign, who saw firsthand the political infighting in Saigon and the pervasive war weariness and burgeoning anti-Americanism throughout the South. Many who had always enthusiastically supported the U.S. commitment to South Vietnam, and who would do so again a few months later after the commitment of American troops, in these months freely asserted that Washington had no obligation to persevere under such circumstances and that there might be no option but to get out. Said *The Washington Post,* later a staunchly hawkish voice on the war, in December 1964, "It is becoming increasingly clear that, without an effective [Saigon] government, backed by a loyal military and some kind of national consensus in support of independence, we cannot do anything for South Vietnam. The economic and military power of the United States . . . must not be wasted in a futile attempt to save those who do not wish to be saved."

A harsh but discerning assessment, and one that John F. Kennedy would have been more likely than his successor to heed.

CHAPTER THREE

THE RIVER STYX

JANUARY 1964–DECEMBER 1965

Two Vietnamese women do their best to get on with their daily lives despite the presence of newly arrived U.S. Marines patrolling near Danang, April 1965.

HE TODAY THAT SHEDS HIS BLOOD

DENTON WINSLOW CROCKER JR. was born June 3, 1947, the oldest of four children. His father and namesake was a biologist. "He was a colicky little baby," his mother, Jean-Marie, remembered. "So we were up night and day with him. My husband was a wonderful dad, very loving and attentive. He'd walk the floor with him. And one day he said, 'He's a regular little mogul the way he rules our lives.' So that's where the name came from. We called him Mogie."

Mogie was raised in college towns: Ithaca; Amherst; Waterville, Maine; and, finally, Saratoga Springs, to which the family moved in 1960, when he was thirteen. He was very close to his sister Carol. "We had a nice big yard where they played," his mother recalled. "And he would often include Carol. And she said to me once, 'Brothers take care of you when you're afraid of dogs.' So she depended on him a lot."

He was an unusual boy. Intelligent, independent minded, and too nearsighted to do well at team sports, he loved books about American history and American heroes. At twelve, he started a diary in which he kept track of cold war events. "I hate Reds!" he wrote, and he admired most those who had proved willing to sacrifice themselves for a cause. President John F. Kennedy's call for all Americans to ask what they could do for their country had mirrored ideas he'd held since he was a small boy.

"One evening," his mother remembered, "when I was reading to Denton before he went to sleep, I chose a passage from *Henry V*: 'He today that sheds his blood with me shall be my brother . . . And gentlemen in England now a-bed shall think themselves accurs'd they were not here and hold their manhoods cheap while any speaks that fought with us upon St. Crispin's Day.' That was the sort of thing that made Denton want to be part of something important and brave."

ABOVE Mogie Crocker reads about one of his many heroes, Winston Churchill. **OPPOSITE** President Lyndon Johnson works the telephone in the Oval Office. "Johnson knew how to woo people," his eventual vice president, Hubert Humphrey, remembered. "He was a born political lover. . . . He knew how to massage the senators. He knew which ones he could just push aside, he knew which ones he could threaten, and above all he knew which ones he'd have to spend time with and nourish along, to bring along, to make sure that they were coming along."

THE ABLEST MEN

TRAGEDY HAD BROUGHT Lyndon Johnson to the presidency in November 1963. And he would not feel himself fully in charge until he had faced the voters the following year. But his ambitions for his country were as great as those of his hero, Franklin Roosevelt. In his first State of the Union address he declared "unconditional war on poverty," and during his years in the White House he would lead the struggle to win passage of more than two hundred important pieces of legislation—the Civil Rights Act of 1964, the Voting Rights Act of 1965, federal aid to education, Head Start, Medicare, and a whole series of bills aimed at ending poverty in America—all components of what he called the "Great Society."

In foreign affairs, Johnson was admittedly less self-assured. "Foreigners are not like the folks I'm used to," he once said. To deal with them, he retained in office all of his predecessor's top advisers—Dean Rusk at State, Robert McNamara at Defense, McGeorge Bundy as his National Security Advisor. "You're the men I trust the most," he told them. "You're the ablest men I've ever seen. It's not just that you're President Kennedy's friends, but you are the best anywhere and you must stay. I want you to stand by me."

Publicly, Johnson pledged that "this nation will keep its commitments from South Vietnam to West Berlin." But privately, the ongoing struggle in Indochina filled him with dread. "I feel just like I grabbed a big juicy worm," he told an aide, "with a right sharp hook in the middle of it."

The president had opposed the coup that overthrew and mur-

dered Ngo Dinh Diem, fearing it would make a bad situation worse. It had. Ambassador Lodge's optimism about the new Saigon leadership had lasted only a few weeks. The generals were bickering. General Paul Harkins, who had opposed the coup, and Henry Cabot Lodge, who had promoted it, were barely speaking. By mid-December, all the news from Vietnam was bad. There were now as many as one thousand violent incidents a week, three times as many as there had been just a year earlier. "When Diem was overthrown we were so excited," Le Cong Huan, the NLF fighter who had helped win the victory at Ap Bac, remembered. "We thought we were close to liberating the whole country. We began attacking the enemy day and night. More and more puppet soldiers surrendered or defected to our side. More and more young people joined our armed forces."

"They had grown so powerful in the Delta that they launched an offensive," Neil Sheehan recalled. "You could *hear* the arming of the Viet Cong because as we made contact with a Main Force unit back in early '62, they only had one machine gun per battalion. It was sporadic fire. Later, when you made contact it would build up into a drumfire of automatic and semiautomatic weapons. They destroyed strategic hamlets, were knocking over one outpost after another."

It had quickly become "abundantly clear," the head of the CIA admitted, that some of Diem's province chiefs and top commanders had simply lied about how well the war was going, deliberately misleading the Americans with cheery statistics that had little to do with reality. By some estimates, 40 percent of the South Vietnamese countryside—and with it more than 50 percent of the people—was now effectively in the hands of the Viet Cong. In one province south of Saigon, only 45 of 219 strategic hamlets still provided security to their inhabitants.

There were problems in the cities, too. Catholics, stripped of the special status they had enjoyed under Diem, feared the future and clashed openly with Buddhists. The Buddhists, whose protests had helped bring Diem's regime to an end, were dissatisfied with the new government, which did not deliver the protection for their faith or the path to peace for which they'd hoped. They were divided among themselves, as well, but a growing faction had come to believe in what came to be called the "Third Force"—a negotiated settlement that would rid their country of its alien American presence.

Robert McNamara pronounced the situation "very disturbing." If it wasn't reversed within two to three months, he warned the president, South Vietnam might be lost. He proposed a four-month program, meant to convince Hanoi it was in its interest to halt its support of the Viet Cong: U-2 flights over North Vietnam; ARVN sabotage teams parachuted in to blow up rail and highway bridges; U.S. destroyer patrols in the Gulf of Tonkin to collect intelligence in support of South Vietnamese

commando assaults along the North Vietnamese coast. All of it was to be kept secret.

Johnson signed on. He was resolved not to be "the president who saw Southern Asia go the way China went," he said. "I want [the South Vietnamese] to get off their butts and get out into those jungles and whip the hell out of some communists," he said. "And then I want 'em to leave me alone, because I've got some bigger things to do right here at home."

ONLY ONE GOAL

THERE HAD BEEN CHANGE and turmoil in North Vietnam, too, just as there had been in Saigon and Washington, though Americans knew little about it. At the Ninth Party Plenum that had coincidentally begun in Hanoi on November 22, 1963, the day President Kennedy was killed, the politburo had argued over how best to proceed with the war. North Vietnam's two "big brothers"—the Soviet Union and China—were offering conflicting advice. The Soviets, now championing peaceful coexistence rather than open confrontation with the West, counseled caution. The Chinese accused Moscow of "revisionism" and continued to call for worldwide revolution.

Ho Chi Minh was most sympathetic to the Soviets; he was still concerned that his country remained fragile, and believed it better to wage a protracted guerrilla war than to step up the conflict in the South and force the Americans to take a more active role in the war. He remained a beloved figure, but now he shared power with younger, more impatient leaders.

First Party Secretary Le Duan, closer to the Chinese, argued that the time was right to strike, and outlined a new military strategy, aimed at ending the war in 1964. In the first "Big Battles" phase, the North Vietnamese would massively increase infiltration into the South while the Viet Cong recruited more men and amassed more arms. Then, employing conventional tactics and large unit formations, they would inflict massive losses on the ARVN "puppets."

By late 1965 or early 1966, when South Vietnamese forces had been sufficiently worn down and demoralized, the second phase, or "General Offensive, General Uprising," would begin—simultaneous attacks on South Vietnamese cities. The weakened South Vietnamese forces would be unable to resist while the people rose up and seized power in conjunction with the military, just as they had during the August Revolution in 1945. A "neutralist" government under NLF control would then ask the United States to leave.

The politburo debated for two weeks. When Ho raised objec-

ABOVE In public, Ho Chi Minh (at the microphone) and Party Secretary Le Duan (at Ho's left) presented a united front. In private, things were more complex.

tions to Le Duan's plan, the younger man argued that he was too timid; the two most momentous decisions Ho had made—not to oppose the French return to northern Vietnam in 1945 and to accept the temporary partition of Vietnam in 1954—were proof of it, he charged. In the end, Le Duan carried the day, and when the votes were about to be cast and Ho saw that he would lose, he stepped out of the room; from then on, while he would always remain the symbol of the revolution, his actual power over day-to-day operations would diminish, while Le Duan's increased.

In the aftermath of the meeting, as regiments of North Vietnamese troops prepared to move south, Le Duan and his allies methodically purged moderate party members who had differed with them. Hundreds of so-called "rightists" and "revisionists" were demoted, dismissed, imprisoned, or sent to "reeducation camps." "Uncle [Ho] wavers," Le Duan said, "but when I left South Vietnam I had already prepared everything. I have only one goal— just final victory."

GET IN OR GET OUT

UNAWARE of what the communists in Hanoi were planning, American planners wrestled with ongoing problems in Saigon. General Duong Van "Big" Minh, the most important member of the military junta now in charge in Saigon, was proving as independent in his own way as Diem had been in his. Minh wanted to replace the U.S.-financed Strategic Hamlet Program with a new scheme that would allow peasants to remain in their homes, and he wanted fewer American advisers visiting the countryside; they reminded people of French imperialism, he said, and suggested that the Saigon government was altogether too close to a foreign power. And, from Washington's point of view, he seemed too sympathetic to a proposal by French president Charles de Gaulle that called for a negotiated settlement and a neutral Vietnam. Most of President Johnson's advisers were against negotiating when South Vietnam's situation seemed so precarious. "*When* we are stronger," Bundy told the president, "*then* we can negotiate." Until then, they needed a South Vietnamese government willing to at least try to win.

On January 30, a group of young ARVN officers, led by General Nguyen Khanh, overthrew Big Minh without firing a shot.

Khanh was profoundly ambitious and thought reliably hawkish. During his gaudy career he had managed to have fought both for and against the French, to have helped rescue Diem from the 1960 coup, and then to have become actively involved in the coup that overthrew him in 1963.

Johnson did not care about the general's consistency or his character. "This Khanh is the toughest one they got, and the ablest one they got," he told a visiting newspaperman. "And [Khanh] said, 'Screw this neutrality . . . we ain't going to do business with the communists. . . . I'm pro-American and I'm taking over.' Now it'll take him a little time to get his marbles in a row, just like it's taking me a little time. . . . We're going to try to launch some counterattacks ourselves. . . . We're going to touch them up a little bit in the days to come."

He sent McNamara to Saigon in mid-March with instructions to show the people of Vietnam that Khanh was "our boy." "I want to see about a thousand pictures of you with General

ABOVE A disbelieving father holds his dead child, killed as South Vietnamese army rangers stormed into a village near the Cambodian border in search of the enemy, 1964.

Khanh," he told the defense secretary, "smiling and waving your arms and showing the people out there that this country is behind Khanh the whole way." At one joint appearance, General Samuel Wilson, then associate director for USAID field operations, remembered, Khanh delivered a long, tedious speech in Vietnamese, ending with, *"Vietnam muôn năm! Vietnam muôn năm! Vietnam muôn năm!"*—"Vietnam, ten thousand years!" At which point, McNamara grabbed one fist and Maxwell Taylor grabbed the other and they held them up, and McNamara leaned over to the microphone and tried to say *"Vietnam muôn năm,"* but, because he wasn't aware of the tonal difference, the crowd practically disintegrated on the cobblestones. What he was saying was something like "The little duck, he wants to lie down."

"No more of this coup shit," Johnson told his advisers. But despite everything Washington tried to do to stabilize the Saigon government, the generals would continue to jockey for power as Buddhists and Catholics clashed in the streets. Over the next fourteen months, Khanh clung to power as president or prime minister, but he would be forced to form and reform his government seven times. One weary Johnson aide sug-

gested that the national symbol of South Vietnam should be a turnstile.

It had quickly become clear that the new policy of clandestine sabotage in and around North Vietnam was having no serious impact on Hanoi's support for the Viet Cong. None of the CIA-trained commandos dropped into North Vietnam were ever heard from again. The Joint Chiefs of Staff urged the president to raise the stakes, to "put aside . . . the self-imposed restrictions which now limit our efforts," and take far bolder action. The war should immediately be broadened beyond the borders of South Vietnam, they said, to include air attacks on North Vietnamese supply routes in Laos and Cambodia and bombing of military and industrial targets in North Vietnam. The Chiefs also called upon the president to deemphasize reliance on North Vietnamese troops and send American soldiers into battle instead.

Johnson resisted, fearing that such aggressive moves would pull China into the conflict, just as it had entered the Korean War in 1950. "They say get in or get out," he complained to McGeorge Bundy, "and I told them . . . we haven't got any Congress that will go with us in the war, and we haven't got any . . .

mothers that will go with us in the war and . . . I'm just . . . a trustee. I've got to win an election . . . and then [I] can make a decision."

But he did agree to increase the number of American advisers from 16,000 to more than 23,000 by the end of 1964. He wanted his own team in Saigon, too. He made Maxwell Taylor his ambassador, and selected forty-nine-year-old General William Westmoreland, a decorated commander from World War II and Korea who had served for six months as General Harkins's deputy, to lead the American military effort. "Have we got anyone with a military mind that can give us some military plans for winning that war?" Johnson asked McNamara.

ABOVE General Nguyen Khanh and Robert McNamara tour the Mekong Delta aboard a helicopter, 1964. The goal of the defense secretary's appearances alongside the general was "to promote him to his own people," McNamara remembered, but "we never realized that encouraging public identification between Khanh and America may have only reinforced in the mind of many Vietnamese the view that his government drew its support not from the people but from the United States."

"Let's get some more of something, my friend, because I'm going to have a heart attack if you don't get me something . . . because what we've got is what we've had since '54. We're not getting it done. We're losing."

A May 27th phone call with McGeorge Bundy made clear that Vietnam continued to fill the president with dread.

LYNDON JOHNSON: I just stayed awake last night thinking about this thing—the more I think of it . . . it looks like to me we're getting into another Korea. It just worries the hell out of me. I don't see what we can ever hope to get out of there with once we're committed. I believe the Chinese communists are coming into it. I don't think it's worth fighting for and I don't think we can get out. And it's just the biggest damn mess I ever saw.

MCGEORGE BUNDY: It is, it's an awful mess.

JOHNSON: . . . I look at this [Marine] sergeant of mine this morning, got six little old kids, . . . and he's getting out my things and bringing me my night reading and all that kind of stuff and I just thought about ordering those kids in there, and what the hell am I ordering him out there for? . . .

BUNDY: Yup. Yup.

JOHNSON: Now of course if you start running, the communists . . . may just chase you into your own kitchen.

BUNDY: Yup. That's the trouble. And that is what the rest of that half of the world is going to think if this thing comes apart on us. That's the dilemma. That's *exactly* the dilemma.

Polls showed Johnson with a commanding lead over his likely Republican opponent, Senator Barry F. Goldwater of Arizona, a blunt uncompromising critic of what he charged was the administration's weakness in the face of communist aggression. But Johnson felt he did not yet have the political capital to take further action in Vietnam, and he didn't want to repeat the mistake he believed Harry Truman had made when he sent troops to Korea without congressional approval. Unless Congress was in at the "takeoff," Johnson told McNamara, they wouldn't take responsibility if there were a "crash landing."

William Bundy—McGeorge Bundy's older brother and the newly appointed assistant secretary of state for Far Eastern affairs—was asked to chair a committee that drafted a congressional resolution, authorizing the president to "take all necessary measures to repel any armed attack against the forces of the United States," to be sent to Capitol Hill when and if the time was right.

GRANDMA'S NIGHTSHIRT

ON JULY 30, 1964, the South Vietnamese, under the direction of the U.S. military, shelled two North Vietnamese islands in the Gulf of Tonkin. The tiny North Vietnamese navy was put on high alert. What followed three days later was one of the most controversial and consequential events in American history.

On the afternoon of August 2, 1964, the destroyer USS *Maddox* was moving slowly through international waters in the gulf, on an intelligence-gathering mission in support of further South Vietnamese action against the North. When the commander of a North Vietnamese torpedo boat squadron spotted the *Maddox,* he moved to attack her. The Americans opened fire and missed. None of the North Vietnamese torpedoes hit the American destroyer either. But carrier-based U.S. planes roared in shortly afterward, damaged two of the North Vietnamese boats, and left a third dead in the water.

Ho Chi Minh was shocked to hear of the attack and demanded to know who had ordered it. The officer on duty was officially reprimanded for impulsiveness. No one may ever know who gave the order to fire the torpedoes—or why he gave it. It may simply have been the action of an overzealous squadron commander. But some believe it was secretly Le Duan's doing, a clumsy attempt at provoking just enough of an American response to transform a civil war into a war of "National Liberation" that would make it easier to draft young men and rally international support. To this day, even the Vietnamese cannot agree.

In Washington, the Joint Chiefs urged immediate retaliation against North Vietnam. The president refused. Instead, the White House issued a warning about the "grave consequences" that would follow what it called "any further unprovoked" attacks—even though Johnson knew the attack had in fact been provoked by the South Vietnamese raids on North Vietnamese islands.

Both sides were playing a dangerous game.

Two days later, on August 4, jittery American radio operators aboard the *Maddox* monitoring North Vietnamese radio traffic thought they heard that a "military operation" was imminent. (Actually, they'd mistranslated the conversation they'd heard; Hanoi had simply called upon torpedo boat commanders to be ready in case of a new raid by the South Vietnamese.)

The *Maddox* and another destroyer, the *Turner Joy,* braced for a fresh attack. So did the White House. Admiral Ulysses S. Grant Sharp, U.S. commander for the Pacific, proposed that in the event of a second attack the destroyer commander be empowered to pursue the North Vietnamese torpedo boats to their base and then destroy it.

Robert McNamara telephoned the president. He thought the admiral's suggestion precipitous. "There will be ample time for us, after a second attack," he told Johnson, "and you can then decide how far you wish to pursue the attacker into his base area." Instead, he said, "I personally would recommend to you, after a second attack on our ships, that we do retaliate against the coast of North Vietnam some way or other."

LYNDON JOHNSON: What I was thinking about when I was eating breakfast: . . . when they move on us and they shoot at us, I think we not only ought to shoot at them, but almost simultaneously pull one of these things that you've been doing, on one of their bridges or something.
ROBERT MCNAMARA: Exactly. I quite agree with you, Mr. President. . . .
JOHNSON: But I wish we could have something that we've already picked out, and just hit about three of them damn quick, right after.

No second attack ever took place, but the sonar operators convinced themselves one had. The attack was "probable but not certain," Johnson was told. Since he believed it had probably occurred, the president decided it should not go unanswered.

That evening, he asked for time on all three television networks. "Aggression by terror against the peaceful villagers of South Vietnam has now been joined by open aggression on the high seas against the United States of America," he told the country. "Yet our response, for the present, will be limited and fitting. We Americans know, although others appear to forget, the risk of spreading conflict. We still seek no wider war."

The next day, Johnson flew to Rochester, New York, where he was to make a campaign speech. Secretary McNamara reached him at the airport with the results of the first American air raid on North Vietnam.

ROBERT MCNAMARA: The reaction from North Vietnam and China is slight so far. Less than I would have anticipated.
LYNDON JOHNSON: How many planes did you lose?
MCNAMARA: We lost two aircraft . . . and possibly a third. . . . Two other aircraft were damaged. One pilot got out of the plane.

That pilot was Lieutenant Everett Alvarez from Salinas, California. He was aboard the carrier USS *Constellation* when his squadron of A-4 Skyhawks was ordered to attack torpedo boat installations and oil facilities near the port of Hon Gai. For the first time, American pilots were going to drop bombs on North Vietnam.

"When we approached the target coming down from altitude," Alvarez recalled, "it was obvious that they could pick us up on their radar. I remember my knees shaking. And, I was saying to myself, 'Holy smokes, I'm going into war. This is war.' I was a bit scared. But once we went in and they started firing at us, the fear went away. Everything became smooth, deathly quiet in the cockpit. My plane was like a ballet in the sky, and I was just performing. And then I got hit."

Alvarez ejected from his spiraling plane and splashed into the Gulf of Tonkin. Coastal militiamen captured him and turned

TOP The USS *Maddox* at sea, four months before her fateful confrontation with North Vietnamese torpedo boats in the Gulf of Tonkin ABOVE In this grainy snapshot taken from the deck of the *Maddox*, three attacking North Vietnamese vessels can be seen on the horizon, July 30, 1964.

The resolution, Johnson told his aides, was like "Grandma's nightshirt—it covers everything." He now felt himself empowered to undertake combat operations in Southeast Asia—whenever he felt such action was necessary.

Goldwater could no longer plausibly claim that Johnson was too timid when dealing with North Vietnam, while those voters concerned that the United States was in danger of becoming too deeply involved admired the president's measured response. Johnson's approval for his handling of the war jumped overnight from 42 percent to 72 percent. The American public believed their president.

Le Duan and his comrades in Hanoi did not. They knew the attacks had not been "unprovoked," and had little faith in the president's claim that he sought no wider war. They resolved to step up their efforts to win the struggle in the South before the United States escalated its presence by sending in combat troops. For the first time, Hanoi began sending North Vietnamese regulars down the Ho Chi Minh Trail into the South.

him over to the North Vietnamese military. "One fellow was "yelling at me in Vietnamese," he remembered. "I started talking to him in Spanish. Don't ask me why. It seemed like a good idea at the time. Anyway, after they discovered 'USA' on my ID card they started speaking to me in English."

He assumed he would be treated as a prisoner of war. "I was sticking to the code of conduct and gave them my name, rank, service number, and date of birth. But they quickly reminded me that there was no declaration of war. So I could not be considered a prisoner of war. And I says to myself, 'You know what? They're right.'"

Everett Alvarez was the first American airman to be shot out of the sky over North Vietnam—and the first to be imprisoned there.

Now, the president sent up to Capitol Hill the resolution he had asked William Bundy to help draft two months earlier. On August 7, 1964, three days after the capture of Alvarez and the president's address to the nation, the Senate passed what came to be called the Tonkin Gulf Resolution. Only Ernest Gruening of Alaska and Wayne Morse of Oregon voted against it. Not a single congressman opposed it in the House.

The diplomat John Negroponte was then a junior official in the Saigon embassy. "Shortly after I got there," he remembered, "we got the first reports of North Vietnamese troops coming into the South. A couple of prisoners were captured from a North Vietnamese unit up near Hue. A lot of us sat back and said, 'Whoa, this is a significant change.' But when our consul in Hue sent his report in about the capture of two North Vietnamese noncommissioned officers, the reaction in Washington was, 'Mr. Hebley shall not communicate directly with Washington anymore. He must vet all his reports through Saigon.' They didn't want that bad news during the 1964 election campaign. Mr. Johnson didn't really want any particular surprises during that period."

But as Johnson and Goldwater campaigned across the country, there were surprises nonetheless. In mid-October, Soviet premier Nikita Khrushchev was overthrown by members of his own party. The next day, China exploded its first atomic bomb. "We can't let Goldwater and Red China both get the bomb at the same time," Johnson told an aide. "Then the shit would really hit the fan."

"There are those who say you ought to go north and drop bombs," he told his campaign crowds. "We don't want our boys to do the fighting for Asian boys. We are not about to start another war and we're not about to run away from where we are. . . . As far as I am concerned, I want to be very cautious and careful, and use it only as a last resort when I start dropping

ABOVE Lieutenant Everett Alvarez, the first American pilot to fall into enemy hands, photographed in Hanoi by a Soviet photographer in 1967. The diminutive guard behind him was called "Elf" by Alvarez and his fellow prisoners.

bombs around that are likely to involve American boys in a war in Asia with 700 million Chinese."

On the last day of October, communist guerrillas shelled the American air base at Bien Hoa. Five Americans died, and thirty were wounded. Five B-57 bombers were destroyed on the ground, and fifteen more were damaged. Senator Goldwater said it was time for the president to admit that the United States was already fighting an undeclared war in South Vietnam—and to get about the business of winning it. Ambassador Taylor urged the president to retaliate with an airstrike against a MiG base in North Vietnam. The Joint Chiefs advised him to go much further—to mount an immediate all-out air attack on ninety-four targets in the North and to dispatch Army and Marine units to South Vietnam, as well.

He refused. Election day was just two days away. On November 3, Lyndon Johnson won the presidency in his own right and by a landslide, with forty-six states to Goldwater's four. It was the largest popular vote and the greatest victory margin in history up to that time.

Within a month, the president would approve what was

The 1964 campaign: For months, the Republican presidential nominee, Senator Goldwater (right) charged that President Johnson (above) was weak and vacillating in Vietnam, but when LBJ ordered airstrikes after the Gulf of Tonkin incident he muted his criticism for a time. "We're all Americans and stick together," he assured Johnson.

called a "graduated response"—limited air attacks on the Ho Chi Minh Trail in Laos and "tit for tat" retaliatory raids on North Vietnamese targets. But he would not undertake sustained bombing of the North until the South Vietnamese got their own house in order. Johnson doubted that airpower alone would ever work and feared that he would eventually have to send in ground troops, though he was not yet willing publicly to say so.

NOTHING EXCEPT
MY OWN CONSCIENCE

MOGIE CROCKER was seventeen in the autumn of 1964 and had been restless since the summer. After the Gulf of Tonkin incident he had confided to his sister Carol that he wanted to join the Navy but knew his parents would not sign the consent form that would allow a seventeen-year-old to enlist. His country seemed to be edging toward war and he saw it as his duty to be part of the worldwide struggle against communism.

"At that point," Carol recalled, "I couldn't understand why this would be so important to him. The war wasn't that prominent in the world I was traveling in. There was some discussion at home. It was on the news. But it seemed like a very distant war at that time. And that was part of the mystery to me of why it was important to him."

Mogie's parents tried to persuade him that he could be more useful to his country with a college education than simply as one more soldier. He was adamant and resolved to run away from home.

"He was home the night before," his mother remembered. "And we had a regular family supper. He said he'd rather be home than go to youth group at church. So that was pleasant. And then Monday morning he left for school. And I watched him leave from the back window. That night he didn't come in for supper and he hadn't called, which was very unusual because all the kids were good about keeping in touch."

Mogie's parents eventually found a letter, addressed to "Mum and Dad": "After weeks of thought I have come to the decision that I must run away and join the service. Please do not search for me! It will only cause many people a lot of useless trouble as I will fight my way out if anyone tries to capture me. Believe me when I say that nothing except my own conscience has made me do this."

Without American military help, he wrote, Southeast Asia was sure to fall to the communists. He wanted to help the Vietnamese "keep their freedom." He was not ready for college, and wanted to earn his own way in the world "while helping people at the same time."

> I still believe that individual freedom is the most important thing in the world and I am willing to die to defend that idea.
> Don't be too upset by my running away and don't pay attention to the jerks who may try to say you're bad parents. I will write you as soon as I am eighteen at which time you could not get me out of the service. My main concern in running away is how it would affect you, so please don't worry.
> Try to understand my decision.
>
> Love,
> Mogie

"When my parents started to share with us that they didn't know where he was," Carol Crocker recalled, "and that they had called the police and that his bicycle had been found, it took on a really unreal feeling for me. I actually remember going into my room and looking under my bed and telling him to come out. I assumed he was hiding somewhere. There was no way he had actually left. I eventually happened to look in my piggy bank and he had taken the money I had and left a note for me. He hadn't indicated where he'd gone or why. But he had promised he would pay me back. I'm not sure he ever did."

The police chief issued a thirteen-state missing-person bulletin. Mogie's parents contacted their congressman, recruiting centers, the FBI. Their church offered special prayers. Mogie did not call, did not write. The Crockers hoped they might hear from him on Christmas, and when they didn't, his mother wrote him a long letter. "I pray, my darling son, that Jesus will strengthen and comfort you in whatever you are doing and fill your heart with love of all that is good," she wrote. "And I shall still be waiting to fly to the door and hug you and call out to our home—and the world—'Mogie is home!'" Then she folded the letter and put it away. She had no idea where to send it.

Mogie was in Montreal. He had hoped to board a ship there and somehow join British forces fighting communists in Malaya. He had left home with only thirty dollars—twenty-five his mother had just given him for painting the front porch and the five he'd stolen from his sister's piggy bank. It hadn't gone far. He'd slept several nights in a church, then landed a job as a stock clerk in a department store, but couldn't earn enough to pay his rent. Shortly after New Year's, he boarded a bus for New

York City. It passed within two blocks of his house in Saratoga Springs, but he was too proud to get off.

He was gone about four months, his mother remembered. "When he finally called us, he was in New York City at a Y. And he told us that he had to give a cigarette lighter to the manager for security to make the phone call. But he still was determined and said that he would not come home unless we agreed to sign for him. And he wouldn't be eighteen until June. Well, we said we'd sign for him. And he did come home. My husband felt it was an honor-bound agreement. I was hoping that I could change his mind."

A LITTLE DIEN BIEN PHU

MARINE LIEUTENANT PHILIP BRADY arrived in Saigon just a few days after Lyndon Johnson's election, one of the new advisers sent to help shore up the South Vietnamese military. He was eager, he remembered, "to get into the first war I could find."

There were still so few advisers in Vietnam that General Westmoreland could greet each batch personally. He was an impressive-looking square-jawed man with an impressive record: some of the men he'd led in Tunisia, Sicily, and Normandy during World War II called him "Superman"; he'd fought with distinction in Korea, commanded the 101st Airborne, and served as superintendent of West Point. *Time* called him "the sinewy personification of the American fighting man."

"General Westmoreland told us that we were down on the five-yard line and we just needed a few more to go to get the touchdown," Brady remembered. Ambassador Taylor briefed the newcomers too. "He said he'd been through battles and wars and he had the clear sense, the professional judgment, that this thing was going to be wrapped up and we were going to carry the day."

Brady was assigned to assist Captain Frank P. Eller, senior adviser to the Fourth Battalion of the South Vietnamese Marine Corps, an elite unit whose members wore distinctive camouflage uniforms and called themselves the "Killer Sharks." Eller had been in country for six months, long enough to come to admire the fighting qualities of the men he helped to lead.

Brady came to admire them too. "You were told that you were going over there to guide, educate, and elevate these little fellows on how to really fight a war. But when you got there you saw that they already knew exactly how to fight. You were there simply, fundamentally, to guide assets they didn't have—Ameri-

can airstrikes, American artillery. They knew exactly what to do. They knew how to fight."

Among the men he came to know best was the platoon leader Tran Ngoc Toan, the son of a trucker, who had escaped life with a hostile stepmother by entering the South Vietnamese military academy at Dalat. He'd been fighting the communists for more than two years, had been among those who'd attacked Ngo Dinh Diem's palace during the 1963 coup, and was frankly suspicious of Americans, who seemed to him to have a "superiority complex." But he liked Philip Brady. "He was a tall guy and big," Toan recalled. "I told him, 'You are not my adviser, you are my helper.' And also, 'You are so tall and big that I want you to

ABOVE Tran Ngoc Toan, still on active duty in 1973, nine years after he nearly died at Binh Gia

General Khanh and four of his rivals. "We Americans are tired of coups," he told them. "You have made a real mess. We cannot carry you forever, if you do things like this." After Taylor's dressing-down, Khanh complained to an American newspaperman that the United States was now acting like a colonial power, and told a national radio audience that he refused ever to fight "to carry out the policy of any foreign country."

Four days later, on Christmas Eve, two guerrillas dressed in South Vietnamese army uniforms managed to drive a car filled with explosives into the parking area beneath the Brinks Hotel, in the heart of downtown Saigon. It was home to scores of American officers. Two died. Fifty-eight were injured.

Clearly, things were not improving for the South Vietnamese regime.

Meanwhile, for weeks, more than two thousand Viet Cong Main Force troops, members of the 271st and 272nd Regiments, had been filing quietly out of the Central Highlands in small groups. Fed and sheltered by village sympathizers along the way, they marched undetected some 125 miles into Phuoc Tuy, a supposedly "pacified" coastal province less than 40 miles southeast of Saigon. Main Force units from elsewhere joined them there, and forty tons of heavy weapons were unloaded on the coast under cover of darkness—mortars, machine guns, and recoilless rifles, capable of blasting tanks. The communists had never attempted anything on this scale before.

Their target was the strategic hamlet of Binh Gia, surrounded by jungle and rubber plantations and home to some six thousand Catholic, anticommunist refugees from the North, many of them the wives and children of South Vietnamese army personnel. The communist plan was to seize the hamlet and then annihilate the forces Saigon was sure to send to retake it.

Before dawn on December 28, their advance units easily overwhelmed the village militia and occupied Binh Gia. When two crack South Vietnamese ranger companies were helicoptered in the next day, they were ambushed and shot to pieces. Another South Vietnamese unit counterattacked, but failed to drive the communists out of the village.

On the morning of the 30th, the Fourth Marine Battalion was flown in to relieve and reinforce the battered rangers. By then, the enemy had withdrawn into a rubber plantation east of the hamlet. Frightened residents crawled out of their hiding places and greeted their liberators with bananas and tea. The South Vietnamese Marines moved through the streets. "We saw things we'd never seen before," Brady recalled, "like commo

stay away from me because if you get too close some Viet Cong sniper will shoot at you and hit me.'"

Brady, Toan, and the Fourth Marine Battalion were stationed near the Bien Hoa Air Base in reserve, waiting to be called into action. Reports reached them of the sudden hit-and-run raids by platoon-sized enemy forces that had plagued the South Vietnamese for years. But there were new rumors now, of larger enemy units moving through the countryside as well. Le Duan's plan for a swift and decisive victory was well under way.

In Saigon, the ruling generals remained preoccupied with vying for power. On December 20, Ambassador Taylor called in

ABOVE Stunned and bloodied, surrounded by shattered glass, an American survivor of the Brinks Hotel bombing in Saigon struggles to comprehend what has happened.

110 | THE VIETNAM WAR

wire used for field phones and all kinds of things that you normally didn't see in the aftermath of a battle with the Viet Cong. They had put together two thousand, twenty-five hundred men, the largest force they ever had. This was new, not an overnight thing, very carefully planned."

That evening, a helicopter with four men aboard, flying above the neat rows of thickly planted rubber trees east of the hamlet, spotted communist positions and came in for a closer look. "It was flying high first, and then lower," Colonel Nguyen Van Tong, a political officer in the NLF's Ninth Division, remembered. "The commander of our antiaircraft company asked for the order to shoot. A minute later [the helicopter] was hit and burning, and fell down on our position."

From Binh Gia, Philip Brady also saw it fall. "All of a sudden, you could see the tracers come out of the plantation, hit the helicopter, and it crashed." Reached by radio, the South Vietnamese colonel in command of the area ordered that a patrol be sent to the crash site to see if anyone had survived. Both Captain Eller and the Vietnamese battalion commander, Major Nguyen Van Nho, argued that it was unlikely. They were ordered to

TOP Under the protection of a U.S. gunship, men of the South Vietnamese Fourth Marine Battalion move toward the strategic hamlet of Binh Gia, just abandoned by the Viet Cong, July 30, 1964.
ABOVE Grateful residents welcome the Marines with cups of tea.

start toward the downed helicopter the following morning anyway.

Meanwhile, Colonel Tong remembered, "I came to the place where the airplane was shot down and I saw four dead Americans. Their bodies were burned. I told my soldiers to bury them. Later on, I would realize how valuable the lives of American advisers were. They sent in a whole puppet battalion to rescue four dead Americans."

At eight a.m., a company-sized Marine patrol set out on foot for the crash site. Captain Eller went along in case an airstrike was needed. They found the charred helicopter and four mounds marking the hastily dug graves of the Americans. The company commander ordered his men to establish a tight perimeter while four men dug up the dead. As they worked, enemy troops appeared among the trees and opened fire. Seventy-five-mm recoilless rifle shells exploded among the rubber trees, scattering branches and shards of wood everywhere. Mortar shells fell among the Marines. Major Eller called in Huey gunships and Skyraiders to provide suppressive counterfire and radioed to the senior American adviser in the area to tell him that he and his men had been ambushed. A bullet struck the rim of Eller's helmet and shattered. Fragments from it tore off most of his nose. Hastily bandaged but bleeding badly, he and what was left of the company started back toward Binh Gia. Twelve dead Marines were left behind.

ABOVE Binh Gia, scene of the 1965 South Vietnamese defeat that helped persuade General William Westmoreland that U.S. combat troops were needed if the Saigon government was to survive

At noon, Major Nho and three companies—326 men—started back toward the crash site. Philip Brady went with them. Tran Ngoc Toan led the first company. Communist snipers appeared between the trees, fired a shot or two, then withdrew, luring the Marines further and further into the plantation. They reached the downed helicopter at about two o'clock. Fearing another ambush, Brady urged Nho to go no further, but the major sent Toan and his men still deeper into the plantation in search of a likely landing zone.

An American chopper soon dropped into the clearing. The crew jumped out and lifted the four American corpses into the helicopter. Toan appealed to them to carry the twelve South Vietnamese dead away as well. They refused—another chopper was on the way, they said, then lifted off and clattered away over the trees.

But no helicopter came. The Marines stayed with their dead comrades. The shadows of the trees grew longer. Rather than wait any longer, Brady suggested they carry the bodies back to Binh Gia. Major Nho refused. "I was getting a little bit antsy," Brady recalled, "because we were losing light and we were outside of our artillery range. I told the battalion commander we had to go. Nho ignored me. At about 4:30 I tried again. Again, he ignored me." One of Brady's Marines spotted shadowy movement among the trees just beyond the plantation's edge. "Clearly, the enemy weren't gone," Brady said. "So at 5:25, I went to the major, and said, 'Major, we have to get out of here now.' And Nho said, 'Don't you forget I am a major and you are a lieutenant.' He turned on his heel and walked away. Ten minutes later all hell broke loose."

Mortar shells rained down on the Marine positions. Bugles blew and wave after wave of enemy troops advanced toward the Marines from three sides. Brady called in Skyraiders and gunships, but the foliage was too dense to spot the communists as they rushed from tree to tree.

Major Nho was killed. So were twenty-eight more of the Fourth Battalion's thirty-five officers.

Toan was shot through the thigh, then through the calf. He kept firing at the figures running toward him through the trees. "I didn't feel any pain at all," he remembered. "I didn't have time to think about it. They kept coming, and I was still fighting as a soldier."

"Ultimately, there were just a few of us left," Philip Brady remembered. "So we tried to get out. Twenty-six of us in the company I was with broke through. I think only eleven of us ultimately made it back to Binh Gia."

Tran Ngoc Toan, unable even to stand, had to be left behind. All that night, the enemy moved among the rubber trees, carrying away their wounded, gathering up American weapons, stripping the dead of their boots and uniforms and shooting any South Vietnamese Marines they found alive. Lying next to a corpse, Toan did his best to play dead. A communist soldier kicked him to see if he was still alive, then fired a burst from his submachine gun. One bullet passed through his side, setting his shirt on fire but somehow missing any vital organs. When the enemy finally began to withdraw into the jungle, Toan was almost exultant. "I'm still alive!" he remembered saying to himself. He lay still until he was sure the enemy had gone. Then, cradling his rifle in his arms, he began crawling toward Binh Gia, just under a mile away. It took him three days to get there. Ants and maggots fed off his wounds. He finally spotted friendly paratroopers.

He hadn't the strength to speak and had to pound on a rubber tree to attract their attention. The first man to reach him recoiled. "His wounds stink!" he said. "He smells like a dead rat." Only when Toan reached what was left of his unit did he allow himself to feel any pain.

When it was all over, 196 South Vietnamese Marines had been killed, wounded, or reported missing out of a 326-man battalion. "I'll never forget those sights," Colonel Nguyen Van Tong remembered. "Everywhere we went we saw corpses of the Saigon soldiers." Just thirty-two Viet Cong bodies were found on the battlefield, though many more are thought to have been killed and carried away.

The big question after Binh Gia, an American officer at headquarters said, was how a thousand or more enemy troops "could wander around the countryside so close to Saigon without being discovered. That tells you something about this war. You can only beat the other guy if you isolate him from the population."

Hanoi was exultant. "The battle at Binh Gia was a historic landmark in the war," Colonel Tong believed. "If the Americans had not got involved, we would have entered Saigon within a year." Ho Chi Minh called Binh Gia "a little Dien Bien Phu." Le Duan was convinced that his new offensive, aimed at drawing South Vietnamese units away from their bases and wiping them out one by one, was working. Once that had been achieved, he hoped to encourage an uprising so widespread and so bloody

that the United States would have no choice but to withdraw and accept neutrality—which could quickly be turned into reunification under communist rule. "The liberation war of South Vietnam has progressed by leaps and bounds," Le Duan said. "After the battle of Ap Bac the enemy knew it would be difficult to defeat us. After Binh Gia the enemy realize[s] that he [is] in the process of being defeated by us."

WE'LL DO WHAT WE HAVE TO DO

MACV AND THE SAIGON EMBASSY were understandably alarmed. "Some kind of action had to be taken to save the situation," John Negroponte remembered. "Most of us saw Saigon as an underdog. There were entire villages being emptied

ABOVE After-action report: Lieutenant Philip Brady explains to a reporter what has just happened at Binh Gia, New Year's Day, 1965. Behind him are some of the South Vietnamese Marines he helped lead out of the trap the enemy had sprung. The communists were so successful by then, Brady recalled, that "the Vietnamese officers I talked to in the [South Vietnamese] Marine Corps figured they had six months before the end."

from the countryside and moving into the provincial and district capitals. The situation was terrible. Our reports were being forwarded to Washington and people were reading them."

On January 27, 1965—twenty-six days after Binh Gia and just a week after President Johnson's inauguration—McGeorge Bundy handed the president a memorandum. The current policy was clearly not working, it said. The Viet Cong were on the move and on the rise, supplied—and now steadily reinforced—by North Vietnam. And Saigon still had no prospect of a stable government. If an independent South Vietnam was to survive, the United States needed to act fast.

The administration faced two choices, Bundy wrote. It could go along as it had been going and try to negotiate some kind of settlement—probably nothing better than the neutral Vietnam they could have had years earlier. ("Surrender on the installment plan," Bundy called it.) Or it could use American military might to force the North to abandon its goal of uniting the country. Bundy and McNamara favored the military option; unless the president chose it, they said, South Vietnam would fall.

Johnson agreed. Stable government or no stable government, he said, "We'll do what we have to do. . . . I don't think any-

thing is going to be as bad as losing." But he wanted a pretext before he ordered further action.

He got one a little over a week later, when guerrillas struck a U.S. helicopter base and barracks at Pleiku in the Central Highlands near the border with Cambodia, killing 9 American advisers and wounding 137 more with mortar fire, satchel charges, and homemade grenades. McGeorge Bundy, in Vietnam on a fact-finding mission, surveyed the damage—wrecked helicopters and body parts strewn across the area—and convinced himself that Hanoi had ordered the attack as a provocation designed to coincide with his mission. He telephoned the White House and urged a retaliatory airstrike on the North. (In fact, Hanoi had had nothing to do with the attack, and the NLF commander who ordered it had never heard of Bundy or his mission.)

Bundy had a receptive audience in Washington. "We have kept our gun over the mantel and our shells in the cupboard for a long time now, and what was the result?" Johnson told the members of the National Security Council. "I can't ask our American soldiers out there to continue to fight with one hand tied behind their backs." He approved an airstrike on an army barracks sixty miles inside North Vietnam.

The clandestine communist radio promised that U.S. servicemen would soon have to "pay more blood debts," and on February 10 the Viet Cong blew up a hotel in Qui Nhon, killing twenty-one Americans and pinning twenty-three more beneath the rubble.

ABOVE Citizens of Hanoi cluster around a New Year's display that hails the recent "Binh Gia Victory" and proclaims that "our army is undefeatable because it is a people's army that our party builds, leads, and educates."

The president called for the evacuation of more than eighteen hundred American dependents and ordered a second airstrike. This time, one hundred U.S. Navy fighter bombers, based on carriers in the South China Sea, as well as Air Force planes based in Thailand and South Vietnam, hit more North Vietnamese military targets—ammunition depots, supply depots, and assembly areas.

Anxiety about what seemed to be happening spread around the world. France, which had spent nearly a century in Vietnam, called for an end to all foreign involvement there. The British prime minister urged restraint. Many leaders of the president's own party agreed, though not yet in public.

In a private memorandum, Vice President Humphrey warned the president that the American public "simply can't understand why we would run grave risks to support a country which is totally unable to put its house in order." The best course would be to reduce, not expand, America's involvement, he wrote. He reminded Johnson that because he had just won a great victory at the polls, "1965 is the year of minimum political risk for the Johnson administration." Escalating the war further would only undercut the Great Society, damage America's image overseas, and end any hope of improving relations with the Soviet Union. Johnson did not respond; instead, he barred his vice president from all discussions of Vietnam policy for several months.

Twenty days later, on March 2, 1965, the United States began a systematic bombardment of the North, code-named Operation Rolling Thunder. It was meant to be a "mounting crescendo" of air raids, Maxwell Taylor wrote, aimed at boosting South Vietnamese morale, providing a substitute for sending in American ground troops—and forcing Hanoi to negotiate a peace on American terms.

"The thesis behind Rolling Thunder," Samuel Wilson, then a deputy assistant to Robert McNamara, recalled, "was that as we ratcheted up the tempo and the volume of this effort against the North Vietnamese sooner or later they would cry uncle, say this is enough. And then there'd be a pause and we would begin to negotiate our way out of this situation. This became an article of faith: if we punish them enough they will want to give up. This article of faith was based on a fallacious assumption: They weren't going to give up. They read us better than we read them."

Once again, the president insisted on strict secrecy. The American people were not to be told that the administration had changed its policy from retaliatory airstrikes to systematic bombing—that the president had, in fact, widened the war. Operation Rolling Thunder would continue on and off for three years, during which U.S. aircraft would fly a million sorties and drop nearly three-quarters of a million tons of bombs on North Vietnam.

Johnson still hoped that he could find North Vietnam's breaking point without having to commit ground troops. "I'm going up old Ho Chi Minh's leg an inch at a time," he assured an early critic, South Dakota senator George McGovern.

But General Westmoreland, who had initially been hesitant about committing ground troops to Vietnam, now asked for two battalions of Marines—3,500 men—to protect the Danang air base from which U.S. fighter bombers were hitting the North.

Ambassador Taylor, who had once called for ground troops, now objected to the whole idea. "Once you put that first soldier ashore," he wrote, "you never know how many others are going to follow him." But the president felt he had no choice but to give Westmoreland what he asked for; he was not prepared to withdraw and knew he would be blamed if more American advisers died. The government of South Vietnam was not to be consulted; the United States of America had larger considerations.

On March 6, Johnson telephoned one of his oldest friends in the Senate, Richard Russell of Georgia, to let him know what was about to happen.

ABOVE At Pleiku, Colonel John C. Hughes of the U.S. Army Fifty-second Aviation Battalion shows McGeorge Bundy and General Westmoreland the extent of the damage done to his command by communist guerrillas. "Like other civilian visitors" confronted with carnage, Westmoreland remembered, Bundy found it hard to "comprehend the primitive countenance of insurgency warfare."

them on." And McNamara and Russell say, "Send them on." . . . What do you think?

RUSSELL: We've gone so damn far, Mr. President, it scares the life out of me. But I don't know how to back up now. It looks to me like we just got in this thing, and there's no way out. We're just getting pushed forward and forward and forward and forward.

JOHNSON: . . . I don't know, Dick. . . . The great trouble I'm under—a man can fight if he can see daylight down the road somewhere. But there ain't no daylight in Vietnam. There's not a bit.

General Khanh had finally been displaced by another military coup just a few weeks earlier. There was a new premier, a civilian this time, Dr. Phan Huy Quat. Before dawn on March 8, Quat placed a call to his chief of staff and liaison with the U.S. embassy, Bui Diem, the mandarin's son who had sided with anticommunist nationalists while still a student at Saigon University. "You have to come to my home right away, because there are urgent things to do," Quat said.

When Bui Diem got to Dr. Quat's home, he found his friend Melvin Manfull, the political officer of the U.S. embassy, waiting for him. "Dr. Quat didn't even ask me to sit down," Bui Diem recalled. "He said, 'There are three Marine battalions landing in Danang right now.' I was flabbergasted. I said, 'But why?' He calmed me down. 'We'll talk about that later. But now I need you to draft a communiqué with Mr. Manfull. Be as brief as possible. Just describe the facts and affirm our concurrence.' We did it but I was very unhappy."

That same day, two Marine battalions landed at Danang, on the coast of South Vietnam, some 100 miles south of the border with the North.

John Flynn, a reporter for *Life* magazine, covered the landing:

As the Americans waded ashore, children broke through lines of Danang police to yell, "O.K.!"—the only English expression they know. And just as the Marines were earnestly digging in along the beach, setting up a defense line against the kind of greeting for which their conventional training had prepared them—an attack by the Viet Cong—along came some pretty Vietnamese girls with garlands of flowers. . . . Happily, the Vietcong did not choose [that] moment to attack. . . .

There have been reports that the Communists are sneaking in heavy artillery pieces to increase their shooting radius around the base. "If the clowns do that," [Brigadier General Frederick J.] Karch growls, "we'll just have to move out to the next ridge."

LYNDON JOHNSON: We're going to send the Marines in to protect the Hawk battalion, the Hawk outfit at Danang, because they're trying to come in and destroy them there, and they're afraid the security provided by the Vietnamese [is] not enough. . . . I guess we've got no choice, but it scares the hell out of me. I think everybody's going to think, "We're landing the Marines. We're off to battle." Of course, if they come up there, they're going to get them in a fight. Just sure as hell. They're not going to run. Then you're tied down. If they don't, though, and they ruin those airplanes, everybody is going to give me hell for not securing them, just like they did the last time they were made afraid.

RICHARD RUSSELL: Yeah.

JOHNSON: So, it's a choice, a hard one, but Westmoreland [comes] in every day saying, "*Ple-e-e-ase* send them on." And the Joint Chiefs say, "*Pl-e-e-ase* send

ABOVE U.S. Marines rush ashore at Danang, ready for combat.

Lieutenant Philip Caputo, from the Chicago suburb of Westchester, Illinois, flew into Danang with the rest of the Third Marine Division a day or two later. Like most of his fellow Marines he was filled with confidence: "We thought that the mere fact that we were there, that the U.S. Marine Corps had landed and our reputation, especially from World War II and Korea, was so ferocious that the Viet Cong were just going to say, 'Well, it's all over, guys, and we quit.' Some people said, 'We'll be out of here in three months.' We actually thought that we're going to go out on a couple of patrols, give 'em a kick in the pants and stomp on 'em a little bit, and that'll be that."

Once Caputo was settled in, he saw that Vietnam was very different from Illinois.

What struck me was how beautiful it was. There were just these endless acres of jade-green rice paddies. And these lovely villages inside groves of bamboo and palm trees. And way off in the distance bluish jungled mountains. It looked like Shangri-La. And I remember seeing this line of Vietnamese women, or schoolgirls I think they were, with

those white *ao dais* flowing in the wind. They actually looked like angels come to earth or something like that. So it was really quite striking but a little unsettling because how can a place like this, so beautiful and so enchanting, be at war?

Seeing foreign troops marching past his village, an old man emerged from his home, shouting, "*Vive les Français!*" He thought the French had returned.

"The problem around here," the U.S. Marine captain leading the patrol told a reporter, "is who the hell is who?"

Many South Vietnamese welcomed the Marines. Duong Van Mai recalled that her father was very pleased that they had come. "We were such a small country and the Americans had decided to come in to save us, not only with their money and resources, but even with their lives. We were very grateful. We thought with this kind of power the Americans are going to win."

ABOVE The reception committee, hastily arranged by the South Vietnamese government

Le Minh Khue was born in 1949 and orphaned as a small child. Her parents were victims of the brutal North Vietnamese land reforms of the mid-1950s. They were village schoolteachers, but, because their grandfathers had been mandarins at the imperial court, they were denounced by the communists as members of the hated landlord class and made prisoners in their home. When Khue's father fell ill and asked permission to go to a hospital, he was refused—and died. Her mother was forced to hand over her child to her sister, who was a loyal party member, and died alone four years later. "They weren't murdered, they weren't beaten," Khue said of her parents. "But they died in sadness, in misery, because of the spiritual violence that was done to them."

Le Minh Khue was brought up in a village in Sam Son, south of Hanoi, that was adjacent to a military encampment. Not long after Operation Rolling Thunder began, she went on a field trip with her schoolmates. That day, American bombers trying to hit the camp hit her village instead. The North Vietnamese were not yet accustomed to bombing and had built no shelters. Khue returned that evening to what she remembered as "the most horrible scene I ever witnessed." People had huddled beneath trees for safety with their children or tried to find shelter in a pond. Scores died. She helped carry their remains to the road, where they were laid out so friends and family could try to identify them. U.S. aircraft returned the next day, and another bomb killed her favorite schoolteacher. "Those were the two worst days of my life," she remembered. "I don't think people can imagine how ferocious the war was."

A recruiter turned up in the village a few days later, calling on young boys and girls to join the revolution and fight the Americans. "My head was full of a spirit of adventure," Khue recalled, "but I was too young. I was sixteen and you had to be seventeen. So I lied about my age and signed up." Her foster parents applauded her decision. They "had pure emotions and loved the revolution," she remembered. "No policy promulgated by the party could be a mistake. They taught me to love my country."

Khue was assigned to a unit called the "Anti-American Youth Shock Brigade for National Salvation," and along with thousands of other young people was sent south to work keeping open the Ho Chi Minh Trail. In her backpack was a gift from her foster father: she and he had always shared a love of American literature, and as she was about to leave he had pressed on her a copy of Ernest Hemingway's novel about the Spanish Civil War, *For Whom the Bell Tolls*. "I liked the resourcefulness of Robert Jordan, the hero who destroys the bridge," she remembered. "I saw how he coped with war, and I learned from that character." She would find herself coping with war for nine harrowing years.

ABOVE Le Minh Khue, second from left, and members of her volunteer unit in 1965

But a good many Americans in country were unhappy. "As a voting member of the Saigon Mission Council," Samuel Wilson remembered, "I was opposed to the entry of American ground combat forces. I felt if the Vietnamese had to beat the Viet Cong off with a bloody stump, they had to do it themselves. We had to do everything we humanly could to help them, but we could not win it for them. I think we crossed the River Styx at that point."

Philip Brady remembered attending the Majestic Theater in Saigon with the young Vietnamese woman who would become his wife, and "seeing the newsreels of the first Marines landing at Danang and saying to myself, 'Go back. Go back.' There was no question that this was a big, big mistake. If we had not intervened, the war would have ended by 1965. And you would not have had the losses of life. Millions of Vietnamese were lost after that. And how many Americans?"

Brady's friend Tran Ngoc Toan, the South Vietnamese Marine who had fought alongside him and survived his wounds after Binh Gia, shared that view. "In the deepest part of every Vietnamese mind is the idea that the foreigner is an invader,"

he said. "So when the Americans came in, the Viet Cong could recruit more people to join the struggle against them."

Le Duan had failed to topple the Saigon government before the Americans intervened. But their arrival infused the North Vietnamese with new patriotic fervor. The party announced its "Three Readiness Campaign," which called for "readiness to join the army, to partake in battle, to go wherever the fatherland deems necessary." Mobilization drives doubled the size of the North Vietnamese army.

"My understanding was that the U.S. Army was the most powerful in the capitalist world," one communist commander recalled. "The war would be cruel. We predicted that it would not be easy. When the Americans came, we had to find a way to fight and beat them. I would not say that I could have foreseen how cruel the war would be. That, I was unable to imagine."

ABOVE A mother rushes her baby to safety as U.S. Marines storm the village of My Son near Danang, April 1, 1965.

THE WEAKEST LINK

"THE AMERICAN PEOPLE," Dean Rusk warned not long after the Gulf of Tonkin confrontation, "are already beginning to ask what are we supporting." President Johnson agreed. "The weakest link in our armor is public opinion," he said.

Most Americans still understood little about Indochina, rarely knew anyone actually involved in the fighting, and saw no reason to question the government's assertion that the United States had vital interests some eight thousand miles from home. The administration was initially most concerned with criticism by those who wanted the war prosecuted more aggressively. Still,

ABOVE When the Students for a Democratic Society organized the first large antiwar demonstration on the Washington Mall on April 17, 1965, they also preapproved the slogans on the placards protestors were permitted to carry.

there was a small but slowly growing number of people who had begun to oppose the war for a number of reasons—because they thought it unjust or immoral, or they believed it was unconstitutional or simply not in the national interest.

The first manifestations of opposition to the war were small and scattered. In Manhattan, a dozen young men burned their draft cards to protest the war. Pickets from the Women Strike for Peace and the Women's International League for Peace and Freedom circled the White House. "The first protest I went to was at a Dow Chemical facility in suburban Chicago," Bill Zimmerman recalled. "Dow was manufacturing napalm. They were dropping napalm on villages in Vietnam. It was a very disappointing experience, because only forty people came. We seemed very out of place and very ineffectual, impotent even, standing outside with just forty people."

But two weeks after U.S. Marines landed at Danang, members of the University of Michigan faculty organized a night-long discussion about the war's escalation between teachers and more than two thousand students. One of the organizers

of the teach-in was a graduate student named Carl Oglesby, who had just been made president of a new national leftist organization, Students for a Democratic Society—SDS. The revolution in Vietnam, he told the crowd, was "inspired by the monied few who exploit their power" over the masses. In backing the Saigon government, the United States was thwarting the people's will and supporting "bureaucratic corruption, governmental indifference, [and] police-state suppression of honest dissent."

The Michigan teach-in was not a one-sided event; seventy-five students marched through the crowd chanting, "Better dead than red." But one young woman, perched on her boyfriend's motorcycle at the back of the crowd, summed up the impact the discussion had on most of those who attended: "I'd never really thought very much about this, but after tonight I think we should get out of Vietnam."

Soon, there were teach-ins on scores of university campuses all over the country. Antiwar feeling was still a minority view among young people. Throughout the war, national polls would show that Americans under thirty were more likely to support the war than those fifty and older.

But when the SDS called for a mass demonstration in Washington that April, it succeeded beyond its sponsors' dreams.

"I didn't want to go," Bill Zimmerman recalled, "because I didn't want to be disappointed in the same way again and go all the way to Washington and stand outside the White House with forty people. Twenty-five thousand people attended that rally." (It was the largest peace demonstration in U.S. history up to that time.) "And that suddenly told me and others I was working with at the time that it might be possible to build an antiwar movement."

ABOVE New Yorkers court arrest by publicly burning their draft cards in Manhattan's Union Square, November 6, 1965. A statute enacted that August—and ultimately validated by the U.S. Supreme Court—had called for anyone who "knowingly destroys [or] knowingly mutilates" his draft card to be punished. Three of the four men were convicted and sentenced to six months in prison.

ENOUGH, AND NOT TOO MUCH

NOTHING Mogie Crocker's parents could say or do since he had come home had shaken his determination to serve, and recent developments in Vietnam had only strengthened his resolve. "It was quite astounding to think that he had that degree of commitment," his mother remembered. "But it made sense in what we knew of him, as drastic as it was."

He'd hoped to become a member of the elite Special Forces, but his age barred him: there were no seventeen-year-old Green Berets, even with their parents' permission. And he turned down the opportunity to attend Army language school. He wanted to become a paratrooper and get into combat. His parents finally, reluctantly, agreed to let him go, and on March 15—less than a week after the arrival of the first Marines in Vietnam—Denton Crocker Jr. entered the U.S. Army. "He bounced down the steps one morning and was off to Fort Dix," his mother recalled. "And it was in a way a sort of relief that the conflict and the anxiety over whether he would or would not go was done. And he was happy. And we just tried to believe that this was the right thing for him to do."

Already by late March, it had been clear that the bombing campaign alone was not working. Troops and supplies continued to steadily filter down the Ho Chi Minh Trail. And in South Vietnam there were more rumors of coups, more riots in the Saigon streets.

"We are faced with waging a war on a cooperative basis in a sovereign country in which we are guests," General Westmoreland told his staff. But he nonetheless felt it was time to "put our own finger into the dike." "The enemy was destroying battalions faster than they could be reconstituted," he recalled. "The South Vietnamese [were] beginning to show signs of reluctance to [fight] and in some cases their steadfastness under fire [was] coming into doubt."

American forces would not guarantee victory, but without them, he warned, "defeat was only a matter of time." He and the Joint Chiefs called for more troops, thousands of them.

The president was cautious. As always, he wanted to do "enough, and not too much." But on April 1, he quietly agreed to send two more Marine battalions—and changed their mission from base security to active combat, "undertaking offensive operations to fix and destroy the VC in the Danang area." For the first time, American troops were formally being asked to fight on their own in Vietnam.

Johnson did not want that fact revealed to the American public. But the bombing of the North and rumors of harsher measures to come had heightened concern around the world. UN Secretary-General U Thant proposed a three-month ceasefire. Seventeen nonaligned nations called for negotiations "without preconditions." Great Britain, America's closest ally, publicly offered to reconvene the Geneva talks that had divided Vietnam in 1954, with the goal of reuniting it. A handful of Democratic senators, including Mike Mansfield, George McGovern, and Frank Church of Idaho, also urged Johnson to negotiate a settlement.

At Johns Hopkins University on April 7, Johnson sought to persuade the world of America's good intentions—and again to calm American fears of a wider war. "In recent months," he said, "attacks on South Vietnam were stepped up. Thus, it became necessary for us to increase our response and to make attacks by air. This is not a change of purpose. It is a change in what we believe that purpose requires." Nothing was said about the new orders sending Marines directly into combat or the ongoing discussions about how many more Americans were going to be sent into battle. Instead, the president called for "unconditional discussions" with Hanoi, and as an old New Dealer, proposed a massive development program for *all* of Southeast Asia.

> The task is nothing less than to enrich the hopes and the existence of more than a hundred million people. And there is much to be done.
>
> The vast Mekong River can provide food and water and power on a scale to dwarf even our own TVA.
>
> The wonders of modern medicine can be spread through villages where thousands die every year from lack of care. . . .
>
> We hope that peace will come swiftly. But that is in the hands of others than ourselves.
>
> We will use our power with restraint and with all the wisdom that we can command. But we will use it.
>
> We have no desire to devastate that which the people of North Vietnam have built with toil and sacrifice. . . . This war, like most wars, is filled with terrible irony. What do the people of North Vietnam want?

Philip Brady would hear the president's speech while hunkered down outside a village from which enemy fire was coming. "I had a little transistor radio," he remembered, "and I'm sitting there listening to LBJ. At the same time we've got to lay some nape on the village. So I'm calling in the nape, and listening to the president talk peace. It was surreal."

"Old Ho can't turn me down," Johnson assured an aide on his way back to Washington. But Hanoi immediately dismissed his offer of talks and development aid as a "wornout trick of deceit and threat." There was a brief flurry of diplomatic activity by both sides, but North Vietnam would not negotiate unless the United States withdrew and Saigon agreed to share power with Hanoi. For its part, the United States would not talk unless Hanoi first recognized South Vietnam as an independent nation.

In early May, while his advisers and the Joint Chiefs debated how rapidly American participation in the war should be escalated, Johnson deployed the 173rd Airborne Brigade Combat Team to Vietnam, the first Army combat outfit to be dispatched and the one to which Mogie Crocker would initially be assigned.

The president was less concerned with Vietnam that month than with a civil war much closer to home, in the Dominican Republic, where rebels sought to overthrow a right-wing dictator friendly to the United States. Johnson sent in eight hundred Marines to protect American citizens—and then another twenty-three thousand to ensure that the Dominican Republic did not "become another Cuba." To justify his action, Johnson claimed that the American ambassador had called him while crouching under his desk as bullets flew through the windows, that "a band of communist conspirators" was leading the uprising, and that "some fifteen thousand innocent people were murdered and shot and their heads cut off." None of it was true. A ceasefire soon brought an end to the fighting, but critics charged the president with indulging in gunboat diplomacy and with being willing to exaggerate and deceive to justify military action. The *New York Herald Tribune* expressed concern over what it called LBJ's "credibility gap," a phrase that would haunt him for the rest of his time in the White House.

ON HIS WAY

THAT SUMMER, before shipping out to Vietnam, Mogie Crocker came home for a visit. "We were at dinner one evening," his mother recalled, "and just talking in generalities about the war. And he said, 'Of course if I were Vietnamese I probably would be on the side of the Viet Cong.' I puzzled over that. And my husband did, too. I suppose Mogie was relating it to our American Revolution, that he saw their need for their own freedom. But as an American citizen, he also saw the larger picture of trying to prevent communism."

Mogie's sister Carol recalled something else. They were watching television together late one evening, sitting on the floor, when Mogie suddenly held his face in his hands. "I don't want to go back," he said. "I was dumbstruck," Carol remembered, "and said to him, 'But this is what you want to do.' It had never occurred to me that he was torn about this, that he was afraid. It confounded me that he had made so many sacrifices and yet was afraid and yet was determined to go."

The whole family turned out to see him climb aboard a bus bound for Fort Dix, New Jersey, the next stop on his way to Vietnam. "Occasionally Mogie looked toward us," his mother remembered, "and we would smile and wave, but already the loud idling of the engine, the barrier of the dark sealed windows isolated him. . . . I blew a kiss and waved again. The bus moved quickly out of sight."

ABOVE Private Mogie Crocker, home in Saratoga just before shipping out for Vietnam, with his youngest sister, Candy, and brother, Randy

MORE HERE THAN WE THOUGHT

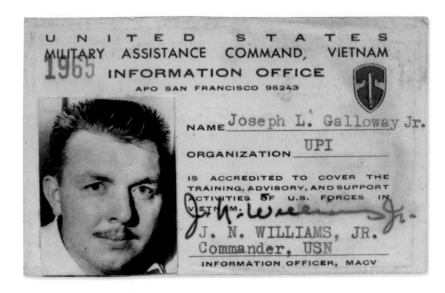

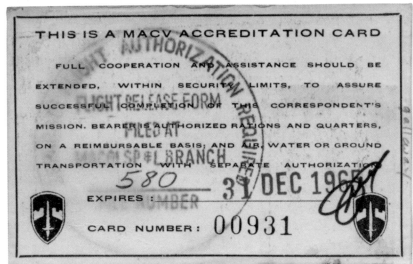

THE GROWING PRESENCE of American combat troops in Vietnam attracted flocks of American reporters, eager to report details about what had until then been a largely secret war. The State Department's strictures on reporting had been eased; there was now no press censorship, as there had been in World War II. Reporters just had to agree to follow military guidelines, so as not to compromise the security of ongoing operations, and were allowed to categorize American casualties only as "light," "moderate," or "heavy."

It would prove to be dangerous work. Seventy-four journalists and photographers would die covering the fighting in Southeast Asia.

Joseph Lee Galloway, a twenty-three-year-old UPI reporter from Refugio, Texas, had arrived in Vietnam that spring. "I thought that if there is going to be a war and if it's going to be my generation's war and I'm a journalist, I've got to cover it," he recalled. "Forty-five years along it'd be a lot easier to explain why I went than if I hadn't gone at all. That'd be like walking out of the movie at the most critical moment to buy a bag of popcorn. And I thought I needed to get there in a hurry, because once the Marines landed I thought this was going to be over and done with and if I'm not careful, I might miss it."

He stopped in Saigon just long enough to sign a form promising not to reveal troop movements or casualty figures while a battle was under way. Then he headed for the air base at Danang, from which American warplanes were taking off daily to bomb North Vietnam under the watchful eye of the Marines. "They quickly figured out you can't just guard an air base," Galloway remembered. "You've got to spread out because the enemy's going to mortar it, they're going to shoot rockets. So you've got to reach out fifteen or twenty miles. And once you're doing that you're no longer guarding an air base, you're operating in hostile territory. The local guerrillas knew the terrain far better than the Marines did, and ran circles around them. So we went on a lot of operations where it was a lot of long hot walks in the sun with not much action except enough to just keep you on edge and keep you running."

Philip Caputo was among the men assigned to those operations. "It wasn't so much the Viet Cong that were intimidating at that point as it was the terrain," he recalled. "Just getting through the jungle, going from Point A to Point B, was so difficult. It was terribly hot. There were snakes and bugs all over the place. The staff officers lived in a world of two-dimensional

maps, and we lived in the three-dimensional world. With their little grease pencils on their maps they would tell you that you were supposed to slash through some area. It once took us four hours to move half a mile, cutting through this bush with machetes. Generally speaking, no military operation ever goes according to plan. But sometimes there's at least a resemblance to what actually happens. These very seldom resembled it. And that's when you began to realize that, you know, there's more here than we thought."

Sometimes Joe Galloway went along on patrol. "You'd get to the bottom of the valley and there'd be three enemy snipers at the top of the hill," he remembered. "And they would fire three rounds and run down the other side while you ran up that hill with a battalion of Marines. And over and over and over until half of the Marines were heatstroke casualties. So there was a lot of wasted effort and energy, it seemed to me."

ABOVE Joseph Galloway's first Vietnam press card, issued by MACV

A BOMBSHELL

NEITHER THE CONTINUING BOMBING nor the growing likelihood of full-scale American intervention seemed to intimidate Hanoi. Le Duan, having failed to win the war before the United States sent in ground troops, hoped that he could still wear his enemy down by waging "Big Battles," and that the American public, like the French public before them, would eventually weary of a costly, bloody war being waged so far from home. By contrast, he said, "the North will not count the cost."

His confidence was bolstered by the stepped-up help American intervention had forced the Soviet Union and China to offer him. Moscow agreed to supply vast amounts of modern weaponry and materiel; Hanoi would one day boast the most formidable air defense system of any capital city on earth. And China agreed to send support troops, freeing North Vietnamese soldiers for combat in the South. In the end, 320,000 Chinese would serve in North Vietnam.

"We will fight," Le Duan promised, "whatever way the United States wants."

Meanwhile in South Vietnam, things were still growing still worse. In May, the Viet Cong—supported now by four regiments of North Vietnamese regulars—were destroying the equivalent of one South Vietnamese battalion every week. The desertion rate among South Vietnamese draftees climbed steadily.

In June, there was yet another Saigon coup. Two ambitious young officers had overthrown the civilian government—Army General Nguyen Van Thieu and Air Vice Marshal Nguyen Cao

Ky. They were, William Bundy remembered, "the bottom of the barrel, absolutely the bottom of the barrel."

Saigon again seemed only weeks from complete collapse.

Westmoreland asked for enough fresh U.S. troops to bring the total to 175,000 and permission to send them into combat wherever they were needed. He also called for planning to begin to "deploy even greater forces if and when required."

His cable was "a bombshell," Secretary McNamara wrote. It "meant a dramatic and open-ended expansion of American involvement. Of the thousands of cables I received during my seven years at the Department of Defense this one disturbed me the most. . . . We could no longer postpone a choice about which path to take."

For seven weeks the president and his advisers argued over how to respond to Westmoreland's urgent request for still more troops, differing mostly over how many should be sent, and how fast. Precisely what political objectives sending reinforcements would or would not achieve received scant attention.

Only Under Secretary of State George Ball argued against further escalation. "Your most difficult continuing problem in South Vietnam," he told the president, "is to prevent 'things' from getting into the saddle, or, in other words, to keep control of policy and prevent the momentum of events from taking over. . . . Before we commit an endless flow of forces to South Vietnam we must have more evidence than we now have that

ABOVE The president and his advisers mull over General William Westmoreland's troop request in the summer of 1965. Left to right: Under Secretary of State George Ball, Secretary of State Dean Rusk, President Johnson, Defense Secretary Robert McNamara, and National Security Advisor McGeorge Bundy.

our troops will not bog down in the jungles and rice paddies—while we slowly blow the country to pieces."

Johnson thanked Ball for his opinion but rejected his counsel.

General Dwight Eisenhower told Johnson that since he'd now "appealed to force . . . we have got to win." Dean Rusk warned that if the United States abandoned South Vietnam, "the communist world would draw conclusions that would lead to our ruin *and almost certainly to a catastrophic war.*"

Johnson convened a bipartisan group of elder statesmen who had served both Republican and Democratic administrations that came to be called "the Wise Men." It included Dean Acheson, Harry Truman's secretary of state; General of the Army Omar Bradley; Arthur Dean, who had helped negotiate an end to the Korean War; and John McCloy, the former American proconsul in occupied Germany. They all but unanimously urged Johnson to stay the course and commit whatever troops were necessary. "We are about to get our noses bloodied," McCloy told McNamara, "but you've got to do it. You've got to go in."

In the end, the president sent Westmoreland fifty thousand more men, pledged another fifty thousand by the end of 1965, and still more if they were needed.

He would not bomb industrial plants around Hanoi, as the

ABOVE General William Westmoreland with three Hawk antiaircraft missiles at Danang, 1965. Once, when asked by a reporter what the answer to insurgency was, he answered, "Firepower."

Joint Chiefs urged him to do, hoping to retain the threat of doing so as a trump card. Nor would he ask Congress for further funds or declare a state of national emergency or impose any new taxes or call up the Reserves or extend the terms of service for those already in uniform. Key Great Society legislation still hung in the balance—the Voting Rights Act, Medicare, aid to Appalachia, the Clean Air Act—and he did not wish Congress to be distracted by an open debate about a distant war.

At a July 28 presidential press conference a reporter asked, "Does the fact that you are sending additional forces to Vietnam imply any change in the existing policy of relying mainly on the South Vietnamese to carry out offensive operations and using American forces to guard American installations and to act as an emergency backup?"

Johnson's answer was terse and dismissive: "It does not imply any change in policy whatever. It does not imply any change of objective."

The president wanted as little attention as possible paid to what he was about to unleash. But Horace Busby, one of his closest aides, spelled out what was really happening. "The 1954–1964 premises, principals, and pretexts no longer apply," he told Johnson. "This is no longer South Vietnam's war. We are no longer advisers. The stakes are no longer South Vietnam's. We are participants. The stakes are ours—and the West's." The eleven-year struggle that had begun with a handful of U.S. advisers under President Eisenhower, and then had become a "partnership" between Saigon and Washington under President Kennedy, was now to become an American war.

General Westmoreland exuded confidence in public, but privately he warned his superiors that the United States was "in for the long pull."

He liked to compare South Vietnam to a wooden house. "Termites"—Viet Cong guerrillas—were chewing away at its foundation, he said, while "bully boys"—Main Force Viet Cong units and regular troops from North Vietnam—were waiting to move in with crowbars to tear the weakened structure down. To keep the structure from collapsing, he planned to use American troops to hunt down and destroy the bully boys, while the ARVN—nearly half a million strong, American armed and trained, supported by regional and local militias—saw to the security of the countryside behind the American shield.

On August 30, Westmoreland outlined a "three-phase sustained campaign."

First, as fresh American forces continued to gather, the "losing trend" that South Vietnam had been experiencing would begin to be reversed, military bases and major cities and towns would be secured, and the ARVN would be rebuilt and strengthened. That phase was already under way.

Phase Two would begin in early 1966—a series of offensive operations that would clear the enemy from the countryside, destroy its Main Force units, and allow for the expansion of pacification—bringing the rural populace under the protection of the Saigon government.

Then, if Hanoi still did not see the hopelessness of its cause, U.S. forces would obliterate the remnants of resistance—a process Westmoreland hoped could be completed by the end of 1967.

To fight the steadily expanding war, Army enlisted men were to serve a one-year tour of duty in Vietnam, rather than serve for the duration, as their fathers and grandfathers had in World War II. Westmoreland explained the reasoning: it "gave a man a goal" and was good for morale, he said; it spread the burden of Army service around; and it would help forestall public pressure to "bring the boys home."

It would also result in higher casualties. Twice as many grunts would die in the first six months of their tours, when they were still learning how to fight, than in the six months that followed. Looking back after a dozen years, a veteran officer would say, "We don't have twelve years' experience in this country. We have one year's experience twelve times."

Officers served only six months in combat, just half as long as the men they led—it was called "punching their ticket," a step up the promotion ladder. One general said that the Army "couldn't have found a better way . . . to guarantee that our troops would be led by a bunch of amateurs."

VIETNAM IN MINIATURE

MOST EARLY TELEVISION REPORTS from Vietnam echoed the newsreels people had flocked to see during World War II: enthusiastic, unquestioning, good guys fighting—and defeating—bad guys. But at dinnertime on August 5, 1965, Americans saw another side of the struggle in which their sons were now engaged. CBS correspondent Morley Safer and his crew went on patrol with Marines near Danang. The mission was to search a cluster of four hamlets from which earlier patrols had been fired upon for caches of arms and rice meant for the guerrillas—and then destroy them all. After the TV screen had been filled with images of weeping children and frightened old people and Marines flicking their cigarette lighters to set fire to the roofs of huts, Safer summed up what Americans at home had just witnessed for the first time.

The day's operation burned down one hundred and fifty houses, wounded three women, killed one baby, wounded

ABOVE CBS correspondent Morley Safer reports from the village of Cam Ne, set ablaze by U.S. Marines. His report so enraged the Johnson administration that Dean Rusk argued, without a shred of evidence, that Safer had staged the whole event because of "ties to the Soviet intelligence apparatus."

one Marine, and netted these four prisoners. Four old men who could not answer questions put to them in English. Four old men who had no idea what an ID card was. Today's operation is the frustration of Vietnam in miniature. There is little doubt that American firepower can win a victory here. But to a Vietnamese peasant whose home . . . means a lifetime of backbreaking labor, it will take more than presidential promises to convince him that we are on his side.

The next morning, President Johnson called his friend Frank Stanton, the president of CBS.

"Hello, Frank, this is your president."

"Yes, Mr. President."

"Frank, are you trying to fuck me?"

Safer had shat on the American flag, Johnson said; he was probably an agent of the Kremlin, and had to be fired. The Marines claimed that the whole event had been staged by the network. A major at the Danang press office called CBS the "Communist Broadcasting System."

But two days after the operation, Safer interviewed one of the Marines who'd burned Cam Ne.

> MORLEY SAFER: Do you have any private doubts, any regrets about some of those people you are leaving homeless?
>
> MARINE: You can't have any feelings of remorse for these people. They are an enemy until proven innocent. . . . I feel no remorse. I don't imagine anybody else does. You can't do your job and feel pity for these people.

When some viewers registered their shock, General Westmoreland admitted, "We have a genuine problem which will be with us as long as we are in Vietnam. Commanders must exercise restraint unnatural to war and judgment not often required of young men."

Philip Caputo remembered taking part in missions like the one Safer's crew had filmed: "You kind of thought at first that it was going to be like the GIs rolling through Paris after the liberation, with all these good-looking girls throwing flowers and kissing you. It sure didn't work out that way. I remember once going into this one *ville* in the middle of the night and finding an entire Vietnamese family cowering in a bunker. They had dug these bomb shelters inside their houses for good reason. And they were terrified of us, and I remember thinking to myself, 'Well, I wonder if, back in the colonial days, when the Redcoats barged into Ipswich, Massachusetts, this is how Americans must have felt, looking at these foreign soldiers barging in. I hated those sorts of operations."

THE ONLY WAY

FROM THE FIRST, General Westmoreland understood that while his most pressing mission was to destroy the North Vietnamese army, his ultimate goal was to win control of the countryside and help foster support for the Saigon government, without which an independent anticommunist South Vietnam could not survive. He and other American officials agreed that pacification was vital but were unable to come to a consensus on how best to implement it.

Multiple official organizations were already at work in rural areas—MACV, the CIA, the United States Information Agency, and the Agency for International Development (USAID). Each had its own agenda. USAID's was the broadest. Its workers were engaged in everything from building schools and hospitals to resettling the steadily growing number of refugees fleeing the battlefield and administering the Chieu Hoi—"open arms"—Program, which encouraged communists to defect.

American reporters, eager for combat stories, generally paid little attention to pacification, but in September, when Jimmy Breslin, a columnist for the *New York Herald Tribune* who spent a journalistic lifetime looking for fresh angles, got to Vietnam, he made a point of calling on Samuel Wilson, then serving as the associate director for field operations for USAID, at his Saigon apartment.

Breslin got an earful. Wilson, only temporarily a civilian, was an authority on guerrilla and counter-guerrilla warfare, a forty-one-year-old veteran who had served three years behind enemy lines in Burma with Merrill's Marauders. He saw the conflict in Vietnam as "a political struggle with violent military overtones," and was openly scornful of those in the military who thought pacification a mere sideshow and believed that simply unleashing conventional American military forces like the First Infantry—the "Big Red One"—would somehow solve things: "'We'll flatten these bastards and then go home.' Oh Christ, what a waste of time," he said. "You roll in the Big One here and do you know what you're doing? Just taking the tarpaulin off the field so you can start to okay a ball game. This is a political fight. . . . Once the Viet Cong get into a hamlet and establish this VC infrastructure, . . . you can roll in the Marines and bring all the firepower in the world with you. For that month that you're in there, you own the hamlet. But when the tail end of that column leaves the hamlet, the VC own it again. So how can you win here with a gun?"

Wilson couldn't help but grudgingly admire the way the communists won the people's loyalty: "They do it with a tight, cohesive organization. They give a man dignity. Even if he's the chairman of the firewood-organizing committee, he gets a chance to conduct a meeting once a month and be on top. . . . The other government, the one that runs [South] Vietnam? It stops at the district level. Saigon? That's [just] a word to most of these farmers. Once in his life the farmer might meet his district chief."

Wilson believed it was his job—and that of the hundreds of civilians currently working for USAID all across the country—to try to bridge the gap between that far-off government and "the man behind a water buffalo," who, he believed, wanted security, schools, social justice, and economic opportunity. Only when real progress was made toward achieving these goals "can you make [the people] understand [that] the only way they can have a decent life is to have a decent government."

"If we don't do that," he said, "we win nothing."

Three young college students who had volunteered to spend a summer working with USAID joined the conversation. All had been shot at. "It's the initiation," one said. He'd signed up, he added, "because it's a much more useful thing to do than student demonstrations."

What did they think they had accomplished?

"Quite a bit," a second worker answered. "The picture changed in our area. Not forever. You've got to remain working, but it did change."

A third said that while in his area they'd managed to boost the monthly numbers of defectors from two to nineteen, he wanted Breslin's readers to know that "the American military . . . should get their ass kicked. The indiscriminate use of airpower here is hurting our effort. A lot of civilians have been killed by airstrikes that don't accomplish a thing except to make some general feel good."

Wilson was fiercely proud of the work his men were doing. "I know there's no sex appeal in it," Wilson told Breslin. "We can't give out big stories about operations we went on and how many people we killed. But I'm going to tell you something. I've tried it both ways. I killed more sons-of-bitches than you've [ever] seen. Killed all the time. . . . And I'm telling you what we're doing here is the only way. . . . You can win a war with these kids, not with any soldiers."

Wilson worked eighteen hours a day, seven days a week, for twenty months, helicoptering from project to project, making sure that promised aid—seed, poultry, pigs, building materials, and the like—reached the rural people for whom it was intended and making it clear to everyone where it came from. At day's end, about to head back to Saigon, he liked to drive that point home by asking the local people, "Tell me, my friends, what have the *Viet Cong* done for you today?" During one inspection tour he found himself in the middle of a fierce firefight. When it ended, the communist battalion commander was found collapsed on the ground with massive wounds to his leg and shoulder. While they waited for a helicopter to evacuate the wounded man, Wilson offered him a cigarette, saw that he was given morphine, and then asked him about himself. He'd begun fighting for the Viet Minh at twelve, he said, had nearly died from fever, been wounded five times. As the evacuation helicopter approached, Wilson asked his customary question, "Tell me, my friend, what did the Viet Cong ever do for you?" The man glared and spat at him: "They gave me the chance to sacrifice."

THE GOOD I HAVE PERSONALLY SEEN

IN SEPTEMBER, Mogie Crocker called his parents from San Francisco just before taking off for Vietnam. He told them he had been assigned to the 173rd Airborne, so when a TV news report showed men belonging to that unit setting up camp, his mother remembered, "we looked desperately, thinking maybe we could get a glimpse of him. But we didn't, and after that, as the battles began to be more severe and serious and the casualties grew greater, we made a conscious decision not to watch the news on television."

ABOVE Eighteen-year-old Private First Class Denton W. Crocker Jr. at jump school, Fort Benning, Georgia, September 1965

Private First Class Mogie Crocker got to Saigon in late September. He'd been reassigned: "I am now with the 1st Brigade, 101st Airborne Div.," he wrote home. "Since the last letters I have seen a lot of Vietnam, and what a beautiful country it is. The jungle highlands were the most breathtaking (that isn't a figure of speech either; our driver was a maniac). Some of the places we passed through are An Lhe, Nha Trang, Qui Nhon, and our present base Cam Ranh Bay."

Three years earlier, Cam Ranh Bay—a vast anchorage conveniently located a little less than halfway between Saigon and South Vietnam's northern border—had been home only to a handful of fishermen living along a pristine beach. Now, thanks to American contractors and a legion of mostly female Vietnamese construction workers, it was a sizable American community—fifteen miles long and almost five miles wide—with twenty thousand residents; five deepwater piers, each capable of offloading four thousand tons of weapons and supplies every twenty-four hours; ten-thousand-foot runways from which bombers took off regularly to hit targets in the North, and a two-thousand-bed hospital, the largest in Vietnam. Similar installations were under construction all along the coast, at Vung Tau, Qui Nhon, Quang Ngai, Chu Lai, and Phu Bai. The United States seemed to be settling in for a protracted conflict.

News of antiwar protests at home disturbed Mogie.

Dear Dad,

Thank you for your letter; it was very interesting, especially the part telling of the demonstrations. We who are in Vietnam find these protests very hard to comprehend, and many people here are quite bitter about them. . . . What is taking place in America, that causes men like Saul Bellow and John Hersey to support these people? It would seem that we are in a period corresponding to the pathetic decade prior to 1939, when intellectuals supported the appeasement of Nazi Germany. Certainly there are mistakes and wrongs committed in Vietnam, however these are dwarfed by the good I have personally seen being done. The belief I have in our present policy has been completely confirmed by what I have seen here, and . . . I am of a mind to extend for another year when the time comes. My chief worry is that these pacifist bleatings might effect even a small change in government policy at a time when we appear close to success.

Much love,
Mogie

At Cam Ranh Bay, Mogie was disappointed to find himself ordered to serve as an armorer—cleaning, repairing, and trouble-shooting weapons—rather than as a regular infantryman in a line company. He hoped, he said, "to find a way to change this situation." He was determined to see combat.

AIN'T NO SUCH THING

THAT SAME SEPTEMBER, the First Cavalry Division—16,000 men, 435 helicopters, and 1,600 vehicles—began arriving at An Khe, its new headquarters carved out of the grasslands at the edge of the Central Highlands, thirty-five miles from the sea. Its heliport was so vast and smooth it came to be called "the Golf Course."

Their numbers would have been still greater and their support wing much stronger if the president had called up the reserves and extended their terms of service; five hundred skilled pilots, helicopter crew chiefs, and mechanics had been left behind because they had too little time left. The division did their best to make up in panache what they lacked in personnel.

"We'd all rather ride to work than walk to work," Joe Galloway recalled. "That applies to soldiers and journalists alike. So we reporters all hustled up there to cover these guys. They were swashbuckling with their Stetsons and their spurs and their boots. They'd been trained in air-mobile warfare using helicopters to the absolute maximum benefit. Moving artillery, leapfrogging troops, chasing the enemy, driving him crazy—this was something new and it was going to change the way we did war."

As the First Cavalry got used to its new surroundings, thousands of North Vietnamese regulars were moving south into the Central Highlands along the Ho Chi Minh Trail.

Lo Khac Tam was a platoon leader in the Sixty-sixth Regiment of the People's Army of Vietnam, one of the first one hundred graduates of the North Vietnamese military academy to volunteer to lead regular troops into South Vietnam. They all had signed their applications in blood. "I had a girlfriend before I went south," he remembered. "She heard I was going to the front and gave me a ring to wear. I just left, did not look back. Tried to forget my life back home. We needed to set that aside. We walked to the Central Highlands—it took two months. I was

OPPOSITE Men of the First Brigade of the 101st Airborne arrive in Cam Ranh Bay, July 29, 1965.

a Communist Party member and a leader and had to keep the men moving. We cooked our rice in the morning, and carried some cooked rice to eat during the day. We had very little salt, and some dried fish. We missed vegetables. We found taro leaf. Back home we fed it to the pigs, but on the trail we ate it. We did not know the exact destination, just to head south. We were excited to be among the first soldiers from the North to fight the Americans, and this kept up the morale. But I worried about the men, how difficult the trip was. It was so simple in the French war—the French did not have such powerful weapons, they were not so scary as what we would be facing from the Americans."

General Chu Huy Man, commander of the gathering forces, had a simple but audacious plan. His troops—the equivalent of a division of North Vietnamese and NLF regulars, more than five thousand soldiers backed by artillery and support units—would establish a base on and around the Chu Pong Massif, a jumble of thickly forested mountains and ravines fifteen miles long that straddles the Cambodian border south of the Ia Drang River.

Then, one regiment would attack Plei Mei, one of several U.S. Special Forces outposts near the Cambodian border. The outpost was defended by a twelve-man team of U.S. Green Berets, an equal number of ARVN Special Forces, and some four hundred militiamen drawn from the indigenous hill people. Meanwhile, two more regiments would ambush the ARVN relief column that was sure to be sent to rescue Plei Mei along the single road running through the region. The rest of Man's troops would wait for the airborne Americans who now seemed sure to follow. "We would attack the ARVN—but we would be ready to fight the Americans," General Man said. "We wanted to lure the tiger out of the mountain."

The fighting began on the evening of October 19. North Vietnamese regulars destroyed a South Vietnamese patrol near Plei Mei, overcame an ARVN outpost, and then opened fire on the camp itself from three sides. Under cover of darkness, sappers had slipped to within forty yards of the perimeter wire, dug trenches for themselves, and set up automatic rifles and 125mm antiaircraft machine guns.

The families of the militiamen lived alongside their men, and when the shooting began women and children fled down into underground shelters. Nine of the twelve Green Berets were hit. Their commander radioed for help. Fifteen more Green Berets and 160 South Vietnamese rangers were helicoptered in two days later, commanded by Major Charles Beckwith, a former college football player and veteran of guerrilla fighting in Malaysia, known to his fellow soldiers as "Chargin' Charlie."

Joe Galloway managed to talk a helicopter pilot into flying him into the besieged camp the next day. "There were mortars landing," he remembered. "There were machine gun bullets whipping all over the place." Major Beckwith was not especially pleased to see him. "I need everything in the world," Beckwith said. "I need ammo. I need medevac. I need someone to carry my wounded out. I need supplies coming in, food. I need medicine. Everything. And what has the Army in its wisdom sent me but a godforsaken reporter?"

Beckwith led Galloway over to a .30-caliber air-cooled machine gun and showed him how to load it and how to clear it when it jammed. "You can shoot the little brown men outside the wire," he said. "You may not shoot the little brown men inside the wire; they are mine." Galloway protested that he was a civilian noncombatant. "Ain't no such thing in these mountains, son," Beckwith replied. Galloway settled in behind the machine gun.

The camp's defenders would endure 178 hours of mortar and recoilless rifle fire and repeated assaults by ground troops trying to get through the wire. They beat them all back, and after American bombs and napalm turned the surrounding terrain into a moonscape, the enemy finally withdrew.

Major Beckwith remembered how hard and how relentlessly the enemy had fought. "I'd give anything to have two hundred

OPPOSITE Brigadier General Chu Huy Man (in the helmet), architect of the North Vietnamese campaign in the Ia Drang Valley, moves through the Central Highlands with his men later in the war. **ABOVE** Defenders of the besieged Plei Mei Special Forces camp watch U.S. airpower blast North Vietnamese positions. **RIGHT** Within the walls, an American adviser prepares a mortar position while South Vietnamese militiamen look on.

VC under my command," he told a reporter. "They're the finest, most dedicated soldiers I've ever seen." (They were not, in fact, Viet Cong; they were North Vietnamese troops.)

Meanwhile, just as General Man had hoped, the ARVN had dispatched a mechanized force to rescue the men at Plei Mei. The North Vietnamese ambushed the column as planned, but after that everything went wrong. Tanks fired heavy canister into the jungle on either side of the road, blasting men and parts of men up into the splintered trees. Artillery was walked methodically along ahead of the column. Airstrikes set the adjacent forest ablaze.

The North Vietnamese retreated from Plei Mei, with First Cavalry helicopters in hot pursuit. "For two weeks they were hopscotching all over that valley," Galloway remembered, "just driving these people like coveys of quail."

ABOVE South Vietnamese rangers, sent to relieve the siege of Plei Mei, run a gauntlet of enemy sniper fire as they enter the camp's perimeter. **RIGHT** Major Charlie "Chargin' Charlie" Beckwith at the siege's end. When it was all over, he remembered, "it was estimated there were eight hundred or nine hundred dead North Vietnamese regulars in front of the camp. I don't know the exact number and I didn't run around counting them. Eventually, a bulldozer came in and just covered everything up."

INTO THE VALLEY

ON THE MORNING of November 14, helicopters belonging to the First Battalion of the Seventh Cavalry—George Armstrong Custer's old outfit—took off from their base at An Khe in the Central Highlands and flew west toward the Chu Pong Massif.

Their commander, Lieutenant Colonel Hal Moore, a forty-three-year-old Kentucky-born Korean War veteran, had been told that there was a large base camp somewhere on its slopes. His orders were to take his understrength unit—29 officers and just 411 men—find the enemy, and kill him.

There were two clearings large enough for Moore to bring in eight choppers at once. He chose the one closest to the mountain—Landing Zone X-Ray, roughly the size of a football field.

Before Moore and his men began setting down in the clearing, twin batteries of 105mm howitzers that had been lifted by helicopter to a fourth clearing six miles away blasted the trees and grasslands around both landing zones to confuse and intimidate any enemy soldiers who might be hiding there.

Moore made a point of leading from the front. He was the first man off the first chopper. He sent four six-man squads one hundred yards in all four directions. The mountain was so beautiful, one soldier remembered, it reminded him of some national park back home.

Within minutes, Moore's men captured a deserter. Terrified and trembling, he said there were three battalions of soldiers on the mountain—sixteen hundred men—who wanted very much to kill Americans, he said, but so far had been unable to find any.

Moore established his command post behind one of the huge termite mounds that dotted the landscape. It would take until midafternoon for all of his men to be ferried in. He couldn't wait. "We had to move fast," Moore remembered, "had to get off that landing zone and hit [the enemy] before he could hit us." He sent two companies up the slope toward the hidden enemy.

Colonel Moore had no way of knowing that instead of sixteen hundred enemy soldiers on the mountain, there were three thousand—seven times his strength. Platoon leader Lo Khac Tam and his unit had only reached the hillside base a day or two earlier, after their two-month trek. "We had put up our hammocks and were supposed to have a few days to rest," he remembered. "But then swarms of helicopters came to our area. Everyone thought we might not survive, but I was a leader and so I had to push that thought away. I had to give orders to my men."

Tam's men—like Moore's men in the landing zone—were new to combat. They were ordered to fix bayonets. "It was going to be a modern battle," Lo Khac Tam recalled, "but we were told the bayonet symbolized our fighting spirit."

Within minutes, the Americans were under attack from hundreds of North Vietnamese soldiers. A platoon leader who found himself fighting his way up a ravine remembered that "at any given second there were a thousand bullets coursing through that small area looking for a target. A thousand bullets a second."

An overeager second lieutenant led his platoon of twenty-eight men too far away from the rest of his company and found himself surrounded. The lieutenant was killed. The sergeant who took over for him was shot through the head. Sergeant Ernie Savage took over and called in a ring of close-in artillery fire that kept the enemy at bay. By late afternoon, only seven of the trapped platoon's men were still capable of firing back.

Repeated efforts to break through and rescue them failed. During one of them, Second Lieutenant Walter Marm Jr., all alone, attacked and destroyed an enemy machine gun and killed the eight men in charge of firing and protecting it before a sniper shot him in the face. He survived and was awarded the Medal of Honor.

By late afternoon, Moore was engaged in three simultaneous struggles—to defend the landing zone, attack the North Vietnamese, and find a way to rescue his trapped patrol. He established a perimeter and radioed for air support and rein-

ABOVE The Ia Drang campaign: North Vietnamese forces, based in the forests that blanketed the Chu Pong Massif, besieged the Special Forces camp at Plei Mei, fought the Americans to a draw at Landing Zone X-Ray, and then successfully ambushed them at Landing Zone Albany.

forcements. As dusk began to fall, a company from the Second Battalion of the Seventh Cavalry was helicoptered in. One of the men aboard caught a glimpse of men in khaki. He thought to himself that "things must be desperate if we're bringing in guys without giving them time to change into their fatigue uniforms. Then, I realized their rifles were pointed at us; that was the enemy."

That night, Joe Galloway asked to be allowed onto a chopper taking ammunition and water to the besieged Americans. Colonel Moore agreed to let him come because he believed "the American people had a right to know what their sons were doing in this war."

As the helicopter approached the battlefield, Galloway was sitting on a crate of grenades, peering out into the darkness. "I could see these streams of light coming down the mountain," he remembered, "little pin-pricks of light. This was the enemy approaching for the next day's attacks. They had little oil lamps tied to the back of their packs so that the guy behind them knew where to follow."

ABOVE Lieutenant Colonel Harold G. Moore was awarded the Distinguished Service Cross for his actions in the Ia Drang Valley. "There is no glory in war," he recalled, "only good men dying terrible deaths."

The chopper dropped into the clearing. Galloway jumped off. The helicopter lifted off again and disappeared into the night sky. Galloway lay belly down in the grass, unsure where to go. A voice came out of the darkness: "Follow me and watch where you step. There's lots of dead people on the ground and they're all ours." American dead, shrouded with ponchos, lay near Moore's command post, where Galloway bedded down.

The night was punctuated by artillery barrages and dropped flares, called in to keep the North Vietnamese from mounting a full-scale attack.

That came at six thirty the next morning. "I had sat up and thought about cooking me a little canteen cup of coffee," Galloway remembered. "But I hadn't quite got to it when the bottom fell out. There was just an explosion of fire, small arms, bombs, artillery, B-40 rockets, AK47s, machine guns. And people are screaming and yelling and calling for medics and for Mother. A din that's unimaginable. You open your mouth to pop your ear-drums. I just flattened out on the ground because all that was being fired seemed to be coming right through the command post at about two, two and a half feet off the ground."

Hundreds of Vietnamese regulars were rushing through the grass and stunted trees toward the Americans. "Look at 'em all! Look at 'em all!" one American shouted. They wore webbed helmets camouflaged with grass, another remembered, and looked like "little trees" as they ran at him, blowing whistles, screaming, firing as they came. "They were trying to overrun us," Galloway remembered. "And they came close. They kept coming. And they were good soldiers. Anyone who didn't understand that was likely to die in that place."

The fighting was close-in and savage, Lo Khac Tam remembered. "We used bayonets, and suffered terrible losses. When an American soldier got wounded they tried to pull him away, but some of their wounded could not be evacuated. The more they retreated, the more we advanced. I did not order it, but some of my soldiers killed the wounded Americans—I encouraged them to take prisoners, but my men did kill some of them, out of hatred, and I could not control all of them."

The North Vietnamese kept coming. Defeat seemed very near. Colonel Moore radioed out a coded message, "broken arrow," which meant that an American unit was in danger of being overwhelmed. "But we had three things going for us," Galloway recalled. "We had a great commander and great soldiers. And we had air and artillery support out the ying-yang. We had it and they didn't."

Each of Moore's units marked its position with colored smoke to keep from being mistaken for the enemy by the American airmen who were on their way. "We knew that the Americans used smoke to signal where their line ended, and we tried to get inside

that line of smoke," Lo Khac Tam remembered. "We had to get close. If we didn't, we would be killed right away."

The colonel would call in eighteen thousand artillery shells over the course of the battle. Some of them landed just twenty-five yards from his men. Helicopter gunships fired three thousand rockets into the enemy. The forward air controller called for every available aircraft in South Vietnam to come to the aid of a unit in trouble. Warplanes were stacked at 1,000-foot intervals above the battlefield, from 7,000 to 35,000 feet, impatiently awaiting their turn to strafe or bomb or burn.

The reporter Neil Sheehan flew in on a helicopter that morning and remembered that from the air Landing Zone X-Ray looked "like an island in a sea of red-orange napalm and exploding shells." "By God," Colonel Moore said, "they sent us over here to kill communists, and that's what we're doing."

At one point, Galloway ducked behind the termite mound where Moore continued to call in airstrikes. "Napalm, seen from afar, has a certain chilling beauty to it," he remembered.

It's blossoms of fire, beautiful reds and oranges and yellows. But in our case we saw it from much, much too close. I looked up and there were two F-100 super-sabers that were supposed to be going north to south. Instead, they were coming east to west, aiming directly at our com-

mand post. The lead aircraft is already lifting off. He's dropped two cans of napalm and it's coming toward us— loblolly—end over end over end. They impacted maybe twenty yards from us on the edge of the clearing. The fire splashed out and these kids, two or three of them plus a sergeant, had dug a hole or two over there. I looked as the thing exploded and I felt the heat on the side of my face and two of them were dancing in that fire. And there's a rush, a roar, from the air that's being consumed and drawn in, as this hell come to earth is burning there, and as that dies back a little then you can hear the screams of these men. I just got up and ran in that direction. I go on over into this burning grass and someone yells "Get this man's feet." And I reach down and the boots crumble and the flesh is cooked off of his ankles. And I feel those bones in the palms of my hands. I can feel it now. You never forget it. We picked him up and we brought him to the

ABOVE Gathering up the dead after the battle at Landing Zone X-Ray. Concerned that enemy snipers might still be in the area, one sergeant ordered his men to drag a corpse to a waiting helicopter. "No, you won't do that," Colonel Moore said. "He's one of my troopers and you will show respect. Get two more men and *carry* him to the landing zone."

aid station. And they shut down the LZ about then. They couldn't bring any more choppers in because the fire was too heavy. And for about two, two-and-a-half hours we had to listen to that man scream. He had sucked the fire down and burnt his lungs. And the doc shot him with all the morphine he had. But all the morphine in the world won't stop pain like that. He died two days later, a kid named Jim Nakayama out of Rigby, Idaho.

By ten o'clock that morning, the North Vietnamese assault had been beaten back. The survivors from the trapped platoon were rescued that afternoon. They had been pinned to the ground and under fire for more than twenty-four straight hours, so long that they had to be coaxed into getting to their feet again.

On the morning of the next day, enemy soldiers hurled themselves against the same sector of Moore's line four more times—and were obliterated by artillery and machine gun fire. "When I saw my soldiers dying I felt deep sorrow for them," Lo Khac Tam remembered. "But I didn't cry. I held back my tears. The war we fought was so horribly brutal that I don't have the words to describe it. I worry, how can we ever explain to the younger generation the price their parents and grandparents paid?"

Unable finally to pierce the cavalry's perimeter, the rest of the North Vietnamese withdrew into the forest and made their way back into Cambodia, leaving behind a ghastly ring of their dead surrounding the landing zone—634 corpses, shot, blasted, blackened by fire. Many more had been dragged away.

Private Jack Smith, a supply clerk with the Second Battalion of the Seventh Cavalry who arrived on the last day of the battle for X-Ray, remembered that dead North Vietnamese lay so thickly in front of the American positions that he could have walked on them for a hundred feet.

After three days and two nights of combat, helicopters began lifting out the American survivors and gathering up the dead. Seventy-nine of Hal Moore's men lost their lives at Landing Zone X-Ray and another 121 were wounded.

A television reporter found Colonel Moore on the battlefield and asked him if he'd like to say something to the people back home. Moore, near tears, did his best. "Please convey to the American people what a tremendous fighting man we have here," he said. "He's courageous, he's aggressive, and he's kind. And he'll go where you tell him to go. And he's got self-discipline. And he's got good unit discipline. He's just an outstanding man. And having commanded this battalion for eighteen months—you must excuse my emotion here, but when I see some of these men go out the way they have . . . I can't tell you how highly I feel for them. They're tremendous."

Neil Sheehan agreed. "I saw them fight at Ia Drang. Here were these young men who'd had no combat experience before, thrown into a ferocious battle, in which they fought like veterans. It always galls me when I hear the World War II generation called 'the greatest generation.' These kids were just as gallant and as courageous as anybody who fought in World War II."

Hal Moore refused to leave until every single man in his command had been accounted for. He had been the first of his men to step onto Landing Zone X-Ray, and he made sure he was the last to leave it. As his chopper lifted off, he recalled, he felt only "guilt that I was still alive."

After the North Vietnamese withdrew from the battlefield, Lo Khac Tam remembered, he and a friend got lost and took shelter in a cave. They were hungry, thirsty, and emotionally drained. They stayed there for two days before rejoining their men. "Nothing could have prepared us for a battle like that," he remembered, and his friend, who had fought the French, said that nothing he'd seen in that war could compare to it. "This was different."

"The [North Vietnamese] units were enveloped in an atmosphere of gloom," one colonel recalled. Some men would not leave their rope hammocks. Some refused to wash. One soldier wrote a poem expressive of their plight: "The crab lies still on the chopping block / Never knowing when the knife will fall."

Still, as Colonel Moore himself said, "The peasant soldiers [of North Vietnam] had withstood the terrible high-tech firestorm delivered against them by a superpower and had at least fought the Americans to a draw. By their yardstick, a draw against such a powerful opponent was the equivalent of a victory."

GRAB HIM BY HIS BELT

COMBAT IN THE IA DRANG VALLEY was not quite over. The morning after the fighting ended at Landing Zone X-Ray, a massive strike by B-52 bombers was scheduled to drop twenty tons of five-hundred-pound bombs on the slopes of the Chu Pong Massif. All American troops were ordered out of the area, and Jack Smith's unit—some five hundred men—made

OPPOSITE Wounded survivors of the "lost platoon"—Second Platoon, Company B, First Battalion, Seventh Cavalry—are helped from the battlefield after their rescue. "They were like men who had come back from the dead," Joe Galloway remembered. "Their fatigue uniforms were ripped and torn; their eyes were bloodshot holes in the red dirt that was ground into their faces."

its way six miles through forest and elephant grass to a second landing zone called Albany, from which helicopters were to fly them back to base.

Just as they reached it, scores of communist snipers tied into the top branches of trees opened fire. So did machine gunners perched atop termite mounds and mortar crews hidden in the tall grass. Twenty men were hit within seconds. Everyone else dove for cover. The Americans did their best to shoot back—and some shot one another because they could not be sure of their targets.

Jack Smith found himself so close to an enemy machine gunner that he was able to poke his rifle through the grass into the man's face and blow his head off. All around him, wounded men were screaming. He tried to help and was soon covered with blood. When ten or twelve guerrillas emerged suddenly from the grass, he played dead. One of them lay down on top of him and started to set up his machine gun. "He probably couldn't feel me shaking," Smith remembered, "because he was shaking so much. He was, like me, just a teenager."

An American grenade killed the gunner—and wounded Smith in the head. Then, a mortar shell damaged his legs. He lay helpless in the grass all night, hoping that the American shells now being fired into the landing zone would not find him, listening to wounded men crying for help and trying not to attract the attention of the Viet Cong who moved through the grass shooting the wounded Americans.

Jack Smith made it out alive. But out of some 425 men involved, 155 were dead and 124 more were wounded.

The battle at Landing Zone X-Ray had demonstrated to the North Vietnamese that they could inflict heavy casualties even when confronted by massive American firepower. The successful ambush at Landing Zone Albany taught them another important lesson: getting close to the Americans negated their advantages in weaponry. "The way to fight the American was to 'grab him by his belt,'" one North Vietnamese commander explained, "to get so close that [his] artillery and airpower was useless." Each suggested to Le Duan that his forces could hold their own in the "Big Battles" that he still believed were the way to victory.

MACV insisted that the battles in the Ia Drang Valley, the first major encounter between American and North Vietnamese forces, constituted a U.S. victory. "It appears the little bastards just don't have the stomach for a fight," one colonel said. "They've had enough and bugged out." But privately, Washington and

Lit by U.S. flares, American wounded huddle with the dead at Landing Zone Albany the night after the ambush when, one injured man remembered, "the woods were left to the dead, the wounded, and the artillery barrage."

Saigon were worried. In spite of the Americans' ever-increasing mobility, the enemy had been able to choose the place and time of battle and only American airpower had saved Moore's battalion from annihilation. From the first, the intelligence on which basic decisions had been made had been uniformly bad. There were now twelve NLF regiments in South Vietnam, not just five; nine North Vietnamese regiments, not three. And, despite months of bombing, three times as many North Vietnamese regulars were now slipping south of the demilitarized zone as originally believed.

ABOVE A member of the U.S. relief force comes upon four dead Americans at Landing Zone Albany. "A new generation of Americans are being thrust into the firing line," wrote the AP reporter Peter Arnett, who covered the fighting in the Ia Drang Valley. "They are discovering that war is as indifferent about who it kills and who it lets live, and as brutal as the history books say all the other wars were."

Meanwhile, American casualties were climbing. When Senator Fritz Hollings of South Carolina visited Saigon shortly after the battles, General Westmoreland boasted, "We're killing these people at a rate of ten to one." Hollings warned him, "Westy, the American people don't care about the ten. They care about the one."

The U.S. Army was still so unprepared to deal with large numbers of casualties that the telegrams stating that someone had been wounded or killed were simply delivered to their stunned families by taxi drivers. When Hal Moore's wife, Julia Compton Moore, learned of it she went personally to every grieving home at Fort Benning, Georgia, consoling widows and comforting distraught children. And she attended every funeral. Her complaints and those of other commanders' wives eventually led the Army to send out two-man notification teams—a uniformed officer and a chaplain.

General Westmoreland sent an urgent cable to Washington,

asking for 200,000 more troops. Again, "the message came as a shattering blow," Robert McNamara remembered. "It meant a drastic—and arguably open-ended—increase in U.S. forces and carried with it the likelihood of many more U.S. casualties"—and even at this elevated level there was no guarantee that the United States would ever achieve its objectives." He hurried to Saigon to confer.

His chronic public optimism was now slightly tempered. "We have stopped losing the war," he told the press before flying back to Washington. But "the decision by the Viet Cong to stand and fight, recognizing the level of force we can bring to bear against them, expresses their determination to carry on the conflict that can lead to only one conclusion: It will be a long war." Aboard the plane he wrote another memo to the president. Once again, he offered Johnson two options: try to negotiate the kind of compromise he had rejected earlier (and abandon hope of an independent, non-communist South Vietnam), or accede to Westmoreland's request and hope for the best. There could be one thousand American casualties a month.

"A military solution to the problem is not certain," he told the president; no better than "one out of three or one in two. Ultimately we must find . . . a diplomatic solution."

"Then, no matter what we do in the military field," Johnson asked, "there is no sure victory?"

"That's right," the secretary answered. "We have been too optimistic."

Johnson chose the second option, anyway.

Meanwhile, hoping the Soviets might somehow help bring Hanoi to the bargaining table, McNamara urged the president to declare a halt to the bombing of North Vietnam. Over the objections of the military, who worried it would give the enemy time to rebuild its defenses, Johnson agreed to stop the bombing on Christmas Eve. If it achieved nothing else, he said, it would show the American people that before he committed more of their sons to battle, "we have gone the last mile."

THINKING OF YOU

ON NOVEMBER 13, the day before the fighting in the Ia Drang Valley began, the Crocker family drove to the WTEN television studio in Albany. The station had offered to record Christmas greetings for local servicemen who were far away in Vietnam. "Christmas always meant a great deal in our family," Mogie's mother remembered. "We had lots of secrets and lots of preparations. And we sent packages to Mogie early. But this was a chance to speak to him directly."

"We dressed up for the cameras," Mogie's sister Carol, then fifteen years old, remembered. "The idea was that we would each just say something about what we were doing and wish him well. It made it so real that he was far away."

The family took their places on a living room set, fitted out for the holidays.

Mogie's father, Denton Sr., spoke first and wished his son a Merry Christmas.

His mother said, "Merry Christmas, darling, we sent your packages and there's one that's waiting for you at home. It's a record of fife-and-drum music that we got for you at Williamsburg." She introduced Mogie's younger sister, Candy, seven, who confided that "my teacher isn't very nice and she always is crabby and I don't like school at all." On the other hand, she said, she was now a Brownie. Eight-year-old Randy stumbled through the Cub Scout oath.

Carol Crocker remembered the experience being almost unbearable. "The awkwardness, the sadness, the strangeness that this was how we were communicating with him, made it very real and very sad and very painful and very frightening for me. I didn't want to think that this was how we had to talk to him. I didn't want to be there."

She managed to say a few words: "Happy Christmas, Mogie. I think I'm getting skis for Christmas, so when you get home we can get together sometime."

Mogie's father assured his son that seven packages were coming in the mail. "I hope you get at least some of them by Christmastime. We do all wish you a very Merry Christmas and we'll be thinking of you on Christmas Day."

His mother signed off for the family. "We miss you, sweetheart."

ABOVE The Crocker family films its Christmas greeting for Mogie.

CHAPTER FOUR

RESOLVE

JANUARY 1966–JUNE 1967

First Cavalry Division medic Thomas Cole, himself badly wounded, refuses to be taken off the battlefield so long as he can help others during Operation Masher/White Wing in early 1966.

COONSKINS ON THE WALL

EARLY IN THE MORNING on Monday, January 17, 1966, Lyndon Johnson placed a call to Robert McNamara. "What's happening to our bombing pause?" he asked. It had been twenty-three days since he had stopped the bombing of North Vietnam and, although diplomats from several countries had suggested that the North Vietnamese were willing to talk, Hanoi had remained silent. Tet, the three-day lunar New Year celebration, was about to begin, and McNamara thought it best to wait until after that before deciding when to resume the air war. There were those at the State Department who wanted the president to hold off longer, he told Johnson, while General William Westmoreland and others within the Pentagon argued that every day that passed without bombing simply allowed the enemy to strengthen its hand. Now persuaded that the pause had been a mistake, Johnson felt trapped; he predicted that

ABOVE South Vietnamese chief of state Nguyen Van Thieu, President Lyndon Johnson, Prime Minister Nguyen Cao Ky, and Ambassador Henry Cabot Lodge dine by candlelight during the Honolulu Conference, February 7, 1966. After meeting Ky for the first time, Johnson told him, "You talk just like an American boy."

hawks would not forgive him for stopping the bombing and doves would blame him when he resumed it.

In the course of their conversation, McNamara told the president that he'd been visited recently by Professor P. J. Honey, an Irish-born scholar of Vietnamese politics, who had told him "that the balance of power in Hanoi [was now] in the hands of . . . hard-liners and particularly in the hands of the first secretary of the Communist Party, a man named Le Duan— L-E capital D-U-A-N." Twelve years after the United States first intervened in Vietnam and ten months after the first American ground troops landed at Danang, the president of the United States was just learning the name of his most powerful antagonist.

Fourteen days later, on January 31, the president reluctantly announced that the United States was about to begin bombing again. "I am not happy about Vietnam," he told his aides, "but we cannot run out."

Johnson's predictions about the public's reaction proved accurate. House Armed Services Committee chairman Mendel Rivers of Mississippi warned that the policy of gradual escalation and limited targets was "getting very unpopular. . . . The American people want this thing over yesterday." Meanwhile, on February 4, Chairman J. William Fulbright of the Senate Foreign Relations Committee, angered by the president's decision to resume bombing, opened his committee's hearings into the conduct of the Vietnam War to television cameras. Once one of the president's closest political allies, Fulbright had become one of his most committed critics, appalled by Johnson's willingness to lie to Congress and the public in order to justify U.S. intervention in the Dominican Republic. Some 2,800 Americans had died in Vietnam; nearly 200,000 were now stationed there, and still more were on their way. Fulbright had become convinced that further escalation of the war was folly, that what was needed was a "way out" of Southeast Asia.

President Johnson was alarmed. Nearly 60 percent of the American people now saw Vietnam as America's most urgent problem, and the television networks would be able to cover the hearings from gavel to gavel.

Johnson had hoped to forge an international coalition to defend South Vietnam—an army of "Free World Forces," he called it, flying "Many Flags." But in the end, it flew very few. Washington's most important allies—Britain, France, Canada, and Italy—refused to take part at all and called instead for peace talks. Australia and New Zealand sent combat troops on their own. The Philippines, Thailand, and South Korea sent combat units too, but only after Washington agreed to foot the bill. Some 320,000 South Koreans would serve in Vietnam over the years, their salaries also all paid by American taxpayers.

To deflect attention from what some of Fulbright's witnesses were likely to say, Johnson suddenly summoned the two military men who headed the junta that had seized power in South Vietnam in June of the previous year to meet with him in Honolulu. Neither had been elected. Neither had constitutional authority. From Washington's point of view it hadn't mattered much; they had forestalled further coups for more than six months. There would be time to legitimate their rule by drawing up a new constitution and holding a presidential election.

Nguyen Van Thieu was the chief of state and chairman of the band of generals who called themselves "the Directory." He was forty-two and a southerner, a convert to Catholicism who had helped overthrow Diem and General Khanh, and was already rumored to be personally corrupt.

The thirty-five-year-old prime minister, Nguyen Cao Ky, spoke fluent English. He was a Buddhist and a northerner, the former head of the South Vietnamese air force, brash and incautious and wary of Thieu. According to one U.S. diplomat, he was "an unguided missile," known for his flamboyant self-designed uniforms and purple scarves, his gaudy private life, and his public pronouncements—he once told a reporter that what Vietnam really needed was "four or five Hitlers." Within weeks of taking office he had formally declared war on North Vietnam, proclaimed a permanent state of emergency, and expanded the draft to meet it. The qualities about Ky that appealed to some

Americans displeased many of his fellow countrymen. He was young and a soldier when they venerated elder statesmen and yearned for civilian leadership, and he was especially close to the Americans when increasing numbers of South Vietnamese were alarmed at the number of American soldiers now pouring into their country.

President Johnson spent most of his time in Honolulu urging Ky and Thieu to undertake the kind of economic and political and social reforms Americans had been urging Saigon to pursue for more than a decade. "The struggle in your country," he told them, "can finally be won only if you are able to bring about a social revolution for your people—while at the same time your soldiers and ours are beating back the aggressor." Johnson wanted American voters and the rest of the world to believe that he was as devoted to "pacification"—earning the loyalty of the South Vietnamese people—as he was supportive of the combat already under way. "Every time I see a picture of a battle in the papers," he told his chief information office in Saigon, "I want to see a picture of a hog."

He wasn't interested in "high-sounding words," he told the Vietnamese; he wanted genuine achievements—what they called in Texas "coonskins on the wall." "Nobody understood what 'coonskins' meant," remembered Bui Diem, then a speechwriter for Ky. "So people in the Vietnamese delegation asked me, 'You understand what it is?' I didn't and had to ask some Americans to explain it to me."

Whatever they may have thought privately, Ky and Thieu saw no reason not to go along in public with everything the president suggested. Their final communiqué, Johnson said, would "be a kind of bible that we are going to follow."

General Westmoreland was given pacification goals, as well. The communists were believed to control nearly three-quarters of South Vietnam. By the end of 1966, Westmoreland was expected to increase the number of people living in secure areas by 10 percent, increase the number of roads open for safe travel by 20 percent, and increase the destruction of NLF and North Vietnamese bases by 30 percent.

But before real pacification could take place, Westmoreland believed, the Viet Cong and North Vietnamese had to be hunted down and destroyed. His principal military mission was to "attrite, by year's end, [enemy forces] at a rate as high as their capacity to put men into the field." His target for the next two years—Phase One of his overall plan—would be reaching what he called "the crossover point," the point at which U.S. and ARVN forces were killing the enemy faster than they could be replaced. If you could do that, one Marine remembered being told, "then you would have crossed over from going uphill in your battle to finally reaching a point where you were winning and it would be downhill and easier from there."

AN ELEPHANT FRIGHTENED BY A MOUSE

WHEN THE PRESIDENT got back from Hawaii, the Fulbright hearings were still in session and George Kennan, the well-known and widely respected author of the doctrine of containment that had for two decades formed the basis of American policy toward the Soviet Union, was about to testify. The president knew Kennan believed U.S. intervention in Vietnam had been a mistake and dreaded the impact of his testimony. He breathed a sigh of relief when, at the last moment, CBS replaced live coverage of the hearings with reruns of *I Love Lucy, The Real McCoys,* and *The Andy Griffith Show.* Fred Friendly, the head of the news division, resigned in protest.

But NBC kept the cameras running. The Honolulu conference had not distracted the public. Millions watched Kennan testify.

ABOVE A television cameraman zeroes in on George Kennan as he testifies before the Senate Foreign Relations Committee. "There is more respect to be won in the opinion of this world by a resolute and courageous liquidation of unsound positions," Kennan told the senators and the vast viewing audience, "than by the most stubborn pursuit of extravagant or unpromising objectives."

"The first point I would like to make is that if we were not already involved as we are today in Vietnam," he told the committee, "I would know of no reason why we should wish to become so involved, and I could think of several reasons why we would wish not to."

The domino theory no longer obtained in Southeast Asia, if it ever had, he continued. Ho Chi Minh was not Hitler. Nor was there any reason to think that if Ho won the war he would be Moscow's or Beijing's puppet. It was unseemly for the United States to "jump around" the world like "an elephant frightened by a mouse," and impossible to defend freedom wherever it was imperiled. Rather, America should follow John Quincy Adams's admonition to "go not abroad in search of monsters to destroy." It was better to abandon an "unsound position," he said, than to stubbornly pursue "extravagant or unpromising objectives" like victory in Vietnam. "Any total rooting out of the Viet Cong . . . could be achieved," he concluded, "if it could be achieved at all, only at the cost of a degree of damage to civilian life and of civilian suffering generally for which I would not like this country responsible."

Summing up, Senator Fulbright asked if it was Kennan's opinion that victory was simply not "a practicable objective," that "we can't achieve it even with the best of wills."

"This is correct," Kennan answered, "and I have fear that our thinking about this whole problem is still affected by some sort of illusions about invincibility on our part."

Within a month of Kennan's testimony, one poll showed, public approval for Johnson's handling of the war had fallen from 63 percent to 49 percent.

WHAT KIND OF FUCKING WAR IS THIS?

EVEN BEFORE the Fulbright hearings began and Johnson met with Ky and Thieu in Honolulu, General Westmoreland had begun the first major offensive of the year.

Some 800,000 people lived in the central coastal province of Binh Dinh, most of them in hamlets surrounded by rice paddies and coconut groves on the narrow plain that set the Central Highlands apart from the sea. It was said that if a person living there did not belong to the Viet Cong, he or she was sure to be related to someone who did. Since World War II, the province had been a bastion, first of the Viet Minh and then of the National Liberation Front. Many of the regroupees who'd moved north in 1955 came from Binh Dinh. When more and more of them filtered back after the NLF was established in 1960, they drove out government officials sent from Saigon, collected their own taxes, drafted young men, fortified hamlets with bunkers and foxholes and communication trenches—and vowed that the sun would rise in the West before the South Vietnamese government was allowed to return.

In recent weeks, NLF forces in Binh Dinh had been augmented by two regiments of North Vietnamese regulars—some eight thousand men in all.

On January 28, Westmoreland sent some twenty thousand American, South Vietnamese, and South Korean troops storming across the region in search of the enemy. The First Cavalry led the way, flying northeastward from its headquarters at An Khe, with ARVN units providing backup. At the same time, Korean troops were to move north from their base at Qui Nhon in search of the enemy, while U.S. Marines came ashore at Duc Pho to annihilate any enemy forces that tried to escape northward; warships from the Seventh Fleet prowled offshore to provide additional fire support. Hal Moore, who had fought in the battle at Landing Zone X-Ray in the Ia Drang Valley, led the initial assault on an enemy supply and recruiting base north of the district capital of Bong Son. He was now a full colonel, in command of the Third Brigade of the First Cavalry.

Three days into the mission, a young CBS reporter named John Laurence talked himself and his camera crew onto one of four medevac helicopters about to set out for a hamlet six miles north of Bong Son. A rifle company had come under heavy enemy fire there. Twenty-three men had been killed or wounded by enemy snipers.

"From the air," Laurence would write, "the land looked wild and angry."

Bright flames from burning houses glowed red beneath clusters of shade trees scattered across the coastal plain. Smoke rose in narrow plumes straight up through the windless heat and dissolved in the high haze. Clouds of dust swirled among circular batteries of U.S. Army field guns firing salvos of artillery shells into the air, the rounds visible as fleeting shadows leaving the tubes, puffs of white smoke spurting from their muzzles. Far away, geysers of earth erupted where the shells exploded, *brraaaak! brraaaak! brraaaak!* booming loud along the length of the sandy plain. Helicopters swarmed over the land buzzing with rockets and machineguns, swooping down into drop zones, disgorging soldiers, kicking out supplies, collecting the wounded and sick, mock assaulting, charging away again, swirling back and forth across the burning land in restless urgent profusion, like furious steel wasps. In the distance, airplanes circled in slow arcs, rolled over on their wingtips and dived at the ground, darting down through the gray air, letting loose shining metal canisters from under their wings that tumbled toward the ground and burst in bright flame-yellow clouds of burning napalm and dense black oil-smoke that stuck to whatever it touched and consumed it in fire. . . . As far as the eye could see the land was under assault, the full expression of the Army's war-fighting fury: all its resources deployed, all its violence unsheathed, as if waging war against the land itself.

Their helicopter came down in a sandy open space that turned out to be a village graveyard. As Laurence, his CBS crew, and the photographer Eddie Adams tumbled out, terrified wounded men were running toward them, risking being hit again to get to the safety of their chopper. Once the four medevac choppers had lifted off again with the wounded men aboard, the soldiers who had helped their buddies to safety took off running for the cover of a dry shallow irrigation ditch that ran along the edge of the hamlet from which hidden snipers were still sporadically firing. Laurence and his crew joined them.

Then, he remembered, there was "a rolling thunderclap of noise," and the air a foot or two above their heads was suddenly filled with "hundreds of bullets breaking the sound barrier at the same time"—machine gun bullets, automatic rifle fire, M79 rounds fired from grenade launchers, all laced with orange tracers. Laurence and his companions lay prone, faces pressed

against the sand, trying to make themselves as small as possible. Overhead, bullets tore through the palm trees. Clipped-off fronds drifted down on the huddled men.

There was no letup in the firing. "So this is how it ends," Laurence thought. "The NVA [North Vietnamese Army] have got us outgunned and are going to overrun us." They were moments away from being shot in the ditch "like helpless animals." He raised his head just enough to see men in dark uniforms, still 150 yards away but moving toward them, muzzles flashing as they came. The deafening sound intensified. Behind the advancing troops was a squadron of armored personnel carriers, each firing five hundred .50-caliber machine gun rounds per minute, eight rounds a second. It was an ARVN unit, not the enemy, sent to relieve the embattled rifle company but unable so far to locate it. A grenade exploded at the edge of the ditch. Shrapnel hit Laurence, the company commander, and all but one of the four other men closest to the explosion. The CBS sound man was severely wounded in the abdomen.

The company commander shouted into his radio, trying to contact the American adviser of the unit that was coming closer and closer to what was left of his company. "Stop-stop-stop— shooting!" he shouted again and again, "Stop, goddamn it!" Finally, contact was made and the gunfire ended.

ABOVE Photographer Eddie Adams caught this group of wounded Americans racing across a graveyard under enemy fire, seeking the sanctuary of the medevac helicopter in which he'd just arrived on the battlefield near Bong Son.
OPPOSITE Cameraman Carl Sorensen and CBS correspondent John Laurence wait for the helicopter that will take the badly wounded sound recordist Vallop Radboon to the evacuation hospital at Qui Nhon. Radboon, who survived, was from Thailand, and Laurence made sure everyone at the hospital understood that he was not Vietnamese for fear he might be ill-treated.

An APC rumbled up to the edge of the ditch. An American adviser called down, laughing. "Guess we shook you up a little," he said.

"Yeah, you sure as hell shook us up," the wounded company commander said. "You killed three of my men."

The adviser paled, horrified at what his men had done. "At that point," Laurence recalled, "the company commander just about to be medevaced asked, 'What kind of fucking war is this?'"

A chopper lifted Laurence and his wounded sound man out before nightfall. When he got back to Saigon, the Army claimed there had been no friendly-fire incident—since no military source had officially reported one. It was at that point, Laurence remembered, that he came to believe what veteran reporters had been telling him: in Vietnam, truth really was the first casualty.

ABOVE A First Cavalry soldier, an M60 machine gun over his shoulder, takes time out for a smoke. Behind him, the village of Lieu An burns. Americans had set it alight after mines hidden on its outskirts killed one GI and wounded two more.

The First Cavalry began moving again, leapfrogging from hamlet to hamlet. Americans had learned as early as the Battle of Ap Bac that infantry assaults across flooded rice paddies yielded heavy casualties. Instead, they dropped leaflets and broadcast from loudspeakers to warn villagers of the terrible fate that awaited anyone who fired on their helicopters, urged them to leave their homes, and promised safe passage to any guerrilla who wished to surrender. Then, rather than risk the lives of American ground troops, they called in airstrikes and artillery and blew the hamlets to bits. Fifteen were obliterated. Five-inch shells fired from U.S. warships splintered the palm trees that had surrounded them. Five-hundred-pound bombs left craters ten feet deep and twenty feet across.

Villages that were not razed were systematically searched for anything that might have been used to support the communists. Lieutenant Michael Heaney, from Basking Ridge, New Jersey, a First Cavalry platoon leader, remembered working his methodical way through one village. "All the young men were gone, which was typical. All the houses were shuttered. I broke into one, knocked the door down, and it was dark inside.

I was freaked out. Was anybody in there waiting for me? The only people inside turned out to be a young mother holding a very young baby. We stood there looking at each other for a while and at first she was very grim and seemed determined. She maintained that for a minute or so, and then she burst into tears and sat down on the bed. I can see her today. And I said to myself, 'Holy shit. I can't even tell her "It's okay. I'm not going to hurt you."' But I had no way of communicating to her. And even then it registered with me: we're not winning any friends. We're just scaring the hell out of these poor peasants, who want us to go away. They want the war to go away."

Hundreds of civilians were caught in the crossfire. Thousands were driven from their homes and camped along Highway 1, South Vietnam's chief north–south artery, swelling a river of internal refugees that had already reached more than half a million. There was a theory behind the forced movement of people. Mao Zedong had famously said, "The guerrilla must move among the people as the fish swims in the sea." General Westmoreland argued that "in order to thwart the communists' designs, it is necessary to eliminate the 'fish' from the 'water,' or

to dry up the 'water' so that the 'fish' cannot survive." "Eliminating" the fish—killing or driving them out—was costly and time-consuming. But relocating the people—the "water"—would quickly "strangle" the fish by denying them the support and sustenance they needed to survive.

"The Americans called it 'generating refugees,'" Neil Sheehan remembered. "Driving people from their homes by bombing and shelling. I was out with Westmoreland one day and I asked him, 'General, aren't you disturbed by wounding all these civilians, the bombing and shelling of hamlets?' He said, 'Yes, Neil, it's a problem. But it does deprive the enemy of the population, doesn't it?' And I thought to myself, 'You cold-blooded bastard. You know exactly what you're doing.'"

The operation had originally been called Masher, but when President Johnson decided that sounded too bellicose it became

ABOVE Operation's end: Men of the First Battalion, Seventh Cavalry, return safely to the First Cavalry base at An Khe at the finish of Operation Masher/White Wing.

Operation White Wing. It lasted forty-two days. When it was all over, the Americans had lost 228 killed and 834 wounded. But 1,342 enemy soldiers were reported killed by the First Cavalry, and the ARVN and South Korean troops were said to have accounted for another 808.

General Westmoreland was pleased. But commanders on the scene noticed that despite all the American firepower brought against them, most of the enemy had still managed to escape into the mountains. And afterward, Colonel Moore remembered, "when we handed over control to the South Vietnamese . . . they flooded into the region with long-absent landlords and tax collectors trailing behind them, trying to squeeze as much rent money and rice as possible out of the tenant farmers. Within a week of our departure, the South Vietnamese and their locust-like camp followers were gone, too, and the enemy had returned and was back in control." A few months later, the First Cavalry would be called upon to sweep the same region all over again. By the end of the year, more than 125,000 civilians in the province had lost their homes, and similar seek-and-destroy and bombing campaigns would produce a total of more than 3 million homeless people all across the country—roughly one-fifth of South Vietnam's population.

There would be eighteen large-scale U.S. offensive operations that year, with mostly all-American names—Davy Crockett, Crazy Horse, Lincoln, Longfellow, John Paul Jones, Paul Revere I and Paul Revere II. They were meant to be "spoiling attacks," Westmoreland said, aimed at keeping the enemy off-balance and allowing the people of South Vietnam to declare their support for Saigon.

But since there was no front in Vietnam as there had been in most of America's other wars, since no ground was ever permanently won or lost, and there was no coherent plan to win and retain the people's loyalty, Washington would never be able to ascertain whether it was winning or losing. From the first, MACV amassed vast quantities of data meant to chart progress, but in the end it fell back, more and more, on a single grisly measure of supposed success: counting corpses—"body count."

General Robert Gard, who served for a time as military assistant to the secretary of defense, remembered that "the genesis of the body count was that Secretary McNamara, when he looked at the estimates from U.S. commanders of the casualties they had inflicted on the enemy, said, 'If these estimates were accurate we would have killed the North Vietnamese army twice. And therefore, I think, we should not claim how many we kill in a battle, unless we've seen the actual body.' Now, if body count is the measure of success, then there's the tendency to count every body as an enemy soldier. And if your success is measured by body count, then there's a tendency to want to pile up dead bodies and perhaps to use less discriminate firepower than you otherwise might in order to achieve the result that you're trying to obtain. The practical result would be killing people who are not enemy combatants and thereby alienating the population."

Colonel John B. Keeley, who commanded an infantry battalion in the Mekong Delta, recalled one whole day spent "beating the bush that flushed and killed four Viet Cong. Another battalion was doing the same thing and killed two VC. We sent the number four and the number two to Brigade for its body count report. There, the numbers were put side by side to make forty-two, instead of the six we actually killed." "The duplicity became so automatic," Major William Lowry recalled, "that lower headquarters began to believe the things they were forwarding to higher headquarters. It was on paper; therefore, no matter what might have actually occurred, the paper graphs and charts became the ultimate reality."

Philip Caputo of the Third Marines remembered being given very specific instructions. "Your mission is to kill VC. Period. You're not here to capture a hill. You're not here to capture a town. You're not here to move from Point A to Point B to Point C. You're here to kill Viet Cong. As many of 'em as you can." But then, he remembered, "there was also the question of how you distinguish a Viet Cong from a civilian—aside from the obvious fact that if a guy's shooting at you, you can be pretty sure he's a Viet Cong. There were, at times, very convoluted rules of engagement given to us. If we were out on an operation and we saw somebody running, that was somehow *prima facie* evidence that he, or even she, was the enemy. Presumably. I guess the idea was if they liked us they wouldn't run, and I remember an officer saying, 'The rule is if he's dead and Vietnamese, he's VC.'"

Caputo had been one of the first American combat troops in Vietnam. He'd survived patrols around Danang, then endured weeks working with Graves Registration, making sure that the bodies of his fellow Marines were identified correctly before being sent home to their families. Once, he found himself responsible for the enemy's dead as well. "A general from Saigon was visiting our battalion. Some high-ranking officer—the colonel or the lieutenant colonel—wanted to show the general that we were killing the enemy. So the general had to be shown the bodies. So I was given the unenviable task of fetching them—not personally, but making sure that they were brought back from the body dump to the headquarters unit and put on display. They were all torn up and the carrier that was towed by the jeep was awash in blood. There were entrails and bones—it was just a goddamn mess, you know. We had to hose this thing out and display the bodies for the general." Dealing with the dead got to Caputo after a time, and he asked to return to combat.

EVEN DEATH BECOMES ROUTINE

FOR YEARS, there had been rumors that North Vietnamese vessels had been quietly smuggling arms to isolated spots along the central South Vietnamese coast, but no one was sure if it was true or where it might be taking place. Then, shortly before the first U.S. Marines landed in 1965, an American medevac helicopter pilot had spotted an unidentified trawler camouflaged with trees and bushes, anchored in a remote inlet on a rocky coast called Vung Ro Bay. South Vietnamese Skyraiders were sent in to sink the ship. One hundred tons of Chinese and Soviet arms were found freshly unloaded on the beach—rifles, grenades, explosives, mortar rounds, and a million rounds of small-arms ammunition.

Still more supplies were quietly being smuggled into the Mekong Delta—among them the weapons that had helped make the communist victory at Ap Bac possible. To deny the North Vietnamese further access to the South China Sea coast, the U.S. Seventh Fleet launched a massive naval patrolling campaign called Operation Market Time, while a second naval operation, Game Warden, employed patrol boats to close off the Saigon River and the multiple river mouths of the Mekong Delta.

Hanoi was forced to alter its plans for resupply. It developed a new seaport, safe from both American and South Vietnamese attack, at Sihanoukville, on the coast of Cambodia. Norodom Sihanouk, Cambodia's ruler, was officially neutral in the war, but after the Americans entered the conflict he cut off diplomatic relations with Washington and—though he publicly insisted he had not done so—secretly agreed to allow arms and supplies to be trucked through his country along what came to be called the Sihanouk Trail.

But most of the men needed for the struggle in the South had to travel overland, through Laos and Cambodia, sovereign nations that Hanoi considered part of the greater battlefield. Americans called it the Ho Chi Minh Trail. The North Vietnamese called it Route 559, after the thousands of men and women of the 559th Transportation Group who first carved a braided web of footpaths through rugged mountains covered with triple-canopy jungle and nearly impenetrable rain forest, and then transformed it into twelve thousand tangled miles of jungle roadways, down which men and materiel streamed south.

When the Viet Minh fought the French, they had depended on tens of thousands of barefoot porters, then on legions of

bicycles specially modified to bear heavy burdens. But now, to offset the growing American presence, the North Vietnamese had turned to more mechanized transport—relays of six-wheeled Russian- or Chinese-built trucks, traveling under cover of darkness.

The trail they followed was a marvel of organization. Way-stations located a day's march apart provided food, medical care, repairs, housing, and air defense for the tens of thousands

ABOVE Heading south, North Vietnamese troops clamber down a cliffside stairway, just above the DMZ, 1966. "The eastern part of the [Ho Chi Minh] trail was very tough," the photographer who took this picture remembered. "Everyone had to carry at least [44 pounds] of equipment in addition to their personal gear."

ON THAT DAY I BECAME A MARINE

The U.S. Marines had been the first American combat troops to fight in Vietnam, and they were expected to fight longer than their Army counterparts—thirteen months, instead of twelve. They came from everywhere.

ROGER HARRIS was born in the Roxbury section of Boston and brought up by his mother and his grandmother. "There were a lot of gangs at the time," he recalled, "and there were those who would recruit you and try to entice you to do things that . . . weren't in the best interests of society. Let's put it like that. One of the fathers on our street had five or six children, and he didn't want to see us drift into negative behavior, so he organized us into a basketball team and a football team. He would take us to games in other neighborhoods, including white neighborhoods. And we'd always want to be in the last car arriving and the first one leaving because we'd get bombarded with stones and sticks and name calling."

Harris dreamed of going to college on a football scholarship but was not big enough to play for his team in high school. The draft was waiting. "I didn't want to risk being drafted by the Navy, or the Air Force, or the Army. I wanted to go with the gladiators, with the tough guys. So I enlisted in the Marine Corps. I felt it was a win-win because, if I died, then my mother would be able to receive the ten-thousand-dollar insurance policy. I thought that was a lot of money, that my mother would be rich if I died. And if I lived then I'd be a hero, you know, and I could come back and get a job. And so I thought it was a viable

employment option and opportunity for me. Naive. Dumb.

"You know, the Marine Corps trains you to fight, to kill. I joined the Marines and volunteered to go to Vietnam to do that. They used to say that if you're a Marine you can't die until you kill three Vietnamese. And I said, 'Oh, I'm from Roxbury. If the expectation is three, I'll do ten.' You know—craziness."

JOHN MUSGRAVE was from the Fairmont neighborhood of Independence, Missouri. He joined the Marines in part because his father and most of the men he'd known and admired had served in World War II or Korea. "I'd always dreamed of being a Marine," he explained, "and my country was at war. When my dad was eighteen and his country was at war he signed. I was seventeen in

Death Row

Your country's protectors! ★ John Wayne ★

The Pride of the Marine Corps!

Skin-head

Look out V.C.

Look out civilians!

eye-opening. When I got to talking to everybody, we were all the same. We were all working class and poor. And we all wanted to be Marines real bad."

BILL EHRHART was raised in an overwhelmingly Republican neighborhood in Perkasie, Pennsylvania. He was fifteen in 1964 and remembered riding around town in a flatbed truck with classmates singing Barry Goldwater campaign songs "because Lyndon Johnson was not tough enough on those communists."

He signed up with the Marines in part because his father, a pastor, had not served. "He went through his entire life feeling like he wasn't a real man because everybody around him, they'd all been there. All those guys in Perkasie dressed up in their American Legion uniforms, marching around on Memorial Day—my dad didn't get to do that. He was constantly being reminded, 'You're not a member of the club.' "

Ehrhart was a gifted student, and in his senior year in high school he was accepted by four colleges. Had he attended any of them he would have been exempt from the draft. But he did not attend: "In the fall was that huge

battle in the Ia Drang Valley, which was the first time it was actually confirmed that North Vietnamese regular soldiers were fighting the Americans. Of course, my way of interpreting that was, 'There it is. That's the proof. The North Vietnamese are the aggressors here. Here they are in South Vietnam.' That's when I began thinking that maybe I don't want to go to college right away. Maybe I'll join the Marines. And it was always the Marines. There was no question. The Marine Corps is full of little guys like me with chips on our shoulder. And it all came down to this notion that I was going to be a hero and have that gorgeous Marine Corps uniform. And the girls would just be draped around my neck and nobody would beat me up again and at the same time I would really be serving my country. It was my chance to be—one doesn't want to trivialize it—but it was my chance to be the star of my own John Wayne movie. It was my chance to do what that WWII generation had done and seemed to be so proud of. Now I had my turn."

But, he recalled, "for about the first five weeks at Parris Island I was convinced that I was going to die. The drill instructors said they were going to kill me. And they certainly sounded serious. But by the time I graduated I felt like I was king of the world. I was God. I could do anything. It was actually a wonderful feeling. On that day I became a Marine."

1966, so my best friend and I went down and enlisted in the Marine Corps. I knew I wasn't going to be a man right away, but I was going to be a Marine and that was enough. And I'd be serving my country. I'd be doing something mature. And I'd be doing something that was important. There was a war on. And I wanted a piece of it."

Training was a revelation to him. "I grew up in segregated neighborhoods all my life. I'd never met a black person till I arrived at boot camp. Never stood next to a black person or a Hispanic or anyone who was Jewish. They just didn't mix where I grew up. So that was just

OPPOSITE, TOP High school portrait of Roger Harris **OPPOSITE, BOTTOM** John Musgrave (on the right) and a friend mug for a photo booth camera. **ABOVE** Bill Ehrhart and his high school sweetheart, photographed just after he got his orders for Vietnam

of workers, many of them teenage volunteers, who labored around the clock to keep the roads open and the traffic moving.

MACV reasoned that if the Ho Chi Minh Trail could somehow be sufficiently damaged, the enemy would be unable to sustain itself. B-52s battered it ceaselessly. Three million tons of explosives would be dropped on the Laos portion alone during the course of the war—three times as much as fell on North Vietnam. Some key choke-points were hit so many times the workers gave them names—"the Gate of Death," "Fried Flesh Hill," "the Gorge of Lost Souls." One important junction was the target of 48,600 bombs within a single eight-month span. To expose enemy traffic, other aircraft dropped chemical defoliants, including Agent Orange, that destroyed thousands of acres of jungle and turned the earth into what one American pilot called "bony, lunar dust."

Le Minh Khue, who had left her home in the North with a novel by Ernest Hemingway in her backpack in order to serve in the Anti-American Youth Shock Brigade for National Salvation, observed her seventeenth birthday on the trail. More than half of those who served in the Shock Brigade were women.

"We all had to endure," Khue remembered. Thousands died—from starvation and accidents, fevers and snakebite and sheer exhaustion, as well as from the relentless bombing. Malaria felled them. Mites caused a form of typhus. Lice and leeches were everywhere, one woman remembered, "black and fat like beans." In the humid forest, nothing dried; clothing rotted, hair fell out.

Rations often failed to reach the volunteers, and they had to subsist for days on thin rice soup, sometimes supplemented by jungle plants and bamboo shoots and gibbon or macaque meat. One veteran of the Shock Brigade remembered that she and her comrades had passed their leisure time working up a list of thirty-two ways to die, ranging from mushroom poisoning to trampling by an elephant.

And always there were the bombs. "We didn't even have time to breathe," Khue recalled. "One group counted and measured craters. Others filled them in. Sometimes, just after we filled the craters, American bombs fell on them again." She and her comrades also had to detonate delayed-action bombs, sometimes five of them a day, sometimes more. The earth from beneath each bomb had to be dug carefully away. Then fused dynamite was packed into the hole and set off. Hundreds of volunteers were killed or maimed.

"Men bury the dead in peacetime," Khue remembered. "During the war, women had to do it. In the morning, they would get up to prepare the white cloth to bury the day's dead, make the coffins, and dig the burial trenches. Getting ready for what was to come. Sometimes, the burial trenches were bombed and they had to take the bodies out and rebury them. Some bodies were in pieces, some had exploded like bombs from the pressure. Sometimes as we walked, we would come upon a skeleton, someone at the rear of a column who had died alone, of malaria or some other disease."

One night, she went to bathe in a stream. "It was dark, and something bumped into me. It was a dead body, floating there. What I feared the most was dying naked, while bathing, or having my clothes blown off by the bombing pressure. It happened to a lot of the girls."

Youth volunteers on the Ho Chi Minh Trail: **ABOVE** A young woman named La Thi Tam counts falling bombs so that those that do not detonate can be located and defused. **RIGHT** This volunteer, filling a rare idle moment on the trail with music, was blown to pieces by a bomb the day after this photograph was taken.

She continued, "But even death becomes routine, and we had to live—so even during airstrikes we chitchatted." In the interest of the revolution, Khue recalled, young volunteers were exhorted to observe the "Three Delays: Don't fall in love. Don't marry. Don't have children." "But in fact," she said, "no one waited. Even in such chaotic times we enjoyed moments of peace and beauty. You know, the jungle was so beautiful. There were about one hundred boys in my unit and fifty girls. We were like classmates. . . . I was too young for love, but when there was no bombing we enjoyed some very romantic moments. . . . It was natural that we girls would have feelings for the soldiers. We saw regular troops all the time. They were young, healthy, muscular, and they looked cute in their uniforms. But they never came back. . . . Relations in wartime were always temporary. Soldiers passed through your life and sometimes sent back letters. I received quite a few and they were a great pleasure to read. The letters remain, but the senders are gone forever."

Despite the relentless air attacks, the rate of infiltration steadily grew, from an average of some fifteen hundred soldiers every month in 1965 to six thousand a month two years later.

A NEW THEORY

B ACK IN JANUARY, Mogie Crocker had received his first taste of the combat he had always hoped for. His headquarters company accompanied fighting men into the field, and he came under enemy fire just long enough to be entitled to a Combat Infantry Badge. But he had soon returned to base—and to the humdrum duties he hated. "My mood is a trifle despondent as I was looking forward to going into action again," he told his parents, "and am now faced with about thirty boring days in the rear area. . . . There is little sense in being over here unless one faces the main objective, the destruction of the VC. Certainly one feels no sense of accomplishment when one's friends are facing all the dangers. . . . I would never even have joined the Army if I had thought they would give me the job of a bloody clerk."

Mogie's parents did not share his disappointment—or his hopes for combat—and struggled to keep up with where he was. His outfit moved so often they called themselves "the Gypsies" and "the Nomads of Vietnam"—Cam Ranh Bay, Nha Trang, Bien Hoa, Phan Rang, Tuy Hoa. "I had a map on the back of the living room door," his mother remembered. "And I put pins in it every time Denton Junior moved. And he moved a lot. I knew those names at one time as well as any other history in the area of our own world."

Finally, after applying for combat duty again and again,

Mogie had deliberately fouled up his work at battalion headquarters so badly that he was reassigned to a fighting outfit, Alpha Company. "It's unfair that things went like they did," he wrote home, "but if I had been conventional I never would have gotten to the line. . . . My squad is good and my platoon excellent. The operations we now conduct are based on a new theory [our] Colonel Emerson developed. It is called the 'checkerboard.' "

Lieutenant Colonel Henry "Hank" Emerson, Mogie's battalion commander, was tough, implacable, and relentless: he once offered a case of whiskey to the first man in his unit to bring him the hacked-off head of an enemy soldier. (When he made good on that promise the photographer Horst Faas immortalized the winner and his grisly trophy.) But Emerson was also an innovative combat officer, the champion of both "checkerboard tactics" and "jitterbug strikes."

Before launching an assault, Emerson divided the terrain into sets of squares and assigned his men to work one after another while in constant radio contact with him, methodically destroying everything they came across—hidden supplies of rice and weapons, whole hamlets, any enemy soldier unwise enough to

ABOVE Lieutenant Colonel Henry Emerson wearing the six-gun that gave him his nickname, "the Gunfighter"

cross their path or try to run. Meanwhile, as his men shot and slashed their way across the landscape, he sent helicopter gunships—"jitterbugs"—clattering overhead to provide cover for flights of other choppers, ready to shoot up thickets or drop in infantry, wherever and whenever they were needed to clear the terrain below.

Mogie Crocker had spent most of his boyhood reading about war—the American Revolution, the Civil War, and World War II, in which his own father had played a part. And he had hoped for a chance to show what he could do in defense of his country. But nothing had prepared him for what he would experience over the next two weeks in remote, mountainous Quang Duc Province on the Cambodian border.

For eleven days, moving mostly under cover of darkness, he and his outfit battled nothing but the terrain—a labyrinth of elephant grass and thorn bushes, bamboo taller than three men, and triple-canopied jungle so thick it sometimes took an hour to move one hundred feet. The monsoon had begun. Sunlight rarely reached the slick, muddy forest floor. Finger-long black leeches caused leg wounds that quickly became infected.

But then a wounded prisoner told Colonel Emerson that four companies of North Vietnamese soldiers were preparing to ambush his men near an abandoned Special Forces camp called Bu Gia Mop. Emerson determined to ambush the ambushers. "My effort," he said, "is to try to beat the damned guerrilla at his own game." He radioed scattered units to help his men encircle the enemy, and on May 11 launched an attack, backed by massive air and artillery strikes.

In the midst of the fighting, Mogie's squad was moving along a narrow path between walls of bamboo when two enemy machine guns opened up on them. Mogie's closest friend, the platoon leader, was hit. Mogie crouched in front of him, radioed for suppressive fire, and then, as both machine guns continued shooting, lifted the fatally wounded man and carried him to safety. For his courage, he would be awarded the Army Commendation Medal for Heroism.

Before the fighting ended, some two thousand artillery shells had slammed into the enemy positions. Blood was everywhere, pooled on the ground, smeared on leaves and grass and bamboo, all of it left by the enemy dead and wounded dragged away by their comrades. There were scores of corpses, too, torn to pieces or driven into the earth, hidden in thickets, half buried in scooped-out graves. The earth-shaking concussions had blown the eyeballs of some of them from their heads. Of the 450 would-be ambushers, only 50 were said to have survived to flee across the border into Cambodia.

Mogie Crocker told his family back home nothing of what he'd done or what he'd seen.

A TARNISHING OF THE NATIONAL SPIRIT

MORE THAN 8,615,000 draft-age men would serve in the U.S. armed forces during the Vietnam War. Most were volunteers like Mogie Crocker or draft-inspired "volunteers" who preferred the Marines or the safer services—the Coast Guard, Navy, and Air Force—to the Army. A little less than a quarter of them—2,215,000—were draftees. Every male citizen had to register at eighteen, and remained in the primary draft pool till he was twenty-six.

Until 1965, when the first Marines landed at Danang and the American buildup began steadily to accelerate, the monthly call-up had been small and uncontroversial. But afterward, the demand for men rose rapidly, from 10,000 to more than 30,000 per month. Of the nearly 27 million American men who came of draft age during the Vietnam War, more than half avoided military service through exemptions and deferments.

A million young men would find a safe haven in the Reserves and National Guard, signing on with the expectation that they would never be sent into combat. Reservists and guardsmen were overwhelmingly white, generally better educated, better connected, and better off than draftees. President Johnson thought it best not to interrupt their lives—which would have required him to obtain a congressional resolution or declare a national emergency—for fear of increasing opposition to the ongoing conflict. So far as possible, as David Halberstam wrote, Johnson wanted a "silent, politically invisible war."

Everyone else was subject to the whims of some 4,080 local draft boards.

Between 1963 and 1966, married men were exempt. (During those years, the marriage rate rose 10 percent among men between the ages of twenty and twenty-one; the director of Selective Service for Georgia remembered that within one week forty-six men who'd been ordered to report for induction got married.) Then the law was changed so that married men had to have a child to be bypassed; afterward, one-third of the young fathers responding to a national survey admitted that the threat of being drafted had influenced their decision to have a child.

Roughly eight out of ten of those who were drafted came from working-class or poor backgrounds. "Any kid with money can absolutely stay out of the Army," a prominent Los Angeles draft attorney said, "with 100 percent certainty." Educational deferments became synonymous with class privilege. At first, simply being enrolled full time in a four-year college program or graduate school exempted young men. (Students who couldn't afford to attend classes full time were out of luck.) "There are certain people who can do more good in a lifetime in politics or academics or medicine," said a corporate lawyer who had been a Rhodes scholar, "than by getting killed in a trench." Of the twelve hundred members of the 1970 Harvard graduating class only fifty-six would serve in the military, and only two went to Vietnam.

"Many of us," recalled Professor Sam Hynes, who had been a decorated pilot during World War II and was teaching English at a small Quaker college in Pennsylvania during the early years of the Vietnam War, "thought that what the exemption for college students did was to bribe the middle and upper classes to be indifferent to the war by guaranteeing that their sons wouldn't have to go fight in it. It made it an undemocratic war. Those of us who remembered the Second World War were troubled by that."

Nearly 500,000 Americans applied for conscientious objector status on religious or moral grounds, six times as many as in World War II. In all, 170,000 were allowed to perform alternative service in hospitals, homeless shelters, and schools. Some were trained as medics and sent to Vietnam. At least two of these were killed; both received the Congressional Medal of Honor.

Educators, too, sometimes faced tough choices about the war. "I remember one of my students coming to me," Sam Hynes recalled, "and asking me to go as a witness to his draft board, and testify that he was a pacifist and that would keep him out of the Army. And I did it. And I talked to the draft board. But I was uncomfortable driving home, that somebody else was going to go in his place, someone who wasn't in college. Did I really know that this student was a pacifist? Not really. Was I even sure that he was a Quaker? Not really. So I had done something that probably in the moral sense I shouldn't have done. Because he was my student. That's why I did it. A redheaded lead singer in a rock band on the campus. I knew him. And I must say I didn't think he'd make a very good soldier. But that's not a reason. No. If you're a teacher you have a certain parental feeling about at least some of your students."

According to one national study, roughly a million potential draftees compromised their health in order to elude the draft. A college football star ate three large pizzas a day so that he could put on 125 pounds and be rejected as obese. One poten-

tial draftee fired a .45 pistol next to his ear nearly one hundred times in order to damage his hearing. Another shot a bald eagle so that he could claim to have committed a federal crime.

Upper- and middle-class youth could often afford to hire lawyers to file appeals against local draft boards, or were able to find physicians willing to say they deserved exemption on medical or psychological grounds. Some orthodontists did a brisk business providing well-to-do potential inductees with unneeded braces.

ABOVE The folk singer and antiwar activist Joan Baez, left, and her sisters Pauline and Mimi Farina do their part for draft resistance.

The writer James Fallows remembered that in college "sympathetic medical students helped us search for disqualifying conditions we . . . might have overlooked."

Poorly educated working-class youth, especially those who were black or brown, had far fewer options. The result was an American military heavily skewed toward minorities and the underprivileged. Racism had a lot to do with it—those who served on America's draft boards were overwhelmingly white—but so did economics. African Americans joined the military in large numbers in part because they saw the service as a source of steady income and a way to move up, and many then volunteered for elite units that provided $55 more a month as combat pay but frequently placed them in danger.

Two potential celebrity draftees made different sorts of headlines. George Hamilton, a second-string Hollywood leading man who earned $200,000 a movie and shared a thirty-nine-room Beverly Hills mansion with his mother, wangled a "hardship" deferment because, his attorneys successfully argued, he was her sole source of support. Meanwhile, the heavyweight champion Muhammad Ali, who told the press, "I ain't got no personal quarrel with them Viet Cong," was denied a deferment despite his assertion that he was studying to become a cleric in the Nation of Islam. Instead, he was convicted of draft evasion and stripped of his championship. (In 1971, the Supreme Court would overturn his conviction on a legal technicality.)

In the autumn of 1966, Robert McNamara launched "Project 100,000," lowering the physical and mental standards for potential inductees. He had twin goals, he said: to deepen the pool of potential draftees, and to allow more of the poor and poorly educated to benefit from military opportunity and train-

OPPOSITE Marine recruits being processed at Parris Island, South Carolina. As the war wore on, even the Marines, which had historically relied on volunteers, had to fall back on conscription. **ABOVE** A military funeral in a small South Carolina town, 1966. Between 1961 and 1966, African American soldiers, a high percentage of whom had voluntarily enlisted, accounted for almost 20 percent of all combat-related deaths. Afterward, commanders worked to lessen black casualty rates, and they were brought down to approximately 12 percent, much closer to their proportion of the U.S. population.

ing. The secretary promised that it would "salvage the poverty-scarred youth of our society at the rate of 100,000 men each year—first for two years of military service and then for a lifetime of productive activity in civilian society."

Forty-one percent of the 240,000 draftees inducted between 1966 and 1968 under the new dispensation were African American. Impatient old hands in the military dismissed the newcomers, white as well as black and brown, as "McNamara's Morons." "We had kids in our platoon that should have been in special ed," one infantrymen remembered, "lots of kids who couldn't read. One kid we had to write 'L' and 'R' on his boots so he'd know which way to go." A disproportionate number of these draftees were assigned to combat. The death rate among them would prove twice the overall rate, and a postwar study of those who survived showed that the training they were supposed to have received actually did little to prepare them for civilian life.

At the same time, the draft law was altered again so that enrollment in college alone was no longer enough to keep students out of the military. "They started drafting people out of college," Bill Zimmerman remembered; a graduate student at the University of Chicago, he'd been an antiwar activist ever since 1963, when he'd seen Malcolm Browne's photographs of a Buddhist monk setting himself on fire. "And that's when the antiwar movement shifted from a moral movement to a self-interest movement, driven by people who didn't want to go to war and their loved ones who didn't want them to go to war. If your rank fell below a certain threshold, the best that could happen to you was that you would lose your chance for a college education and the worst that could happen was that you would be killed in Vietnam. So we protested that the University of Chicago, by agreeing to supply those rankings to the draft boards, was complicit in the war. We took over the administration building. This was the first time that students had seized a building on a college campus. We removed everybody, wouldn't let anybody in who wasn't with us, and held that building for three days. And we became a national news story. Some of us were asked to speak, and our voices were being projected to the entire nation. That was quite a high. We thought for the first time that we were really having an impact."

Within weeks, students would seize buildings and make similar demands at the University of Wisconsin and the City University of New York. When the deferment for graduate school was eliminated in 1967, the percentage of college graduates serving in Vietnam rose from 6 percent to 10 percent.

The way conscription worked during the Vietnam War, wrote Kingman Brewster, the president of Yale, "was a cynical avoidance of service, a corruption of the aims of education, a tarnishing of the national spirit, . . . and a cops and robbers view of national obligation."

WHO *ARE* THE VIET CONG?

DUONG VAN MAI and most of her family had been part of the flood of refugees who fled North Vietnam for the South back in 1954. They settled in Saigon, where her father, who had been an important official in the French colonial regime, became a minor one in the Finance Ministry. Mai did well in school, won a scholarship to Georgetown University in Washington, D.C., spent three years there, and returned to Vietnam with an American fiancé, Army Sergeant David Elliott.

In 1964, Robert McNamara—genuinely puzzled by the stubbornness of the communists in the face of American power—had commissioned the RAND Corporation to do a study of defectors and enemy prisoners, seeking to know "Who *are* the Viet Cong? And what makes them tick?"

The Elliotts signed on with RAND, and Mai began interviewing subjects. She remembered that she'd been "brought up to believe that the communists were people who destroyed the family, destroyed religion, had no allegiance to our country but only to international communism."

"My mother would describe them as *đầu trâu mặt ngựa*" she recalled. "Brutal subhumans with the head of a water buffalo

and the face of a horse. But I knew that they also included people like my sister, Thang, and a lot of my cousins. I couldn't quite reconcile the two images, but of the two, my mother's image was stronger because I was so scared of them. That was the frame of mind I had when I started doing research into the communist movement. I remember my first interview. I was by myself. I was very young. I was going to this grim prison to interview this high-ranking cadre who had been captured. I went in thinking, 'I'm going to meet this beast—this guy with a head of a water buffalo and the face of a horse'—but when I walked in he did not look like a brute."

Instead, he was a dignified middle-aged man, she remembered, "with the authoritative demeanor of someone used to leading others." She offered him an American cigarette, but he refused it—"he did not want to touch anything so American." He answered her questions fully and patiently, and "had more integrity than anyone I had met in Saigon in a long time.

"He believed that the [Viet Cong] would free his country from foreign domination and reunify it under a regime that would bring social justice and equality to the poor," she recalled. "He looked at himself as poor: a poor peasant who had been elevated to a position of leadership. Of course, one interview could not change my views right away. But it did raise troubling questions in my mind. Who were the good guys and who were the bad guys? I thought I knew. Now, the situation no longer seemed so black and white."

When the first RAND report was presented to McNamara's top deputies at the Pentagon, describing the Viet Cong as a dedicated enemy that "could only be defeated at enormous costs,"

OPPOSITE Duong Van Mai Elliott at the Can Tho Airport, on her way home after interviewing enemy prisoners and defectors, 1965 **ABOVE** Five proud soldiers belonging to an NLF artillery company that had recently been awarded the title of "Hero Unit" one of them said, "If what you say is true, we're fighting on the wrong side, the side that's going to lose this war."

In the summer of 1966, Mai Elliott was asked to act as translator for the veteran American journalist Martha Gellhorn on a visit to an American hospital in South Vietnam. "I saw for the first time what the weapons were doing to real human beings," she recalled. "I saw children and adults who had lost limbs. I saw eyes staring out of heads swathed in bloody bandages. I saw a woman who had been burned by a phosphorus bomb, with peeling skin showing pink and raw flesh underneath. I knew this was only a fraction of the toll in human misery. I left shaken and more convinced than before that it was unfair to make the peasants bear the brunt of the suffering to save my family and other middle-class families from a communist system they felt they could not live under."

Still, Mai couldn't bring herself to wish for an American withdrawal. "I hated the war and I wanted peace, but a peace that would keep the communists from winning. I feared that once the shield of American power was removed, the communists would sweep the hapless Saigon regime aside and my family would suffer with nowhere else to run and hide. I began to wish that the group of people dubbed 'the Third Force,' who were neither pro-America nor pro-communist, would succeed in rallying the people."

CONTACT IS A MOTHER

I WAS WITH A REALLY GOOD UNIT," First Cavalry Division platoon leader Michael Heaney recalled. "They believed in Army traditions, they believed in honor, they believed even in treating your enemy humanely once he was a POW." Heaney had arrived late in 1965 and was assigned to a densely populated section of Central Vietnam, where he found himself surrounded by NLF fighters, North Vietnamese infiltrators, and villagers whose loyalties were unclear.

"We never really figured out how to determine who the enemy was," he remembered. "Being normal, decent American boys, you don't just put your rifle up and take a shot at a guy and try to kill him unless you're pretty sure this is an enemy. And if he wasn't armed, or wasn't menacing you in any way, we wouldn't shoot him. We'd go through a village in which there would be no people we could identify as enemy soldiers, and we'd find a big cache of rice. So the standing instructions were 'Blow that up, burn it, destroy it, poison it,' whatever. We really didn't want to do that, because you didn't have to be a rocket scientist to look around and say these people are depend-

ing on this. This is their food. We were told sometimes to burn thatched dwellings. And guys would unenthusiastically try to light a roof. And as soon as the flame burned out they weren't going to try again. Our hearts really weren't in trying to destroy civilian food, civilian homes. It gave us an uneasy feeling about what this war was about."

Large-scale operations like Masher/White Wing and its successors made the most news back home. But most of the fighting in Vietnam was the kind Heaney and his men were about to experience—relatively small scale and closeup, and initiated by the elusive enemy. The military called it "contact." "War is hell," grunts liked to say, "but contact is a mother."

American infantrymen found themselves being used as "bait"—though military spokesmen were expressly forbidden to use that word when speaking with the press. The hope was that if U.S. patrols were unable to locate the enemy, the enemy could locate *them*—and then be annihilated by the massive firepower the Americans were able to call in. "We were acting as bait," Heaney recalled. "At some level we knew that. Go walk in the woods and draw fire. And then, when you draw fire, return fire."

Six months into his tour, Heaney undertook what he and his men thought would be a relatively easy assignment: climb a slope not far from their base at An Khe and drive an enemy mortar unit off a ridgeline. "As soon as we started out we started to get some bad vibes," he remembered. "We found some boot prints in the mud at the edge of this landing zone. And a nice trail, a well-used trail going up the ridge. And then we found some communication wire—'commo' wire, we called it—black wire, that came on a reel. We didn't use that stuff. But they did. I remember talking to one of my squad leaders about this. And we were both sitting there, 'Well, shit. This sucks.' But, you know, we got the mission and we'll go up and maybe nothing'll happen. My platoon pulled the point position.

"I had about twenty-six guys that day out of forty-five. And all of a sudden the point man, the first guy in the column, Sergeant Mays, good soldier, without saying anything, just put his M16 up to his shoulder and fired off a round. Then he turned around and said, 'VC on the trail. VC on the trail.' And before I had a chance to digest this he went down, shot right through the chest. Boom! And all of a sudden what was a very well-laid ambush erupted. And we started taking a very heavy volume of fire, heavier than I'd ever experienced. And it was so loud and so unexpected I was stunned for a little bit, you know. 'What the fuck is going on?'"

Terry Carpenter, Heaney's radio operator, got the company commander on the line. "We've run into something bad," Heaney shouted into it. A bullet hit Carpenter in the head.

"I knew Terry was down," Heaney recalled. "I knew Sergeant Mays was down. I had asked the first machine gun crew to come

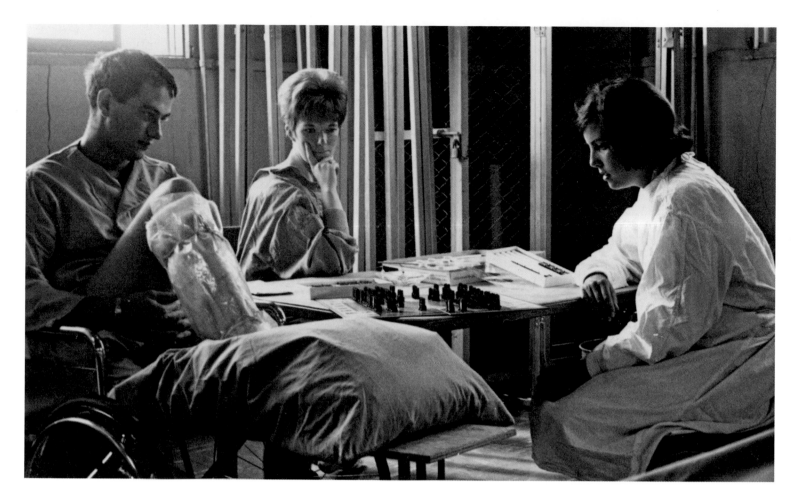

up and start laying down machine gun fire. They got blown away pretty quickly. They never really had a chance to lay down much fire.

"Right after the ambush happened and I knew I'd lost a bunch of guys, I said a prayer to God, saying basically, 'If you need any more guys from my platoon, take me. Don't take any more of my men.' As soon as I said it I freaked myself out and said, 'Holy shit. Can I take that prayer back?' But it was too late. I'd said it. And as it turns out, not one more man in my platoon died after that prayer."

Heaney continued: "Now, we saw numbers of North Vietnamese regular soldiers—PAVNs, we called them, People's Army of Vietnam—running along back toward where our column was and trying to surround us. And they did surround us finally and placed us under siege."

Heaney's men set up a perimeter and called for support. Low-hanging clouds prevented Skyraider pilots from seeing the struggle clearly enough to strafe or rocket the enemy. Helicopter gunships did what they could. They tried to call in artillery, but the North Vietnamese remembered the lesson they'd learned in the Ia Drang Valley: Grab on to the Americans' belt and hold on, and get close enough so they can't call it in.

Night fell. Heaney's company braced for the assault they assumed would come at dawn. "I was lying there on the perimeter," he remembered. "I was right next to a dead enemy soldier. It was kind of my face and his feet and I kept looking back at him, because I couldn't see any wounds on him. And you know, the strange things you think—'This guy's going to kill me. He's faking it. He's waiting until the assault and then he's going to jump up on me and kill me.' And I almost shot him again, just to make sure he was dead. And I said, 'Well, that's pretty stupid, shooting a dead guy.' I remember his face. He was young."

Then the enemy began to hurl mortar shells among the men.

"As I was lying there, there was a boom, a detonation in the tree canopy," he recalled. "And I felt like somebody had taken a bat and hit me on my right calf as hard as he could. A piece of mortar shell about the size of a quarter went clean through

ABOVE Michael Heaney, recovering from his wounds, plays chess with an American nurse. "I was almost glad I'd been wounded," he remembered, "because it proved to me, 'Okay, you don't need to have survivor guilt. You got wounded too.' I still feel I'm lucky. I came home. I can still walk around. I can still play sports. The guys I was with got killed. I keep their memory alive on purpose. I try not to be morbid about it or obsessed with it. But it's important to me. I'm living my life in a sense for them, because they didn't have that chance."

my calf, severed the small calf bone, missed the shin bone fortunately or it would have taken my leg off. And I just drew in a deep breath and I started to claw at the mud in terrible pain. I couldn't speak."

Heaney was bleeding badly. He crawled to the center of the perimeter and found a medic who still had a few bandages. "Nobody had any morphine left by this point. I said, 'Take my pant leg off and bandage that wound. Got to stop the bleeding.' He did. And I started to go into shock."

American artillery finally managed to zero in on the enemy mortar section. The survivors of Heaney's company stumbled down the hill to safety. He was carried to a hospital. His war was over. "The wound hurt a lot because the nerve had been severed," he remembered. "I was lying on my bed sobbing as quietly as I could, just from the pain. A brand-new nurse came over. I found out later she'd only been there a couple of days. She bent over and she said, 'Lieutenant, your men are all over the place. You've got to stop crying.' And at that point my platoon sergeant—a huge black guy from Detroit whom I loved dearly, Sergeant Sam Hunt, he came over and sat down next to me and he took my hand and he said to this nurse, 'Ma'am, this here lieutenant don't have to stop doing anything.' And he said, 'Sir, you're going to be just fine.'"

WORSE THAN FOLLY

ON MAY 15, 1966, the day after Mogie Crocker and his exhausted unit were helicoptered back to their base, the government of South Vietnam, the country for which they had risked their lives, once again seemed on the brink of collapse.

The trouble had begun with the ascendancy of Air Vice Marshal Nguyen Cao Ky to the prime ministership and the Catholic Nguyen Van Thieu to the office of chief of state the previous June. For the activist Buddhists who had helped topple the Diem regime and continued to hope for a civilian, democratically chosen government in which they could play a major role, this had seemed a disastrous development.

Thich Tri Quang, a charismatic monk who had emerged as one of the chief spokesmen for the Buddhist uprising during the months leading up to Diem's fall in 1963, sent his followers into the streets again and again, demanding the resignations of Ky and Thieu, calling for an end to the war through a transition to popular democracy and representative government. Ky's government met the protestors just as Diem's had, with tear gas grenades and helmeted police with clubs and wicker shields.

Despite his apparent cockiness, Ky knew his grip on power depended on support from the generals who commanded South Vietnam's four military regions, or corps. Each wielded political as well as military power within his area. Saigon could do little without their cooperation. Three of them were reliable, if pragmatic, Ky allies: since Washington was backing him, aligning themselves with him assured them of an uninterrupted stream of American military assistance.

But Major General Nguyen Chanh Thi, the commander of I Corps, made up of the five provinces farthest from Saigon, was different. Flamboyant, tough talking, and independent minded, he was an aggressive field commander, beloved by the men of the ARVN's crack First Division and the local militias that he led. General Lewis Walt, the commander of the Third Marine Amphibious Force, headquartered at Danang, thought his leadership "exceptional."

Thi got along well personally with Walt, but he was deeply suspicious of Washington. Not long after Joe Galloway arrived in Vietnam, he was taken to meet the general and got an earful. How serious were the Americans? Thi asked, wagging his finger. They seemed to be in a great hurry. Were they in this for the long run? If things didn't go the way they thought it ought to, would they simply leave? "If you come here and draw us into

a much more violent and destructive war and then decide to get on your helicopters and fly away," he warned, "you're going to be under fire. And it won't be the Viet Cong shooting at you, it'll be me and my troops."

Thi was also a devout Buddhist, careful to cultivate good relations with activist Buddhist leaders, some of whose goals he shared. Thich Tri Quang and others had hoped that he, not the Catholic Thieu, would become chief of state. "We cannot be so dependent upon the Americans," he told Ky. "We cannot be puppets. We must do something to have freedom and democracy." In part because Thi believed Ky was too willing to do the bidding of the Americans, he was openly contemptuous of him; once, when Ky called upon him at his headquarters, Thi asked his subordinates in a loud voice, "What is this little man doing here, anyway?"

Humiliated and furious, Ky saw Thi as a potential rival and wanted him removed. Henry Cabot Lodge, now back in Saigon as ambassador, agreed, fearing that Thi might lead a secession movement in the northern provinces, but he urged Ky to move against him only when he thought the time was right. Ky assured him there would be no public outcry.

In early March, Ky convinced the generals who made up the ruling Directory to dismiss Thi, then provided the press with a cover story: the corps commander had requested a "vacation," he claimed, so that he could go abroad and have his sinuses treated. No one was fooled. "The only sinus condition I have," Thi said, "is from the stink of corruption." Ky placed him under house arrest.

Ky had badly miscalculated. Thousands of Buddhists poured into the streets of Danang and Hue to protest Thi's dismissal. They formed an organization that came to be known as the "Struggle Movement." Students took over the Danang radio station and began broadcasting antigovernment messages. ARVN units loyal to their dismissed commander abandoned the struggle against the enemy and headed for Danang to lend their support to the dissidents. So did thousands of local militiamen.

Thich Tri Quang was again the best-known spokesman of the Buddhist movement. "If the Americans do leave" thanks to

OPPOSITE Thich Tri Quang, who became a central figure in the Buddhist "Struggle Movement" of 1966. Opaque and changeable, he opposed both communism and the military government in Saigon, believing that "only religions count in Vietnam." **ABOVE** Backed by tanks, ARVN troops loyal to the Saigon government move into Danang to crush the Buddhist uprising, May 15, 1966. It would take them more than a week to subdue the city.

peaceful demonstrations, he said, "I will have achieved passively what the Viet Cong have been unable to do by killing people."

Hoping to defuse the crisis, Thieu, as head of state, convened a National Political Congress of all factions, and on April 12 signed the document that emerged from it, promising elections for a constituent assembly within three to six months. Once that vote had been taken, he pledged, he and Ky would hand over power to a new civilian government.

Things calmed down. Thich Tri Quang toured the northern provinces urging his followers to return to their homes and begin preparing for the coming vote. Then, a month later, Ky casually told a roomful of reporters that whatever happened, he planned to stay in power for at least another year.

Ky's change of heart was "an act of treachery," one Buddhist leader said; surely "it will lead to civil war." Angry Buddhists returned to the streets of Danang—3,500 of them, joined by 1,000 ARVN troops loyal to Thi. They declared a general strike that paralyzed the city and closed down the wharves where U.S. war materiel was unloaded. Nonessential U.S. personnel were

ABOVE When rebel ARVN troops threatened to blow up this bridge across the Danang River in order to deny it to troops loyal to the Saigon regime at the other end, the U.S. Marines intervened, for fear U.S. installations on Danang's outskirts would be cut off from the city itself.

evacuated. General Walt stepped up security around the important Marine base just outside the city.

Ky now declared that communists, not Buddhists, had captured Danang. The demonstrations spread to Hue and Saigon, where marchers chanted, "Down with Americans!" as they passed the U.S. embassy. Lodge insisted that the protestors were being manipulated by "a VC Fifth Column . . . utilizing signs of communist techniques"—the evidence, he said, was "everywhere." (The CIA could find no such evidence; there were surely communist agents among the Buddhists—just as there were within the Saigon government, for that matter—but they were not in charge.)

Once again, the whole American effort in Vietnam seemed in peril. Just fourteen months after ordering the first American troops into Vietnam, President Johnson was afraid he might have to pull them out again. The United States should do everything it possibly could to keep Ky in power, he told his aides, but should also "be ready to make terrible choices. . . . If necessary, the U.S. should be prepared to get out of . . . Vietnam."

Some advisers urged him to do just that. John Kenneth Galbraith, the former ambassador to India, saw in Ky's potential fall "an opportunity only the God-fearing deserve and only the extremely lucky get"—to stage "an orderly withdrawal." Jack Valenti, the president's closest aide, agreed; he saw "no reasonable hope" in Vietnam, and told Johnson he needed to find "some way out" for fear the war would overshadow all the things he'd done for the country.

But most of the president's men urged him to hold on, and in the end he resolved to "continue roughly along the same lines" he'd been following, though he did demand "more planning on how to pick a man before he takes over so we won't have to get out when the wrong man gets in. . . . The way I see it, Ky is gone. . . . Let's get a government we can appoint and support." It was clear that for all of Washington's talk of defending freedom and democracy around the globe, when it came to South Vietnam, the need for order took precedence over self-determination.

In the end, Ky would survive, but not without more chaos. Before dawn on May 15, he sent four battalions of South Vietnamese Marines and paratroopers storming into Danang to crush the rebellion. Their commander was the head of the national police force, Colonel Nguyen Ngoc Loan, a veteran paratrooper with no sympathy for dissidents of any kind.

The city exploded in gunfire as ARVN troops loyal to Ky faced their fellow soldiers wearing orange armbands as a sign of their fidelity to the Buddhist cause. Neil Sheehan covered the fighting for *The New York Times.* At first, he wrote, "soldiers on each side appeared reluctant to kill each other and fired into the air or into trees and buildings." But as the day wore on things got more serious—and more surreal. The heaviest fighting took place early in the evening when an observation plane flew over the central market and was fired upon by rebel soldiers. Within minutes, two fighter bombers swooped in and strafed the marketplace. A column of pro-government troops led by two tanks moved into the square and a pitched battle began that went on for almost two hours. "While this battle was in progress," Sheehan reported, "150 Buddhist youth and priests and girl and boy scouts sat praying on the pavement in front of a major pagoda 800 yards up an adjacent street. Some of the girls wept as a priest harangued them over a loudspeaker and bullets cracked through the treetops and splattered into the walls and roofs of the pagoda." Inside the shrine, rebel soldiers set up mortars and prepared for a siege.

That same evening, Lieutenant Philip Caputo, at the U.S. Marine command post on a hilltop outside the city, watched in disbelief as two battles unfolded simultaneously: "Looking to the west we could see Marines fighting the VC; to the east, the South Vietnamese army fighting itself. . . . I saw tracers flying over the city, heard the sound of machine gun fire, and then, in utter disbelief, watched an ARVN fighter plane strafing an ARVN truck convoy. It was incredible, a tableau of the madness of the war. One of the plane's rockets fell wide of the mark, exploding near an American position and wounding two

Marines. The prop-driven Skyraider roared down again, firing its rockets and cannons once more into the convoy, packed with South Vietnamese soldiers. And I knew then that with a government and an army like that in South Vietnam, we could never hope to win the war. To go on with the war would be folly—worse than folly: it would be a crime, murder on a mass scale."

Thich Tri Quang cabled President Johnson, asking him to intervene. Johnson did not reply. Dean Rusk did instead, blandly urging all South Vietnamese to unite against the communists. The monk, who had seen the Americans as allies during the struggle to overthrow Diem, felt abandoned. General Walt cabled his own alarm: "Certain factions in Saigon have carefully planned this attack in order to wipe out the Buddhist resistance and opposition. As a result, there is going to be bloodshed and a lot of bitterness among the population in I Corps area."

The fighting went on. In Danang itself, the ARVN dissidents, outnumbered and outgunned, took refuge in pagodas, surrounded by civilians. When the Vietnamese air force commander ordered his warplanes to bomb and strafe these last pockets of resistance, General Walt vehemently objected, fearing that more stray bullets and errant bombs or rockets might damage his airfield or injure more of his men. When Vietnamese planes took off anyway, Walt ordered two American jets to fly above them, prepared to shoot them out of the air "if they fired one rocket, dropped one bomb, or shot one single round into the city." In that case, the Vietnamese commander said, he'd send four of his planes still higher, Walt recalled, so that "if my jets fired on his planes beneath them, his planes above would shoot them down." Walt immediately sent up two more jets with orders to fly still higher. "For two hours, this four-layer aircraft sandwich circled Danang . . . [until] the Vietnamese tired of this waiting game and returned to base."

Meanwhile, on the ground, Ky's men encircled the pagodas and took them, one by one.

After the shooting stopped, Neil Sheehan visited one of the pagodas. "It was deserted," he wrote, "except for two monks wearing white mourning bands around their heads who chanted prayers and beat hollow wooden blocks before the gilt statue of Buddha. . . . Pools of congealed blood still lay on the tile floors. The front of the shrine was heavily pock-marked by bullets. The yard outside was littered with Buddhist Boy Scout hats."

It took a little over a week to crush resistance in Danang. Some 150 ARVN troops on both sides had been killed. At least 100 civilians died in the crossfire. A total of 700 South Vietnamese soldiers were wounded, along with 23 American Marines.

Ky next turned his attention to Hue, where he hoped by cutting off access to food and water he could force the dissidents to surrender without further bloodshed. Americans were now targets of Buddhist wrath in that city because, as one monk

ABOVE Premier Ky arrives in Hue in triumph after the last Buddhist rebels surrendered to his forces. "From that day," he exulted, "Vietnam's Buddhists . . . displayed no further political passion."

told Sheehan, "the government used all the American aid and American weapons to attack the people." Six thousand marchers roamed the city with banners reading "End the Foreign Domination of Our Country, Down with the American Protectors of the Ky Clique, End the Oppression of the Yellow Race." Crowds burned the United States Information Service Library and sacked the U.S. consulate. One hundred and twenty-five monks and nuns began a fast. Ten Buddhists—two nuns and eight monks—burned themselves alive. But the dissident ARVN in the city eventually realized that the odds against them were now hopeless, and when Ky sent four hundred policemen into the city on June 8, they met little resistance. Thich Tri Quang was placed under permanent house arrest.

The last hope for a civilian government of South Vietnam seemed to have died.

Jean Marie Crocker, Mogie's mother, remembered reading about the anti-American demonstrations that spring and think-

ing, "Vietnam is in total chaos. Why, why, why are we there?" She spoke for a good many Americans. General Earle Wheeler, chairman of the Joint Chiefs of Staff, wrote to General Westmoreland, "Even if we get some semblance of solidarity and common purpose among the contending factions, we have lost irretrievably and for all time some of the support which until now we have received from the American people. . . . [R]egardless of what happens of a favorable nature, many people will never again believe that the effort and the sacrifices are worthwhile."

WE'LL LOVE EACH OTHER AND WE'LL BE ALRIGHT

NOT HEARING [FROM MOGIE] in those days was so difficult," his mother remembered. "It wasn't quite as bad as during World War Two when my husband was overseas. But there'd be at least eight to ten days between letters. So knowing he was in action I just didn't know what might be going on.

And one day when I was at the post office mailing something I asked the clerk, 'How do they let you know if your son is wounded?' It was very hard for me to form those words. But I just felt, I've got to know. I just felt so suspended in space and anxiety. And the man said, 'Now, don't ask that. Don't think about that.' I said, 'Well, I have to know.' And he said, 'Don't worry. They'll tell you.'"

On May 16, Mogie Crocker wrote to his parents. He gave no details about the fighting he'd just been through, said nothing about the bravery he'd shown under fire. But this letter was different from all the others: bitter, cryptic, worrying. He had had his fill of patrols, he said, and worried that more and more of them were being "thrown at us." He might take a fifteen-day leave in Japan soon, he wrote, "to keep from cracking up."

The letter filled his mother with apprehension. She remembered thinking, "Mogie had been through something very terrible, and, exhausted and lonely, he might have been sent out again since he had written." "That letter showed a kind of despair," his sister Carol said. "It echoed back to the day he said to me, 'I don't want to go back.' It was very hard to realize that he had gone back and it was getting painful for him, too."

When a second letter arrived from Mogie a few days later, saying he was now in a Saigon hospital recovering from a minor leg infection, his parents felt they could relax a little. For the moment at least, he was out of danger. "I was beginning to feel that, oh, it's not so long now," his mother recalled. "Maybe three months and he'll be home again, so I mustn't let myself be too anxious."

To Duff Thomas, an old high school friend, Mogie was more forthcoming. His nerves were shot, he wrote. "A number of exciting but terribly unpleasant events have occurred, the worst of which was being pinned down by two Chinese light machine guns firing 900 rounds a minute . . . and having my best friend killed more or less beside me. . . . Someday I may tell you the whole story if my nerves aren't completely shot by then. Actually, the latter is just wishful thinking in false hope they will take me off the line. I was fantastically religious for a while, sending up various and sundry prayers mainly concerned with trying to stay alive, but back in the hospital I am once again an atheist until the shooting starts again—or maybe I'll hold out longer next time."

June 3, 1966, was Mogie Crocker's nineteenth birthday but he'd had no chance to celebrate. He'd been released from the

Denton W. Crocker Jr., 19, Killed in Viet Nam

"He had so much to give. We couldn't believe he wouldn't come back, so he could give it here."

Mrs. Denton Crocker was speaking of her son, Pfc. Denton W. Crocker, Jr., who died of wounds in Viet Nam June 4, one day after his 19th birthday.

Young Crocker, a member of the Class of 1965 at Saratoga Springs High School, was the first Saratoga Springs boy to be killed by enemy action in Viet Nam and the third in Saratoga County.

Wanted to Help People

Determined from the time the American involvement in Viet Nam started to grow to "help the Vietnamese people," Denton finished high school early so that he could enlist in the Army.

He joined the 101st Airborne Division, volunteered for duty in Viet Nam and managed to get a transfer from supply services to a line infantry company. There he saw weeks and weeks of combat action with the "Gypsies," an elite force of "shock troops," sent on one mission after another against the Viet Cong.

And on June 4, his family was notified by telegram he "died of wounds received from hostile arms fire while on a combat operation."

Recall His Determination

In their home at 118 White St., Mrs. Crocker and his father, Dr.

press for permission to enlist. Finally, it was agreed that he should graduate from high school, and then could enter service.

And so, he was graduated in March, 1965. On the way, he had scored the highest of any Saratoga High senior and fourth in the county on the Regents scholarship exam. But use of that scholarship, he figured, could wait more important affairs.

"I asked him whether he

He wrote and asked that his family recruit some assistance for the Vietnamese civilians through the Marine Civic Action Program, affiliated with CARE. The Marines, stabilized as a garrison force, had more opportunity to do that sort of thing, he explained. They could provide, with Care, the tools, food, clothing and other things the villagers needed.

Was There 8½ Months

Private Crocker had arrived in Viet Nam 8½ months ago, after basic training at Fort Dix and paratroop training at Fort Benning, Ga.

Originally he was in the supply services, although even there he earned the Combat Infantryman's Badge. But, said a high school classmate who had stopped to share a letter with his family, Denton had written, "You couldn't sit and see friends risking their lives."

"I guess this (The Infantry Badge) wasn't enough for him," said his father." He managed to get transferred to a line company.

He had written once that he had been on 13 combat patrols. A last letter to his classmate had said that he had been on combat missions for five weeks, mostly near the Cambodian border.

Left Hospital

When he wrote, he was hospitalized in Saigon, for what cause his family does not know.

Denton W. Crocker Jr.

hospital just in time to rejoin Company A and take part in Operation Hawthorne, yet another campaign aimed at finding and killing North Vietnamese troops filtering into the Central Highlands from Laos. Its first objective was a besieged ARVN outpost at a place called Tou Morong. As night fell on June 4, Mogie and his squad were ordered to move up toward the crest of a hill overlooking the outpost so that artillery could be brought up and positioned to shell the enemy in the morning.

They moved slowly, warily, up the slope in the dark. Mogie was the point man. A machine gun opened up. Mogie never made it to the top of the hill.

In his hometown of Saratoga Springs "June 4 was just a lovely day to be out in our garden," his mother remembered. "And

ABOVE *The Saratogian* reports the death of Mogie Crocker, June 6, 1966.

Candy, our little girl, had gone to a birthday party. The other children were just around the house. But shortly after lunchtime I stepped out onto the porch, looking for my husband to come home from doing some errands."

Instead, she saw two men in uniform coming across the street, accompanied by the family's Episcopal priest, Father Ben Holmes.

"I just knew that they must have bad news. I ran down the steps, and I just grabbed hold of one of them and said, 'Don't tell me. Don't say it. Not my beautiful boy.' And he just said, 'Yes.' And then I said, 'But he was in the hospital.' And he said, 'He was killed by small-arms fire.'"

Mogie's sister Carol was sitting on the living room couch. "I suddenly heard my mother screaming for my father. And she said, 'It's Father Holmes.' I knew what she meant. Like in a movie, here came a priest up the stairs with a soldier and she's going, 'Oh no.' And she's calling my dad. My reaction was to leap up off the couch and grab my little brother's hand. 'You have to come with me,' I said. 'I have something to show you.' We raced out the back door and I just started walking. I have no idea why. I just said to myself, 'No. This isn't going to happen.' And somehow I felt I had to protect my little brother from it. And then I heard my father bellowing my name from the backyard and just screaming, 'Carol! Carol!' And something made me turn around and I walked up to the back of the house. And my dad was standing there. And I fell into his arms and I said, 'Don't let it be true. Dad, is it true?' And he said, 'Yes.' I was still clinging to my little brother's hand. And we went in the house. My mother was collapsed on the stairs. I'd never seen that kind of sadness in grownups before. She just grabbed me and hugged me. I somehow knew that things had changed forever. That my mom as my mom and my dad as my dad were never going to be quite the same again. And I'd never be quite the same again."

"I remember sitting on the couch," her mother recalled, "and I put my arms around them and I said, 'We'll love each other and we'll be alright.' But I don't know how far it carried. We all tried. I just felt so thankful for the gift of Denton Junior's life. I know Carol asked me, probably that very day or the next day, 'How can you believe in God?' And I said, 'Because we had Mogie.' A friend wrote to me that our children are really only on loan to us. Which I guess is true. But, of course, we were blessed that we had three [other] lovely children. I can't imagine somebody losing an only child. I just can't picture how that would be survivable."

Neighbors came to commiserate, bringing casseroles and cakes.

"One evening," Carol said, "I remember my mother letting out a scream in the kitchen, so angry that somebody had brought another chocolate cake. That cake at that moment symbolized

the absurdity of all this food in any way nourishing the emptiness that she was feeling. It's a scary thing to see your parents feel so fragile."

Ten days later, an Army captain escorted Mogie's body to a funeral home in Saratoga Springs, operated by a family friend named Dick Stone.

"When my mother asked me if I wanted to see my brother's body," Carol recalled, "one of the things she said to me was, 'He looks just like himself and very peaceful. It's hard to tell that he was injured so badly.' I felt if I didn't go I was bad; I felt to go would be the undoing of me. I ended up not going. I'm grateful my mother told me he looked peaceful. The funeral is very vivid to me still. The casket was draped with a flag. The church was packed. And, being who I am and who my family is, I felt it was important for me to hold my head up high, and be strong and be brave. That was the best way that we could honor my brother at that moment."

The family priest had suggested that Mogie be buried in Saratoga Springs so that his parents could easily visit his grave. But they chose Arlington National Cemetery, in Washington, because, his mother recalled, "a corner of my heart knew that if he were buried near us, I would want to claw the ground to retrieve the warmth of him."

ABOVE Mogie Crocker's headstone at Arlington National Cemetery. "We have always sent a wreath to his grave," his mother said, "partly in remembrance of him but also thinking of other grieving people or just people that are visiting to pay their respects. It's good for them to know that the soldiers are remembered."

THE HEIGHT OF MY AMBITION

ON JUNE 8, 1966, four days after Mogie Crocker's death, Vice President Hubert Humphrey spoke to the graduating class at West Point. He had long since swallowed his private doubts about the course President Johnson had chosen to follow in Southeast Asia. In Vietnam, he now said, "we are tested as never before. We face a situation of external aggression and subversion against a postcolonial nation that has never had the breathing space to develop its politics or its economy. In South Vietnam, both defense and development—the war against the aggressor and the war against despair—are fused as never before. Vietnam challenges our military courage, our political ingenuity, and our ability to persevere. If we can succeed there—if we can help sustain an independent South Vietnam, free to determine its own future, then the prospects for free men throughout Asia will be bright indeed. We know this. Our friends and allies know it. And our adversaries know it. That is why one small country looms so large today on everyone's map of Asia."

No parent in the listening crowd that day was prouder of his graduating son than Colonel Matthew Clarence Harrison. He had always believed that Matt Jr., the oldest of his three boys, would one day become an officer, too. Matt's nickname within the family was "Chips" because he seemed such a chip off the old block. "I was born at West Point when my dad was on the faculty there," he remembered. "From my earliest recollection, West Point was what I wanted to do. It was kind of the height of my ambition."

The Harrisons and their five children had moved from base to base—West Point, Fort Leavenworth, the Canal Zone—and the military was always at the center of things. "My dad was an Army officer and all that came with that," Matt's sister Anne recalled. "You addressed your parents as 'sir' and 'ma'am,' and you said 'yes' and not 'yeah.' And you answered the phone, 'Colonel Harrison's quarters.' We got up every Saturday morning and dusted the house. My dad would put on a record by the West Point Marching Band and my sister and I would dust around the living room."

It seemed to Matt's parents—and his siblings—that he could do no wrong. "He was the adored golden son," Anne said, "the captain of his football team, the president of his high school class. It was clear that he was special. Everything he did seemed wonderful to me." Their sister Victoria agreed. "He was the oldest. He was named after my father. He was following in my father's footsteps. He was doing all of the right things, setting the bar. I think every one of us just thought, you know, 'I want to be able to do that,' or 'I want to make Mom and Dad proud. I want to do good.' Now, of course, we were also kids. And there

were times when we would sit there and go, 'Whew, why does he have to be such a goody-two-shoes?' You know, 'Great. Thanks. None of us can live up to him.'"

He joined the infantry after West Point and volunteered for Vietnam. "I would have been surprised if he didn't go," Victoria remembered, "and I certainly understood his desire to go. It made perfect sense to me, because I believed that if you were going to serve your country and you were going to be in the military, then that means you are going to go forth and follow orders and serve your country."

Harrison and his fellow graduates all seemed to feel that way. "The strongest impression I have of my classmates was that they just were idealists," he recalled. "You needed to serve your country and you needed to be a patriot. It was a time before anyone questioned American exceptionalism. We didn't question it. We believed in what this country stood for, and we believed that people who had the ability to lead soldiers should do that. I remember discussing with my classmates how horrible it would be to serve in the Army if everybody just a year ahead of us had served in combat and we didn't have the opportunity. It's as though you had trained to be a surgeon and all of a sudden all diseases were conquered, and you never had the chance to treat them. You don't hope to have people get cancer but, on the other hand, if that's what you spent your life training to do you'd be disappointed if you didn't have that opportunity. I was afraid we were going to win the war too quickly and I wouldn't have a chance to experience it."

Before Harrison shipped out he was to serve four months with a stateside outfit. He endured nine weeks of the most rigorous officer training the Army had to offer—as a ranger. The man in charge was Major Charlie A. Beckwith—"Chargin' Charlie"—the cigar-chewing hero of the siege of Plei Mei the year before. He had survived a machine gun bullet through his stomach during Operation Masher/White Wing and been brought home to toughen up Ranger training before returning to combat. "If a man is bloody stupid," he told each group of newcomers, "his mother will receive a telegram and it will say, 'Your son is dead because he's stupid.' Let's hope your telegram only reads, 'Your son is dead.' With the training we're going to give you here maybe your mother won't receive any telegram at all. So pay attention."

They had no choice. To make it through they had to survive days without sleep; were deprived of food and water, forced to march up mountains until their feet bled, and patrol through swamps that harbored copperheads and cottonmouths; had to learn how to detect booby traps and outmaneuver battle-hardened veterans masquerading as Viet Cong. "Expect the unexpected," Beckwith told his trainees again and again. "Life is unfair."

Of the 212 men who began training alongside Matt Harrison, only he and 161 others received the coveted gold-and-black Ranger uniform patch that symbolized their toughness. Harrison was eager now to get to Vietnam and put into action the survival and leadership skills he'd been absorbing for five years.

I LOVE A PARADE!

B Y THE END OF JUNE 1966, MACV claimed to have killed fifty-seven thousand NLF and North Vietnamese troops since the beginning of the year. But the secured civilian population had grown by just one-tenth of 1 percent, and the enemy's numbers were still steadily increasing; men and supplies continued to stream south along the Ho Chi Minh Trail. There was no sign that either the large-scale American ground operations or the small-scale firefights or the more than twenty thousand air sorties against North Vietnam had shaken Hanoi's will.

General Westmoreland's "crossover point" seemed no nearer. From the first, the Joint Chiefs had urged the president to be more aggressive—to permit ARVN troops and their American advisers to pursue the enemy into Laos and Cambodia and to expand the target list for bombing in North Vietnam. Johnson still would not allow borders to be officially crossed by ground troops for fear of bringing China into the war (though reconnaissance patrols were secretly operating against the Ho Chi Minh Trail). And he was wary of heavier bombing. "I seem to be the only one," he said, "that's afraid that they'll hit a hospital . . . or a school or something." But he did now agree to "systematic and sustained bombing of facilities that refined petroleum, oil, and lubricants" concentrated around the cities of Haiphong and Hanoi. The Joint Chiefs assured him this would be a mortal blow to the enemy.

Johnson gave the go-ahead but continued to worry. Only the most experienced pilots were to take part in the attacks. The weather had to be clear. And, above all, no pilot was to fire on any vessel for fear of inadvertently hitting a Soviet tanker and triggering a nuclear confrontation.

On June 28, orders were flashed to the Air Force and Navy commands in Southeast Asia to launch their strikes the following day. Johnson called Secretary McNamara, seeking some reassurance about the way things were shaping up "Things are going reasonably well in the South, aren't they?" he asked.

McNamara's answer was disappointingly qualified. "We think we're taking a heavy toll of them, but it just scares me to see what we're doing there . . . with God knows how many

ABOVE West Point classmates (left to right) Matthew Harrison Jr., Richard Hood, and Donald Judd. Only Harrison would survive the war.

HERO PILOT

"Fighting the Americans was difficult because they always had more planes than we did," North Vietnamese fighter pilot Nguyen Van Bay remembered. "But I liked those odds." Bay defied them—and downed seven American jets in air-to-air combat, to become one of North Vietnam's sixteen wartime aces.

The seventh of eleven children, Bay was born to a landowning farmer and his wife in the Mekong Delta. He left school at nine; there seemed no point in further study, since he planned to farm just as his father had. But when his father insisted he marry at seventeen, he ran away from home and joined the Viet Minh. "It seemed exciting and adventurous—like a game," he said. "I was never 'enlightened.' It wasn't political for me."

In 1955, he withdrew to the North, where a selection team eventually picked him to undergo pilot training in China.

Learning to fly wasn't easy. "I just had studied through the third grade," he remembered. "I could do some basic addition and subtraction but nothing else. I could not read a newspaper. I didn't even know how to ride a bicycle." Worse than that, he was chronically airsick. "As soon as the plane took off I would start to throw up. And so I took a soccer ball and cut it in half, put a string around my neck, and hung it under my mouth. I would tell the pilot instructor to take over and then puke into the ball."

A visit by Ho Chi Minh to the Chinese camp inspired Bay to stick with it—and to master the MiG-17 fighters provided by the Soviets. When Ho asked if there were any southerners among the students, Bay and several others raised their hands. Ho urged them to persevere so that on the day of victory

one of them might fly the plane that carried him south.

On October 7, 1965, Bay faced combat for the first time. It was almost his last. His plane and three others were patrolling the skies over northeastern North Vietnam when an American fighter on his tail fired a missile. Bay took evasive action, but it detonated off his left wing and the force of the explosion flipped his fighter upside down. Shrapnel ripped through the cockpit canopy. "There was a huge hole in my right wing. Right in front of me there was a hole, as well. I told the air controller that my plane was damaged and had to return to base." Somehow, he made it back safely. When he examined the plane he realized how close he'd come to disaster. The wings were shredded. The fuselage was riddled with eighty-two bulletholes.

Within two years, he was a full colonel and had shot down seven U.S. planes—two of them over Haiphong on the same day. "Our MiG-17s were fairly slow," he recalled. "The American F-4s were very, very fast. But in order to fight

us they had to slow down to our speed. I was happy when I could get into an enemy formation and fire at the enemy."

Ho Chi Minh himself designated Bay as a "Hero Pilot" and grounded him because he feared the death of such a celebrated flyer would be bad for morale. But before he could receive his award, Bay remembered, he had to provide a short autobiography. He wasn't a good writer, he recalled—"my syntax and grammar wasn't good. So I had to have a cadre who was a better writer tell my story. And I was forced to say that the reason I wasn't well educated was because my family had been exploited by the imperialists and the feudalists. It wasn't true, but I didn't argue. After all, that's what the party wanted. But at the end of the day, the real reason I didn't read well was because I was lazy."

ABOVE Seated on what's left of a downed American warplane, Colonel Nguyen Van Bay uses model planes to show three would-be pilots how he shot down a U.S. Phantom.

airplanes and helicopters and firepower . . . going after a bunch of half-starved beggars. . . . And this is what's going on in the South. And the great danger . . . is that they can keep that up almost indefinitely. The only thing that'll prevent it, Mr. President, is their morale breaking. . . . There's no question but what the troops in the South, the VC and North Vietnamese, . . . they know that we're bombing in the North. . . . And we just have a free rein. . . . And when they see they're getting killed in such high rates in the South, and they see that the supplies are less likely to come down from the North, I think it will just hurt their morale a little bit more. And to me that's the only way to win, because we're not killing enough of them to make it impossible for the North to continue to fight. But we are killing enough to destroy the morale of those people down there if they think this is going to have to go on forever."

"All right," Johnson answered. "Go ahead, Bob."

The president was still worried over what was to come. That evening, his daughter Lucy came upon him sitting alone in the family quarters. She asked him what was wrong. He was still fearful that an errant bomb might hit a Soviet ship, he said. "Your daddy may go down in history as having started World War Three. You may not wake up tomorrow."

The next day, June 29, 1966, 116 U.S. military aircraft from Air Force bases in Thailand and Navy carriers in the South China Sea roared into the airspace above North Vietnam's capital and its biggest port for the first time and dropped one hundred tons of bombs and rockets. "The whole place was going up," one of the mission's Air Force commanders reported when he returned to base. "Every bomb that went in set off a secondary explosion." No Soviet vessel was hit. North Vietnam's oil-storage facilities in and around the two cities were virtually obliterated.

For months, the North Vietnamese had threatened to try as war criminals the American airmen they'd shot from the sky. (There were now more than one hundred of them, locked away in three prisons; over the course of the war, the North Vietnamese would hold some eight hundred Americans in fifteen prisons and prison camps.) Hanoi had published *U.S. War Crimes in North Vietnam*, a seventy-seven-page pamphlet chronicling in grisly detail the deadly impact of American weaponry gone astray—dead children, destroyed hospitals, wrecked homes. From London, the British mathematician, philosopher, and political activist Bertrand Russell was planning an international war crimes tribunal, hoping to put American leaders as well as American pilots in the dock. The intensification of American bombing only intensified Hanoi's denunciation of it. Radio Hanoi charged that the United States was carpet-bombing the North, just as Nazi pilots had carpet-bombed Europe during

World War II. Angry crowds were roaming the streets of Hanoi, it said, chanting, "Death to the U.S. imperialists!"

Among those who heard the broadcasts was Lieutenant Everett Alvarez, the first U.S. pilot to have been shot down over North Vietnam. He was then locked up with fifty-two other Americans in a prison they called "the Briarpatch," thirty-five miles west of Hanoi. News of the stepped-up bombing caused the prisoners to tap encouraging coded messages to one another, he remembered: "Should be over pretty quick!" "We'll be out of here pretty soon if they keep this up!"

Their eagerness was understandable. Alvarez had been a prisoner now for twenty-three months. At first, he and the other pilots captured early on had been treated relatively well. The men were kept in strict isolation, food was meager, and there were rats everywhere, but at least they had been permitted to write and receive letters from home and to get packages from the International Red Cross in Geneva, filled with toothpaste and Nescafé, Swiss chocolate and Sunbeam soap. But as their numbers grew, along with the damage American bombs were doing in the North, conditions for the prisoners grew increasingly grim. Their captors withheld Red Cross packages, withdrew mail privileges, and told the men that their country had forgotten them. They were forced to bow to their jailers, and were subjected to day after day of relentless interrogation, frequent beatings, and pitiless torture—all aimed at forcing them to admit their guilt and record statements denouncing the war. "When that cell door would open," Alvarez recalled, "and they would say, 'Your turn,' the bottom just fell out of you, and you knew that you might not come back. The manacles, the ropes, the beatings, they broke bones. They did everything. My arms turned black from the cuffs that cut off all circulation. And they didn't let me die. They just kept the pain going. That's when I realized that I was not superhuman. The first time I broke and gave them something I felt so low, I felt so little."

And so, when he and fifteen of his fellow prisoners were taken out of their cells on July 6, blindfolded, handcuffed together two by two, and loaded onto two trucks, some dared hope that thanks to the intensified bombing, the war was actually coming to an end, that they were being taken to Hanoi to be released.

But as they approached the city, air raid sirens split the air. Clearly, the war was not over. After dark they were driven to a park in the heart of the city, where they found thirty-six more

OPPOSITE From the relative safety of his personal concrete-pipe air raid shelter, a Hanoi resident scans the sky for American bombers, in June 1967. By then, similar shelters were everywhere in North Vietnam's cities and towns, one survivor remembered, and "every house had a supply of bandages, alcohol, and cotton for first aid."

shackled Americans who had been ferried in from another prison, called "the Zoo."

The men were ordered to fall in line at the end of a narrow street that led toward a stadium two miles away. Tens of thousands of North Vietnamese already lined the street, chanting anti-American slogans. In the middle of the street was a flat-bed truck fitted out with spotlights and filled with Eastern Bloc cameramen ready to film the spectacle.

One prisoner shouted, "Oh boy, I love a parade!"

A big-eared guard whom the men from the Briarpatch called "Rabbit" ordered the men to move out. They must lower their heads as they marched as a sign of contrition, he said. The senior-most prisoner on hand, Navy Commander Jeremiah Denton Jr., ordered them to stand tall instead.

They did their best. Within a few yards, the crowd began to press in around them, spitting, shouting, trying to get at the stumbling, shackled men, half blinded by the spotlights. "As I passed this one fellow with a megaphone," Everett Alvarez recalled, "he yelled to the crowd, 'Alvarez! Alvarez! Son of a bitch! Son of a bitch!' The people started pressing in, throwing things—bottles, shoes. By this time, the guards were having a hard time keeping the people away. I started to pray. That took my attention away from what was happening to me physically. And I just remember plodding through and plodding through."

The men were kicked, pummeled. Handcuffs made fighting back almost impossible. Several lost teeth or had their noses broken. By the time the last two men made it through the stadium door the ordeal had gone on for an hour.

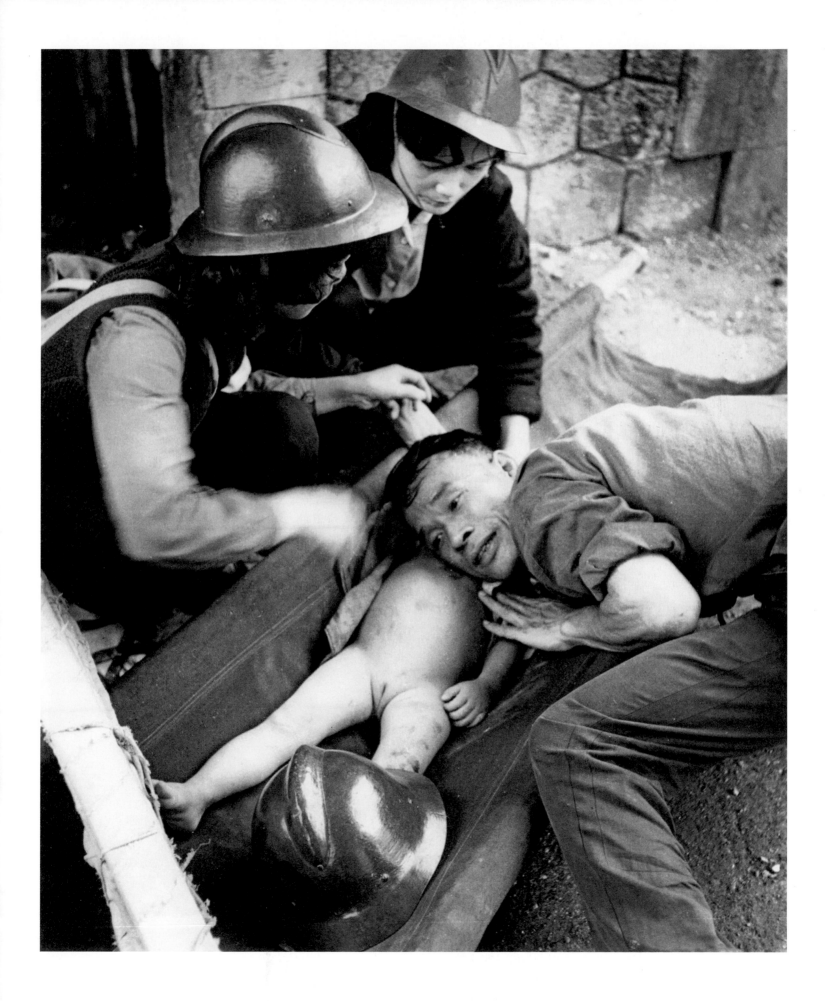

As the men sprawled on the stadium grass, trying to stanch their wounds and catch their breath, one Navy officer, captured just two weeks earlier and bleeding over both eyes, managed to joke, "Do they do this often?"

"You have just seen the wrath of the Vietnamese people," a voice over the public address system shouted overhead. "Those of you who have seen the light and want to apologize for your crimes and join the Vietnamese people will receive lenient and humane treatment. If you are true Americans, you will follow the way of Fulbright, the way of Morse, the way of Mansfield."

PREVIOUS SPREAD, LEFT PAGE Protected by a specially equipped B-66 Destroyer aircraft that jams North Vietnamese radar systems, Air Force F-105 Thunderchief bombers hit military targets just north of the DMZ, 1966. **PREVIOUS SPREAD, RIGHT PAGE** Medical workers struggle to save an infant injured in an American bombing raid on Haiphong. The target was an oil depot, but the bomb fell on a nearby residential district. **ABOVE** As angry Hanoi citizens chant their hatred of the Americans they blame for bombing their country, Navy Lieutenant Everett Alvarez (left), handcuffed to Air Force Colonel Robert Risner, waits for the order to begin the POW parade in Hanoi, July 6, 1966.

None took the bait—and when they were trucked back to their cells later that night several were beaten.

Hanoi had somehow hoped this staged parade would draw attention to the damage American pilots were doing to North Vietnam. Instead, people everywhere—even many of those who opposed the war—sympathized with the helpless beleaguered men. Richard Russell, chairman of the Senate Armed Services Committee, pledged to make North Vietnam "a desert" if Hanoi dared put American pilots on trial, while eighteen senators who opposed further escalation of the war, including William Fulbright, George McGovern, and Eugene McCarthy, sent a letter to Hanoi warning that further violence toward its captives would only ensure "swift and sure" American retaliation.

Hanoi quickly thought better of its plans for the prisoners. Ho Chi Minh declared that North Vietnam's policy "with regard to the enemies captured in war is a humanitarian policy." There would be no public trials.

ABOVE The crowd began by shouting slogans but quickly turned to violence against the prisoners as they marched. "We inched ourselves forward with no apparent goal other than to escape the mob," Alvarez remembered. "It seemed interminable."

CHRISTMAS IN NAM DINH

THE BOMBING CONTINUED, regardless. Tens of thousands of sorties were flown. One hundred and twenty-eight thousand tons of bombs would be dropped by the end of the year. But by August, the North Vietnamese had shifted most of their oil to underground tanks that could not easily be targeted from the air and hundreds of thousands of fifty-five-gallon barrels that were strung out along the roads. And more oil was arriving every day from China and the Soviet Union by rail and tanker.

The bombing steadily expanded to include most of North Vietnam's limited industrial plant and transportation infrastructure—match factories and sugar refineries, power plants and railroad yards, roads and ports and bridges. But the North Vietnamese had never made their own weapons, they imported them, and the bombing did little to interfere with that traffic.

Three hundred and eighteen American planes were lost in 1966 getting it all done, most of them shot down in thickets of antiaircraft gun fire and surface-to-air missiles, all supplied by Moscow and Beijing. And very little of the bomb damage proved permanent. Factories were broken down and reassembled far beyond the cities. Workers switched from electricity to manual labor, and small diesel generators.

"The people in North Vietnam hated the bombing," Master Sergeant Nguyen Van Mo remembered. "They were enraged about the air raids. In the beginning the Americans carried out their attacks very carefully. . . . We used to watch them, to see how accurate the bombers were and to judge how good the pilots were at avoiding antiaircraft fire and rockets. We had to admit that during the early attacks they hit proper military targets and that their flying techniques were pretty good. If they hadn't been, our ground fire would have shot down a great number of them. But later . . . the Americans dropped them all over the place. . . . [In Hanoi] large groups [of people] would gather to watch the attacks. At one point the pilots dropped a couple of beehive bombs . . . [that] contained hundreds of little steel balls. A large number of civilians were unexpectedly killed. After that, people began to hate the Americans. If the local authorities hadn't intervened, they would have beaten shot-down American pilots to death."

Mo continued, "In my opinion, in the early days the Americans didn't have any intention of bombing populated areas. Later, because the antiaircraft fire had gotten so heavy, the pilots had to escape themselves, and they dropped their bombs carelessly without paying any attention to the lives of the people. They were afraid of dying, and they didn't think about the adverse political effect."

Half of Hanoi's million citizens scattered into the countryside. "Our lives were turned upside down by the bombing," the future novelist Bao Ninh remembered. "People were killed, their houses were destroyed. I couldn't go to school in Hanoi; I had to evacuate to the rural areas. All of it aroused indignation. I was fourteen in 1965. I wasn't scared; I was agitated."

Throughout North Vietnam, enough crude air raid shelters were fashioned from concrete pipe buried five feet beneath the

OPPOSITE A lone cyclist spins past what is left of a Hanoi neighborhood devastated by American bombs, 1966. **ABOVE** Harrison Salisbury of *The New York Times* at work in the North Vietnamese capital. He asked a local official why he thought the Americans had done so much unexpected damage to his town. "Americans think they can touch our hearts," the man answered.

ground to accommodate some eighteen million people. Thousands living near the DMZ spent most of their daylight hours underground, emerging only at dawn and dusk to tend their fields and do their marketing. Children attended school underground and ate communally cooked meals.

Meanwhile, over a million people were said to be working around the clock to fix the damage American bombs had done to the transportation system. When key bridges were destroyed, they fashioned pontoon bridges overnight to keep vital traffic moving. Road crews waited along the roads with heaps of gravel and stone and stacks of wood to fill bomb craters. They worked under a simple slogan: "The enemy destroys, we repair. The enemy destroys, we repair *again*."

Samuel Wilson, then back home from Vietnam and in command of a Special Forces group at Fort Bragg, remembered that "Secretary McNamara was too intelligent an individual not to learn as the war progressed and not to see that things were going wrong that he had been told were going right. I recall one instance when I went by to see him and he asked me how I thought our strategic bombing program was affecting the course of the war.

"I said, 'It's not gaining us anything. Indeed, it's counter-productive.'

"'What do you mean?' he asked.

"I said, 'Mr. Secretary, these people know that at some point we're going to get tired of killing them. And they think they can outlast us. And they also are very much aware of the fact that we have to keep the public behind us in order to continue to prosecute the war. The sledgehammer approach is not working.'

"'Why don't people tell me these things?'

"'Mr. Secretary, you don't ask.'"

But when McNamara did ask about the bombing, the answers he got disturbed him.

Reports of the damage it was inadvertently doing to civilians had been filtering out of North Vietnam for months. Many Americans dismissed them as propaganda. But when Harrison Salisbury, the deputy managing editor of *The New York Times,* traveled to North Vietnam and reported what he had seen—bombs meant to destroy roads and railroad lines had obliterated the villages that stood alongside them; an attack on a supposed "truck park" destroyed a school three-quarters of a mile away—public doubts about Operation Rolling Thunder and the war itself continued to grow. Salisbury wrote,

Christmas wasn't a joyous occasion for Nam Dinh, although strings of small red pennants decorated the old, gray stucco Catholic Church and a white Star of Bethlehem had been mounted on the pinnacle of the tower.

Few Americans have heard of Nam Dinh, although

until recently it was the third largest North Vietnamese city . . . essentially a cotton-and-silk textile town, containing nothing of military significance.

Nam Dinh has been systematically attacked by American planes since June 28, 1965. The cathedral tower looks out on block after block of utter desolation; the city's population has been reduced to less than 20,000 because of evacuation; 13 percent of the city's housing, including the homes of 12,464 people, have been destroyed, 89 people have been killed and 405 wounded.

No American communiqué has asserted that Nam Dinh contains some facility that the United States regards as a military objective. It is apparent, on personal inspection, that block after block of ordinary housing, particularly surrounding a textile plant, has been smashed to rubble by repeated attacks by Seventh Fleet planes . . .

Whatever else there may or may not have been in Nam Dinh, it is the civilians who have taken the punishment. . . . President Johnson's announced policy that American targets in North Vietnam are steel and concrete rather than human lives seems to have little connection with the reality of attacks carried out by United States planes.

The brutal facts outlined in Salisbury's report were seen by some in the Pentagon as a "national disaster"; the Defense Department's press secretary dismissed Salisbury as gullible and denounced his paper as "The New Hanoi *Times*." But *The Economist* said the administration was "making an ass of itself by not admitting much earlier what it knew perfectly well, that some of the bombs were missing their targets. It is not what [Johnson] does, it's the way he does it." The credibility gap widened.

SPOOFED

EARLY IN 1967, General Westmoreland mounted two more major operations, aimed at tracking down and eliminating the enemy within its sanctuaries.

The first, Cedar Falls, involved sixteen thousand U.S. troops and an equal number of ARVN soldiers. Its target was a cluster of enemy installations within the Iron Triangle, forty-six square miles of jungle just eighteen miles from Saigon that had provided a safe haven and staging area for guerrillas since the time of the French. MACV was concerned that troops gathering there might be planning an imminent assault on Saigon.

To minimize civilian casualties and separate out the Viet Cong they resolved to clear the entire population of the area—and to

empty and destroy the town of Ben Suc on the jungle's western edge whose people had supported the NLF since the settlement had been seized from the ARVN three years earlier. Once the area had been emptied it was to be declared by the province chief a "free-fire zone" in which any adult civilian found there would be considered an enemy combatant or supporter.

Four days of intense bombing by B-52s preceded the ground assault. Then, specially built plows tore fifty-foot swaths through the vegetation, clearing some 2,700 acres of jungle to deny the enemy further sanctuary. Villages were razed. MACV reported that U.S. troops had killed 750 enemy soldiers, destroyed 1,100 bunkers and 400 tunnels and captured 3,700 tons of rice and almost 500,000 pages of enemy documents. Meanwhile, 60 helicopters and 500 troops descended on Ben Suc. Bulldozers crushed every building. Almost 6,000 civilians—mostly women, children, and old people—were herded onto trucks and taken to a place called Phu Loi, where there was supposed to be a refugee camp. But the province chief in charge had not been told the civilians were coming, for fear the plan would be

betrayed to the enemy. When the camp was finally completed, a sign was hung on the barbed wire. "Welcome," it said, "to the Reception Center for Refugees Fleeing Communism."

Major General William DePuy, commander of the U.S. First Division, claimed that his men had dealt "a blow from which the VC in this area may never recover." But within two weeks, an American commander admitted that the Iron Triangle was once again "literally crawling with . . . Viet Cong."

Junction City, the second big operation of the new year, was the largest in the war so far—an eighty-day sweep north of Sai-

ABOVE Residents of Ben Suc gather what belongings they can before being forced from their homes during Operation Cedar Falls. An American reporter asked an elderly refugee what she thought of the refugee camp to which she'd been taken. "We were forced to come here," she said. "The enemy came to our old village four times. Twice it was the men from the jungle and twice it was you foreigners. Each time we suffered. You came last and brought us here. You ask me what I want. I want to be left alone. I want to grow rice."

gon by more than thirty-five thousand U.S. and ARVN troops, intended to annihilate the Ninth NLF Division and to locate and eliminate COSVN, the communist headquarters from which insurgent activities were directed. Some of the fighting was fierce—MACV claimed to have killed nearly 3,000 communists with a loss of 282 Americans killed in action. But COSVN was not where American planners had thought it was. "There is a possibility that we have been spoofed by the enemy," Westmoreland admitted. The headquarters—really just a small stall and an easily movable collection of maps, files, and radio equipment—along with most of the Ninth Division, slipped across the border into Cambodia, where Westmoreland's troops were forbidden to go.

"One of the discouraging features of both Cedar Falls and

ABOVE Weary GIs from the 173rd Airborne Brigade with a communist flag they had seized from an underground enemy bunker within the Iron Triangle

Junction City was the fact that we had insufficient forces . . . to prevent the Viet Cong from returning," a U.S. commander concluded. "In neither instance were we able to stay around, and it was not long before there was evidence of the enemy's return."

I'M HERE TO LIBERATE YOU

MARINE PRIVATES John Musgrave from Independence, Missouri, Roger Harris from Boston's Roxbury, and Bill Ehrhart from Perkasie, Pennsylvania, all arrived separately at Danang in early 1967. Each had high hopes, for himself and for the cause for which he expected to fight.

"There were kids selling sex books and cokes," John Musgrave recalled of his first glimpses of Vietnam. "And there were girls giving out flowers. The units had trucks with big signs. I found the truck from my unit and climbed aboard. We drove

188 | THE VIETNAM WAR

through Danang, which is a big city. The first thing that assaulted me was the foreign smells, and then watching people relieve themselves by the side of the road and seeing animals I'd never seen before—the big water buffaloes. It was like being on Mars because it was totally foreign to me. But honestly, in my dumb Missouri kid kind of way, I thought, 'Look at all those foreigners.' And it didn't dawn on me for a little while that the only foreigner in that area was me."

"Certainly when I got there," Ehrhart recalled, "I'm thinking I'm involved in a winning enterprise. America doesn't lose. We never lose. I had sort of not really known much about the War of 1812, which was pretty much of a draw, or the Civil War, in which half of America lost, and the Korean War, where we won the first half and lost the second half. But I'd been taught America never loses. So it never occurred to me that we would not ultimately achieve the goals we set out to achieve."

"The feeling was that we were going over to rescue folks," Harris remembered. "The communists were taking over this country and the South Vietnamese needed help, but then when we got there we realized it wasn't exactly like that. Many of the Vietnamese would spit at our trucks and tell us to go back to America. And so we began questioning ourselves. These people don't want us here. Why are we here?"

John Musgrave was initially stationed with B Company, First Military Police Battalion, with the First Marine Division at the Danang Air Base. Roger Harris was assigned to G Company, Second Battalion, Ninth Regiment of the Third Marine Division at Phu Bai, north of Danang. And Bill Ehrhart joined the First Battalion of the same division near the coastal city of Hoi An. "I had visions of American troops rolling through France in 1944 and young women giving them bottles of wine and flowers and kisses," he said. "And I remember driving down this dirt road to our battalion command post on the day after I got to Vietnam, and I'm sitting there in the jeep waving like Douglas MacArthur, and nobody's paying any attention to me. And I'm thinking, 'Wait a minute. I'm here to liberate you.' It was puzzling to me. And that was only the beginning."

Private Ehrhart was given a desk job, collating snippets of information for the daily intelligence summary. But from the first, combat seemed close. Sleep was elusive. Three artillery batteries fired salvo after salvo into the darkness all night long, every night of the week, part of the countrywide campaign of "Harassment and Interdiction" fire ordered by General West-

moreland. Its object was to keep the enemy off guard, but the random shelling of the countryside also took countless civilian lives—and sometimes American lives as well. In 1966, only 15 percent of all the artillery shells expended by the U.S. Army were fired in support of troops; all the rest fell on targeted areas where the enemy might or might not have been.

Three days after Ehrhart arrived in Hoi An, he got word that a group of civilian detainees was being brought into the compound. He was expected to take charge of them when they got there. "Now, a prisoner is defined as an armed combatant caught with weapons," he recalled. "A detainee is a civilian who is detained for questioning. There was one set of rules for how

ABOVE Marine Corporal Bill Ehrhart and detainees on Barrier Island, twenty miles south of Danang, August 1967. The island was repeatedly swept by the U.S. Marines. The fishermen and their families who made up its population were twice forcibly removed, but they slipped back again, rebuilt their homes, and maintained their loyalty to the NLF throughout the war.

you treat prisoners and another for detainees." Ehrhart hurried to the place where amphibious tractors—"amtracks"—parked. He was just in time to see two of them rumble through the gate. "These vehicles, eight or nine feet tall, are flat-topped. There's a bunch of people bound hand and foot on top. The Marines start pushing them off. Their hands are tied. Their feet are tied. They have no way to break their fall. People are screaming. You can hear bones snapping, shoulders dislocate."

Ehrhart grabbed the corporal in charge. "'What are they doing? What are they doing? These are detainees!'" This guy looks at me and he looks down at my hands grabbing his upper arm. And he looks back at me again and he says in the flattest, hollowest voice I had ever heard, 'Ehrhart, you better keep your mouth shut and your eyes open till you understand what's going on around here.' I said, 'Oh, okay.' And then he says, 'Untie their feet.' So we marched this band, there must have been about twenty to thirty people, old men, women, children, no young men. As we're marching them up to the prisoner compound, he says to me, 'Listen, pal, those trackers, the guys who operate the amtracks, are hitting mines out there on the sand flats every week. Fifty-pound box mines, seventy-five-pound box mines. They're getting killed; they're getting maimed. And these people know where those mines are. You treat these people nice in front of the trackers and those trackers will rearrange your head and ass for you and walk away laughing.' Well, at that point, three days into Vietnam, I'm thinking, 'Whoa. What the hell is going on here? This ain't what my high school teacher told me was going to be going on.' And it just went on from there."

NO OTHER CHOICE

ON SATURDAY, January 14, 1967, Dr. Martin Luther King Jr. and his closest aide and traveling companion, Bernard Lee, arrived at New York's John F. Kennedy International Airport to catch a flight to Jamaica. King was exhausted and deeply conflicted. For a dozen turbulent years he'd been the most prominent civil rights spokesman in the country. He'd been jailed, mobbed, stabbed, hounded by the FBI, and denounced by white supremacists and black separatists alike, and he looked forward to four weeks in the sun, the first vacation he'd allowed himself since the Montgomery bus boycott that had turned him into a national figure.

At an airport newsstand, King picked up a handful of magazines for the flight. Then he and Lee found a restaurant and ordered breakfast. King began leafing through a copy of the leftist magazine *Ramparts*. The lead article was a photo-essay called "The Children of Vietnam" by a human rights activist named William Pepper. King's friend Dr. Benjamin Spock, the best-loved pediatrician of his time and an early and unremitting opponent of the war, had written a preface.

For two years, the war in Vietnam had filled King with what he called "anxiety and agony and anguish." Nonviolence was a matter of principle, not politics, with him: segregation was wrong and so, he believed, was the war. But when his conscience told him to speak out against it, black and white allies alike had urged him to keep his own counsel about the war. They argued that it was folly to risk alienating the president who, by winning passage of the Civil Rights Act of 1964 and the Voting Rights Act of 1965, had done more for black people than any president since Abraham Lincoln. "Johnson needs a consensus," Whitney Young, president of the National Urban League, said. "If we are not with him on Vietnam, then he is not going to be with us on civil rights."

King's food came, but he ignored it, continuing to flip through the article, twenty-four pages of harrowing color photographs of the youngest victims of the war, orphaned, maimed, hideously disfigured by napalm. "Martin pushed the plate of food away," Lee remembered. "I looked up and said, 'Doesn't it taste any good?' and he answered, 'Nothing will ever taste any good for me until I do everything I can to end that war.'"

While in Jamaica, King would recall, "I spent a lot of time . . . in prayerful meditation. I came to the conclusion that I could no longer remain silent about an issue that was destroying the soul of our nation."

On his return he became a full-throated critic of the war. On April 4, at the fashionable Riverside Church on Manhattan's Upper West Side, he spoke of what he thought the war was doing to Vietnam—and to the United States. "I come to this magnificent house of worship tonight because my conscience leaves me no other choice," he said, his resonant voice echoing through the vast vaulted space. He could never again speak "against the violence of the oppressed in the ghettoes," he continued, without first having spoken clearly to "the greatest purveyor of violence in the world: my government."

It had been wrong not to recognize Vietnamese independence in 1945, he said, wrong to back the French in their colonial war, wrong to send young Americans to bolster a corrupt and autocratic regime in Saigon. The war was corroding the national character—"If America's soul becomes totally poisoned, part of the autopsy must read 'Vietnam'"—and it made a mockery of the ideals the United States professed to be defending.

"All the while the people read our leaflets and receive regular promises of peace and democracy and land reform. Now they

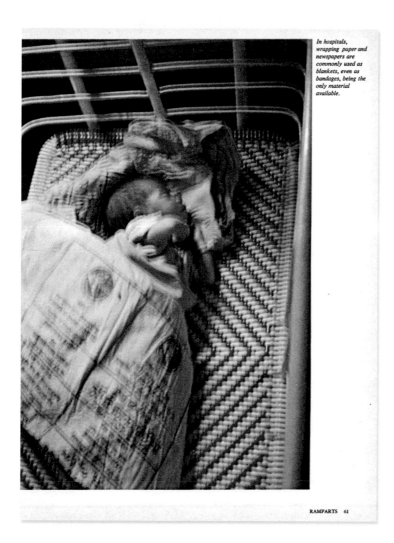

In hospitals, wrapping paper and newspapers are commonly used as blankets, even as bandages, being the only material available.

languish under bombs and consider us, not their fellow Vietnamese, the real enemy. They move sadly and apathetically as we herd them off the land of their fathers into concentration camps. . . . They know they must move on or be destroyed by our bombs. . . .

"I should make it clear that while I have tried to give a voice to the voiceless in Vietnam and to understand the arguments of those who are called our 'enemy,' I am as deeply concerned about our own troops there as anything else. For it occurs to me that what we are submitting them to in Vietnam is not simply the brutalizing process that goes on in any war where armies face each other and seek to destroy. We are adding cynicism to the process of death, for they must know after a short time there that none of the things we claim to be fighting for are really involved. Before long they must know that their government has sent them into a struggle among the Vietnamese, and the more sophisticated surely realize that we are on the side of the wealthy, and the secure, while we create a hell for the poor.

"Surely this madness must cease. We must stop now. I speak as a child of God and Brother to the suffering poor of Vietnam.

I speak for those whose land is being laid waste, whose homes are being destroyed, whose culture is being subverted. I speak for the poor of America who are paying the double price of smashed hopes at home and death and corruption in Vietnam. I speak as a citizen of the world, for the world as it stands aghast at the path we have taken. I speak as one who loves America, to the leaders of our nation: the great initiative in this war is ours; the initiative to stop it must be ours."

King called upon Washington to end the bombing, declare a ceasefire, include the National Liberation Front in negotiations between North and South, cease clandestine activities in Laos, and set a date for the withdrawal of all foreign troops. "If we do not act," he said, "we shall surely be dragged down the long, dark, and shameful corridors of time reserved for those who possess power without compassion, might without morality, and strength without sight."

The public reaction to King's address was mostly hostile. *Life* compared it to "a script for Radio Hanoi." *The Washington Post* charged that King had "diminished his usefulness to his cause, to his country and to his people." The black *Pittsburgh Courier* criticized him for "tragically misleading" African Americans. The NAACP declared any effort to merge the civil rights and peace movements "a serious tactical mistake." Ralph Bunche and Jackie Robinson publicly agreed. And J. Edgar Hoover told the president that King's speech was proof that "he is an instrument in the hands of subversive forces seeking to undermine our nation."

King felt liberated, nonetheless. He may have been "politically unwise," he told an aide, but he had been "morally wise." Eleven days later, he joined Dr. Spock and some 400,000 other protestors at a massive Manhattan demonstration organized by a new umbrella organization, the National Mobilization Committee to End the War in Vietnam—"the Mobe." It was an ideologically diverse throng. Stokely Carmichael of the Student Nonviolent Coordinating Committee led a phalanx of marchers carrying NLF flags. Protestors burned two hundred draft cards. Uniformed antiwar World War II and Korean War veterans carried placards: "Vets Demand Support for G.I.'s! Bring Them Home Now!" But there were also thousands of everyday citizens marching that day, impelled for the first time to express their opposition to the war.

ABOVE A Vietnamese infant wrapped in newspapers and orphaned by the war, from *Ramparts* magazine **OVER** In front of the United Nations secretariat in Manhattan, Dr. Martin Luther King Jr. speaks to the largest gathering of war protestors yet assembled, April 15, 1967. "I think," he told the crowd, "this is just the beginning of a massive outpouring of dissent."

"That was the biggest crowd any of us had ever been in in our lives," Bill Zimmerman recalled. "It started in Central Park and we marched twenty blocks to the United Nations. We took up the whole avenue, and when the front of the march got to the UN, the back of the march had not yet left Central Park. That's how many people we were. It gave us a sense of empowerment. Because not all of the people on that march were students. And as a result we all felt we have a chance now, you know. There was a path that we could see to ending the war."

The antiwar movement was growing, in numbers and in militancy. A draft resistance organizer, inspired by the New York demonstration, said, "We [now] speak of squads, escalation, campaigns. The terminology is no accident—it fits our attitude. We are no longer interested in merely *protesting* the war; we are out to stop it."

"At that time," Zimmerman remembered, "people who supported the war were fond of saying, 'My country right or wrong' or 'America, love it or leave it' or 'Better dead than red.' Those sentiments seemed insane to us. We didn't want to live in a country we're going to support whether it's right or wrong. We want to live in a country that acts rightly and doesn't act wrongly. And if our country isn't doing that, it needs to be corrected. So we had a very different idea of patriotism. So we began an era in which two groups of Americans, both thinking that they were acting patriotically, went to war with each other."

WHERE DOES IT ALL END?

ON APRIL 28, 1967, thirteen days after the Manhattan protest, General Westmoreland addressed a joint session of Congress—the first general in history ever to be ordered home from a battlefield to do so. His task was to rally flagging support for the war. "As I have said before," he said, "in evaluating the enemy strategy it is evident to me that he believes our Achilles' heel is our resolve. Your continued strong support is vital to the success of our mission. . . . Our soldiers, sailors, airmen, Marines, and coastguardsmen are the finest ever fielded by our nation. . . . Those men understand the conflict and their complex roles as fighters and as builders. They believe in what they are doing. They are determined to provide the shield of security behind which the Republic of Vietnam can develop and prosper for its own sake and for the future and freedom of all Southeast Asia. Backed at home by resolve, confidence, patience, determination, and continued support, we will prevail in Vietnam over the communist aggressor."

Behind the scenes, neither Westmoreland nor the administration that had called him home was confident the United States would prevail. Westmoreland reported to the president that according to the latest statistics, the crossover point had finally been reached, except in I Corps, the military sector just south of the DMZ, but overall victory was still elusive.

Ellsworth Bunker, the latest American ambassador in Saigon, summed up the problems the United States faced after a decade of deepening involvement. "Much of the country is still in VC hands, the enemy can still shell our bases and commit acts of terrorism in the securest areas, VC units still mount large-scale attacks, most of the populace has still not actively committed itself to the government, and a VC infrastructure still exists throughout the country."

To change things, Westmoreland and the Joint Chiefs now wanted to wage an even more ambitious war. They called upon the president to call up the reserves, and provide another 200,000 troops with which to step up the land war.

But "when *we* add divisions," Johnson asked, "can't the *enemy* add divisions? Where does it all end?"

Westmoreland had no satisfactory answer.

There was more. The Chiefs wanted the president to permit American bombers to hit targets still closer to Hanoi and Haiphong and the region just below the Chinese border—and to mine North Vietnamese harbors to keep Hanoi's Soviet ally from resupplying her by sea, as well. They also wanted permission to send troops into Laos in search of enemy sanctuaries, and some among the president's advisers called for a seaborne invasion of North Vietnam itself. If all those requests were met Westmoreland believed the United States might be able to hand the war over to South Vietnam in two years.

Meanwhile, Robert McNamara, the chief architect of American strategy in Vietnam, had grown less and less confident in its ultimate success—and in the repeated calls for more men and more bombing made by the military he oversaw. In a private memorandum to the president, McNamara told Johnson that "the picture of the world's greatest superpower killing or seriously injuring 1,000 non-combatants a week, while trying to pound a tiny backward nation into submission on an issue whose merits are hotly disputed, is not a pretty one."

He urged Johnson to limit troop levels, not expand them, and to declare an unconditional end to all bombing north of the 20th parallel—a suggestion that so angered the Army chief of staff, General Harold K. Johnson, that he considered resigning in protest and urging the other Chiefs to join him. McNamara was unmoved. "The war in Vietnam is acquiring a momentum of its own that must be stopped," he wrote. "[D]ramatic increases in U.S. troop deployments . . . [and] attacks on the

North . . . are not necessary and are not the answer. The enemy can absorb or counter them, bogging us down further and risking even more serious escalation of the war."

The debate within the administration went on, but McNamara was now privately convinced that something had gone terribly wrong with the war he had helped to plan and oversee. He wanted to understand what had happened, and placed a call to his executive assistant, General Robert Gard.

"My phone rang," Gard remembered, "and the little light showed it was the secretary on the line. I picked it up and said, 'Yes, Mr. Secretary.' And Mr. McNamara said, 'Bob, I want a thorough study done of the background of our involvement in Vietnam,' and hung up the phone."

Leslie Gelb, then a thirty-year-old member of the International Security Affairs staff, was tasked with overseeing the top-secret analysis of how key decisions had been made, going all the way back to the Truman administration, that would one day be called the Pentagon Papers. "McNamara gave us full access to his closet," Gelb recalled, "the famous closet in his office, which was like a room. All his private papers were there. And I rummaged through the closet, picking out the memos, a lot of which I helped to write. But there were others in there that I had never seen. And in those memos you began to see Robert McNamara communicating with the president, alone, his doubts. It stunned me."

ABOVE Antiwar demonstrators circle the White House while President Johnson, General Westmoreland, cabinet members, and congressional leaders lunch inside following the MACV commander's speech to Congress, April 28, 1967.

CORDS

THE BUDDHIST CRISIS that nearly toppled Nguyen Cao Ky had been yet another setback for pacification—the painful, frustrating process of somehow controlling the countryside and gaining popular support for the government in Saigon. Pacification remained primarily a South Vietnamese program. Hamlet security was supposed to be handled by the Regional and Popular Forces—known to the Americans collectively as "Ruff-Puffs." Separate American efforts were run by the military, the State Department, the CIA, and the United States Agency for International Development. Progress was slow, spotty, and hard to measure.

Hoping to streamline and somehow speed up the process, President Johnson appointed Robert Komer, an ex–CIA officer and member of the National Security Council, to head a brand-

ABOVE At MACV headquarters in Saigon, CORDS officials attempt to assess the latest statistics on NLF violence in South Vietnam's villages. "There is no independent absolute criterion of truth about pacification," one official admitted. In the end, "all we can measure is how the degree of pacification as it appears to advisers corresponds to the degree of pacification as it appears to other observers such as the villagers themselves."

new coordinated program called CORDS (Civil Operations and Revolutionary Development Support) to consolidate and oversee the entire American effort, military as well as civilian. General Westmoreland made Komer one of his three deputy commanders; he was given the title of ambassador and the rank of a three-star general. Komer was tough-minded, aggressive, impatient—his nickname was "Blowtorch"—and close to the president. He began with a staff of 4,980 and within six months had nearly doubled it.

Pacification's tangible results were impressive: 30,000 new classrooms and 40,000 newly trained teachers; U.S.-funded hospitals and clinics in areas that had never seen a physician; inoculations for some 2 million children; 2,500 miles of paved roads; "miracle rice" that boosted South Vietnamese production; and much more.

Accurately assessing pacification's intangible results in forty-four provinces and thirteen thousand hamlets was something else again. To measure it, CORDS came up with the Hamlet Evaluation System. "Each province and district adviser had a series of questions," recalled Donald Gregg, who worked for the CIA. "Does the hamlet chief sleep in the village? What's the price of rice? Are the schools open? Has the bridge been repaired? How many people were captured or killed that week? These answers were computerized. Each hamlet had a red, orange, and green light. And according to the sum total of these

answers you'd push a button and ta-da! Vietnam would light up with a series of either red, yellow, or green buttons."

Soon, more than 220 overworked U.S. district advisers were required to produce some ninety thousand pages of data every month, far more than anyone could usefully analyze, and much of it gathered from Vietnamese sources less interested in accuracy than in pleasing Americans.

"Everything was supposed to be quantified," recalled Philip Brady, who had survived the deadly battle of Binh Gia, served out his thirteen months as a Marine, and then returned to Vietnam to work for USAID. "So you could literally say, How pacified is this *ville*? It's thirty-seven-point-five percent pacified. Well, what does that mean? Does it mean that the Viet Cong are still levying taxes? Yes. Does it mean that they're still assassinating? Yes. Does it mean they're still recruiting? Yes. Does it mean that they're still infiltrating? Yes. Even so, an American would tell you, 'We haven't had an incident in this village. The incident rate's going down. Therefore, we're winning.' Now, the reality was that the government presence was restricted to the barbed wire they were hiding behind. There is no conflict inside there because they already own it. 'What's the problem? We don't have a war here anymore because it's ours.'"

"Many people no longer like the Viet Cong," the South Vietnamese minister for rural pacification said, "but this does not mean they like us. We must not try to force people to cooperate. We must convince them."

That would never be easy.

"There were many Vietnam wars," recalled intelligence officer Stuart Herrington. "I saw a different war from my friends who were in infantry units. We lived in the villages. Our war and the infantry war canceled each other out. We worked to create a safe environment, with clean water, schools, etc. We advised the ARVN military how to protect themselves, got to know the people in the villages. We tried to insulate the hamlets from the VC, tried to help the government do things so the villagers would have a stake. We'd do that for a year. Then the infantry would come in and set up a bivouac. The VC would fire at them, and they would level the village. That ruined everything we'd been working on. We'd go through the adviser's chain of command to complain. All the way up to MACV. We'd tell them this cavalry unit in our area is antithetical to what we're trying to do—too much firepower, running over chickens. The infantry set us back from the day they walked into our province. This happened time and time again."

ABOVE South Vietnamese farmers work their paddy beneath a vast South Vietnamese flag, flown so that ARVN and American troops conducting sweeps in the area harbor no doubts about their loyalty.

A FAIRY TALE

IN JUNE, First Lieutenant Matthew Harrison Jr. got his orders to join the 173rd Airborne—the first Army unit to have landed in Vietnam and known as General Westmoreland's "Fire Brigade"—ready to rush to any spot the commander felt it was needed. Harrison believed in his mission: "I thought the war was important strategically. Just as France had provided us with support during our revolution, we were providing the South Vietnamese with support during their revolution. I really felt as though I was uniquely qualified to lead American soldiers and that there was nothing more important than what I was going to be doing."

Harrison's arrival at the air base at Bien Hoa was a reunion of sorts. He and seven West Point classmates all found themselves serving in the Second Battalion, including two of whom he was especially fond: Rich Hood and Donald Judd. "As young lieutenants," he remembered, "as twenty-two-year-olds, we really were idealists and Boy Scouts. I understood theoretically what it meant to be in a war. But, of course, no one can really understand that until they've done it."

Within a few days, Harrison, Hood, Judd, and the rest of Second Battalion were helicoptered into the heart of the Central Highlands, where North Vietnamese regulars were said to be threatening a Special Forces camp at Dak To.

Harrison was assigned to Charlie Company as a platoon leader. His friends served with Alpha Company. They were all airlifted into landing zones hacked out of the steep, jungle-blanketed slope of a mountain named Hill 1338 on American maps for its height in meters, with orders to hunt down the enemy.

They walked for two days, following a well-worn enemy trail, constantly on the lookout for booby traps or ambushes. Low-hanging monsoon clouds yielded a steady mist punctuated by sporadic showers. The heat was intense, humid, enervating. Mahogany and teak trees eight feet around and lofty clattering stalks of bamboo shut out the sky.

On the evening of June 21, Harrison's Charlie Company settled in for the night while his friends in Alpha Company set up camp a little less than two miles to the south, further along the same slippery jungle path. No one knew that an entire North Vietnamese battalion—perhaps five hundred men—was encamped on the other side of a ridgeline just a few hundred yards to the east.

A scout for Charlie Company sent out to survey the area was shot through the throat by an enemy soldier and killed. Then a nervous American sentry shot and killed a GI who had stepped outside the perimeter to relieve himself. Both corpses were wrapped in ponchos to be carried out at daybreak; the foliage overhead was too dense for a helicopter to drop in and pick them up.

At 6:58 the next morning, as most of the men of Alpha Company finished their breakfast, a patrol stumbled into a squad of North Vietnamese, opened fire, then pulled back to a small clearing. Within minutes, they were under attack by AK-47 automatic fire. Over the coming hours, the enemy mounted three attacks, drawing closer and closer each time.

Alpha Company radioed for air and artillery support, but the triple-canopy jungle blocked the spotter's view. They called for "dust-off" helicopters to lift out the growing number of wounded, shouted coordinates for artillery, most of which exploded harmlessly in the treetops, and described the well-armed enemy as it closed in.

ALPHA 6: This is Alpha 6.
PARAGON 6: Paragon 6, over.
ALPHA 6: We have an extremely large force moving in the gully to the west of us now. We need airstrikes. . . . Put something all around this hill, but stay off the ridgeline, over.
PARAGON 6: This is Paragon 6, you say you have large forces moving toward you from the west, over.
ALPHA 6: We've got heavy movement and firing on our left.
ALPHA 6: We've got some real heroes and I'm damn proud of them. . . . But be advised that these people [the North Vietnamese] all got black berets on, they got AK-47s, every one of them, and they got so damn much ammunition. They got twice as much as I got.
PARAGON 6: We'll be there as soon as we can, over.
ALPHA 6: Appreciate it. Just do the best you can.

At around noon, Harrison's unit was ordered to go to Alpha Company's aid but to avoid contact with the enemy: "Don't throw good money after bad," the battalion commander told them.

"It was mountainous," Harrison recalled. "We were carrying the two bodies along with a bunch of engineer equipment." The going was steep and slippery. The distant shooting died down. North Vietnamese troops, now entrenched along both sides of the trail, prevented Harrison and his men from reaching Alpha Company. At dusk, Harrison and his men dug in at the top of a ridge and did their best to sleep. "We lay there on the night of June 22nd and we could hear the screams of the wounded down the hill as the North Vietnamese went around and shot them," Harrison remembered.

By dawn, the enemy had melted away. Once again, they had chosen the time and place for battle—and then vanished. Harrison and his platoon crept down the hillside and reached what was left of Alpha Company. Out of 137 men, 78 were dead, sprawled along the path. Forty-three had been shot in the head at close range, executed by the enemy. Ears had been cut from some; eyes were gouged out; ring fingers were missing. Twenty-three more men were wounded.

Harrison found his classmates, Don Judd and Rich Hood, among the dead. "This was my introduction to war. This was my welcome to Vietnam. We spent the rest of the day putting those bodies into body bags and getting them out of there. Getting killed is forever. That was something that I had known theoretically but I now understood, particularly when I put my two classmates in body bags—guys that I had gone to school with for four years. Just the week before we had been drinking beer and ribbing each other and now these guys were gone."

The paratroopers found just nine or ten North Vietnamese corpses, half buried nearby in shallow graves. Harrison and his men were ordered to search the nearby hillsides for more enemy dead, presumably fallen to U.S. artillery. "We never located them," Harrison remembered many years later, "and I believe today that we didn't locate them because they weren't there. I think we just took a terrible loss on June 22nd. For reasons of

ABOVE First Lieutenant Matthew Harrison Jr. in the field, 1967. "We just could not conceive," he remembered, "that the army that had won World War II, that had had a two-hundred-year track record of success, couldn't defeat a guerrilla movement in a backward country in Asia."

morale, for reasons of prestige, to admit that a rifle company in the 173rd had been wiped out by the North Vietnamese was not something our leaders were prepared to say. So we had to sell ourselves—and we had to sell the public—on the idea that we had inflicted casualties on the North Vietnamese as severe as those they had inflicted on us."

An officer told a reporter in Saigon that the shattered rifle company had somehow killed 475 enemy soldiers. When another officer suggested to Westmoreland that the figure seemed too high to be believable, the general replied, "Too late. [It's] already gone out."

A few days later, Harrison recalled, "Westmoreland came up to speak to 'his brigade.' He hopped up on the hood of a jeep in very crisp fatigues, looking every inch the battle commander. And he gave us a pep talk and told us how proud he was and what a magnificent job we had done." A sergeant who had survived the fighting leaned over and muttered to a friend, "Wonder what *he's* been smoking?"

"A pep talk after we'd spent the day putting dead bodies into body bags was not something that appealed to my soldiers," Harrison remembered. "By then, I had more than just a suspicion that this was a fairy tale, that Westmoreland was wrong, and I didn't know whether he knew he was wrong or whether he believed what he was being told and wanted to believe it. But this was the first time that I had to come to grips with the fact that our leadership was either out of touch or lying."

A VERY DIFFICULT CONVERSATION

IN SARATOGA SPRINGS, Mogie Crocker's family continued to struggle with his loss. He had been the first local boy to die in combat, his sister Carol recalled, and his death had forced others his age to begin to think for the first time about their own vulnerability, about whether the war was worth fighting. "I remember a very difficult conversation I had with a girl who had really been a best friend of mine. She and I were sitting on the front steps of our home on White Street as we always did. And the talk turned to Vietnam. And I remember her looking at me and saying, 'My father says that you can't listen to people who've lost someone in the war because they're going to support it to justify that person's death.' I felt like she'd hit me in the stomach. But I knew at that moment that factions were developing, that this wasn't going to be an easy path to walk; that people were going to have opinions about my brother's death that had nothing to do with his death for me."

CHAPTER FIVE

WHAT WE DO

JULY–DECEMBER 1967

From the hilltop at Con Thien, men of Mike Company, Third Battalion, Ninth Regiment, Third Marine Division watch U.S. airstrikes on enemy positions hidden within the supposedly neutral DMZ in the autumn of 1967. Beyond lies North Vietnam and the distant hills from which shells rained down on the Marines. "The NVA absorbed everything the Marines fired at them," the journalist John Laurence wrote, "and kept coming back. No one was winning. Both sides were sacrificing their best young men."

A SOLID FOUNDATION
OF MUTUAL RESPECT

B Y THE SUMMER OF 1967, almost half a million American military personnel were already in South Vietnam, and tens of thousands more would soon be on their way. Along with boots and uniforms and duffel bags and all the other paraphernalia of war, each man was issued a little book, published by the Department of Defense, called *A Pocket Guide to Vietnam*. It was a sort of mini manual, offering a handful of facts about Vietnamese life and culture, and outlining how U.S. military personnel were supposed to behave in South Vietnam.

"The growing American commitment in Vietnam makes it ever more important for us to maintain the good relations that exist between Americans and the Vietnamese," it said. "Wherever you go, remember that Vietnam is a land of dignity and reserve. Your good manners, thoughtfulness, and restrained behavior will be appreciated by the Vietnamese. You will benefit, as will the country you represent, in terms of the job you are there to do and in terms of friendship built on a solid foundation of mutual respect."

The book set forth "nine simple rules" to follow:

- Remember we are special guests here; we make no demands and seek no special treatment.
- Join with the people! Understand their life, use phrases from their language, and honor their customs and laws.
- Treat women with politeness and respect.
- Make personal friends among the soldiers and common people.
- Always give the Vietnamese the right of way.
- Be alert to security and ready to react with your military skill.
- Don't attract attention by loud, rude, or unusual behavior.
- Avoid separating yourself from the people by a display of wealth or privilege.
- Above all else you are members of the U.S. military forces on a difficult mission, responsible for all your official and personal actions. Reflect honor upon yourself and the United States of America.

Many years later, Bruns Grayson, an ex–Army captain who had served in Vietnam, was asked to write the introduction for a reprint of the book. He still admired its earnest tone, but questioned how much impact it could ever have had on "the behavior of the average American soldier—about twenty years old,

not well educated . . . very often on his first trip away from the United States. I don't know what the Vietnamese equivalent of 'overpaid, oversexed, and over here' was, but . . . such a phrase would have described almost all of us. We were curious, scared, open, friendly, and preoccupied with how much time we had left before we could go home. We were no more loutish and noisy than any similar collection of young innocents would be, but certainly no less."

Some new arrivals did their best to follow the guidebook's suggestions—and many of those who worked at pacification in the countryside or served as advisers to the South Vietnamese forces did master at least the rudiments of the Vietnamese language, came to understand Vietnamese customs, and made lasting friendships among the people alongside whom they worked. But for many men, both those about to face combat and the far larger number who would provide combat soldiers with support, the training they had received back home combined with the sheer foreignness of Vietnam itself soon erased the memory of many of the guidebook's admonitions.

In training, troops were encouraged to call the Vietnamese "gooks"—a term first used by U.S. Marines for the people of Haiti and Nicaragua during the American occupation of those nations, and then applied to the Asian enemy in Korea. "They taught you that you were going to be fighting gooks," an Army medic recalled. "That was part of the song you sang as you jogged down the road. As you went through bayonet training you were stabbing gooks. You were not talking about Vietnamese. Vietnamese might be people, but gooks are close to being animals."

There were other contemptuous names for Vietnamese as well, including "slopes," first employed during the Korean War, and "dinks," a word apparently coined in Vietnam itself. Troops learned to call Vietnamese homes "hooches"—a corruption of the Japanese word for dwellings that GIs had learned during the battle for Okinawa in World War II—and to refer to older Vietnamese women as "mama sans," the name GIs used for women who ran whorehouses in occupied Japan.

Virtually nothing was done to teach new soldiers about the people against whom—or for whom—they had been asked to fight. Instead, "the Army just gave you the opinion that all Vietnamese were bad," an Army infantryman remembered. "I never heard anything about a friendly Vietnamese." "I went to fight

OPPOSITE Army basic trainees head for the Quick Kill Reaction Course at Fort Bragg, North Carolina. "I want to go to Vietnam," they chanted in cadence as they marched. "I want to kill a Viet Cong." Sergeants led them down a trail lined with concealed trip wires, simulated booby traps, and pop-up silhouettes of the caricatured enemy at which they were to shoot with BB guns shaped like M16s.

for America, not for the Vietnamese," Marine John Musgrave recalled. "I never thought about them as anything other than my future enemy. I didn't know anything about the country. So to say that I went over there uninformed would be an understatement. I didn't know anything about the Vietnamese, and I didn't care."

First impressions of Vietnam did little to alter preconceptions formed in training. Everything seemed strange. City streets were crowded and chaotic. There were unfamiliar smells—exotic cooking odors combined with the reek of raw sewage. The roads along which newcomers were driven to their bases were lined with makeshift shacks in which people seemed to live in a kind of squalor never encountered at home. Small children played in the dust half naked. Rural families shared their quarters with livestock. People relieved themselves in the open. Rice paddies turned out to be fertilized with human feces. "I didn't think, 'Boy, I'm going to get over here and win this war for these people,'" one infantryman recalled. "It was more a reaction of 'Boy! I wouldn't want to live here.'"

Furthermore, many newcomers expected to find the South Vietnamese grateful for their presence and instead were often met with indifference or fear or open hostility toward the new foreigners, who reminded many of them of the hated French. A poll taken among urban South Vietnamese later in the war found that most saw the Americans as "drunkards, haughty, licentious, . . . indifferent to accidents for which they were responsible."

General William Westmoreland shifted thousands of American troops to bases as far from Saigon as was practicable in order to reduce the likelihood of what he called "incidents" between Americans and Vietnamese. He succeeded in doing that, but one result was that most of the troops confined to the bases came to know Vietnamese only as translators, cooks, maids, interpreters, bar girls, or prostitutes. Meanwhile, grunts in the field often found it impossible to separate friends from enemies. "Charlie, VC, gook," one soldier remembered being taught. "If he had slant eyes he also had an AK-47. If it was a woman, she would have a grenade stuck up under her dress someplace."

"My time in Vietnam," recalled one infantryman, "is the memory of ignorance. I didn't know the language. I knew nothing about the village community. I knew nothing about the aims of the people—whether they were for the war or against the war."

Ignorance and fear alienated a good many American soldiers

Contact of a different kind: A U.S. Marine tries to get to know some village children.

pass the time. The temple's there, so let's wreck it. I wrecked that temple for no reason at all. I took a little vase that they used for holding the joss sticks. I brought that vase home with me. Forty-four years later I still have it. I've kept it all these years to remind myself of what I'm capable of."

HUBRIS

IN THE SUMMER OF 1967, Le Duan was in trouble. His aggressive strategy, aimed at destroying the Saigon regime before the Americans could intervene on its behalf, had actually accelerated that intervention. The war in the South had stalled ever since, with high casualties and little progress. American bombing of the North had not shaken his people's resolve to resist, but it had disrupted their lives and destroyed much of the infrastructure the communist regime had painstakingly built since 1954. Two of the North's most revered figures, Ho Chi Minh and General Giap, opposed the kind of large-scale war championed by Le Duan and urged caution and a return to protracted guerrilla warfare. Meanwhile, Hanoi's communist patrons, now more antagonists than allies, offered diametrically opposed counsel: Moscow, supplier of the antiaircraft batteries and heavy weapons without which continuing the war would be impossible, urged Hanoi to seek a negotiated settlement, while Beijing, which controlled the logistics of delivering those weapons and was providing hundreds of thousands of support troops, wanted North Vietnam to hold out for victory no matter how long it took.

To silence his critics and break the stalemate, Le Duan began to promote a new and far riskier version of the plan for victory he had first outlined in 1964. He had called then for mounting a "General Offensive, General Uprising," only after a series of "big battles" decimated the ARVN. That had not happened, but he was now determined to launch it anyway.

It would come in two phases. First, Main Force North Vietnamese and NLF units would combine forces to make simultaneous coordinated attacks on scores of South Vietnamese cities and towns and military bases.

That offensive, Le Duan believed, would ignite the second phase, when Le Duan expected South Vietnamese civilians to rise up—just as Ho Chi Minh's call for the Viet Minh and its sympathizers to revolt against a return to French rule had been answered in August of 1945. "We believed the cities were oppressed by the Americans and South Vietnamese, so the people there were ready to rise up," the writer and ex-soldier Nguyen Ngoc recalled. "We were told the cities were like pregnant fish,

from the people they were supposed to be defending. Sometimes, so did simple adolescent boredom.

In the summer of 1967, Marine Lance Corporal Bill Ehrhart's outfit was conducting operations in an area called the Horse Shoe in Quang Nai Province: "We were sweeping a company-sized search-and-clear operation. (They used to call those operations 'search and destroy,' but they changed the name to 'search and clear' because 'search and destroy' sounded a little too harsh.) At one point the column got held up for some reason. We're stopped for a fair amount of time and there's this little Buddhist temple there. Very small. One room. Had an altar with a vase on it for burning joss sticks. They'd been doing repairs to the roof so there was a sawhorse there. We pick this up and we take turns using the sawhorse as a battering ram and we just start knocking in the sides of the temple about waist height until we've knocked in enough of these concrete walls that the whole damn structure collapses. Just because we were bored. We're a bunch of teenage kids. It's not much different from wrecking the sandcastle at the beach. Okay, we're Marines. We're fighters. We've got these guns. But we're still a bunch of kids and we were bored. It was stinking hot; we're going nowhere. And we're just looking to

ABOVE Marines with nothing better to do while away an afternoon using a sawhorse to destroy a Buddhist temple.

filled with eggs. We just needed to tickle the fish a little, and all the eggs would pour out."

These twin blows were meant to "finish off" the enemy, destroy the Saigon regime, and so horrify the American people that they would demand that their sons be withdrawn from Vietnam. Washington would then have no choice but to sue for peace and negotiate a settlement favorable to Hanoi.

If the first two phases failed, Hanoi planned further attacks, but Le Duan was so confident of initial victory that he ordered new police uniforms made for the day when the communists took over southern cities.

"We talk about our own hubris," said the historian James Willbanks, who served as an adviser in Vietnam later in the war. "But there's some hubris on their side as well. And once they had convinced themselves that this was going to be a great success, it's what some wags have called drinking their own bathwater. They decided it's going to be a victory even though there are

people saying, 'Hey, this is not a great idea.' These people are essentially charged with 'subjectivism' and told to shut up and keep rolling."

Le Duan ruthlessly neutralized those who dared oppose his plan. Over the next few months, he undertook a massive purge remembered in Vietnam as the "Revisionist Anti-Party Affair." Hundreds of people suspected of having doubts about the upcoming offensive—journalists, students, even highly decorated heroes of the French war—were denounced as "revisionists," spies, "pro-Soviet traitors." Some were locked away in the old French prison that the Vietnamese called Hoa Lo, or "Fiery Furnace," and American POWs called the "Hanoi Hilton."

ABOVE The people of a village in the coastal Thanh Liem district of North Vietnam turn out to cheer local boys on their way to join the army. "Morale among the young recruits was high," the photographer recalled. "Those who were accepted brought honor to their families."

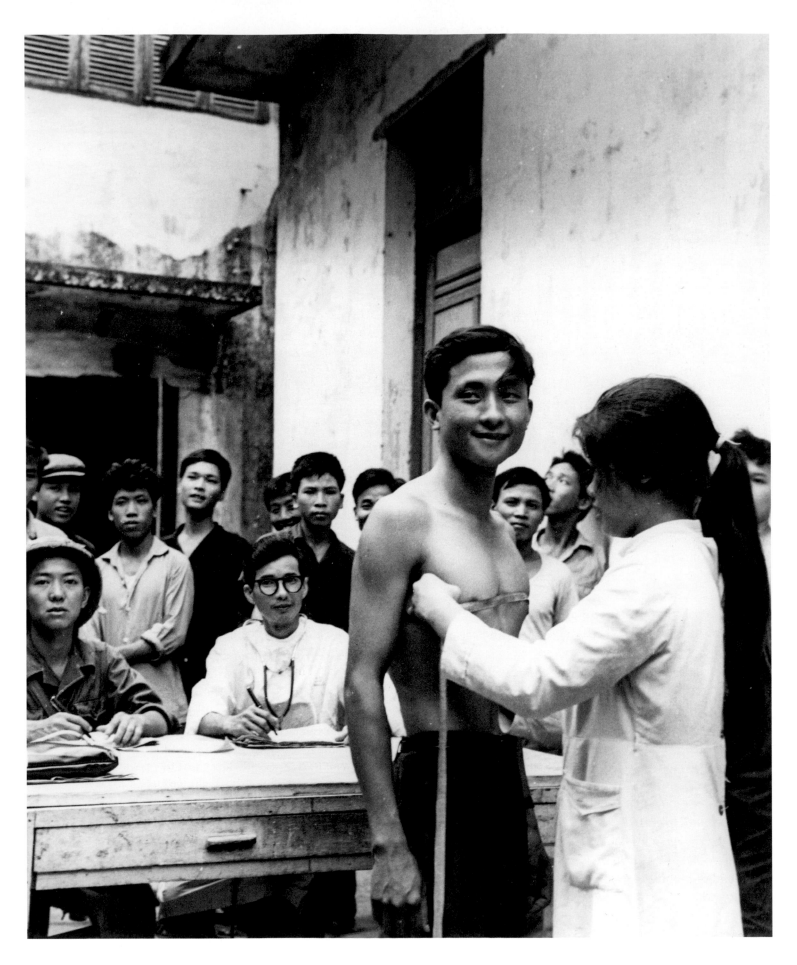

JUST A GIRL

Mrs. Nguyen Thi Hoa

"I was fired up, excited at the thought that maybe we would at last be liberated," Mrs. Nguyen Thi Hoa remembered, when, in the late fall of 1967, word filtered down to her that the long-awaited General Offensive, General Uprising was soon to begin. She was just nineteen but she'd already been a revolutionary for several years. Her village, Vong Tang, was just three miles from Hue. During the day, it seemed to be under the control of the Saigon government. ARVN troops camped nearby and were sometimes stationed within the village itself. But once the sun went down each day, Hoa and five other girls retrieved their snugly wrapped weapons from the duck pond in which they kept them hidden, so they could guard visiting cadre and drill in preparation for the revolt they had been assured was only weeks away.

Secrecy was everything; Hoa knew the names of just three of her superiors. Not even her mother knew what she was doing. She traveled to the city daily to sell the straw conical hats she and her friends wove, but also to gather intelligence. "I learned the positions of the puppet troops—ARVN, American, Korean—where they went, where they were stationed," she remembered. She was small, soft-spoken, always dressed in an *ao dai*. "I would pretend to be very weak," she said, "so that the Saigon soldiers would say, 'Oh, she's just a girl.' "

General Giap was alleged to be in poor health and went to Hungary for medical treatment in mid-July—and then was encouraged to stay there. While he was gone, soldiers on his staff were arrested. So was Ho Chi Minh's former secretary. Ho himself was sent to China for medical treatment in September.

The date for the offensive was still to be determined, but by late summer, hundreds, then thousands, of North Vietnamese regulars in civilian clothes had begun slipping southward to join the tens of thousands of NLF and North Vietnamese troops already in place. "Suddenly we were ordered to recall our soldiers from the battlefield," recalled Colonel Ho Huu Lan, who had been fighting U.S. Marines just below the DMZ. "We were supplied with more weapons, ammunition, food, rice, salt, and dried fish, even sugar and condensed milk. We were told we were going to the southern front for a long period of time. We were very excited. We had the feeling that this time we would bring the war to an end."

Nguyen Van Hoang was studying art in Haiphong that summer when an American bomb killed his fiancée. "Immediately afterwards," he remembered, "I decided that I had to go south to fight. At the time . . . I thought that the Liberation Army was riding the crest of a wave. If I didn't join up right away I'd miss my chance to take revenge. I reasoned that the Americans must be bombing the North in retaliation for their defeat in the South. I thought the NLF was on the verge of winning the decisive battle and that they would take Saigon in the very near future. I desperately wanted to go and kill a couple of Americans to relieve the bitterness I felt." When an uncle who was a highly placed cadre took him aside to warn him that the war in the South represented "a colossal sacrifice of troops," that if he insisted on signing up he was likely to die "a meaningless death," he paid no attention.

"The farewell ceremonies I saw in my village were really enthusiastic affairs, organized by the communists," remembered the journalist Huy Duc, who was a boy then, living in his village in Ha Tinh Province. "The soldiers were so excited to go to the South to fight. My eldest brother shouted with happiness when he got the results of his physical exam and was accepted into the army. There were young men in my village who didn't weigh enough, so they put rocks in their pockets to increase their weight. No one was sad, no one thought about the fact that they might not return, about the tragedy that might befall them.

OPPOSITE Medical staff examines a future soldier at a Haiphong recruiting station in the summer of 1967. "Nowadays," said a North Vietnamese sergeant who defected to the South that year, "many young men lie about their age, making themselves older, so that they can be accepted into the army. The morale of the young men in the North is very high. Many seventeen-year-olds volunteered and, when refused, came home crying."

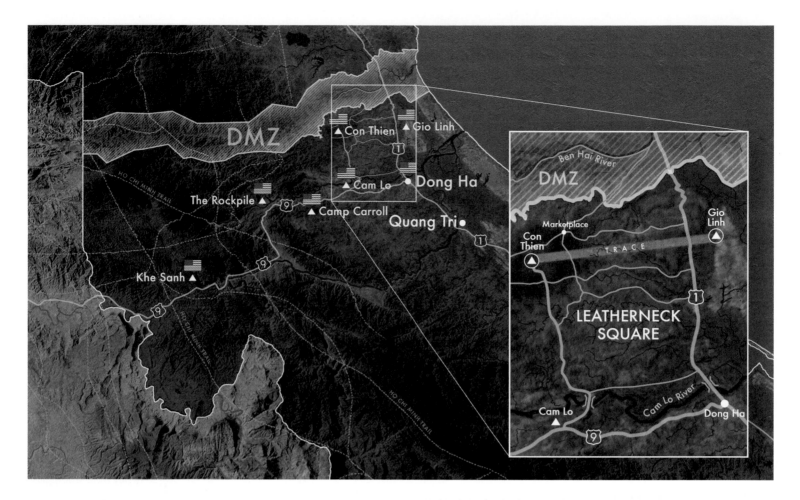

THE DEAD MARINE ZONE

E ARLY IN THE WAR, an American general had marveled at the complexity of the conflict in which he found himself. The NLF and the North Vietnamese seemed to be carrying on "a different kind of war in each of South Vietnam's forty-four provinces," he said. One province might endure ceaseless warfare, both large scale and small, while the province next door remained apparently at peace.

MACV had divided South Vietnam into four tactical zones. By the summer of 1967, Americans were fighting in all of them.

In IV Corps, Army and Navy forces patrolled the rivers and canals and marshes of the Mekong Delta, searching for the elusive enemy.

In III Corps, the Army continued to sweep the Iron Triangle, the NLF sanctuary near Saigon that was supposed to have been permanently denied to the enemy by big American operations earlier in the year.

In II Corps, a series of bloody battles in the Central Highlands around Dak To would temporarily drive North Vietnamese troops back into Cambodia and Laos.

But the central focus of the fighting would soon be in I Corps—made up of the five northernmost provinces of South Vietnam—where the U.S. Marines had taken the lead.

More than two and a half million people lived there, all but 2 percent of them within the narrow rice-growing river valleys along the South China Sea. The Marines initially wanted to focus on those lowland areas, and, working with the local South Vietnamese Popular Force, to eradicate the guerrillas there and provide security to the people, village by village, hamlet by hamlet, methodically choking off the rice and supplies and extorted taxes the NLF needed to keep fighting. The vast, largely empty highlands that stretched westward all the way to Laos, the Marines argued, could safely be left to the enemy. "The real war is among the people," said Marine Lieutenant General Victor Krulak, "and not among the mountains."

But General Westmoreland worried that leaving large swaths of territory in enemy hands could fatally undermine Saigon's legitimacy, and he feared that thousands of North Vietnam-

OPPOSITE South Vietnam, divided into four U.S. tactical zones
ABOVE U.S. Marine outposts in the northernmost section of I Corps, just below the DMZ, and (inset) the area called "Leatherneck Square," where thousands of U.S. Marines were stationed and more than 1,400 died

coast all the way west to the Laos border. The initial section to be cleared by Marine bulldozers was the 6-mile-long, 218-yard-wide "Trace," sewn with mines, barbed wire, and detection devices, which ran from Gio Linh to Con Thien. In addition, somewhere between thirteen thousand and eighteen thousand Vietnamese men, women, and children would have to be driven from their homes to create a vast free-fire zone.

The Marines who were ordered to construct and man the barrier that became known as "McNamara's Line" thought it was madness. "With these bastards," one officer said, "you'd have to build [the barrier] all the way to India, and it would take the whole Marine Corps and half the Army to guard it. . . . Even then they'd probably burrow under it." A North Vietnamese soldier named Le Van Cho confirmed their view: "It was nothing to us. Every night, we would go across it."

Monitoring the border would tie down thousands of Marines and subject them to almost ceaseless combat. Between March 1967 and February 1969, 1,419 Americans—U.S. Marines and Navy corpsmen—would lose their lives within just four miles of Con Thien and inside the rough rectangle that came to be called "Leatherneck Square." Nearly ten thousand more were wounded.

"For the Marines in northern I Corps in the Third Marine Division in the summer of 1967," Private First Class John Musgrave, of Fairmont, Missouri, recalled, "we called the DMZ the 'Dead Marine Zone,' because we lost so many people up there."

Musgrave could have missed the fighting along the DMZ altogether. He had initially been assigned to an MP battalion with the First Marine Division at Danang. While he was there, he found time to teach English in a village school and distribute books to the children provided by his church back home.

But his unit was a reinforced rifle platoon, and he soon found himself patrolling the countryside around the main Marine base. He came under fire for the first time when his patrol was ambushed at night. "They fired on us with automatic weapons. I got down and I didn't get up. I was the automatic rifleman for the squad, and my squad leader had to come over and kick me and suggest to me that it would behoove me to get that rifle working. I was more afraid of him than I was of anybody else at that point, so I brought the rifle up and did my job—which meant I shot off twenty rounds into the dark. It was just a very brief contact. But it scared the living shit out of me. Later, I was to wish every ambush would be like that."

Not long after that patrol, Musgrave found himself in another firefight. This time, his bullets found their mark. "I only killed one human being in Vietnam," he remembered. "And that was the first man that I ever killed. I was sick with guilt about killing that guy and thinking, I'm going to have to do this for the next thirteen months. I'm going to go crazy. And then I saw

ese army regulars were planning to seize the two northernmost provinces. Finding, fixing, and destroying the North Vietnamese remained his principal goal. He insisted the Third Marine Division move inland to meet that challenge, establish a base at Dong Ha, and man strongpoints at Gio Linh, Con Thien, Cam Lo, Camp Carroll, the Rockpile, and Khe Sanh, overlooking Route 9, the east-west highway that Westmoreland hoped would one day carry American and South Vietnamese troops across the border into Laos to cut off the flow of North Vietnamese men and supplies coming down the Ho Chi Minh Trail.

Meanwhile, Secretary Robert McNamara, disappointed that American bombing had failed to stop traffic on the trail, hoped that an electronic barrier below the narrow DMZ might somehow do the job. It was an ambitious scheme—three to five billion dollars, five million fence posts, fifty thousand miles of barbed wire, thousands of mines, and sonic and seismic sensors meant to detect enemy movements—stretching from the

ABOVE Private First Class John Musgrave, photographed near Danang before he asked to be sent north to I Corps because that was where the action was **OPPOSITE** A Marine CH-53 Sea Stallion heavy-lift transport helicopter hovers above a smoke marker, preparing to drop a sling-load of ammunition and C-rations to the besieged men at Con Thien. The Marines were wholly dependent on resupply from the air. Medevac helicopters meant to carry away the wounded dared land only momentarily for fear of being hit by incoming shells.

a Marine step on a Bouncing Betty mine [designed to launch upward when triggered and explode at chest level], and that's when I made my deal with the devil and I said, 'I will never kill another human being as long as I'm in Vietnam. However, I will waste as many gooks as I can find. I'll wax as many dinks as I can find. I'll smoke as many zips as I can find. But I ain't going to kill anybody.' Turn the subject into an object. It's Racism 101. And it turns out to be a very necessary tool when you have children fighting your wars, for them to stay sane doing their work."

Meanwhile, news of the bloody fighting along the DMZ was filtering down to him—his best buddy was stationed there—and in May when a recruiter from the Third Marines turned up asking for volunteers to replace men killed and wounded further north, Musgrave had stepped forward. "Part of it was I didn't like operating around civilians around Danang. There were too many restrictions, you know. 'Don't fire until fired upon.' That's a really bad idea. I joined the Marine Corps to be in the varsity. And I felt like I wasn't varsity unless I was up north fighting the NVA. I have never regretted that decision. There were times when we were under artillery fire, when I thought, 'What were you thinking?' But that's where I had to be. I was a Marine rifleman. Here it is in a nutshell: if I lived to be sixty-three years old I didn't want to look in the mirror some morning and have a guy looking back at me that hadn't done everything for what he believed, who let somebody else do the harder part."

Musgrave was assigned to Third Platoon Delta Company, First Battalion, Ninth Marines, Third Marine Division—"The fightingest Marines in Vietnam," he said—and sent to Con Thien, a Marine strongpoint strung along the tops of three knolls two miles south of the DMZ and twelve miles from the coast. The easternmost anchor of the Marine outposts, raised just 518 feet above the surrounding flat terrain, it afforded the Marines unobstructed views in all four directions—eastward along the Trace for six miles to the Marine firebase at Gio Linh, southward ten miles to the I Corps logistical complex at Dong Ha, westward across the hills and ridges that stretched away toward the Truong Son range and harbored enemy artillery, and, finally, northward across the supposedly neutral DMZ that harbored still more, and on into North Vietnam itself. In Vietnamese, Con Thien means "Hill of Angels"; the U.S. Marines who endured life there came to call it "the Bull's-Eye" and "the graveyard."

A member of Musgrave's new outfit remembered that for a full month no one bothered to learn the names of newcomers like him. They were all known as "FNGs"—"Fucking New Guys." "Nobody counted, nobody was part of reality unless

OPPOSITE Under enemy fire, a Marine helps a wounded comrade to safety during Operation Prairie IV, somewhere in Leatherneck Square, May 13, 1967.

they'd stayed alive that long," he remembered. "If they had . . . you could count on them to do their job."

The unit had already suffered so many casualties in a series of bloody sweeps over roughly the same ground—Operation Prairie I, Prairie II, Prairie III, Prairie IV—that it was believed to be a hard-luck outfit. "If it could go wrong, it would go wrong," a tanker who had carried their corpses from the battlefield remembered. "Wherever they went, they stepped into the shit." The men of the First Battalion called themselves "Walking Death," and "Death Dealers"; fellow Marines called them "Dying Delta."

The North Vietnamese regulars they faced were small, wiry, tough, well armed, and determined. "My hatred for them was pure," Musgrave recalled. "I hated them so much. And I was so scared of them. I was *terrified* of them. And the scareder I got the more I hated them. They didn't have a thirteen-month tour like we did. They fought from the time they were old enough to pick up a rifle until they were dead. Every major contact I remember with the NVA was initiated by them ambushing us. They wouldn't hit us unless they outnumbered us. And we were fighting in their yard. They knew the ground; we didn't. They were just really good."

The enemy mirrored Musgrave's emotions. "When we and the Americans faced one another," North Vietnamese Colonel Ho Huu Lan recalled, "they were determined to kill us and we were determined to kill as many of them as possible. Sympathy and hatred were interwoven, but in a battle the hatred was dominant."

The North Vietnamese were armed with Soviet-made, seemingly indestructible AK-47s. The Marines had to fight with newly issued M16 rifles that had for a time a potentially fatal design flaw: they needed constant cleaning and often jammed in the middle of firefights. "Their rifles worked; ours didn't," Musgrave said. "The M16 was a piece of shit. You can't throw your bullets at the enemy and have them be effective. That rifle malfunctioned on us repeatedly."

The tropical heat was intense and relentless, Musgrave recalled, and the fighting was close in and deadly. "The enemy knew if they would pop the ambush close and then get amongst us, we would hesitate to call in air on ourselves. Firefights like that we called 'brawls.' They were very intimate. And they were very deadly. And they were absolutely terrifying." On one early patrol, Musgrave watched an American A-4 Skyhawk swoop down to drop napalm on enemy troops hidden behind a hedgerow. He could hear their AK-47s firing at the plane until the instant they were engulfed in flames. "If the enemy is willing to die like that," he thought, "this is going to be one very long war."

The Marines were spread too thin to hold any of the territory

I DON'T WANT A WOMAN SEEING ME DIE

Her nickname in Vietnam was "Sam," because, as one soldier told her early in her stint as a freelance war correspondent, her real name—Jurate Kazickas—was too hard to pronounce. She had escaped with her parents from Lithuania just before Soviet troops rolled in during World War II, worked after college at a Catholic mission in Kenya and as a researcher for *Look* magazine in New York, and then resolved to go to Vietnam and try to cover the war. When no one would hire her—she was just twenty-four, had never published a word, and covering battle was still considered mostly men's business—she won $500 on the TV game show *Password*, used it to buy a one-way ticket, and set out for Vietnam, hoping to provide copy for a handful of relatively small publications.

Some women reporters stuck to human interest stories, but from the first Kazickas was determined to cover combat. It wasn't easy. Many commanders disliked the idea of women in the field. They were a distraction, couldn't keep up, would have to be protected, they said. "But women reporters in Vietnam did just what men did," Kazickas and a fellow journalist wrote. "We were killed, wounded, shot at and captured by the enemy. We jumped out of planes, slept in foxholes, went on patrol, humped through the boonies, looked out for land mines, and wondered how we could ever try to put it all in words. Could we really make them see, feel, and understand?"

The Army placed few restrictions on her—though General Westmoreland tried for a time to bar female reporters from remaining in the field overnight—but the Marines insisted on providing her with an escort wherever she went. On one early patrol close to the Cambodian border she easily outwalked the overweight desk clerk who had been sent to accompany

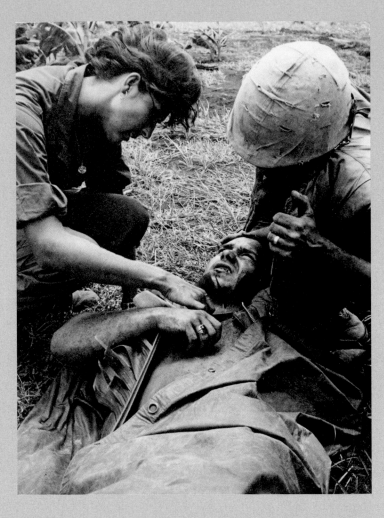

her, and when the exhausted man suffered a groin injury and had to be evacuated by helicopter she was furious to find herself obliged to go with him.

Her "first encounter with war at its most obscene," she remembered, came at Con Thien in early July 1967, as John Musgrave's unit gathered the dead after the Marketplace Massacre. "What shook me to the core was the devastating sight of so many dead Marines who had been lying in the sun for three days—their bodies bloated, their faces black as if charred by fire." "It's getting so bad, I'm afraid to make friends anymore," one corporal told her. "I talk to a guy one minute, the next thing they bring him back in a poncho."

That November, during the jungle fighting around Dak To, she would spend a terrifying day pinned down by enemy snipers and photographing men of the 173rd Airborne as they fought back. When an enemy rocket exploded in the midst of the clearing, wounding so many Americans the medics could not deal with them all, she put her camera and notebook aside and went to work with gauze and bandages trying to do what she could to help them. When she got back to Saigon a TV correspondent taunted her. "Well, well, we heard you were playing Florence Nightingale at

Dak To." She never regretted it for a moment.

"I don't want a woman seeing me die," one wounded soldier told her. "War is a man's business." She understood: many of the young soldiers with whom she spoke believed they were in Vietnam so that their women and children would never have to experience war in their own country. "But," she said, "they were also saying, 'I don't want you to see me scared, I don't want you to see me cry the way I cry. I don't want you to see me bleed the way I bleed. And I don't want you to see me kill the way I like to kill.'"

ABOVE Jurate Kazickas tries to comfort a Marine wounded near Con Thien.

they fought so hard to take. Again and again, they were sent out from one stronghold or another along the DMZ, looking for enemy soldiers. Again and again, they found them—often hidden in the same thickly grown hedgerows and irrigation ditches or concealed in the same bunkers and tunnels and spider holes from which the same Marines had driven them days or weeks or months before.

"The disillusionment for me began when I was going back to fight at places we'd already fought before," Musgrave recalled. "We had fought, captured, and then left them, and the NVA came right back. You don't like getting wounded in places you've already been before. War is a real estate business. We're supposed to take real estate away from the enemy and then deny the enemy access to that real estate."

On the morning of July 2, the First Battalion launched Operation Buffalo, a sweep of an area between the Trace and the southern edge of the DMZ, less than a mile and a quarter northeast of Con Thien. They had swept the same terrain just a few days earlier. Bravo Company moved along a narrow dusty cart track walled with three-foot hedgerows near a crossroads the Marines called "the Marketplace." At about nine fifteen, the North Vietnamese opened fire from three sides. Thirty mortar rounds fell among the Americans within three minutes. A single shell killed the company commander, two platoon leaders, the radio operator, and the forward observer. Then the enemy used flamethrowers to set the brush and dry elephant grass on either side of the road on fire and shot the Marines as they tried to flee the flames.

Bravo Company was virtually annihilated in what came to be called the Marketplace Massacre. The men of Alpha Company, sent to rescue the survivors of Bravo Company, were themselves soon pinned down in the open. "The Americans were not very shrewd," Colonel Ho Huu Lan remembered. "One soldier

ABOVE The men of John Musgrave's platoon escort some of the dead of Alpha and Bravo Companies back to Con Thien after the Marketplace Massacre, July 2, 1967.

would be killed, and another one would run up to carry away his body, so many of them were shot. If they had attacked us first so we would have to retreat and then gone out to collect their wounded or dead, they would have taken fewer casualties."

At about ten thirty that morning, John Musgrave's platoon, escorted by four tanks, set out from Con Thien to do what they could for their fellow Marines. As they tried to clear and defend a landing zone so that the wounded could be evacuated, eleven men were hit by enemy artillery. So were several of the already wounded.

It was one of the worst days the Marine Corps endured in Vietnam: 51 dead and 166 wounded were carried off the battlefield under fire. Thirty-four more dead had to be left behind—and when Marines fought their way back two days later to retrieve their bodies, they found that a number had died because their M16s had jammed as the enemy closed in. All of the wounded had been executed, shot in the face or back of the head at close range. Some bodies had been booby-trapped, others hideously mutilated.

In the immediate aftermath, at least, the savagery of combat intensified. "Marine Amphibious Force headquarters was so desperate to get North Vietnamese prisoners that they offered us three-day in-country R&R if we'd bring a prisoner in," Musgrave remembered. "'Good luck,' we said. 'Don't you know what we're doing up here? Do you know who we're fighting? You think we're going to take somebody prisoner that's mutilating our wounded? You really think we're going to do that?' I want to make this clear. We did not torture prisoners. And we did not mutilate them. But to be a prisoner you had to make it to the rear. If an enemy soldier fell into our hands he was just one sorry fucker. I don't know how to explain it that it would make sense to anyone who wasn't there."

By the time the two-week operation ended, headquarters would claim that the Marines had killed 1,290 enemy troops. Musgrave and other Marines in the field were not so sure. "We were supposed to determine victory by the yardstick of the body count—which we called 'counting meat.' The unit got rewarded not for how much property you took but how much meat it could stack. We knew it was no way to win a war. If we sent in a body count of fifteen to the headquarters for the Marine Corps in Vietnam, it would turn into twenty or thirty and by the time it got to MACV in Saigon it would turn into fifty or sixty. We'd see an article in the *Stars and Stripes* about a battle we were in that said we'd killed a lot more people than we ever saw. We'd just go, 'What the fuck? This is bullshit.' It wasn't that we didn't do enough for you? If you guys think this is so easy, come out here and get that extra meat. We're doing the best we can here. This is a dirty job."

A LOT OF DEATH AND CRAZINESS

PRIVATE ROGER HARRIS of Roxbury, Massachusetts, had joined the Marines in part, he said, because he wanted to be "a gladiator," a killer of his country's enemies. But once he got to Vietnam and was plunged into combat in Leatherneck Square he was rattled, at least at first. "You go over there with one mind-set," he recalled, "and then you adapt. You adapt to the atrocities of war. You adapt to killing and dying. After a while it doesn't bother you. Well, it doesn't bother you as *much*. When I first arrived in Vietnam, there were some interesting things that happened and I questioned some of the Marines. I was made to realize that this is war, and this is what we do. And after a while you embrace that. This is war. This is what we do."

On the morning of July 28, fourteen days after Operation Buffalo ended and John Musgrave's badly mangled First Battalion of the Third Marines was pulled back to Camp Carroll to rest and recover, Harris and the Second Battalion moved out of

ABOVE Marine Private Roger Harris, proud son of Boston's predominantly black neighborhood, Roxbury **OPPOSITE** Marine survivors of Operation Kingfisher return to Con Thien following the dirt track called Route 606 that had led them into the DMZ and disaster two days earlier.

Con Thien, across the Trace, and into the southern half of the DMZ itself. Operation Kingfisher was intended to be a "spoiling attack," meant to get at the North Vietnamese and disrupt any plans they might have to cross into Quang Tri Province.

The column, reinforced by five tanks, three armored personnel carriers, and three massive M50 multiple-cannon antitank vehicles, was forced to stay close to Route 606, a rough cart track that led north toward the Ben Hai River, because the jungle on either side of the road was especially dense.

The heat was intense, well above 100 degrees. At first, everything was quiet. The Marines camped for the night in and around an abandoned hamlet and prepared to continue along the road the next morning as it looped eastward and back out of the DMZ. But planners had failed to see that the concrete bridge over an otherwise impassable stream was too narrow and too weak to carry armored vehicles. The Marines had no choice but to violate a cardinal rule of infantry tactics—turn around and try to go back the way they had come.

The enemy was waiting for them. The two lead platoons had gone just a little more than 100 yards when they set off a 250-pound bomb hidden beneath the road during the night. Several Marines were killed. Parts of them hung in the trees beneath which their fellow Marines now had to advance.

Farther down the road, combat engineers stopped the column to explode a second hidden bomb. At that moment, enemy soldiers concealed in bunkers and spider holes along both sides of

the road began shooting. "That's when everything broke out," Harris recalled. "Massive ambushes. A lot of death and craziness."

The Marines were forced to run a bloody one-thousand-yard gauntlet of mortars, machine gun bullets, and rocket-propelled grenades. Some men who sought cover off the road landed on punji stakes (sharpened bamboo spears smeared with feces to ensure infection) and booby traps planted there under cover of darkness. "There's an old saying among Marines," one survivor remembered. "They never retreat. They just advance in the opposite direction. Bullshit! We were retreating, getting the hell out of there!"

A tank was set on fire. A grenade smashed its way through an APC. Three crewmen trying to man the guns on their antitank vehicles were killed. Infantrymen found themselves trying to protect the cumbersome armored vehicles that were supposed to be protecting them. American planes dropped napalm: one Marine would never forget what he called the exposed enemy's "cry of horror" as they saw the silver napalm tanks tumble toward them.

The column broke into separate sections, each fighting to keep from being cut off from the others. Roger Harris's G Company held up the rear, hounded by enemy soldiers on all sides. He and his comrades killed at least two dozen enemy troops before the fighting ended, and the Marines staggered back out of the DMZ alongside the battered armored vehicles heaped with dead and wounded Americans.

The Second Battalion suffered 214 casualties—23 dead, 191 wounded and evacuated, 45 suffering from heatstroke. Thirty-two dead North Vietnamese were left on the battlefield but Marine commanders estimated they had killed another 175.

Harris mourned the loss of his friends. "It wasn't a good day for the Marines," he said. But he also remembered the ferocity of the enemy. "I have the utmost respect for the North Vietnamese army soldier. When you see someone jump out and confront a

tank, with a big fifty-caliber machine gun on it and a ninety-millimeter cannon on it—that says something about him. They traveled for weeks just eating rice and drinking water. They were incredible soldiers."

THE SCARIEST THING

ABOVE Registering the dead after Operation Kingfisher. "We showed no emotion over dead Marines," a corporal at Con Thien remembered long after the war. "It was just a fact of life, and when you put bodies on helicopters it was just like resupply going the other way—you were just putting something on to be taken out, and you didn't think . . . that it was a dead friend—a dead brother—because you did not have time to grieve. Maybe we should have taken the time to grieve, because it seems to be catching up with us now."

IN AUGUST, John Musgrave's squad was in the Ba Long Valley, dug in on a hilltop, guarding an outpost that relayed radio messages back to headquarters from Special Forces probing the jungle in Laos. "That was like getting a death sentence," he recalled. "Because that's just three Marines out there with a radio at night. That's the scariest thing I did. You're listening for the enemy. And they call you on the radio every hour,

'Delta, Lima, Papa, 3, Bravo, Delta, Lima, Papa, 3, Bravo, this is Delta 3. Delta, Lima, Papa.' (Delta company, listening post, Third Platoon, second squad, was three Bravo.)

" 'If your sit rep is Alpha Sierra, key your handset twice.' (If your situation report is all secure, break squelch twice on the handset.)

"And if it's not all secure, they think you're asleep, so they keep asking you until it finally dawns on them that maybe there's somebody too close for you to say anything. So then they say, 'If your sit rep is negative, Alpha Sierra, key your handset once,' and you damn near squeeze the handle off, because they're so close you can hear them whispering to one another.

"That's real scary stuff. I'm scared of the dark, still. I've still got a nightlight. When my kids were growing up, that's when they really found out that Daddy had been in a war, when they said, 'Well, why do we need to outgrow our nightlights? Daddy's still got one.' "

A few weeks after his terrifying nights on the hilltop, Musgrave's squad was encamped south of Cam Lo, providing security for a reconnaissance team. He had just climbed out of his fighting hole when the North Vietnamese opened fire and hurled grenades in among the men. He was hit by shrapnel and knocked senseless. Risking his own life, Navy corpsman George Shade left his fighting hole, ran out, and carried Musgrave back to safety. When he regained consciousness, he was temporarily deafened and terrified that he had been seriously hit. He never forgot the care with which Shade calmed him down or the skill with which he tended to the wounds in his arm and hand.

A STEP FORWARD

LIKE LE DUAN, Lyndon Johnson found himself in trouble during the summer of 1967. He had always maintained that the United States was "rich enough and strong enough" simultaneously to fight both the Vietnam War and the War on Poverty. That no longer seemed to be true. The steadily climbing cost of the war had sparked worrisome inflation. To offset it, Johnson proposed a 10 percent income tax surtax. Before conservatives in Congress would approve it, they forced him to accept cuts in the antipoverty programs that meant the most to him. Two of the most important domestic achievements of his administration—the Civil Rights Act of 1964 and the Voting Rights Act of 1965—had brought a measure of true democracy to his country, but they had not materially affected the fundamental conditions of African American life. During that spring and summer, 159 cities and towns saw violent uprisings against the glacial pace of

change. At least 67 people died. And a backlash had simultaneously begun to grow among white blue-collar workers who felt the pace of societal change somehow was too rapid, that they were being passed by.

Meanwhile, talks in June between Johnson and Soviet premier Alexei Kosygin that at first seemed to suggest Hanoi might be prepared to negotiate if Johnson stopped bombing the North had come to nothing. A Gallup poll completed in July showed that for the first time a majority of Americans—52 percent—

ABOVE A Saigon vendor sells fruit beneath an election poster proclaiming "The Government of Nguyen Cao Ky Is the Government of the Poor," in July 1967. The poster was soon removed—along with hundreds like it—when Ky's fellow generals forced him to withdraw from South Vietnam's presidential race in favor of his bitter rival, Nguyen Van Thieu.

stalemate is complete fiction," the general said. "It is completely unrealistic. During the past year tremendous progress has been made."

Three weeks later, the president publicly ended the nine-week internal debate over how to respond to the latest troop request made by the Joint Chiefs of Staff. They had hoped for 200,000 men and had urged the president to call up the Reserves to provide some of them. He agreed to send only 45,000 to 50,000 troops, which would bring the total to just over 525,000 by mid-1968. The Reserves were to remain at home, for fear their deployment would spur more criticism of the war.

The administration was at least outwardly united in its optimism. General Harold K. Johnson, Army chief of staff, was asked if this latest increase in troops might also be the last. He said he thought so: "This should be, with circumstances substantially as they are now, adequate to provide a degree of momentum that will see us through to a solution in Vietnam."

Then, on August 7, 1967, just four days after the president revealed how many fresh forces would soon be on the way, a front-page story in *The New York Times* called into question every optimistic assumption about the war the administration and the military had expressed. Headlined "Vietnam: The Signs of Stalemate," it was reported and written by R. W. Apple, the widely respected chief of the newspaper's Saigon bureau. Almost 13,000 Americans had now died, Apple wrote. Nearly 75,000 had been wounded. The war was costing $2 billion a month. Within a year, there would be more than half a million Americans in country. "And yet," Apple wrote, "in the opinion of most disinterested observers, the war is not going well. Victory is not close at hand. It may be beyond reach." He continued,

Stalemate is a fighting word in Washington. President Johnson rejects it as a description of the situation in Vietnam. But it is the word used by almost all Americans here except the top officials, to characterize what is happening. They use the word for many reasons:

—Because the Americans and their allies, having killed by their own count 200,000 enemy troops, now confront the largest enemy force they have ever faced, 297,000 men, again by their own count.

—Because the enemy has progressed from captured rifles and skimpy supplies to rockets, artillery, heavy mortars, a family of automatic weapons, flamethrowers and antibiotic drugs—brought into South Vietnam despite unchallenged U.S. airpower.

—Because 1.2 million allied troops have been able to secure only a fraction of a country less than one and a half times the size of New York state. . . .

—And above all, because if the North Vietnamese and

disapproved of the president's handling of the Vietnam War. The same poll revealed that 41 percent believed that American troops should never have been sent to Vietnam in the first place and, still worse from the administration's point of view, 56 percent thought the allies were either stalemated or actually losing the war.

Trying to rebuild public confidence, Johnson called a press conference on July 13. "We are generally pleased with the progress we have made militarily," he assured reporters. "We are very sure that we are on the right track." General Westmoreland was on hand so the president could ask him to dismiss what he called this "stalemate creature." "The statement that we are in a

ABOVE A young mother casts her first vote for president of South Vietnam, Bien Hoa Province, September 3, 1967. At the right is one of the U.S. observers sent by President Johnson to assess the election's fairness. One of them, Governor Richard J. Hughes of New Jersey, dismissed the idea that the vote had been rigged: "We could all possibly have been bamboozled, but it would have taken a minimum of twenty-five thousand character actors and about eleven thousand stagehands to put on the production we have seen."

U.S. troops were magically whisked away, the South Vietnamese regime would almost certainly crumble within months, so little have the root problems been touched.

It is true, as General Westmoreland has often said, that the United States has built an awesome logistical empire in Vietnam, that the enemy seldom wins a major battle, that more highways are open than before, that U.S. bombers have severely hampered Hanoi's war effort, that the Viet Cong are suffering.

But the enemy continues to fight with tenacity, imagination and courage, and no one knows when he will stop.

Apple reported that many officers considered General Westmoreland delusional when he talked of soon being able to turn the struggle over to the South Vietnamese. "Every time Westy makes a speech about how good the South Vietnam army is," a general told him, "I want to ask why he keeps calling for more Americans. His need for reinforcements is a measure of our failure with the Vietnamese." ARVN troops were "tough, willing and courageous," Apple wrote, but still poorly led by a "corps of young officers, often incompetent and more often corrupt." The

government was incompetent and corrupt, too. "The problem isn't the North Vietnamese army," an out-of-favor Saigon politician told him. "It's the South Vietnamese government."

The story made Johnson livid. He called Barry Zorthian, the embassy public affairs official in Saigon, and told him that Apple was clearly a "communist" and should be thrown out of Vietnam. Zorthian was not to so much as speak to Apple again. America was at war; American reporters needed to "get on the team."

Johnson's ire was exacerbated because Apple's story appeared just as a long-delayed presidential election campaign was get-

ABOVE Nguyen Van Thieu takes the oath of office as South Vietnam's president; Vice President Nguyen Cao Ky reluctantly stands in the background. The most serious problem facing the new Saigon government, *The New Yorker*'s Robert Shaplen wrote, "is that of conflicting personalities. The two men are almost completely different in character and behavior. Thieu is withdrawn, suspicious, and highly cautious. . . . Ky has always been gregarious, incautious, and flamboyant, with a political style entirely in keeping with his career as a pilot."

ting under way in South Vietnam. From the moment in 1963 when the United States raised no objection to the generals who overthrew and then murdered South Vietnam's first president Ngo Dinh Diem, many in Washington had worried about the legitimacy of the Saigon government American troops were being asked to defend. The Buddhist uprising that had threatened to topple Prime Minister Nguyen Cao Ky in 1966 had forced him to promise at least tentative moves toward democracy—election of a national assembly, a new constitution, and elections for president and vice president. Despite communist intimidation, 81 percent of South Vietnam's registered voters had turned out in September of that year to vote for the assembly, which then drew up a new constitution and scheduled the presidential election for September 3, 1967. "When they have that election," Johnson told a reporter, "that's when South Vietnam stops crawling and begins to walk—when they get a democratic government."

It seemed to the White House that real progress toward at least the appearance of democratic rule was finally being made. Ky assumed he would run for president. Washington pledged official neutrality, but behind the scenes it believed he and the military junta that appeared to support him were most likely to provide the stability South Vietnam needed. Ten civilians signed up to run against him. Ky saw to it that anyone who advocated peace was barred from the ballot, including two potentially serious rivals, General Duong Van "Big" Minh and An Truong Thanh, a former member of Ky's cabinet, both of whom now favored opening talks with Hanoi.

Then things seemed to go off the rails. General Nguyen Van Thieu suddenly announced his candidacy. Shrewd, politically skilled, and seven years older than Ky, he was popular among his fellow soldiers, many of whom found his rival's boastful swagger hard to tolerate. At a smoke-filled meeting of fifty high-ranking officers, Thieu outmaneuvered his opponent. He would be the junta's candidate for president. Ky had to settle for being his vice presidential running mate.

To strengthen Saigon's hand as election day approached, Johnson decided to increase pressure on the North. The Joint Chiefs were eager to do that too. They had already urged him to mine North Vietnam's harbors, permit large numbers of allied troops to cross the Laos and Cambodia borders in search of the enemy, and authorize new bombing targets. Johnson felt that border crossing and the mining of harbors still carried too great a risk of Chinese or Soviet intervention. But he eagerly expanded the target list around Hanoi and Haiphong. "Our strategy, as I see it," he told his national security team, "is that we destroy all we can without involving China and Russia by September 1st [two days before election day]. The [American] people will not stay with us if we do not [destroy]

all we can, so let's find the least dangerous and most productive targets."

During the final week of the campaign, the communists did everything they could to intimidate potential voters. They mortared Hue and shelled Can Tho, briefly took over the provincial capital of Hoi An, dynamited bridges to keep voters from village polls, and stopped the show in four movie theaters in the Chinese Cholon district of Saigon to warn audiences not to vote. In a single day, some four hundred South Vietnamese are thought to have been killed from one end of South Vietnam to the other.

Roughly a third of all South Vietnamese lived in areas controlled by the NLF and thus were unable to vote. Many Buddhists, still angry at the treatment they had received from the Saigon government, boycotted the polls. Still, more than 83 percent of South Vietnam's registered voters went to vote.

Thieu and Ky won, but their margin was just 35 percent, well short of the majority for which Washington had hoped. Truong Dinh Dzu, a civilian lawyer who had revealed himself as an advocate of peace negotiations after the campaign began, came in second, with 17 percent, and in Saigon and other urban areas Thieu and Ky lost to another civilian candidate, former premier Tran Van Huong. The winners' strength turned out to lie in the countryside, where military commanders quietly controlled much of the vote. One American reporter described the election in some rural areas as "Chicago politics, with circumspection." As soon as the results were in, Thieu had his nearest rival, Dzu, clapped in jail, along with some twenty other prominent South Vietnamese who had dared express doubts about continuation of the war.

Nonetheless, the State Department declared the election an important "step forward," and in a television address, President Johnson used it as further evidence that "the grip of the Viet Cong on the people is being broken."

But it was soon clear that neither the election of a new president in Saigon, the accelerated bombing of the North, nor the behind-the-scenes offers made by Johnson to stop it was having any discernible effect on the men who ran North Vietnam.

TIME IN THE BARREL

IN THE LATE SUMMER and early fall of 1967, North Vietnamese and NLF forces made a series of coordinated attacks on American outposts below the DMZ and along the Cambodian border that became known as the "Border Battles."

Con Thien would be the first. In early September, North Vietnamese ground troops tried and failed again to take the

outposts. Beaten back by Marines, they stepped up their shelling, beginning a relentless two-month siege. In one nine-day period, three thousand mortar, artillery, and rocket rounds landed among the huddled Marines.

Roger Harris and the Second Battalion, recovered and rebuilt since the Operation Kingfisher disaster, returned to Con Thien on September 10, just in time to suffer the consequences. "The most terrifying thing was being under siege by rockets," he remembered. "There's nothing you can do. You just listen to the sounds of the rockets coming over. You just pray that they don't land on you. And there's always one in each barrage that's louder

than the others. You know it's coming. It just screams. It gets louder and louder and louder and then it hits, maybe ten yards away. I've never been as afraid as I was then. That's why I'm not afraid of anything now."

"Marines who survived at Con Thien developed senses as

ABOVE A Marine at Khe Sanh tries to outrun an incoming 152mm shell. He had been loading Marine dead onto a helicopter when the enemy zeroed in on the landing zone. "I cringe as each [shell] hits and explodes," one trapped Marine wrote. "They are striking the ground around this hole. It is almost as though the enemy are looking for me."

acute as wild animals,'" remembered the CBS correspondent John Laurence, who spent a terrifying few days there during the siege. "They had extraordinary sensitivity to sound; their hearing warned them, like deer, when an NVA shell was closing in. New guys and journalists didn't have it. We'd hear the scream of the shell and the explosions almost simultaneously. Veterans at Con Thien picked up the faint *pop* of a round leaving its tube many miles away, tracked it moving through the air, and knew before it crashed roughly how close it was going to hit. Sometimes they got the warning from a slight compression of air in their ears, a tiny change in atmospheric pressure, a signal on the wind."

After one barrage ended, Laurence recalled, he heard sobbing. He left the hole in which he'd huddled and made his way to the side of a Marine lying motionless out in the open, wounded in the leg by shrapnel. "'Hey man, don't cry,' I said, surprised at the words coming out of my mouth. 'You're a Marine!' The wounded kid stopped crying, and looked at me with an expression of genuine pity that anyone, even this strange dude in the area, could say something so ridiculously lame. . . . 'He's not scared,' [another] Marine said. 'He's cryin' cause it's his third wound. He's gotta go back to the rear. And he can't come back now, with three wounds. He's cryin' cause he's got to leave all his buddies here.'"

In retaliation, the American high command had unleashed Operation Neutralize—forty-nine straight days of coordinated pummeling of North Vietnamese positions by B-52 bombers and tactical aircraft, naval guns fired from warships offshore, and Marine and Army artillery. Before it was over, some two thousand enemy troops were said to have been killed.

The monsoon added to the men's misery, week after week of rain—seventeen inches in a single day—that filled foxholes and trenches, ruined supplies, caused painful trench foot, and turned Con Thien into a sea of red mud. The constant explosions—shells coming in, shells going out, bombs dropping on the nearby enemy—deafened some men and drove others mad.

"Almost every hour there'd be a barrage," Roger Harris remembered. "And at the end of the barrage, somebody always got caught outside their holes.

"Then, you had to police up the bodies. You've got to try to remember whose hole this was, you know. If you find dogtags, that's great. But many times you find nothing. People get blown to bits, literally blown to bits. There's a crater. It's raining. So now it's a big puddle of blood. And there's pieces of bodies.

But you can't identify any of the bodies. So you have to try to remember whose position was this? You find a boot with a leg in it. So is the leg white or black? So who was the white Marine that was here? Who was the black? So then you try to remember and you tag it and put that in the green bag. And that's what goes back, you know, as 'Marine Lance Corporal so and so.' And sometimes you're not even sure because the body has literally been blown to bits and the only thing that's left is a foot or a piece of an arm. Those kinds of things, they stay in your mind. They're haunting. They're haunting."

For Harris, it went on for nearly a month. At some point during the siege, the ingenious men in the communications bunker managed to patch together a telephone connection so the men could speak briefly with their families back home. When Har-

OPPOSITE An exhausted Marine catches a few moments of sleep in his water-filled trench at Con Thien. "Our holes would fill with water," a Marine machine gunner named Jack Hartzel recalled. "We'd have to bail them out four or five times a day. We also had immersion foot and your feet would bleed and hurt like hell. Then there was the damned mud! You walked in it, you sat in it, you slept in it, and you even ate it. There was just no escaping it." **ABOVE** Sitting out the rain. The monsoon's single saving grace was that the thick fog that accompanied it and kept Marine helicopters grounded also kept the enemy's forward observers, huddled within the DMZ, from calling in accurate fire.

ris's turn came, he told his mother that she shouldn't believe the upbeat stories about Con Thien that were appearing on television and in the newspapers. "'Because we're losing the war,' I said. 'You'll probably never see me again because we're the most northern outpost the Marines have. We can literally look right into North Vietnam. We can see the sparks when the guns fire on us.' And I said, 'Everybody in my unit is dying and I probably won't be coming back.' Ma said, 'No, you're coming back.' She said. 'I talk to God every day, and you're special. You're coming back.' And I said, 'Ma, everybody's mother thinks they're special. I'm putting pieces of special people in bags.' And she said, 'No, you're coming back.' She tried to joke about it. And I was feeling that my mother's in denial. She just doesn't want to face the fact that her only son is going to die in Vietnam. And so I said, 'Ma, this isn't a joke.' I said, 'Everybody's dying over here.' And she said, 'You're not going to die. You're not going to die.' And the last thing she said to me was, 'God has a plan for you.' And I said, 'Yeah, right.' And I hung up."

Harris and the Second Battalion were finally relieved on October 7, replaced by John Musgrave's First Battalion. The rains did not let up. "Mud is everywhere, covering everything," Musgrave wrote home to his mother and father. "It ranges from toe-deep to waist-deep. . . . I'm living in a hole about 4½ foot deep and 5 feet wide. . . . It's just a little wider than shoulder-width, but with my flak jacket and fighting gear on, which we never take off, it's a pretty tight fit. I can think of other places I'd rather live. What bugs me is my walls aren't big enough to hang things on. I wish I was home in my own room instead of this one."

"I sat in water," Musgrave recalled. "I slept in water. I ate in water, because our holes were full. A flooded foxhole can drown a wounded man. The mud was real sticky and it could just grab onto you and pull your boots off. It's hard to run in that stuff. And running, when you're at a place where they're firing heavy artillery at you, is pretty important."

The peak of the siege had passed by the time Musgrave returned to Con Thien, but shells still fell every day. "Time at Con Thien was 'Time in the Barrel,'" he remembered. "We were the fish; they had the shotguns; they stuck it in the barrel and blasted away. They were going to hit something every shot. Because Con Thien was such a small area, they couldn't miss.

Changing of the guard: Amid the muddy chaos of Con Thien, the First Battalion, Ninth Marines, replaces the Second Battalion, October 7, 1967. "The most noticeable first impression of Con Thien is mud," one man recalled, "and a unique smell of mud, human waste, and decomposing flesh—not overwhelming, but there all the time. . . . One cannot go very far without seeing (and smelling) various small body parts."

We were getting newspaper articles in the mail from our families and we were being called 'the Alamo.' Hey, we knew what the Alamo was. We knew what happened there!"

On October 13, just a week after his unit replaced Harris's, it was Musgrave's turn to get hit a second time. He was ordered to help unload supplies from helicopters dropping into the Con Thien landing zone—a duty the men hated because the enemy could be counted on to step up their artillery fire whenever a helicopter appeared. Musgrave heard a shell coming in and tried to run but was slowed down by the mud and the heavy cans of water he was carrying. Shrapnel hit him in both legs. George Shade, the Navy corpsman who had tended his wounds a few weeks earlier, patched him up again.

Far worse was to come that evening. "We had a clear night," Musgrave recalled. "Big moon—what my dad said was called a 'bomber's moon' in World War II. It was around eight thirty. That was what one of the guys told me later, because his watch stopped. Two Marine Phantoms bombed my platoon. We thought it was MiGs—because who would be stupid enough to bomb Con Thien? They walked the bombs right through our area. One of them, a five-hundred-pound bomb, hit our command post bunker and blew away the wire in front of our position. It blew my rifle out of my hands. All the mines went up. So did the trip flares. The dirt fell and fell and fell until I got up on my hands and knees on the bottom of my hole because I was afraid I was going to be buried. Dirt just kept falling on us. In the midst of this chaos we're trying to find out who's standing around. How many guys are left? And you're trying to figure out how many guys were in the bunker. The bunker was now just a big hole with twelve-by-twelve beams coming out of it."

Musgrave and his buddies worked feverishly to dig men out of the earth before they suffocated. He heard a familiar voice screaming from somewhere inside the bunker. "I couldn't make myself go in there," he recalled. "I just ran out of guts. The person in the bunker that I was closest to that we lost was the corpsman who ran from his well-protected position to my little hole to treat me back in August, 'Doc' Shade. I liked him a lot. He never let us down. To be killed by our own jets after he'd been through Operation Buffalo and other operations, it wasn't right." The military kept secret the fact that U.S. bombs had killed Musgrave's buddies; parents were told that their sons had died from fragmentation wounds from enemy artillery.

A few days after the bombing, Musgrave wrote home to tell his father what had happened. He'd never be able to forgive the errant American pilots, he said. "I'll never cheer another airstrike again, even though it's against the gooks. I know what they're going through and I don't wish it on anybody. When I see one now all I do is shudder and say a simple prayer: 'God have mercy on us all and bring this war to an end.'" He continued:

Every Marine that's left in Delta Co., 3rd platoon, says much the same prayer also. . . .
Don't worry because God is with me.

     Your Loving Son,
John

SHUT IT DOWN

AS RAIN AND ENEMY SHELLS continued to fall among Con Thien's filthy, exhausted defenders, the men still somehow found time to pass around a copy of the October issue of *Playboy*. It was "obviously very important to us," Musgrave remembered. "There was an article on Haight-Ashbury with pictures of girls running around without their tops, you know, free love. They were 'hippies,' it said—and we thought it was pronounced 'hip-peye' because it had two *p*s. Hey, I'm going home and these hippy girls don't wear no clothes. And they'll go to bed with anybody. Even I could score!"

During that summer, the Haight-Ashbury neighborhood in San Francisco had been the center of what became known as the "Summer of Love." Thousands of young people from all over the country had congregated there, eager to join the new and growing California counterculture—its music, its ubiquitous drugs, and the bright promise of promiscuity. It seemed to be a rebellion against everything, and its impact would soon be felt throughout the antiwar movement.

As the war had escalated, so had the frustration of those Americans actively opposed to it. "There was a major demonstration either in New York or in Washington every fall and every spring," remembered Bill Zimmerman, by then an assistant professor of psychology at Brooklyn College, and when yet another giant rally in Washington was planned for October 21, he and many others wanted to do something "more militant than simply stand around and make speeches opposing the war, which is what these demonstrations had become." One of the organizers, the longtime antiwar activist David Dellinger, put it best. The time was long overdue, he said, for a shift "from protest to resistance." Since the Pentagon represented "the murder of people throughout the world," the Yippie leader Jerry Rubin said, "the only thing to do with [it] is shut it down."

The October 21 march was also meant to be the culmination of a national "End the Draft" week that had seen a protestor burn herself alive on the steps of the Federal Courthouse in Los Angeles; the public burning of draft cards in Boston; students

OUR BEST INTERESTS

Eva Jefferson was the daughter of an Air Force officer and grew up overseas, on military bases—in "desegregated settings," she remembered, though "I was usually the only little black girl in the class. If you look at my class pictures I look like the little chocolate chip in the vanilla ice cream. I was always a good student. I remember people saying, 'Oh, you speak so well.' The unstated part was, 'for a black girl,' probably a 'Negro girl' or 'colored girl' at that point. I was a Girl Scout. I was on the debate team. I played the organ in choir. I babysat. I was just your little wholesome little 'Negress.' Didn't cause trouble. I was just wholesome beyond belief."

Eva's father served a year in Vietnam, overseeing MPs at Tan Son Nhut and Cam Ranh Bay, and returned home convinced that the United States had no business being there. But when his daughter entered Northwestern University in the Chicago suburb of Evanston in September 1967, race, not Vietnam, became uppermost in her mind. "My first roommate was a white woman from California," she remembered. "Big bushy hair, very friendly. Then another woman, a blond woman, came in. Nothing against blondes, but I just remember her being very blond and Nordic looking. Anyway, she came in, took one look at me, left, spent the night in a hotel, and then got a single down the hall. So that was my welcome to Northwestern."

The Vietnam War still seemed very far away. "Northwestern called itself 'the Harvard of the Midwest,'" Jefferson remembered. "It was a school that had extraordinary wealth. And the war was not really an issue there yet. I still supported the war. The notion of even questioning the war was nothing that ever entered my consciousness. I found it so odd that some of my college classmates were questioning the war.

It was like, 'Well, no, the president has our best interests at heart. He, of course, would only prosecute a war that made sense.' And I think most of America still felt that way."

Meanwhile, at the University of Nebraska, Jack Todd also supported the war. In fact, he had felt so strongly about it in 1966 that he had signed up for Marine officer training. "I went into the Marine Corps thinking this was all I wanted to do. My goal was to be a platoon commander in Vietnam."

But as time went by and the war went on, Todd and many of his fellow students began to change their minds. "All young people go through changes," he remembered. "But we were going through astronomical changes at a rapid rate. All the music, the culture, everything that we listened to, everything that we thought was transforming—and the core of it all was Vietnam, Vietnam, Vietnam. It just kept going in the background. First, it was kind of like a background noise, and then it got to be the elephant in the room. And then it was the elephant sitting on your head, and we couldn't escape it."

When Todd attended Officer Training School at Camp Upshur in Quantico, Virginia, doubts about the war followed him there, too. "I guess the emotional things that were happening on the

ground, the photographs that we saw, the television news images, and the fact that there was no discernible progress started to eat away at what we thought. Napalm really bothered a lot of people. The fact that babies were being hit with napalm—even if it was one child who died that way—was enough to galvanize a lot of the feeling on the campus. In the summer of '67, I was at Camp Upshur, you know, wanting to go kill Vietnamese people. And by October, I was completely against the war."

TOP Eva Jefferson (third row, center) and primary school classmates at the Chateauroux-Déols U.S. Air Force base, France **ABOVE** Jack Todd (right) and a high school friend

tear-gassed, beaten, and arrested while trying to close down induction centers in Oakland, Chicago, Madison, and Brooklyn; and antiwar protests from Tokyo to Tel Aviv to London, where three thousand antiwar demonstrators stormed the U.S. embassy.

At noon on Saturday the 21st, tens of thousands of protestors gathered at the reflecting pool between the Washington Monument and the Lincoln Memorial. Crowd estimates ranged wildly from 50,000 to 100,000. Earlier antiwar demonstrators had been decorous, by and large, mostly older men and women.

This time there was "only a sprinkling of Americans past the age of thirty," *The New York Times* reported, and they were "shaggier" than their predecessors. The "sweet smell of marijuana"—still novel to older reporters—seemed to be everywhere. Three giant NLF flags flew above the crowd, and vendors did a brisk business selling miniature versions of them for a dollar each. There were angry chants—"Hey, hey, LBJ, how many

kids did you kill today?," and no less angry placards: "War Is Good Business; Invest Your Son," "No Viet Cong Ever Called Me a Nigger," "Where Is Oswald Now That We Need Him?"

Peter, Paul, and Mary sang a new song by Phil Ochs, "I Declare the War Is Over." Dr. Spock assured the crowd that America's enemy was not North Vietnam. It was "Lyndon Johnson," he said, "whom we elected as a peace candidate in 1964, who betrayed us within three months, [and] has stubbornly led us deeper and deeper into a bloody quagmire."

David Dellinger and Jerry Rubin helped lead roughly half the demonstrators across the Arlington Memorial Bridge toward the north parking lot of the Pentagon. "We marched unimpeded toward what we saw as the enemy," Bill Zimmerman remembered. "To us, the Pentagon was the brain of an evil monster, and we burned with the need to confront it. Nevertheless, we had no idea what to do when we got to the building. Most of us intended to simply stand in front of it in silent protest and defiance. A few were determined to get inside and ransack it. Others wanted to deface its outer walls. The more whimsical spoke of 'levitating' the building and 'exorcising' the evil spirits inside."

The squat, sprawling building was protected by concentric rings of U.S. marshals and military MPs with truncheons, two lines of temporary wire fencing, and some 2,500 soldiers

ABOVE Ranks of nervous MPs stand ready to defend the Pentagon against antiwar demonstrators, October 21, 1967. They weren't sure what to expect. March organizers had promised to blend "Gandhi and guerrilla": "We will fill the hallways and block the entrances," they said. "This confrontation will be massive, flexible, surprising."

carrying rifles—without live ammunition, at McNamara's orders—but with sheathed bayonets. Large numbers of protestors simply sat down in front of the marshals and refused to move. While loudspeakers blared "Demons out! Demons out!," hippies chanted incantations meant somehow magically to lift the Pentagon off the ground. Shouts of "*Sieg Heil*" alternated with choruses of "America the Beautiful." Some demonstrators urinated on the Pentagon walls; others made love in full view of the Pentagon's defenders. Some hurled bottles at the soldiers; still others placed flowers in the barrels of their rifles.

"It was the first time that antiwar demonstrators had confronted active-duty military personnel," Zimmerman remembered. "We didn't consider them the enemy. We considered them victims of the war. But we began to see our own government as the enemy." He joined others intent upon ripping down the fences. Some thirty demonstrators managed to make it through one of the doors, only to be beaten back with clubs and tear gas.

"Inside the Pentagon," Leslie Gelb recalled, "the secretaries who were working in my area were frightened by what these protestors might do. They thought they were going to come into the building and rape them. It was a sense of revolution." Robert McNamara, watching from his third-floor office, was anxious

too. "Of course I was scared: an uncontrolled mob is a frightening thing," he said.

Six hundred and eighty-two people were eventually arrested. Forty-seven people were hurt—demonstrators, soldiers, and U.S. marshals. The press was generally scornful of the march. *U.S. News & World Report* charged that it had been "cranked up in Hanoi." On NBC television, David Brinkley called it "a coarse, vulgar episode by people more interested in exhibitionistic displays than any redress of grievances." *The Washington Post* dismissed it as "an intercollegiate jamboree. . . . They came and they confronted and by the end of the day everyone was fulfilled and nothing changed. The war goes on."

To many men like John Musgrave, caught up in unimaginable violence and cut off completely from their peers back home, antiwar demonstrations like the Pentagon march were simply inexplicable. "The only information I had about the peace movement came from *Stars and Stripes*," Musgrave recalled. "That wasn't a real objective newspaper. So I hated them before

ABOVE Protestors face sheathed bayonets. "You are our brothers," one demonstrator shouted to the soldiers. "We want you to come home to us. You don't belong to them, the generals who are going crazy up there in the top part of the Pentagon because we're talking to you."

I ever knew anything about them. They were against what we were doing. They were calling us some pretty terrible things. We couldn't begin to understand. What were they thinking? This was America. You don't turn your backs on your warriors. We grew up watching the World War II movies and the newsreels and the way people reacted then. That's what we expected. That's what we wanted. That's what we thought we'd earned."

For his part, President Johnson was convinced that Ho Chi Minh himself, in collusion with Moscow and Beijing, had somehow directed the demonstration. He instructed the CIA to come up with the evidence—and was furious when it found none. Secretary of State Dean Rusk claimed they just hadn't looked hard enough—and then told the press, "We haven't made public the extent of our knowledge of subversion" for fear of setting loose "a new McCarthyism."

Several days after the Pentagon march, Johnson shared his fears with his Republican predecessor Dwight Eisenhower on the telephone. "We just had hell [with] these college students," he said. "I've had [FBI chief J. Edgar] Hoover in after them. . . . They marched here, and we arrested 600 of them, and we gave 29 of them pretty tough times. We found most of them really were mentally diseased. Hoover's taken 256 that turned in supposedly their draft cards. . . . So you're dealing with mental problems, . . . I think that we talk too damn much about civil liberties and constitutional rights of the individual and not enough about the rights of the masses."

The ex-president offered sympathy. Whenever people criticized Johnson to him, he said, he told them he'd "been in the same position of responsibility. I might've done some things differently but that's a question of judgment. . . . We have freely elected [our] people and we've got to stand behind them."

Johnson thanked him for his support. "I think your government's in trouble, general," he said. "I think it's—I don't want to say this—but I think we're in more danger from these left-wing influences now than we've ever been in the thirty-seven years I've been here. And they're working in my party from within."

ABOVE Allard Lowenstein, caricatured by David Levine. "He had what other people . . . in the antiwar movement did not," a peace campaigner remembered, "which was a sense of political strategy. There were a lot of activists who didn't see beyond the semi-annual mobilizations. Allard was not only extremely articulate about [how the administration was] lying to you . . . but he [also] had an idea of how to stop it."

What Johnson had in mind was the fledgling "Dump Johnson Movement," led by Allard Lowenstein, a thirty-eight-year-old attorney from New York who hoped to end the war by replacing the president who was waging it. A onetime student leader who had worked against segregation in Mississippi and apartheid in South Africa, Lowenstein shared the antiwar fervor of the protestors, but he believed the most effective way to end the fighting was to work within the political system, not outside it.

He had traveled the country all year in search of someone willing to challenge the president in the upcoming Democratic primaries. He asked Senator Robert F. Kennedy of New York, who had begun to separate himself from the Johnson administration over the war. He asked Lieutenant General James Gavin. He asked Senator George McGovern. They all turned him down. Unseating a president still seemed a hopeless cause.

Lowenstein vowed to keep looking.

THERE *ARE* NO FRIENDLIES

FOR NINE MONTHS, Private Dennis Stout served as a line soldier with Company B of the First Battalion, 327th Infantry, 101st Airborne. He was wounded three times, twice by bullets and a third time in June 1967, when a mortar round hit an ammunition dump at Buc Pho. He was treated for concussion and temporary deafness at a medical station. While he was recuperating, someone among his superiors learned that he'd wanted to be a freelance writer before entering the service, and made him public information officer, tasked with writing up and photographing the men in the field for the battalion newspaper, *The Diplomat and the Warrior.*

As long as he turned in two stories a week, he was free to accompany any unit he liked. Not long after he was back on his feet, the men of one company he covered captured a teenage Vietnamese girl. They interrogated her, then everyone in the platoon except for himself, the medic, and one other man—some twenty men in all—raped her repeatedly over a two-day period. Afterward, she was murdered. Later, Stout would report what he said he had witnessed to the battalion sergeant major, who told him things like that happened in war and that he should forget about it. He then told the chaplain, who went with him to confront the sergeant major again. Stout remembered that "the sergeant major told the chaplain to stick to religion, sent him away, and then told me to keep quiet, that I did not have to return from the next operation."

Meanwhile, Stout often chose to cover the activities of a unique commando platoon called "Tiger Force" because, he remembered, "that's where the action was"—small hand-picked teams, capable of remaining in the jungle for weeks at a time, fast moving and deadly, intended to "out-guerrilla the guerrillas." In a little under two years, Tiger Force had fought in six different provinces, repeatedly suffering heavy losses. Some at MACV had worried that such a freewheeling outfit, operating on its own, would be difficult to control. But General Westmoreland and commanders in the field admired Tiger Force for its reliable ferocity.

In the summer of 1967, Tiger Force was sent into the fertile Song Ve Valley. Stout went with them. The entire population had already been herded from their homes and crowded into a refugee camp. But some had come back to resume the farming they had always done. Tiger Force was ordered to stop them. The valley had officially been declared a free-fire zone—and its officers were to take that literally. "There *are* no friendlies," one team leader told his men. "Shoot anything that moves."

They sometimes did. Not long after joining the company, Stout and several soldiers spotted two men in North Vietnamese uniforms running toward them down a hill. They were waving leaflets and shouting, "No shoot, GI!, No shoot, GI!" They appeared to be unarmed. Two U.S. soldiers raised their M16s and opened fire. The men fell dead.

"It happened so fast," Stout recalled. "They just shot them. I couldn't believe it." Another soldier, disgusted, asked his sergeant to explain what had happened. The sergeant reiterated that the valley was a "damn free-fire zone, and you don't question that."

Stout left Vietnam at the summer's end. But Tiger Force continued to work its deadly way across the valley. Among the scores of unarmed victims were two blind brothers; an elderly Buddhist monk; women, children, and old people hiding in underground shelters; and three farmers whose only crime was trying to plant rice in the paddy their family had farmed for generations. All were reported as "VC." When two soldiers dared to complain to their superiors about what the other men were doing, they were transferred out.

Years later, a rice farmer remembered how hard it had been to bury his friends and neighbors killed by Tiger Force. "We couldn't even have meals because of the smell. I couldn't breathe air sometimes. There were so many villagers who died, we

couldn't bury them one by one. We had to bury them all in one grave."

In August the First Battalion got a new commander: Lieutenant Colonel Gerald Morse. He was thirty-eight, a decorated veteran of combat in Korea, whose enthusiasm for killing seemed to match his new command. His radio moniker was "Ghost Rider." After bloody combat between elements of the 101st Airborne and North Vietnamese regulars as part of Operation Wheeler, Tiger Force was about to be sent into Quang Nam Province in the Central Highlands with orders to find and destroy every remaining vestige of the enemy—base camps, supply depots, sympathetic villages. At some point along the way, Morse radioed the battalion, "You're the 327th Infantry. We want 327 kills."

The mission was already under way in early October when Private Rion Causey, a medic from Perry, Georgia, joined Tiger Force. He was excited. "I had an uncle that stormed the beach on D-Day," he remembered, "and I had always dreamed that I could do something like that."

It was quickly clear that this was to be nothing like D-Day. Tiger Force had recently been caught in a series of ambushes. Five men were killed, and the survivors vowed vengeance.

ABOVE The hand-lettered sign ordered up in September 1967 for Tiger Force's headquarters near Duc Pho in Quang Ngai by a new battalion commander, Lieutenant Colonel Gerald Morse, set the tone for its activities. "Above the Rest" was the First Battalion's motto, but the cowboy on the winged horse, symbolizing his radio alias, "Ghost Rider," and the alarming names for the force's constituent parts were all Morse's creations.

ABOVE Tiger Force members surround a wounded North Vietnamese soldier near Tou Morong in the Central Highlands, June 16, 1966. Five days earlier, eleven of the unit's forty-five men had been killed in action. The First Brigade of the 101st Airborne, of which Tiger Force was a part, was awarded a Presidential Unit Citation for extraordinary heroism as part of Operation Hawthorne.

"Everybody was bloodthirsty," Causey remembered, "saying, We're going to get them back. We're going to even the score." But he still had no idea what that would mean. "A decision had been made by Ghost Rider and by the captain in charge of Tiger Force," Causey quickly learned, "that in the interest of removing anyone who might grow rice for the NVA, we were to kill all the males between the age of approximately sixteen and sixty.

"It was my first experience of combat. This was getting late into the operation, so as we flared out into a village we were surprised to find seven men. We rounded these people up. And we called back to the captain, Captain [Harold] McGaha, and said, 'Well, what are we supposed to do with these people?' And so the CO called back to battalion headquarters and said, 'Well,

we have seven all at one time. What are we supposed to do with them?' And the word came back, 'Field expediency. Deal with them as you're supposed to.' So we lined the people up against the wall and several of the people in the squad immediately opened fire and killed all seven."

Causey could not bring himself to fire. He was surprised later to read in *Stars and Stripes* that only three men had been killed, that weapons had been found proving that they had been Viet Cong, and that Tiger Force was to be commended for the action. That was not what he had witnessed.

"I think when mothers send their sons off to war they anticipate that there'll be officers who have a sense of dignity, that have a sense of responsibility, of morality," Causey remembered. "If you've lost your best friend and you want revenge, it's the officers who should say, 'No, you can't do that. And if you do it, there are consequences.' But when the officers—and in this case it included the platoon leader and the battalion commander—are telling you that this is what you're supposed to do, then it gets completely out of hand. There was a young man, the same age I was, who joined Tiger Force the same time I did. And I

was surprised about three weeks into the operation, when we came into a small hooch area, that he came running up to the front saying, 'It's my turn. It's my turn!' And I knew then that things had just completely gotten out of hand. It was his turn to execute the people."

Tiger Force moved on. "If I walked into a village and everyone wasn't lying prostrate on the ground," one team leader remembered, "I shot those standing up. If they didn't understand fear, I taught it to them. . . . The way to live is to kill because you don't have to worry about anyone who is dead." In one eleven-day period, Tiger Force claimed to have killed forty-nine "VC," most of them allegedly shot while "running from a hut." Not a single weapon was captured from any of them, yet no one questioned the unit's claims or looked into its tactics. At least one member of Tiger Force wore a necklace of dried human ears, cut from the heads of men he had killed.

One afternoon, Causey remembered, a patrol came upon a young man who was found to be carrying separation papers from the ARVN. They were unsure at first what should be done even with someone who clearly had been allied with the Ameri-

cans. Causey was sitting nearby when a member of the company slipped up behind the man with a knife. The CO had given him permission to "take care of this person," Causey recalled, and so "right in front of everyone in the platoon," he seized the man from behind and slit his throat, sawing back and forth until his victim stopped kicking.

In November, Tiger Force fulfilled their battalion commander's grisly quota—327 dead. No one knows how many more people they killed while in the field—or how many of those killed were unarmed civilians.

Years later, thanks in part to a sergeant named Gary Coy, whose conscience would not allow him to remain silent about

ABOVE The men of Tiger Force photographed at the end of Operation Wheeler. Long after the war, a sergeant refused to answer directly if he had ordered the rounding up and execution of unarmed civilians. "But if I gave the order to kill those people," he said, "it was to keep my men alive. You don't have to worry about the dead. You know what I mean? Those farmers were farmers by day and VC at night." Medic Rion Causey kneels, fourth from left.

what he had heard Tiger Force had done, an Army investigation would find probable cause to try eighteen members of the unit for murder or assault. But no charges were ever brought— "nothing beneficial or constructive could result [from] prosecution at this time," said the Army brief—and six men, including an officer, were allowed quietly to resign. The official records were buried in the archives.

"I'm sure Ghost Rider thought that he was doing a good job of fighting the war," Causey remembered. "But what he didn't realize was what he was doing to the people that were doing it. It absolutely made every one of them a victim too. At the time, it may seem like a normal reaction to simply go out and shoot someone. You don't have time to think about it. You're trying to stay alive. But when you get home, either then or ten years, fifteen, twenty years later, it comes back. You can't get away from it. The death and the fact that you were there and watching, it just comes back, it comes back, it comes back. And people like Ghost Rider, Colonel Morse, should know what they did."

"They should have all gone to jail," James Willbanks said. "They were guilty of murder. Period. At the same time, I felt as if that incident, which was an aberration, not the norm, tarred all veterans. There are hundreds of thousands of veterans who went and did their duty as honorably as they possibly could, and they're tarred with the same brush."

"One of the things that I learned in the war is that we're not the top species on the planet because we're nice," concluded Karl Marlantes, who would later serve as a Marine first lieutenant in Vietnam. "We are a very aggressive species. It is in us. People talk a lot about how the military turns kids into killing machines. But I'll always argue that it's just finishing school. What we do as a civilization is that we learn to inhibit and rope in these aggressive tendencies. But in war we have to recognize them. I worry about a whole country that doesn't recognize that. Think how many times we get ourselves in scrapes as a nation because we're always the good guys. Sometimes I think if we thought we weren't always the good guys, we might actually get into fewer wars."

TRIAGE

THROUGHOUT THE EARLY FALL, monsoon rains had continued to make life miserable for John Musgrave and the other Marines huddled together at Con Thien. But by November, the worst of the shelling had finally ended and some battered North Vietnamese units had withdrawn northward. MACV credited the American airstrikes, artillery, and Navy shelling with driv-

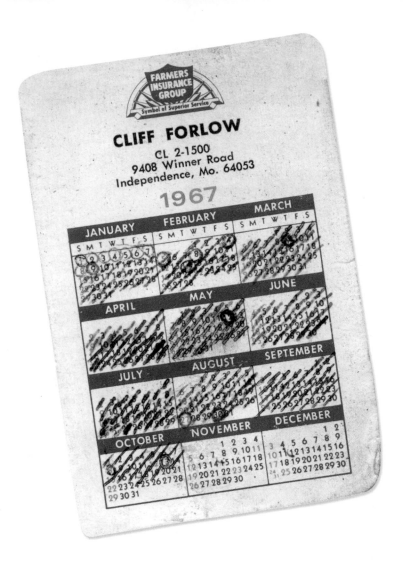

ing them away. Actually, most were pulled back in order to ready themselves for the major offensive, now less than three months away.

Still, the North Vietnamese had not all disappeared, and before dawn on November 7, two companies of Musgrave's outfit were sent half a mile into the countryside northwest of the base to conduct yet another sweep. Calling upon his own disjointed memories and what eyewitnesses told him later, Musgrave painfully reconstructed what happened next: "We got into an area that was old hedgerows grown over with jungle. Very difficult to see very far. In the clear area, three NVA showed themselves and started spraying thirty rounds out of their AKs and then booking. The company commander himself said,

ABOVE John Musgrave's wallet calendar, given to him by his father's insurance agent for him to carry in Vietnam. "I marked off each of the days religiously," he remembered, "and then in October, we went up to Con Thien again and I just stopped marking the days off because I thought: This is pointless. I'm not going to go home. I'm not going to make it home. You know, what's the point? So I just quit marking them off."

'I want their bodies. Bring me their bodies.' Everything's about body count, right? We said, 'Man, this is as old as Custer. These guys are showing themselves to draw us into an ambush. Lieutenant, don't do this, you know. Please, these guys are bait.' But the skipper says, 'We've got to go. We've got to go.'

"And we went. I can't tell you a whole lot about the ambush. I was one of the first people to be shot. One round put me down. And my grenadier was down. From the first day in boot camp you learn that Marines don't leave their dead—and they never, never leave their wounded. And that's why I'm alive today.

"I was lying on my face when the first guy came for me. He reached down and stuck his arms under my shoulders and lifted me up and the machine gun was maybe nine feet—ten feet at the most—away from me. This is a very intimate ambush. It's a brawl. He fired a burst into my chest that blew me out of the Marine's arms and then he was shot. Another very brave young Marine—an eighteen-year-old from Louisiana, his first firefight—had seen what happened and still came for me. He reached for me, and he was shot, I think in the forearm. He was lying beside me. I've got a hole through my chest big enough to stick your fist through, and I'm dying and I know it. And I heard this horrible screaming going on, and I was trying to figure out who was screaming like that because it sounded so—and then I realized it was me.

"When they began to drag us out, they were being pursued by the North Vietnamese and they would drop us and lay on top of us. They knew we were both dying. The grenadier had been shot in the right side of his chest. They knew we were both dead. But we were still alive. So they weren't going to leave us. They would die before they left us. They covered us with their bodies and fired back at the NVA and then they'd jump up and drag us a little farther and then drop us and lie back on top of us. I kept telling them to leave me. And I meant it, I meant it. But all of a sudden I got scared that they might really leave me.

"I was triaged three times. The senior corpsman said, 'He's either shot through the heart or the lungs. There's nothing I can do for him.' He just turned away. I went, 'Well, okay.'

"Then a helicopter came in. They threw me into the bird.

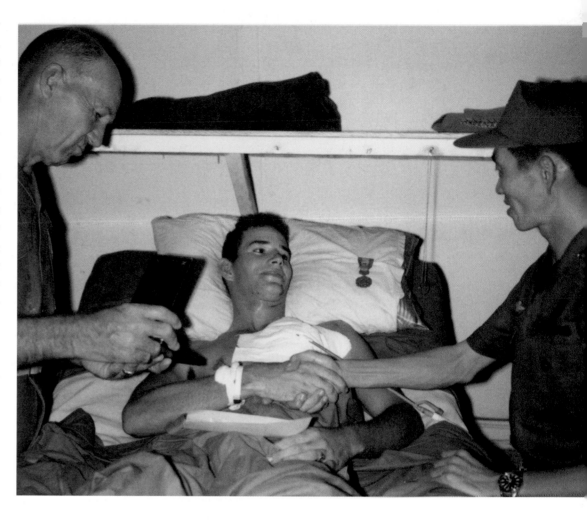

The corpsman on the bird straddled me, stood over me and looked down at me, and then looked up at the door gunner and said, 'Get him out of the way.' Because he couldn't work on me. I was a dead man.

"They flew me to Delta Med at Dong Ha. And I thought, Okay, I made it this far. But then this doctor comes over and looks at me and I'm conscious. I'm lucid. He checks a couple of things. I've got this huge hole in me. He looks me right in the eye and he says, 'What's your religion, Marine?' And I said, 'Well, I'm a Protestant.' He says, "Get a chaplain over here, I can't help this man." And then he walked away.

"Another surgeon walks by, and he looked at me, and I was raised always to be nice to people so when he looked at me I smiled at him and nodded. And he said, 'Why isn't somebody

ABOVE Recuperating from his wounds in an Army hospital at Phu Bai, Musgrave receives his Purple Heart from General Bruno Hochmuth, commanding officer of the Third Marine Division, and General Tru Vuong, commanding officer of the Eleventh ARVN Division. General Hochmuth would die in a helicopter explosion the following year, the first general officer and the first and only Marine Corps division commander to be killed during the war.

helping this man?' And inside I'm going, 'Yeah, why isn't somebody helping this man?'

"When they put me to sleep, I thought, 'Boy, this is really it.' You know. It was kind of 'Okay, God. Into your hands I deliver my spirit.' I thought that was it. So when I woke up in the surgical care intensive care ward, which was a Quonset hut, I thought, 'Holy mackerel.' I just couldn't believe it."

THE THIRD CIRCLE OF HELL

ALL THROUGH THE FALL OF 1967, the North Vietnamese and NLF forces continued their series of "Border Battles."

The siege of Con Thien was followed by an assault on the ARVN base at Song Be. The South Vietnamese outpost adjacent to the provincial capital of Loc Ninh was next. There, large units of North Vietnamese and NLF regulars mounted a coordinated attack—and then fought for five days to hold on to the ground they'd gained, something they had never done before. American commanders were puzzled. Later, North Vietnamese commanders claimed they'd been practicing for the urban warfare they knew lay ahead.

Then, in early November, reports reached MACV that five North Vietnamese regiments and one NLF battalion—some seven thousand men in all—had again begun massing in the Central Highlands around the U.S. Special Forces camp at Dak To.

Among the North Vietnamese regulars was Colonel Nguyen Thanh Son, a political officer who had been so eager to fight that he, too, had filled his pockets with rocks to pass his physical. "Our commanders' strategy was to lure American troops up there to fight," he remembered, "so we could deplete and destroy them in the Central Highlands."

As the NVA deployed their troops, Westmoreland sent his to Dak To—exactly what the enemy wanted him to do. Operation MacArthur was named for General Douglas MacArthur, the hero of the Pacific War—who had once warned President Kennedy that American boys should never be asked to fight in the jungles of Southeast Asia.

Among the Americans were the men of the elite 173rd Airborne—Westmoreland's "Fire Brigade." First Lieutenant Matthew Harrison was now with Alpha Company of the Second Battalion, the same rifle company that had been ambushed and so badly shattered back in June on the slopes of Hill 1338, just fourteen miles to the east. "We all knew in a general sense that we wouldn't be brought back if there wasn't something big going on," Harrison recalled. "You just knew the area was crawling with North Vietnamese and that they were there not to avoid contact with us, but to have contact with us. This wasn't like the Viet Cong, where if you could find them, you could kill them. Our problem wasn't finding them, our problem was what to do with them once you found them."

The fighting had begun in early November. By the time Harrison's oufit reached its firebase, U.S. troops—supported by artillery and airpower—had driven the North Vietnamese off two mountains.

But the 174th NVA Regiment was still waiting for the Americans. Nguyen Thanh Son and his men were already dug in on Hill 875, the high ground he and his superiors knew the Americans would want to command. "We got there a month earlier," Son recalled. "The men were puzzled and asked, 'The forest is so peaceful and beautiful. Why are we here?' We told them, 'Keep working, they'll come.'" The North Vietnamese were hidden within a network of fortified trenches and bunkers heavily reinforced with thick teak logs and ten feet of earth, all linked by tunnels.

On Sunday morning, November 19, 1967, Alpha, Charlie, and Delta Companies were ordered to take Hill 875. Matt Harrison had an infected shrapnel wound in one hand from an earlier fight and was not permitted to accompany his men, but he anxiously followed their progress over the radio.

Heavy artillery and flights of F-100s blasted the hillside ahead of the Americans, meant to knock out enemy positions before the paratroopers ever got within range. "The top of Hill 875 was bald, there were no trees left," Son remembered. "The Americans destroyed them all. But while the bombs and shells fell, we were safe in our bunkers."

The three companies began moving warily up the slope—Charlie and Delta in the lead, Alpha bringing up the rear, following the "two up and one back" assault tactic that had worked well in the mostly open European terrain during World Wars I and II but was unsuited to the dense triple-canopy jungles of the Central Highlands. The point men found leaflets in English scattered among the splintered trees. They urged every American soldier to sit down, hold his weapon over his head, and surrender. "You will not be shot," they promised.

Eventually, the paratroopers stepped warily into a clearing littered with fallen trees from the morning's bombardment and only a little over three hundred yards from the summit. "As they were scrambling up the hill, we held our fire," Son remembered. "They made it just five meters from our trenches. When we could see their faces, we yelled, 'Open fire!'"

Several men fell. The others ran to the right and left and stumbled into minefields. The rest fell back. Thousands of automatic weapon rounds ripped through the air. Chinese-made grenades came rolling and bumping down the slopes.

The Americans sought what cover they could find behind fallen trees. Some scrabbled at the earth with their helmets, trying to dig fighting holes.

Charlie and Delta Companies were pinned down and being torn to pieces.

Meanwhile, near the foot of the hill, other North Vietnamese troops surprised Alpha Company from behind. They were first spotted moving up through the trees by a private from the Bronx named Carlos Lozada. As the men of his company scrambled up the slope, dragging their wounded with them, Lozada provided what cover he could, firing his M60 machine gun from his hip—until a bullet hit him in the head. He would be awarded a posthumous Medal of Honor.

"By early afternoon," Harrison remembered, "the three companies had basically been decapitated. The company command-ers were dead; most of the officers and most of the NCOs were dead." The survivors from all three companies clustered in the clearing and did their best to set up a defensive circle. At its center was an aid station where officers and NCOs were bunched up, surrounded by wounded men.

ABOVE Using shattered trees for cover, paratroopers of the 173rd Infantry Division struggle up the slope of Hill 875 in the face of fire from enemy bunkers. "The Americans made a mistake when deciding to come to that hill, which didn't have any military and economic value," North Vietnamese Colonel Nguyen Thanh Son told an American interviewer after the war. "We tried to lure you to the hill, and we succeeded. You came. Your first assault was unsuccessful. Why did you carry out the following assaults?"

Enemy mortars and snipers hidden in the trees took a steady toll. The huddled men called in artillery and air support. U.S. artillery routinely hit within fifty feet of them—and sometimes closer. "The napalm engulfed our trenches and burned like a dragon," Son recalled. "Most of our position was completely burned out. I was burned myself. My face, nose, hands, and feet were on fire. I became a torch. I was running around. My soldiers threw dirt on me to smother the flames."

American bombs and napalm continued to pound enemy positions until it grew almost too dark to see.

A full moon rose.

Then, at 6:58, an American fighter bomber roared in from the northeast—the opposite direction from which earlier air support had come.

Two five-hundred-pound bombs fell from beneath its wings. One landed among the hidden enemy troops.

But the other fell directly onto the American aid station. In a fraction of a second, forty-two men were blown apart. Forty-five more were hideously wounded. A badly hit lieutenant from Alpha Company named Tom Remington crawled among the corpses and the screaming, moaning wounded men until he found a working radio. "No more fucking planes," he shouted into it. "You're killing us up here."

The fighting and the horror on the hillside continued all the next day—some of the most furious combat since the Ia Drang Valley battles two years earlier. The men ran out of water. The ammunition supply ran dangerously low. Helicopters that tried to ferry in supplies were shot down.

Matt Harrison was not able to chopper in to take command of what was left of Alpha Company until late that afternoon. Snipers were still picking off Americans. North Vietnamese mortar crews crouched so close the men could hear rounds leaving the tubes. "Just after I got in there," Harrison remembered, he came across "one of my platoon leaders—a great young lieutenant named Tom Remington. Despite the fact he'd already been shot twice he'd kept pushing on and was shot twice more. He was lying there beside the trail when I got in. And he just croaked at me, 'Matt, do you have some water? My canteen's been dry for two days.' I gave Tom some water and moved on.

"It was chaos—collections of guys who had tunneled and dug down behind trees. It was not a real defensive position. And these were guys who had gone without water in that heat for two days, had gone with very limited resupply of food and ammunition. And almost every one of them was wounded. And all

After four straight days of combat, exhausted men of the 173rd slump atop an abandoned North Vietnamese bunker on the summit of Hill 875, Thanksgiving Day, November 23, 1967.

POOLAW

At Fort Still, Oklahoma, on November 17, 1967, friends and family of a fallen soldier gather for a funeral—one of five military funerals held there that month. First Sergeant Pascal Cleatus Poolaw Sr. had been killed as he tried to drag one of his wounded men off the battlefield near the village of Loc Ninh.

He was a remarkable soldier, and was awarded forty-two medals, including one Silver Star in World War II, two more in Korea, and a fourth, posthumously, for his gallantry in Vietnam. He was also a Kiowa. He and three of his sons were among the 42,000 Native Americans who would serve in Vietnam, the highest per capita service rate of any ethnic group in the United States. Sergeant Poolaw's widow spoke at the ceremony. "He has followed the trail of the great chiefs," she said. "His people hold him in honor and highest esteem. He has given his life for the people and the country he loved so much."

TOP Kiowa dance, held at Carnegie, Oklahoma, in honor of Sergeant Poolaw upon his return from the Korean War in 1952
RIGHT Sergeant Poolaw's funeral at Fort Sill. His widow is at the left, next to her three sons.

around were bodies. Guys who had been shot and blown up. It was the third circle of hell.

"Once we got the situation stabilized I was determined I was going to find every one of my guys. Nobody was going to be left behind. There were guys that I never found because they had essentially been completely blown apart. I had a copy of the company roster in my pocket. I found the living guys quickly. I would find the dead guys and check them off on my roster. I remember there was one really good sergeant. I couldn't find him and I couldn't find him. And finally I found a pair of legs. He was still wearing his fatigue pants. I pulled the wallet out

from his pocket, so I knew that that was my NCO. The rest of him had been pulverized. There were two or three guys I was just never able to find a body for."

On Thursday, two fresh battalions of the 173rd finally made it to the top of the hill for which so many had died. But the night before, the surviving North Vietnamese troops had slipped down the other side and disappeared into Cambodia and Laos.

Harrison remembered that "the powers that be decided it would be important to our morale for us to be in on the taking of the top of the hill. I had twenty-six guys left out of a company that started out at a hundred and forty, and all twenty-six had been wounded." He and those of his men who were still mobile dutifully dragged themselves up the slope. Reporters and camera crews descended on the battlefield. A reporter asked a survivor what had happened. "What the fuck do you think happened?" the paratrooper answered. "We got shot to pieces. Make that 'little pieces.'" One hundred and seven Americans had died taking Hill 875; another 282 were wounded. Ten more were missing. The number of North Vietnamese casualties is unknown, but their losses are thought to have been staggering.

Harrison and his exhausted men spent no more than half an hour on the hilltop, "just trying to gather ourselves," he remembered, before they were helicoptered to the top of yet another hill.

It was Thanksgiving. Chinook helicopters clattered down out of the sky, carrying huge containers of hot turkey and mashed potatoes and cranberry sauce so that the 173rd could have their Thanksgiving dinner. As they ate, a TV news crew set up for a holiday spot, using them as a backdrop. "I was really angry," Matt Harrison recalled. "It was as though we were entertainers."

Back in June, Harrison had lost two West Point classmates on Hill 1338. He lost two more on Hill 875. Of the eight with whom he had served in the Second Battalion, four were now dead and two had been wounded. "To take tops of mountains in a triple-canopy jungle along the Cambodian-Laotian border accomplished nothing of any importance," he remembered. "The battle for Hill 875 was a microcosm of what we were doing and what went wrong in Vietnam. There was no reason to take that hill. And I doubt that there's been an American on Hill 875 since November 23. We accomplished nothing."

THE END BEGINS
TO COME INTO VIEW

IN THE WEEKS leading up to the battle on Hill 875, fearful that public support for a prolonged war was slipping away, the Johnson administration had been waging what one national security advisor called a "multimedia public-relations campaign . . . to persuade the American public that the war was being won." In a July cable to the Joint Chiefs, General Westmoreland had proposed a coordinated administration-wide effort to persuade Americans that all the talk of "stalemate" was nonsense, that the United States was winning the war. It should all be organized quietly, he wrote, "to avoid charges that the military establishment is conducting an organized propaganda campaign, either overt or covert."

Robert McNamara did not take part. Instead, he sent the president another eyes-only memorandum. To the public, the defense secretary was so closely identified with the Vietnam conflict that it was sometimes called "McNamara's War." But he himself had grown increasingly disillusioned with it—so disillusioned and so anguished that the president and others within the administration feared he might collapse, might even kill himself.

McNamara made the strongest case he could. "Continuation of our present course of action in Southeast Asia would be dangerous, costly in lives, and unsatisfactory to the American people," he wrote in a cover note to the memorandum. There was no longer any reason to believe that the prolonged "infliction of grievous casualties, or the heavy punishment of air bombardment, will suffice to break the will of the North Vietnamese and Viet Cong," he told the president. Instead, he said, the United States should cap troop levels, curtail ground operations to lessen the damage being done to South Vietnam, and declare a "unilateral and indefinite halt to the bombing of North Vietnam in order to bring about negotiation."

Johnson never responded. McNamara had already angered him by testifying before a Senate committee that, in his view, no bombing that had already taken place nor any he could foresee in the future would "significantly reduce the . . . flow of men and materiel to the South." Later that month—and without giving McNamara advance warning—the president would announce that his defense secretary was leaving the administration on March 1, 1968, to become head of the World Bank. Robert Kennedy, a friend and former colleague of McNamara's, rushed to his office and urged him to make public his opposition to continuing the war and go out "with a hell of a bang." McNamara would not do it. Although he had harbored doubts about the conflict since the first U.S. Marines landed in Vietnam in 1965, he would keep silent about those doubts for thirty-one years. His successor as defense secretary would be Clark Clifford, a prominent Washington lawyer and trusted counselor to Democratic presidents, whom Johnson assumed would be more supportive of the war.

Meanwhile, Johnson had asked the Wise Men to reconvene at the White House to assess the war and how it was being waged. After two days of discussion, they concluded that the ground war was still worthwhile, that the bombing of the North should be continued, that there was no point in calling for peace talks since the communists would never seriously negotiate, and that under no circumstances should the United States withdraw. In order to rally greater support for the war, they urged the administration to find "ways of guiding the press" to hopeful conclusions about prospects for victory.

The president started the ball rolling, ordering the embassy in Saigon to discover and publicize "sound evidence of prog-

ress," and it dutifully fell in line, again praising the recent elections, claiming that security in the countryside was improving, that ARVN morale was on the rise.

Vice President Humphrey was dispatched to the *Today* show to assure viewers that "we are beginning to win this struggle. We are on the offensive. Territory is being gained. We are making steady progress."

On the CBS Sunday morning program *Face the Nation,* Ambassador Bunker employed a metaphor first used thirteen years earlier by the French commander in Vietnam, not long before France's great defeat at Dien Bien Phu.

> ELLSWORTH BUNKER: I think we're now beginning to see light at the end of the tunnel.
> BERT QUINT: Mr. Ambassador, you talk about light at the end of the tunnel. How long is this tunnel?

ABOVE General Westmoreland reports to the White House, April 27, 1967. Left to right: Special Assistant for National Security Affairs Walt Rostow; Westmoreland; Under Secretary of State Nicholas Katzenbach; Secretary of State Dean Rusk; President Johnson; Deputy Secretary of Defense Cyrus Vance; and Chairman of the Joint Chiefs of Staff General Earle G. Wheeler.

> BUNKER: Well, I don't think that you can put it into any particular time frame.

General Westmoreland himself was summoned home again to assure the National Press Club that the enemy was now "unable to mount a major offensive. . . . I am absolutely certain that whereas in 1965 the enemy was winning, today he is certainly losing. . . . A new phase is now starting. We have reached an important point when the end begins to come into view." The recent battles around Dak To—including the struggle for Hill 875—constituted the "beginning of a great defeat for the enemy." He also told reporters that the impressive body counts his commanders reported were "very, very conservative"; the figures probably represented, he said, "50 percent or even less of the enemy that has been killed."

As if to prove it, MACV released a new and surprisingly low estimate of enemy forces to show how much damage the United States had done to them. It was only two-thirds of the total suggested by the CIA, in part because, after a bitter and prolonged debate behind the scenes, General Westmoreland had chosen to exclude from it the part-time guerrillas—farmers, old men, women, even children—who helped place mines, grenades, and booby traps that accounted for many American casualties.

Robert Komer, the head of CORDS, chimed in too. All trends in pacification were "significantly upward," he said: two-thirds of South Vietnam's people now lived in "secure" areas; there'd been a bountiful rice harvest; the growing number of tractors at work in the fields and motor scooters plying the roads were evidence that life in the countryside was steadily improving.

For the moment, the administration's PR offensive seemed to succeed. A Harris poll taken that winter showed that the American people, by a margin of 63 percent to 37 percent, now favored escalating the war rather than limiting it; the previous summer a majority had preferred deescalation. Lou Harris thought there were three reasons for the change: the tactics of the antiwar movement; the failure of the war's opponents to offer a persuasive alternative; and the optimistic reassurance offered by Humphrey, Bunker, Westmoreland, Komer, and others.

Meanwhile, Allard Lowenstein's yearlong search for a Democratic challenger to the president had finally succeeded. On November 30, 1967, Minnesota senator Eugene McCarthy announced that he would enter the New Hampshire Democratic primary and try to unseat the president of his own party. "There are some things that are just so wrong you have to take a stand," McCarthy said, "no matter what."

LIVING IS THE DIFFICULT THING

CAPTAIN HAL KUSHNER was twenty-six years old and married when he arrived in Vietnam that fall, the father of a three-year-old girl with another baby on the way. A recent graduate of medical school, he had volunteered to serve as a flight surgeon with the First Squadron, Ninth Cavalry—the "tip of the spear" for the First Air Cavalry.

Every few days, he tape-recorded his impressions for his family back home. Kushner complained about living conditions at Landing Zone Two Bits, in the center of the Bong Son Plain, worried he hadn't been adequately trained to carry out the inves-

ABOVE Minnesota senator Eugene McCarthy (center) and some of the well-dressed student followers who got "clean for Gene" campaign in downtown Manchester during the New Hampshire primary. "We're involved in what has become a major war," McCarthy told the voters. "The fact is there's no economic justification . . . for the continuation of the war. There certainly is no diplomatic justification for it. It's not militarily defensible, as we can see in the evidence being presented to us every day. And in my judgment, it has long since passed the point [at] which it can be morally justified."

tigation of aviation accidents that was part of his new job, wished he was allowed to tend to the most seriously wounded men who were helicoptered out to bigger hospitals in the rear—and was initially appalled by the people whose independence he believed he was helping to defend. "Went downtown today—they call it a town—to get a haircut. The town consists of a bunch of filthy hovels. Just couldn't believe how the people live. These little kids running around begging, and they're about the same age as Toni-Jean. It just makes me want to vomit. Everything is dirty, filthy. There's no sewage. There's no sanitation. There's nothing. People defecate right in the middle of the street. It's just very, very depressing. . . .

"I don't know if the country's worth saving or not. I'm sure that if we do anything for them it'll have to be long range. I mean a hundred to a hundred and fifty years because apparently the French didn't do anything with them when they were here. And it's really going to take at least two or three generations to raise their standards and their levels of intelligence, their understanding of sanitation and preventive medicine and politics and

ABOVE Captain Hal Kushner before setting out for Vietnam

everything up to an acceptable American standard, if we want to help this country."

On November 30, the same day Eugene McCarthy announced that he was going to challenge the sitting president, Kushner flew to the air base at Chu Lai to deliver a lecture on the dangers of night flying. Afterward, he planned to head right back to his outfit. He never got there. "We had terrible weather that night. I asked the aircraft commander, Major Steve Porcella, who was from Massachusetts, if I could make a call to my family on the MARS station. There were people waiting in line. You had to wait in line for an hour or so and then you could talk for two minutes. He said, 'No. We can't. We have to get the airplane back.' I said, 'The weather is so bad.' There was wind and rain. 'Why don't we wait out the weather and go back in the morning,' Steve said. 'Our mission is not so important. But we have to get the airplane back for operations tomorrow.' I'll never forget the dedication of that very brave young officer.

"It was dark and rainy and windy. Aboard were Major Porcella and myself, Warrant Officer Gifford Bedworth from Connecticut, the co-pilot, and the crew chief, who was a Sergeant McKee, whom I didn't know well. As we were flying, I saw that we had drifted west of Highway 1 because I could see trucks. I knew that was wrong. So Steve called Duc Pho on the radio and he said, 'I think we're lost.'"

The helicopter slammed into a jungle-covered mountainside.

"The next thing I knew I was hanging upside down in a burning helicopter. I remember yelling, 'Is anyone alive? Is anyone alive?' I heard some groaning and I couldn't tell where it was from. At first, I couldn't unbuckle my seatbelt because I couldn't move my left arm. When I managed to unbuckle myself I fell out of the helicopter and almost broke my neck. I didn't realize that I'd been hanging upside down. I was completely disoriented.

"In the firelight I could see that Porcella was dead, jammed up against the console. He was kind of crushed. I just jumped away from the helicopter and it didn't explode but it just went shwoosh and burned up. There was an M60 machine gun on the helicopter and the rounds were cooking off and it was exploding. One or several of the rounds went through my left shoulder. I could feel that. And I knew that my face had been cut and I knew that I had broken some teeth. I ran my tongue over my teeth.

"From the ground, I saw Warrant Officer Bedworth, who was still in his seat. The whole seat had come through the chin bubble of the aircraft. He had a broken tibia and fibula. The bones were sticking through the nylon of his jungle boot. He was conscious. And he was hurt very badly. Very brave. I took some branches and splinted his legs with his Army belt.

"So I just sat there with Warrant Officer Bedworth. I assessed

my own wounds. I had some burns on my buttocks and burns on my back. I had a broken left wrist; a broken collarbone; and a bullet wound in my shoulder from the cooked-off rounds. I had lost seven teeth. I had no glasses. We had no first aid kit; no flares; no nothing. Everything had burned up in the airplane. We had no food or water.

"That was the situation. So the rule is you wait with the aircraft until you get rescued. We waited one day. We waited two days. And poor Bedworth was in pain. On the morning of the third day he died, he just slipped away. It was very, very sad.

"I had to decide whether or not to stay with the helicopter. I had no idea whether it was going to keep raining. I had no idea where the enemy was. I thought that my best choice was to leave the aircraft and try to go down the mountain. So I used my Army belt to tie my left arm to my body. (That's the way you treat a fractured collarbone.) And I tried to make my way down the mountain."

It took Kushner four hours to stagger down the slope. When he finally reached level ground he looked back up—and saw two American helicopters hovering above the crash site. Their pilots did not see him. He was too exhausted and in too much pain to scramble back up the slope in hopes of catching their eye. "I just didn't think I could make it. So I kept going. I saw this peasant working in a rice paddy. And he saw me. I had captain's bars and a caduceus, the medical symbol, on my collar. And he said, '*Dai uy bac si. Dai uy bac si.*' 'Captain, doctor.' He took me about another mile to a little hooch, and he sat me down on the front of it and he brought out a can of condensed milk and a plastic C ration spoon. It was the first thing I had had to eat but rainwater for three days. I opened the can and it was just the best stuff I've ever eaten in my whole life.

ABOVE Hal Kushner visits a village near Landing Zone Two Bits.

"Then, I heard another person say, '*Dai uy bac si. Dai uy bac si.*' There was a squad of Viet Cong. The squad leader said, 'Surrender, no kill,' and he put his arms up. And I put my right arm up. The left one was still tied to my side. I think he was more nervous than I was, and he shot me with an M2 carbine, right where the M60 had shot me. It went right through my neck and came out the back. It just knocked me over. They went through my wallet and the squadron leader took my Geneva Convention Card, which was white with a red cross. He tore it up and he said in English, 'No POW. Criminal. Criminal.'

"I thought that I would receive different treatment because I'd seen all these war movies where doctors had hospitals and treated their own patients and had instruments and got Red Cross packages. My father had given me a medallion before I left—a Star of David on one side and St. Christopher's medal on the other. The squad leader tore that off and he took my dogtags and my watch. I had a wedding ring and he tried to take that too. I fought for the wedding ring. He made a motion like he was going to cut my finger off if I didn't give it to him. But he finally let me keep it.

"So then they took my boots and we started marching. I was weak and I was sick and I was hurting and I was burned. It was bad. And they took me to this little village. The squad leader told me that the American airplanes had bombed this village, and there'd been many people killed there. The people came out and they tied me to a big block of wood, like a door. And this kid, a teenager, beat me with a bamboo stick.

"We stayed that night in that village. They fed me. And then we walked for a month, almost always at night. I was barefoot and my feet were just lacerated. I had maggots infesting my wounds. I had a fever. I was really sick. We kept going always higher in the mountains. I was weak and I asked to stop a lot. And most of the time they didn't let me stop. I didn't think I could possibly survive, I just didn't think I could. And I didn't care."

Hal Kushner and his captors kept walking deeper and deeper into the Central Highlands, moving at night so as not to be spotted from the air. Once, he was taken to what he took to be a hospital. "It was just a series of caves but there were a lot of wounded lying around in hammocks. This female nurse came out and inspected my wounds. She laid me down and she gave me this bamboo stick to bite on. Then she took a rifle-cleaning rod and she heated it up in a fire until it was red hot. I was watching this and I was thinking, 'Oh my God. What are they going to do with this?' I didn't know whether they were going to blind me with it or what. She put it through my wound, through and through. And it really hurt. It really, really, really hurt. And then she put Mercurochrome on the wound. And she gave me

an aspirin tablet. I thought, 'What else can they do to me?' And I was to find out."

Kushner spent the daylight hours at a series of way stations, a day's march apart. "We stopped at this one place and this old man came out and he took my fatigue jacket. And I thought he wanted it. I kind of resisted him taking it. But he just pulled it away from me. And he went over and he washed it in the river and dried it. He dried it over a fire. And he brought it back to me. It was such an act of kindness that I get emotional thinking about it because it was just an island of kindness in this sea of cruelty."

At another way station, Kushner met a North Vietnamese army officer who spoke English. "He had a little reel-to-reel battery-powered tape recorder. And he asked me to record a message to my family to let them know that I was safe. He said I could do that if I would make a statement against the war. And I told him with great bravado that I would rather die than make a statement against my country. And he said to me, 'You will find dying is very easy. Living is the difficult thing.' And those were probably the most profound words I had ever heard in my whole life, although I didn't realize it at the time."

Kushner and his captors kept going. It was raining heavily now. The jungle paths were slippery, the rocky hillsides so steep Kushner had to be pulled along by a rope. Finally, he was led up another hill and saw the outline of several huts hidden among some trees. At first, he thought it was another way station. But it turned out to be Prison Camp One, the first of six camps hidden in the Central Highlands of South Vietnam that he would survive over the course of the next five years.

"I expected to see a camp, to see Stalag 17, to see Hogan's Heroes—barbed wire, searchlights, guards up in guard towers, a camp commander, Red Cross packages, maybe a hospital where I could see some prisoners. What I saw was a little clearing by a little muddy creek, a group of hooches, and four of the worst-looking Americans I have ever seen in my life. Their hair was matted. Their teeth were black. They had no shoes. The guards tore the rank off my uniform. They said that there would be no rank structure in this camp. Everybody is equal. I was not a doctor. I was the latrine orderly."

WE'RE NOT GOING TO SHIMMY

AT YEAR'S END, public opinion polls delivered a distinctly mixed message for the White House: while most Americans still disapproved of the president's handling of the war,

more than 60 percent favored further escalation over reducing America's effort.

In December, President Johnson flew to Australia to attend memorial services for Prime Minister Harold Holt, who had won Johnson's personal loyalty by supporting the American effort in Vietnam when his countrymen were deeply divided about the war in which their sons were dying alongside American boys. President Thieu attended the services too, and Johnson took the occasion to urge him to begin informal talks with representatives of the NLF, hoping that it might somehow be persuaded to separate itself from Hanoi. Thieu publicly refused; so long as they were intent on toppling his government, he said, he would never sit down with them.

On his way home, Johnson stopped over at Cam Ranh Bay. "The enemy is not beaten," he told thousands of servicemen gathered to hear him, "but he knows that he has met his master in the field. . . . We're not going to yield. And we're not going to shimmy." He also surprised General Westmoreland with the

Distinguished Service Medal and credited him with having brought South Vietnam "from the valleys and depths of dependence to the cliffs and heights where we know now that the enemy can never win."

With nearly half a million troops in Vietnam—and despite the deaths of more than 11,363 Americans during the year—Westmoreland remained convinced that he was grinding the enemy down. The recent Border Battles had all been American triumphs, he argued, since thousands of enemy troops had been killed. Now it was time, he said, for an "all-out offensive on all fronts"—political, military, economic, and psychological. But the enemy was just a month away from launching an all-out offensive of its own.

ABOVE President Johnson surrounded by U.S. military personnel at Cam Ranh Bay, December 23, 1967. Behind him is Vice President Ky. "Please know that we are with you," Johnson told his listeners. "We are for you. We will be there until the end."

CHAPTER SIX

THINGS FALL APART

JANUARY–JUNE 1968

Citizens of Hue, carrying what few belongings they'd been able to take away with them when they fled the battle for their city, return to what's left of their homes and shops in late February 1968.

SOMETHING'S GOING TO HAPPEN

AS 1968 BEGAN, Lieutenant Tobias Wolff from Newhalem, Washington, was serving as an adviser to an artillery battalion with the ARVN Seventh Infantry Division, stationed just outside the provincial capital of My Tho in the Mekong Delta, thirty-seven miles southwest of Saigon. Despite the presence of U.S. troops and intensified pacification efforts, three out of four of the surrounding hamlets were believed to be under NLF control, but the city itself—with its broad, tree-lined streets, ancient fishing fleet, and crumbling French-era homes overlooking the Mekong River—was a relatively serene place, and when, in late January, Wolff learned that a carnival had been set up in a riverfront park as part of the days-long Lunar New Year celebration called "Tet," he and his sergeant decided to go into town and have a look around.

The streets seemed more crowded than usual, Wolff remembered, but he had no inkling that some of the strangers he passed were NLF fighters waiting for the signal that would soon launch Le Duan's General Offensive, General Uprising. "They had been coming into My Tho for weeks," Wolff wrote years later. "The [South] Vietnamese didn't know, the American advisers didn't know. The town was full of them and nobody said a word. I wouldn't forget that afterward—not a word of warning from anyone. For weeks they were all around us, on the streets, in the restaurants, gathering for the great slaughter and tasting the pleasures of the town until it began."

In the park, Wolff and the sergeant wandered among "the puppet shows, the jugglers and fire-eaters" until, he wrote, he decided to try his hand at a "dinky shooting gallery with a couple of antique .22s. . . . A stoop-shouldered man, tall for a Vietnamese, took the place to my right. A pair of younger fellows stood behind him and cheered him on. He shot well. So did I. We didn't acknowledge that we were competing but we were, definitely. Then I missed some and quit for fear I'd miss more. 'Good shooting,' I said to him. He inclined his head and smiled. It might have been an innocent smile, but I think of it now as a complicated, terrible smile."

Some three and a half weeks earlier, on the evening of January 1, Radio Hanoi had broadcast a poem, written by Ho Chi Minh.

This spring far outshines the previous springs,
Of victories throughout the land come happy tidings.
Let North and South emulate each other in fighting the
    U.S. aggressors!
Forward!
Total victory will be ours.

The broadcast was filled with static. The reader's voice was muffled. But for communist commanders, its message was unmistakable. The General Offensive, General Uprising that Le Duan and his allies on the politburo believed would end the war was drawing closer.

Tens of thousands of North Vietnamese troops were already in place in South Vietnam. The NLF had infiltrated dozens of cities and towns. Tons of smuggled Chinese- and Soviet-made weapons had been spirited toward intended targets in sampans and flower carts, coffins and false-bottomed trucks, then hidden in pagodas and churches and barbershops and buried in paddy fields and garbage dumps and cemeteries until the signal came for them to be retrieved.

And the communists had quietly developed a new warmaking technique with which to fight the ARVN and the Americans, aimed at taking as many allied lives as they could while losing as few of their own as possible—specially trained "spearhead" or "special operations" sapper units made up of both men and women, meant to prepare the way for conventional troops rushing along behind. "The training was elaborate," one sapper recalled. "We learned how to crouch while walking, how to crawl, how to move silently through mud and water, how to walk through dry leaves. . . . In teams of seven men, we practiced moving in rhythm to avoid being spotted under searchlights, synchronizing our motions, stepping with toes first, then gradually lowering heels to the ground." Barefoot, their bodies often painted green to blend in with foliage, sappers slipped through or beneath barbed wire, carrying rocket launchers, AK-47s, and explosive charges with which to breach fortified defenses.

MACV saw no special significance in Ho's verse; each year, after all, he broadcast a patriotic New Year's poem that was repeated on the eve of Tet. In a classified cable sent the day after the broadcast, General William Westmoreland again assured Washington that things in Vietnam were on the upswing. "The enemy did not win a major battle in Vietnam in 1967," he wrote, and "through careful exploitation of the enemy's vulnerability and application of our superior firepower and mobility, we

OPPOSITE A few days before the Tet Offensive begins, NLF commanders study the target they've been assigned. According to the man who took this picture, several of the men in it died in the subsequent fighting.

should expect our gains of 1967 to be increased many-fold in 1968." Meanwhile, he assured his superiors, U.S. forces would continue to be able to "detect impending major offensives and mount spoiling attacks.

There were more than ten thousand American military and civilian intelligence officers at work in South Vietnam, so many amassing so much data that it was impossible to analyze it all adequately. Still, here and there hints of what was to come filtered up the chain of command: enemy units were detected moving around in inexplicable ways; enemy defections were down, a sign of high morale; captured enemy reports described coming attacks on several cities; eleven cadres were caught in the city of Qui Nhon carrying prerecorded tapes calling on the local people to rise up against the Saigon government. Joint Chiefs Chairman General Earle Wheeler thought the North might be readying something along the lines of the "desperate efforts of the Germans in the Battle of the Bulge in World War II." Lyndon Johnson told the Australian prime minister to expect last-ditch "kamikaze" attacks in the coming weeks. "All of these things were saying to us, 'Something's going to happen,'" Philip Brady, now working for USAID, remembered. "But we didn't know exactly what."

ABOVE NLF fighters and local sympathizers form a human chain to smuggle weapons across a river. The coming struggle, they were told, "will be the greatest battle ever fought throughout the history of our country. It will bring forth worldwide change but will also require many sacrifices."

SIDESHOW

GENERAL WESTMORELAND thought he knew. "I believe that the enemy will attempt a country-wide show of strength just prior to Tet," he told Washington, "with Khe Sanh being the main event."

Khe Sanh Marine Combat Base was the westernmost of the American strongpoints established below the DMZ in 1966 to prevent the enemy from seizing South Vietnam's northernmost provinces. It occupied a treeless plateau, honeycombed with cement bunkers and defensive positions and ringed with thickly wooded hills. Its location—just eight miles east of Laos—made it an important base from which to monitor and hinder enemy infiltration down the Ho Chi Minh Trail, as well as a potential jumping-off point for the cross-border invasion Westmoreland still hoped he could one day persuade the president to underwrite.

Lieutenant General Lewis W. Walt, the top Marine commander in Vietnam, had never wanted to send men there. "It's too isolated," he said, "too hard to support." Its only overland link to other Marine bases was Route 9, an old dirt road that in places was no wider than a driveway, subject to washouts during monsoons and ideally suited for ambushes. Replacement and resupply would have to be brought in by air in a mountainous region where blankets of fog often made landing and taking off all but impossible. "When you're at Khe Sanh you're not really anywhere," said Brigadier General Lowell English, assistant commander of the Third Marines, whose men would be tasked with defending the base. "You could lose it and you really haven't lost a damn thing."

Westmoreland overruled them. In 1967, in a series of bloody battles remembered as the "Hill Fights," Marines successfully beat back repeated North Vietnamese attempts to seize one or another of the summits overlooking the base.

That fall, Marines patrolling near Khe Sanh had come upon new enemy bunkers, freshly dug fighting positions, and freshly created roads. It was clear that North Vietnamese troops were massing in the hills—eventually, there would be somewhere between twenty thousand and forty thousand of them. Westmoreland believed that North Vietnam wanted to isolate and destroy a major U.S. force at Khe Sanh—just as the Viet Minh under General Giap had done to the French at Dien Bien Phu fourteen years earlier. (The American assumptions seemed plausible, because U.S. commanders assumed that Giap was in command; in fact, he remained in temporary exile in Hungary.)

Any attacks mounted elsewhere in South Vietnam, Westmoreland was sure, would only be a diversion. Attrition was finally having the impact he'd hoped for; the communists had simply suffered too many casualties to focus serious attention on more than one target at a time. "The most logical course for the enemy," he said, was to overrun the northern provinces, "coupled with lesser attacks throughout the rest of the country to tie down American forces that might be moved to reinforce the North."

To thwart that plan, Westmoreland reinforced Khe Sanh with four battalions of Marines belonging to the Twenty-Sixth Regiment—some six thousand men, augmented by three hundred ARVN rangers—and sent unit after unit northward to I Corps, until, by January's end, half of all American combat maneuver battalions were stationed there, ready for any eventuality.

One Army commander, Lieutenant General Frederick C. Weyand, was less sure of the enemy's intentions. Responsible for defending the approaches to Saigon, he had been overseeing combat along the Cambodian border, and when the enemy there seemed suddenly to have vanished, he got permission to reposition a third of the troops under his command—fifteen combat battalions—closer to the South Vietnamese capital. Had he not done so, the character of the upcoming battle for that city might have been very different.

On January 2, the day Westmoreland sent his latest upbeat report to his superiors, his prediction about Khe Sanh seemed to have been confirmed. Sentries manning an advance outpost just west of the base camp spotted six men in U.S. Marine uniforms strolling along a path beyond the defensive wire. Twice ordered in English to stop, they didn't respond. The Marines opened fire, killing five and wounding a sixth, who managed to stagger away into the jungle. The men turned out to be a North Vietnamese regimental commander and his staff, apparently scouting the area in preparation for an assault.

Ever since taking command in South Vietnam, Westmoreland had hoped the enemy would somewhere mass his troops so he could destroy them with overwhelming American firepower. Khe Sanh now seemed to provide the perfect opportunity. He adopted a two-part plan he called Operation Niagara "to evoke an image of cascading bombs and shells." First, reconnaissance aircraft would photograph every inch of the surrounding terrain to pinpoint enemy positions while helicopters carpeted the countryside with acoustic devices to detect voices and seismic sensors to record truck and tank vibrations. Then, he readied a giant flight of more than two thousand warplanes, prepared to hit the enemy when the time came.

Just after midnight on January 21, North Vietnamese troops attacked Hill 861A, one of the summits that overlooked the base camp, and nearly captured it, then began pounding Khe Sanh itself with rockets, mortars, and artillery shells.

Marine Private John Corbett, from Nyack, New York, who had only recently arrived, took cover with two other men in his fighting hole, roofed with sandbags and dirt-filled ammunition boxes. An enemy rocket hit the main Marine ammunition dump. "It sounds as though all the Fourth of July fireworks of my youth have come back to blow up altogether," Corbett wrote. "The . . . noise starts to disorientate us. . . . [I]t hurts our eardrums so badly that in desperation we tear the filters off cigarettes and plug them into our ears. . . . Dirt continues to filter down on us from shaken sandbags on the roof." The initial explosion set off smaller ones that went on for forty-eight hours, filling the air with shrapnel.

Although the continuous explosions were terrifying, Corbett wrote, the Marines did their best to fight back.

Even with our base's ammunition dump exploding, with fires burning all around us, with our mortar's barrel still glowing and overheating, with an unexploded enemy mortar round sticking out of the dirt several feet away, the men in my squad are singing. Though I am undoubtedly the most scared Marine in Khe Sanh at the moment, I am also the proudest because of the song we are singing: *The Marine Corps Hymn.* "From the Hall of Montezuma to the shores of Tripoli, we will fight our country's battles on land or on the sea." I join in. This singing together, under these circumstances, keeps our courage up. I am very proud to be here with these Marines.

The explosions had destroyed 90 percent of the Americans' ammunition. The enemy had cut off Route 9. Big C-125 and C-130 transport planes lumbered in to replenish supplies. Their cargo included four large crates addressed to "Fifth Graves Registration Team, Khe Sanh"; each contained one thousand pounds of body bags. When enemy gunners zeroed in on the single landing strip, helicopters had to take over the dangerous task of resupply.

Private Corbett and his buddies soon saw that they were bait, meant to lure enemy troops out into the open so they could be blasted from the air. Major Mirza Baig, the target selection offi-

LEFT A foggy morning at Khe Sanh. "The digging of defensive positions is not what the Marines have trained me for," a veteran recalled. "The Corps didn't instruct us on how to build a bunker or dig a trench line. . . . We were trained to attack and destroy, to always be the aggressor, to never spend a second night on the same piece of real estate when there is more to attack." ABOVE Early in the struggle to hold the base, a Marine who has survived several days of savage combat on Hill 861A seeks solace in his Bible.

far enough to fire at him. With his machine gun, Ferrizzi managed to take out all five crew members. On another occasion, when a U.S. helicopter was shot down and burst into flame, Ferrizzi jumped from his chopper to free the trapped crew. As he struggled, the wrecked chopper exploded, blowing him into the air. When he came to, he was bleeding and badly burned and the enemy was close enough that he could hear them talking. A machine gun opened up, but somehow he managed to clamber back aboard his chopper. For his bravery under fire he was awarded the Silver Star.

Combat was traumatic, but life between firefights in the thickly forested Central Highlands was sometimes surreal. From the air, Ferrizzi and another crew chief once shot a tiger, said to have been menacing a Marine detachment. He was also expected to keep an eye out for elephants. "If we spotted any we had to land the aircraft, pick up elephant turds, and bring them back to the base to find out what they were eating. If the elephant was being used as a pack animal for the North Vietnamese its diet might include plants from another part of the country and it would be gunned down." If not, they were to be left alone.

Vietnam was the first real helicopter war. Chopper pilots flew more than 36 million individual sorties before it was over. They scattered propaganda leaflets over the enemy and poured lethal fire into their positions; carried troops and supplies and artillery pieces into battle—and lifted the wounded off the battlefield so swiftly that most reached a field hospital within fifteen minutes. It was a perilous business; U.S. Army aviators suffered the highest casualty ratio of any contingent of U.S. combat troops in Vietnam.

In 1968, Ron Ferrizzi, a policeman's son from the Swampoodle neighborhood of North Philadelphia, was a helicopter crew chief with the First Air Cavalry, Charlie troop, First Squadron, Ninth Cavalry, initially flying out of Two Bits,

the same Central Highlands landing zone where Hal Kushner had been stationed before his capture by the NLF. Ferrizzi flew in light observation helicopters—"like riding around in a lawn chair," he remembered, "we were so exposed"—that were expected to be the infantry's eyes in the field. They flew so low and so slowly, Ferrizzi remembered, that he could sometimes see the eyes of the enemy. "My job was to get shot at, to draw enemy fire, to see where the enemy was," he remembered. "I got shot at a lot."

Determined to destroy a North Vietnamese anti-aircraft gun during the siege of Khe Sanh, the pilot of his chopper flew so close to the ground the gun's crew couldn't depress the barrel

ABOVE Ron Ferrizzi and a Hughes OH-6 Cayuse light observation/attack helicopter OPPOSITE Huey (UH-1 Iroquois) helicopters belonging to the 199th Light Infantry Brigade ferry ARVN and American troops into battle somewhere in the Mekong Delta.

Messages: **TOP LEFT** A Marine hunkers down as a shell comes in, wearing a helmet with a few words for the journalists who fly into Khe Sanh and then can fly out again. **ABOVE** This Marine's helmet includes both his blood type, in case he is wounded, and a calendar marking off the months till he can go home. **LEFT** Another Marine protects himself with cards he considers lucky.

"It was never easy to guess the ages of Marines at Khe Sanh, since nothing like youth ever lasted in their faces for very long," wrote the journalist Michael Herr. "It was the eyes: because they were always either strained or blazed-out or simply blank, they never had anything to do with what the rest of the face was doing, and it gave everyone the look of extreme fatigue or even a glancing madness."

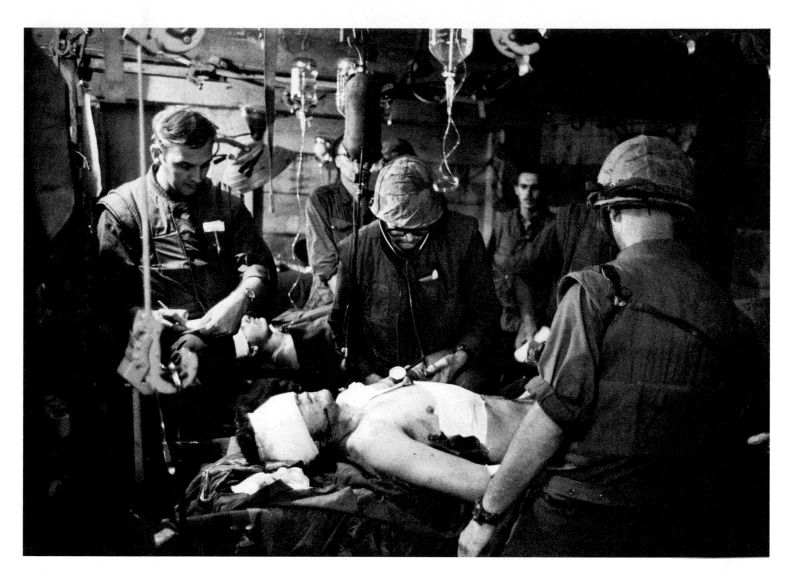

cer at Khe Sanh, explained Westmoreland's tactic. "Our entire philosophy [is] to allow the enemy to surround us closely, to mass about us, to reveal his troop and logistic routes, to establish his dumps and assembly areas, and to prepare his siege works as energetically as he desires. The result [will be] an enormous quantity of targets . . . for heavy bombers."

Reporters and photographers choppered in and out as the siege began, and the imperiled, surrounded men at Khe Sanh quickly caught the imagination of the American public. Unlike most combat in Vietnam, here was a struggle civilians could understand: surrounded U.S. Marines holding on, though heavily outnumbered. During the sixty-day period between February and March, Khe Sanh was the subject of one-third of all the AP stories filed from Vietnam, a quarter of the Vietnam clips on the network nightly news, and seventeen days' worth of Vietnam headlines in *The New York Times*.

Khe Sanh consumed President Johnson's attention, too. Ninety sixty-eight was an election year. "I don't want any damn 'Dinbinphoo,'" Lyndon Johnson said. He asked again and

again if General Westmoreland had all the men and materiel he needed, ordered a scale model of the battlefield installed in the White House so he could follow the fighting there hour by hour, and often wandered down to the situation room in the early morning hours insisting on the very latest news. To allay his anxiety, General Earle Wheeler, chairman of the Joint Chiefs, signed a document on behalf of his colleagues assuring the president that Khe Sanh would never fall. So concerned were U.S. commanders about the possibility of failure that if things began to look bad, Westmoreland recommended the use of "tactical nuclear weapons or chemical agents." Later, he would explain that since the area around the base was "virtually uninhabited," civilian casualties would have been minimal. How the Marines would have been shielded remains unclear.

It never came to that. As part of Operation Niagara, 2,700

ABOVE In a makeshift underground aid station hung with bags of saline solution, doctors in flak jackets do their best to keep wounded Marines alive until they can be medevaced out of Khe Sanh.

B-52 sorties would drop a total of 110,000 tons of bombs during a siege that would last 77 days. "Some Marines open their mouths and scream to equalize the effects of the bombs' concussions," Private Corbett wrote.

> The planes are above us and dropping bombs close to our lines. They fly so high we can't see them or hear their jet engines. . . . We hear a horrific screeching, tearing noise—the sound of bombs falling. They sound as though they are ripping the sky. . . . [It] is a frightening but beautiful sound, because the bombs will kill many enemy soldiers. Shock waves ripple from the bombs' impact. The valley trembles. . . . A single two-thousand-pound bomb can leave a crater thirty feet deep. Everyone has jumped from the trenches and foxholes clapping, whistling and cheering for the bombers. It was as if it's a ball game and our team has just scored. I guess it has.

No one knows how many North Vietnamese died in the hills surrounding Khe Sanh before the siege was finally lifted: MACV's estimate was between ten thousand and fifteen thousand. The precise number of Americans killed and wounded is unclear, too, but if the entire Khe Sanh campaign is taken into account, roughly 1,000 died and 4,500 more were wounded.

ONCE EVERY THOUSAND YEARS

FROM TIME TO TIME over the coming weeks the North Vietnamese would probe Khe Sanh's defenses, but the all-out assault that Westmoreland was sure was coming would never materialize. His basic assumption turned out to be spectacularly wrong: Khe Sanh would be the sideshow; the attacks on cities and towns and military installations about to begin all across South Vietnam would be "the main event." "Even if I had known exactly what was to take place," Westmoreland's intelligence chief, Brigadier General Phillip Davidson, recalled, "it was so preposterous that I probably would have been unable to sell it to anybody. Why would the enemy give away its major advantage . . . its ability to be elusive and avoid heavy casualties?"

In Hanoi, Party First Secretary Le Duan's basic assumptions were about to be tested, too. For the coming offensive to succeed, two monumental things would have to take place simultaneously: the South Vietnamese "puppet army" would have to collapse, and the people of the southern cities would have to rise up and join the revolution.

"All our thinking was focused on finishing off [the enemy],"

one North Vietnamese general remembered. "We were intoxicated by that thought." Another recalled that "no one was allowed to harbor any doubts or to even think about the possibility of winning a partial victory. . . . Never once did we discuss . . . what would we do [if] the enemy counterattacked?" "The slogan was, 'An opportunity like this comes once every thousand years,'" remembered Le Cong Huan, who had fought with the NLF at Ap Bac. "We were confident. We were told to bring only our newest uniform to wear when we seized Saigon." "In some units," the journalist Huy Duc recalled, "enthusiasm was so high that before heading toward their assigned targets they destroyed their cooking pots and burned their huts because they were so sure they'd never have to come back."

The general outline of the plan for the offensive had been shared with regional-level commanders three months earlier, but precise targets and the exact date on which the attacks were to be launched were not finally set until January 15. It was to be midnight on January 31, the night between the first and second days of Tet, then just two weeks away. Even then, only those at the very top were let in on the secret, for fear of alerting the enemy.

Tet is the most important holiday in the Vietnamese calendar, observed in different ways by people of every faith, a festive three-day interval between the end of the arduous harvest season and the beginning of spring planting. Special markets go up overnight, selling candied fruit and marigolds and peach and kumquat trees. Homes are cleaned to eliminate any trace of misfortune that might have marred the previous year. Children get new clothes and auspicious red envelopes filled with cash. Special foods are prepared and special offerings made to the ancestors. Above all, it is an annual coming-together of the family, and tradition dictated that both sides observe a cease-fire to allow troops not stationed at too-distant points to rejoin their families for the festival. By January 30, an informal thirty-six-hour truce agreed to by both sides was to go into effect. Thousands of ARVN troops would be at home for the holidays.

General Huynh Cong Than was an NLF subregional commander in Long An Province, in the western part of the Mekong Delta. A veteran of the war against the French, he'd been working for weeks getting his forces ready to attack Saigon. He knew what his men were supposed to do but not yet when they were supposed to do it. "There were mountains of work to be done," he recalled. Some units were undermanned, and he had to scour the countryside for youths to fill them out, some as young as thirteen. There were not enough arms to go around. Reinforcement units promised by NLF higher-ups failed to appear. The geography of the city his men were meant to help capture was a mystery to many of them. "We did not know the situation in the city outskirts and in the inner city," he remembered, "so we had to send cadres to contact our people who were operating in those areas."

Despite all the obstacles he faced, General Than had faith in those directing the revolution. "Even though problems of every sort confronted us, . . . the atmosphere was very enthusiastic. . . . Our enthusiasm was based on our understanding that, this time, total victory was certain. Even though we had not found solutions for all our problems, everyone believed that these were just local difficulties encountered only by our own individual units. . . . Our national-level leadership, our superiors, had made careful calculations for this offensive. Certainly they would only have made this decision if it were certain we could win, because this was a major decision—it was not just one single battle to be fought in just one locality. . . . While our preparations were carried out on an urgent basis, no one yet knew the exact date of the offensive. . . . [When] both Liberation Radio and Radio Saigon announced a cease-fire that would last several days to allow the population to celebrate the new year in the traditional manner, [we] thought this meant any attack would have to be launched after Tet."

Meanwhile, U.S. and ARVN forces continued to conduct business more or less as usual. Since arriving in Vietnam, Marine Corporal Bill Ehrhart had patrolled around Hoi An and Dong Ha, survived fighting in Leatherneck Square, and endured thirty-three days under sporadic shelling at Con Thien. "Toward the end of January, they pulled us back to Phu Bai, to the big Marine base there, just south of Hue," he remembered. "We'd been out in the field continuously for about four months. So we were going to go back and rest and refit, re-equip ourselves. I'm figuring at that point I've got a month to go. I'm home free. When you got down to being a 'double-digit midget' and you had ninety-nine days to go, you'd make a short-time calendar—which was usually a *Playboy* centerfold—and you'd literally draw these ninety-nine little segments on it. And every day you'd fill in a segment. They were numbered. And the idea was that when you'd filled in your short-time calendar you'd take it back to the world [the United States] and trade it in for a real one. So I had this short-time calendar. Our operations officer, Major Murphy, had the same rotation date as me. Then we got this new S2 officer, Captain Black. And the very first thing he does is say, 'That's inappropriate. Take that down.' Well, Major Murphy turns around and he goes, 'Captain, that's *my* short-time calendar. Corporal Ehrhart maintains it for me.'

This captain looked like he'd just sucked a lemon. But there was nothing he could do."

Time was almost up for Marine Corporal Roger Harris, too. In fact, he was scheduled to fly out of Vietnam on January 29. He and his unit were still hunkered down under enemy shelling at Camp Carroll, just south of the DMZ. But he had his orders, and he was determined to get out. He said goodbye to his friends and headed for the landing zone. "When the helicopters came in, I helped put the body bags on the helicopter. And I got on with the bodies. We landed in Dong Ha, which was division headquarters. When we got about two hundred meters from the airstrip, the airstrip started getting hit. I'm just thinking personally that God realizes that He made a mistake because some of the guys that got killed that were with me were good Christians that never had sex, didn't swear. And I had been this sinner. God realized He made a mistake: He killed the Christians and I got away. So now Death is following me. They told us that in another hour or so a plane was going to come in. When it did come in the artillery started coming in again. We jumped on and took off. We landed at Danang and boarded airplanes again, finally on our way home. We were sitting there. Everybody's slapping five. We made it. Then, all of a sudden, *whump, whump, whump,* Danang airstrip starts getting

ABOVE Women of the NLF hurry along a village path, carrying crates of ammunition toward Saigon. The coming attacks on the cities, Party Chairman Le Duan said, would constitute a "sharp dagger through the throat of the enemy."

ABOVE Enemy rockets and mortar rounds hit the airfield at Danang early in the morning of January 30, 1968. Hanoi Radio falsely claimed that the attack was meant to "punish the U.S. aggressors . . . who insolently slighted the traditional Lunar New Year festival of the Vietnamese people" by canceling the ceasefire.

hit, artillery's coming in. And I'm thinking it's all coming after me. It's all about me, you know. God doesn't want me to make it out of here."

The plane managed to take off despite the barrage, and as Harris headed home he had no way of knowing that the shells that had seemed to pursue him everywhere were the opening salvo of what came to be called the Tet Offensive.

Confusion about the calendar had caused NLF and North Vietnamese forces in several places, including Danang, to jump the gun. Long after the war, a Vietnamese military history explained what had happened:

The orders stated that region and province leaders were to be informed of the exact day and hour seven days before the attack and that district leaders and the commanders of independent regiments, spearhead battalions, and

urban commando groups were to be informed forty-eight hours ahead of time. In 1968 North Vietnam announced a change in the lunar calendar. According to the new calendar, the first day of Tet would be one day earlier than the date on the old calendar [used in the South]. In [Central Vietnam] and the Central Highlands our forces were already hidden in place right outside the target objectives and were unable to delay their attacks.

And so, between midnight and three a.m. on January 30—a full twenty-four hours before the agreed-upon jumping-off time—the communists shelled and attacked seven towns and cities: Nha Trang, Ban Me Thuot, Hoi An, Kon Tum, Qui Nhon, and Pleiku, as well as Danang. Each assault was beaten back within hours, but the element of surprise was badly undercut.

"This is going to happen in the rest of the country, tonight or tomorrow morning," intelligence chief Davidson warned Westmoreland. President Thieu had already canceled the ceasefire and recalled all ARVN personnel on leave. Westmoreland placed U.S. forces on "maximum alert." But since the summer of 1967, U.S. forces had been placed on some kind of heightened alert about half the time and for the most part nothing untoward had happened, so most officers were not unduly concerned. With half his combat forces concentrated in I Corps, and still convinced that any potential attacks elsewhere would be purely diversionary, there wasn't much more Westmoreland could do. He did not pass up his afternoon tennis game at Saigon's Cercle Sportif.

News of the surprise attacks confused NLF commanders, too. General Than, who'd been readying his troops for an attack on southern Saigon that he had assumed was not to begin until after Tet, was asleep in the early-morning hours of January 30 when a cadre from the local NLF headquarters burst into his room.

"The situation is extremely critical," he said. "We have orders that Saigon must be attacked tonight!"

Than was appalled. At first, he remembered, all he could do "was stand there moaning, 'Oh my God! Oh, my God!'" He now had just twenty hours in which to rally ten battalions of fighters, issue three-days' rations and arms sufficient for the coming struggle, and then march his soldiers toward the city in broad daylight, hoping that they would somehow not be spotted by the enemy and that the guides who were needed to lead them to their targets would be in place and ready when they got there. He did his best.

SPLIT THE SKY AND SHAKE THE EARTH

THE MAIN THRUST of the Tet Offensive began shortly after midnight on January 31. Over the next forty-eight hours, some eighty-four thousand NLF and North Vietnamese troops would hit 36 of 44 provincial capitals, 64 of 245 district capitals, more than fifty hamlets, dozens of ARVN and American bases, and five of the six largest cities in the country, including three that Hanoi called the "focal point targets"—Hue, Danang, and Saigon. Their goal, their commanders told them, was to "split the sky and shake the earth."

To the people of Saigon, asleep in their beds, the first mortar barrage was not especially disturbing. The sound of distant explosions was commonplace in Saigon. ARVN and NLF forces frequently exchanged fire in the city's outskirts; in any case, President Thieu, anxious to reassure his people that he was fully in charge and that the Saigon government was stable at last, had authorized four days of Tet fireworks.

Eventually awakened by an aide, General Westmoreland stayed by his telephone as reports of fresh attacks came in from all over South Vietnam. Their scale was stunning. MACV had expected assaults of some kind, but nothing like this. Never

before had communist troops dared to enter South Vietnamese cities; nor had so many ever been committed to such a broad, coordinated campaign.

Years later, Westmoreland would claim that the attacks had been "a surprise to the American people but not to us on the battlefield." His peers did not agree.

"Boy, it was a surprise, let me tell you," Robert Komer, the head of CORDS, recalled. "I was at Westy's elbow." "My God," said General William A. Knowlton, assistant division commander to the Ninth Infantry Division, "it's Pearl Harbor all over again." Some two hundred officers were attending a New Year's pool party when the shooting began. Not a single top commander was present at "Pentagon East," the sprawling MACV headquarters at the Tan Son Nhut Air Base on the northern edge of Saigon. At first, aides to General Creighton W. Abrams Jr., Westmoreland's second in command, did not bother to wake him. Ambassador Bunker was attending a party to celebrate "the light at the end of the tunnel"; Marine security guards had to hurry him into an armored personnel carrier and rush him to a secure location. "There was an intelligence failure," he privately admitted later. "We had no inkling of the scope, the timing, or the targets of the offensive."

For maximum impact, the communists had chosen a handful of targets in Saigon they considered central to the American and South Vietnamese cause. Sapper squads were to seize and hold each of them for forty-eight hours until a relief force could reach them. Simultaneously, U.S. military installations in the city's outskirts would be attacked in an effort to keep American troops occupied and unable to rush into the city. (In the end, virtually all the opposition that NLF fighters faced within Saigon during the first two days of fighting would come from ARVN troops, augmented by some seventeen thousand armed members of the National Police.)

General Weyand, whose last-minute foresight had circled the city with U.S. forces, remembered that the map showing the reported attacks in and around the city soon reminded him of "a pinball machine, one light after another going on as it was hit." He would spend hours shifting nearly five thousand mechanized and airborne U.S. troops from place to place to thwart the enemy's assaults.

Sappers slipped through the wire at Long Binh, eleven miles northeast of Saigon, the site of the largest U.S. installation in Vietnam, and managed to blow up a huge ammunition dump. A mushroom cloud rose above the airfield so vast that some Americans thought there had been a nuclear explosion. But when NLF troops followed along behind, they were virtually obliterated by gunships, airstrikes, and artillery.

The NLF attacked Bien Hoa, South Vietnam's busiest air base, too. Sleeping above the nearby USAID office, Phil Brady

and his wife and a colleague named Bob Mellon awakened to gunfire. "All hell broke loose," Brady remembered. "There were VC moving on the house, moving everywhere. A lot of shooting, a lot of confusion. We were shooting back out the window and my wife was reloading. When we ran out of ammunition we'd slide the magazine down the tiles and she was down there at the other end filling them up and sliding them back. Tells you how tough she is." These attackers, too, were quickly wiped out.

From three sides, three communist battalions blasted their way onto the Tan Son Nhut Air Base, threatening the MACV complex and the headquarters of the Seventh Air Force as well as hundreds of airplanes and helicopters. They were met by a motley but determined assortment of allied troops: U.S. Air Force Security Police, security guards assigned to MACV and to Vice President Ky, whose home was on the base; a battalion of ARVN paratroopers who happened to be there waiting for a plane; and a squadron of tanks summoned by General Weyand from Cu Chi, fourteen miles away; flares dropping from their commander's control helicopter to light their way. NLF fighters were eventually driven into a nearby textile mill, where allied airpower eliminated them. When it was all over, 162 bodies were found inside.

ABOVE NLF reinforcements rush through a Saigon suburb toward the city. Most arrived too late. Many never got there at all.

Many years later, Bui Hong Ha, an NLF mortar man who managed to survive the struggle at Tan Son Nhut, recalled what had happened to him and his unit: "My battalion crossed the Vam Co River and advanced toward Saigon, but we still had not been told what target we were supposed to attack. The fact that a General Offensive was about to be launched was kept absolutely secret. When we reached the approaches to Saigon we finally were given the important mission of attacking and capturing Tan Son Nhut Air Base. . . . We were very happy, and we had no fear of danger or of being killed. My 82mm mortar team was ordered to shell the air base. We used 'Charge 3' on our mortar rounds. With such a large propellant charge the recoil was very powerful, and the explosion of the mortars firing made our ears ring. The ground was so dry and hard that we were unable to dig in to build protected firing positions. Every time we fired our mortar we had to have two of our soldiers stand on the . . . base plate to hold it down. After firing for a while, we ran out of ammunition, so we then began to fight with infantry weapons. At that very moment a swarm of enemy helicopters suddenly filled the sky. They swept down on us, pelting us with bullets. Because the ground was so hard we could not dig foxholes, so many of our men died very tragically. We had only a few dozen men left out of our entire battalion. That night we withdrew. Local residents gave us food and water and carried our wounded away for medical treatment. In 1995, we finally found a mass grave where 181 of the battalion's officers and enlisted men were

buried. Every year when the Tet Lunar New Year arrives I go to the cemetery to light incense sticks in memory of my fallen comrades-in-arms."

As the fighting raged at American bases outside Saigon, small NLF commando squads, under the direction of superiors housed in a noodle shop on Yen Do Street, moved toward hand-picked targets within the city.

Nothing would go according to plan.

A squad ordered to seize the Chi Hoa Prison and release its five thousand inmates never got there; the guides meant to lead them to it had all been killed by the police.

The sappers who attacked the ARVN Armored Command and Artillery Command headquarters fared no better: the tanks they'd hoped to steal had been moved elsewhere; artillery pieces had been rendered useless by removing the breech locks; a promised ARVN mutiny meant to have been instigated by NLF agents failed to materialize. All the trespassers were killed or captured.

Twenty men dressed as policemen shot their way into the government radio station, hoping to broadcast prerecorded tapes proclaiming Saigon's liberation by the NLF. But as the shooting started a technician radioed to the transmitting tower fourteen miles away and ordered the wires between it and the station cut, and the station broadcast Viennese waltzes and Beatles songs instead. ARVN troops set the station on fire and shot most of the sappers as they tried to flee.

The two most spectacular attacks took place in the heart of the city, within easy walking distance of the hotels in which newspaper and television reporters were housed.

Thirty-four sappers, dressed in South Vietnamese army uniforms, blasted through the gate of the Presidential Palace only to be killed or driven out again. The survivors took refuge in an unfinished apartment building across the street and held out there for two days before ARVN troops and American MPs wiped them out. TV crews captured it all on film.

Meanwhile, just three blocks away, nineteen sappers used a satchel charge to blow a hole in the wall of the U.S. embassy compound. There were supposed to be twice as many men but half never turned up. As they wriggled through the gap, an American MP radioed his headquarters: "They're coming in! They're coming in! Help me! Help me!" He and another MP managed to shoot several intruders, including their leader, before they were themselves killed. With no one to give them orders, the surviving sappers seemed confused as to what to do next. They did not try to enter the gleaming new six-story chancery building—though an AP reporter wrongly reported that they had done so. Instead, they took what cover they could

ABOVE A hastily assembled group of men belonging to the 377th Combat Security Police Squadron fire at NLF forces trying to capture Tan Son Nhut airport.

behind pillars and concrete planters as American MPs and chopper-borne paratroopers picked them off, one by one. The last NLF fighter, badly wounded but still firing his AK-47, staggered inside a villa at the corner of the compound and was shot to death by a retired army colonel with a pistol tossed to him through the window by an MP. That gunfight, too, was filmed.

All nineteen sappers were killed or captured. Five Americans died, and five more were wounded. Three innocent South Vietnamese civilian employees were also killed, at least one of them shot by an American while he frantically waved his embassy ID card. The front of the embassy was pocked with bullet and shrapnel holes. The Great Seal of the United States had been blasted from over the entrance. Bloody Vietnamese and American corpses lay sprawled on the immaculate lawn—"like a butcher shop in Eden," one reporter wrote.

At nine thirty that morning, fifteen minutes after the final shots were fired, General Westmoreland toured the grounds, then did his best to reassure the stunned reporters who had watched it all. "The enemy's well-laid plans went afoul," he said. The attacks across the country had been "very deceitfully calculated" both to undercut public confidence in the war's steady progress and to divert attention from the major assault on Khe Sanh he was still sure was imminent. "The enemy exposed himself by virtue of his strategy and he suffered great casualties. . . . As soon as President Thieu . . . called off the truce, American troops went on the offensive and pursued the enemy aggressively."

With gunfire still echoing across the city, and with more reports of communist attacks cascading in from everywhere, Westmoreland's relentless optimism struck some reporters as surreal, even delusional.

A later appearance at the embassy by Ambassador Bunker did little to change their minds.

ABOVE American MPs close in on the last enemy sappers trapped within the U.S. embassy compound in Saigon. Beside them lie two American soldiers killed during the first moments of the enemy attack.

REPORTER: Is Saigon secure right now?
ELLSWORTH BUNKER: Saigon's secure as far as I know.

REPORTER: There's no more fighting in the streets?
BUNKER: There may be some in the outskirts still. I'm not sure. Don't know.

Saigon was far from secure, and would not be fully secure for more than a week. And neither Bunker's reassurances nor Westmoreland's could blunt the impact of television footage of bloody combat in the symbolic heart of the American effort in Vietnam. If the United States was winning the war, as administration spokesmen had been saying for months, how could this possibly have happened?

The NLF may have failed to achieve its primary objectives, but its fighters were still in the streets, still seeking revenge on the Saigon regime, still hoping the people of the city could be persuaded to rise up in their support.

Duong Van Mai Elliott and her husband, David, had been asleep in the RAND Corporation villa on Pasteur Street near the Presidential Palace when the assault on the embassy began. "We heard gunfire, and our first reaction was 'Must be another coup d'état,'" she recalled. "Then we heard that the Viet Cong had attacked Saigon and were still attacking. It came as a total shock because we always thought Saigon was safe, the safest place in all of South Vietnam." She hurried to her parents' house and found them huddled inside, "the doors and windows shut, very dark. They were afraid because our house was located near a slum. And we always assumed that there were a lot of Viet Cong agents living among the poor where they could hide very easily and that they were going to come out and look for government officials and military personnel to kill."

Her parents' fears were justified. NLF assassination squads, guided by spies, were moving through the back streets armed

ABOVE Accompanied by press and armed security, U.S. ambassador Ellsworth Bunker (center, in short sleeves) gazes in disbelief at a dead NLF sapper sprawled in the embassy garden. *The Vietnam Courier*, an English-language propaganda newspaper printed in Hanoi, would later claim that the infiltrators had suffered "practically no losses" and, after seizing the embassy itself, had successfully withdrawn. In truth, no sapper ever entered the embassy building, and all nineteen who entered the compound were killed or captured.

with lists of "blood debtors of the people" marked for assassination—bureaucrats, intelligence officers, ARVN commanders, ordinary soldiers home on leave and their families. They went from house to house. People hid their family albums for fear a snapshot would give away their connection to the Saigon regime. Nguyen Tai, a North Vietnamese spy who supervised operations of the murder squads in Saigon, was pleased. "The armed scouts of our security network did a number of excellent jobs in assassinating traitors," he remembered.

An assassination squad captured an ARVN colonel at his barracks, tied his hands, led him behind a church, and shot him. His widow was captured at home. "A young fellow about eighteen years old held a [machete] to my neck," she remembered. "He was about to chop it but I begged for my life. My children . . . screamed and screamed. The leader was waiting outside. He yelled through the door, 'What are you waiting for? Just liquidate her so we can go. Don't waste time talking.'" The younger man took pity on the woman and told her to hide but warned that if he saw her again he would have no choice but to kill her.

A taxi driver remembered that when the guerrillas came to his street, "they decapitated three people and left their bodies and heads lying at a coffee shop." They killed three more the next day. "I don't know what crimes these people committed. I only saw the VC throw their corpses in the street and forbid anyone's passing that place."

In one neighborhood, another resident recalled, they forced everyone out of their homes to act as jurors at so-called "people's courts," before which they brought those they accused of collaborating with the government. "The VC addressed the people: 'If you say these men are guilty, we shall punish them; if you say they are not guilty, we shall release them.' The people said, 'Not guilty,' so the VC did not kill anyone in our area."

Propaganda squads with megaphones chanted: "Compatriots, arise and give us a hand in getting Ky and Thieu down." "Nightly they came to every house," one man recalled, "exhorting the people . . . to take to the streets and go for demonstrations. They told the people to take the [South Vietnamese] flags down and hoist the NLF ones because they had already liberated the capital. No one responded to their calling. Nobody took to the streets, and nobody hoisted the NLF flag." The wife of a pedicab driver spoke for a good many people: "This is a

war between the two sides, and it is their business. We will obey both sides when asked."

"The civilian population had a very good attitude toward our troops when they encountered our men," the NLF commander General Huynh Cong Than recalled, "but we never saw any large demonstrations. . . . We were not playing a supporting role for an uprising of the masses as we had thought. . . . The rate of advance of our spearhead battalions began to slow. . . . Our ammunition supplies decreased, day by day. . . . Meanwhile, the political struggle, which was to have been launched by the students and the masses, still had not appeared. . . . What were the conditions among the masses and the students in Saigon that led our people to the conclusion that millions of people were boiling over with revolutionary zeal and were prepared to sacrifice everything for the cause of independence and freedom?"

Some Saigonese, stunned to find the war now being fought in the supposedly safe streets of their capital, assumed that there must be a sinister explanation: otherwise, how could the United States, with all its firepower, have let it happen? A rumor spread that the Americans had deliberately allowed the enemy to enter Saigon and other cities in order to force President Thieu to negotiate with the NLF so U.S. forces could go home. This baseless story was so widespread that Ambassador Bunker would have to broadcast an official denial.

A CONTINUOUS NIGHTMARE

THE WHITE HOUSE had been as stunned by what was happening in Vietnam as were the commanders in the field. The president was presiding over his regular Tuesday lunch meeting when he got the news. "Principals only" were present—Dean Rusk, Robert McNamara, Walt Rostow, CIA chief Richard Helms, General Wheeler, and, on this occasion, Clark Clifford, just confirmed as the new secretary of defense but not officially set to take charge until March 1.

The lunch discussion centered on Khe Sanh—the president's "obsession," Clifford remembered. General Wheeler proposed that General Westmoreland be authorized to tell the Saigon government he was planning a waterborne invasion of North Vietnam. Wheeler was sure that communist spies within the South Vietnamese high command would inform their masters in Hanoi—who would then rush troops from Khe Sanh to defend their coastline. Clifford opposed what he called "this strange idea"—"it could easily leak, backfire, or lead to actual ground combat in North Vietnam." But McNamara thought the idea worth exploring. So did the president.

OPPOSITE, TOP NLF fighters armed with AK-47s escort three captives along a Saigon street during the Tet Offensive. No one knows the prisoners' fate. OPPOSITE, BOTTOM A South Vietnamese army captain, his wife, and their son, executed in Saigon by an NLF assassination squad. The motto of the assassins was "Kill the Wicked and Destroy the Oppressors to Promote Mobilization of the People."

A CALLOUS DISREGARD

The AP photographer Eddie Adams was roaming the Saigon streets on the second day of the Tet Offensive when he happened upon several South Vietnamese marines escorting a man wearing shorts and a checked shirt toward the An Quan pagoda. The man's hands were tied behind his back, and he appeared to have been beaten. Adams fell in behind them, snapping an occasional picture as they moved along. An NBC film crew followed them, too.

A cluster of soldiers stood in front of the pagoda. Adams recognized Brigadier General Nguyen Ngoc Loan, the head of the South Vietnamese National Police. Loan was a tough-minded anticommunist, close to Marshal Ky, who had overseen the crushing of the Buddhist revolt in 1966 and saw the

Americans as insufficiently committed to the South Vietnamese cause.

The prisoner was brought before him. He was an NLF agent named Nguyen Van Lem and may have been the head of an assassination squad. (He had been found with a pistol adjacent to a hastily dug grave that held the bodies of seven South Vietnamese policemen and their families.) He and Loan exchanged words that no one else heard. Loan ordered one of the soldiers to shoot the prisoner. When the men hesitated, Loan drew his own pistol and shot him through the head. Then he spoke a few words of explanation to Eddie Adams: "They killed many of my people, and yours, too," and strode away.

Adams had photographed the whole thing. So had the TV crew.

The White House hoped that the

next day's American newspapers would be dominated by a second press conference held by General Westmoreland that was meant to put as much positive spin as possible on what was happening in South Vietnam's cities. Almost 6,000 enemy troops had been killed, Westmoreland assured reporters, compared to 530 Americans and South Vietnamese. The offensive had been "characterized by treachery and deceitfulness. It showed a callous disregard for human life."

But the front page of most papers that day also featured Eddie Adams's photograph of the shooting by General Loan. It, too, seemed to show a callous disregard for human life—but on the side of America's ally. "The man was wearing a checked shirt," Professor Sam Hynes remembered. "And the photographer

had come up very close and had pressed his shutter just as the officer pulled his trigger. So camera and gun went off together and you could see the man's head bulging at the side where the bullet was about to come out. We were there, face-to-face with this man who was dying. Right now. *Dead.*"

Two nights later on the *Huntley-Brinkley Report*, the NBC cameraman's color footage of the same public execution would be seen by some twenty million people.

"It was a devastating thing to [witness]," James Willbanks remembered. "And I think many Americans began to ask themselves, 'Are we supporting the wrong guys here?' And it sort of bought home to the dinner table—or the breakfast table if you saw it in the

newspaper—the brutality of this war and the fact that it looked like it was never going to end."

Dean Rusk berated newsmen for reporting such a brutal act, implying that the killing of a bound prisoner by a high government official, in broad daylight on a Saigon street, in front of journalists, was somehow not newsworthy. "Whose side are you on?" he asked. "I don't know why people have to be probing for the things that one can bitch about, when there are two thousand stories on the same day about things that are more constructive."

In Saigon, Phan Quang Tue, the son of the opposition leader Dr. Phan Quang Dan and now himself a fledgling politician, understood the impact the photograph and footage had on South Vietnam's American allies. "We paid a

big price for that picture. It was a turning point because it made Americans think, 'Do we want to spend our money and the lives of our sons to protect a system that allows that?'"

OPPOSITE AND ABOVE The photograph that won Eddie Adams the Pulitzer Prize and the contact sheet from which it came. "The general killed the Viet Cong," Adams said later. "I killed the general with my camera. . . . Photographs do lie, even without manipulation. They are only half-truths. What the photograph didn't say was, 'What would you do if you were the general at that time and place on that hot day, and you caught the so-called bad guy after he blew away one, two, or three American soldiers?'"

An aide entered and handed Walt Rostow a note. Rostow left the room and returned with what Clifford recalled as "a dramatic announcement": "We have just received a flash message from the National Military Command Center. We are being heavily mortared in Saigon. The Presidential Palace, our military installations, the American embassy, and other parts of the city have been hit."

Silence followed, broken by the president: "This could be very bad."

General Wheeler assured everyone that there was nothing to worry about. This sort of thing happened all the time in Saigon: "This is about as tough to prevent as a mugging in Washington."

On February 2, forty-eight hours after most of the attacks began, President Johnson called a White House press conference intended to calm public anxiety about what they had begun to see on their television screens. He assured the room full of reporters that "we have known for some time that this offensive was planned by the enemy. The ability to do what they have done has been anticipated, prepared for, and met. . . . The biggest fact is that the stated purposes of the General Uprising have failed. Communist leaders counted on popular support in the cities. . . . They found little or none."

True, "services" in the cities had been disrupted—just as they sometimes were in the U.S. if there was a riot or a serious strike—but they would soon be restored. The president struck a note of caution: the situation remained "fluid," he said; "a massive attack" on Khe Sanh was still "imminent," but "we feel reasonably sure of our strength."

Johnson was asked if "this present rampage in South Vietnam" would lead to a change in strategy."

The answer was no. Nor, the president said, had he received any requests for more troops. General Westmoreland had assured him that he had all the men and materiel needed to get the job done.

Critics in and out of Congress were not persuaded, either by the president or by his doggedly sanguine spokesmen in Saigon. "If this is a failure," Republican Senator George Aiken of Vermont said, "I hope the Viet Cong never have a major success." "Something enormous has gone wrong," said the editors of *The Cleveland Press,* "and it cannot be shrugged off with the kind of flimsy explanations given so far." The editors of *The Baltimore Sun* agreed: "If we expected attacks, why were we caught utterly by surprise?"

Despite the confident air the president tried to convey to the press, the days immediately following Tet were a time of "frustration and genuine anguish," he remembered; he sometimes felt as if he "were living in a continuous nightmare."

Compounding the president's anxiety was another cold war confrontation in another part of Asia. The same day the Khe Sanh siege began, thirty-one North Korean commandos had attacked the South Korean executive mansion in Seoul; twenty-six South Koreans and three Americans died before all the would-be assassins were killed or captured. Two days later, the North Korean navy seized an intelligence-gathering vessel, the USS *Pueblo,* along with eighty-three members of her crew. Johnson was convinced that the two events were closely connected, and that Moscow was colluding with North Korea in an effort to make Washington divert its forces from Vietnam—and force Seoul to withdraw its troops from there as well.

Hawks in Congress demanded military action to rescue the captives; Congressman L. Mendel Rivers of Louisiana, chairman of the House Armed Services Committee, urged Johnson to threaten the use of nuclear arms if the crew were not immediately let go. Johnson called almost fifteen thousand reservists to active duty to be sent to Korea, but the last thing he wanted was a second war in Asia. Delicate negotiations between Washington and Pyongyang were already under way at Panmunjom, aimed at getting the Americans back without further conflict. Seoul resented being excluded from the talks—the Americans did not wish the assassination attempt on the South Korean president and the potential release of the crew to be conflated. The leader of the South Korean opposition warned that the U.S. must never admit that its ship had been in North Korean waters, for fear it would only lead to further aggression, and someone leaked to a CBS reporter a false story that a deal had been reached in which, in exchange for such an admission, the prisoners would be released. (Secretary of State Rusk would soon publicly admit that Washington wasn't "one thousand percent sure" the ship hadn't intruded into North Korean waters, but it would be eleven months before the crew was released.)

On the morning of February 5, Garnett D. "Jack" Horner, a veteran White House correspondent working for *The Washington Star,* called the president for clarification. The two men began by talking about Korea, but the Tet Offensive and the American public's reaction to it was now uppermost in the president's mind.

LYNDON JOHNSON: Hello.

JACK HORNER: Good morning, Mr. President.

JOHNSON: Hi, Jack.

HORNER: We need guidance this morning, sir.

JOHNSON: Guidance? Is that all you want?

HORNER: Yes, sir.

JOHNSON: No quotation.

HORNER: That's right.

JOHNSON: No attribution. No connection. Give it absolutely none.

HORNER: Absolutely none.

JOHNSON: Your press is lying like drunken sailors every day. First thing I wake up this morning was trying to figure out after seeing CBS, . . . watching the networks, reading the morning papers, was how can we win—possibly win—and survive as a nation and have to fight the press's lies.

There was no quid pro quo agreement with the North Koreans, he told Horner, his voice quivering with anger—"not one goddamned thing to it." And by falsely suggesting that there was one the press had further complicated an already tense situation. There were other dangerous rumors floating around Washington, he continued. The columnist Drew Pearson, for example, claimed General Westmoreland was on his way out. "That's just as untrue as it could be," Johnson said. "There's nobody that works for me that's been more satisfactory all the time."

JOHNSON: Now the truth of the business is, he has done an expert job. Anybody that can lose four hundred [Americans] and get twenty thousand [enemy dead] is pretty damn good. [Casualty figures seemed to shift with every spokesman.]

HORNER: Yes, sir.

JOHNSON: And I don't admit that this is a communist victory, and I don't think anyone but a goddamn communist admits it. That's what I think. . . . It's just like a quarterback on a football team playing for your side, and you getting out and whipping the hell out of him. . . . I'm trying to protect my country, and they're all whipping me. Not a son of a bitch said a word about Ho Chi Minh. . . . He hasn't been elected to nothing. He's a dictator if there ever was one. . . . They talk about us bombing, yet these sons of bitches come in and bomb our embassy and nineteen of them try a raid on it—all nineteen get killed—and yet they blame the embassy. I don't understand it. . . . We think we killed twenty thousand; we think we lost four hundred. We think that of course it's bad to lose anybody—any one of the four hundred—but we think that the good Lord has been so good to us that it is a major, dramatic victory. And I think, what would have happened if I lost twenty thousand and they lost four hundred? I ask you that.

IT BECAME NECESSARY

THE AMERICAN PRESS, headquartered in Saigon, understandably focused almost exclusively on the fighting in that city; the war had never come so close to them before. But the Tet Offensive seemed to be happening everywhere. ARVN and American forces quickly blunted most assaults. The enemy was suffering terrible losses. The same weaknesses that undercut their attack on Saigon were evident elsewhere, as well.

Plans for the attack on My Tho, for example, called for an initial artillery and mortar salvo of between one thousand and two thousand rounds, but the necessary shells never turned up. In the end, just thirty-six were actually fired. Sappers led four battalions—some two thousand NLF soldiers—into town, intent on seizing the headquarters of the Seventh ARVN Division. One American who was quartered in the city never forgot waking up and watching from his bedroom window as they streamed along the street below. "I've seen a lot of scrawny little Viet Cong prisoners and corpses," he said, "but that night the Viet Cong outside my window looked seven feet tall."

They quickly shrank to size. The guides meant to take them

ABOVE Photographic overkill on the outskirts of Saigon during the Tet Offensive. "The death of a sapper is dreadful," recalled an NLF commander who trained hundreds of them. "His corpse is most often left on the road. . . . Often the ARVN will expose his body so that his relatives passing by can see it."

to their target got lost. ARVN tanks drove many back toward the edge of town. Gunfire drowned out the voices of the propaganda squads with megaphones calling upon the citizenry to rise up. U.S. Navy SEALS with sniper rifles picked off enemy soldiers from the third floor of their barracks. "I think it's great," one said to another. "All our trips into the jungle, and now they are coming to us." Boats from the Mobile Riverine Force ferried in American infantry. "Pockets of enemy resistance had to be wiped out to prevent the Viet Cong from closing in behind the allied troops," one commander recalled. To do that, airpower and artillery were called in.

The ARVN Artillery Battalion based outside the city to

ABOVE Twisted steel, all that remains of a market building in Ben Tre after some fifty hours of allied bombing and artillery. "It is always a pity about the civilians," an Air Force major who'd taken part in the assault told a reporter. They "don't know where the lines are . . . don't know where to hide, and some of the weapons we were using were area weapons." But "there could have been many more dead," he said. When he'd been ordered to napalm "a thousand Viet Cong" said to be retreating from the city, he flew down low enough to see that they were not soldiers but terrified women and children and called off the attack. "I think I saved hundreds of civilians," he said.

which Lieutenant Tobias Wolff was attached kept firing around the clock. "The process by which we helped lay waste to My Tho seemed not of our making and at all times necessary and right," he recalled. "As the ARVN battalions in town came under more and more pressure we began to drop shells on the buildings around them. We bombarded the old square surrounding [the ARVN division commander's] headquarters where he and the province chief were holed up with their staff officers. There were pockets of terrified government officialdom and soldiery huddled throughout the town, and every time one of them got through to us on the radio we put our fire right where we wanted it, no questions asked. We knocked down bridges and sank boats. We leveled shops and bars along the river. We pulverized hotels and houses, floor by floor, street by street, block by block. I saw the map. I knew where the shells were going, but I didn't think of our targets as homes where exhausted and frightened people were praying for their lives. When you're afraid, you will kill anything that might kill you. Now that the enemy had the town, the town was the enemy."

U.S. Phantom fighter bombers screamed in over the burning city, strafing and bombing the already damaged buildings. A third of My Tho was destroyed, and half the populace was rendered homeless. "The place was still smoldering two weeks later," Wolff recalled, "still reeking sweetly of corpses. The corpses were everywhere, lying in the streets, floating in the reservoir, buried and half-buried in collapsed buildings, grinning, blackened, fat with gas, limbs missing or oddly bent. Some headless, some burned almost to the bone, the smell so thick and foul we had to wear surgical masks scented with cologne, aftershave, deodorant, whatever we had, simply to move through town." A taxi driver who had burned to death inside his charred vehicle was still behind the wheel; someone had put dark glasses on him and stuck a cigarette in his mouth.

Still more destruction was done to the nearby city of Ben Tre. There, Americans, outnumbered by an NLF regiment, called in massive air and artillery firepower to dislodge it. Forty-five percent of the dwellings were destroyed. Afterward, a reporter quoted an American major as having said, "It became necessary to destroy the town to save it."

"A lot of people knew that the country could never be won, only destroyed," the journalist Michael Herr wrote. "After Tet, we took space back quickly, expensively, with total panic and close to maximum brutality. Our machine was devastating. And versatile. It could do everything but stop."

John Paul Vann, now back in Vietnam as commander of all civilian and military advisers in the Third Corps Tactical Zone, warned that civilian resentment of the inadvertent damage both U.S. and ARVN forces were doing was growing at an alarming rate. "Unless stopped," he said, "the destruction is going to exceed our capability for recovery and battles we win may add up to losing the war."

It took ten days to subdue Saigon. A twenty-four-hour curfew was imposed. (An exception was made for coffin makers, whose hammers and saws could be heard around the clock as they rushed to fill the steadily growing demand.) Eventually, surviving NLF fighters were cornered in and around a racetrack in Cholon, the western neighborhood populated largely by poor Chinese. Residents were ordered from their homes, creating a free-fire zone, so that the last remaining guerrillas could be blasted from their hiding places. Much of the area was burned or blown apart, but the threat was finally lifted.

AN ENTIRELY DIFFERENT KIND OF FIGHT

THE LONGEST, BLOODIEST BATTLE of the Tet Offensive was fought in the streets of one of the country's loveliest cities, Hue, Vietnam's onetime imperial capital and still a center of Vietnamese culture and intellectual life.

For months, just outside the city, nineteen-year-old Nguyen Thi Hoa and the four young women in her village NLF cell had been putting aside rice and salt for what she was told was only "something big being planned." Then, two weeks before Tet, she and her friends were asked to guide Main Force fighters disguised as ordinary citizens to rendezvous points within the city. "It was very compartmentalized," she remembered, "so we still didn't know what the plan was. For those two weeks they were supposed to avoid enemy forces and not engage." On the eve of Tet, with NLF fighters already in place, North Vietnamese units appeared, in uniform and armed far more heavily.

Colonel Ho Huu Lan, fresh from months spent fighting the U.S. Marines south of the DMZ, remembered that he and his men "had had to move fast in order to arrive at Hue by the 30th of January. We marched at what we called the 'magic speed,' and it took us only ten days. When we were going through the jungles, the local soldiers had cut trails for us and at night local fighters lit the way."

Nguyen Thi Hoa was one of those who guided them toward their objective. "Everywhere we went," she remembered, "people brought Tet food out to them, sweet cakes and rice cakes. But our troops did not have time to stop and eat. So they were eating while walking, one hand holding their weapons. They were very excited. We were even more excited."

The city they were about to try to seize was divided in two by the Perfume River. The south side was occupied by the bus-

ABOVE On the outskirts of Hue, a commander entrusts an NLF flag to a Main Force unit the day before the attack on the city is to begin. This flag, or one just like it, would soon fly above the old walled city, called the Citadel.

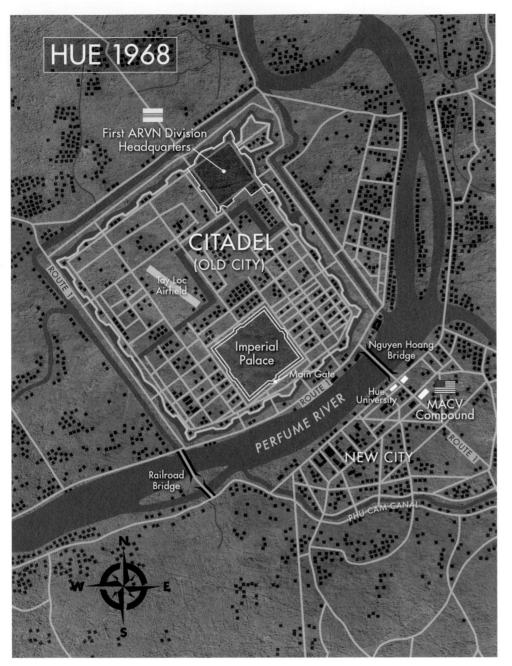

HUE 1968

First ARVN Division
Headquarters

CITADEL
(OLD CITY)

ROUTE 1

Tay Loc
Airfield

Imperial
Palace

Nguyen Hoang
Bridge

Main Gate

ROUTE 1

Hue
University

MACV
Compound

PERFUME RIVER

ROUTE 1

NEW CITY

Railroad
Bridge

PHU CAM CANAL

N
W E
S

At 3:40 in the morning on January 31, First Lieutenant Tran Ngoc Hue—Harry Hue to his American advisers—was asleep at his home just inside the western wall of the Citadel when the sound of explosions woke him. As a boy, he had witnessed firsthand the cruelty of the French and the Viet Minh and, like his father before him, had enlisted in the South Vietnamese army, convinced that both colonialism and communism were alien to his homeland. Trained at the Dalat Military Academy, he had risen quickly to command the Hac Bo, or "Black Panther," company, the elite all-volunteer reaction force of the First ARVN Division. At first, he thought the sounds he'd heard were fireworks, but as they grew louder and more insistent, he realized they were rockets and mortar shells.

He dressed quickly and set out on a bicycle for the airstrip. Hundreds of North Vietnamese soldiers were already moving through the dark streets. One entire battalion was fanning out to occupy the residential area of the walled city; a second was supposed to overrun the airstrip and then seize the compound housing the ARVN headquarters in the Citadel's northeastern corner. Hue, like all the men in his company, was a son of the city and fiercely protective of his hometown. As he pedaled, he recalled, "there were VC running all around me. I'd watch them go down one street and I would head the other way. I knew where I was going. They didn't."

He found his men already engaged with the enemy at the airstrip, took charge there, and, grabbing a light anti-tank weapon (LAW), fired a rocket into a dozen enemy soldiers, killing three and scattering the rest. Together, he and his unit and an ordnance company then held their ground until word reached him that the ARVN division commander, Brigadier General Ngo Quang Truong, wanted them to withdraw to the headquarters compound. Half of Truong's troops were on leave; most of the rest were stationed outside the city. He needed help. Hue rallied his men. "The enemy has pushed us into a corner!" he shouted over the sounds of battle. "We must fight for our own survival, for the survival of our families, the survival of Hue City, and the survival of our fatherland! Will you fight with me?"

tling New City, site of the local MACV headquarters. Across the river was the Old City, or Citadel, where two-thirds of the city's people lived. Surrounded by water on all sides—by the river as well as a moat ninety feet wide and twelve feet deep—with walls forty feet thick, thirty feet feet tall, and more than a mile and a half in length, it was large enough to contain a maze of narrow streets, shops, residences, pagodas, parks, an airstrip, the headquarters of the First ARVN Division, and the walled Imperial Palace, from which the Nguyen dynasty once ruled.

ABOVE Hue, split by the Perfume River between the Citadel and the New City

He finished by shouting, "Hac Bao!" His men shouted it back at him and fell in as he raced toward the compound. When they got there, Hue remembered, "I . . . saw that the enemy had set up three machine guns overlooking the gate to support an attack. I brought up some LAWs, and we blew away the machine guns. Then we threw down a smokescreen and dashed into the compound. We were very lucky." "Harry Hue was bigger than life in the field," his American adviser remembered, and "utterly fearless." Had he not taken charge at the airstrip and then rallied his men to defend the compound, it might well have fallen—and with it the entire Citadel.

At roughly the same time the communists were attacking the walled city on the river's north bank, they rained rocket and mortar shells on the MACV compound on the south side. Behind its six-foot walls were a two-story, twenty-room hotel annex, a dispensary, a chapel, a barbershop, an officer's club, and canvas tents, housing some two hundred U.S. advisers and Australian warrant officers. "It was a typical rear-echelon billet, heavy on the steaks and shrimp and light on the heavy weapons," one resident remembered. "The occupants were advisers and support personnel, not killers."

The barrage eventually ended, but due to apparent confusion among the sappers waiting to attack, five minutes ticked by, time enough for the men inside to gather up their weapons and prepare to fight. They beat back two assaults. North Vietnamese troops took up positions in the surrounding buildings and prepared to wait the allies out.

By eight in the morning, only the ARVN headquarters within the Citadel and the MACV compound on the south side of the river remained in allied hands, and both were under siege, while a vast gold-starred, blue-and-red NLF flag flew above the Imperial Palace, a sign that unlike any other South Vietnamese city, Hue had actually fallen to the enemy. As if to prove it, NLF political officers with megaphones accompanied by armed guards moved through the streets of the Citadel reading out from pre-prepared lists the names of those they considered enemies of the revolution. Those named—denounced as "surviving functionaries of the puppet administration and officers and men of the puppet army who were skulking"—were ordered to report to a certain school. Many would never be seen again.

The Americans in the MACV compound radioed for help. With so many reports of so many attacks in so many places flooding in at once that morning, and unaware that the equivalent of an enemy *division* was now occupying Hue, the base commander at the First Marine Division Forward Headquarters at Phu Bai dispatched a single undermanned company to reinforce the men holding the MACV compound—A Company, First Battalion, First Marines, First Marine Division—Bill Ehrhart's company.

Ehrhart was at the end of his tour and could have stayed back, but he chose to go. "Won't be nothing to do around here with everybody else gone," he explained to his gunnery sergeant. "I'll go nuts sitting around here all alone."

"We loaded into the trucks," he wrote, "and rumbled into the darkness up Highway One toward Hué, eight miles north." Highway One was the old colonial highway that ran from Saigon all the way north to close to the Chinese border. During the French war, the stretch near Hue was called "the Street Without Joy" because so many convoys had been ambushed there. It was about to live up to its reputation once again.

The Marines, joined by four tanks, rolled past half a dozen abandoned ARVN tanks stopped earlier that morning by enemy fire as they had tried and failed to blast their way to the embattled force trapped within the Citadel.

"Less than an hour after we had awakened," Ehrhart wrote, "with dawn just breaking, the convoy entered the south side of the city, the silhouettes of two- and three-story buildings visible ahead of us. We passed a Shell gasoline station. And then all hell broke loose."

Enemy soldiers dug in close by on either side of the road behind walls and inside buildings and on rooftops, let loose a withering fusillade that struck against the sleepy convoy with the force of a sledgehammer crushing a cockroach: automatic weapons, small-arms, rockets, recoilless rifles, mortars, grenades. Everything. All at once. Men began to topple over in the trucks. . . . Marines scrambled pell-mell out of the trucks, diving wildly for anything that offered cover. . . . I lay in a ditch, pushing the barrel of my rifle up over the . . . top and firing wildly, not daring to look for a target, only trying to make somebody duck out there."

A second company was sent to relieve them, armed with two self-propelled twin 40mm guns. Together, they fought their way out of the ambush and along the street to the besieged compound. Ten Marines died getting there, and thirty more were wounded. "I could never imagine there could be so many NVA in the whole world," Ehrhart recalled. "And they had to be NVA. The Viet Cong never had anything like this: the recoilless rifles, the heavy machine guns; not in these numbers. The mythical NVA were real, and they were all in Hue City, and they were all trying to kill me."

Marine headquarters still had no idea of the odds they faced. Some of the exhausted men were ordered to keep going, to cross the Perfume River and break through to the ARVN compound. Their commander warned that he had too few men. He was ordered to "go anyway." He tried. As his men stepped onto the Nguyen Hoang Bridge, a machine gun at the other end opened

up. Ten men fell. Lance Corporal Lester A. Tully made it across and hurled a grenade that knocked out the machine gun. (He would be awarded a Silver Star.) Two platoons followed him but came under withering fire from what their commander remembered as "virtually every building in Hue City" north of the river. He had no alternative but to pull back across the river. Forty-nine men had been lost. Nothing had been gained.

As the scale of the struggle grew clearer, reinforcements began to arrive. The ARVN were to clear the Citadel while the Marines drove the enemy from the New City. "I could feel a knot developing in my stomach," one Marine captain remembered as

ABOVE Marines take up positions inside a house on the south side of the Perfume River. It would take five days of house-to-house combat to fight their way four blocks between the MACV advisers' compound and the municipal hospital. "In each garden," an eyewitness recalled, "from street to street, everywhere—manholes, walls, or anything that was somewhat a good place to hide—contained soldiers." **OPPOSITE** Marines take cover from sniper fire in Hue. "On the worst days no one expected to get through it alive," Michael Herr wrote. "They all knew how bad it was, the novelty of fighting in a city had become a nasty joke, everyone wanted to get wounded."

his unit entered the battle. "Not so much from fear—though a hell of a lot of fear was there—but because we were new to this type of situation. We were accustomed to jungles and open rice fields, and now we would be fighting like it was Europe during World War II. One of the beautiful things about the Marines is that they adapt quickly, but we were going to take a number of casualties learning some basic lessons in this experience."

"It was ugly, ugly fighting," Ehrhart remembered. "But it was exhilarating. I was scared utterly witless—but it was the greatest adrenaline high I'd ever experienced: to have real armed targets to shoot at; to be able to say, 'We're going to go over there and take that house away from them,' and then proceed to do it—and to stay there and hold it. Instead of turning around immediately and going back where you came from; at last, to be able to fight back!"

Slowly, the Marines—now reinforced by several more companies—pushed farther and farther out from the MACV compound. Small squads moved from house to house. They blew holes through walls with rocket launchers or recoilless rifles, then sent in fire teams to clear the structure room by room, firing M16s and lobbing grenades.

On the sixth day, Ehrhart was in a second-floor bedroom of a former official's residence when an enemy B-40 rocket hit within a few feet of him. "I was utterly stone deaf," he recalled. "Under any other circumstances I would have been evacuated. But I could see, I could walk, and I could shoot. So I stayed."

The fighting continued. Civilians, driven from their homes by one side or the other, sought sanctuary wherever they could find it. Hundreds made their way to the campus of the University of Hue, filling its dormitories and classrooms, stairwells and hallways with frightened men, women, and children. "They had all gone there to get the hell away from having grenades thrown into their living rooms," Ehrhart remembered. "And one of the guys comes in and says, 'I found this girl who will fuck us all for C rations.' And I'm thinking, 'Wait, we're in the middle of this big battle.' But I'm nineteen years old and my buddies are going to. And once again I demonstrated to myself how little courage I actually had. I've lived with it ever since, but I did it because I

wasn't going to say, 'You guys, we shouldn't do something like this.' Even more than the killings, it's the thing I think I'm most ashamed of when I think back on the time I spent in Vietnam. I think it's because my mother's a woman, my wife's a woman, my daughter's a woman. Somebody gets shot? Not a good thing. You see somebody running away? It could've been a VC. But that woman? Nah. I had every opportunity to say no."

The next day, in the midst of still another firefight, a lieutenant in a jeep pulled up in front of the building from which Ehrhart and five fellow Marines were firing at the enemy. "Come on, Ehrhart!" he shouted. "Chopper's on the LZ right now. You want to go home or not?" From the helicopter that lifted him up and away from the ruined, smoking city he could see a farmer and his water buffalo working a flooded field and women in conical hats carrying twin baskets hurrying along between the paddies as if there were no war.

Back in Hue, the fighting went on. When the Marines had finally cleared the south side of the river, they turned their attention to the Citadel. By then, John Laurence noted,

ABOVE Marines peer into what's left of the nineteenth-century Citadel. On February 10, with the south side of the river more or less secure, they'd been ordered to cross the river and go to the aid of the ARVN forces fighting to regain the Old City.

the Americans and North Vietnamese were like two exhausted boxers in the final round of an ugly fight that

had already been decided, trying to hang on long enough to get in a few last shots without getting killed, waiting without hope for someone to stop it. Each day the Marines advanced a few more meters across the burned ground, and each day the two sides sent back another load of battle dead. . . . And yet after twenty days, the Marines in Hue seemed to have adjusted to the noise and smoke and death. To most of them, it had become normal, a background to the blighted landscape. When shells came, some of them no longer bothered to duck.

The weather added to the grimness. "The days were cold and dark," Laurence continued.

Monsoon rain fell on the city in a slow drizzle that kept everything but the barrels of the guns cool and wet. Fog crept in and cast a blanket of mist across the blasted houses, broken walls, and fractured trees of no-man's-land. Low clouds cut the light and trapped the lingering smoke from burning rubble and campfires. The Citadel was enveloped in a wet gloom that gathered early and haunted the morning like the memory of a bad dream.

From the roof of the ARVN headquarters, Army Captain George W. Smith watched the relentless allied bombardment of enemy positions within the Citadel: "It was almost like watching a thunderstorm. I could see the explosions a split second before I heard the rumble. Chunks of mortar flew a hundred feet in the air after the delay fuses exploded and then fell to earth in all directions. Training my binoculars to the east, I could see the lightning flashes of the naval guns of the U.S. Seventh Fleet. The naval shells sounded like freight trains roaring past a crossing on some midwestern plain. . . . It was later reported that the U.S. Navy had fired over 4,700 shells into Hue and surrounding areas. . . . When the naval guns were not firing, the heavily loaded Skyraiders and jets roared in with high-explosive bombs, napalm, and tear gas. It was hard to imagine anyone surviving this continuous bombardment—but the enemy soldiers did. In

ABOVE Within the ruined Citadel, exhausted Marines barely register that napalm is being dropped just over the horizon. Initially, hoping to preserve the former imperial capital, Saigon forbade air and artillery attacks. But it quickly became clear that without them, the NLF could never be blasted from their positions, and much of the city, old as well as new, was reduced to rubble.

ABOVE After twenty-six days of combat, the South Vietnamese flag again flies above a battered Citadel gate.

fact, some of them popped out of their holes to fire rounds at the departing planes in a show of defiance, . . . a glowing testament not only to the enemy's fortitude and resilience but to the builders of this nineteenth-century fortress as well."

Harry Hue and his Hac Bao company seemed everywhere at once. They hurled back repeated assaults on ARVN headquarters, escorted the first South Vietnamese relief force into the Citadel, and led a successful fight to retake the airstrip, flew from place to place plugging gaps in the defense perimeter, and broke the encirclement of two different South Vietnamese units. On February 22, Hue and his men were given the honor of retaking the palace compound. "It was an emotional moment," he recalled. "There were a lot of enemy bodies lying around . . . but there were no enemy soldiers." A few months later, Harry

Hue—now a captain—would be awarded first the Bronze Star and then the Silver Star, the highest award for valor that can be bestowed by the United States on an allied soldier.

Finally, on March 2, with the flag of South Vietnam once again flying above the Imperial Palace, the fight for Hue was officially declared at an end. Two hundred and twenty-one Americans had died and another 1,364 had been badly enough wounded to be medevaced from the battlefield. The ARVN had lost 384 dead and another 1,800 wounded—and 30 more were listed as missing in action. The allies estimated that 5,000 enemy troops had been killed fighting within the city and another 3,000 in the surrounding countryside.

The surviving North Vietnamese and local NLF fighters had finally been permitted by their commanders to withdraw from the city and return to their hidden jungle bases. Nguyen Thi Hoa, the young woman who had acted as a spy and guide for North Vietnamese troops before the battle, retreated with them.

She had initially been occupied with carrying the wounded away from the battlefield, but as the fighting went on she had found herself and her comrades fully engaged. "When the Americans charged, if we didn't shoot them, surely, they would shoot us," she recalled. "So I had to shoot first. When I found them, I shot them. An American, not that far away, about ten feet, opened fire. So I raised my AK. I aimed. And I dropped him." She hadn't wanted to leave the area. "We wanted to stay in our villages," she remembered, "but we had to follow orders. The retreat was terrible." Fighter planes strafed them. Navy shells rained down on the road. "We had to hide during the day. We withdrew a bit, then hid, then continued to withdraw." When they finally reached their forest sanctuaries, food was scarce: "A very small bowl of rice once a day with tree ferns and weeds foraged from the forest. 'If you just want to follow a happy road,' we used to say, 'you shouldn't be a revolutionary.'"

In the city they had left behind, some 6,000 civilians had died. Of the city's 135,000 residents, 110,000 were homeless, and stood by helplessly as ARVN troops—and a scattering of Americans—systematically looted the abandoned buildings. "All remnants of shops were emptied," a Dutch resident of the city remembered. Looters were everywhere, "dragging bags of rice, furniture, tables, chairs, and an ancestral altar, clothing, radio sets, anything that could be carried. . . . Two-and-a-half-ton army trucks were parked in front of the ruined houses, warehouses, and stores, and quickly loaded with rice, furniture, refrigerators, desks, motor scooters, bicycles, anything at all."

In the end, little was left of Hue, one reporter wrote, except "ruins, divided by a river."

ABOVE After the battle, the people of Hue stream back through the Citadel's pulverized south wall to pick up the pieces of their lives. "Hue has nothing now, nothing," a medical student said. "It is not only the loss of our buildings and monuments, it is the loss of our spirit. It is gone."

A SMEAR AGAINST THE REVOLUTION

In early March, two weeks after Hue had finally been recaptured, Second Lieutenant Phil Gioia of the 82nd Airborne Division was leading his platoon along the sandy bank of the Perfume River on the outskirts of the ruined city, looking for caches of weapons that might have been buried by the enemy before the battle began.

Gioia's sergeant, Reuben Torres, saw something sticking up from the ground. He thought it was a root. It turned out to be an elbow. The Americans got out their entrenching tools and began to dig. The smell quickly became unbearable, even when the men put on protective masks. Some men vomited.

At first, Gioia and his squad assumed they'd found a spot where the retreating enemy had buried their dead comrades. "But when we found the first body, it was a woman," he recalled. "She was wearing a white blouse and black

trousers. She had her hands tied behind her back. She'd been shot in the back of the head. Next to her was a child, who'd also been shot. The next person to come up was another woman. At that point it was clear that this wasn't the enemy." Gioia's men uncovered 123 bodies in two shallow ditches, men, women, and children. Some, their mouths filled with sand, appeared to have been buried alive.

Over the months that followed the battle other mass graves around the city would yield other bodies—at least 2,800 of them—including Catholic priests and Buddhist monks, civilian volunteers from Canada, the Philippines, and the United States, schoolteachers, and South Vietnamese government and military officials, their wives, and their children.

Hanoi would always deny that innocent civilians had been killed at Hue. And it became almost an article of faith

among some antiwar protestors that the killings at Hue had either never taken place at all, had been fabricated to serve Saigon's propaganda purposes, or had simply been the spontaneous acts of a few retreating soldiers bent on vengeance.

But evidence subsequently showed that many of these deaths had been systematic rather than spontaneous. In the first hours of the communist occupation of the city, NLF cadre went from house to house with carefully prepared lists of names of "blood debtors"— men and women opposed to the revolution and therefore deserving of revenge. Many were tried before hastily assembled "people's courts" that meted out on-the-spot punishments ranging from ostracism to execution. Some were shot publicly to serve as object lessons; others were led away and killed just out of sight. Still others were murdered late in the battle, because NLF fighters feared if they were allowed to live they would betray their captors once Saigon was back in charge. "When our forces withdrew from Hue, if they'd released the people they'd arrested, their former prisoners would have denounced the revolutionaries," the soldier and historian Nguyen Ngoc remembered. "I don't know whether the order to kill them came from the local commanders or higher up. But they killed the people they'd arrested. Some had worked for the South Vietnamese government or for the Americans, but there were people who were wrongly arrested, too, maybe because of some personal grievance, and they were all killed. This is a smear against the revolution, a stain on the revolution's record."

OPPOSITE Second Lieutenant Phil Gioia (foreground) and men from his platoon
TOP Garbed in mourning white, widows grieve at a mass reburial of some of those executed by the communists at Hue.
RIGHT Workers unearth bodies from one of at least nineteen mass graves discovered in and around the city. A communist report on "the victory of our armed forces in Hue" boasted that while the city had been "the place where reactionary spirit had existed for over ten years . . . it took us only a short time to drain it to its root."

MIRED IN STALEMATE

IN THE MIDST OF THE FIGHTING in Hue, some marines had looked up to see an unexpected visitor: Walter Cronkite, the anchor of the *CBS Evening News* and the most trusted newsman on television, wearing a helmet and flak jacket and carrying a notepad, picking his way among the ruined buildings, interviewing infantrymen and officers, trying to understand what was happening.

Cronkite was no stranger to war. During World War II he had landed with the first U.S. troops in North Africa and Normandy, parachuted into Holland, flown in B-17 bombers over Berlin, and covered the Battle of the Bulge. (The fighting in Hue reminded him of the fight for Bastogne, he said.) He had first visited Vietnam in 1965, shortly after the first Marines landed there, and came back applauding the men who had sent them. Theirs had been "a courageous decision," he said. "The communist advance must be stopped in Asia and . . . guerrilla war as a means to a political end must be finally discouraged." What impressed him most was the notion of simultaneously waging a war and building a nation, something no one had ever dared try before.

Nine million Americans tuned in to hear him every evening, in part because of his reputation for scrupulous objectivity; his personal opinions, he often said, had no place on the *Evening News*. He had loyally backed Morley Safer when he came under attack for his early report showing Marines burning a village, and he was unflinching in his willingness to include in his nightly news reports combat footage of a kind rarely seen by the general public during World War II. "In a war situation every American ought to suffer as much as the guy on the front lines," he believed. "We ought to see this. We ought to be *forced* to see it." But, as another veteran CBS newsman recalled, Cronkite remained one of the "World War II guys" who thought it "unseemly to not be 100 percent behind the troops," and he had been summoned to the White House three times so that President Johnson and other officials could assure him that steady progress was being made. "They kept telling me there was light at the end of the tunnel," he remembered.

Tet changed everything. "What the hell is going on?" Cronkite had asked when the first reports came in. "I thought we were winning the war." Eleven days after the offensive began, he and a CBS crew landed in Saigon to see for themselves.

General Westmoreland assured him that the communists had suffered a great defeat; even in Hue, he claimed, the enemy was on the run. The next day, Cronkite set out to see for himself. He and his crew tried first to go to Khe Sanh but were turned away; it was thought too dangerous. Instead, they joined a convoy of trucks headed for Hue. There, it quickly became clear that Westmoreland had misled him. No one was on the run. The Marines were still fighting house to house; incoming artillery shook the building in which he and other reporters lay curled up on the floor trying to snatch a few minutes' sleep. When Cronkite and his companions left for their next stop they shared their chopper with a dozen dead Marines in body bags.

Before returning to Saigon, Cronkite spent an evening at the Phu Bai combat base with General Abrams, Westmoreland's deputy commander and an old acquaintance from the war in Europe. Abrams was "remarkably candid" about the shock the offensive had been and the damage it had done, Cronkite recalled, but when the general and his staff began to discuss what to do next he was appalled: "It was a highly and brutally technical discussion of firepower and kill ratios and the like. How, in effect, we could kill more Vietnamese." "It was sickening to me," Cronkite remembered. "They were talking strategy and tactics with no consideration of the bigger job of pacifying and restoring the country. This had come to be total war, not a counterinsurgency. The ideas I had talked about in 1965 were gone."

Back in Saigon and about to fly home, he dined on the roof of the ten-story Caravelle Hotel with three CBS correspondents who'd been covering the war—Peter Kalischer, Robert Schakne, and John Laurence. Again, he'd been told Saigon was secure, though four of its nine districts were still officially considered "red"—unsafe and off-limits—and he could see black smoke rising from the burning docks downriver and helicopter gunships pouring fire into areas on the city's outskirts said still to be harboring the NLF. He kept asking how it could have happened. MACV had told him Tet had been an American and South Vietnamese victory because so many enemy soldiers had been killed. "I acknowledged the huge numbers of deaths," John Laurence said, "but pointed out that the northerners would replace their losses and come back at us again. And again, and again. And the sooner we realized the fact that we were not going to win this fucking war, the better for everyone, especially the Vietnamese and the Americans who were being butchered by the thousands. For no good purpose." On the way to the airport, Cronkite's driver had to take a circuitous route to avoid enemy mortar fire.

At ten o'clock on the evening of February 27, Eastern Standard Time, twenty million Americans tuned in to watch an hour-long Cronkite special, "Report from Vietnam." At its end, he did something he'd never done before: he stepped forward to express his own views on the Vietnam War and America's role in it. He was careful to say that his remarks were "speculative, personal, subjective." "We have been too often disappointed by the optimism of the American leaders, both in Vietnam and

Washington, to have faith any longer in the silver linings they find in the darkest clouds. They may be right, that Hanoi's winter-spring offensive has been forced by the communist realization that they could not win the longer war of attrition, and that the communists hope that any success in the offensive will improve their position for eventual negotiations. It would improve their position, and it would also require our realization that we should have had all along, that any negotiations must be that—negotiations, not the dictation of peace terms. For it seems now more certain than ever that the bloody experience of Vietnam is to end in a stalemate. This summer's almost certain standoff will either end in real give-and-take negotiations or terrible escalation; and for every means we have to escalate, the enemy can match us, and that applies to invasion of the North, the use of nuclear weapons, or the mere commitment of one hundred, or two hundred, or three hundred thousand more American troops to the battle. And with each escalation, the world comes closer to the brink of cosmic disaster.

"To say that we are closer to victory today is to believe, in the face of the evidence, the optimists who have been wrong in the past. To suggest we are on the edge of defeat is to yield to unreasonable pessimism. To say that we are mired in stalemate seems the only realistic, if unsatisfactory, conclusion. On the off chance that military and political analysts are right, in the next few months we must test the enemy's intentions, in case this is indeed his last big gasp before negotiations. But it is increasingly clear to this reporter that the only rational way out then will be to negotiate, not as victors, but as an honorable people who

lived up to their pledge to defend democracy and did the best they could."

President Johnson was traveling that evening and unable to watch the report. The well-worn story that he said, "If I've lost Cronkite, I've lost the country," or some variant of it, is probably apocryphal. But George Christian, the president's press secretary, remembered that "shock waves rolled through the government," nonetheless.

I SHALL NOT SEEK, AND WILL NOT ACCEPT

THE INITIAL IMPACT of the Tet Offensive on American opinion was mixed. Neither Walter Cronkite's public doubts about the war, nor night after night of grisly combat footage on the evening news, nor the widely reproduced image of the commander of South Vietnam's National Police executing a bound prisoner in the street initially appeared to damage American support. Just before Tet, according to George Gallup, 45 percent

ABOVE Walter Cronkite (with microphone) and a CBS camera crew interview Lieutenant Colonel Marcus J. Gravel, commander of the First Battalion, First Marines during the battle of Hue. "I was assured by our leaders back in Saigon that we had the enemy just where we wanted him," Cronkite remembered. "Tell that to the Marines, I thought."

of his respondents believed U.S. entry into the war had been a "mistake"; immediately afterward, that number remained unchanged. More Americans still saw themselves as "hawks" than "doves"; support for continued bombing actually rose from 71 to 78 percent, while the numbers favoring a bombing halt fell from 26 to 15 percent.

Most Americans did not yet want to give up on a war in which American boys were so heavily engaged, but Tet did badly shake their faith in how the president was *waging* that war. Disapproval of his handling of it rose from 47 to 63 percent in February, and would rise still further in March.

The administration continued to insist that the Tet Offensive had been "a devastating defeat for the communists." The basic assumptions on which the North Vietnamese mounted their offensive had been proved wrong, after all. Hanoi's leaders had assumed that the ARVN would crumble, that South Vietnamese soldiers would come over to their side. Instead, not a single unit defected. The civilian populace Hanoi had expected to rise up may have been dissatisfied with their government, but they had little sympathy for communism, and when the fighting began, most people simply hid in their homes to escape the fury in the streets.

General Vo Nguyen Giap, who had opposed the offensive and did not return from Hungary to resume his post as supreme commander of the armed forces and minister of defense until it was well under way, later admitted that it had been a "costly lesson, paid for in blood and bone." "Giap wasn't the only one to see that the Tet Offensive was a defeat," the journalist Huy Duc said. "Many members of the General Staff, and certainly the generals who commanded troops in the field, shared General Giap's point of view because they had suffered unimaginable losses. Several very high-ranking officers of the People's Army surrendered. That had never happened before. No units emerged intact. Some companies existed only on paper, because they had just a couple of soldiers still alive."

Of the 84,000 NLF and North Vietnamese troops who are estimated to have taken part in the Tet Offensive, more than half are thought to have been killed, wounded, or captured, perhaps 20 percent of the total communist forces then stationed or living in the South. Nguyen Van Tong, the political officer who had helped win the NLF Main Force victory at Binh Gia, watched in sorrow during Tet as his comrades tried and failed to take an army training center in Saigon; he remembered that his Ninth Division "lost over three thousand soldiers killed, and around eight or nine thousand soldiers wounded. Up to 1968 we had only southerners. However, after the first phase of Tet, we had to ask for replacements from the North."

"The American military command celebrated the Tet Offensive as a victory," John Laurence remembered. "They said, 'They finally came at us, and we blew them away.' Which was basically true. But the administration had been telling the American public for months that the war was being won; that the NLF and the North Vietnamese were ground down to such an extent that we could see the end of the war—a victory. So when Tet hit, it contradicted everything that the administration and the Saigon country team had been telling the American public."

"Despite their retrospective claims to the contrary, the reaction of our most senior military leaders approached panic," Clark Clifford remembered. General Harold K. Johnson, the Army chief of staff, admitted that "we suffered a loss, there can be no doubt about it." Robert Komer reported that pacification had been drastically undercut: "In terms of hamlets, we lost 38 percent of our pre-Tet holdings"; just 4,500 of South Vietnam's 12,500 hamlets were now "secure"; nearly 3 million South Vietnamese were no longer even nominally loyal to Saigon. General Westmoreland's hope that the ARVN would soon be able to take over the bulk of the fighting had been dashed. South Vietnamese troops had generally performed well in meeting the Tet attacks, but the desertion rate was high, they had lost more than nine thousand men, and the average battalion strength was just 50 percent. It would take at least six months to get them back into the shape they'd been in before Tet.

"Well," the president complained to his advisers, "it looks as if you all have counseled, advised, consulted, and then—as usual—placed the monkey on my back again. I don't like what I am smelling from those cables from Vietnam." At a February 8 meeting that included the Joint Chiefs, he wanted to know how the United States was going to deal with further attacks. (The chiefs' initial suggestion had been stepped-up airstrikes on new targets around Hanoi and Haiphong, even though month after month of bombing had obviously had little effect on the enemy's ability to mount an offensive in the South.) Johnson wanted to be sure Westmoreland had all the men he needed, and wondered if he should call up the Army Reserve and even ask Congress for a declaration of war.

Johnson's apparent willingness to consider taking unprecedented action spurred Joint Chiefs Chairman Wheeler into action. Since 1965, he and the other chiefs had pushed for a wider war—more frequent and less-restricted airstrikes on the North, incursions into Laos and Cambodia to destroy enemy sanctuaries and cut off reinforcements and resupply, even a possible landing in North Vietnam itself. Beyond that, Wheeler believed that U.S. forces overseas were stretched too thin to deal simultaneously with potential crises in Korea or Berlin or elsewhere. Up to now, their repeated efforts to persuade the president to replenish them by calling up the strategic reserve had failed. But now, if Westmoreland were to request enough more troops, Wheeler thought, he might be able to force Johnson's hand.

Westmoreland fell in line, sending a cable to Wheeler whose tone seemed almost diametrically opposed to all the optimism he'd expressed immediately after Tet. Whereas he'd claimed then that the offensive was merely a "diversion" and a "last gasp," that he had matters "well in hand," he now said that since the enemy "had launched a major campaign signaling a change of strategy of protracted war to one of quick military/political victory during the American election year . . . we are in a new ballgame where we face a determined, highly disciplined enemy, fully mobilized to achieve a quick victory. He is in the process of throwing in all his military chips to 'go for broke.' We cannot permit this. I need reinforcements of combat elements. Time is of the essence. A setback is fully possible."

To meet the emergency, the president agreed to send 10,500 men right away, but still balked at calling up the reserve.

Wheeler flew to Saigon. The report he submitted on his return only added to the sense of crisis. It now turned out that the enemy offensive had been a "near thing." Nor was there any reason to believe it had "run its course." The enemy's determination appeared to be "unshaken." By contrast, South Vietnam's government, suffering from low morale and the demands of a flood of new refugees, was incapable of meeting fresh attacks. "In many areas pacification is at a halt. The Vietcong are prowling the countryside and it is now a question of which side moves fastest to gain control. The outcome is not at all clear. I visualize much heavy fighting ahead. . . . General Westmoreland does not have theater reserve."

For all those reasons, he was now requesting 205,000 fresh troops in three phases—108,000 by May 1, 42,000 by September 1, and 55,000 more by year's end—plus an additional call-up of 280,000 reservists. (The second and third tranches would be used to rebuild the strategic reserve unless communist gains in Vietnam required their presence.)

The scale of the request astonished the administration, Clifford recalled, and the president "was as worried as I [had] ever seen him." Johnson now faced a terrible dilemma: If he agreed to the generals' request, he risked greatly expanding the Americanization of the conflict during an election year and at a time when the voters' confidence in his handling of the war was already declining. But if he rejected it, he could be accused of going back on his pledge to provide everything his field commander asked for while the war would likely drag on as it had for the last three years with no victory in sight.

Exhausted, unsure what to do, and impatient with his generals, who seemed incapable of coming up with new ideas, the president asked Clifford to form a task force and begin what Dean Rusk would call an "A to Z Reassessment" of the war effort. "Give me the lesser of evils," Johnson told Clifford. "Give me your recommendations."

The president liked and trusted Clark Clifford. Washington's best-known, best-paid corporate lawyer, he was courtly, persuasive, discreet, and hugely knowledgeable about how things were done in Washington. As counsel to Harry Truman, he'd helped persuade his chief to adopt George Kennan's concept of containment of the Soviet Union, drafted the legislation that brought both the CIA and the Department of Defense into being, and helped engineer Truman's come-from-behind victory in 1948. He'd supervised the presidential transition for John Kennedy,

ABOVE Using a specially prepared terrain map of the Khe Sanh area installed in the White House Situation Room, Walt Rostow explains the situation to President Johnson and Air Force General Robert N. Ginsburgh of the National Security Council staff. Even after the Tet Offensive, General Westmoreland continued to tell the commander in chief, "I still see the enemy position in Khe Sanh as the greatest threat."

and chaired his Foreign Intelligence Advisory Board after the Bay of Pigs. He was among the first people Johnson asked to see after Kennedy's assassination, directed his election campaign in 1964, and had been offered the Defense Department because Johnson wanted someone at the Pentagon who could get along better with the military than Robert McNamara had. To be sure, in 1965 Clifford had warned the president that Vietnam "could be a quagmire," and he had sided with George Ball in opposing General Westmoreland's initial request for tens of thousands of troops that same year. ("If we lose fifty thousand men it will ruin us," he'd told Johnson then; far better to "moderate our position" and seek a way out.) But once Johnson had committed to a ground war, he'd been a self-styled "full supporter of our policy," convinced that the best way out of Vietnam was to continue to "hit them hard."

That was about to change.

"Politely but firmly," using his status as a supposedly naive newcomer, Clifford seized the opportunity to ask the military fundamental questions that hadn't been asked since the ground war began to see if they could justify the troop request. In his view, they could not. Notes were not taken, but Clifford later reconstructed the gist of those conversations.

Will 205,000 more men do the job? *They could give no assurance that they would.*

If 205,000 might not be sufficient, how many more troops might be needed—and when? *There was no way of his knowing.*

Can the enemy respond with a buildup of its own? *He could.*

Can bombing stop the war? *No. Bombing was inflicting heavy personnel and materiel losses, but by itself it would not stop the war.*

Will stepping up the bombing decrease American casualties? *Very little, if at all. Our casualties are a result of the intensity of the ground fighting in the South.*

How long must we keep on sending our men and carrying the main burden of combat? *We do not know when, if ever, the South Vietnamese will be ready to carry the main burden of the war.*

Clark Clifford, Dean Rusk, and Lyndon Johnson confer in the Oval Office, March 26, 1968. Clifford, not yet installed at the Department of Defense, was already growing skeptical about the possibility of victory in Vietnam. "How do we gain support for major programs if we have told people things are going well?" he asked. "How do we avoid creating the feeling that we are pounding troops down a rathole? What is our purpose? What is achievable?"

This exchange and many others like it disturbed me greatly. The military was unable to provide an acceptable rationale for the troops increase. Moreover, when I asked for a presentation of their plan for attaining victory, I was told there was no plan for victory in the historic American sense. Although I kept my feelings private, I was appalled: nothing had prepared me for the weakness of the military's case.

The Clifford task force's report to the president, delivered on March 4, recommended that he send Westmoreland an additional 22,000 troops on an emergency basis and urged him to approve a call-up of 262,000 men to replenish the strategic reserve. But it also suggested that a final decision about the full request be delayed until the completion of a "complete review of our political and strategic options in Vietnam."

Clifford told the president that the new request had brought him to a "watershed." "Do you continue down the same road of more troops, more guns, more planes, more ships?" he asked Johnson. "Do you go on killing more Viet Cong and more North Vietnamese? There are grave doubts that we have made the type of progress we had hoped to have made by this time. As we build up our forces, they build up theirs. The result is simply that we are fighting now at a higher level of intensity. . . . We seem to have gotten caught in a sinkhole. We put in more, they match it, put in more, they match it. . . . I see more and more fighting with more and more casualties on the U.S. side, and no end in sight." With a weak government in Saigon and a badly depleted ARVN force, there was "no reason to believe" that 205,000 more men—"or double or triple that quantity"— could drive the communists from South Vietnam.

On March 10, a front-page *New York Times* story by Hedrick Smith and Neil Sheehan headlined "Westmoreland Requests 206,000 More Men, Stirring Debate in Administration" laid the ongoing argument within the administration bare. Worse, from the administration's point of view, were anonymous quotes from "high administration officials." One said Vietnam was a "bottomless pit"; another confessed that Tet had shown him and his colleagues that "all we thought we had constructed was built on sand."

That same day, a fresh Gallup poll revealed that 49 percent of Americans, more than ever before, now thought the United States should never have become ensnared in Vietnam; only a third believed progress was being made in the war, down from 50 percent during the public relations offensive of the previous fall.

More and more Americans were now asking if the United States had been winning the war—if Tet had been such a disaster for the enemy—why were still more men needed? Dean

Rusk was called before the Senate Foreign Relations Committee and grilled for eleven hours. "We are in the wrong place," Senate Majority Leader Mike Mansfield said, "and we are fighting the wrong kind of war." Senator Frank Church of Idaho warned that the U.S. seemed "poised to plunge still deeper into Asia, where huge populations wait to engulf us and legions of Americans are being beckoned to their graves." One hundred and thirty-nine members of Congress sponsored a resolution demanding a complete congressional review of U.S. policy in Vietnam. The editors of *Newsweek* declared that "the war cannot be won by military means without tearing apart the whole fabric of national and international relations. . . . Accordingly, unless it is prepared to indulge in the ultimate, horrifying escalation—the use of nuclear weapons— . . . the U.S. must accept the fact that it will never be able to achieve decisive military superiority." NBC anchor Frank McGee warned that "the enemy now has the initiative, he has dramatically enlarged the area of combat. . . . [T]he war as the administration had defined it is being lost."

On the evening of March 12, President Johnson watched the returns come in from the New Hampshire Democratic presidential primary, where he was facing an unexpected challenge from Eugene McCarthy. Johnson had dismissed his challenger as "the type of fellow who did little harm and damn little good . . . always more interested in producing a laugh than a law in the Senate." And the most recent poll had suggested he would crush his upstart rival, two to one. But the president was not a declared candidate, so the president's supporters had had to depend on a massive write-in campaign. They didn't get it. Johnson won just 49.6 percent of the vote against 41.4 percent for his opponent. The result was generally reported as evidence of growing antiwar feeling—though many of those who had voted against the president actually wanted him to prosecute the war more vigorously.

Johnson tried to laugh it off. "The New Hampshire primary," he said, "is the only race . . . where a candidate can claim 20 percent is a landslide and 40 percent is a mandate, and 60 percent is unanimous." But he knew he was in trouble, and there was more to come.

Ever since he had inherited the presidency, Johnson had both feared and hated the late president's brother, Robert, whom he privately called "a grandstanding little runt." The feeling was mutual: Kennedy saw Johnson as a usurper, could not bear to call him "president," considered him "mean, bitter, vicious—an animal in many ways." Kennedy had left Johnson's cabinet in 1964 to run for the Senate from New York and had been distancing himself from the president's Vietnam policy ever since. He accused Johnson of transforming his brother's limited guerrilla war into an all-out one, called for peace negotiations even

if they resulted in a "compromise government," and denounced American bombing of the North.

The Tet Offensive had intensified Kennedy's antiwar feelings. It had "finally shattered the mask of official illusion," he said, because it had shown that "no part or person of South Vietnam was secure." He confessed that he had himself once been one of those who had reported progress toward victory when none was really being made. But he was no longer able to pretend that it served the interest of the people of South Vietnam to devastate their country and wage war in their streets. Nor was it in the interest of the United States to conduct a war so cruel and so destructive as to cause "our oldest friends to ask, more in sorrow than in anger, what has happened to America?"

Antiwar friends and supporters had repeatedly urged Kennedy to challenge Johnson for the presidency and he had always turned them down, fearing that the cause was hopeless, that voters would simply think he was acting out of anti-Johnson pique, that he might fatally divide the Democratic Party. But accelerating events and McCarthy's unexpected success changed his mind, and now, on March 16, just four days after the New Hampshire primary, Robert F. Kennedy declared his candidacy for the presidency

The next day, before a packed field house at Kansas State University, he made his case against the war. "Every night," he said, "we watch horrors on the evening news. Violence spreads inexorably across the nation, filling our streets and crippling our lives." The administration had no answer to the war—"none but the ever-expanding use of military force . . . in a conflict where military force has failed to solve anything. Can we ordain to ourselves the awful majesty of God—to decide what cities and villages are to be destroyed, who will live and who will die, and who will join the refugees wandering in a desert of our creation? . . . In the next months we are going to decide what the country will stand for—and what kind of men we are."

The audience of fifteen thousand exploded in applause. "The field-house sounded as though it was inside Niagara Falls," one reporter wrote. "It was like a soundtrack gone haywire." Polls would soon suggest that Kennedy was more popular than the president.

"It was the thing I feared from the first day of my presidency," Johnson recalled. "Robert Kennedy had openly announced his intention to reclaim the throne in the memory of his brother. And the American people, swayed by the magic of the name, were dancing in the streets. The whole situation was unbearable for me."

His initial reaction to Kennedy's announcement was to dou-

ABOVE Robert Kennedy on the campaign trail. Despite the huge exuberant crowds he drew, one of his advisers wrote, "[h]e always looked so alone . . . standing up by himself on the lid of the trunk of his convertible—so alone, so vulnerable, so fragile you feared he might break."

ble down on Vietnam. The same day the senator launched his campaign in Kansas, the president appeared before the National Farmers Union in Minneapolis: "Your president has come to ask you people, and all the other people of this nation, to join us in *a national effort* to win the war. . . . We will—make no mistake about it—*win*. . . . We are not doing enough to win it the way we are doing it now."

Clark Clifford was worried. With skepticism about the war growing steadily, speeches like that could lose the president the election. In a speech delivered at San Antonio the previous year, the president had expressed willingness to stop "all aerial and naval bombardment when this will lead promptly to productive discussions." The Tet Offensive had seemed to signal that Hanoi was uninterested in talks. But it was suggested that now might be the time to test that notion again.

Dean Rusk agreed: "We could try stopping the bombing during the rainy season in the North. It would not cost us much militarily since our air sorties are way down at that time anyway." He doubted the temporary halt would actually bring about talks, but at least it would make the United States seem less bellicose when the bombing began again.

Clifford took the suggestion much more seriously. He saw it as a possible way out of the war and urged a halt above the 20th parallel, hoping for reciprocal action by the enemy. When the president called him to talk about the upcoming election, he used the opportunity to make his case.

LYNDON JOHNSON: I think what we've got to do . . . is get out of the posture of just being the war candidate that McCarthy has put us in, and Bobby's putting us in, the kids are putting us in, and the papers are putting us in. . . . We've got to come up with something. . . . Our right hand is going after [Hanoi's] jaw . . . on the war front, but we ought to have a peace front, too, simultaneously, and use both fists, not just one, not just fighting with one hand behind us, so that we can say we're the peace candidate, but we're the true peace candidate. We're not the [Neville] Chamberlain peace. We're the Churchill peace. We're not the guy who's going to throw in the towel and let them take Athens, we're the Truman who stands up and finally saves Greece and Turkey from the communists. . . . The course they [Kennedy and McCarthy] have of temporary peace . . . , why, you'd have peace until [the communists] got their government installed, and then, by God, you'd have—

CLARK CLIFFORD: Another war . . .

JOHNSON: A bigger one than ever. Now . . . we've got to come up with something . . .

CLIFFORD: What it is: We're out to win, but we're *not* out to win the war. We're out to win the *peace*.

JOHNSON: That's right.

CLIFFORD: And that's what we give them and . . . our slogan could very well be: "Win the peace with honor," and I think we've got to get that thought over. Now I've been giving some consideration to offers of de-escalation . . .

The president said he might be willing to stop the bombing of Hanoi and Haiphong for "a period that didn't really hurt us." Then, if Hanoi reciprocated by, say, recognizing the neutrality of the DMZ, "we're willing to sit down and pull our troops out of there as soon as the violence subsides and willing, as well, to take our treasure and go back and help rebuild . . . as we did with the Marshall Plan. But we've got to have something new and fresh that goes in there along with the statement that we're going to win."

CLIFFORD: Right. But we have to be very careful what it is we say, "We're going to win."

JOHNSON: That's right.

CLIFFORD: I think we frighten the people if we just end with "and we're going to win." They think, "Well, hell, that means we're just going to keep pouring men in until we win militarily." And that isn't what we're after, really.

JOHNSON: We're not going to get these doves, but we can neutralize the country; that way, it won't follow them, if we can come up with something . . .

CLIFFORD: Yes, that's right, I think you've put your finger on it. We have a posture now in which Kennedy and McCarthy are the peace candidates and President Johnson is the war candidate. Now we must veer away from that, and we can do it.

What was needed, Clifford argued, was a "consistent, far-ranging policy that we don't have."

CLIFFORD: I think we have to keep in mind that maybe before the [Democratic] convention—and if not before the convention, before the election—I think we have to work out some kind of an arrangement where we start some negotiation.

JOHNSON: Well, you can't do that one-way, you know. And these folks [the North Vietnamese] are not wanting to do that.

CLIFFORD: I know.

JOHNSON: They wanted to get rid of us.

CLIFFORD: Yeah, that's right. But I think there's a good chance to do that if [the plan] is prepared properly. . . . All I'm saying is we don't have such a plan, and the major . . . task now is to come up with such a plan, and I intend to give a good part of my time and effort to seeing if we can't come up with such a plan.

The first tangible sign that Johnson was beginning to see that the way the war had been waged was not working, that something new was needed, came on March 23, when he announced that he was summoning General Westmoreland home to become Army chief of staff. It was a promotion, but many saw it as punishment for his having failed to see the Tet Offensive coming. The headline in a Saigon English-language newspaper was "Westmoreland Kicked Upstairs."

The president's speechwriters were at work on a report to the nation, planned for the evening of March 31. Johnson was still blowing hot and cold about the proposed bombing pause. Eager to nudge him closer to that strategy, Clifford suggested that the Wise Men, the veteran cold warriors who had twice urged Johnson to hold steady in Vietnam, return to the White House for another briefing. Clifford knew that Dean Acheson, the senior-most member of the group, had already shifted his view; the military, he'd told the president, "are leading you down the garden path." Discreet phone calls to several other members of the informal group suggested to Clifford that they had also shifted away from their initial hard-line positions.

The group convened at the State Department on March 25 and was briefed by Philip Habib of the State Department, George Carver of the CIA, and Major General William DePuy. They were stunned by what they heard. Tet appeared to have changed everything. How long would it take to win the war? "Maybe five, maybe ten years," they were told. Could victory be won at all? "Not under present circumstances," said Habib. "What would you do?" he was asked. "Stop bombing and negotiate." When DePuy boasted that the enemy had lost more than 80,000 troops during Tet, UN Ambassador Arthur Goldberg asked about the ratio of killed to wounded. Three to one would be a conservative estimate, the general thought. "How many operatives do you think they have operating in the field?" DePuy cited the official MACV figure: 230,000. "Well, gen-

eral," Goldberg said, "I am not a great mathematician, but with 80,000 killed and a wounded ratio of three to one, or 240,000, for a total of 320,000, who the hell are we fighting?"

McGeorge Bundy, who had left the White House to become president of the Ford Foundation, came back for the meeting and summarized the participants' deliberations for the president: "The majority feeling is that we can no longer do the job we set out to do in the time we have left and we must begin to take steps to disengage. When we last met we saw reasons for hope. We hoped then there would be slow but steady progress. Last night and today the picture is not so hopeful."

Johnson did not comment as the Wise Men weighed in, but he took notes. "Can no longer do the job we set out to do. . . . Adjust our course. . . . Move to disengage."

The president was shaken, Clifford remembered: "The men who had helped lay down the basic line of resistance to communism in the world, the statesmen of Berlin and Korea, had decided they had had enough in Vietnam. The price was not

ABOVE At the head of the luncheon table, President Johnson presides over the fateful final meeting of the Wise Men, March 26, 1968. Left to right: General Creighton Abrams, George Ball, Maxwell Taylor, McGeorge Bundy, Dean Rusk, General Matthew Ridgeway, Dean Acheson, the president, General Omar Bradley, Averell Harriman, Clark Clifford, Cyrus Vance, Walt Rostow, and Dean Rusk

commensurate with the goal." The cold war was still worth waging, they believed; China and the Soviet Union still needed to be contained. "Their opposition to the war was based solely on the belief that Vietnam was weakening us at home and in the rest of the world. And they were right."

And there was still more bad news for the president. With no end to the war in sight and the budget deficit soaring, European investors had begun cashing in their dollars for gold. The dollar itself—and the U.S. economy—now seemed under threat.

On the evening of March 31, 1968, seated behind his Oval Office desk and squinting into the television lights, dark rings beneath his eyes, Johnson looked grim and weary. Neil Sheehan, covering the White House then, remembered the toll the war seemed to be taking on him: "His face was a mask of exhaustion and defeat. It was very sad to see the man. He was broken by it."

He wanted to talk of peace, he said. "There is no need to delay the talks that could bring an end to this long and this

ABOVE President Johnson announces a partial bombing halt of North Vietnam—and his own unwillingness to run again for president, March 31, 1968. "I was never surer of any decision I ever made in my life," he told the press afterward." I have 525,000 men whose very lives depend on what I do, and I can't afford to worry about the primaries. Now I will be working full time for those men out there."

bloody war. . . . So tonight, in the hope that this action will lead to early talks, I am taking the first step to de-escalate the conflict . . . unilaterally and at once. . . . I have ordered our aircraft and our naval vessels to make no attacks on North Vietnam, except north of the demilitarized zone, where the continuing enemy buildup directly threatens allied forward positions." Even this limited bombing could come to an early end, he said, "if our restraint is matched by restraint in Hanoi."

He praised the South Vietnamese for showing new signs of resolve—Saigon had ordered the mobilization of 135,000 new troops, extended ARVN tours of duty for the duration of the war, and was about to start drafting eighteen-year-olds. He was sending just 13,500 more men to Vietnam—support troops to back the small emergency combat force he'd recently dispatched. No mention was made of Westmoreland's call for 205,000 men; though no one could have known it then, the era of apparently open-ended escalation was over.

The president asked "all Americans, whatever their personal interest or concern, to guard against divisiveness and all its ugly consequences."

Then, Johnson stunned the nation and the world: "With America's sons in the fields far away, with America's future under challenge right here at home, with our hopes and the world's hopes for peace in the balance every day, I do not believe that I should devote an hour or a day of my time to any personal partisan causes or to any duties other than the awesome duties of this office—the presidency of your country," he said. "Accordingly, I shall not seek, and I will not accept, the nomination of my party for another term as your president."

After thirty-seven years in public life, Lyndon Johnson had become a casualty of his own war. The *Chicago Tribune*—no friend of Democrats or the Democratic president—hailed his decision as "an act of self-abnegation unparalleled in American history." William Fulbright, his old friend turned antagonist, described it as "the act of a very great patriot."

Four days later, Radio Hanoi announced that it was willing to begin talks. The Chinese accused their ally of "disappointing the world" by even considering compromise with the Americans. But the Soviets backed the proposed negotiations, and governments around the globe expressed hope for an end to the fighting.

"The rancorous, near hysterical atmosphere of the Tet offensive has been entirely transformed since the President's speech," a British correspondent wrote from Washington. "Most appear to believe that whoever captures the presidency [this November] will be obliged to end the conflict within a matter of months. How this is to be done or what concessions are to be made is very much a matter of detail."

MERE ANARCHY IS LOOSED UPON THE WORLD

JOHNSON'S WITHDRAWAL from the 1968 presidential contest and Hanoi's willingness to negotiate robbed Robert Kennedy of his most important issue. His rivals for the Democratic nomination were now McCarthy, and—although he would not announce his official candidacy until late April—Vice President Hubert Humphrey. Before he could hope to claim the Democratic nomination and take on the likely Republican nominee, former vice president Richard M. Nixon, whom his brother Jack had defeated eight years earlier, he faced a gauntlet of must-win presidential primaries.

Indiana's was first, and on the evening of April 4 Kennedy was flying to Indianapolis when R. W. Apple of *The New York Times* told him that Dr. Martin Luther King Jr. had been shot in Memphis. Kennedy "sagged," Apple recalled. "His eyes went blank." When they landed, Kennedy learned that King had died. He was scheduled to make an outdoor speech in a black neighborhood. The mayor and the police chief told him not to go. It was too dangerous. His wife begged him to stay away, too.

"I'm going to go there," he said. "That's it." He asked that no police accompany him.

"I'm only going to talk to you for a minute or so this evening," he told the crowd of a thousand waiting in the dark, "because I have some very sad news for all of you, and, I think, sad news for all of our fellow citizens, and people who love peace all over the world, and that is that Martin Luther King was shot and was killed tonight in Memphis, Tennessee."

Some among his listeners moaned. Others began to weep. Kennedy went on, speaking without notes. "He was up there," a reporter remembered, "hunched in his black overcoat, his face gaunt and distressed and full of anguish."

"Martin Luther King dedicated his life to love and to justice for his fellow human beings," Kennedy said, "and he died because of that effort.

"In this difficult day, in this difficult time for the United States, it's perhaps well to ask what kind of a nation we are and what direction we want to move in. For those of you who are black . . . you can be filled with bitterness, with hatred and a desire for revenge. We can move in that direction as a country. In greater polarization—black people amongst black, white people amongst white, filled with hatred toward one another.

"Or we can make an effort, as Martin Luther King did, to understand and to comprehend, and to replace that stain of bloodshed that has spread across our land, with an effort to understand with compassion and love. . . .

"We've had difficult times in the past. We will have difficult times in the future. It is not the end of violence; it is not the end of lawlessness; it is not the end of disorder.

"But the vast majority of white people and the vast majority of black people in this country want to live together, want to improve the quality of our life, and want justice for all human beings who abide in our land.

"Let us dedicate ourselves to what the Greeks wrote so many years ago: to tame the savageness of man and to make gentle the life of this world. Let us dedicate ourselves to that, and say a prayer for our country and our people."

That night, Indianapolis was one of the few urban centers that did not experience chaos. Over the next week, African Americans—grieving, frustrated, angry—poured into the streets of more than one hundred cities and towns, including New York and Oakland, Newark and Nashville, Chicago and Cincinnati—and in Washington, D.C., where, for the first time in history, the Situation Room monitored combat in American streets. Forty-six Americans died, and 2,600 more were injured. Twenty thousand were arrested. Twenty thousand regulars and 34,000 National Guardsmen were called out to restore order.

Marine Corporal Roger Harris would not be one of them. He had come home in early 1968, a veteran of thirteen months

of savage combat below the DMZ. He landed in California and took a plane home to Boston. "I was feeling good," he recalled, "because I survived and I fought for my country. I got off the plane at Logan and I stepped out there in my uniform with my

ABOVE An infantryman patrols a ruined section of the nation's capital in the wake of the assassination of Dr. Martin Luther King Jr. "When white America killed Dr. King, she declared war on black America," Stokely Carmichael told a news conference. There could be "no alternative to retribution. . . . Black people have to survive, and the only way they will survive is by getting guns."

duffel bag and I'm just happy to be home. I walked out to the curb and the cabs just kept going by me. And there was a state trooper standing there. And I didn't realize what was happening, but he stepped in the street and he stopped a cab and he said, 'You have to take this man. You have to take this soldier.' And the driver looked over at me and he said, 'I don't want to go to Roxbury.' They don't see me as a soldier, you know. They see me as a nigger coming home. I'm thinking I'm a Marine. I just fought for my country thirteen months in the combat zone. And I can't get a cab to get home. You know, sad, sad."

Now, he was stationed at Quantico Marine Corps Base, just

thirty-six miles from Washington. When his unit was called out to help quell the riots in the nation's capital, he recalled, "I was ready to go until I saw what they were giving out. I thought they were going to give us billy clubs and I thought we were going to stand in front of buildings and protect businesses. But they were passing out flak jackets, helmets, M16s with live ammunition—the same things we had in Vietnam. And when I saw that I said, 'I'm not going. I'm not going.' And my company commander said, 'What did you say?' I said, 'I've got family in Washington, D.C.' And he said, 'So what does that mean? Get on the truck, Marine.' I said, 'I'm not going. So I got Article 15—non-judicial punishment—and I didn't make sergeant because I refused to go."

Roger Harris's feelings echoed those of many African Americans serving overseas. The Vietnam War was fought by the first fully integrated American military in history—in Korea, there had still been some all-black and all-white outfits—and in units actually engaged in combat it had been working well. After spending a month talking with black troops in Vietnam, a black reporter for *The Chicago Daily Defender* found that "the men in the line companies who are fighting and dying . . . have pushed through the barriers of racial and ethnic prejudice." Robert Sanders, a black paratrooper from San Francisco who served with the 173rd Airborne, agreed. He remembered feeling closer to the men in his integrated unit "than I do my own blood sisters and brothers. . . . We was so close it was unreal. That was the first time in my life I saw that type of unity and I haven't seen it since. . . . It was beautiful. It sort of chills you, brings goose bumps just to see it, just to feel it."

Dr. King's death—and the reaction of some white troops to it—threatened to destroy that unity. At Cam Ranh Bay, a group of white sailors hoisted a Confederate flag over the naval headquarters and paraded around in makeshift Ku Klux Klan robes. At Danang, one black Marine wrote home, "when Martin Luther King was killed, a group of about 150 Negro soldiers went to the chapel, which always had been open 24 hours a day, to say a prayer for him." MPs refused them entry. When some of the men moved on to the enlisted men's club and began talking about Dr. King, armed guards were called "as though we were rioting. We are supposed to be American soldiers fighting a war in Vietnam. But it seems as though the white man thinks we're still at home."

When the news of King's death reached the Fourth Infantry Division at Kon Tum, a black noncommissioned officer named

Allen Thomas Jr., remembered, "the young guys wanted to hurt somebody." He and a group of other African American noncoms led hundreds of black soldiers to a field, where they camped for several days. "We went to the officers, asked them to back off," Thomas remembered. "The last thing you wanted was to set [the men] off. . . . Let them get over their anger and hurt."

Reports of anger and hurt seemed to be coming from everywhere that spring, as young people took to the streets. Their motivations were many, but opposition to the war in Vietnam was a common denominator. In Italy, students shut down the University of Rome. London police arrested two thousand demonstrators outside the U.S. embassy. In Paris, tens of thousands

ABOVE Beneath North Vietnamese and NLF flags, Parisian students take to the streets in opposition to the war.

marched, chanting, "Johnson Assassin." West Germany endured the worst street rioting since the rise of Adolf Hitler. There were similar scenes in Madrid, Rio, Jakarta, Tokyo.

Tet deepened antiwar feeling on American campuses, as well. There were more teach-ins, more demonstrations. At the university of Wisconsin–Madison, students planted four hundred white crosses. "We thought the campus ought to look like a graveyard," one ex-student said, "because that's where most of the seniors are headed."

At Columbia University in Manhattan, students occupied several campus buildings to protest the university's collaboration with a think tank that advised the military. The administration eventually called in the police, who drove the demonstrators out of the buildings—arresting 712 people and sending more than 100 students and faculty members to the hospital. The SDS saw it as a triumph, proof that determined protestors could bring a great institution to a halt. "The Columbia strike more than any

ABOVE A Columbia University professor arrives for class to find the hallway blocked by antiwar protestors, April 1968. "At a time when the radical movement was the most disheartened and dispirited," recalled Mark Rudd, a leader of the campus uprising, "the Columbia student rebellion broke through the gloom as an example of the power a radical movement could attain."

other event," one student leader said, "has given the radical student movement the belief that we can really change this country." Tom Hayden called for "two, three, many Columbias."

Earlier that year, Robert Kennedy had published an op-ed in *The New York Times* in which he warned that the bleak vision of William Butler Yeats now seemed to be being fulfilled: "Things fall apart; the centre cannot hold; / Mere anarchy is loosed upon the world."

The euphoria that had followed Johnson's partial bombing halt and Hanoi's expressed willingness to talk had rapidly died away. Washington and Hanoi bickered for more than month over where negotiations should take place. Geneva, Phnom Penh, Rangoon, New Delhi, and Warsaw were each proposed by one side or the other, only to be rejected. Indonesia, impatient to see an end to the bloodshed, offered a battleship in international waters. That, too, was rejected.

Finally, the two sides agreed on Paris. There, beneath a vast crystal chandelier in the *grande salle* of the Hotel Majestic, Hanoi's spokesman, Xuan Thuy, declared that the sole purpose of meeting was to arrange for the "unconditional cessation of the U.S. bombing raids and all other acts of war so that talks may start."

The seventy-seven-year-old head of the U.S. delegation, W. Averell Harriman, replied that Washington was willing to stop the bombing completely—but only if Hanoi agreed to a mutual troop withdrawal along the DMZ, ceased attacks on Saigon and other cities, and agreed to "prompt and serious talks" thereafter.

Xuan Thuy rejected that notion: only the United States had violated the buffer zone, he said. If the talks failed, "the American side would bear the full and entire responsibility."

Weeks would go by. Neither side budged. "Never," one member of the American delegation confided to a reporter, "have I heard two nations call each other sons of bitches so politely." President Johnson began to consider calling his delegation home. Clark Clifford helped talk him out of it. The American people had high hopes for the talks, he said, and "if we do anything to wreck [them] Bobby [Kennedy] shoots up and public opinion goes against us." (By "us," he simply meant the Johnson administration; the president had pledged to remain neutral in the upcoming presidential contest.)

Meanwhile, the politburo had begun implementing a policy it called "fighting-while-talking, talking-while-fighting."

BRINGING THE FLAMES OF WAR

ARMY LIEUTENANT VINCENT OKAMOTO arrived in South Vietnam on April 30, 1968 and bunked down at the 90th Replacement Batallion compound at Bien Hoa, awaiting assignment to one outfit or another. He'd been born during World War II in a Japanese American war relocation camp at Poston, Arizona, the seventh son of Japanese immigrants. All six of his brothers had served in uniform—two fought with the celebrated 442nd Regimental Combat Team, the most highly decorated unit of the war—and so, when his country went to war again in Vietnam, he believed he should go, too. He took reserve officer training at UCLA, endured training as an elite airborne ranger at Fort Benning, and had been stationed at Fort Bragg, North Carolina, when flag-draped coffins began to come home after the Tet Offensive.

"If a paratrooper was killed in Vietnam and his family lived within driving distance of Fort Bragg, there was a set routine," Okamoto remembered. "The padre or the chaplain or the rabbi and a young lieutenant would check out a car, and drive to that location. Eventually, my turn came up. It took a while to find the location, and when we finally did, it was something out of *Tobacco Road*—broken-down house, old dog sleeping on the porch. I followed the padre. He knocked on the door, and an elderly African American woman answered it. I think she knew the instant she saw us why we were there. She didn't say a word,

but she stepped back, and let us come in. The padre said, 'I'm terribly sorry to inform you that your son was killed in Vietnam.' And she just sat down. Didn't say a word. And then her husband called from somewhere in the back, saying, 'What's going on?' And he came in, and said, 'What do you gentlemen want?' And again, the padre said, 'I'm sorry to tell you this, but your son was killed in Vietnam.' The wife is still stoic, not saying a word. He says, 'No, there's a mistake.' He leaves the room and comes back with this letter. He said, 'Look, see? We got it yesterday, my son was still alive yesterday.' The chaplain looked at the letter, and said, 'It's a week old. I think your son was killed . . . on the day he wrote this letter.' The father broke down and started weeping. We offered whatever service we could and we left.

"I just felt like a lowlife, because I'd been playing soldier at Fort Bragg, going to the officers' club at night, having dinner, knocking back a couple of shots of tequila. And here's this poor couple, I think they were sharecroppers; their only son gets killed in Vietnam. So as soon as we got back to the post,

ABOVE Training to become an airborne ranger, Vincent Okamoto prepares to jump.

I said, 'I'm never going to do this duty again.' So I walked to the adjutant's office, and I said, 'Give me my request for transfer. I want to go to Vietnam.' And that was the first time that I really saw the Army work with efficiency. They said, 'Sure, man.' And about a week later, I got my orders to go to Vietnam."

On his second night in South Vietnam, mortar rounds hit the base, Okamoto remembered, and he took shelter in a darkened bunker. "It was hot. It was crowded. Everybody's sweating, everybody's scared. A near miss shook the bunker with a concussion. Everybody got quiet. The guy sitting right next to me lit a cigarette with an old Zippo lighter. And all of a sudden, I hear someone say, 'There's a gook in here!' And I start looking around. It's dark. The light goes out. And people say, 'What?' 'Where?' 'Who?' And it just happened that another second lieutenant that I had met the day before said, 'Hey, Okamoto, is that you?' I said, 'Yeah.' And he said, 'Be at ease, people, he's an American.' And then another voice, with a distinct southern drawl, said, 'Hey, no offense, partner; but if I was you I'd dye my hair blond and whistle 'Dixie' when it gets dark.'"

The mortar shells that hit Bien Hoa that night were part of a second attempt to initiate the General Offensive, General Uprising that Le Duan and the other leaders in Hanoi somehow hoped would achieve what the Tet attacks had not achieved months earlier. There had been major engagements since Tet. ARVN and American sweeps had successfully hunted down enemy forces in the Mekong Delta. A combined force of U.S. First Cavalry, U.S. Marines, and ARVN airborne troops reopened Route 9 and lifted the 77-day siege of Khe Sanh. But

OPPOSITE A resident of the Cholon neighborhood watches helplessly as fire creeps toward her home during the fierce fighting that engulfed parts of Saigon during "Mini-Tet" in May 1968. Some thirty thousand homes were destroyed, many by U.S. and South Vietnamese air attacks meant to blast NLF fighters hidden within them. "The Viet Cong has no air force of its own," said the Saigon police chief, "so he uses ours." **ABOVE** Refugees crowd together, surrounded by the few household objects they've managed to salvage, on the grounds of a Catholic church in Saigon. Mini-Tet displaced nearly eighty-seven thousand Saigonese.

HEROIC MOTHER

Few families made more sacrifices for the NLF cause than that of Nguyen Thanh Tung, one of some 47,000 women honored by the Vietnamese government after the war as "Heroic Mothers."

She was born in 1930 into a family already fully committed to the revolutionary struggle. The French burned her village just east of Saigon, and killed many of those who lived there. Her mother died at the hands of French captors in 1945. Her father died in the notorious prison on Con Son Island. She had eight brothers. Four died fighting the French. Four more would die fighting the Americans.

Given the chance to go north after the Geneva agreement in 1954, she resolved to stay in the South, instead, ready to resist the Diem regime when called upon

ABOVE Madame Nguyen Thanh Tung in uniform **OPPOSITE** On the eve of Mini-Tet, NLF fighters, all women, plot their attack on the Chu Y Bridge, which connects southern Saigon with outlying districts. The fighting in its vicinity would be among the fiercest in the city.

to do so. And when that signal came in 1959, she was more than ready. "At the time, we had no arms," she recalled. "We asked our superiors for weapons, but they didn't provide them. Our superiors told us, 'We don't have arms to give you. Why don't you steal our enemy's arms to fight?' I was upset and asked them, 'Do you want us to become thieves?' But as the only woman in my unit, with four older men, I had an advantage in being able to move around. The men usually had to keep hidden. Step by step, I made friends with those in our enemy's outposts. I made friends with the soldiers' relatives and found out where their arms were stored, what they looked like, found ways to get them.

"I started to steal arms. I could not steal big guns. I only stole grenades and small guns. At first, I stole two grenades, then two more, then I got four."

Her responsibilities steadily grew. "Whatever duty was assigned to me, I performed," she recalled. "I worked as a temporary worker, a street vendor, and disguised myself as a local resident.

Wherever my superiors needed me to go, I always tried to blend in to approach our targets."

Her superiors introduced her to her future husband, Pham Van Tam, a fellow NLF fighter who had also resolved to stay in the South. "I hadn't wanted to get married," she recalled. "But they persuaded me, 'If you focus only on fighting, without reproducing, who will be our future fighters? When we get old, and can no longer fight, the younger generation, your children, will take over the responsibility.'"

Husband and wife would have little time together: "Our first son was born in 1956 in a tunnel on the outskirts of Saigon, and I bore our second son in one of the tunnels at Chu Chi in 1958. My husband only heard the news a month later, when he came back from an assignment." Even the naming of their boys was dictated by the cause they shared. "My older son's name was Pham Quoc Nam," she recalled. "The younger one was Pham Quoc Trung. The names we chose came from our decision to stay in the South instead of moving to the North. 'Quoc' means 'Nation.' 'Nam' means 'the South.' We named the younger one 'Trung' so that he would always remember that no matter what happened, the blood of loyalty ran in his veins."

Her husband was killed in battle in 1967. She and her two sons took part in the Tet assault on Saigon the following year. Her boys were in the sapper unit that tried to take the offices of Radio Saigon, and when the ARVN surrounded it, managed to escape and then flee the city. "After that we communicated only through letters," she remembered. "They encouraged me. They always wrote at the beginning of their letters: 'Our father sacrificed his life, and now

we only have you left. Please, take care of yourself, and do your duty. We want to be worthy of being your sons.'"

In May, when the NLF attacked the South Vietnamese capital again as part of Mini-Tet, Nguyen Thanh Tung found herself part of a commando unit that tried for six days to take and hold the Chu Y Bridge, the southern entrance-way to downtown Saigon. "The enemy counterattacked. Some of my colleagues were killed. First, Miss Hong got injured. I was next to her. She shouted, 'I am hit.' I crawled over to her and hugged her. She told me: 'I have finished my assignment. Please fight and get revenge for me. When the peace comes, please go to my village, and take care of my mother.' I embraced her when she died.

Then, Miss Tram was killed. An hour later, I was injured. There is still shrapnel in my leg. There were seven pieces of shrapnel in my head. Four have recently been removed. I still have three fragments of shrapnel. It still hurts, especially when it gets cold." Still more sacrifices lay ahead.

this was different. The enemy hit 119 targets between May 5 and the end of the month, in what the Americans would call "Mini-Tet."

General Huynh Cong Than, the NLF commander who had scrambled to get his troops ready for the first attack on Saigon in February, received new "guidance" from his superiors. The General Offensive, General Uprising had never been meant to be a single definitive event, he was now told; instead, it was "a process." Nor had there been any changes in tactics or armaments or orders since the first assault. He and his men were now to try to do what they had failed to do with far greater numbers three months earlier. "Our assigned mission . . . called for our forces to penetrate as deeply as possible into the very heart of the city," he recalled. "At that time this tactic was called 'bringing the flames of war into the enemy's own lair.' In truth, we went into the second wave of the Tet Offensive with the attitude of suicide troops. The fighting . . . was extremely violent, but our troops could not penetrate any deeper than they had during the first offensive, and in places didn't even get as far as they had the first time." Morale among the NLF plummeted.

One hundred and twenty-five thousand more South Vietnamese civilians were driven from their homes. American tanks and American gunships again pounded every structure in which NLF fighters were thought to be hiding. "These weapons create more problems than they solve," an ARVN officer told a *Newsweek* reporter. "We cannot go on destroying an entire block every time a Viet Cong steps into a house."

The North Vietnamese and NLF suffered 36,000 more casualties and failed to capture a single one of their key objectives. But for the United States, May 1968 proved the bloodiest month of the Vietnam War—2,416 Americans lost their lives. If the enemy had suffered such terrible losses at Tet, how could they be taking such a toll on the U.S. forces afterward? Nearly half of those Americans interviewed by Gallup now believed U.S. entry into the Vietnam War had been a mistake.

THE MURDEROUS SPRING

FOR A TIME THAT SPRING, it looked as if Robert Kennedy might be on his way to winning the Democratic presidential nomination. He had conducted a remarkable campaign—frenetic, exhausting, pledging an end to the war and seeming to embody the hope of bridging the growing gulf between white and black Americans. It was an uphill fight—McCarthy's followers were bitter about his late entry into the race, Johnson loyalists within the Democratic Party shared the president's

antipathy toward him, and white southerners were unforgiving of his civil rights record—but Kennedy won Indiana, Nebraska, and South Dakota. He lost Oregon to McCarthy—the first time any member of the Kennedy family had lost an election anywhere—but on June 4 he scored dramatic victories in South Dakota and California and seemed poised to drive his rival from the race. Shortly before midnight, he declared victory. He called on his fellow countrymen to "end the division, the violence, the disenchantment. . . . We are a great country, an unselfish country, and a compassionate country. So my thanks to all of you," he said, "and now it's on to Chicago and let's win there."

Moments later, he was shot by a delusional Palestinian. He died the next day. His body lay in state at St. Patrick's Cathedral in New York for two and a half days, then was carried by slow-moving train to Washington past thousands of mourners, black and white, and finally laid to rest at Arlington.

For those who lived through the "murderous spring of 1968," the journalist Jack Newfield wrote, there had been a terrible lesson. "Things were not really getting better . . . we shall not overcome. We had already glimpsed the most compassionate leaders our nation could produce, and they had all been assassinated. And from this time forward things would get worse. Our best political leaders were part of memory now, not hope."

"People were stunned, and people were scared," recalled Mogie Crocker's sister Carol, who was then soon to leave for college. "The people we'd looked up to were being taken away from us. It definitely put those of us who were heading off on our own on a path that felt uncertain."

The United States now appeared to be more divided than at any time since the Civil War.

By that June, Captain Hal Kushner had been a prisoner of the Viet Cong for six months, hidden away in a remote jungle camp deep in the Central Highlands of South Vietnam. "When Martin Luther King was assassinated and Bobby Kennedy was assassinated," he remembered, "they said that was part of the struggle of the American people against their government. And that there were riots in the streets. The camp commander actually told us, 'You can kill ten of us to one of you, but your people will turn against this. We will be here for ten years or twenty years or thirty years—as long as it takes. Unless you kill every one of us we're going to win this war.'"

OPPOSITE Philadelphians gather at Union Station to say goodbye, as Robert Kennedy's funeral train passes by on its way to Washington. Clark Clifford attended the funeral and "wondered again how our nation would survive the most serious challenge it had faced since the Civil War. . . . Perhaps Bobby Kennedy had been the last Democrat who could have united the factions of the party, which was beginning to unravel; but now we would never know."

CHAPTER SEVEN

THE VENEER OF CIVILIZATION

JUNE 1968–APRIL 1969

North Vietnamese troops
climb through the Truong Son
Mountains in Quang Binh,
South Vietnam's northernmost
province, 1969. Sent south
to refill the depleted ranks of the
NLF after the Tet Offensive, one
draftee remembered, they were
told "to move fast or there will
be nothing left to liberate."

NO DEADLINE FOR RETURN

At FIRST, Radio Hanoi had portrayed the Tet Offensive as a series of "tremendous and all-sided victories" in which "hundreds of thousands of people have risen up and destroyed enemy positions, [and] wiped out whole fragments of the puppet administration."

ABOVE Somewhere along the Ho Chi Minh Trail, North Vietnamese soldiers struggle to carry two comrades felled by malaria. Some units are said to have lost eight out of ten men to the life-threatening blood disease.

"But after a couple of weeks," one Hanoi resident remembered, "we didn't hear any more news. The Saigon regime was still there and the U.S. planes were still bombing. It was obvious the radio wasn't telling the truth."

Casualty figures were never revealed, but to North Vietnamese citizens, secretly listening to reports on the BBC and Radio Saigon, it was clear that they had been heavy. Parents had no idea whether their sons and daughters who had gone south were still alive. "Nobody was allowed to talk about deaths or rumors of deaths," a fisherman's wife remembered, "not until the official death notification came from the army. Up until then, if you talked about things like this it was considered anti-state. You were undermining people's morale. You would get into trouble or be sent to jail." Wives or mothers might get word indirectly, she continued, "from messages sent by friends who were in the army or by other soldiers from their village. . . . So sometimes a woman knew her husband was dead, but she couldn't mourn out loud or she and the rest of her family would be in trouble with the police. That's why my mother and I couldn't tell my sister."

"It was as if the nation were in mourning," a North Vietnamese journalist wrote, "searching for its children. [The war] began to seem like an open pit. The more young people who were lost there, the more they sent." Thousands of NLF Main Force troops had been lost during Tet. Thousands of fresh troops had to be rushed south to replace them.

Just as in the United States, conscription fell unequally on the country's youth. "Some leaders sent their children to the front, but they were the minority," the journalist Huy Duc recalled. "Most leaders' children, like Le Duan's children, were sent to the Soviet Union to study." People with money bribed recruiters to overlook their offspring or paid physicians to declare them unfit to serve.

Most draftees were poor people from the countryside, especially receptive to the slogans and promises of the revolution. Nguyen Van Hung's father had been a deputy village chief under the French and—even though he was just four when his father died—he remained stigmatized as a "middle farmer element" and therefore "undesirable" as a soldier of the revolution. He was also an only son and the head of his household and therefore thought himself unlikely to be drafted on all three counts. But there was such a desperate need for new troops to fill the NLF Main Force ranks that the draft laws were altered and

in the spring of 1968 he got his notice: "I knew I was destined to go south. And I knew the chances of coming back were very slim. About a hundred guys from my village had gone, starting in 1962, and none had returned. Their parents and wives were waiting for them up to their eyes in fear. But nobody had gotten any news. The government was very explicit about it. They said, 'The trip has no deadline for return. When your mission is accomplished, you'll come back.' Uncle Ho had declared, 'Your duty is to fight for five or ten years or even ten to twenty years.'"

Nguyen Van Hung was bitter when he left home, he remembered. His wife had urged him to file a petition against being called up. But he'd gone anyway. Those who resisted had their rations cut off. Basic training turned out to be two-thirds political. "Fight the Americans and save the country," was the slogan.

He was taught that the Americans were a hundred times crueler than the French; that soldiers were part of the proletariat; that it was their duty to liberate the southern population that lived in misery under the domination of the U.S. imperialists. "After a continuous week of this," he remembered, "my morale was a lot higher than it was when I left my village."

During the spring and summer of 1968, tens of thousands of replacements like him would make their way down the Ho Chi Minh Trail in infiltration groups of four to five hundred

ABOVE Two NLF fighters help a third who has been wounded, following a firefight near the Cambodian border. "There's no doubt that 1969 was the worst we faced," one communist veteran recalled. "There was no food, no future—nothing bright."

men. It was an arduous two- to three-month trek through the Truong Son Mountains of Laos and western Vietnam where, one diarist wrote, one day "has four seasons. The morning is spring; at noon it is summer; in the afternoon it is autumn; and at night it is winter."

President Johnson's decision to halt the bombing of most of the North meant that U.S. airpower could focus more single-mindedly on the infiltration routes in Laos and Cambodia. One unit, picking its way toward the South, claimed to have dodged sixty-six separate B-52 bombloads in six hours. When rice and

salt ran short, some men survived on roots, moss, ferns, and leaves. Malaria ravaged their ranks. "I have a constant fever," one soldier wrote, "my body is emaciated, my wrists are thin, my eyes are sunken, my hair falls out, but I must still carry a load weighing over thirty kilograms."

As they neared South Vietnam they passed burned-out vehicles and military graveyards, the stones neatly marked with the names of the dead and the date each had died. They encountered small groups of wounded men moving in the other direction. Those without arms walked. Legless men rode in camouflaged trucks. There were blinded soldiers, too, and others who had been hideously burned by napalm.

"You'll see all *kinds* of pleasures in the South," the war-weary wounded told the frightened men moving toward the war.

When anyone seemed overly anxious approaching the South, a platoon's political officer remembered, "the answer was that war always brings death and that we shouldn't bother ourselves with morbid thoughts. No one argued with the cadres. But everyone was frightened, especially when we met those men. . . . It was like looking at our future selves."

ABOVE LEFT This photograph, entitled "Heroic Soldier from Anti-aircraft Company #5 Loads Artillery," became the basis for a North Vietnamese postage stamp and was meant to spur the people's support for the war. It was actually taken in a Hanoi suburb where no American bomb ever fell. **ABOVE RIGHT** A visiting government official rations out *nuoc mam*, the staple Vietnamese fish sauce, among the people of a village in the North Vietnamese province of Nam Ha. Because the scene suggested scarcity this image was suppressed during the war.

I LOOK FOR MORE FIGHTING

WHEN THE REPLACEMENTS reached the South they would be facing a new American commander. On June 10, President Johnson announced the appointment of General Creighton Abrams. He was a soldier's soldier, a combat leader, one reporter wrote, who "could inspire aggressiveness in a begonia." His tank battalion had been the first to break though the German lines and relieve Bastogne during the Battle of the Bulge. He had served as chief of staff to three different corps in Korea, commanded Army regulars and National Guardsmen to quell the riots that followed the desegregation of schools and colleges in Alabama and Mississippi, and served for a year in Saigon as General Westmoreland's top deputy, earning a reputation as "the godfather of the ARVN" because of his determination to improve the performance of South Vietnamese forces.

On the surface, at least, he and his predecessor could not have been more different. Westmoreland had been crisp, controlled, perpetually confident—one reporter noted that he breakfasted in his underwear in order not to muss his perfectly pressed uniform. Abrams was very different: "Chances are," one observer wrote, "if he were in civilian clothes, sitting on a park bench, a cop would tell him to move along." "Even in appearance the men are opposites," a *Time* reporter wrote: "Westy, the handsome, square-jawed, picture poster image of a U.S. general; Abrams a kind of middle-aged Joe Palooka, an ever-present Dutch Master cigar between his teeth enhancing the tough-guy image. His manner follows his face. Where Westy is a soft-spoken, courtly gentleman from the South, Abrams is the no-nonsense hard guy from Massachusetts."

The hard-guy demeanor was not a pose. He was tough-talking, hard-drinking, a "slumbering volcano," one general remembered, who "suddenly erupts in an earthy profane way when necessary to straighten someone out or to spur lagging performance." He did not insist that his subordinates invariably report progress: "Occasionally," one officer said, "we are allowed to state frankly that we didn't do a damn thing this month." Unlike his predecessor, Abrams thought it unwise to issue perennially hopeful bulletins. "The overall public affairs policy of this command," he told his subordinates, "will be to let results speak for themselves. We will not deal in propaganda exercises but will portray all of our activities in a low key. Achievements, not hopes, will be stressed." And while commanders were free to speak with reporters, he continued, "considerably more extensive use could be made of the phrase 'No comment.'"

The Christian Science Monitor hailed his appointment as likely to "open the way to further new approaches to strategy," and two early changes Abrams made did seem to signal a promising shift: he ordered Khe Sanh abandoned and plowed under, and, while ringing Saigon with U.S. and ARVN forces in order to stop the enemy from rocket attacks on the city, he prohibited the tactical use of artillery, bombing, and gunships anywhere in its environs without his express permission.

ABOVE General Creighton Abrams salutes the flag for the first time as MACV's new commander, June 1968. Behind him, hand on heart, is U.S. ambassador Ellsworth Bunker.

IS THAT WHY I DID THAT?

The Vietnam War forced young men from all over the country to face questions and choices their fathers and grandfathers had rarely had to face when asked to fight in other wars: What obligation did a citizen owe his country? What should one do when asked to fight a war in which one did not believe?

Tim O'Brien grew up in Worthington, a small farming community in southern Minnesota that liked to call itself "the Turkey Capital of the World." "Small-town America, at least my small town, had great virtues," he remembered. "It was a safe place to grow up. There was Little League baseball in the summer, and hockey in the winter. Everybody knows everyone else's business and their faults and what's happening in their marriages and where the kids have gone wrong. It was full of the Kiwanis boys and the Elks Club and the country-club set and the chatty housewives and the holier-than-thou ministers."

But, as O'Brien recalled, the specter of the war haunted unmarried young men of draft age, including him: "I remember the day my draft notice arrived. It was a summer afternoon, maybe June of '68. And I remember taking that envelope into the house and putting it on the kitchen table where my mom and dad were having lunch. They just looked at it and knew what it was. The silence of that lunch: I didn't speak, my mom didn't speak, my dad didn't speak. It was just that piece of paper lying at the center of the table. It was enough to make me cry to this day, not for myself, but for my mom and dad, both of whom had been in the Navy during World War Two, and had believed in service to one's country and all those values.

"On the one hand I did think the war was less than righteous. On the other hand I love my country. And I valued my life in a small town and my friends

and family. So I wrestled with what was, for me, at least, more tortuous and devastating and emotionally painful than anything that happened in Vietnam. Do you go off and kill people if you're not pretty sure it's right? And if your nation isn't pretty sure it's right? If there isn't some consensus, do you do that? In the end, I just capitulated, and one day I got on a bus with other recent graduates, and we went over to Sioux Falls about sixty miles away, and raised our hands and went into the Army. But it wasn't a

decision; it was a forfeiture of a decision. It was letting my body go, turning a switch in my conscience, just turning it off, so it wouldn't be barking at me saying, 'You're doing a bad and evil and stupid and unpatriotic thing.'"

O'Brien underwent basic training at Fort Lewis, Washington, just a ninety-minute bus ride from Canada. "I wrote my mom and dad from there and asked for money," he recalled. "I asked for my passport. They sent them to me with no questions like, 'What do you want the

bullets. It's that failure of nerve that I so regret."

Karl Marlantes wrestled with the same decision that tormented Tim O'Brien. Born in Astoria, Oregon, the son of a veteran of the Battle of the Bulge, he'd joined the Marine Reserve in high school, eager to prove himself and defend his country. But questions about the Gulf of Tonkin, stories of civilian casualties, the shock of the Tet Offensive, the suspicion that American officials had misrepresented what was happening, had nagged at him at Yale and afterward as a Rhodes Scholar at Oxford University.

He loved it at Oxford, "drinking beer, hanging out with the girls, and having a grand old time." But, he remembered, in the end "I couldn't do it. I felt that I was sort of hiding behind privilege, and that I had to make a choice. I was very torn. And there was another kid there, Mike Fredrickson, and we spent one whole night debating what to do. And Mike decided to turn his draft card in and go to Canada. And I decided to send my letter in to the Marine Corps. I'd taken an oath, 'so help me God.' I took that seriously. But I think more importantly it was my friends, guys that I trained with. I felt like I was going to sort of let the side down. That by not joining in with them and sharing the burden that I wouldn't be a decent person. The thing about patriotism had faded enormously. So it was more my personal oath, my own honor at stake. And you know, I think about that. It's a mixed bag because I went over there and killed people. Is that why I did that?"

passport for?' They just sent it. And I kept all this stuff, including civilian clothes, stashed in my footlocker, thinking, maybe I'll do it. It was this kind of maybe thing going on all throughout this training as Vietnam got closer and closer and closer. What prevented me from doing it? I think it was pretty simple and stupid. It was a fear of embarrassment, a fear of ridicule and humiliation. What my girlfriend would have thought of me and what the people in the Gobbler Cafe in downtown Worthington would have thought. The

things they'd say about me: 'What a coward and what a sissy for going to Canada.' I would imagine my mom and dad overhearing something like that. I couldn't summon the courage to say no to those nameless, faceless people who really in essence represented the United States of America. I couldn't say no to them. And I've had to live with it now for, you know, forty years. That's a long time to live with a failure of conscience and a failure of nerve. And the nightmare of Vietnam for me is not the bombs and the

OPPOSITE Tim O'Brien at home at Christmastime in Worthington, Minnesota, with his brother, Greg, and sister, Kathy **ABOVE** Karl Marlantes and a girlfriend at Oxford

guage as his own. The enemy already understands, he said, "that this is just one, repeat, *one* war. He knows there is no such thing as a war of big battalions, a war of pacification, or a war of territorial security. Friendly forces have got to recognize and understand the one-war concept and carry the battle to the enemy, simultaneously, in all areas of conflict."

But earlier that spring, while the White House was still wrestling with the questions raised by the Tet Offensive, President Johnson had asked Abrams, "Is there anything we should be doing that we aren't doing?"

"Our basic strategy is sound," Abrams answered. "I don't think we need to change strategy. We need to be more flexible tactically inside South Vietnam."

The new commander inherited unchanged the multifaceted mission his predecessor had outlined more than three years earlier: Main Force enemy units were to be destroyed; insurgents were to be disrupted and eventually defeated; cities and towns were to be protected; pacification was to be advanced in order to enhance Saigon's control of the population—all this while readying South Vietnamese forces so they could one day assume responsibility for their own independence. And he was being asked to do it all at the same time and within strict new limitations. The era of American escalation was over; Defense Secretary Clark Clifford had made it clear that there was "no plan to ask for any more American troops."

"Abe knows damn well that he wasn't sent here to win the war," a senior U.S. officer said, "but to hold the fort until the Indians make peace."

Some observers also took comfort in the new way Abrams talked about the war. Lyndon Johnson often spoke of pacification as "the other war," a phrase Ambassador Bunker particularly disliked. "To me," he said, "this is all one war," with a host of interlocking parts. The new commander adopted Bunker's lan-

When, shortly after Abrams took command, a reporter asked if he had in mind any major changes in strategy, he would only say, "I look for more fighting." The memoranda he issued to his commanders that summer were virtually indistinguishable from the exhortations produced by his predecessor: they were to "accommodate the enemy in seeking battle and in fact to anticipate him wherever possible"; their aim should be to "defeat his forces, then pursue them and destroy them"; they were to launch "spoiling and preemptive operations" against Main Force units as well as the NLF infrastructure. All summer, Abrams would keep his troops prowling South Vietnam, seeking out the enemy

ABOVE Private First Class Robert Whitworth of Albany, Oregon, and the Americal Division after three days in pursuit of the enemy south of Danang, 1968. "There was no way we could stand up to the Americans [that year]," a communist fighter remembered. "Every time they came in force we ran from them. Then when they turned back, we'd follow them."

and hoping to provide a shield behind which the South Vietnamese government could restore its grip in the wake of Tet.

The communists would mount yet another costly countrywide offensive in August. Like its predecessors, it would fail. Enemy planners had hoped that attacks on several border towns would lure U.S. forces away from the cities. They did not. An assault on Danang was thwarted before it could begin. Some planned attacks failed to materialize; others were broken by massive U.S. firepower or lack of food and supplies. In five weeks of fighting, MACV claimed to have killed another twenty thousand enemy troops.

During the second half of 1968, the number of battles fought by battalion-sized forces would fall sharply, a sign some observers saw as evidence of a fresh Abrams strategy. But by and large it was the enemy that had begun to change its ways. Tet and Mini-Tet had taken a fearful toll on North Vietnamese and NLF forces alike. "When the Tet campaign was over, we didn't have enough men left to fight a major battle," North Vietnamese colonel Huong Van Ba recalled, "only to make hit-and-run attacks on posts. . . . Morale was very low. We spent a great deal of time hiding in tunnels, trying to avoid capture. We experienced desertions, and many of our people filtered back to their homes to join local guerrilla forces." Most Main Force units that did remain more or less intact retreated to bases hidden in the Central Highlands or slipped across the border to sanctuaries in Laos and Cambodia.

After Tet, Mini-Tet, and the August offensive—despite new leadership at MACV, despite the loss of thousands of American and South Vietnamese lives, despite the deaths of tens of thousands of enemy troops and the displacement of tens of thousands of innocent civilians—the war remained what it had been for months: a stalemate.

The talks in Paris were stalemated too, and Lyndon Johnson had begun to regret ever having declared a partial bombing halt. Hanoi had yet to make even a remotely reciprocal gesture. The president felt "hornswoggled," he told Clifford, and now wished he could "knock Hanoi and Haiphong off the map."

There was little good news from Saigon, either. In June, Thieu had signed the General Mobilization Law, which would eventually expand the South Vietnamese armed forces from 600,000 to over a million. But Clifford was not encouraged. Visiting Saigon in July, he warned Thieu that the American public was fast wearying of the war, that "if we could not achieve a settlement in Paris, we expected the South Vietnamese gradually to take over."

"Saigon's weakness was the major cause of our dilemma," Clifford recalled, "and I saw no reason to indulge it. [Ambassador] Bunker may have perceived growing stability in the government and discovered 'statesmanlike' qualities in [Thieu]—clearly his favorite among the South Vietnamese leaders—but I saw a group of squabbling and corrupt generals selfishly maneuvering for their own advantage while Americans and Vietnamese continued to die in combat." He reported to the president that he was "now 'absolutely certain' that Saigon did not want the war to end—not while they were protected by over 500,000 American troops and a 'golden flow of money.'" He was especially appalled, he said, by the "shocking and outrageous list" of military hardware Thieu had requested, "including between three hundred and four hundred helicopters and T-39 trainer jets to be used as private aircraft for senior officials."

Back in Washington, Clifford argued that, since the United States had fulfilled its obligations to Saigon "many times over," the South Vietnamese were unlikely to establish an honest and effective government before the U.S. public gave up on it, and the North could not be bombed into submission, it was time to move the Paris talks along by declaring an unconditional halt to the bombing—reserving the right to resume it if the North took advantage of American forbearance.

Johnson would not do it.

Clifford appealed to Dean Rusk to help him persuade the president to reconsider.

Rusk would not.

Clifford was angered. "All you are suggesting," he said, "is that we keep on fighting and having our men killed indefinitely."

Rusk answered with what Clifford remembered as "maddening . . . blandness": "You never can tell when Hanoi will break and give in."

When *The New York Times* reported that the secretaries of defense and state were at loggerheads, Johnson complained to Clifford, "Every day I read something in the papers about deep policy differences between you and Dean. I am telling both of you that I want it stopped."

It did not stop. The president remained caught between his key advisers—and between his own conflicting desires simultaneously to end a war and to keep from being the first president to lose one.

WHEN THE MORNING COMES

EVERY AFTERNOON at five o'clock, the staticky voice of the radio propagandist Trinh Thi Ngo, whom the Americans called "Hanoi Hannah," brought the news of at least some of these developments to Captain Hal Kushner, who was locked away with other American captives in the first of several remote prisoner-of-war camps in the Central Highlands. But for the most part Kushner and his fellow prisoners were shut off from the outside world.

Not long after Kushner arrived, two Puerto Rican captives, Marine Corporal Jose Agosto-Santos and Army PFC Luis Ortiz-Rivera, were to be set free by their captors as alleged proof that prisoners were receiving "lenient and humane" treatment. Kushner took the opportunity to smuggle out word that he was still alive: "It was about the only time I had a pencil in my whole captivity. I had some paper. I think it was a paper towel. I wrote down the names, ranks, and serial numbers of the men who had been freshly captured, as well as my own. And when I said good-bye to one of the Puerto Ricans I shook hands and I had this paper all balled up. The Vietnamese let it go or they had lousy security. Anyway, I passed him the paper. I told him in Spanish to give that paper to the authorities. My father and my father-in-law, who spoke Spanish, went down to Fort Bragg. And they were allowed to speak to these two prisoners. And my father identified my handwriting. So he knew that I was at least able to write on that particular date."

Kushner received no word of how his family was faring. His family would hear nothing further about him for more than a year. "I'd been married five years when I went to Vietnam. I had a child who was two and a half, a little girl, who I adored, and I knew my wife was pregnant and I knew that she was going to have a baby in April. So I got captured in December. And I never knew whether he was a boy or a girl. But I thought about my parents and my siblings and my wife and my little girl. And one of the things that bothered me, and I think this is not an unusual dynamic, is that I couldn't really remember what they looked like after a while. I remembered what their pictures looked like. And when I imaged them in my mind's eye I would image a picture, a photograph."

There was nothing either lenient or humane about the treatment Kushner and his fellow prisoners received over the months that followed. They lived crowded together in one grass hut, surrounded by dense jungle. Their "kitchen" was a hole in the ground surrounded by rocks. "We had one blanket per person, if you could call it that," a fellow prisoner remembered—"a burlap bag split and sewn together, the kind of bag in which the U.S. Agency for International Development shipped free rice and bulgur wheat to Vietnam." Each bag featured the clasped-hands symbol of international friendship.

Sheets of monsoon rain fell for weeks at a time, leaking through the straw roof, turning the clearing into a sea of mud. The men slept on a large bamboo pallet, sometimes as many as eighteen of them, Kushner remembered: "And we were sick.

We were very sick. And we discharged our functions on this pallet. And we defecated and urinated and vomited and did all these things next to each other. We had no change of clothing, no shoes, no mosquito nets, no blankets. And we were in the mountains. No toothpaste, no soap, none of the things that we consider almost necessary for survival. Our food ration was three cups of rice per day, coffee-cup size. In the rainy season, which was three or four months, it was cut down to two coffee cups of rice. And they gave us a ration of [*nuoc cham*], which is a rotting fish sauce. It's dead fish that ferments and it makes a kind of gravy that smells just like you would expect it to smell and tastes worse. And we would put that on the rice. And the rice was not white rice. It was old rice that had been cached in the mountains for years. . . . It was shot through with weevils and rat feces and things like that. We got no protein and we were vitamin deficient. And we got no vitamin C. We swelled up. We got what was called in World War Two hunger edema. It's hypoproteinemia—lack of protein. We got beriberi from lack of vitamin B_1. We got every vitamin deficiency one could get. We had terrible skin diseases. We had scabies. We had everything."

In order to survive, Kushner repeated his own mantra over and over again during the night: "I'll be here when the morning comes. I'll be here when the morning comes." He could not always convince himself that it was true.

DID WE COME ALL THIS WAY FOR THIS?

BY THE TIME the Republicans gathered in Miami Beach for their national convention in early August, Richard Nixon was the front-runner for their presidential nomination. That fact in itself was remarkable. Just six years earlier he had issued his own political epitaph. A California congressman and senator, best known for fierce anticommunism, equally fierce partisanship, and a sinuous air that early on earned him the contemptuous epithet "Tricky Dick," he served for eight years as Dwight Eisenhower's vice president. John Kennedy defeated him for the presidency in 1960, and, when he was defeated again trying to become governor of his own state two years later, he had bid a bitter televised farewell to politics. "For sixteen years," he'd told reporters then, "you've had an opportunity to attack me. But as I leave you . . . just think how much you're going to be missing. You won't have Nixon to kick around anymore, because, gentlemen, this is my last press conference."

Kennedy's death revived Nixon's ambition. In 1964, he

began to rebuild his reputation within his party, campaigning in thirty-six states for Barry Goldwater and the Republican Party. He did it again for congressional candidates two years later, winning the gratitude of party stalwarts all over the country, methodically building support for his presidential nomination.

Two of his rivals, both moderates, self-destructed: Michigan governor George Romney, seeking to explain newfound skepticism about the war, said he'd been "brainwashed" by the military, became a laughingstock, and withdrew before the first primary; while New York governor Nelson Rockefeller entered the race too late to stop Nixon's momentum. California governor Ronald Reagan failed to declare himself a candidate until the convention, and then proved unable to peel away enough southern conservatives from the front-runner to make a difference.

When Nixon won the nomination on the first ballot, James Reston of *The New York Times* called it "the greatest comeback since Lazarus." For his running mate Nixon picked Spiro Agnew, the once-moderate governor of Maryland, who had won conservative support for the hard and dismissive line he'd taken toward African American leaders after the Baltimore riots following the death of Dr. King.

In a masterful acceptance speech, Nixon made the case for himself as the man who could bring a badly divided country together and both "end the war and win the peace." "A party that can unite itself will unite America," he said. "As we look at America we see cities enveloped in smoke and flame. We hear sirens in the night. We see Americans dying on distant battle-

ABOVE The 1968 Republican ticket: Richard Nixon (right) and his running mate, Maryland governor Spiro Agnew, accept their party's nomination.

fields. We see Americans hating each other; fighting each other; killing each other at home. Did we come all this way for this? Did American boys die in Normandy, and Korea, and in Valley Forge for this?

"The problem," he said, was that Washington had stopped listening to "the quiet voice in the tumult and the shouting . . . the voice of the great majority of Americans, the forgotten Americans—the non-shouters; the non-demonstrators." He promised to be their president.

When the strongest nation in the world can be tied down for four years in a war in Vietnam with no end in sight;

When the richest nation in the world can't manage its own economy;

When the nation with the greatest tradition of the rule of law is plagued by unprecedented lawlessness;

When a nation that has been known for a century for equality of opportunity is torn by unprecedented racial violence;

And when the President of the United States cannot travel abroad or to any major city at home without fear of a hostile demonstration—then it's time for new leadership for the United States of America. . . .

I pledge to you tonight that the first priority of our next administration will be to bring an honorable end to the Vietnam War. . . .

For five years hardly a day has gone by when we haven't read or heard a report of the American flag being spit on, and our embassy being stoned, a library being burned, or an ambassador being insulted. If we are to restore prestige and respect for America abroad, the place to begin is at home, in the United States of America.

The editors of *The Boston Globe* wrote that there really was a "new Nixon." "Gone is the lack of self-confidence, gone the scarcely concealed conviction that he was just a political accident who really did not belong in the Big Time, gone the almost self-evident apprehension that he would be found out sooner or later as an upstart tyro. . . . What Mr. Nixon has done and done superbly is to list the problems confronting the nation. His testing period will come when (and if) he spells out what he proposes to do about them."

ATTABOY

SECOND LIEUTENANT Vincent Okamoto, whose introduction to Vietnam had been a mortar attack at Bien Hoa on his second night in country, was now a platoon leader with Bravo Company, Second Battalion, Twenty-seventh Regiment, Twenty-fifth Infantry Division—based at Cu Chi, some fourteen miles northwest of Saigon, an area honeycombed with miles of Viet Cong tunnels. "My parents are Japanese immigrants," he said. "I had rice literally every day of my life until I went into the military. We were conducting a cordon and search of a village. Didn't find any weapons, didn't find any communist literature. So we took a prolonged lunch break. Everybody wants to get out of the sun. Well, my RTO [radio telephone operator], my medic, and I went into this particular house. There were three women in there, and a babe in arms, and a kid about four years old. And one woman was cooking rice. Well, here's Okamoto, Mrs. Okamoto's son, who hadn't had rice—hot, steamed rice—for months. I'm looking at it. It looks pretty good to me. I get my interpreter, 'Hey, tell this woman, the grandma, that I'll give her a pack of cigarettes, my C-ration turkey loaf, and a can of peaches for some of that steamed rice and that fish and vegetables.' It was great. And I asked for seconds. My RTO said, 'Damn, ain't these people poor enough without you eating their food?' I said, 'Hell, they got enough rice here to feed a dozen men.' And then it dawned on me: they *did* have enough rice to feed a dozen men. So I had my interpreter ask the woman, 'Who's all this rice for?' And she said, 'No *biết*, no *biết*, no *biết*,'—'I don't know, I don't know, I don't know.' So we started looking around again, and we found a tunnel mouth. I was given a phosphorous grenade. After the smoke cleared, we pulled, I think, seven or eight bodies to the town square. You couldn't identify these charred bodies. So we wanted to see who would cry over these people. Then we'd have more people to question. The women that lived in that house, whose rice I had eaten, they're all squatting down, wailing. I think that was the first time I knew that I personally had killed people. I got an 'Attaboy' from the supervisor. But it wasn't something that had any glory in it, or made you feel a real sense of accomplishment."

Over that summer, Okamoto was wounded twice and made twenty-two helicopter assaults, four of them as commander of Bravo Company. The success or failure of a given mission was still measured largely as it had been under General Westmoreland. "You were told very succinctly," Okamoto remembered. "We need to rack up as much body count as we can. How many gooks did you kill today? A kill ratio determined whether or

not you called a firefight a victory or a loss. If you killed twenty North Vietnamese and lost only two people, they declared it a great victory."

On the morning of August 23, he made his twenty-third assault. Nineteen helicopters ferried the first and second platoons to a new landing zone just thirteen miles from the Cambodian border. Their task was to dig in, stay put, and somehow block a *battalion* of some eight hundred North Vietnamese troops, who were trying to escape back across the border.

Okamoto's unit was reinforced by a platoon of mechanized infantry, three APCs, and a tank, but they were still badly outnumbered. He and the fewer than 150 men under his command spent the rest of that day and all of the next preparing for an attack as best they could—setting Claymore mines and hanging coils of razor wire.

At about ten o'clock on the night of August 24, Okamoto remembered, "we got hit with a very heavy mortar barrage. Within the first ten seconds, all three of those armored personnel carriers and tanks were knocked out with rocket-propelled grenades."

Trip flares briefly lit up the landscape. Scores of enemy troops were running at the Americans through the elephant grass. Enemy mortar shells blasted two gaps in the razor wire. If Okamoto and his outnumbered men couldn't plug them, they were

sure to be overrun. He and the four men closest to him held their M16s above their heads and fired blindly.

The enemy kept coming. "I had my four people. And through the light of the flares, I said, 'A couple of you guys go and man the machine guns out on those APCs.' Well, the response I got was, like, 'Fuck you, I ain't going up there.' So I ran to the first armored personnel carrier, and I pulled the dead gunner out of the turret. I jumped in there, manned the machine gun, and fired until it ran out of ammo." Okamoto moved to the second disabled APC, then the third, emptying their guns.

"They were still coming at us," he remembered. "So I crawled out there, till I was about ten meters from them. I killed them with hand grenades." Two enemy grenades fell near him. He managed to throw both back. But a third landed just beyond his reach. Shrapnel fragments peppered his legs and back.

"I just knew for sure I was going to die," he remembered. "'Hey Okamoto, you're not going to make it out of here. Mom's going to take it hard, but you're not going to make it out of here.' That's liberating. When you know you're going to die, the fear

ABOVE On August 23, 1968, Second Lieutenant Vincent Okamoto's outfit faced a near-impossible task. From their base at Cu Chi, he and his men were helicoptered northwestward to block a battalion of North Vietnamese troops from escaping across the border into Cambodia.

REMFs

Eight out of ten Americans in Vietnam never heard a shot fired in anger, never saw a bomb dropped or a village burned. They were the men in combat support and service support units—clerks, cooks, mechanics, MPs. These were the jobs nearly everyone wanted.

But combat soldiers had a name for them. "They're REMFs—rear-echelon motherfuckers," Vincent Okamoto remembered. "These are the dudes that . . . never go out beyond the barbed wire of base camp. They sleep in a bed, with sheets. They have showers every day. They drink cold beer at night. Their only danger is every once in a while, they might be . . . hit with rockets or mortars. They're not humping the boonies every day in hundred-degree weather, carrying a sixty-pound pack, thinking that if you don't get shot, you may die from heatstroke. They were totally alien."

Private American contractors constructed one hundred airfields in South Vietnam—including fifteen big enough for jets to land on and take off from—and they created seven deep-draft ocean ports for the loading and unloading of supplies and men. Six giant dairy plants produced 17 million gallons of milk substitute for GIs. More than forty ice cream plants—including one aboard a floating barge in the Mekong Delta—turned out hundreds of thousands of gallons in a dozen flavors every month.

Long Binh, twenty miles north of Saigon, was the biggest of all the American bases. Roughly the size of Manhattan, it was so large, one colonel said, that "if we ever really got attacked, the VC would have to use the scheduled bus service to get around." As many as sixty thousand Americans made it their home. Tens of thousands of South Vietnamese filed through its gates each day to see to the Americans' needs. Vietnamese cooks prepared their meals. Vietnamese maids and laundresses tidied up their barracks and made sure their uniforms were clean and crisply ironed.

"Here at Long Binh," the operations officer told CBS correspondent Morley Safer, "we have about the same facilities you might find stateside. We have eight Olympic-sized swimming pools. We have ranges for archery and skeet shooting. For golf we have putting and driving ranges. And we are building a couple of bowling alleys. And, of course, there is basketball. We have only four football fields and right now we don't have enough people to referee the games. There's a lot of roads to run around for people who want to keep in shape. They have to use their initiative, you know, and go to special services and find things to do. There's plenty to do: there's no real cause for complaint."

Long Binh also housed a military jail that held hundreds of prisoners and forty separate air-conditioned clubs at which officers and enlisted men could drink and eat, a bakery that produced 180,000 loaves of bread a day, a Chinese restaurant, a go-cart track—and a "massage parlor," operated by an independent contractor and open twenty-four hours a day.

Since most of the men who lived and worked on the base rarely moved beyond the barbed wire and never saw combat, the Army built for them what was officially called "the Nature of the War Museum," a replica of a Viet Cong–held village—a hut, a Buddhist temple, artificial booby traps, and a hollowed-out haystack with an opening at the side and a helpful sign reading "Hiding-Place in Haystack."

There were forty-six "main store" PXs in South Vietnam, each the size of a big, one-story, fully stocked department store—and 168 smaller "troop and base" stores at which GIs could buy everything from refrigerators and color television sets to hairspray for their Vietnamese girlfriends.

"There was an ongoing cottage industry between the grunts and the rear-echelon motherfuckers," Okamoto remembered. "The base camp commandos were hungry for souvenirs. AK-47s became the coin of the realm. We would be filthy with AK-47s. So when you ran out of the small creature comforts of life, you'd say, 'Okay, pack them up in a trailer, or ship them to Tan Son Nhut Air Base.' I made a run one time. And when we got there, it was surreal. I just left Cu Chi, and two and a half hours later, I am at Tan Son Nhut, at the main PX. It's air-conditioned. They are playing soft music. They had everything in stock, from refrigerators to a jewelry counter, where you could buy diamonds and Rolex watches. And you see these Air Force types wearing starched khaki uniforms. You see civilian workers, all shopping in the PX. They have a snack bar where you could buy hamburgers and chocolate milk and malts and cherry Cokes. But you have to say to yourself, 'Damn; this is a different universe. Two and a half hours away people are killing each other. My people are risking their ass. And here, they're playing taped music of the Mamas and the Papas in the PX.'"

OPPOSITE Just a portion of Long Binh, the largest U.S. base in South Vietnam, seen from the air **TOP LEFT** Soldiers tan themselves alongside one of eight swimming pools on the base. **TOP RIGHT** Film star Raquel Welch stirs up the men at Danang during one of Bob Hope's annual USO Christmas shows. "Sending girls like me to Vietnam to entertain the troops is like teasing a caged lion with . . . raw meat," she said. "Those boys want relief, not more frustration." **ABOVE** Precious cargo, at fifteen cents a can

died—nineteen-, twenty-year-old high school dropouts. Most were draftees. They didn't have escape routes that the elite and the wealthy and the privileged had. They looked upon military service as like the weather: you had to go in, and you'd do it. But to see these kids, who had the least to gain—there wasn't anything to look forward to. They weren't going to be rewarded for their service in Vietnam. And yet, their infinite patience, their loyalty to each other, their courage under fire was just phenomenal. And you would ask yourself, 'How does America produce young men like this?'" Before his tour of duty ended, Vincent Okamoto would become the most highly decorated Japanese American to survive the Vietnam War.

THE WHOLE WORLD IS WATCHING

THE SIRENS IN THE NIGHT and the spectacle of Americans hating and fighting one another, of which Richard Nixon had spoken in Miami sixteen days earlier, would be all too evident during the Democratic convention that opened in Chicago on August 26, the day after Okamoto and his men were lifted off the battlefield.

The Democratic Party was as deeply divided as the country. Vice President Hubert Humphrey was now the most likely nominee: mayor of Minneapolis, senator from Minnesota, champion of civil rights, and a friend of labor, he had once been a hero to the liberal wing of his party. But because, as vice president, he had unswervingly supported the president and the war in public, many of his old admirers had come to despise him, and his official announcement of his candidacy, promising to practice "the politics of joy," had made him seem hopelessly out of touch with his troubled country.

A sizable but vocal minority of the delegates—those won by Senator Eugene McCarthy, as well as those loyal to the memory of Robert Kennedy, who would find a new potential standard-bearer in Senator George McGovern—was determined to add a plank to the party platform calling for an unconditional and immediate end to all bombing of North Vietnam, and a phased withdrawal by both American and North Vietnamese forces leading to talks including the NLF and aimed at the creation of a coalition government.

Humphrey worked to create a vaguely worded compromise peace plank that at least some of the antiwar delegates might support: "Stop all bombing of North Vietnam," it said, "unless this action would endanger the lives of our troops." Since it included no demand that Hanoi reciprocate in any way, Johnson vetoed it. "This plank just undercuts the whole policy," he

leaves. At least in my case, I was no longer afraid. I was just mad because here are all these little guys trying to kill my ass. And if that's the case, then I'm going to make it as tough on them as I possibly can before I go down. I killed a lot of brave men that night. And I rationalized that by telling myself, 'Well, maybe what you did—just maybe—it saved the lives of a couple of your people.'"

During the night, the enemy slipped over the border into Cambodia, dragging as many of their dead with them as they could. A third of Okamoto's company had been lost.

For his efforts that day, Vincent Okamoto received the Distinguished Service Cross, the Army's second highest honor. "You know what?" he asked. "The real heroes were the men who

ABOVE Second Lieutenant Vincent Okamoto and his M16. "The Twenty-fifth Infantry Division," he remembered, "had responsibility for guarding the Cambodian border. These had been North Vietnamese–Viet Cong strongholds for years. We would go there, and some of those places, we wouldn't have to look for them. They'd come out, gunning for us. The old-timers would throw away their C-rations to carry more ammo, because they knew it was going to be a real battle."

told his vice president. "By God, the Democratic Party ought not be doing that to me and you ought not be doing it; you've been a part of this policy." Humphrey gave in and threw his support behind a plank that explicitly praised the president for his efforts at peacemaking and offered a bombing halt only if there were a matching gesture by Hanoi. The stage was set for an epic floor fight.

Meanwhile, in city parks and the streets surrounding them, protestors had been gathering for days, most to register their anguish over the war, some bent on disrupting the proceedings. "It was a wild array of different people with different strategies and different tactics," Bill Zimmerman recalled. Rumors of coming trouble were everywhere: "black militants" were planning to attack white neighborhoods; radicals were going to shell the convention; yippies threatened to lace the city's drinking water with LSD and kidnap delegates and orchestrate a nude "swim-in" in Lake Michigan by ten thousand men and women.

The threats were empty, but Chicago mayor Richard J. Daley chose to take them all seriously. During the uprising that followed Dr. King's death, he'd ordered his police force to "shoot to kill" anyone seen looting. "As long as I am mayor of this city," he said, "there's going to be law and order in Chicago." He ran his city—and his party's statewide Democratic machine—with an iron hand. "If Daley instructs his [118] delegates to vote for Ho Chi Minh," a veteran Chicago politician said, "all but twenty votes will go to Ho Chi Minh without a question." The mayor had refused to back any of the likely nominees, unpersuaded that any of them could defeat Nixon, and even encouraged Lyndon Johnson to fly to Chicago and get back in the race, promising that enough delegates would rally to him to snatch the nomination. But the Secret Service warned Johnson it could not guarantee his safety, and when the pollster Lou Harris informed him that the Republican candidate held a sizable lead over him as well as over every other potential Democratic candidate he reluctantly abandoned the idea.

The mayor remained unsure whom to support—he would try and fail to persuade Senator Edward Kennedy, the lone surviving Kennedy brother, to run before he finally threw his support behind Humphrey—but he was determined that there would be no trouble in his city. He put twelve thousand Chicago policemen on twelve-hour alert, and saw to it that six thousand armed National Guardsmen were stationed in the city, alongside one

thousand intelligence operatives from the FBI, the CIA, the Army, and the Navy. Another six thousand Army troops stood by at air bases across the country in case they were needed. Daley also created a one-square-mile security area around the amphitheater and surrounded it with chain-link fences topped

ABOVE Chicago mayor Richard J. Daley, seated on the floor of the 1968 Democratic convention alongside the Illinois delegation he controlled. Many of the demonstrators gathering outside the Chicago Amphitheater, he told the delegates, were "extremists . . . who have been successful in convincing some people that theatrical protest is rational dissent."

by whorls of barbed wire. Manhole covers were sealed with tar. Helicopters chattered constantly overhead. The mayor also refused to issue permits for protest marches and forbade anyone from remaining in a city park after 11 p.m.

When Rennie Davis, one of the protest's organizers, was asked if he planned to go ahead with demonstrations anyway, he was adamant: "Given the fact that for many months we have notified this city and this nation that we wish to hold an assembly in Chicago to register our convictions about the war, the tens of thousands of people coming to the city . . . *constitute* a permit. . . . Our fight is with the militarism that is developing in this country in the response to legitimate political and social grievances . . . by bringing in troops rather than dealing with the real issues and real problems."

Walter Cronkite, anchoring the CBS convention coverage, was appalled at what Daley was doing. "In the name of security, freedom of the press, freedom of movement, perhaps as far as the demonstrators themselves are concerned even freedom of speech, have been severely restricted here," he told his viewers on opening day. "A Democratic convention is about to begin in a police state. There just doesn't seem to be any other way to say it."

"To go to Chicago," Tom Hayden remembered, "was a matter of finding out how far you were willing to go for your beliefs, and finding out how far the American government was willing to go in suspending the better part of its tradition to stop you." "You stayed away if you wanted to avoid trouble, and you went if you couldn't stay away," Todd Gitlin recalled. "The fear, the squabbling, maybe above all the lack of permits, took their toll. The tens of thousands of demonstrators once trumpeted did not materialize. A few thousand did, three or four thousand on most days, up to perhaps eight or ten thousand at the peak on Wednesday, August 28."

"Never before," wrote *Chicago Sun-Times* columnist Mike Royko, "had so many feared so much from so few."

Twice, the police drove demonstrators out of Lincoln Park with clubs and tear gas, then chased them through the fashionable streets of Old Town, clubbing fleeing protestors and spectators alike. Phil Caputo, who had been among the first Marines to serve in Vietnam and was now a cub reporter for the *Chicago Tribune,* saw it happen and thought he knew what accounted for the officers' ferocity. "The cops were all guys from the neigh-

borhoods," he remembered. "Mostly ethnic guys, Italians, Polish guys, Irish guys. Probably some had been in Vietnam—and if they hadn't been they certainly had cousins or brothers who were. And, like a lot of guys from the neighborhood, they had a certain image of what college students ought to be like. Now, all of a sudden, the streets are filled with these kids who don't look to them like college kids are supposed to look. Some are breaking windows and yelling obscenities. I think a lot of policemen saw that as abusing their privileges and scorning them, the cops." Whatever their motivation, whether they were acting out of personal resentment or under direct orders from their superiors, the Chicago police seemed intent on brutalizing demonstrators.

There was trouble inside the amphitheater, too. Fights erupted over credentials and procedures. Television reporters were manhandled. On Wednesday the 28th, delegates began debating the party platform. Humphrey supporters argued that adopting the peace plank would jeopardize the lives of American troops and undermine the talks going on in Paris. Tennessee senator Albert Gore Sr. was among those who spoke in favor of it. "The American people think overwhelmingly we made a mistake," he said, "and yet in the platform we are called upon not to only approve this unconscionably disastrous policy but to applaud it."

The peace plank was defeated by a vote of 1,567 to 1,041, but even before the tally was completed hundreds of delegates had donned black armbands and broken into chorus after chorus of "We Shall Overcome." An astonishing 40 percent of the Democratic delegates had expressly voted against the policy of their own president.

By then, some three thousand demonstrators had left Lincoln Park for Grant Park, just across Michigan Avenue from the Chicago Hilton, where both Humphrey and McCarthy had their headquarters. When word spread that the Humphrey forces had won the battle over the platform, a skinny shirtless young man shinnied up a flagpole and tore down the American flag. The police dragged him down, sprayed the crowd with tear gas, and again attacked individual demonstrators. Rennie Davis was beaten unconscious. Tom Hayden exhorted the crowd to "move out of this park in groups throughout the city and turn this overheated military machine against itself. Let us make sure that if blood flows, it flows all over the city."

As night fell, blood was about to flow at the intersection of Michigan Avenue and Balbo in front of the Hilton. Permit or no permit, demonstrators started drifting out of Grant Park, headed for the amphitheater, where the balloting for the presidential nomination was about to get under way. Some sang "America the Beautiful." Others chanted, "Peace now!," "Fuck you, LBJ," and "Dump the Hump."

Hundreds of policemen in blue helmets and an unknown

OPPOSITE In Grant Park on the late afternoon of August 28, 1968, antiwar demonstrators fly an NLF flag from atop a bronze statue of Civil War General John A. Logan. The Conrad Hilton Hotel, where many convention delegates were staying, stands just across Michigan Avenue. "They have decided they are going to march on the amphitheater," Jack Perkins of ABC News reported, "despite police determination to stop them short."

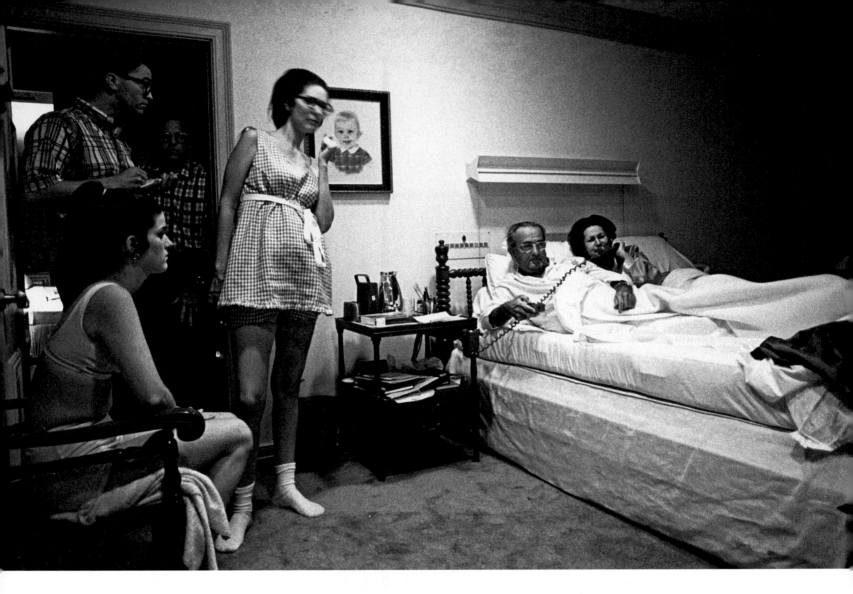

number of plainclothesmen were waiting for them. At a signal, they charged into the crowd, swinging their nightsticks. Television cameras and lights had been set up around the main entrance to the Hilton to capture the comings and goings of the delegates. The garish lights were turned on. The crowd began chanting, "The whole world is watching! The whole world is watching!"

The novelist Norman Mailer was looking on from the nineteenth-floor of the hotel when "the police attacked with tear gas, with mace and with clubs. They attacked like a chain saw cutting into wood, the teeth of the saw the edge of their clubs, they attacked like a scythe through grass, lines of twenty and thirty policemen striking out in an arc, the clubs beating, demonstrators fleeing. [The police cut] through the crowd one way, then cut through them another. They chased people into the park, ran them down, beat them up; they cut through the intersection at Michigan and Balbo like a razor cutting a channel through a head of hair, and then drove columns of new police into the channel who in turn pushed out, clubs flailing, on each side to cut new channels, and new ones again. . . . Police cars

rolled up, prisoners were beaten, shoved into wagons and driven away."

For seventeen floodlit bloody minutes, network cameras captured it all. Down below, Jack Newfield, reporting for the *Village Voice,* found himself in the middle of it.

At the southwest entrance to the Hilton, a skinny, long-haired kid of about seventeen skidded down on the sidewalk, and four overweight cops leaped on him, chopping strokes on his head. His hair flew from the force of the blows. A dozen small rivulets of blood began to cascade

ABOVE From the bedroom of their ranch in Stonewall, Texas, the Johnsons watch the chaos in Chicago unfold on television. Left to right: Luci Johnson Nugent, staffer Tom Johnson, unknown, Linda Johnson Robb, the president, and Lady Bird Johnson **OPPOSITE, CLOCKWISE FROM TOP LEFT** Lit by TV lights, demonstrators chant, "Join us! Join us!" A defiant demonstrator, bloodied by a policeman's nightstick, gives the peace sign. Chicago police charge into the crowd in front of the Hilton.

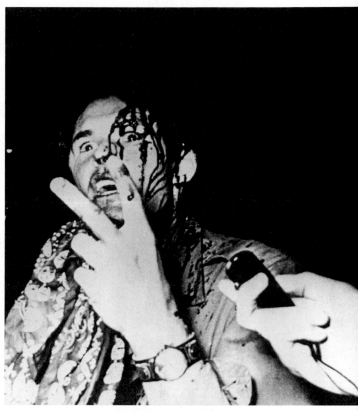

down the kid's temple and onto the sidewalk. He was not crying or screaming, but crawling in a stupor toward the gutter. When he saw a photographer take a picture, he made a V sign with his fingers.

A doctor in a white uniform and Red Cross armband began to run toward the kid, but two other cops caught him from behind and knocked him down. One of them jammed his knee into the doctor's throat and began clubbing his rib cage. . . .

A few feet away a phalanx of police charged into a group of women reporters and young McCarthy activists standing idly against the window of the Hilton Hotel's Haymarket Inn. The terrified people began to go down under the unexpected police charge when the plate glass window

shattered, and the people tumbled backward through the glass. The police then climbed through the broken windows and began to beat people, some of whom had been drinking quietly in the hotel bar. . . .

The defiant kids began a slow, orderly retreat back up Michigan Avenue. They did not run. They did not panic. They did not fight back. As they fell back they helped pick up fallen comrades who were beaten or gassed. Suddenly, a plainclothesman dressed as a soldier moved out of the shadows and knocked one kid down with an overhand punch. The kid squatted on the pavement of Michigan Avenue, trying to cover his face, while the plainclothesman punched him with savage accuracy. Thud, thud, thud. Blotches of blood spread over the kid's face. Two photographers moved in. Several police formed a closed circle around the beating to prevent pictures. One of the policemen then squirted mace at the photographers, who dispersed. The plainclothesman melted back into the line of police.

ABOVE The press was not immune from police attacks on Michigan Avenue; here, photographer Burton Silverman, working for *The New York Times,* is roughed up before being placed under arrest.

At least 800 demonstrators and passersby—including 20 reporters and photographers—were beaten seriously enough to require medical attention during the convention week, and 668 persons were jailed. One hundred and fifty policemen would report injuries, too.

The balloting got under way while television sets scattered through the amphitheater broadcast tapes of the chaos on Michigan Avenue. Speaker after speaker denounced what one called Mayor Daley's "Gestapo tactics," but, as expected, Humphrey easily won the nomination on the first ballot. Afterward, he assured the press how pleased he was and pleaded with his fellow Democrats to unite behind him. But he later confessed that he left Chicago "heart-broken, battered, and beaten," and he told his wife he felt as if they'd been in a shipwreck.

Helicopter crew chief Ron Ferrizi happened to be in Australia during convention week. He'd been flying combat missions in Vietnam for ten months. Earlier that year, he'd nearly been killed when the ammunition aboard a downed and burning helicopter exploded as he was trying to pull out the wounded pilot. Afterward, he was awarded the Silver Star, but he'd eventually begun to go "a little crazy," he remembered, and his first sergeant insisted he take a few days in Australia for rest and recreation—R&R. "So I turn on the TV in my hotel room," he remembered. "The first scene was a closeup over the shoulder of this storm trooper who had a kid by the scruff of his shirt. And he smacks him with his bat. And there's blood and everything and all this jumble. And then the camera pans out and it's far away. And there's a riot and there's fighting going on. And I go, 'Oh my god. The Russians invaded Czechoslovakia.' [Soviet tanks and troops had in fact crossed into Czechoslovakia just a few days earlier, crushing the reform government led by Alexander Dubček.] And then [I read at the bottom of the screen] "Chicago Democratic Convention. United States of America." And at that moment I was politicized. At that moment I realized that anybody who really cared for America was sent halfway around the world chasing some ghost in a jungle killing somebody else's grandmother for no reason at all. And in the

meantime my country's being torn apart. So I saw somebody who looked like my dad hitting somebody who looked like me. Oh my God, whose side would I be on?

A day or two later, Professor Sam Hynes was to start a new

ABOVE Antiwar delegates express their displeasure after Hubert Humphrey captures the Democratic presidential nomination. "I was a victim of that convention," Humphrey said later. "I could've beaten the Republicans anytime—but it's difficult to take on the Republicans and fight a guerrilla war in your own party at the same time."

THE VENEER OF CIVILIZATION | 335

job, teaching English at Northwestern University in the Chicago suburb of Evanston. "We drove out together from Pennsylvania," he recalled, "my wife, Liz, and my daughters, Mandy and Jo and I. As we approached downtown Chicago, I said, 'I'll get off the expressway and take you up Lakeshore Drive so that you can see the beauty of this city built along the lake.' But when we turned into Grant Park what we saw wasn't a beautiful, urban cityscape. What we saw was garbage, debris, floating paper, a chaos of disorder that looked like a battlefield after a battle. And indeed that's what it was. The Democratic convention had just ended the day before. And on that field, in Grant Park, the army of protestors had fought against the Chicago city police. It was a scene of ruination. We drove through all that drifting paper up Lakeshore Drive until we came to a pedestrian bridge over the drive and there was a banner attached that read 'Mayor Daley Welcomes You to Chicago.' When we got to Evanston, I remember one of my new colleagues invited us to a cocktail party and the other people there were in a state of shock, very quiet. They were shocked because they were liberals, as Liz and I were, my daughters, too, for that matter, and something terrible had happened to their idea of liberalism—it had been invaded by violent forces. And what should they do? They didn't know. And I didn't know either. Nobody knew."

Events in Chicago had further deepened American divisions. Antiwar demonstrators left the city more alienated from their government than ever, and some saw in the violent street clashes they had experienced the need for a full-scale violent revolution.

A presidential commission would declare what had happened in Chicago a "police riot," but 56 percent of those Americans responding to a nationwide Gallup poll actually approved of the way the police had handled the demonstrators.

"To our innocent eyes," Todd Gitlin remembered, "it defied common sense that people could watch even the sliver of the onslaught that got onto television and side with the cops—which in fact was precisely what the polls showed. As unpopular as the war had become, the antiwar movement was detested still more—the most hated political group in America, disliked even by most of the people who supported immediate withdrawal from Vietnam. McGeorge Bundy had been right to tell Lyndon Johnson, in November [1967], just after the [March on the Pentagon]: 'One of the few things that help us right now is public distaste for the violent doves. . . .' Apparently, the majority agreed with Bundy that whoever swung the clubs, we were to blame."

Five days after the convention ended, when Richard Nixon chose to open his campaign with a motorcade through the Chicago Loop, nearly half a million Chicagoans would turn out to cheer him.

A DIFFERENT DEMEANOR

ON AUGUST 29TH, the day after police and demonstrators clashed in Chicago, twenty-year-old Private Michael Holmes arrived in Vietnam. He was an only child, born and brought up in the tiny town of Williamsville, in the heart of the Missouri Ozarks. His father and mother ran the general store where Michael worked every day after school. He rode horses, floated the rivers, hunted deer and squirrels, and went steady with a girl named Darlene. But he had trouble keeping up in high school, did not complete community college, and soon found himself in the Army.

In Vietnam, he was assigned to F Troop, Seventeenth Armored Cavalry, 196th Infantry Brigade, stationed at an isolated firebase twenty-two miles south of Da Nang, called "Baldy." Holmes used a tape recorder to communicate with his family back home. "Baldy isn't too much," he told them, "about as big as Williamsville, maybe bigger."

He began as a gunner on an armored personnel carrier, one of twenty-seven heavily armed APCs belonging to his brigade that patrolled the nearby countryside, looking for Viet Cong and those who supported them.

Until he was drafted, he had never been far beyond the borders of Missouri. Everything was new and strange: "The people are something else. They're ignorant. Filthy and everything. Hardly no clothes on at all. I mean they've got clothes on but just real shorts and a blouse or shorts and a shirt. Hardly nothing at all. They're really little and ugly. Teeth are all black. But they work pretty hard. You've seen these pictures where they carried this rice on their shoulders, and have it balanced. Well, we stopped this one to check his ID. And I tried to pick that thing up. Why, that like to broke my back before I got it stood up. That thing weighed about two hundred pounds. And one of them little bitty dinks—just little ole bitty, about five-three—carrying that thing. Why, he could have broke me in two if he wanted to.

"I really can't tell you too much about this country except the rice paddies stink. And it's just miles and miles of nothing but rice paddies. And they got dikes in them. Real cool looking. We go through with our APCs and tear them down. And they's bound to get all hacked off at us for tearing down their rice fields."

Life at Firebase Baldy was tedious. It rained steadily. There were endless sandbags to be filled and repairs to be made, supplies to load and unload. Holmes and his friends looked for ways to relieve the boredom: "One night we were out and the lieutenant started shooting [his M16] so everybody started shooting sixteens. Then the [M60 machine guns] and then the [50mm

machine guns], then everything all at once. It was at night. The tracers going. Oh, it really did look good. We killed a couple of [water] buffalos that night, ducks and everything else. But no one got hurt. And we were just doing it for the heck of it. That's what's so great. You know it's not really that bad [being here]. In a way, I like it. It's just being away from home and everything that I don't like."

In Williamsville, family and friends gathered in his parents' living room to listen to Michael's reports from Vietnam—and to fill him in, on tape, on what he was missing back home. It was autumn, and the Ozarks looked beautiful. Squirrel hunting was in full swing. Signs of deer were everywhere. A fellow draftee planned to get married, but not until he came home from the service. A friend named Ricky had broken up with his girlfriend and was "really prowling now." Another friend had bought himself a Chrysler, and still another was driving a brand-new Bonneville.

"I miss you a lot," his mother said, "and I'm really looking forward to the day when you come home. I guess that's what mothers are for, just to worry and look forward to their children coming back home once they're away. Maybe I'll get used to it someday, but I don't know. It sure is lonely sometimes with just Dad and I."

His father offered what he hoped would be helpful advice:

"Mike, this is your dad talking. I think you was probably really lucky in getting attached to the APC division. I don't think that they're necessarily 100 percent safe, but I believe you're a lot safer, and you get to live a lot better and cleaner life than you would if you was in the infantry. And we think you'll be okay, just don't be nosing around where you don't have any business and get hold of a booby trap or something. Keep your eyes open, and be careful. This is about the end of this tape, so goodbye for now."

Holmes was disappointed that during mission after mission, the enemy remained elusive. "We burned down a whole lot of hooches today of these people who don't cooperate with us," he told his parents. "We just burn down their houses and everything. I don't really understand it because if they are not VC and we do that to them—you know, treat them bad—then they're going to turn VC. The Army does everything backwards."

ABOVE LEFT Private Michael Holmes and one of the dogs, specially trained to locate hidden mines, that accompanied his armored unit's patrols into the countryside. "I'm growing a moustache," he told his parents. "It's a little thin but I'm getting it there. If it don't work out within another two or three weeks I'm going to cut it off." **ABOVE RIGHT** The APC, overturned by a bomb, in which Holmes was wounded and his best friend was killed.

One morning that autumn, several APCs from F Troop moved cautiously up Highway One toward Danang. Mike Holmes and five of his closest buddies rode in the second vehicle. "When we go out this time we won't be going out real far," he'd assured his mother and father. "We'll be on a road sweep. That's where these guys are in front with these mine detectors trying to find mines in the road. It isn't any big thing. Nothing ever comes of that. So far hasn't. We've been on a lot of them."

At five minutes before noon, their APC hit a three hundred-pound bomb buried beneath the road. The explosion hurled the massive vehicle into the air and turned it belly up. Three men died instantly. Holmes was thrown clear but knocked unconscious and woke up five hours later in the hospital.

To reassure his parents he tried to make light of what had happened: "Really isn't no worse than when I fell off my bike when I was little and got all skinned up. That's about how I feel. I don't think I'll have any scars except maybe on my behind. That's where I think I landed. Got a great big sore right on my butt . . . where I skidded on the ground when I fell off or something. It may sound funny but it does hurt. Up to this point I didn't know if there was really a war going on over here. I just thought maybe they was playing a game or something. But I could've reached out and touched two of those people. I knew them real good, not real good, but I did know them. One of them I knew very good."

In fact, one of those killed that day had been his closest friend in the platoon, Corporal Jimmy Howard, the son of the country singer Jan Howard, whose spoken "letter" to "My Son" was a country hit when he died. After Jimmy's death, the other men in his outfit remembered, Holmes seemed different. "Once you lose a few friends over there you take on a different demeanor," one recalled. "You have almost a grudge at that point, that you want to maintain. And because you've lost these friends and they've taken them from you, you want the opportunity to get back at them. He shared that. I shared that."

AN ACCEPTABLE RISK

THE DISASTER of the Democratic convention haunted Hubert Humphrey's campaign for president. Comfortably ahead in the polls, the Republican candidate refused to debate him. Eugene McCarthy, to whom many antiwar Democrats remained loyal, refused to endorse him. A third-party candidate, George Wallace, the segregationist former governor of Alabama, was stealing away traditional Democratic voters. (His campaign would eventually collapse in October, in part because

his running mate, former Air Force Chief of Staff General Curtis LeMay, suggested using nuclear weapons in Vietnam.) Democratic Party coffers were empty; the Humphrey campaign could not afford to buy a single radio or television spot. And everywhere he tried to speak, protestors did their best to drown him out, chanting, "Fascist! Fascist! Dump the Hump!"

Nixon reveled in Humphrey's troubles. He hinted that he had a plan to end the war but was careful to say nothing substantive about it, other than to promise "peace with honor," by which he meant an end to U.S. military involvement and an autonomous South Vietnam that would justify four years of American sacrifice. In keeping silent, he was mirroring the counsel of a young campaign aide named Kevin Phillips: "Non-specificity is desirable. . . . The lack of an ideological position helps make RN [Richard Nixon] a rallying point for a cross-section of voters disgusted with the war." Only an unexpected breakthrough toward peace, the candidate believed, could "cut down a lead as big as ours."

In 1965, Humphrey had expressed grave doubts to the president about the wisdom of sending American troops to Vietnam but in public he had never been anything but faithful to Johnson's policies. Now, his advisers told him, if he wanted to win he had to break with the president and make some gesture toward ending the conflict. Johnson warned him against it. "He told me that it would endanger American troops like his son-in-law [Charles Robb, a Marine serving in combat in Vietnam] and cost lives," Humphrey remembered. "I would have blood on my hands. He would denounce me publicly for playing politics with peace." Twice, the candidate tried to put at least a little daylight between himself and the administration; he said some American forces could start coming home in 1969, whatever happened at the Paris peace talks, and he claimed that he could have run on the peace plank that had been defeated in Chicago, evidently forgetting that it had called for an unconditional bombing halt. Johnson rebuked him both times.

On September 27, Gallup showed Humphrey fifteen points behind his Republican rival. Something had to be done. Three days later, without consulting the White House, Humphrey gave a televised address from Salt Lake City. For the first time, the vice presidential seal was not affixed to the lectern; Humphrey was speaking for himself, not for the administration he had served. He called for a *total* halt to the bombing of the North as "an acceptable risk for peace," accompanied by a move toward "de-Americanization" of the war, an immediate cease-fire, and the "supervised withdrawal of all foreign troops."

Johnson felt betrayed. It was a "fool speech," he said, and wondered privately whether Richard Nixon might not make a better president.

But Humphrey's crowds grew larger overnight. Heck-

lers began staying home. Money flowed into the campaign. McCarthy voters—though not McCarthy himself—rallied to Humphrey. He started to rise in the polls. The race was tightening.

ACCELERATED PACIFICATION

A S THE AMERICAN ELECTION drew near, Saigon found itself facing new challenges. President Johnson had refused to send more U.S. troops. Clark Clifford's visit in July had made it clear that Washington was fast losing patience with President Thieu. No one knew who would win the American presidency or what impact that victory might have on the prospects for peace. And it was at least possible that the stalled Paris peace talks—in which Saigon still had no voice—might yet call for

a cease-fire in place and a freeze on force levels. Hanoi and the NLF already seemed to be preparing for that possibility—they had stepped up terrorist attacks and the creation of "people's committees" in the villages in order to strengthen their claim to political power in the negotiations to come.

If the Saigon regime were to survive, concluded Ambassador Bunker, Robert Komer, the outgoing head of CORDS, and William Colby, the former CIA station chief who was about to succeed him, it needed to expand its political control over as much of the countryside as it could as fast as it could. The old strategy of slow consolidation needed to be replaced by what

ABOVE Hubert Humphrey gets a warm welcome in front of his father's drugstore in Huron, South Dakota, where he had worked as a pharmacist before going into politics. Elsewhere, he was booed, heckled, jeered, drowned out. "These people are intentionally mean anarchists," he complained. "They do not believe in anything. . . . They will never live long enough to run us off the platform because basically they are just cowards."

they now called "accelerated pacification." The program they drew up was hugely ambitious. They proposed to upgrade a thousand contested hamlets (the number was later upped to over thirteen hundred); "neutralize" three thousand communist cadre (by which was meant persuade to defect, capture, or kill them); talk five thousand communist fighters into abandoning the NLF under the Chieu Hoi program; and create a new armed force of tens of thousands of volunteers pledged to defend their villages. And they proposed to do all of it within ninety days.

President Thieu was reluctant at first, fearing that he hadn't enough Regional and Popular Forces on hand, that the Americans were trying to do too much too fast. He disliked the idea of calling any villages "contested," too, and eventually insisted that they be divided into just two categories: "areas or hamlets controlled by the government," and "areas or hamlets not yet controlled by the government." But the Americans pushed hard, and in the end Thieu felt he had little choice in the matter.

Progress for the accelerated pacification program was to be measured by a revised version of the original CORDS Hamlet Evaluation System. More than half the HES categories used in grading hamlets were dropped—those having to do with schools and health and land reform, for instance—in favor of focusing on those having to do with security. But their accuracy did not improve. Some villages were never actually assessed. Both American advisers and South Vietnamese officials often exaggerated progress. And permanent security would not be possible unless what the Americans called the "Viet Cong Infrastructure"— the tax collectors and sympathetic village chiefs, runners and spies and suppliers and sympathizers who made NLF activity possible—could be broken up. To do that, the CIA had created the Phoenix Program.

After recovering from his wounds, Lieutenant Vincent Okamoto became attached to that program as an intelligence offi-

TOP William Colby, the former CIA official who succeeded Robert Komer as head of CORDS, examines an antiquated country-made shotgun carried by a member of a self-defense militia. **BOTTOM** Another militiaman, armed with an up-to-date M16 provided by the accelerated pacification program

cer. "[The Phoenix Program] was premised on the fact that the North Vietnamese coming down the Ho Chi Minh Trail were strangers in the South, just like the Americans," he recalled. "They didn't know the terrain. They didn't know the people. So in order for them to function operationally, they needed the Viet Cong infrastructure. And so the project was to eliminate those guys. I think it made a great deal of sense."

Stuart Herrington, an intelligence officer who took part in the Phoenix Program later in the war, explained how it was meant to work: "It was a simple attempt to collect in one place the intelligence that was in the hands of the police, the military intelligence community, the civilian intelligence community, the revolutionary development cadre, and everyone who worked in the villages and hamlets as a part of pacification, about who most likely were the cadre who should be targeted. Let's communicate, let's set up an office, everybody brings in all their information, and pretty soon we have a target list."

The program's targeting was only as good as the intelligence

upon which it was based—and that varied widely. Americans served only as advisers. Day-to-day enforcement was left to the South Vietnamese Provincial Reconnaissance Units—the PRUs—who sometimes were more interested in settling old scores than in rooting out communists. "It was subject to abuse, and was abused," Okamoto remembered. "You'd get the list, and you'd check with other intelligence officers in the district. And you tried to pool that information. Next night, or a couple nights later, a bunch of cowboys from the PRUs would go out there. And, you know, knock on the door: 'April Fool, mother-fucker!' And, boom. There wasn't any real accountability."

Critics would denounce the Phoenix Program as little more than a campaign of assassination—and in 1971 William Colby

ABOVE Villagers on the Ca Mau Peninsula, allegedly under Saigon's control, feel free to attend an outdoor exhibition of North Vietnamese propaganda posters organized by local cadre.

would testify to Congress that there was no way to know how many of the more than twenty thousand that had been killed under its auspices to that point might have been innocent.

But the program's champions pointed to the fact that more than two-thirds of the 81,740 supposed cadre neutralized between 1969 and 1972 had been captured, not killed. "Regardless of how effective the Phoenix Program was or wasn't, area by area," Stuart Herrington recalled, "the communists thought it was very effective. They saw it as a significant threat to the viability of the revolution because, to the extent that you could take a sharp pointed knife and carve out the shadow government, their means of control over the civilian population was

ABOVE A terrified twenty-year-old named Pham Van faces an NLF-organized people's court in Long An Province. Charged with helping South Vietnamese forces uncover hidden weapons, he was sentenced to two years' imprisonment. His codefendant was executed.

dealt a death blow. And that's why, when the war was over, the North Vietnamese reserved special treatment for those who had worked in the Phoenix Program. They considered it a mortal threat to the revolution."

"The [accelerated pacification program] is really the most important thing we are doing," Creighton Abrams told his commanders at one meeting. "If we are successful in bashing down the VC and the government can raise its head up, the villages and hamlets can maintain their RF/PF units and keep a few policemen around and people are not being assassinated all the time, then the government will be where it belongs—out in the villages. Pacification is the 'gut' issue for the Vietnamese." On paper, it did seem to be working. By the end of January 1969 only 195 of the 1,317 hamlets that had been targeted were found to be still contested or controlled by the NLF, and nearly 1.7 million more people were said to be living in areas controlled by Saigon. More than 8,600 NLF fighters had defected, exceeding the target by well over 3,000.

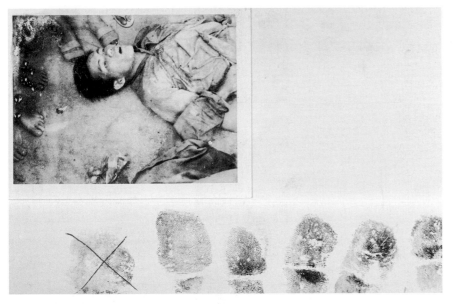

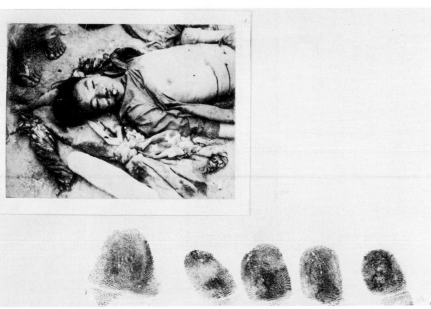

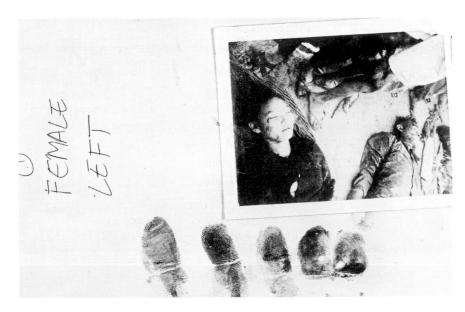

But that did not mean that the Saigon government had grown more popular with the people in its tenuous grip. A poll taken in the Delta Province of Long An in 1970 would show 35 percent of the people ready to vote for Thieu, and 20 percent willing to admit they favored the National Liberation Front—while 45 percent backed someone, anyone, opposed to both the NLF and the United States. "We were losing because of ourselves," Duong Van Mai Elliott recalled. The communists had an ideology, strict discipline, and effective leaders. "We had been unable to come up with a system, an ideology, and a leadership that could tap the same qualities in the same direction to win the struggle."

TREASON

LYNDON JOHNSON knew that it was now too late to negotiate an end to the war before he left office, but he still hoped that serious talks might get under way before that deadline. And on October 9—after five frustrating months without progress at the conference table—there was at least a hint that this goal might actually be within reach. During a tea break in Paris, a North Vietnamese delegate told one of his American counterparts that if the U.S. stopped bombing, Hanoi might agree to let Saigon take part in the negotiations. Three days later, Moscow—the prime supplier of weapons to the North Vietnamese—let it be known that the offer was serious.

The president was wary. The United States had consistently insisted that before ordering a total halt to the bombing the enemy had to meet three conditions—tactfully called "facts of life," in order to make them more palatable to Hanoi—respect for the neutrality of the DMZ, an end to the shelling of South Vietnamese cities, and peace talks in which Saigon was a full partner. He sent Ambassador

LEFT, TOP TO BOTTOM Three file photographs of alleged communist cadre "neutralized" by members of a Provincial Reconnaissance Unit under the auspices of the Phoenix Program. The bare feet around the bodies suggest that their corpses were displayed before their fellow villagers in hopes of confirming their identities. The fingerprints presumably offered further proof.

Buker and General Abrams to talk things over with President Thieu. Provided that all three terms were met—and the bombing could begin again if they were not—the South Vietnamese president said he saw no objection. "After all," he said, "the main problem is not to stop the bombing but to stop the war, and we must try this path to see if they are serious." Nor did he object to the presence of NLF representatives at the negotiating table, so long as they were not considered an entity separate from North Vietnam.

Meanwhile, in Paris, Ambassador Harriman read aloud the "facts of life" to the North Vietnamese, and when they did not object to any of them, Washington took it as acquiescence. (To be on the safe side, this process would be repeated nearly a dozen times, and was always met with the same encouraging silence from the Hanoi delegation.) Dean Rusk told the president that since the enemy had now at least tacitly agreed to every one of his terms he had no choice but to stop the bombing. Johnson remained cautious. He wanted to end the war, but he also did not want to be criticized for being the first president to have lost one, and he feared that calling a last-minute halt to the bombing might be perceived by the voters as a cynical political maneuver meant to keep the White House in Democratic hands. He polled the Joint Chiefs of Staff. They all agreed it was worth a try, in part because for two months monsoon weather would make it difficult to bomb the current targets, and U.S. aircraft could be better employed hitting the Ho Chi Minh Trail.

So far, everything had officially been kept secret—or so the White House hoped. Johnson had agreed to keep all three candidates apprised of developments—and they had all pledged to say nothing that would complicate his peace efforts in Paris—and since no agreement had yet been signed, he assured them that nothing had yet changed.

But the Nixon campaign had a mole within the administration, and while visiting Paris, Harvard professor Henry Kissinger, who had been a foreign policy adviser to Nelson Rockefeller, had also learned that "something big was afoot." Both reported to Nixon's campaign manager, John Mitchell, that it seemed likely that the president would announce a total bombing halt before election day. Nixon, whose lead in the polls had now been halved, saw it as a political trick intended to put Humphrey over the top, and set out to undermine it.

Nixon on the campaign trail. Early on, it seemed likely that he would win the presidency by a landslide—a quarter of a million people turned out to see him in San Francisco; thirty thousand heard him in Houston; national polls ran heavily his way. But he was haunted by the fear that President Johnson would unleash an "October surprise"—a last-minute promise of peace in Vietnam—that would obliterate his lead and hand the presidency to Humphrey.

RW - how do you want him to hit HH?
how hard shld he go?

V.N. bomb halt news

Harlow - have Dirksen & Tower blast this
Dirksen call LBJ & brace him w/this
- any other way to monkey wrench it?
Anything RN can do.

Rose - get her fd Louie Kemp
zing on the SVN - tell him told him

Dirksen - or someone

Rebozo - have Smathers threaten J
N has learned that stoppers are dealing w/ H
& N is going to blast him -
the lets are off & N very disappted
hard evidence W House is giving H
stuff he's not giving N
will blast in major speech in N.Y.
on Thurs

Harlow - try Bude, Radford, Greenthu
find out what's going on
Les Arends - Mel said
have Dirksen call J

Har - Scranton call Vance
heard rumor - N very distressed
what's going on

Har - tell Dirksen if don't get 3 conditions
N will blast bomb halt

Agnew - go see Helms -
tell him we want the truth -
or he hasn't got the job.

RN since military not for it.
- this might make SVN govt. fall

- Tomorrow RN blandly say US shld pause
under condition J laid down in N Orle
ie go further than present position
if conditions are met that J laid down
then we would approve bomb paus
but H is wrong in saying pause period
to give away our trump card w/o
getting this much would be bad

they're selling out SVN - leave new admin to hld
make a communist Asia -
wld have to go into Thailand.

be - N mad as hell -
W House staffers (name) Clifford, Califano
& L. Thompson
are now talking to H
giving info they're not giving N
that that at Al Smith dr.

RN
10/22
late   - indicate tomorrow
preparing & recording 2 radio speech

Harlow - Harlow monitoring V. Nam

RN - Andrews - if take a poll - inform us immy

Rhodes says we've dropped on older p
done - use radio for G & Sen spot
& a major ad - nail the

RW - sit down w/ RW + Moore etc -
in terms of their thot on tempo & co
how do you want him to hit HH - how ha

? maybe have to bite V.N.

UN - keep Chennault anna working on SVN
- insist publicly on the 3
Johnson conditions

- say for Fri - doing 3 hrs of TV sp

Moore - elect - get a reading on how they thk we're

He had already appointed Anna Chan Chennault to act as his secret liaison with the South Vietnamese regime. The wealthy, Chinese-born widow of General Claire Chennault, she was a prominent Republican fund-raiser, a member of the so-called "China lobby" who continued to blame the Democrats for having "lost" China, and was well connected in Saigon. Now, it became her task to privately communicate Nixon's message to Bui Diem, the South Vietnamese ambassador, and to President Thieu himself: Stay out of the Paris talks; the Democrats were planning to sell out South Vietnam; a Nixon administration would stand by America's ally. To cover Nixon's own tracks, Chennault was to communicate only with Mitchell, Spiro Agnew, and Bui Diem, using pay phones in case her own telephone was tapped. Nixon's instructions to his closest aide, H. R. Haldeman, scribbled down after a late-evening phone call on October 22, suggest how hard the candidate was working behind the scenes to scuttle the talks: "Keep Anna Chennault working on SVN"; "Any other way to monkey wrench it?"

In a statement to reporters three days later, Nixon sought both to cast doubt on Johnson's motives and to paint himself as a selfless observer. "I am told that officials in the administration have been driving very hard for an agreement on a bombing halt," he said, "accompanied possibly by a cease-fire, in the immediate future. I have since learned these reports are true. I am also told that this spurt of activity is a cynical, last-minute attempt by President Johnson to salvage the candidacy of Mr. Humphrey. This I do not believe." The speech got under Johnson's skin. "[Nixon] came out here," he told a friend, "and said, 'Now they say Johnson's a thief, but I knew his daddy and I don't think he's a thief, and they say he's a son of a bitch, and I knew his mother, she's not a bitch.' Well, hell, he advertised all over the country and he . . . planted the idea and he knew goddamn well I'd been fair to him."

Progress toward meaningful talks in Paris inched forward. Johnson remained chary, still worried he'd be accused of playing politics: "I would rather be viewed as stubborn and adamant than be seen as a tricky, slick politician." Clifford, still determined to stop the bombing, offered advice gleaned from Mark

OPPOSITE The scrawled notes H. R. Haldeman made during a rambling late-night telephone call from his boss, Richard Nixon, on October 22, 1968, hint at the Republican candidate's near-obsessive fear that peace might break out before election day. Not only does he want Anna Chennault to keep working to persuade President Thieu to stay away from the planned peace talks, and is looking for ways to throw another "monkey wrench" into the negotiations, but he also wants Spiro Agnew to call upon Richard Helms, the head of the CIA, and threaten him with dismissal if he doesn't reveal what Johnson is up to.

Twain: "When in doubt, do right. This will gratify some people and astonish the rest."

The president ordered General Abrams home for one more consultation.

He assembled his senior advisers at the White House at 2:30 in the morning of October 28 and in front of all of them interrogated his field commander. "I am going to put more weight on your judgment than that of anyone else," he told him.

LYNDON JOHNSON: General, do you think they will violate the DMZ and the cities?
GENERAL ABRAMS: I think they will abide by it on the DMZ, Mr. President. On the cities, I am not so sure. I am concerned about Saigon.
JOHNSON: If the enemy honors our agreement, will this be an advantage militarily for us?
ABRAMS: Yes, Mr. President.
JOHNSON: Will it compensate for lack of bombing north of the 19th parallel?
ABRAMS: Yes sir, it will.
JOHNSON: Can we return to full-scale bombing easily if they attack?
ABRAMS: Yes sir, very easily.
JOHNSON: In August you said that stopping the bombing would increase enemy capability severalfold. Why can we stop the bombing now?
ABRAMS: First, our interdiction in the panhandle [of North Vietnam] has been successful. Second, they haven't replaced their losses in the region. He cannot cause the mischief he could have caused in August.
JOHNSON: Can we do this without additional casualties?
ABRAMS: Yes sir, we can.
JOHNSON: If you were president, would you do it?
ABRAMS: I have no reservations about doing it, even though I know it is stepping into a cesspool of comment. It is the proper thing to do.

With Abrams aboard, the president polled his senior advisers, one by one. They were now unanimous in urging him to proceed. At 5 a.m., word came that an NLF delegation had just taken off for Paris. Everything seemed to be going smoothly.

Then, at 6:04, a cable arrived from Ambassador Bunker in Saigon. President Thieu had suddenly said he needed more time to consult his National Security Council. Johnson was livid—and had been tipped off that the Republicans had been at work behind the scenes. "It would rock the world," he told his advisers, "if it were said that Thieu was conniving with the Republicans. Can you imagine what people would say if it were known

that Hanoi has met all these conditions and that Nixon's conniving with them kept us from getting [the talks started]?"

Clark Clifford urged the president to go ahead anyway; it was "too late to turn back." Richard Helms agreed: "It is undesirable to allow these people to believe they have hijacked us out of this." General Abrams was indignant: "Thieu was unequivocal. I was there. He took it, understood it, marched right up to the plate, and swung." The president reluctantly agreed to give Thieu twenty-four more hours, but he also sent him a strongly worded message: If Americans ever came to blame him for blocking a peace settlement, he said, "God help South Vietnam,

ABOVE Lyndon Johnson and Hubert Humphrey appear together for the only time during the campaign, in the Houston Astrodome, November 3, 1968. Theirs had been an often stormy relationship— Johnson had even expressed private doubts about his vice president's readiness for the White House—but the president now told his listeners that "for the sake of our union," Humphrey "should and must become the thirty-seventh president of the United States."

because no president could maintain the support of the American people."

Ambassador Bunker spent hours at the Presidential Palace, trying to get Thieu to live up to his earlier promise. The South Vietnamese government, Thieu responded, "is not a car that can be hitched to a locomotive and taken anywhere the locomotive wants to go." "Anyone who still thinks the South Vietnamese are our puppets after this," an embassy official said, "is crazy."

Meanwhile, for all the effort he was putting into getting Saigon to the negotiating table, Johnson remained ambivalent about the prospects for an end to the fighting. When Abrams returned to Vietnam the following day, he carried with him a handwritten letter from the president addressed to "Dear Abe." It urged him to "follow the enemy in relentless pursuit. Don't give them a minute's rest. Keep pouring it on. Let the enemy feel the weight of everything you've got. With luck and with Abe we shall conquer ourselves a peace in the next three months."

On Thursday, October 31, Johnson called all three candidates to tell them he was going ahead with the bombing halt.

Negotiations were to begin in Paris on November 6—the day after election day. The next president—no matter who he was—would take office with negotiations already under way. Nixon joined Humphrey and Wallace in saying, "We'll back you up, Mr. President."

That evening, in a taped address broadcast by all three networks, the president announced that "all air, naval, and artillery bombardment of North Vietnam is to cease as of 8 a.m., Washington time, Friday morning." "The representatives of the government of the South are free to participate" in the subsequent talks, he added, and while representatives of the NLF would be present, "their attendance in no way involves official recognition of them" as distinct from the government of North Vietnam. He did not know who was going to win the presidency, he concluded, but he promised over the next few months to "do everything in my power to move us toward the peace that the new president—as well as this president and, I believe, every other American so deeply and urgently desires."

Humphrey's poll numbers surged. By the weekend, he had pulled almost even with his rival—and Lou Harris had him slightly ahead.

Then, disaster: in an address to the South Vietnamese national assembly on Saturday, President Thieu declared that "the government of South Vietnam deeply regrets not being able to participate in the present exploratory talks." The Nixon campaign had successfully scuttled the negotiations. "Through the confusion of those last three days," the journalist Theodore White wrote, "it became apparent that the bombing halt, begun on Friday morning, would not end the killing of Americans in Asia; and the tide of opinion that had begun to flow to Hubert Humphrey began, at the end of the weekend, to flow back to Nixon."

The president now had a clear picture of what Nixon's agents had been up to. The National Security Agency had intercepted cable traffic between Saigon and its Washington embassy. The CIA had placed a bug in President Thieu's office. The FBI had tapped Bui Diem's telephone at the South Vietnamese embassy. The president ordered the Bureau to tail Mrs. Chennault and record who came and went at the embassy. Saturday evening, with just three days before election day, Johnson called his friend and former colleague Everett Dirksen of Illinois, the Senate minority leader and the highest elected Republican official in the country, trusting that he would tell Nixon that the president was on to him and was considering telling the voters what he knew.

LYNDON JOHNSON: I want to talk to you as a friend and very confidentially because I think we're skirting on dangerous ground and I thought I ought to give you the facts and you ought to pass them on if you choose.

He explained that until October 28, President Thieu had seemed to be on board.

JOHNSON: Then we got some of our "friends "involved.

EVERETT DIRKSEN: Uh-huh.

JOHNSON: Some of it your old China crowd.

DIRKSEN: Yeah.

JOHNSON: And here is the latest information we got. The agent says that she's just . . . talked to the "boss" in New Mexico. [Spiro Agnew was campaigning there, and was thought to have spoken with Anna Chennault.]

DIRKSEN: Uh-huh.

JOHNSON: And that he says that "You must hold out . . . just hold on until after the election." Now, we know what Thieu is saying to them out there [because the CIA had bugged the South Vietnamese president's office].

DIRKSEN: Yeah.

JOHNSON: We're pretty well informed on both ends.

DIRKSEN: Yeah.

JOHNSON: Now, I'm reading their hand, Everett. I don't want to get this in the campaign.

DIRKSEN: That's right.

JOHNSON: And they oughtn't to be doing this. This is treason. [The 1799 Logan Act forbids any American citizen from negotiating with a foreign government without authorization.]

DIRKSEN: I know.

JOHNSON: I know this, that they're contacting a foreign power in the middle of a war.

DIRKSEN: That's a mistake.

JOHNSON: And it's a damn bad mistake. Now, I can identify them, because I know who is doing this. I don't want to identify it. I think it would shock America if a principal candidate was playing with a source like this on a matter this important.

DIRKSEN: Yeah.

JOHNSON: I don't want to do that.

DIRKSEN: Yeah.

JOHNSON: But if they're going to put this kind of stuff out, they ought to know that we know what they're doing. I know who they're talking to and I know what they're saying.

DIRKSEN: Yeah.

JOHNSON: And my judgment is that Nixon ought to play it just like he has all along, that I want to see peace come the first day we can, that it's not going to affect the election one way or the other. The conference is not even going to be held until after the election.

DIRKSEN: Yeah.

JOHNSON: They have stopped shelling the cities. They have stopped going across the DMZ. We've had twenty-four hours of relative peace. Now, if Nixon keeps the South Vietnamese away from the conference, well, that's going to be his responsibility. Up to this point, that's why they're not there. I had them signed on board until this happened.

DIRKSEN: Yeah. Okay.

JOHNSON: Well, now, what do you think we ought to do about it?

DIRKSEN: Well, I better get in touch with him, I think, and tell him about it.

JOHNSON: I think you better tell him that his people are saying to these folks that they oughtn't go through with this meeting. Now, if they [the South Vietnamese] don't go through with the meeting I don't think it's going to be me who's hurt, I think it's going to be whoever's elected, and, it'd be my guess, him.

DIRKSEN: Yeah.

JOHNSON: And I think they're making a very serious mistake, and I don't want to—I don't want to say this.

DIRKSEN: Yeah.

JOHNSON: And you're the only one I'm going to say it to. . . . Well, you just tell them that their people are messing around in this thing and if they don't want it on the front pages, they better quit it.

Dirksen managed to contact Nixon—who called the president the next day.

RICHARD NIXON: I just wanted you to know that I got a report from Everett Dirksen with regard to your call. I just went on *Meet the Press* and I said that . . . I had given you my personal assurance that I would do everything possible to cooperate both before the election, and if elected, after the election. And that . . . I felt . . . Saigon should come to the conference table, that I would—if you felt it was necessary . . . go to Paris, anything you wanted. I just wanted you to know that I feel very, very strongly, about this and any rumblings around about somebody trying to sabotage the Saigon government's attitude—certainly have no, absolutely no credibility as far as I am concerned.

JOHNSON: . . . I'm very happy to hear that, Dick, because that is taking place. Now here's the history of it.

The president explained again how everything had seemed to be moving forward until Saigon suddenly balked because Thieu had been told he'd do better with Nixon as president. "I didn't say that it was with your knowledge," he told Nixon. "I hope it wasn't."

NIXON: Ah, no. . . . They think Nixon will be tougher, and I understand that. And I think that's one of the reasons you felt you had to go forward with the pause. But my point that I'm making is this: My God, I would *never* do anything to encourage Hanoi— I mean Saigon—not to come to the table because, basically, that was what you got out of your bombing pause, that, good God, we want them over in Paris. We've got to get them to Paris or you can't have peace. . . . I just want you to know, I'm not trying to interfere with your conduct of it. I mean I'll only do what you and Rusk want me to do, but I'll do anything . . .

JOHNSON: Well, that's good, Dick.

NIXON: We've got to get this goddamned war off the plate. . . . I think you've gotten a bad rap on this thing. . . . The war . . . now is about where it could be brought to an end, and if we can get it done now, fine, that's what it ought to do. Just the quicker the better and the hell with the political credit. Believe me, that's the way I feel about it.

JOHNSON: Thank you, Dick.

Nixon was lying: he was determined that Johnson get no political credit for peacemaking, and at his personal direction and in secret had done everything he could to make sure it didn't happen.

On Monday morning, the day before Americans went to the polls, *The Christian Science Monitor* asked the White House to confirm or deny a story from their Saigon correspondent that said "political encouragement from the Richard Nixon camp" had been "a significant factor" in President Thieu's sudden decision to stay home. At first, Johnson wasn't sure what to do. He thought it likely Nixon had lied to him but had seen no absolute proof of his *personal* involvement. (That would not be made public for thirty-nine years, in the form of H. R. Haldeman's notes of the candidate's October 22 late-night telephone call.) He didn't want to be accused of making a baseless charge or

playing politics on the eve of an election, but he also didn't want to be charged with keeping to himself information the public needed to know.

Walt Rostow encouraged Johnson to "blow the whistle" and "destroy" Nixon. Dean Rusk urged him to keep silent: since the story came from someone in Saigon, the White House need say nothing, he argued, and to confirm it would expose the "special channels that we don't make public." Clark Clifford shared Rusk's concern, and added another: he found "some elements of the story . . . so shocking that I'm wondering whether it would be good for the country to disclose the story, and then possibly have a certain individual elected. It could cast his administration under such doubt that I would think it would be inimical to our country's interest."

In the end, the White House refused to comment. The story of the Nixon campaign's role in keeping Saigon from the peace table was not published. His secret was safe. The American people were never told that the president of the country for which thirty-five thousand Americans had died had been willing to boycott peace talks to help elect Richard Nixon—or that a can-

didate for the American presidency had been willing to delay an end to the bloodshed in order to win it.

On election day, Nixon was elected president with 43.4 percent of the vote to Humphrey's 42.7 percent, a margin of just seven-tenths of 1 percent. Clandestine maneuvering may have helped him win that narrow victory—"Nixon probably would not be president if it were not for [President] Thieu," his speechwriter William Safire once admitted—but Nixon's fear that the maneuvering might someday be exposed would eventually help bring about his undoing.

Johnson still remained determined to get the talks started. Three days after the election, he spoke by telephone with the president-elect. Pleasantries were exchanged. Then, Johnson got to the point. Careful not to explicitly accuse Nixon of having interfered personally with the peace talks, he revealed enough of what he knew to make the president-elect anxious. Agnew and Mrs. Chennault, the president told him, had "been quoting you

ABOVE President-elect Nixon and Lyndon Johnson at the White House

to Paris before it's too late. I can also give you firm and unequivocal assurances that under no circumstances will the United States recognize the National Liberation Front as a separate entity. I absolutely affirm that the United States does not contemplate a coalition."

With the survival of his regime wholly dependent on support from the United States and both the president and the president-elect now pressuring him, Thieu reluctantly agreed to send a delegation to the Paris talks—which would promptly stall over the seating arrangements. Saigon was adamant that the North Vietnamese and NLF delegates be seated together, since from its point of view the NLF was just a creature of Hanoi. For its part, Hanoi insisted that the NLF be treated as a separate independent party to the talks, with its own flag and nameplate.

Round tables, square tables, oblong tables, diamond-shaped tables—all were proposed and rejected. It was "a famously stupid argument," Clark Clifford remembered. "In one meeting at the White House we looked at nine different table arrangements. I thought it was one of the silliest discussions in which I had ever participated." One U.S. diplomat predicted that the next winner of the Nobel Peace Prize would be a furniture designer. The standoff went on for ten weeks. It was the Soviets who finally helped come up with an acceptable solution: a circular table at which all four delegations were to sit, with a pair of rectangular tables on opposite sides for secretaries and support personnel, symbolizing Saigon's wish for negotiations between "two sides." The new talks would not begin until January 25, 1969—five days after Richard Nixon's inauguration as president.

indirectly that the thing [the South Vietnamese] ought to do is just not show up at any conference and wait until you come into office. . . . Now they started that, and that's bad." Meanwhile, he said, the enemy was "killing Americans every day. I have that documented." "It's a sordid story, Dick," he added. "Now, I don't want to say that to the country because that's not good. . . . You won't have ten men in the Senate support South Vietnam when you come in if these people refuse to go to the conference."

Nixon got the point. "There's nothing I want more than to get those people to the table," he now said. "Is there anything we can do right now?" There was: he must make it clear to Thieu that he wanted him to agree to join the Paris talks. The president-elect agreed to do so.

The next morning, Everett Dirksen turned up unannounced at the South Vietnamese chancery to deliver Nixon's message directly to Bui Diem. "I am here on behalf of two presidents, President Johnson and President-elect Nixon," Dirksen told the startled diplomat. "South Vietnam has got to send a delegation

ABOVE President Nixon and National Security Advisor Henry Kissinger pose in the Oval Office with Anna Chennault, the woman who helped put them in power, 1971. Nixon always denied that she had played any part in his election, and two years later, when Mrs. Chennault wrote asking that she be made "special ambassador to the Far East," he brushed her off.

A REVOLUTION WAS COMING

THE WAR—and the growing opposition to it—was affecting more and more of America's youth. Carol Crocker had still been grieving for her brother, Mogie, that fall when she entered Goucher College in Baltimore, an all-women's school with a long conservative tradition.

"We dressed for dinner," she recalled. "We had an eleven o'clock curfew. Obviously, no boys or men were allowed in the dorms. That was the rule. It could not have even been any later than the beginning of the second semester that most of the rules that were in place and had been in place for many, many years no longer existed. The challenge to campuses countrywide was how do we encourage our student body to behave in a civil manner, and teach them, and not have them try to burn us down? If that means not dressing for dinner, so be it. Our guy friends were scared and worried about the war. And they weren't sure what they were going to do. More discussion was happening about whether this was a valid war. And for me, this was the first time I opened my ears to the war in a way other than that it was about my brother's death. I honored him. I respected him for doing what he believed in. But I did not agree with him."

That was not an easy decision. "Moving away from one's family's ideologies is a scary balance on a very tricky precipice," she recalled, "because they have been the focal point of how we judge how we're doing. And I was now trying to judge my decisions and my actions on the basis of my own ideas and own thoughts."

Young people all over the country were undergoing the same process.

Eva Jefferson was now a sophomore at Northwestern. A serviceman's daughter, she had entered college convinced that the American government would never mislead its citizens. But for her, too, things had begun to change. Earlier that year, when a handful of black Northwestern students decided to occupy the bursar's office demanding African American studies, she joined them, then called her parents to tell them what she'd done. "I said, 'Mom and Dad, guess where I am? We just took over the bursar's office.' They were horrified. And upon reflection, *of course* they were horrified. And they said, 'If you don't get out of there we're going to cut off your money.' So that was the moment in my own consciousness when I became independent. I thought, 'Well, they're going to cut off my money. *C'est la vie.*'"

But "the university met all our demands in three days," she remembered. "At that time, if you asked for black studies on Friday, you got it on Monday. It felt like something was happening that was profound, that was irreversible. I was eighteen, nineteen years old. It was exciting. I felt as though a revolution was coming. And I thought the revolution would be won by our side."

Relations between parents and children, brothers and sisters, were changing everywhere. Captain Matt Harrison Jr.—"Chips" to his military family—who had graduated West Point, served a tour in Vietnam, and taken part in two of the war's bloodiest battles (Hill 1338 and Hill 875), was back stateside

in the autumn of 1968, when the family began to worry about his younger brother, Bob, whom his siblings sometimes called "Robin."

"He and I were just great pals growing up," Matt Harrison recalled, "because we moved every year or two years and had to make a new set of friends but I always had my brother."

"When we lived in the Panama Canal Zone, Bob was in the ROTC," his sister Anne remembered, "and polished and buffed his shoes and had short hair, and said, 'Yes sir' and 'Yes ma'am,' but then we moved to California his senior year in high school. And he became the consummate blond surfer boy and cut school. And was immediately very popular and having a great time."

Robin did not follow family tradition and enter West Point. Instead, he went to Marin Junior College, and then further shocked his Army family by signing on with the *Marine* Reserve. "Mom and Dad were very upset," his sister Victoria remembered. "They felt that he ought to have enlisted in the Army. That's the branch that our family serves in. I remember him coming home

ABOVE Carol Crocker in her dormitory room at Goucher College. "There were a few people at school who knew that my brother had been killed in Vietnam," she remembered, "but I never talked about that when we were organizing to get out petitions or organizing marches."

a seasoned veteran. I was going to go command a company. My chances of getting hurt were a lot less than Robin's were. And if I did choose to make the Army a career, the fact that I had had a second tour as a rifle company commander was going to be good for me. And so it wasn't entirely selfless."

The senior Harrisons were satisfied with this arrangement. "I think they felt like if Robin had gone, he would have been killed," Anne Harrison remembered. "Whereas, I think they felt that Chips was going to be okay. I can't imagine, having had a son now go to Iraq, how my mother could have gotten through a single day, without believing very firmly that he was going to be fine."

When Matt Harrison assumed command of Alpha Company, Second Battalion, Fourteenth Regiment, Twenty-fifth Infantry Division, he was the only regular Army officer in his company. "The squad leaders were just kids who knew nothing," he recalled, "and we were at three-quarters strength most of the time. By now it was '68–'69. The war had lost whatever support it had had," he remembered. "I was now commanding a company of draftees . . . almost none of whom wanted to be there. They didn't want to be in the Army and they certainly didn't want to be an infantryman in Vietnam.

"There were times when it was very difficult to keep the men under control . . . particularly if we had taken casualties on the way into a village. One of the things that I learned is that the veneer of civilization is very thin on me, probably on you and I think on everybody. I just saw over and over again some nice young guy out of, say, Huron, South Dakota, who back in Huron helped old ladies across the street and went to church every Sunday. It did not take long for that veneer of civilization to erode. And he was now capable of doing things that just simply are inhuman. I was not willing to allow it to happen on my watch and I didn't think it was good for the soldiers to do those kinds of things. Now, I'm not saying that we didn't do some horrific things—we did. But there's a difference between being spontaneous and being premeditated."

Matt Harrison's decision to serve a second tour did not, in the end, protect his brother. Robin went AWOL, was court-martialed, and was sentenced to three months' hard labor. The sentence was suspended. He returned to the Marines, served as a chaplain's assistant, applied for conscientious objector status—and then went AWOL again.

and he looked good in uniform and appeared to be very proud of it. The issue of the Marines moved to the background and it was no longer a big issue in the family anymore. We were just very proud of him and very happy that we had another member of our family who was serving the country."

But Robin's attitude toward the war began to shift. "At some point, Robin became convinced that the war was wrong—not only wrong but immoral," Matt Harrison recalled. "So he quit going to the Reserve weekends, and because of that he was activated. And it was very likely now that he was going to be going to Vietnam as a Marine Corps rifleman. I didn't think being a Marine Corps rifleman was a very safe occupation. And I didn't think Robin would be a particularly good Marine Corps rifleman. I just thought that this was a very bad outcome, for him and for the family."

Matt Harrison knew that under military regulations, if one brother was already in a combat zone, a second brother did not need to accept assignment there. So to keep Robin out of the war, he volunteered for a second tour in Vietnam. "I was back in Vietnam, I think, in less than thirty days," he recalled. "I was

ABOVE Matt (left) and Robin Harrison with a sailfish the older brother had just boated

"I was a junior in high school," his sister Anne remembered. "And I remember walking in the living room and it was dark, which was odd. And Robin was on the couch. I remember being startled because he wasn't supposed to be home. I knew instantaneously, I could just feel it, that something wasn't right. I don't remember if he just came out and said, 'I'm going to Canada.' I think he did. And I was worried about my dad coming home and what would happen."

The FBI arrived first. Robin's sister Victoria answered the door: "They asked if Robert Harrison was there and I just knew this wasn't good and said no and slammed the door. And Bob went out the back and ran out to the main street and, as I understand it, got in a car and left and that was the last I saw him."

His parents grieved, Anne remembered: "My dad was quiet. I'm certain he felt disgraced. I'm certain he was shocked and did not know how to transmit that information to anybody in his family or any of his West Point classmates. I don't think a military mom at the time would want to announce, 'My son has gone AWOL. My son has run to Canada.' My son is . . . all the words that were associated with it, 'deserter,' 'coward'—all of the things these guys were called. I don't think that's what those guys thought they were doing. I do not think they thought they were deserting. I do not think they thought they were cowards. In fact, I think they thought they were very brave."

Many years later, Robin Harrison, still adrift, got caught up in the world of drugs and died, ten thousand miles from home in a hotel room in Hong Kong, another casualty, his brother Matt came to believe, of the war in Vietnam.

THE TRAGEDY OF IT

DURING HAL KUSHNER'S TIME in jungle prison camps, thirteen of his fellow prisoners would die. It was a source of perpetual pain for him that he was a doctor but had no medications, no antibiotics or saline solution with which to treat his fellow prisoners. "The fall of 1968 was probably the toughest time we had," he recalled. "Four people died within a month. And two more died very shortly after that." All Kushner could do was bury each in a bamboo coffin and make sure the spot was marked with a heap of stones daubed with mercurochrome.

The already meager food rations shrank further. The sick, weakened men were sent into the surrounding forests to search for cassava roots to supplement their diet. "I thought that I was just going insane," Kushner remembered. "It was the rainy season and we were starving. Nothing to eat. We were sitting up one night and we saw the camp commander's cat, that had free

rein of the camp. And he came down to our area. And we were starving to death. So someone suggested, 'Let's eat the cat.' So we killed the cat and we cut the head off and we cut the paws off and we skinned and dressed out the cat. And we had this little carcass of about two pounds."

Before they could begin cooking the cat, a guard came by. They told him they'd killed one of the weasels that often raided the camp's flock of scrawny chickens. He complimented them, Kushner recalled, "and then he looked around and someone had neglected to bury one of the paws. And he saw the paw. And he knew instantly that it was the camp commander's cat. And things got very serious. He went up and told the guards. The officers, the cadre came down with sidearms. The guards had rifles. And they lined us up and they said, 'Who did this? Who killed the cat?' Nobody said anything. And I thought they were going to kill us all. Just shoot us. Execute us. And one of the people who was a ringleader in this said he did it. And I said that I did it also. And we all said we did it. 'I am Spartacus,' you know? It was that. So they called that person and me out. The guard kicked him and beat him to the ground, just beat him unmercifully. They hit me in the face with fists and didn't beat me as badly as they beat him. Then they tied me with commo wire very tightly onto a hooch and left me for a day with the carcass of the cat draped around my neck. I was so crazy I thought, Maybe they're going let me eat this cat, you know. But I had to bury it. And they kept telling us, you know, 'You Americans think you're so superior to us in culture and so forth. And here you go killing this house pet of the camp commander.' It was not the type of situation where I would remind them, 'Well, we only did that because you reduced us to this starving, dying mass of humanity where we had to do anything to survive.' That wasn't the appropriate place to remind them of that. The fellow that they beat very badly died two weeks later. And it was just a horrible situation. But I would have eaten the cat. To me, the tragedy of it was we didn't get the cat."

On Christmas Eve, the camp commander permitted his prisoners a small celebration. They were presented with a banner sewn with a single Christmas star, and were allowed to decorate a small tree with bits of paper and to sing carols and repeat the Lord's Prayer. In the afternoon, one of Kushner's fellow prisoners remembered, they listened to Radio Hanoi "as several captive pilots read warm messages about how they missed home and the children who were growing up without them. We allowed ourselves to linger over thoughts of our families."

That evening, the camp commander spoke to them: "You are allowed to enjoy Christmas because of the Front's lenient and humane policy," he said. "We are sorry you are not with your family. But Johnson prolongs the war. Maybe next year you will be back home."

"He didn't promise," the prisoner remembered, "but he sounded almost certain that Nixon, who had been elected the month before, would end the war. We clutched at his optimism, and our spirits rose."

BRUTE FORCE

THE ENTHUSIASM for pacification that General Abrams had begun to show did not immediately alter the behavior of some of his commanders. The first months of 1969 saw several big-unit operations that were indistinguishable from those undertaken under his predecessor at MACV.

In the northern part of Quang Ngai Province, the American Division attacked NLF forces entrenched among civilians with fearsome firepower; a single hamlet received 648,000 pounds of bombs and 2,000 artillery rounds in two days. Afterward, bulldozers wiped flat what little remained—the Vietnamese had come to call this "ironing" a village. In two months, the Quang Ngai hospital struggled to treat 2,452 injured civilians, and even the Saigon-appointed province chief suggested that nearly half of them had been hurt by friendly fire. Fifteen thousand people lost their homes, bringing the total number of refugees in that one province to more than 100,000.

In another multi-battalion operation in the same province, thousands of U.S. Marines, U.S. Army soldiers, and Korean troops, backed by firepower from the sea and air, swept the Batangan Peninsula of the NLF, killing 239, capturing 102, and helicoptering all 12,000 civilians who lived there to a holding center for interrogation. Those not found to be NLF cadre were resettled at four new sites, where they were expected to build themselves new homes. The operation was considered a success: an NLF stronghold had supposedly been cleared of the enemy, and more than eleven thousand civilians had been placed under the control of the South Vietnamese government. But their loyalty to the government that had destroyed their homes was questionable, a dusk-to-dawn curfew had to be imposed because the NLF remained active at night, and an Army after-action report concluded that the operation demonstrated that "a highly contested area is a poor environment for community development."

Three densely populated provinces in the Mekong Delta—Dinh Truong, Go Cong, and Kien Hoa—had long been centers of NLF activity. (Kien Hoa had been the site of the first of the "concerted uprisings" against the Diem regime in 1960.) At first, MACV had resisted sending American forces into the region for fear the massive firepower that invariably accompanied them would alienate the population. Laced with a thousand miles of tidal rivers and canals, the Delta was a terrible place to fight—leeches, immersion foot, mud, swarms of malarial mosquitoes, and red ants whose bite was so painful, one soldier recalled, "you'd stand up in the middle of a firefight." There was the constant threat of ambushes and booby traps, too, hidden beneath the water as well as on land.

The Ninth Infantry had eventually been given the task of bringing the region under control. It had begun in 1967 by joining forces with two Navy assault squadrons to form the Mekong Delta Mobile Riverine Force—part of the "Brown Water Navy"—meant both to deny the enemy access to the region's maze of waterways and to ferry infantry into combat. In the months following Tet, NLF units in the region, like those elsewhere, had broken down into small groups and sought to avoid combat while they rebuilt.

In December 1968, the division commander, Major General Julian J. Ewell, commander of the Ninth Division, launched a new operation, Speedy Express, that promised relentless pursuit of the elusive enemy. Ewell was a career infantry officer, a hero of World War II who had parachuted into Normandy and Holland. He had fought alongside his friend Creighton Abrams, but did not share his belief in the importance of pacification. "I guess I believe that the 'hearts and minds' approach can be overdone," he once explained. "In the Delta the only way to overcome VC control is by brute force applied against the VC."

In his view, nothing measured progress like body count: "Jack up that body count or you're gone, Colonel," he was overheard shouting at a subordinate. He flooded all three Delta provinces with small infantry units whose commanders were told they would not be extracted from the field until they had killed an acceptable number of the enemy. "All the battalion commanders," one colonel recalled, "had to carry a three- by five-inch card with an up-to-date, day-to-day, week-to-week, and month-to-month body count tally, just in case General Ewell showed up and wanted to know. And woe to the commander who did not have a consistently high count."

To deny the countryside to the enemy at night as well as during the day, Ewell instituted a program called Night Hunter. UH-1 troop transport helicopters worked in unison with two Cobra gunships. The transport helicopter flew a couple of hundred yards off the ground. In its belly was a "people sniffer," an instrument that could detect traces of carbon and ammonia that meant human beings were below them—though not which side they were on or what they might be doing. Three snipers lay in the back with night scopes also looking for targets. If some were spotted, the snipers would open fire with tracer bullets that showed the gunships hovering three hundred yards above them precisely where to direct their fire.

Day or night, men in black pajamas were targeted. A major

remembered skimming low over a rice paddy with Colonel Ira Hunt, Ewell's chief of staff. "He said something to the pilot, and all of a sudden the door gunner was firing a .50-caliber machine gun . . . and I said, 'What the hell is that?' He said, 'See those black pajamas down there? They're Viet Cong. We just killed two of them.'"

How could he recognize VC from a helicopter?

"Because they're wearing black pajamas."

"Well, sir, I thought workers in the fields wore black pajamas."

"No, not around here. Black pajamas are Viet Cong."

Anyone seen running was targeted too, though no warning was ever given telling civilians that to remain safe they needed to hold their ground.

A sergeant reported that "gunships and loaches [light observation helicopters] would hover over a guy in the fields till he got scared and run and then they'd zap him," while GIs on the ground would "see people in a field and start toward them and they'd run and get killed."

"If someone was told that anyone who runs away should be assumed to be an enemy, that's totally improper," remembered Robert Gard, who served for a time under Ewell as artillery division commander. "People run away because they're afraid. I've seen instances of farmers when you descend in a helicopter suddenly, first they freeze but they're frightened and they run. You can't just make a blanket judgment that anybody that runs away is an enemy."

"Most of the people [the Americans] killed were civilians, because civilians would run," recalled Le Quan Cong, an NLF platoon commander who had fought at Ap Bac, survived the aborted Tet assault in Saigon, and was now struggling to hold his weakened unit together. "We soldiers held our fighting positions. They couldn't get us easily. There always seemed to be helicopters overhead, day and night. They wiped out whole villages—there was often nothing left. If they saw even a shadow of a person they opened fire, and if guerrillas shot at them, they brought even more firepower. The people would try to get into their bunkers, but sometimes they couldn't get there in time."

Ewell was proud of his nickname within the military—"the Butcher of the Delta"—and of his unit's statistical

ABOVE Operation Bold Mariner, February 5, 1969: U.S. Marines drive children and women, with their hands bound, from the tunnel in which they'd been hiding on the Batagnan Peninsula. **OVER** To fulfill General Julian Ewell's desire to kill "four thousand of these little bastards a month," the Ninth Infantry Division applied relentless pressure to three Delta provinces as part of Operation Speedy Express. **LEFT** Landing craft belonging to the Mobile Riverine Force patrol a winding waterway; when the enemy was spotted, troops rushed ashore while the ships laid down covering fire. **RIGHT, TOP** A Cobra gunship pulls out of a rocket and strafing run on an abandoned rice paddy already cratered by repeated air attacks. **RIGHT, BOTTOM** An Army gunner who stood six foot five bears his M60 machine gun across a river, part of one of the infantry squads that patrolled the region, day and night.

THE VENEER OF CIVILIZATION | **359**

WE DO NOT REGRET YOUR BEING HERE

record—10,899 Viet Cong killed in six months, with a loss of only 242 Americans—an astonishing kill ratio of forty-five to one. Some officers were skeptical. "The idea that we killed only enemy combatants is about as gross an exaggeration as I could imagine," Robert Gard remembered. "But to talk about ratios of forty-five to one simply defies my imagination."

Later, when critics, inside the military as well as outside, pointed out that Ewell's men had managed to capture only 688 individual and 60 crew-served weapons from all those supposed enemy dead—perhaps the lowest ratio of weapons seized to body count tallied during the war—Ewell claimed it was because so many deaths occurred at night and because "many of the guerrilla units were not armed." (Four years later, the Army inspector general would estimate that somewhere between five and seven thousand of the roughly eleven thousand kills claimed by the Ninth Infantry Division had been unarmed civilians.)

General Abrams hailed the Ninth Infantry's performance as "magnificent, . . . unparalleled and unequaled." Ewell was made a three-star general and given command of II Field Force, the largest Army combat command in Vietnam. But when the Ninth Infantry finally withdrew from the Delta, one seasoned American journalist would write, it "left as many enemies as friends among the South Vietnamese."

ABOVE General Creighton Abrams hands the colors of the II Field Force to its new commander, Julian Ewell, promoted to lieutenant general because of the supposed success of Speedy Express, April 3, 1969.

IN EARLY JANUARY, with Richard Nixon's inauguration and the start of the new Paris peace talks just days away, Robert Shaplen of *The New Yorker* reported that not since the fall of Diem five years earlier had "there been such a mood of impending change in Saigon." He had been covering Vietnam off and on since the French war and remembered that the weeks following the 1963 coup had been a hopeful time. This was not. The consuming worry among Saigon's elite was that President Thieu was being railroaded, forced by the Americans to participate in talks about the future of the country before it was ready.

"Even if the government's claim that it now controls some [seventy-five] per cent of South Vietnam's population—forty per cent of which, including refugees and other displaced persons currently lives in the cities—is statistically accurate," Shaplen wrote, "the statistics do not provide a true picture of the situation. The remaining thirty per cent is about equally divided between people living in 'contested' areas and people living in areas that are admittedly controlled by the Communists." The cities were not safe, either: just in the past few weeks, some four hundred communist sappers had been captured in Saigon itself, and MACV believed still another enemy offensive was in the offing, most likely during the Tet festivities in February.

Ambassador Bunker reported to the White House that same month that while the current South Vietnamese government was "the best and most effective I have seen . . . it is still not strong enough" to stand on its own, and was still "plagued by inefficiency and corruption."

Colonel Tran Van Hai, the new director general of the National Police, had recently drawn up for the CIA a list of weaknesses he felt were undermining the Saigon government: a continuing inability to control hamlets and villages; a failure to connect with schools and universities where many teachers and "the best and most dedicated students [were] also dedicated communists"; an unwillingness to compromise with the Buddhists; and unthinking arrogance among government officials, both in Saigon and in the countryside, where many treated peasants and refugees with open contempt.

Corruption continued to riddle the regime too. "The Vietnamese had a saying," U.S. adviser Stuart Herrington recalled. "'The house leaks from the roof on down.' That was their way to elliptically refer to the ever-present, nagging problem of corruption." And South Vietnam's ever-greater dependence on the United States only made it worse.

Before U.S. troops arrived, eight out of ten Vietnamese lived in villages; by 1970, almost half would be crowded into urban

areas. (Their absence from the rural areas where they once had lived accounted for many of pacification's supposed statistical successes; virtually empty landscapes were counted as under Saigon's control.) Perhaps a third of the country's population had been displaced, and hundreds of thousands trekked to Saigon and other cities, some in search of work, others because they had nowhere else to go.

As parts of the countryside emptied, Saigon's population tripled to three million. Half the newcomers had no permanent shelter. Many neighborhoods were without a sewage system. Cholera and typhoid killed thousands. One hundred and fifty thousand hungry children roamed the streets, scavenging, begging, searching for jobs to do or pockets to pick.

Meanwhile, some five thousand American contractors, construction workers, and businessmen occupied many of the villas and apartment buildings where the French had once lived. A single consortium of contractors employed some sixty thousand Vietnamese, most of them women because their men had been drafted into the ARVN. They unloaded ships, drove forklifts, spread gravel, swept floors.

The U.S. military employed ninety thousand more Vietnamese as day laborers, allowed onto military bases in the morning and escorted out again at night.

According to one study, as many as 300,000 young women became bar girls and prostitutes in cities and towns and around the military bases scattered across the country.

"The people who collected garbage in Saigon quit and went to work for the contractors on the American bases, where they made more money," Neil Sheehan remembered. "The garbage piled up in the streets, and at night when you walked by, it would move on top from the rats feeding on it down below. One day I was walking by a pile of garbage and I noticed writing in chalk on the sidewalk. I was with a Vietnamese, so I asked him, 'What does it say?' He said it said, 'This is the fruit of American aid.' The society was rotten. It was not going to stand. It was as simple as that."

Government officials were on the take. Policemen could not be trusted. Tons of American goods piled up on Saigon's docks. Building materials intended for refugee housing were sold back to Vietnamese contractors building high-priced housing for U.S. personnel.

Some Americans made money too. One liquor dealer used bribery to corner amusement sales to U.S. officers' clubs and made $40 million before he got caught. In just one year, the black market cost the U.S. military $2 billion. Warehouse guards were paid to overlook pilferage. American goods flowed out the back doors of PXs. Middlemen sold to the enemy antibiotics, surgical instruments, sophisticated weapons, and dry cell batteries used to set off land mines.

ABOVE One of Saigon's thousands of bar girls catches a GI's eye on Tu Do Street. Some were refugees from the war-ravaged countryside who had nowhere else to go and could find no other work. Others gravitated to the city for other reasons: to escape unwanted marriages or rural drudgery or in search of excitement and an income they could never have matched in their village.

"They were stealing from us and selling to anybody," Joe Galloway recalled. " 'Two-man helicopter? You want one of those? They've got one in a box in the back.' You could probably get it for twelve thousand bucks if you negotiated strongly. The corruption was endemic. And we tolerated it."

"Who benefited most from the financial aspect of the war?" Phan Quang Tue asked. "The generals. Don't deny that. They got the money, became richer and richer. From Thieu and Ky down to every echelon, they were all war profiteers."

Mai Van Duong Elliot remembered that her father considered Thieu and his cronies both incompetent and corrupt. "With leaders like that," he used to say, "the Americans must be very frustrated and might just pack up and leave."

Edward Landsdale, who'd been involved in Vietnam since the advent of Ngo Dinh Diem and was now an official in the Saigon embassy, assessed the pervasiveness of the corruption. The ARVN Corps commanders employed intermediaries—aides, staff assistants, often their wives—to sell the most important posts in their regions: division officers, and province and district chiefs. The grateful buyers were expected to continue making regular payoffs to their superiors while themselves collecting payoffs from less important officials whom they, in turn, had appointed. "No businessman can operate without at least the acquiescence of the government," Lansdale wrote. "Thus virtually all substantial businessmen operating in provincial capitals pay a regular sum under the table . . . to stay in business, and some pay more to obtain special privileges. The same system . . . is in effect at the district level in most districts and at the village level in many villages. Village chiefs pay part of the money collected to district chiefs as do the latter to province chiefs." Lansdale insisted that this crude system had more to do with how the Saigon regime actually functioned "than the institutional channels of authority which appear on organizational charts. Its damaging effects in terms of weakening discipline, esprit, and the overall effectiveness of the [government and armed forces] are obvious. It has become . . . a system with its own momentum, entrapping most senior soldiers and most middle-level managers."

Lieutenant Colonel Hoang Duc Ninh, the chief of Bac Lieu Province in the Delta, was among the most egregious offenders. A first cousin of President Thieu, he demanded that anyone in his province who bought a pack of cigarettes or burned a gallon of gasoline come up with a tax payable to him personally. According to Neil Sheehan, he also extorted blackmail payments from innocent people rounded up under the Phoenix Program, doubled his fees to free NLF fighters from prison, and "sold artillery barrages to imperiled garrisons; no bribe, no artillery." At one point, John Paul Vann—now back in Vietnam as CORDS commander in IV Corps—tried to get him promoted to command of a regiment because, he said, "He'll steal less with a regiment." CORDS personnel compiled lists of corrupt officials who hampered their work, and Ambassador Bunker made repeated trips to the presidential palace to discuss them with President Thieu—seventy-eight such visits, by one count—but officials removed from one high post were too often put back in charge somewhere else. "Win the war first," Thieu said, "*then* make far-reaching social and economic plans."

A Vietnamese friend of Robert Shaplen's once tried to explain to him why his country seemed so slow to be able to fend for itself.

There is much we must blame ourselves for, but much of what has happened is your fault. At the end of the Second World War, you decided who should go where in Asia and occupy what. The French returned here—and you helped keep them here, with your guns and your money—for nine more long years. It was natural enough that the French should try to manufacture fake nationalism with mandarin officials, but why did you have to do the same when you moved in, in 1945? You came to Vietnam without any preparation and therefore without understanding, yet you forced us to adjust to your anti-communist objectives without helping us develop our own democratic ones. You were afraid of Diem, until it was too late to get him to change his ways and to get rid of his brother Nhu. You ended by creating a vacuum the communists were best prepared to fill. The strongest non-communist political party in the country became USAID and now you wonder why so many Vietnamese are corrupt. You brought an American army here, and you made a western army out of ours, but it has never been a national army and it still doesn't know how to fight a war of insurgency or how to deal with the people. We are no longer the makers of our own destiny. We are the victims of your global policy.

Despite all the U.S. failings, Shaplen's friend continued, "If the Americans had not come to South Vietnam, we would have gone Communist long ago, so we do not regret your being here—and we will do everything we can to keep you here, because we need you even more, economically, without a war."

OPPOSITE Black-market sales in Saigon: "People were selling pilfered goods," Duong Van Mai Elliott remembered. "People began to have favorite brands. I remember Prell shampoo, Colgate toothpaste, Johnny Walker whiskey. They remained very loyal to those brands. So life was good, and the people who were working for the Americans or doing business with the Americans were making money hand over fist."

THE PEACE WE SEEK

IF RICHARD NIXON had his way, the United States would not be kept in Vietnam much longer. "I'm not going to end up like LBJ, holed up in the White House afraid to show my face on the street," he told an aide. "I'm going to stop that war. *Fast*. I mean it!"

On January 20, on the steps of the U.S. Capitol, he took the oath of office as the thirty-seventh president of the United States, his left hand resting on a family Bible, held open by his wife, Pat, to Isaiah 2:4—"They shall beat their swords into plowshares and their spears into pruning hooks; nation shall not lift up sword against nation, neither shall they learn war anymore." He made no mention of Vietnam in his inaugural address, but the overall theme was peace, at home and abroad:

> The greatest honor history can bestow is the title of peacemaker. . . . We find ourselves rich in goods, but ragged in spirit; reaching with magnificent precision for the moon, but falling into raucous discord on earth. We are caught in war, wanting peace. We are torn by divisions, wanting unity. . . . America has suffered from a fever of words; from inflated rhetoric that promises more than it can deliver; from angry rhetoric that fans discontent into hatreds; from bombastic rhetoric that postures instead of persuading. We cannot learn from one another until we stop shouting at one another—until we speak quietly enough so that our words can be heard as well as our voices. . . . Let this message be heard by strong and weak alike: The peace we seek—the peace we seek to win—is not victory over other people, but the peace that comes with healing in its wings, with compassion for those who have suffered; with understanding for those who have opposed us.

But as it had with Johnson, the ongoing war in Vietnam threatened to derail Nixon's plans. As the new president and his wife rode along the inaugural parade route down Pennsylvania Avenue toward the White House, protestors mixed in with the cheering crowds, chanting, "Ho, Ho, Ho Chi Minh, the NLF is going to win." Some burned miniature American flags passed out by the Boy Scouts. At Twelfth Street, protestors waved an NLF flag and hurled rocks, bottles, and beer cans at the president's limousine. No inaugural parade had ever been attacked before in the history of the presidency, and when the limousine reached Fifteenth Street, Nixon ordered the sunroof opened so that he and Pat could stand up and be seen by the crowd, the president with his arms raised in the V-for-Victory sign President

Eisenhower had pioneered in American politics. It was clear that the divisions Nixon hoped to heal had not narrowed.

Like Lyndon Johnson, Nixon had an ambitious agenda for his presidency, but, unlike Johnson, events overseas interested him more than challenges close to home. "I've always thought the country could run itself domestically without a president," he'd told a newspaperman. "You need a president for foreign policy." He hoped to create a more stable international order in which the United States retained its central position while easing a quarter of a century of tensions with the Soviet Union and opening the door to China, whose existence the United States had refused to recognize since the communists took over in 1949.

As his national security advisor, he chose a man who shared both his ambition and his vision, forty-five-year-old Henry Kissinger. On the surface, Nixon and Kissinger didn't appear well suited to one another. "The combination was unlikely," the president himself would write, "the grocer's son from Whittier [California] and the refugee from Hitler's Germany, the politician and the academic." In private, each often derided the other; Kissinger sometimes referred to his boss as "our meatball president"; Nixon called his national security advisor "my Jew-boy."

Nonetheless, they worked closely together throughout the Nixon presidency. Each saw himself as a hardheaded realist and both favored secrecy over openness. Each agreed that foreign policy should be run from the White House, and had little but scorn for the bureaucrats with whom they had to work: "We've checked," Nixon once explained, "and 96 percent of the bureaucracy are against us. They're bastards who are here to screw us." The president routinely avoided consulting William Rogers, the former law partner he'd made secretary of state, while the Joint Chiefs of Staff so rarely found themselves within the policymaking loop they assigned a Navy yeoman to steal White House documents just to find out was going on.

Both Nixon and Kissinger were convinced that Vietnam was foreign policy "problem no. 1." The president had been an early and enthusiastic advocate of intervention there and had been critical of his predecessors for not being more aggressive against the enemy, but he now had no illusions about winning a conventional victory in Vietnam. "I've come to the conclusion that there's no way to win the war," he told aides during the campaign. "But we can't say that, of course. In fact we seem to have to seem to say the opposite, just to keep some bargaining leverage."

Kissinger agreed. In fighting the Vietnam War, he wrote, "we lost sight of one of the cardinal maxims of guerilla war; the guerilla wins if he does not lose. The conventional army loses if it does not win." Both men had come to share the views of the Wise Men who, after Tet, had told President Johnson that the U.S. "could no longer achieve its objectives within a period or with force levels politically acceptable to the American people." Nonetheless, Kissinger wrote, the United States "could not simply walk away from an enterprise involving two administrations, five allied countries, and 31,000 dead, as if we were switching a television channel."

It was not South Vietnam's independence that mattered most to Nixon and Kissinger. They believed that the credibility of the United States was at stake. This was not a new notion. In a 1965 memorandum, written before the first Marines ever landed at Danang, Assistant Secretary of Defense John T. McNaughton set forth his understanding of the underlying rationale for intervention: avoiding "a humiliating U.S. defeat (to our reputation as a guarantor) comprised 70 percent of it," he wrote, while allowing "the people of SVN to enjoy a freer and better way of life" accounted for only 10 percent.

But Kissinger made what had been one element of an internal argument the central public rationale for the Nixon administration's policy toward Southeast Asia:

> The commitment of 500,000 Americans has settled the issue of the importance of Vietnam. What is involved now is confidence in American promises. However fashionable it is to ridicule the terms "credibility" or "prestige," they are not empty phrases; other nations can gear their actions to ours only if they can rely on our steadiness. . . . In many parts of the world—the Middle East, Europe, Latin America, even Japan—stability depends on confidence in American promises.

But American promises to Saigon, Kissinger and Nixon believed, did not need to be perpetual pledges. Neither saw South Vietnam's survival by itself as vital to American interests. Their approaches differed slightly. What Kissinger hoped to do was find a way gradually to withdraw U.S. forces while strengthening the South Vietnamese so that they could hold on long enough that if they eventually collapsed it would be because of Saigon's weaknesses, not Washington's. Nixon shared that hope but never wholly abandoned the notion that the application of American military power might somehow bring about an early conclusion to the war on American terms.

The new president's plan of action was to proceed on several fronts simultaneously. He extended preexisting programs—including accelerated pacification of the countryside, and the expansion and strengthening of the South Vietnamese armed forces begun as "de-Americanization" by Clark Clifford, and renamed "Vietnamization" by his successor, former Wisconsin Congressman Melvin Laird. Newer elements of his program were intended to reassure the American public that the war really was coming to an end: he let it be known that he had ordered up a study of ending the draft in favor of an all-volunteer army,

ABOVE Henry Kissinger in his White House office as national security advisor.

and he waited impatiently for the moment to announce the first withdrawal of U.S. troops.

The four-party Paris talks began just five days after Nixon's inauguration and promptly stalled. Hanoi continued to insist that before there could be peace the United States would have to withdraw from South Vietnam unilaterally and the government of Nguyen Van Thieu, whom they called the "American puppet," would have to be deposed. For its part, the United States insisted on the opposite: North Vietnamese troops would have to leave the South first, and President Thieu could only be removed from power by free elections.

"The state of play in Paris is completely sterile," Nixon said. Nonetheless, he remained convinced that Vietnam was a

"short-term problem" and acted quickly to try to solve it. When Moscow signaled it was interested in beginning Strategic Arms Limitation Talks (SALT), the president responded that he was willing to get started, but only if Moscow persuaded Hanoi to soften their demands for a settlement.

Meanwhile, he said, he was "convinced that the only way to move the negotiations off dead center is to do something on the military front. That is something [Hanoi] will understand." He believed his reputation as a fierce anticommunist could be used to his advantage. "I call it the 'Madman Theory,'" he told Bob Haldeman, now his chief of staff. "They'll believe any threat of force *Nixon* makes because it's Nixon. We'll just slip the word to them that 'for God's sake, you know Nixon's obsessed about communism. We can't restrain him when he's angry and he has his hand on the nuclear button'—and Ho Chi Minh will be in Paris in two days, begging for peace."

Ho Chi Minh seemed no more likely to buckle under future Nixon threats than he had been to accept the allegedly irre-

ABOVE Quakers hold a "meeting for worship" outside the White House, July 7, 1968, while a delegation meets with Henry Kissinger inside. "Give us six months," he told them, "and if we haven't ended the war by then, you can come back and tear down the White House fence."

sistible economic blandishments Lyndon Johnson had offered at Johns Hopkins in 1965. Ho was old and ailing now, in any case, and largely a figurehead, while Le Duan and the other men calling the shots in Hanoi had fought too long against too-great odds to consider abandoning the struggle. They thought it would take them two to three years to rebuild the forces that had been hit so hard during the Tet Offensive, but they also believed that time was on their side, that the American public would steadily grow more weary of the war.

Nonetheless, all Nixon needed, he thought, was a pretext for him to unleash the kind of "irresistible military pressure" President Johnson had been reluctant to use and that he believed would intimidate the enemy.

JUST A SAVAGE JOY

MEANWHILE, the war went on. In early 1969, twenty-four-year-old First Lieutenant Karl Marlantes, who a year earlier had been a Rhodes Scholar at Oxford, found himself executive officer of Charlie Company, First Battalion, Fourth Marines, Third Marine Division, just south of the DMZ at the western edge of South Vietnam. It was a mountain region so remote, he remembered, that during all his time there he never saw either an American reporter or a Vietnamese village. The enemy was plentiful, however, well-trained, well-armed troops belonging to two North Vietnamese divisions. The first day coming into the area, he remembered, "holes appeared in the chopper I was in and I realized, 'My God, I'm being shot at.' I hadn't even landed yet."

His unit was fighting the same sort of war over the same chain of steep, jungle-covered hills Marines had been fighting now for more than two years. "You would hear the name of the latest operation—Operation Purple Martin 1 or Operation Scotland 2," Marlantes remembered, "and it was like, 'Yeah, whatever.' All that meant to us was that someday soon some choppers are going to show up and drop us into the jungle someplace and then we'd be humping, as we called it. Days and days of being on an operation trying to find the enemy. If you did, then you got into a fight; and if you didn't, you'd just hump until you did. There was no sense of strategy."

At the beginning of March, Marlantes's company was sent to the aid of Marines under fire from North Vietnamese regulars dug in on a hillside. "We were supposed to be the anvil to their hammer. It turned out that we had been inserted in the middle of a major movement of a North Vietnamese army regiment. We made an attack on Hill 484. And we took that hill." But the North Vietnamese force they'd driven off the hill regrouped, poured mortar fire into their ranks, and drove them off again. "We'd been fighting seven days, something like that," Marlantes recalled. "It was a long fight. And then we were ordered to take the hill back again. At that moment I thought things had gotten crazy. First of all, we had been fighting there for all that time. There was another unit that was fresh. Why didn't they send them up the hill? And the word that I got—and I'll never know if this is true or not—was, 'Well, you guys abandoned the hill, so you have to take it back.' We were in the middle of this horrible shit sandwich.

"We had moved up in the dark and waited in the jungle, strung out on line as the jets roared in to bomb the enemy defenses at first light. But because of a screw-up the jet hit the wrong hilltop. We came out of the jungle and started forward. The NVA were in bunkers up above us. It was a very steep hill, hard to climb. Now, you don't charge because you're carrying a lot of weight—a lot of ammunition, water. Going uphill you'd exhaust yourself if you tried to run. So you *walked* into an assault. The discipline is to walk and walk until things start happening. We probably got about a third of the way up when they unleashed on us."

The Marines took what cover they could. Marlantes realized that they would face machine gun fire if they continued up the slope, but if they stayed where they were, mortar shells would surely find them. "It's just inconceivable that Marines would turn around. So now what? It was like I left my body and I looked down. I saw the whole situation. I saw where the machine guns were placed, where the vulnerable point would be. I came back down into my body and I started organizing people to take some of the bunkers under fire. Then I stood up and went up the hill. I thought I was all by myself. I was running zigzag at this point because I wanted to cover that ground as fast as I could without getting hit. I caught some movement out of the corner of my eye and I rolled to the ground to come up with my rifle to shoot the person. It was a kid from my platoon. And then I looked behind him and there were more kids. They had all come behind me. I mean I think it felt to me like I was there for a week but I think I was probably by myself four seconds, five seconds. The entire platoon just stood up and up they came. It remains to me a moment that is just almost inexpressible of the heart that these kids had. And then we just hit those bunkers."

The Marines cleared them, one by one. "Two NVA had retreated to a hole behind the line of bunkers." Marlantes recalled. "I was down on the ground so that I wouldn't get hit. One had been killed. The other one stood up and saw me. I was very close. And I had the rifle laid right on him. He had a grenade in his hand. And we locked eyes. And when you lock eyes it all breaks down that this is an animal. I can remember

looking at this kid's eyes and thinking, 'I wish I could speak Vietnamese.' So I started to just sort of just whisper fiercely, 'Don't throw it. Don't throw it. If you don't throw it, I won't kill you. If you don't throw it, I won't pull the trigger. Don't do it.' And I wouldn't have. But I remember him snarling at me. And he threw the grenade right at me. I pulled the trigger and it hit the lip of the hole he was in and the bullet went up through his chest, I'm pretty sure. And two other guys who were with me came running around the corner. My radio operator had his rifle on full automatic and finished the job off. But those two eyes stayed with me a long, long time."

Moments later, an enemy grenade peppered Marlantes with shrapnel and knocked him momentarily unconscious. Minute shards of metal and dirt thrown up by the explosion temporarily blinded him. His radioman managed to clear one eye by pouring Kool-Aid into it from his canteen. Marlantes found the strength to rejoin his men, as they continued to fight their way toward the summit. "I've often used the expression that combat is like crack cocaine," he said. "It's an enormous high,

but it has enormous costs. No sane person would ever do crack because of what it's going to do to them. But from what I've heard you can't deny that crack is an incredible high. Combat is like that. You're scared, you're terrified, you're miserable, but then the fighting starts and suddenly everything is at stake— your life, your friends' lives. And it's a complete experience of almost transcendence because you're no longer a person. You lose that sense. You're just the platoon. And the platoon can't be beat. Maybe people will get killed, but the platoon can't be beat. You're beyond that. There's an enormous exhilaration in it. You lose yourself. Everything in your body is sacrificed for other people. And there's a savage joy in overcoming your enemy, just a savage joy. And I think that we make a big mistake if we say, 'Oh, war is hell.' We all know the war-is-hell story. It is. But there's an enormously exhilarating part of it."

When the hilltop had finally been cleared, Marlantes insisted that his men's wounds be seen to before he received treatment. For the "heroic actions and resolute determination" he displayed on that day, Karl Marlantes was awarded the Navy Cross. "The official commendation makes it sound as if I took a bunch of bunkers all alone," he wrote later. "I did lead the charge, but I often remind people that none of those kids who wrote the eyewitness accounts could have done so if they hadn't been right

TOP LEFT Karl Marlantes's platoon just before the battle for Hill 484 **TOP RIGHT** Marlantes recovering from his wounds

there with me." Charlie Company suffered fifteen casualties, including five men killed in action. Fighting for Hill 484 and the adjacent summits would go on for months.

BREAKFAST

THE OPTIMISM with which Nixon and Kissinger had set about trying to bring a speedy end to the war did not last long. Moscow never bothered to respond to their repeated requests for Soviet help in persuading North Vietnam to soften its negotiating position; Nixon and Kissinger had clearly overestimated the degree of control the Soviet Union exerted over Hanoi.

Hanoi's intransigence, in turn, kept the president from announcing the troop reduction that he hoped would help begin to defuse the antiwar movement.

On February 22nd, at the end of yet another Tet cease-fire, the North Vietnamese launched a new offensive from their jungle sanctuaries in Cambodia. Four hundred and twenty-five Americans died within the first week; two weeks later the total would be nearly eleven hundred.

Nixon was eager to retaliate but did not feel he could resume the bombing of the North for fear of provoking protest at home. And so on March 18, when the Joint Chiefs brought him a proposal to bomb North Vietnamese sanctuaries in a jungle-covered area of neutral Cambodia—a proposal President Johnson had repeatedly rejected for fear of widening the war—Nixon signed on. He saw it as the chance he'd been waiting for to unleash the kind of "irresistible military pressure" his predecessor had been hesitant to use, the kind he assumed would startle and intimidate the enemy. General Abrams applauded the decision. He knew troop withdrawals were coming soon and hoped his men would see the bombing as "evidence of support" for "their spirit and their morale and their determination."

In fact, Abrams's men would learn nothing about the bombing because the president imposed unprecedented secrecy on the whole operation. The secretary of the Air Force was not informed. Neither the secretary of state nor the secretary of defense was told anything about the bombing before the decision was made. B-52 pilots were given false targets within South Vietnam that were corrected by ground-based radar only after they had left the ground. Paperwork was falsified.

The first target was labeled "Breakfast." Nearly sixty B-52s dropped more than thirteen hundred tons of ordnance on a single sanctuary that was supposed to include COSVN head-

quarters. The bombing would go on for fourteen months—an average of 100 sorties a month through the summer, several hundred a month after that—dropping well over 100,000 tons of bombs on other jungle targets named "Lunch," "Snack," "Dinner," and "Dessert."

When *The New York Times* finally discovered what was happening and published a front-page story about it, the White House denied that any bombing was taking place—and Kissinger persuaded FBI bureau chief J. Edgar Hoover to place illegal wiretaps on the telephones of seventeen reporters and government officials in a fruitless effort to find out who had leaked the story.

No one knew how many enemy troops or Cambodian civilians were killed during the bombing campaign. But the everelusive COSVN again remained unscathed, a neighboring nation struggling to stay out of war had been destabilized, and, according to the CIA, the so-called "Menu" attacks had had "no appreciable effect on enemy capabilities in target areas."

Hanoi had not been intimidated. There would be no quick end to the war. "We will not repeat the same old mistakes," Henry Kissinger had joked to an aide shortly after coming to Washington. "We will make our own."

I WASN'T SUPPOSED TO LIVE

WHEN GARY POWELL, from Akron, Ohio, joined the second platoon of the Seventeenth Armored Cavalry early in 1969, Michael Holmes, now a Spec 4 and back in action after the roadside bomb that had injured him and killed his best friend, went out of his way to make him feel welcome. "I didn't know anybody," Powell recalled. "I'm the 'FNG'—the Fucking New Guy. Holmes came right up to me. He was tall, dark-complexioned, a little bit of a pencil mustache, kind of a Zorro type of thing. He was a good old country boy, and right off the bat we just liked each other. So he began to tell me, 'All the training you had will serve you to some degree. But it's not what you're going to need to live if you stay over here. You need to learn as you go from the guys around you.' And he was the one to teach me. He was a super-nice guy—other than he just had this thing that he wanted to kill gooks, and he wanted to get revenge for his buddies because he was really tight with the young guy that was killed. I remember him saying, 'I should have died on that track. I am going to go out and waste all those gooks that did this. I wasn't supposed to live.'"

His anger only seemed to deepen when Darlene, his girlfriend back home, stopped writing. "He used to talk about her quite a bit," another member of his outfit remembered, "but then he quit talking about her all of a sudden. So I don't know if it was a breakup or a 'Dear John' letter or what it was, but it seemed like he wasn't the same anymore."

The second platoon spent weeks at a time in the field, searching for the enemy, seizing rice and supplies, and destroying villages suspected of aiding the NLF. Eight APCs, accompanied by artillery, infantry, and dogs trained to sniff out mines patrolled during the day, then drew into a defensive circle at night. Before settling down, a squad was sent to patrol around the perimeter. Holmes clamored again and again to be the pointman. "Michael always volunteered," Powell remembered. "He wanted to get out there. He was looking for the enemy. It was unheard of. I would certainly not do that."

A fellow soldier thought that Holmes had accounted for seven enemy soldiers, the highest body count in the platoon. He reported some of his kills on tape. One day, he told the folks back home, "I told my sergeant, 'There's some people out there with packs and they ain't us because we don't carry packs.' He said, 'No, they ain't.' So I run down there and wounded one. . . . Now don't get the wrong idea about me shooting another human being. If I hadn't saw them they might have got me because they had weapons. . . . There were about two weapons with them. But then after I got through firing, the Sarge asked, 'Why did you fire? Why didn't we let them go?' Well, that's what we're over here for." A few days later, Holmes spotted two uniformed North Vietnamese eating rice beneath a big rock. He killed one and wounded the other.

Encounters with the local populace were often brutal and heedless. "The villagers were never happy to see us," recalled Herman Conley, from Independence, Kansas, another member of the platoon. "A couple of guys threw someone down a well—an old man, no reason for it—I knew he couldn't get out of that well. We weren't the best people when we went over there."

Uniformed South Vietnamese who often accompanied the Americans—most of them members of the poorly trained Popular Forces—rounded up Viet Cong suspects and those thought to sympathize with them for interrogation. "Some of them," another member of the platoon, Bruce Austin, remembered, "were mean, mean individuals. You look in their eyes and you didn't see a soul. They had no qualms about doing whatever was necessary to get their information and they'd have done it to us, too, if they had got us. I remember they caught two women and they whipped them with canes. That just made me sick. I'd never seen anybody abusing women. I'm from Pontotoc, Mississippi, and down there we respected women. I remember I went

around behind the hooch and prayed. And I thought, 'I hope don't nobody find this out. They'll think I'm a wimp.' But I prayed for those ladies. They were hurting, you know. He beat them pretty bad. And I never liked him. I don't know who he was. Don't care to know who he was. But maybe somewhere in life fate has dealt him something that will make him remember that.'"

Beatings, torture, and rape by Popular Force personnel were common. Americans rarely intervened. After all, the platoon's lieutenant said, "it was them getting intelligence from their people the way they do it." Some captives were murdered.

In April, Holmes's platoon was sent to Antenna Valley, so named because so many U.S. helicopters had been shot down there. "There had been no friendlies for over a year when we got there in April," Bruce Austin remembered. "The Ho Chi Minh Trail ran right through the valley and there was a lot of activity." Like Gary Powell, Austin was a newcomer to the platoon whom Michael Holmes had befriended.

The mountainous terrain made maneuvering APCs difficult, and the few paths they could follow were strewn with mines. On April 13, the men were ordered to park their APCs in a dry riverbed and move on foot up a mountainside, hoping to make contact with enemy troops coming down it. "There was a river running down the mountain," Austin remembered. "So we decided we'd go up the riverbank and hit the Ho Chi Minh Trail up top. It was hard, but it was beautiful. If we weren't in a war it would have been a beautiful place to take pictures and just get to know."

They caught three North Vietnamese troops coming down the path and killed them. When the Americans spotted more enemy troops farther up the hill, the men were pulled back so an airstrike could be called in. They planned to return to the hillside the next morning.

That night, Herman Conley noticed that Michael Holmes seemed unusually restless, especially anxious to get at the enemy: "It was like he was worried about something. It was my turn to go out on patrol. But he told me to stay back, and he got permission to take my place. He wasn't supposed to be out there. I was supposed to be out there."

On the morning of April 14, the platoon halted at the foot of the mountain. APCs could go no farther. The platoon started up the hillside on foot

Michael Holmes was where he insisted on being—walking point.

The recollections of his fellow soldiers differed about precisely what happened next. His lieutenant, Charles Garefin, remembered that Holmes spotted several NLF troops and "was chasing them down. For Michael it was kind of instinctive."

Gary Powell was sure that Holmes had managed to shoot several of them: "He did get a body count that day." Bruce Austin was equally convinced that Holmes had been ambushed by a single NVA soldier, hidden just twenty feet from him.

Whatever happened, the outcome was the same: an AK47 burst smashed into Michael Holmes's brain.

American bullets riddled the North Vietnamese soldier who shot him.

"It was over quickly," Austin recalled. "When we knew we had cleared the slope, we took our shirts and made a stretcher. Holmes was my friend, so I carried one end of him all the way

down. We wrapped his head in a shirt to keep it together, but his brains ended up on my boots. It was the worst thing I ever encountered in my life. We put him on a chopper. And I'm thinking, you know, 'He's gone. And his mother and daddy

ABOVE Michael Holmes (center) and his crew enjoy a beer in the field. "We weren't like infantry," his fellow platoon member Gary Powell remembered. "We could carry cases of beer, fifths of whiskey. What are they going to do, check you? At night, when things calmed down, people got a little tanked up occasionally. Never enough to make stupid decisions."

MISTY

MAJOR MERRILL MCPEAK was a crack fighter pilot when he arrived in Vietnam, a veteran of some two hundred air shows with the death-defying Air Force Thunderbird aerobatic team. But it was combat flying he was after. "I got to the war late, as a professional fighter pilot. And the feeling I had was, in a sense, relief, that I got to the war, finally. I didn't want to be the only fighter pilot in the known universe not to get to fight in Vietnam."

He was quickly disillusioned with the way the war from the air was being waged. "An air war needs to be organized according to a common-sense idea of what we're doing; and it needs to be executed under the command of somebody who understands air operations. None of that was true in Vietnam."

The Army was in charge. At first, McPeak remembered, he helped provide air support for Army battalions with a guaranteed number of sorties per day, "whether or not they had anything in front of them worth blowing up. At the end of any sortie where we dropped bombs on what we called 'trees in contact'—because there was nothing important down there—we would always get back a bomb-damage assessment from the forward air controller. It would read 'Twelve supply sources destroyed. Two structures collapsed.' All these metrics were modern management approaches to war. It was phony, just a waste of time. I think that was clear to most junior lieutenants wearing wings in Vietnam. This is not something I had to be a genius to discover. We talked about this a lot. At night we'd go to the bar, and commiserate with each other. The only good part was occasionally some Army Special Forces guy would come drifting into the bar, and say, 'Thank you, guys. You know, you saved our bacon.'

"The best result I achieved in a year was a result of a gross miss from what I was aiming at. I dropped a bomb one afternoon that must have had a broken fin or something. It just went crazy, went over and hit a mile away from where I was aiming and started a series of secondary explosions, meaning that I had hit an ammunition dump, or a cache of ammunition. So it cooked off for fifteen minutes. As we were leaving, the thing was still blowing up. Now, that's the exact reverse of how you want to use airpower."

Then, in early 1969, McPeak was assigned to Project Com-

don't even know this yet. And it'll be days before they do.' I just thought this would be the case with me, too."

Twelve days later, the Department of the Army awarded Michael Holmes a posthumous Bronze Star. The citation mentioned that before he was killed he had heroically knocked a buddy out of the way of a North Vietnamese bullet—something no member of his platoon recalled having happened.

April 1969—the month Michael Holmes was killed—marked the high point of the United States commitment to South Vietnam—543,482 men and women were now in country, and tens of thousands more were stationed at air bases and aboard ships beyond its borders. A total of 40,794 had died, and more than $70 billion had been spent.

ABOVE Michael Holmes's helmet, rifle, and several weapons he'd captured from the enemy form the centerpiece for a brief memorial service held in his honor.

mando Sabre, piloting a two-man F-100 fighter bomber flying high-speed forward air control, seeking to pinpoint men and supplies moving on the Ho Chi Minh Trail. McPeak and his fellow pilots called their outfit "Misty," after its radio call sign. "I spent four months in Misty," he recalled, "and that was the best four months of the war, as far as I was concerned, because what we were doing was simple, straightforward, and made sense. We wanted to stop traffic from A to B down this dirt road. That, I can understand. Somebody in Saigon wasn't saying, 'Go bomb trees at such-and-such a location.'"

In his memoir, McPeak described the challenge he and his fellow pilots faced:

North Vietnam was shaped like a funnel, bounded on the east by the South China Sea and on the west by the Annamite Mountains. A heavily fortified demilitarized zone corked the bottom of the funnel, so supplies moving through North Vietnam's southern panhandle had to side-step across the mountains into Laos. Here, with unbelievable effort and at great risk, the North took over a piece of real estate the size of Massachusetts and on it built and maintained an extraordinary infrastructure that in many ways mirrored the one constructed by Americans in country, complete with hundreds of miles of highways, communications centers, ammo dumps, stockpiles of food and fuel, truck parks, troop bivouacs—altogether enough to sustain a field army, and all of it out of sight, except for the trace of the road itself. We went out and actually found the target. And then we designated it, and we had somebody else bomb it, and that's the kind of thing you should do with airplanes.

Finding targets beneath the trees was not easy, and it was dangerous work. Thirty-five of the 157 Misty pilots were shot down. Two were shot down twice. Seven men were killed, and three were captured. Misty put up seven sorties a day, from dawn to dusk, on the lookout for signs of human activity—gardens, roadside trees coated with dust, or wet roads on either side of fords that signaled a truck convoy had recently passed through. "The truck drivers drove in stages," McPeak recalled. "So they knew fifteen, twenty clicks [kilometers] of the road. They drove from A to B, and back to A. They rested during the daytime,

and then the next night, they drove from A to B and back to A again. They had memorized the road, which was very important, because they were running without lights, at night. They drove very good Russian trucks, sturdy but pounded pretty hard by the trail, and by us. And so occasionally one of them would break down in a spot where the trucks behind it would get trapped and couldn't back out of there. One time I stumbled across a bunch of trucks backed up. That was a great morning for me. Usually, you don't have to worry about the lead truck in a deal like that, because it's broken down and can't move. So you try to strafe the last truck, so that it can't move. These are one-lane roads, often on the side of a cliff. So once you get the back truck disabled, you just call in fighters and you're shooting fish in a barrel. We stopped a lot of them, we killed a lot of them. I have enormous

ABOVE Major Merrill McPeak just before he joined Misty

LEFT Under cover of darkness, a member of Group 599, the North Vietnamese unit tasked with building and maintaining the Ho Chi Minh Trail, helps supply-laden trucks, their roofs crudely camouflaged with leaves and branches, find their way around a tricky curve. **ABOVE** The Ho Chi Minh Trail: "Originally, it was just a footpath," recalled General Dong Si Nguyen, commander of Group 559 from 1966 to 1975. "Gradually it was built to become a road for vehicles and the critical artery for transporting supplies and troops. It ran along both the east and west sides of the Truong Son Mountains, spreading over the three Indochina countries. It was not an ordinary road; it became a sophisticated battlefield."

YOUR BEAUTIFUL IMAGE REMAINS IN MY HEART

Nguyen Nguyet Anh was a teenage Youth Volunteer, helping to build an air base north of Hanoi, when she met Tran Cong Thang in 1965. "It was in a very rural area where there was nothing to do," she recalled, and when a troupe of traveling entertainers turned up at a nearby army camp she and her friends resolved to go and see them perform.

A guard stopped them. "I noticed Anh right away," Thang remembered. "She was tall and striking." He convinced the guard to let her and her friends in, managed to get her address, and began calling on her every other week at her barracks. "She seemed a very likable and attractive young woman, a girl from the countryside," he said.

"When I met Thang for the first time,"

she recalled, "I found him kind and helpful. He showed up a couple of weeks later, asked about the location of my squad, and came in to talk to me. From that point on he used come to visit me. We gradually became close to each other."

"But both of us were shy," Than remembered. "We didn't know anything about kissing. We saw each other every two weeks for two years, but when I just held Ánh's hand, my hands were shaking. Of course, I felt in my heart that I really wanted to know what kissing a young woman would be like. Later, I felt that it would be a great loss if I went to the front, a man in love, if I died without finding out what a kiss is like."

In 1967, Thang received orders to go

south to work on the Ho Chi Minh Trail. "He came to see me," Anh recalled, "and said, 'My unit is going to the southern front.' He wanted to make it clear he hoped we could wait for each other if we could promise to find each other after the war. I said to him, 'Okay, please don't worry and go to fight. I'll wait for you. If both of us survive, we'll get married.' Even if he came back handicapped, if he were wounded, I'd definitely wait for him because I loved him. And I'd marry him."

"At that moment," Thang remembered, "I really wanted to hug and kiss my sweetheart, but I didn't dare to show my emotions, I was shaking. It was sad, but I just kept silent. Anh cried, just cried. She didn't say anything to me. We couldn't say anything to each other. So we shook hands. . . . I ran back to my unit, which departed at midnight."

Thang found himself on the Laos section of the trail, part of a combat engineering brigade, moving from one bomb-battered choke point to another, filling bomb craters in the road, getting damaged trucks rolling again, doing his best to stay alive under relentless bombing. One day, while he was at work elsewhere on the road, an American bomb destroyed the bunker in which he had slept the night before. Everything he owned was obliterated, including the only photograph he had of Nguyen Nguyet Anh.

Eight months after Thang came under fire in Laos, Anh became a truck driver on a section of the trail far to the north. Communication with Thanh was almost impossible. Still, whenever he could, he sent her messages with soldiers traveling north and she did the same with troops heading south.

"I got two or three letters from him. No more," she recalled. "The other letters were lost. The distance was very far, the roads were unsafe, so letters were often lost." Through it all, she thought of him constantly. "I was worried for him every single day. Whenever I saw a truck that was carrying wounded soldiers to the North, I would ask whether there was anyone from Hanoi on the truck, and if there was, I would look for him. It was a very difficult time because if I worried too much, I might not be able to fulfill my duties."

Month after month went by. In 1972, Thanh wrote Anh an anguished letter:

My darling!

. . . I have carried your love in my heart through the long years of our being far from each other. Four years are the measurement of your faithful love for me. We love each other so much, but are unable to see each other, to say

gentle words to each other which cannot be written in a letter. . . . I love you with all my heart and mind. . . . I understand that as a soldier, my life is full of hardships and may bring you many sorrows. The distance between us makes our life so miserable that I have to try to understand why life is so

OPPOSITE and **ABOVE** Tran Cong Thang and Nguyen Nguyet Anh, during their years on the Ho Chi Minh Trail

Anh happened to be there. "The feeling was like that at the moment when we said goodbye to each other," Thanh recalled. "I had thought that when seeing her again, I would leap to her and kiss her. All the time at the front I dreamed of kissing her when we saw each other again. But at first I didn't dare to do that either. We looked each other in the eyes, and we were crying. We were sitting next to each other, so I held Anh's shoulder and then her neck and I kissed her. I was extremely happy because I had the feeling that it was a kiss I was given by God."

When the war finally ended two years later, they married and had two children. "We tell our children today what it was like when their mother and father fell in love," Thang recalled. "Not like what they do today!"

unfair to us. One year went by, two years went by, three years went by, and now we have not seen each other for almost four years. My belief is that I can endure all of it because I am a soldier who is . . . encouraged by your love.

I have spent many nights without sleep . . . thinking of you, thinking of your future. I do not want to lose you, but I do not want to be selfish either. . . . I say your name to myself at the most serious moments in battle. Your name, Anh, always makes me happy. . . . I do not want to lose such a generous love as your love for me. However, your generous love requires me to make a great sacrifice. I do not want to bind your life with the life of a soldier. You should find another man. You deserve to be happy. You cannot wait for me forever. Our love for each other has made us better. I do not want your young years to go by in your waiting

for me. If you are happy, I will be happy, too.

The year of 1972 has arrived. Spring brings hope to people, including me. I wish you a Happy New Year. I cannot say exactly when we will see each other again, but I believe we will get together someday in our homeland.

Your beautiful image remains in my heart.

Yours,
Thang

"I never got that letter," Anh remembered. "If I had, I couldn't have forgotten him. I wanted to wait for him because I believed that we would see each other again. It wouldn't be possible for me to give up on him and love someone else."

Tran Cong Thang and Nguyen Nguyet Anh remained apart but faithful to one another for nine years. At the end of 1973, Thang was ordered to Hanoi.

ABOVE Tran Cong Thang and Nguyet Anh united at last, in 1973 **OPPOSITE** For months, American airstrikes peppered this single crossing on the Ho Chi Minh Trail, but trucks continued stubbornly to splash their way across the river.

respect for those guys. They left their homes in the North and they didn't know if they were ever going to go home again. The food, when they got it, was not much good. It took a month to deliver a letter to their wives in Hanoi and it could take a whole season to get an answer. We ended up having a lot of respect for them."

Although McPeak and his fellow Misty pilots did not know it, among the truck drivers threading their way through the forest below them by night were scores of women. "I think it was greatly regrettable that women had to participate in the war in that manner," Major Nguyen Quang Khue, an engineer who worked alongside them, remembered. "But we desperately

ABOVE A panoramic view of a section of the trail, fashioned from six negatives, shows North Vietnamese trucks rumbling through a devastated landscape, its once lush forests destroyed by defoliants and napalm.

needed manpower. So the upper levels had no other way but to bring women in. I really admired the women, but I was probably more sad than anything because people shouldn't be born to have to live through that."

"It's not that they were lacking in truck drivers," Nguyen Nguyet Anh, one of the women, believed, "but they wanted to buck up the men so that they would be brave. They thought if some women were doing the same job they were doing, then they would be more fired up and their morale would improve."

For three years, Anh drove her section of the trail, ferrying arms and supplies south, then heading back north with cargoes of wounded men. "The roads were bombed every day," she recalled, "and so the roads were never in good condition. You had to be very alert to what was around you, because if there was a crater on one side of the road, you had to quickly move to the other side to get around it. Sometimes we'd be

driving and a plane would drop a flare. Then we'd have to turn around and follow a subsidiary road to make sure the convoy got there before dawn, because if we didn't get there on time, we'd be caught in the daylight when the airplanes could find us."

Tens of thousands died along the Ho Chi Min Trail—seventy-two military cemeteries would eventually be required to hold their remains. But despite everything the Americans did to try to choke off the stream of men and supplies flowing south along the five main roads, twenty-five branch roads, and countless bypasses, the flow never stopped. McPeak described the frustration he felt:

We attacked choke points, and bypasses appeared. We rolled avalanches into the roadbed, and it slithered to the other side of the hill. We made mud and soon found corduroy. We cratered fords that somehow filled and wid-

ened. More a maze than a road, the trail expanded, split, reunited, vanished, materialized. We blasted a big chunk of Laos, the six-hundred-year-old monarchy, the Land of a Million Elephants, to bony, lunar dust. Yet somehow the Ho Chi Minh Trail, itself the enemy, was always there. Killing it was like trying to put socks on an octopus.

"We did not stop traffic down the trail," he recalled. "That is a big disappointment for me. To this day, it irritates me. The real failures were made at the policy level. Now the fact is—it sounds bad now, and I don't mean this to be bad—we were fighting on the wrong side. The government in the South was corrupt. And its people knew it. And we knew it. And they didn't fight very well. I'll tell you something: those truck drivers fought very well. I would have been proud to fight with them. One of the things you've got to do when you go to war is pick the right side, get the right allies."

CHAPTER EIGHT

THE HISTORY OF THE WORLD

MAY 1969–DECEMBER 1970

At the height of antiwar
fury over student deaths at
Kent State and U.S. atrocities
at My Lai, demonstrators fill
Boston Common, May 1970.

BRAVE AND COURAGEOUS THINGS

SECOND LIEUTENANT JOAN FUREY had wanted to be a nurse ever since she was a small child in Brooklyn when she and her older sister watched a movie on television called *So Proudly We Hail!* It starred Claudette Colbert, Paulette Goddard, and Veronica Lake as three of the nurses who faced enemy fire while ministering to American forces on Bataan and Corregidor during World War II. "It was probably the first time in my life that I realized that women could do brave and courageous things," she remembered. "It wasn't just something men could do. That was a pretty dramatic experience for me."

She was the second of five children of a grocer who, along with four of his seven brothers, served in the armed forces in World War II. A book about his infantry unit rested on the living room coffee table. His Bronze Star with Oak Leaf Cluster hung on the wall. From earliest childhood, Furey remembered, she'd been "aware of the whole issue of service in our family."

ABOVE Joan Furey and two adopted pets. Behind her is the building in which she and several other Army nurses lived at the 71st Evacuation Hospital at Pleiku, its thin walls reinforced by sandbags against the mortar and rocket fire that hit the compound from time to time.

Four of her high school classmates were drafted and sent to Vietnam while she was attending nursing school at Pilgrim State Hospital on Long Island. One was killed at Khe Sanh. The student protesters who took over the Columbia University campus in the spring of 1968 filled her with contempt. "They were going to this great school," she said, "and had all this money and shouldn't be acting out like this. If America was in Vietnam, we must be there to do good. I felt that as an American I had a responsibility to do something. I made the decision, and on my way home from work I stopped at the Army recruiter's office in Patchogue and said, 'Hi, I'm a nurse. I want to go to Vietnam.' Needless to say, they said, 'Okay, sign right here.' When she got home and told her parents what she'd done, there was silence at first. "My mother began to cry. Even my father got a tear in his eye. They were very frightened but very proud."

Volunteering to become a nurse in Vietnam was not a cause for universal admiration, Furey recalled. "There were people in those days who thought, 'Well, if you're in the military, you either must be out to get a husband or get a man, or you're gay.' It never occurred to those people that you might make that choice because you really wanted to make a difference, that you could be motivated by patriotism."

Some eleven thousand American women would serve in the military in Vietnam, eight out of ten of whom were nurses. Ten nurses died in country, eight women and two men: seven were killed in air accidents; two died from illness; and one, First Lieutenant Sharon Lane, was killed by an enemy rocket that hit the ward in which she was working at Chu Lai.

Joan Furey was assigned to the intensive care unit of the three-hundred-bed 71st Evacuation Hospital at Pleiku, in the heart of the Central Highlands. The hospital itself, she remembered, was "better than I'd expected": semipermanent Quonset huts linked by covered walkways and adjacent to a helipad where patients arrived by chopper.

She quickly became accustomed to the facilities, but nothing in civilian life could have prepared her for what she saw and did over the next twelve months. Wounded men, mostly belonging to the Fourth Infantry Division, the Mobile Strike Force Command of the Special Forces, and the indigenous mountain people who fought alongside them, were choppered in at all times of the day and night. "Amputations, dismemberment, head wounds, chest wounds," she remembered. "Some were blinded or had their faces blown off—and all of them were my age or younger." One man had been pulled from his tent by a tiger and badly mauled. Women and children caught in the

crossfire or burned by napalm or phosphorous were flown in for treatment, too. So were North Vietnamese soldiers and NLF guerrillas—one less than fifteen years old—who sometimes spat at the medical personnel trying to save their limbs or lives.

A triage officer stationed outside the operating room made the grim decisions as to who might be saved and those for whom there was no hope.

"I think one of the things that initially was so difficult was what we called 'expectant' patients—expected to die," Furey remembered. "These were patients who, it was determined, had no chance to survive. But they weren't dead yet. So somebody had to take care of them. Now, you're given a patient who is breathing but you're not supposed to do anything for him except try to make him comfortable. That's just contrary to everything you emotionally want to do. One day, they brought in a young soldier who had a head injury. He had a large field dressing on the back of his head. They said, 'He's expectant.' That was written on his tag, which meant you don't give him blood. His pupils were fixed and dilated. I kind of freaked out and I decided, 'No, they're wrong.' I was going to take care of this patient. I told the corpsman to get me blood. And he's saying, 'Well, Lieutenant, this patient is expectant. You're not supposed to be using blood.' I said, 'Get me the blood.' He went and got

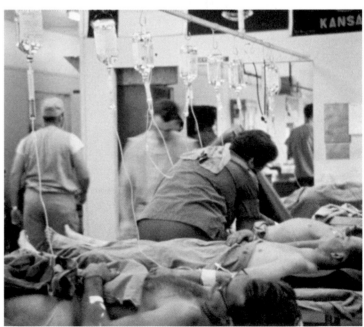

TOP Helicopter-borne wounded arrive at the hospital. **ABOVE** Nurses and doctors at work in the intensive care unit to which Joan Furey was assigned. "We had all these guys come in with little tags on them that said they were taken off hill such-and-such," she remembered, "and two weeks later we'd get another group in—same thing, same hill."

it and I hung the blood on the patient and I decided to change his dressing. Meantime, I'm ignoring everything else going on around me. It was like I was in this zone. I took off the dressing. The whole back of his head was gone and all the blood I had been giving him came out. Now, I didn't freak. I just put a nice dressing back on. It was almost robotic. A friend of mine came over and said to me, 'You just have to walk away. Come on, you can't give him any more blood. We have all these other patients.' And he just walked me out of there. We went out and had a cigarette. A few minutes later we walked right back in and got back to work. You had to learn to be detached, to push down those overwhelming emotions to get the job done."

The hospital's main goal was to stabilize each wounded man within three days so that he could be flown to a hospital in Japan for more sophisticated care. Anyone staying longer was likely to develop an infection that might prove fatal. "With every cell in your body you were just focused on taking care of these guys," Furey remembered. "Sometimes we would try to evac patients who didn't even meet the criteria for evacuation because we just wanted to get them the hell out of Vietnam."

The hospital was sandwiched between the Pleiku Air Base and the American communication center for the Central Highlands and so frequently found itself in danger from mortar and rocket fire. As soon as the red-alert siren was heard, Furey recalled, "if we had empty beds we'd grab mattresses off them, pull the side rails up, and put them over the patients. These were mostly infantry guys lying there practically naked and totally helpless during a rocket attack. They were just terrified. We had flak vests and helmets so we could crawl from one bed to the next and do what we could to help them. They still had pain. Some of them could still hemorrhage. You couldn't leave them unattended. So we just had to kind of swallow our own fear.

"Being an American woman in a war zone was a very unique thing," she remembered. "You did become the center of attention. As nurses, we were treated with a great deal of respect, but you also had a lot of pressure on you to fraternize and to socialize and to enter into intimate relationships with the men around you. The older I get the more I see that the relationships brought a piece of sanity into this crazy world that both the men and we were living in. But a lot of women left Vietnam with broken hearts, in one way or the other.

"I did meet a pilot and kind of fell in love. He told me his wife had died in a car accident a couple of years before, and, you know, he talked about the loss and the grieving and da-da-da-da-da-da. One night there was an attack on the air base. I was in bed in our hooch [the wooden hut with a tin roof that housed Furey and several other nurses] when the phone rang and one of the other girls answered it and said, 'Joan, Becky's on the phone for you.'

"So I answered, and she says, 'Joan. I just want you to know that so-and-so came in. He's very, very badly injured.'

"'How?'

"She told me. And then she said, 'I think there's something else you need to know.'

"I said, 'What's that?'

"'His next of kin is his wife.'"

He was now in the ICU. Furey's shift started there at seven a.m. "So I had to go," she recalled. "It wasn't like I could say, 'Oh, I think I'd like to have the day off.' You don't get to do that. So I went. He had a massive crushing injury to the back and shoulders. And he was in and out of consciousness. I went over to see him. And, you know, what can you say? You have someone who's critically injured and you just found out that there's been this incredible betrayal. And—it was so many years ago—but I really think that he did look up and just say, 'I'm sorry.' And what could I say? But I remember just feeling so violated and betrayed by this. It was like everything else in Vietnam."

NOT NEGOTIABLE

BY MAY 1969, it was clear to Richard Nixon that something new was needed if his hope of bringing a swift end to the war that had destroyed his predecessor was going to be fulfilled. Moscow had not persuaded Hanoi to soften its negotiating stance. News of the supposedly clandestine ongoing bombing of enemy sanctuaries in Cambodia had embarrassed the administration but was doing little to slow the North's preparations for further offensives. Accelerated pacification and the Phoenix Program were showing some signs of progress but had neither eradicated the Viet Cong infrastructure they were meant to destroy nor appreciably bolstered support for the Saigon regime.

Like Lyndon Johnson, the new president put as bright a public face on things as he could. The military and diplomatic team in Saigon was "especially fine," he told *Time* magazine; President Thieu was an able leader, and, militarily, "There is light at the end of the tunnel. If we are losing the war we are losing it in the U.S., not Vietnam." But privately, he knew, as Johnson had known, that he faced three seemingly unsolvable problems: Hanoi would not settle for less than communist control of all of Vietnam, from the Chinese border to the Ca Mau Peninsula; Saigon remained incapable of defending itself on its own; and Americans were no longer willing to go on indefinitely supporting an apparently endless war. The latest Gallup poll had found that a majority of those responding—52 percent—now believed that sending troops to fight in Vietnam had been a mistake.

Henry Kissinger hoped he could persuade the enemy to accept a "two-tiered" approach to the talks in Paris: while Washington and Hanoi worked out the details of a mutual withdrawal of "external forces"—allied and North Vietnamese—from the South, Saigon and the NLF could negotiate a settlement to the civil war between them. (If those negotiations failed, at least the Americans could come home.)

Neither North nor South liked the American plan. Although Hanoi was participating in the peace talks, communist leaders treated the negotiation as "talking while fighting"—an opportunity to gauge the enemy's intentions while preparing for a new offensive. In public, they insisted that mutual withdrawal was impossible because, they claimed, there were no North Vietnamese forces in the South. Instead, the Americans would have to pull out all of their forces and remove the hated "Thieu-Ky clique" before any agreement could be reached.

President Nguyen Van Thieu of South Vietnam was equally displeased by Kissinger's plan. He wanted the North Vietnamese out of South Vietnam, Laos, and Cambodia. Only when that was achieved would he be willing to permit individual members of the NLF to participate in South Vietnamese political life—and then only if they renounced communism. To make his stance clear he had billboards set up setting forth his position:

> Everything is negotiable. Everything except my four "No"s.
> One, coalition government. Not negotiable.
> Two, territorial integrity. Not negotiable.
> Three, the Communist Party in the Republic of Vietnam. Not negotiable.
> Four, neutralism. Not negotiable.

Even had Thieu been tempted to yield on any of these points, the generals who backed him would not have allowed him to waver. If there was so much as a hint of a coalition government, Vice President Ky warned, "there would be a coup inside ten days."

On May 14, Nixon spoke to the country for the first time about Vietnam. He portrayed himself, as he often did, as above politics: "The easy thing to do," he claimed, would be to "simply order our soldiers home," but to do so, he claimed, would constitute a "betrayal" of his presidential responsibilities. He had "ruled out," he said, "a one-sided withdrawal." Instead, he proposed an eight-point program that included *mutual* troop withdrawal, followed by internationally supervised elections that would include "each significant group" in South Vietnam and would allow its people to adopt any form of government they freely chose. Further, the United States had no objection

to unification "if that turns out to be what the people of South Vietnam and North Vietnam want."

Henry Kissinger said Nixon's offer represented a "quantum advance" over Washington's earlier proposals. Hanoi did not agree: it was a "farce," the North Vietnamese delegates said; they were prepared to stay in Paris "until the chairs rot" and the Americans came to their senses.

President Thieu was dismissive too. The U.S. proposal negated two of his "no"s, he believed: it failed to bar the NLF from the "significant" groups permitted to participate in elections, and it implied that if the communists won seats in the National Assembly the result might be a coalition government. There'd been no time for his government to object to any of Nixon's proposals, South Vietnamese ambassador Bui Diem recalled, "only to accept them. The game of imposition and attempted finesse that would become the Nixon administration's trademark in dealing with its ally had begun with a bang." Thieu asked for a personal meeting with Nixon. "The policies of the two nations cannot be solved very easily over 100,000 miles of water," he said.

WAS IT WORTH IT?

THAT SPRING, still struggling with the losses and dislocation suffered during Tet and its successor offensives, the communists had officially altered their strategy. "Never again and under no circumstances are we to risk our entire military force for just an offensive," COSVN decreed in April. "On the contrary we should endeavor to preserve our military potential for further campaigns." A few weeks later, COSVN's orders were still more explicit: "We secure victory not through a one-blow offensive, and not through a phase of attack, not even through a series of attacks culminating in a final kill. . . . Victory will come to us, not suddenly, but in a complicated and torturous way." With the talking continuing in Paris, and with their own conventional forces in need of rebuilding and resupply, it seemed wisest for the communists to limit most of their battlefield activity to small-scale mortar and sapper attacks. The result would be an overall lull in the fighting that would last, with some grisly exceptions, for several months.

Earlier that same spring, General Creighton Abrams had issued a new MACV Objectives Plan, meant to provide guidelines for fighting his "one war." Its basic premise was that American patience with the war was thinning fast. "Time . . . is running out," it said, and set June 30, 1972—before the U.S. presidential and congressional elections would be in full

ABOVE Medical personnel check the weight of a North Vietnamese soldier at one of many clinics hidden along the Ho Chi Minh Trail, part of the intricate enemy infrastructure U.S. commanders tried again and again to disrupt.

swing—as the date that "should mark the termination of major commitment of military resources in Vietnam. Additional time for achieving a 'win' beyond that date cannot be reasonably expected."

Battle would always remain a key component of MACV strategy, but Abrams hoped to deemphasize his command focus on enemy Main Force units and the "preoccupation" with body counts and instead renew emphasis on "meaningful, continuing security for the Vietnamese people in expanding areas of increasingly effective civil authority." Destruction of the "Viet Cong infrastructure," already under attack by accelerated pacification and the Phoenix Program, was to be stepped up still further, because without it enemy units "cannot obtain intelligence, cannot obtain food, cannot prepare the battlefield, and

cannot move unseen." Moreover, there should be the closest possible coordination with South Vietnamese forces, while the use of American firepower needed to be curtailed so as not to kill or injure or force from their homes the people whose independence U.S. forces were defending.

Some U.S. commanders enthusiastically adopted Abrams's principles, and there was some evidence that they were working. When a seasoned NLF cadre whose responsibility had been to block the ARVN from reaching unpacified areas in My Tho instead was captured by them, he was remarkably candid with his captors: there was no question that accelerated pacification was having "a powerful negative impact" on the NLF, he said. "During the Tet Offensive, [our] plan was to seize land and expand out from it like an oilspot. Unexpectedly, the pacification program shrank these areas bit by bit, like a piece of meat drying in the sun. . . . Both cadres and people lost their confidence gradually, until . . . the cadres and units fled from one place to another, but there were no safe havens. . . . The situation . . . deteriorated alarmingly, just like soap bubbles exposed to the sunlight. . . . We felt really let down. My life was miserable and my struggle was really worthless. I couldn't hold the territory and I myself had to be exiled like a sacrificial beast."

Not all of Abrams's commanders were persuaded by his fresh precepts. They resented being told to cut back on firepower; its lavish use had spared American lives, they insisted. One commander denounced what he called the "primitivization" of U.S. armed forces. "I'll be damned," another said, "if I permit the United States Army, its institutions, its doctrine, and its tradition to be destroyed just to win this lousy war." A third objected to what he dismissed as "windshield wiper tactics . . . going, going, going back and forth to keep the countryside clear."

When the colonel who headed the task force that drew up the MACV plan was sent to brief General Julian Ewell, mastermind of Operation Speedy Express and now in command of II Field Force, things didn't go well. "Ewell sat there during the briefing," his visitor recalled. "He chewed up and spat out an entire yellow pencil in the course of listening. When it was over he stood up, turned around to his staff, and said, 'I've made my entire career and reputation by going 180 degrees counter to such orders as this,' and walked out."

Nor was the zeal for body counts ever wholly exorcized. "Our battalion commander, in my opinion, is a very poor leader," a radio operator in the Ninth Infantry Division complained to an Army historian in April 1969. "Very poor. Every fifteen minutes he's on the horn asking me what the body count is. . . . He never fails. I don't even need a watch out there in the field because I know every fifteen minutes the man is going to be on the horn asking where his body count is."

While emphasizing pacification, Abrams had never stopped urging his generals to engage with enemy Main Force units

ABOVE A squad of Ninth Infantry troopers crosses an irrigation canal in the Mekong Delta, on the lookout for the enemy. "You weren't seeking anybody out," one veteran recalled. "They were there. If they came to you, you had a chance, but there was very little seeking out of Charlie. Charlie knew where you were before you knew where he was."

whenever they could be found, and so when intelligence revealed renewed North Vietnamese activity in the A Shau Valley—a twenty-eight-mile-long natural funnel, leading from a terminus of the Ho Chi Minh Trail along the Laotian border toward the cities of Hue and Quang Tri and Danang—elements of the 101st Airborne, the Ninth Marines, and the First ARVN Division were helicoptered in on May 10 with orders to disrupt the communist buildup and destroy the crack Twenty-ninth North Vietnamese regiment known as "the Pride of Ho Chi Minh," which was said to be camping there. In overall charge was Major General Melvin Zais, commanding general of the 101st Airborne and a veteran of mountain combat in the Maritime Alps during World War II.

The valley was a beautiful but forbidding place—steep slopes covered with double-canopy forest and all-but-impenetrable

ABOVE Hamburger Hill: In the midst of a bamboo thicket at the foot of the hill, a trooper from the 101st Airborne, photographed at the instant he is hit in the back by enemy shrapnel **LEFT** Under fire, paratroopers land higher up the slope.

stands of bamboo that led up to five-thousand-foot ridgelines. The northeast and southwest monsoons overlapped here, so clouds routinely hung over the valley and some 120 inches of rain drenched its walls each year. The valley floor and lower slopes were covered with eight-foot stands of sawtooth elephant grass, honeycombed with ancient animal trails and leech-filled streams and ponds. "Over 97 percent of the snakes in the A Shau are deadly poisonous," the Army warned. "The other three will eat you."

The valley had long been an enemy staging area, and U.S. forces had been sent in to clear it out five times over the past three years, seizing vast quantities of supplies only to find them replenished a few weeks or months later. Operation Delaware Valley, the previous spring, had cost 142 American lives and left 731 wounded. During the fifty-six-day Operation Dewey Canyon that had begun in late January, 130 Marines died and nearly 1,000 more were wounded.

This time, paratroopers belonging to the Third Battalion of the 187th Infantry regiment of the 101st Airborne came in contact with what they initially thought was a relatively small enemy force—no more than a company—dug in high on a steep, thickly forested stand-alone peak that dominated the north end of the valley. In fact, more than two enemy battalions were waiting for them. The local hill people called the hill "Dong Ap Bia"—"the mountain of the crouching beast"—and it was tagged on U.S. maps as Hill 937, but it would be remembered as "Hamburger Hill" because of all the men ground up trying to take it.

It took the better part of eleven days. Although they were eventually reinforced, three companies of the 187th did the bulk of the fighting, led by Lieutenant Colonel Weldon F. Honeycutt, a famously aggressive officer known by his radio moniker, "Blackjack." Ten assaults were beaten back. The fighting was furious—sometimes so loud and relentless that radios proved useless. Five times U.S. gunships misdirected their fire, killing

ABOVE Surrounded by U.S. dead and wounded, a paratrooper awaits medical evacuation at base camp, May 19, 1969. "They just kept sending us up there," one survivor remembered, "and we weren't getting anywhere. They were just slaughtering us like a turkey shoot, and we were the turkeys."

and wounding Americans. By the 17th, Honeycutt's battalion had been reduced to below 50 percent combat readiness: two companies had lost half their men, two others had lost eight out of ten. General Zais proposed to pull them back and send others up the slope. Honeycutt talked him out of it; it would be bad for his men's morale, he said, for anyone else to seize the summit.

Meanwhile, word of the ongoing battle had reached Saigon—prolonged large-unit combat was now a rarity in Vietnam—and reporters began flying in to cover the big story. On the 18th, Honeycutt's exhausted men fought their way back up the hill, only to have a sudden rainstorm turn the slope into a muddy quagmire in which it was impossible to maintain one's footing. Jay Charbutt of the AP interviewed exhausted men of the 101st Airborne as they slid back down the hillside.

The paratroopers came down from the mountain, their green shirts darkened with sweat, their weapons gone, their bandages stained brown and red—with mud and blood. Many cursed Lt. Col. Weldon Honeycutt, who sent three companies to take this 3000-foot mountain just a mile east of Laos and overlooking the shell-pocked A Shau Valley. They failed and they suffered. "That damn Blackjack won't stop until he kills every one of us," said one of the 40 to 50 101st Airborne troopers who were wounded.

Charbutt's report was syndicated to newspapers throughout the United States. To many readers it epitomized the apparent pointlessness of so much of the fighting in Vietnam.

Three days later, U.S. and ARVN forces finally fought their way to the hilltop, after it had been pounded by 20,000 artillery rounds, 1 million pounds of bombs, and 152,000 pounds of napalm. An ARVN unit got to the top first but was hastily ordered to withdraw so that the survivors of Blackjack Honeycutt's outfit could have the honor of being the first to reach the summit. They found the enemy bunkers mostly empty. The North Vietnamese had slipped down the backside of the mountain and vanished into Laos. One weary GI nailed the cardboard bottom of a C ration carton, with "Hamburger Hill" written on it, to a charred tree trunk. Another American stopped to scrawl a question, "Was It Worth It?"

Senator Edward Kennedy of Massachusetts did not think so.

OPPOSITE Tending to the wounded in a torrent on May 21, the day after the summit of Hamburger Hill was finally taken. Even some senior officers questioned the wisdom of sending soldiers up the slope again and again. "We can get ourselves into another Korean War situation if we keep losing men on hills that don't have to be taken today or tomorrow," one colonel said. "What's wrong with cordoning off a place and pounding the hell out of it [with B-52s]?"

It was "senseless and irresponsible to continue to send our young men to their deaths to capture hills and positions that have no relation to ending this conflict," he said. "President Nixon has told us . . . that we seek no military victory, that we seek only peace. How then can we justify sending our boys against a hill a dozen times or more, until soldiers themselves question the madness of the action? . . . I would ask him now to issue new orders to the field—orders that would spare American lives and . . . advance the cause of peace." Even *The Wall Street Journal* called for reducing the level of violence in Vietnam.

General Zais saw nothing to apologize for. "That hill was in my area of operations, that was where the enemy was, that's where I attacked him," he said. "If I find him on any other hill in the A Shau Valley, I assure you I'll attack him. . . . You can't go into the A Shau and leave the hills alone. . . . If we just sit, they try to overrun us. They'd kill us. It's just a myth that we can pull back and be quiet and everything will settle down. . . . They'd come in under the wire and they'd drop satchel charges on our bunkers and they'd mangle and maim and kill our men. The only way I can in good conscience lead my men and protect them is to insure that they're not caught up in that kind of a situation."

A reporter pointed out that 72 U.S. soldiers had died taking the mountain and 372 more had been wounded. Zais said that he "didn't consider [those casualties] high at all." The bodies of 633 enemy troops had been found on the battlefield, and it was assumed that many more had been dragged away. That was a ten-to-one kill ratio, he said, "a tremendous, gallant victory. We decimated a large North Vietnamese unit and people are acting as if it were a catastrophe. . . . I've never received orders to hold down casualties. If they wanted to hold down casualties then I'd be told not to fight."

But "they" did now want American casualties held down, and General Zais's public pugnacity did not make the administration's job easier. "We're fighting a limited war," an anonymous official told *The New York Times*. "Now clearly the greatest limitation is the reaction of the American public. They react to the casualty lists. I don't understand why the military doesn't get the picture. The military is defeating the very thing it most wants—more time to gain a stronger hand." And when the public learned in early June that U.S. commanders had chosen to abandon the mountain for which so many American lives had been sacrificed and that North Vietnamese troops were once again occupying the hillside bunkers as if no battle had ever taken place, the public clamor for a new policy intensified.

Hamburger Hill had not been the most costly engagement of the war, but it marked a milestone, nonetheless. It would be the last large-scale battle after which body count and kill ratios would be offered as the official measure of success.

CALCULATING THE COST

The June 27 issue of *Life,* including the names and photographs of all 242 Americans who had died in Vietnam during the week of May 28–June 3, caused a sensation. It included an excerpt from a letter evidently written during the battle for Hamburger Hill—"I'm writing in a hurry," it said. "I see death coming up the hill." So a good many readers confused that costly battle with the

casualties the issue chronicled. (In fact, only five of those whose images appeared in the magazine had been mortally wounded on those slopes.) "It was an issue to make men and women cry," David Halberstam recalled: it "probably had more impact on antiwar feeling than any other piece of print journalism" during the war; "almost nothing else . . . brought the pain home quite so fully."

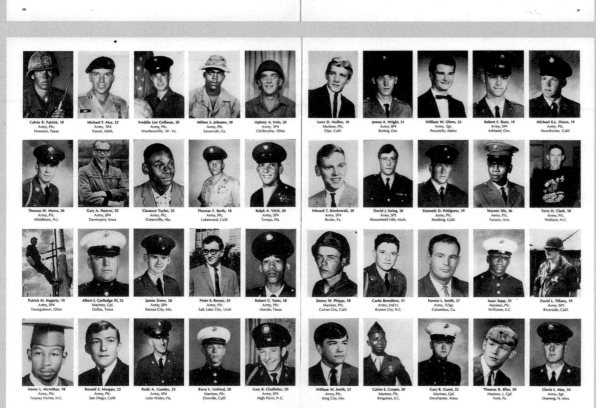

Dennis L. Babcock, 19
Army, Pfc.
Pacific Grove, Calif.

Johnnie L. Brigman, 23
Army, Pvt.
North, S.C.

Donald J. Deevers, 19
Army, Pfc.
Hinton, Okla.

Douglas J. Sommer, 18
Army
Kearns, Utah

Joe T. Conkle, 25
Army, 1st Lt.
Hampton, Ga.

Clarence Creaghead, 21
Army, SP4
Detroit, Mich.

Keith A. Kohlstorf, 20
Marines, Pfc.
Britt, Iowa

Michael A. Powell, 19
Marines, L. Cpl.
Atlanta, Ga.

Byron B. Bowden, 21
Army, SP4
Arcata, Calif.

Chris M. Pyle, 21
Navy, HM2
Hardesty, Okla.

Elmer E. Fields, 20
Army, Pvt.
Fairfax, Okla.

Jeffery A. Richardson, 20
Army, Pfc.
Red Lion, Pa.

Russell Evans, 20
Army, Pfc.
Sylvania, Ga.

Emmett L. Davis, 18
Army, Pfc.
Lakeland, Fla.

Charles A. Jones, 29
Army, Sfc.
Modesto, Calif.

Patrick M. Dixon, 23
Army, 1st Lt.
Dixon, Ill.

Joseph C. Chisholm, 24
Army, SP4
Union Lake, Mich.

Robert A. Pitts, 21
Army, Pfc.
Galveston, Texas

Albert O. Nelson Jr., 20
Marines, 2nd Lt.
Alexandria, Va.

Gary McCollough, 20
Army, Pfc.
Charlotte, N.C.

John H. Platt, 20
Army, Pfc.
Early, Iowa

Chris R. Martinez, 21
Army, Cpl.
Alameda, Calif.

James M. Leonard, 20
Army, Sgt.
Edmond, Okla.

Michael M. Hatzell, 19
Army, Pfc.
San Jose, Calif.

Iran C. Brown, 19
Marines, L. Cpl.
Roanoke, Va.

Charles D. Ervin, 18
Marines, Pfc.
Lemont, Okla.

James Titmas III, 19
Army, Pfc.
Glendale, Calif.

William J. Thornhill, 20
Army, Pvt.
Baltimore, Md.

John M. Randall, 20
Army, SP4
Phoenix, Ariz.

Max Lisenby, 21
Marines, Cpl.
Lawton, Okla.

Thomas E. Hays, 20
Army, WO
Oklahoma City, Okla.

Raiford J. Jackson, 20
Marines, Pfc.
Tuba City, Ariz.

Timothy K.P. Foster, 18
Marines, Pvt.
Honolulu, Hawaii

Virgil V. Hamilton, 20
Army, Pfc.
Brooksville, Fla.

Donny R. Lawson, 21
Marines, L. Cpl.
Grandview, Wash.

Gail G. Sanderson, 19
Marines, Pvt.
Anthon, Iowa

Robert P. Scibilia, 21
Army, SP4
Nashua, N.H.

William A. Seigle, 20
Army, Pfc.
Sapulpa, Okla.

Gerald W. Posten, 20
Army, Pfc.
Placerville, Calif.

Howard S. Hill, 22
Army, Sgt.
Irwin, Pa.

26

27

Calvin R. Patrick, 18
Army, Pfc.
Houston, Texas

Michael F. May, 22
Army, SP4
Vassar, Mich.

Freddie Lee Coffman, 21
Army, SP4
Wardensville, W. Va.

Milton S. Johnson, 20
Army, Pfc.
Savannah, Ga.

Ophrey A. Irvin, 25
Army, SP4
Chillicothe, Ohio

Larry D. Mullen, 18
Marines, Pfc.
Ojai, Calif.

James A. Wright, 21
Army, Sgt.
Boring, Ore.

William W. Olsen, 22
Army, Sgt.
Pocatello, Idaho

Robert F. Rose, 19
Army, SP4
Ashland, Ore.

Michael K.L. Dixon, 19
Army, Pfc.
Hawthorne, Calif.

Thomas W. Myers, 26
Army, Pfc.
Middlesex, N.J.

Gary A. Neavor, 25
Army, SP4
Davenport, Iowa

Clarance Taylor, 25
Army, Pfc.
Greenville, Ala.

Thomas F. Barth, 18
Army, Pfc.
Lakewood, Calif.

Ralph A. Vitch, 20
Army, SP4
Tampa, Fla.

Edward T. Kierzkowski, 20
Army, Pfc.
Butler, Pa.

David J. Ewing, 20
Army, SP4
Bloomfield Hills, Mich.

Kenneth D. Pettigrew, 19
Army, Pfc.
Redding, Calif.

Warren Nix, 26
Army, SP4
Tucson, Ariz.

Terry D. Clark, 18
Army, Pfc.
Wallace, N.C.

Patrick M. Hagerty, 19
Army, SP4
Youngstown, Ohio

Albert J. Cartledge III, 23
Marines, Pfc.
Dallas, Texas

James Drew, 20
Army, SP4
Kansas City, Mo.

Peter S. Borsay, 24
Army, Pfc.
Salt Lake City, Utah

Robert C. Yates, 18
Army, Pfc.
Hondo, Texas

Jimmy W. Phipps, 18
Marines, Pfc.
Culver City, Calif.

Curtis Breedlove, 31
Army, 2nd Lt.
Bryson City, N.C.

Forrest L. Smith, 27
Army, S/Sgt.
Columbus, Ga.

Isaac Sapp, 21
Marines, Pfc.
Williston, S.C.

David L. Tiffany, 19
Army, SP5
Riverside, Calif.

Henry L. McArthur, 18
Army, Pfc.
Fuquay Varina, N.C.

Ronald E. Morgan, 22
Army, Pfc.
San Diego, Calif.

Rudy A. Camley, 23
Army, SP4
Lake Wales, Fla.

Barry L. Unfried, 20
Marines, Pfc.
Oroville, Calif.

Gary R. Clodfelter, 20
Army, Pfc.
High Point, N.C.

William W. Smith, 21
Army, Pfc.
King City, Mo.

Calvin E. Cooper, 20
Marines, Pfc.
Kingstree, S.C.

Gary R. Guest, 22
Marines, SP4
Dorchester, Mass.

Thomas R. Bliss, 20
Marines, L. Cpl.
York, Pa.

Clovis L. May, 24
Army, Sgt.
Deming, N. Mex.

24

25

On the *NBC Nightly News,* two days after the *Life* issue appeared, anchor David Brinkley introduced his report of the week's casualty statistics by paraphrasing President Nixon, who had said at his latest news conference that "the only thing that had been settled when he came into office was the shape of the table." "Well," Brinkley continued, "in the five months since then, they have used the table in the shape agreed on, settled nothing, and in Vietnam the war and the killing continues. Today in Saigon they announced the casualty figures for the week. And, though they came in the form of numbers, each one of them was a man, most of them quite young, each with hopes he will never realize, each with families. Anyway, these are the numbers. . . ."

David W. Kinney, 20, Army, Pfc., Charleston, W. Va.

Ernest C. Munoz, 26, Army, S/Sgt., San Antonio, Texas

Cordell B. Rogers, 30, Army, Capt., Remsen, Iowa

Larry E. Boyer, 22, Marines, Cpl., Williamstown, W. Va.

Ronald A. Brown, 20, Army, Pfc., Huntington Park, Calif.

Edison R. Phillips, 19, Army, Pfc., Plymouth, Pa.

Gary C. Towle, 26, Army, Pfc., Concord, N.H.

Douglas R. Matheson, Army, Columbiaville, Mich.

Santiago V. E. Quintana, 20, Santa Fe, N. Mex.

Charles A. Hilbert, 20, Army, Pfc., Parksville, Ky.

John Winters, 18, Marines, L. Cpl., Clark, N.J.

Floyd E. Barber, 23, Army, SP4, Franklin, Ohio

Marvin C. Briss, 20, Army, SP4, Binford, N. Dak.

Garey L. Grubbs, 20, Army, Pfc., Denver, Colo.

Merlin J. Laber, 21, Army, SP4, Sykeston, N. Dak.

Robert L. Anderson, 21, Army, Pfc., Middletown, N.Y.

James Troy Ralph, 21, Army, Sgt., Hobart, Ind.

Orville Hampton, 37, Army, Sgt., Lawton, Okla.

Cris Holliday, 20, Army, Pfc., Meridian, Miss.

Billy W. Pettis, 21, Army, Pfc., Castleberry, Ala.

John M. Hohman, 22, Army, CW2, Leominster, Mass.

Gordon D. Perry, 19, Marines, Pfc., Morgantown, W. Va.

James J. Wise, 20, Army, SP4, Detroit, Mich.

Robert T. Bensberg, 28, Army, Capt., Columbus, Ga.

Kenneth M. Seward, 22, Army, SP5, Greeley, Colo.

William H. Darden, 20, Army, Pfc., Lanett, Ala.

Jan Rauschkolb, 22, Marines, Cpl., Denver, Colo.

Steven C. Owen, 22, Army, SP4, Long Beach, Calif.

John W. Abbott, 23, Marines, 1st Lt., South Bend, Ind.

William J. Peterson, 23, Army, 2nd Lt., Ephrata, Wash.

Edward Frowner, 20, Army, Sgt., Manila, Ala.

James S. Colombero, 24, Army, SP5, McCloud, Calif.

Donald P. Seburg Jr., 19, Army, Pfc., Jackson, Mich.

Milford E. Cobb, 33, Army, S/Sgt., Tempe, Ariz.

Ronald A. Yashack, 21, Army, Pfc., Diagonal, Iowa

Wayne E. Garven, 21, Army, Pfc., Mt. Vernon, Ohio

William H. Beske, 21, Army, Pfc., Lathrup Village, Mich.

Ralph H. Crowley, 20, Army, Sgt., Remus, Mich.

Yvon E. Girouard, 20, Marines, Pfc., Littleton, N.H.

Errol W. Pereira, 21, Army, Pfc., Hilo, Hawaii

Harold James Warmsley, 24, Army, SP4, Mansfield, La.

Allen M. Graff, 21, Army, Sgt., West Covina, Calif.

Robert Sigholtz Jr., 23, Army, Capt., Annandale, Va.

Edward F. Clennon, 23, Army, Pfc., Joliet, Ill.

Billy L. Thomas, 19, Army, Pfc., Stinnett, Texas

Derrill L. Price Jr., 20, Army, SP4, El Dorado Springs, Mo.

Richard L. Brumfield, 21, Army, Sgt., Denham Springs, La.

Steven K. Sprinkle, 20, Army, SP4, Winston-Salem, N.C.

Steven E. Murray, 19, Army, SP4, Indianapolis, Ind.

Euan J. Parker, 22, Army, Pfc., Brigham City, Utah

Emerson Martin, Marines, Pfc., Gallup, N. Mex.

Farrell J. Vice, 21, Army, SP4, Abbeville, La.

Scott E. Cochran, 18, Army, Pfc., Eugene, Ore.

Philip L. Gamble Jr., 26, Army, 2nd Lt., Newport, R.I.

James W. Clark, 21, Army, 1st Lt., Reno, Nev.

James D. Johnson, 20, Marines, L. Cpl., Bedford, Texas

Kenneth D. Shoaps, 20, Army, Sgt., Grosse Pointe Woods, Mich.

Joey L. Boles, 21, Army, SP4, Wingate, Texas

Bobby G. Newby, 21, Army, Pfc., Winchester, Ky.

Thomas B. Paynter, 21, Army, SP4, Seattle, Wash.

Terry V. Miller, 23, Army, Pfc., Ottumwa, Iowa

Herman L. Judy Jr., 23, Army, Pfc., Alexandria, Va.

James Hebert III, 20, Marines, Pfc., New Orleans, La.

Willie L. Kirkland, 20, Army, SP4, Avon Park, Fla.

James F. Hilliard, 23, Army, Sgt., Kalamazoo, Mich.

Michael E. Gerber, 20, Army, SP4, Conway Springs, Kan.

Donald W. Ide, 25, Army, 1st Lt., Beirut, Lebanon

Gary M. Paul, 19, Marines, L. Cpl., Norway, Mich.

Gary W. Leighton, 19, Marines, Pfc., Washington, Pa.

Thomas A. Nebel, 20, Army, Pfc., Keota, Iowa

Jim J. Walters, 20, Marines, Pfc., Sioux City, Iowa

Dick E. Whitney, 22, Army, SP4, Newberg, Ore.

Robert L. Boese, 22, Army, Pfc., Marion, Kan.

During the week of May 28–June 3 these men were also reported killed in action.

Earl A. Godman, 21, Army, Sgt., Baltimore, Md.

John P. Karr, 21, Army, 1st Lt., Clearwater, Fla.

Gary K. Smith, 20, Army, Pvt., Detroit, Mich.

James S. Luckett II, 28, Army, 1st Lt., Columbus, Ohio

Claude R. Van Andel, 19, Army, Sgt., Norfolk, Neb.

Charles E. McMillion, 20, Army, Pfc., Jefferson, Ohio

Albert C. Walls Jr., 22, Army, Pfc., Elmsford, N.Y.

Richard L. Cox, 21, Navy, HM3, Shakopee, Minn.

Valarian L. Finley, 21, Marines, L. Cpl., Mansfield, N. Dak.

Peter R. Adams, 19, Marines, L. Cpl., Dorchester, Mass.

Kenneth W. Smith, 20, Army, SP4, Detroit, Mich.

David T. Chapman Jr., 20, Army, SP4, Dumas, Miss

Charles R. Jones, 29, Army, SP4, Calhoun City, Miss.

James E. Workman, 22, Army, Pfc., Harts, W. Va.

Wesley G. Ice, 21, Army, Pfc., Bridgeport, W. Va.

Richard N. White, 21, Army, Pfc., Golden Valley, Minn.

James P. Duffy Jr., 29, Army, Sgt., Brunswick, Ohio

Jack L. Johnson, 20, Marines, Pfc., Elkhart, Ind.

John M. Stenberg, 20, Marines, Pfc., Pasco, Wash.

Thomas J. Orr, 20, Marines, Pfc., Garden Grove, Calif.

James B. Smith, 19, Marines, L. Cpl., Louisville, Ky.

Robert G. Schmidt, Marines, L. Cpl., Levittown, N.Y.

Pedro A. Rios, 40, Army, Sfc., Mount Holly, N.J.

Gary W. Cox, 19, Army, Pfc., East Gary, Ind.

Ronnie E. Parker, 23, Army, Pfc., Fullerton, Calif.

THERE IS NOTHING I CAN DO

PRESIDENT NIXON reluctantly agreed to see the increasingly anxious president of South Vietnam. His first thought was to meet Thieu in California, but he felt that antiwar demonstrations there might embarrass them both. Thieu suggested Honolulu, but Nixon didn't want to stage their meeting in the same place where Thieu had first met Lyndon Johnson. Nixon finally chose Midway Island, a tiny isolated coral atoll in the western Pacific. It had lent its name to the great U.S. naval victory fought nearby during World War II, but had since become little more than a refueling stop, best known as the home of tens of thousands of black-footed albatrosses whose eccentric, rattling, head-bobbing mating dance and comically awkward attempts to take flight gave them their nickname, "gooney birds."

President Thieu had been delighted by Nixon's election victory. "This is nice," he'd told an aide when he heard the results. "Now at least we have bought ourselves some time." And he'd initially hoped that during his meeting with the president he could take advantage of the gratitude he was sure the new U.S. president must be feeling for his last-minute behind-the-scenes help in defeating Hubert Humphrey. But, as Bui Diem wrote, it quickly became clear "that [the Americans] wanted to use Midway for one purpose only: to get Thieu's formal consent on troop withdrawals. It would be the briefest of talks (five hours all told) at an obscure place, meant solely as a ceremonial gesture of agreement on one issue."

That issue was Nixon's unilateral decision to announce that he was going to withdraw twenty-five thousand U.S. troops from Vietnam by the end of August, and perhaps eighty thousand more by the end of the year. Even before his election, Nixon remembered, "it was no longer a question of whether the next president would withdraw troops but of how they would leave and what they would leave behind." Despite the president's recent pledge that the United States would never withdraw unilaterally, he and his closest advisers believed they would eventually have to do just that, whether or not South Vietnam was ready to defend itself. They differed only as to when to begin and at what pace they should proceed. Henry Kissinger was for going slow. "Withdrawal of U.S. troops will become like salted peanuts to the American public," he warned at a meeting of the National Security Council. "The more U.S. troops come home, the more will be demanded." Secretary of Defense Melvin Laird, a former Wisconsin congressman with seventeen years of experience on Capitol Hill and a seasoned politician's keen understanding of the steady pace at which patience with the war was fraying there, was eager to get on with it. The defense budget was far too high, he believed—and he would impose cuts even as the fighting continued in Vietnam—while the war's prolongation threatened to undercut the rest of the president's agenda just as it had weakened his predecessor's Great Society. The president himself seemed most concerned with the potential domestic impact of bringing soldiers home. With talks under way in Paris and a new administration in charge, the antiwar movement was still relatively quiescent. Sam Brown, an antiwar activist who had headed Youth for McCarthy in 1968, explained the reasons for temporarily lying low: "There was a political sense that you couldn't attack [Nixon] until he'd been in office long enough that he owned the war. To go after him [during the winter] would have been silly. People would have looked at you and said, 'Wait a minute. This guy says he's got a plan. Let's give him a chance.'" A sign of apparent progress like a presidential announcement of a troop withdrawal could help keep the protest movement under control, at least for a time.

En route to his meeting with Thieu, Nixon stopped in Honolulu to give his Vietnam commander new marching orders. "It was painful to see General Abrams," Henry Kissinger remembered, "epitome of the combat commander, obviously unhappy, yet nevertheless agreeing to a withdrawal of 25,000 combat troops. He knew then that he was doomed to a rearguard action,

ABOVE President Thieu and Nixon meet the press at Midway Island: "I know that you are going to go," Thieu told the U.S. president privately, "but before you go, leave something for us as friends. Leave something to help me out."

that the purpose of his command would increasingly become logistic redeployment, not success in battle. He could not possibly achieve the victory that had eluded us at full strength while our forces were constantly dwindling."

President Johnson's mission statement had called upon MACV to "defeat" the enemy and "force" him to withdraw from South Vietnam. Nixon's was far more modest. In the end, Nixon reiterated, the war would have to be won or lost by the South Vietnamese themselves. To that end, Abrams was to "provide maximum assistance to strengthen" Saigon's forces so that they could eventually take over from his, speed up still further the pace of pacification, and reduce the flow of men and supplies coming down the Ho Chi Minh Trail. Meanwhile, he was to do all he could to "hold down" American casualties. U.S. losses like those suffered on the slopes of Hamburger Hill must never happen again.

When the president told the general he planned to bring the first troops home as early as July, Abrams asked for more advance warning in the future; the whole process should be at least "reasonably deliberate," he said, and he hoped to be consulted and "given a chance [to express his concerns] as the services cut and run." He thought the South Vietnamese might possibly one day be able to defeat the NLF, but he saw no possibility that without continued American support they could ever defeat both the NLF and the North Vietnamese. Still, he would do his best to carry out the president's wishes. "I do not want to be an obstructionist to this thing," Abrams explained to an associate. "It's going to happen whether you and I want it to happen or not . . . but I want it to be done in a way that does not completely bug out on the Vietnamese and leave them flat and unable to defend themselves."

Nixon and his five hundred–person entourage of officials, security men, journalists, and hangers-on moved on to Midway on June 8, just in time to greet President Thieu and his entourage, who arrived aboard a chartered Pan American jet flying an American flag on one side of the cockpit and a South Vietnamese flag on the other. The Marine band from Pearl Harbor was there to play the national anthems of both countries. More than twenty limousines had been flown in from Washington to ferry the two presidential parties around an island that measured less than three square miles.

Nixon and Thieu were all smiles in public. In private, within the freshly painted naval commander's house where their meeting was held, things were tense. The American president explained that he was under such enormous pressure from Congress, the press, and the antiwar movement to demonstrate real progress in Vietnam that he had no choice but to begin bringing some troops home. It was just a ploy, he assured Thieu, an effort to buy time. America was not abandoning its ally. He continued to insist that he would never settle for anything less than mutual withdrawal of American and North Vietnamese forces; by the time the last U.S. troops went home, he assured Thieu, the North Vietnamese would long since have left South Vietnamese soil. To show his continuing support for the Saigon regime, Nixon promised four years of "military Vietnamization" to ready South Vietnamese forces, followed by four more years of "economic Vietnamization" during his second term.

Thieu had known of Nixon's decision in advance—news of it had been leaked to the press—and understood that it was irrevocable. He therefore didn't formally object, though he did ask that in order to minimize panic among the South Vietnamese, when Nixon made his announcement he would say he was "redeploying" troops rather than "withdrawing" them. It was his hope, Thieu said, that the war would eventually end as the Korean War had ended, with a DMZ separating the two antagonists and a large residual U.S. force to ensure that the North did not invade the South. In addition, he asked that Washington arm and train two new mobile South Vietnamese divisions capable of coping quickly wherever northern aggression occurred.

Nixon would not commit himself. Instead, he said he had made another nonnegotiable decision—to start secret high-level talks, separate from the ongoing Paris negotiations between Washington and Hanoi. Thieu had no objection, he said, provided he was consulted as they went along.

Once their conversation had ended, Nixon and Thieu were driven to an airplane hangar where more than 150 members of the White House press corps were waiting. The American president told them he was redeploying twenty-five thousand men within thirty days—and that he was doing so at the "recommendation" of President Thieu and General Abrams. (This last, the president later admitted, was something of a "diplomatic exaggeration"; neither man wanted him to do it.)

Flying home, Kissinger recalled, "Nixon was jubilant. He considered the announcement a political triumph. He thought it would buy him the time necessary for developing our strategy. His advisers, including me, shared his view. We were wrong."

Aboard Thieu's plane headed for Saigon, the South Vietnamese president did his best to seem pleased at how things had gone, but he was worried. When a friend asked him why he hadn't objected to the American president's plan, he was bleakly philosophical. "When Nixon decides to withdraw, there is nothing I can do," he said. "Just as we could do nothing about it when Eisenhower, Kennedy, and Johnson decided to come in. Once you know you cannot change the American decision, it is better to make the best of it."

Despite Nixon's assurances, Thieu understood that the troop withdrawal signaled there was no going back. The situ-

ation reminded him of a Vietnamese saying: "If the head slides through easily, the tail will follow." "Perhaps most of all," Bui Diem recalled, Thieu "rankled at having been compelled to meet with Nixon in this desolate and gooney bird–ridden place. As did we all. It was impossible not to reflect on the difference between the treatment we were receiving and that accorded the North Vietnamese by the Russians. We knew that in private the Soviets referred to the northerners as 'those stubborn bastards,' but in public, at least, Moscow rolled out the red carpet for visitors from Hanoi. Yet our own meetings were relegated to such places as . . . Midway, almost as if we were regarded as lepers by those in whom we had placed our security and with whom we shed so much blood. Circumstances forced us to swallow such things, but we did not forget them. . . . Thieu especially did not forget."

Thieu's confidence in Washington was shaken further not long after Nixon got back to Washington. Former Defense Secretary Clark Clifford had just published an article in *Foreign Affairs* in which he urged the president to pull 100,000 combat troops out of Vietnam by the end of the year and commit to bringing them all home by the end of 1970. When he was asked about it at a press conference, Nixon said that he planned to make another decision to withdraw troops as early as August, provided there was evidence of real progress both in Paris and in building up South Vietnamese forces, and hoped to "beat Mr. Clifford's timetable." Asked if he was "wedded" to the Saigon government, he added that, while "there is no question about our standing with President Thieu," the United States would never grant veto power to any foreign government.

The same week that Nixon and Thieu met on Midway Island, eighty-eight representatives of the NLF and other allied anti-Thieu organizations gathered in a hastily constructed meeting hall hidden in the forest on the Cambodian border.

ABOVE News of Nixon's plan to reduce the American presence in South Vietnam reaches Saigon on the front page of the semi-official *Saigon Times*, June 9, 1969. "The magic word is 'Vietnamization,'" wrote *The New Yorker*'s Robert Shaplen, "which may be defined as a process surrounded by difficulties comparable to those of carrying out a successful heart transplant."

Their objective was to form a new Provisional Revolutionary Government (PRG) to compete with the hated Saigon regime, and replace the NLF at the Paris peace talks. NLF Main Force units formed a perimeter to safeguard the meeting. Banners proclaimed "Strengthen the Great United Solidarity" and "South Vietnam Is Independent, Democratic, Peaceful, and Neutral." The president of the NLF presided alongside the president of the Alliance of National, Democratic, and Peace Forces—a recently formed noncommunist organization that worked with the NLF but many of whose members worried that too-great reliance on the North was undercutting the struggle's southern character.

The object of the gathering in part was to "upstage" the Midway meeting, explained Truong Nhu Tang, a prominent alliance leader who agreed to serve as justice minister in the new shadow government. But there was more to it than that. "Our goal was to influence public opinion: domestically, where a noncommunist government would give us added credibility with the

South Vietnamese populace; internationally, where we would be able to compete with Saigon for formal recognition (and the potential support that would come with it); and in the United States, where we would enhance our claim of representing the southern people, giving the peace movement additional ammunition. . . . From here on in we would be able to wage full-scale diplomatic warfare."

Tang was a nationalist, not a communist. A French-trained banker and businessman who loathed what he called the "Saigon dictatorship," he had helped found the NLF in 1960 and had endured several years in a South Vietnamese prison for opposing the Thieu regime. He saw the PRG as a vehicle for achieving southern independence, from Hanoi as well as from Washington—a "coalition government . . . immune to outright North Vietnamese domination." (Madame Nyuyen Thi Binh, the PRG's foreign minister, who soon took over from the chief delegate to the Paris peace talks, was less naive about its provenance; after the war she admitted that "real decision making regarding the negotiations" always came from Hanoi.) Ho Chi Minh and North Vietnamese Premier Pham Van Dong immediately sent telegrams declaring the the PRG was henceforth to be considered "the legal government and the true representa-

ABOVE Between ranks of uniformed NLF guards, members of the new Provisional Revolutionary Government enter the hastily constructed meeting hall on the Cambodian border in which the PRG was formed, June 8, 1969.

TAXIWAY

tive of the people of South Vietnam." Within a day or two, the Soviet Union, China, and their communist allies had followed suit.

The PRG constructed a thatched-hut capital of sorts along the Vam Co River, just a few miles south of COSVN headquarters and close enough to the Cambodian border to make escape across the border easy. Food was scarce, so guerrilla hunting parties emptied the surrounding jungles of wildlife. "Elephants, tigers, wild dogs, monkeys," Tang recalled, "none of them were strangers to our cook-pots." U.S. B-52s were an ever-present threat, he remembered. "From a kilometer, the shockwaves knocked their victims senseless. Any hit within a half kilometer would collapse the walls of an unreinforced bunker, burying alive the people cowering inside. . . . It was something of a miracle that from 1969 through 1970, the attacks, though they caused significant casualties generally, did not kill a single one of the military or civilian leaders in the headquarters complexes." Part of the explanation was that as soon as Soviet trawlers plying the South China Sea detected bombers flying from Okinawa and Guam they contacted COSVN, which, in turn, relayed the message to those in harm's way in time for them to take shelter.

"Hours later," Tang remembered, "we would return to

find . . . that there was nothing left. It was as if an enormous scythe had swept through the jungle, felling the giant teak trees like grass in its way, shredding them into billions of scattered splinters. On these occasions—when the B-52s had found their mark—the complex would be utterly destroyed: food, clothes, supplies, documents, everything. It was not just that things were destroyed; in some awesome way they had ceased to exist. You would come back to where your lean-to and bunker had been, your home, and there would simply be nothing there, just an unimaginable landscape gouged by immense craters. The terror was complete. One lost control of bodily functions as the mind screamed incomprehensible orders to get out. On one occasion a Soviet delegation was visiting our ministry when a particularly short-notice warning came through. When it was over, no one had been hurt, but the entire delegation had sustained considerable damage to its dignity—uncontrollable trembling and wet pants: the all-too-outward signs of inner convulsion. The visitors could have spared themselves their feelings of embarrassment; each of their hosts was a veteran of the same symptoms."

ABOVE B-52s at Andersen Air Force Base on the island of Guam prepare to fly to targets in South Vietnam, some 2,500 miles away.

STAND TALL AND BE PROUD

LINED UP on the baking tarmac at Tan Son Nhut Air Base on July 8, 1969, 814 men of the Third Battalion, Sixtieth Infantry, of the Second Brigade of the Ninth Infantry Division, waited for permission to board nine C-141 Starlifter transport planes. They were bound for McChord Air Force Base in Tacoma, Washington—and home. They were the first of the 25,000 U.S. troops President Nixon had promised to withdraw from Vietnam by summer's end.

Some of the men couldn't believe their luck. "I don't think anybody is going to believe it until they get back," one platoon sergeant said. "You ain't never lucky until you leave this place."

Young Vietnamese women held up signs reading, "Farewell to the Old Reliables," the division's cherished nickname. Actually, fewer than two hundred of the men present had fought with the division's Third Battalion. When the transfer order came, those with time left to serve in Vietnam had been moved to other outfits, their places filled with men ready to rotate home. General Abrams had hoped that in the interest of unit cohesion units would be redeployed as intact outfits with the men currently assigned to them. But long-standing military policy held that the only "fair and equitable" method of deciding who was to go home first was to choose those individual soldiers who had served longest in the field. Tradition prevailed, and commanders would soon find themselves without their most experienced troops. "Our fear was that the turbulence would be so high that units would become ineffective," said a member of Abrams's staff. "And that's what happened. I believe it caused most of the indiscipline in units which plagued us later." In the end, he continued, that decision "caused leaders to go forth to battle daily with men who did not know them and whom they did not know."

The men lined up on the tarmac at Tan Son Nhut did not concern themselves with questions of policy. They were just eager to be on their way out of Vietnam. A second group of young women hung plastic garlands around their necks and handed each man a folded South Vietnamese flag. General Abrams called them a "credit to your generation." President Thieu helicoptered in to express his country's gratitude, handed out cigarette lighters emblazoned with his signature and seal of office, and expressed the hope that one day the men might come back to South Vietnam as tourists.

Following their eighteen-hour flight, they received an all-American welcome at McChord. A brass band played "The Stars and Stripes Forever." One hundred Little Leaguers in uniform greeted them. So did Miss Tacoma. "You men can stand tall and be proud," General William Westmoreland told them.

"You can look any man in the eye knowing that you have served your country when you were called." An elderly woman moved through the crowd of happy friends and family members with a picture of her son, asking the returning men if they'd known him. He had been killed in Vietnam the year before.

Thousands of people turned out to cheer the men as they paraded for eight blocks through downtown Seattle. It rained steadily. The soldiers didn't mind: "We would have marched in snow," one captain said. Pretty girls threw them roses. Antiwar demonstrators across the street from the reviewing stand set up in front of the public library did their best to drown out Stanley R. Resor, the secretary of the army, chanting, "Hell no, we won't go!" and "Bring them all home now!" Some in the crowd shouted back, "Go home, you commies!" Others held up a sign saying, "Students for Victory in Vietnam." But there was no violence.

Afterward, the men boarded buses that were to take them to a salmon bake organized by local people. As they pulled away, demonstrators held up the two-fingered peace sign, hoping the returning soldiers would respond in kind. Some men on each bus did, and, a reporter noted, "one GI reached under the collar

OPPOSITE The homecoming parade honoring the first U.S. troops brought back from Vietnam ends in front of the Seattle Public Library, July 10, 1969. Moments after this photograph was taken, an angry supporter of the war ripped down the large banner that read, "WELCOME HOME. WE'LL STAY IN THE STREETS TILL ALL THE G.I.S ARE HOME." **ABOVE** Most of those who turned out in the rain that day, like this weeping woman, were just glad to see the soldiers return.

of his fatigues, pulled out the three-pronged peace symbol hanging from his neck and waved it with a sly grin."

The promise of Vietnamization had not persuaded the peace movement that an end to the war was any nearer. "It seemed that [Nixon] was going to get out of Vietnam as slowly as possible," Sam Brown said, "while selling the idea that he was getting out as fast as possible." With other veterans of the McCarthy campaign, Brown set up a "Vietnam Moratorium Committee" and opened an office in Washington, D.C., to begin planning an ongoing monthly series of nationwide protests against the war to begin on October 15. It was their goal, Brown told the press, to demonstrate to the country that the young people who wanted an end to the war were not "crazy radicals" but "your sons and daughters."

WHAT ARE WE FIGHTING FOR?

THOMAS JOHN VALLELY was born in Boston, the son of a judge, and brought up in the suburb of Newton. Undiagnosed dyslexia kept him from doing well in school. "I was not a good student, but I was ambitious," he remembered. "I did not have a lot of options. My father had been a naval officer in the

ABOVE Marine radio operator Tom Vallely in South Vietnam. Going to war, he remembered, "is not a pleasant experience. But there's some camaraderie and there's friendship and there's smiling and there's laughter—and at the same time great sadness. I don't know how to describe it better than that."

Second World War. I used to wear his flight jacket around the house and I began to think, 'Okay, this is how I'm going to create a path forward for myself. I'm going to go to Vietnam and I'm going to try to excel there and be a hero.'"

The Marine Corps gave him a chance to start over. "America always did good," he believed, "and I wanted to do good. Like the people that went to World War II, I would get to wear the uniform, do something people would respect. Part of going to war in Vietnam I enjoyed. If you survive, it's quite thrilling. It's the history of the world. Where I was, survival was an issue. There were times I would have loved to have been in the National Guard. Period." By the summer of 1969, Vallely was a radio operator in the Marine Corps, part of a massive search-and-clear mission in Quang Nam Province in the northern part of South Vietnam.

On August 13, his company was ambushed and came under heavy machine gun fire. "It was a grab-'em-by-the-belt type of situation," he remembered. "We lost a lot of people, so did they. Lot of people lying around."

Vallely radioed for reinforcements. Then he picked up a rifle and ammunition from a wounded Marine and, firing as he went, took up a position no more than ten feet from an enemy machine gun. He hurled a smoke grenade to mark its position, and then, as enemy fire swept back and forth across the field, he moved from Marine to Marine, pointing out targets among the trees and encouraging his comrades.

For his "conspicuous gallantry," Tom Vallely was awarded the Silver Star.

"You want to tell your grandchildren it has a lot to do with courage," he recalled. "But it's really quite reactive. It's survival. There's no choice there. You react or you're not going to *have* grandchildren."

Two days after the battle in which Tom Vallely distinguished himself, and while half a million Americans were still in Vietnam, roughly the same number of young Americans gathered on a dairy farm in upstate New York for a music festival— "Woodstock Music and Art Fair, an Aquarian Exposition." For three days, a muddy six-hundred-acre dairy farm near the little town of Bethel was transformed into the third largest city in the state. Everyone who was anyone in the world of American rock and roll and popular music performed: Joan Baez and Janis Joplin, Richie Havens and Jimi Hendrix, Santana and Sly and the Family Stone, the Who and the Grateful Dead, Crosby, Stills & Nash—and Country Joe & the Fish, whose "I-Feel-Like-I'm-Fixin'-to-Die Rag" became a singalong favorite of the antiwar movement.

And it's one, two, three,
What are we fighting for?

Don't ask me, I don't give a damn,
Next stop is Vietnam;
And it's five, six, seven,
Open up the pearly gates,
Well there ain't no time to wonder why,
Whoopee, we're all gonna die.

"We used to think of ourselves as little clumps of weirdos," Janis Joplin recalled. "But now we're a whole new minority group." The antiwar activist Bill Zimmerman and his girlfriend of the time were there and were inspired: "That many people celebrating the new rock music, and the new culture growing up around it, made us feel that our point of view was on the ascendancy, and that despite our differences with the larger society, history might be on our side." Some four hundred people were treated for drug or alcohol overdoses, but not a single act of violence was reported.

The New York Times was scornful at first: "What kind of culture is it that can produce so colossal a mess? . . . The adults who helped create the society against which these young people are so feverishly rebelling must bear a share of the responsibility for this outrageous episode. . . . The dreams of marijuana and rock music . . . had little more sanity than the impulses that drove lemmings to the sea. They ended up in a nightmare of mud and stagnation." But the next day, the *Times* had reconsidered: "The rock festival begins to take on the quality of a social phenomenon. . . . And in spite of the prevalence of drugs it was essentially a phenomenon of innocence."

"The late '60s," Air Force pilot Merrill McPeak recalled, "were a kind of confluence of several rivulets. There was the antiwar movement itself, the whole movement towards racial equality, the environment, the role of women. And the anthems for that counterculture were provided by the most brilliant rock and roll music that you can imagine. I don't know how we could exist today as a country without that experience—with all of its warts and ups and downs—that produced the America we have today, and we are better for it. And I felt that way in Vietnam. I turned the volume up on all that stuff. That, for me, represented what I was trying to defend."

ABOVE High times at Woodstock: "Everyone was fist pounding and angry about the war," the singer Stephen Stills remembered, "and our music gave them something to do besides just be mad at everything."

AGENT ORANGE

By the spring of 1970, American and South Vietnamese forces had sprayed some twenty million gallons of herbicides over roughly one-quarter of South Vietnam—and border areas in Laos and Cambodia, as well. The idea had been to reduce casualties by clearing areas around U.S. installations and denying crops and forest cover to the elusive enemy. Five million acres of upland forest and 500,000 acres of crops were destroyed, but more than 3,000 villages were also sprayed. One RAND study found that for every ton of rice denied to the NLF, five hundred civilians went hungry.

The most frequently used chemical was Agent Orange. Its manufacturers were aware that it contained a toxic chemical—dioxin—that in large doses caused birth defects in mice and produced a disfiguring skin disease in men and women who came in contact with it. But they kept those facts from the Defense Department.

From the first, Hanoi accused the United States of waging chemical warfare. MACV dismissed the charges as propaganda. But at home, environmentalists eventually convinced the administration that the chemicals present in Agent Orange presented such serious potential hazards to humans and to the environment that they should be banned from use on American farms.

On April 15, over the objections of the military, President Nixon ordered an end to all herbicide operations in Vietnam by the end of the year. The *ecological* damage herbicides did to Vietnam is undeniable; the amount of damage it did to Vietnamese civilians and American military personnel would be the subject of angry debate for decades to come.

OPPOSITE Two Fairchild C-123K Provider aircraft blanket a mangrove forest, twenty miles southeast of Saigon, with Agent Orange. **BELOW** An NLF guerrilla poles himself through a denuded forest on the Ca Mau Peninsula after it had been sprayed. Mangroves traditionally provide protection from serious flooding during tropical storms and seasonal monsoons.

A TOTALLY DIFFERENT ARMY

MERRILL McPEAK was clear about what he was fighting for. Others serving in Vietnam were no longer sure. Vincent Okamoto remembered the difficulty many of the men he knew had in defining their mission. "When a nineteen-year-old high school dropout says, 'Why are we here?'" he recalled, "the standard response, at least on an official level, was, 'To prevent international communism from conquering the world.' The men would say, 'Hey, that's bullshit.' The other reason put forth, at least in the latter days of the war, was to maintain America's international credibility with our allies, and our enemies. No nineteen-, twenty-year-old kid wants to die to maintain the credibility of Richard Nixon. And so, within a relatively short time, the guys were saying, 'Look, we shouldn't be here, but we are. So my only function in life is to try and keep you alive, buddy; and to keep my precious ass from being killed; and then to go home, and forget about this.'"

"If Nixon is going to withdraw, then let's all go home now," one First Infantry Division soldier told a reporter. "I don't want to get killed buying time for the gooks." A medic in the First Cavalry, serving his second tour in Vietnam, said, "The first time I was here, we were more aggressive. Then people felt that if we really went at it, we could finish the war. Now we know that it will go on after we leave, so why get killed?"

"I was there for about eighteen months, from May of '69 until November, '70," remembered Wayne Smith, an African American medic from Providence, Rhode Island, who served with the Ninth Infantry in the Mekong Delta. "The morale was terrible. No one wanted to be the last guy to die in Vietnam. The military broke down. It wasn't about this nonsensical 'pacification of the enemy' or 'Vietnamization,' or winning the so-called 'hearts and minds.' It was about trying not to let any of my men be the last one to die on that shitty piece of earth. That's how most of us thought."

Worried commanders, including General Abrams, called it "short-timers' fever." It was not the only problem now plaguing U.S. forces. "Vietnam was a microcosm of everything that was happening in America," Smith recalled. "It was all happening in Vietnam, really, in one way, shape, or form." An earlier generation of African American soldiers, who saw in the military advantages not easily found in civilian life, had often swallowed racial slights in the interest of advancement. But the young draftees who had now followed them to Southeast Asia were different. The urban rebellions of 1967 and 1968, anger and anguish at the death of Dr. King, the rise of the Black Power and Black Panther movements—all found echoes among American forces in Vietnam.

Sergeant Allen Thomas Jr. was an African American lifer who served three tours in Vietnam. In 1965, he remembered, "war was what the military did, and I was anticommunist so I pretty much supported the war." When he returned in 1967, things had already begun to change: "It was a lot of draftees. . . . There was more disobedience. Third tour was just survival, everybody just wanted to stay alive."

"There were very serious racial issues," Wayne Smith recalled. "But what it was largely was summed up by, 'Hey, I'm here in Vietnam. No one's going to call me a nigger. I'm not going to take any shit from anybody.' I mean it was almost that simple. I remember talking with friends about whether African Americans should serve in Vietnam or not. That was a big question for me, too. I was of two minds like so many young African Americans. Should we kind of adhere to the philosophy of Dr. King—of passive resistance but also of participation, to serve with white Americans? Or should we follow the next generation like Malcolm X and Stokely Carmichael? Those conversations were everywhere. And I remember some brothers being

ABOVE The Confederate battle flag on the wall of Annie's Bar, run by a Vietnamese woman not far from the Danang Air Base, signaled that it catered to a mostly white clientele.

very militant. And sometimes the loud voice simply dominated. I was very confused, I will tell you."

African American grievances were many. Only roughly 2 percent of the officer corps was black. Black personnel caught flouting military discipline were far more likely than whites to be jailed or court-martialed. Adherents of the Nation of Islam incarcerated in the Army prison at Long Binh were forbidden Korans. "Black men didn't want to get skinhead haircuts like the Army liked," Sergeant James T. Gillam of the Fourth Infantry Division remembered. "They wanted to grow an Afro. Some officers wouldn't allow even a little one, yet white guys could have a 'Beatle' haircut." "Black is Beautiful" stickers were ordered removed from inside foot lockers while white soldiers were allowed to display the Confederate flag. "I mean, of all things to have over here, man," one black GI complained. "There ought to be some goddamn law to outlaw them goddamn flags. The fucking Confederacy is gone." Hoping to ease tensions, the Pentagon had the Stars and Bars banned. But when southern congressmen complained, permission was granted to fly state flags that included versions of it, a distinction lost on embittered African American troops, some of whom now flew green-and-black Black Power flags of their own.

Some African American soldiers wove "slave bracelets" from black bootlaces, carried ebony canes with carved Black Power

fists as handles, and created elaborate, time-consuming "dap" handshakes that symbolized the special bond between black troops and often angered white troops waiting behind them in the chow line. In May 1969 at Cam Ranh Bay, two white sailors burned a twelve-foot cross in front of a mostly black barrack. At Chu Lai the same month black soldiers beat up white officers who had refused to pick them up in jeeps. Black self-defense groups were formed—the Blackstone Rangers, De Mau Mau, Ju Ju—in order to present a united front against white groups claiming to be linked to the Ku Klux Klan. There were fights over women and name-calling and whether soul or country music should be played on the jukebox.

The Army inspector general's report for 1969–1970 listed well over two hundred serious racial incidents in Vietnam. Eighty percent were concentrated in "built-up military bases." In the field, things were still different. James Gillam's war was fought in the Central Highlands, where survival depended on sticking together: "I had people in my unit, in my squad and in my platoon, who were racists, or who were racially inexperienced," he recalled. "There were black people from Harlem who had never really dealt with white people. There were people in

ABOVE Off-duty at Chu Lai, African American Marines offer Black Power salutes at an outdoor bar that caters predominantly to them.

growing steadily slimmer, the niceties of military discipline struck many as pointless. Some took to wearing helmets emblazoned with "Fuck the Green Machine," their derisive term for the military. To a good many it all seemed senseless. "Charlie had a philosophy," one GI remembered. "I would wonder what provoked a woman or a little kid to get out there and fight . . . unless they honest to God felt that their beliefs were right. It was scary to me, waking me up, making me ask what I was doing there. I mean, what *were* we doing there?"

Anxiety, alienation, longing for home—all played their parts. The desertion rate climbed: in 1965 just fifteen soldiers per thousand had deserted, fewer than had done so in Korea; by 1972, the rate would be seventy per thousand, the highest in U.S. history. The rate of alcoholism rose. So did marijuana use. Some units were permanently split between "juicers" and "dopers."

Marijuana was grown everywhere in Vietnam and sold almost everywhere, too. "When a man is in Vietnam," a brigade officer reported, "he can be sure that no matter where he is, who he is with, or who he is talking to, there are probably drugs within twenty-five feet of him." An MACV investigation found that nearly every shop of any kind in Saigon sold it. Children stationed along the roadside outside military installations offered loose "number one cigarettes" to any soldier passing by. More sophisticated salespersons peddled for just five dollars sealed cartons of Salems and Kools in which every cigarette had been meticulously refilled with pot. A 1967 study found that 29 percent of returning soldiers admitted to having smoked marijuana in Vietnam at least once, but only 7 percent had done so more than twenty times. By 1969, fully half were smoking it, and 30 percent considered themselves heavy users.

"We'd get together in a hooch or sometimes we'd sneak out to this Buddhist temple near the base," one soldier remembered. "It was very powerful stuff and everybody got real happy. At first we'd laugh and joke and talk about silly shit. But after a while it got real mellow and we might even talk about things that bothered us. Or we'd lay back and get off on the designs in the temple. Most of the time I hated everything about Vietnam. But when I was stoned I could really appreciate the beauty of the country. You'd look out over the valley and everything seemed really peaceful. And even if there was a firefight going on out in the jungle we wouldn't think, 'Hey, there are people getting blown away out there.' It was more like, 'Wow, man, take a look at those colors!'"

Since its earliest days in Vietnam, the U.S. military had complained that the ARVN too often seemed to lack the motivation needed to engage the enemy. Now, the same complaint was being lodged against some American outfits. "Back in 1967," one colonel said, "officers gave orders and didn't have to worry

my unit from odd corners of the South who had never seen a live black person. And there I am, a squad leader, and this guy from Arkansas told me he would not carry the radio for me. He said, 'I will not follow you like Cheetah follows Tarzan. It's not going to happen, Sarge.' He's a PFC. I'm a buck sergeant. And I thought, 'Well, this is going to be a really long year.' He evolved a little bit. He kind of got the idea that the enemy's bullets are color-blind. They would shoot anybody, not just me. So we ended up actually getting along after a couple of weeks."

Race friction affected black and white troops alike. So did frustration. "There is malaise among the troops in Vietnam," a *Newsweek* reporter noted. "Hatred for the war runs deep, especially among the younger draftees. As more and more younger soldiers arrive from the U.S., the antiwar spirit mounts. And at a time when the Administration seems bent, however cautiously, on withdrawal from Vietnam, the soldier inevitably asks himself why he should risk his neck in a war nobody wants to win."

With the possibility of a traditional victory on the battlefield

ABOVE GIs smoke marijuana at an off-base apartment in Saigon in 1971. By then, one study found, some 15 percent of the U.S. forces in South Vietnam had become addicted to heroin, which was cheap, pure, and ubiquitous.

about the sensitivities of the men and find new ways of doing the job. Otherwise you can send the men on a search mission, but they won't search."

They called it "sandbagging." Ordered to patrol an area, men would head out into the countryside, settle down somewhere just out of sight of their superiors, and then radio back false coordinates that suggested they were climbing hills, crossing streams, sweeping jungles. "Whenever we can get away with it," one young lieutenant admitted, "we radio the old man [the commander] that we are moving our platoon forward. . . . But if there is any risk of getting shot at, we stay where we are until the choppers come to pick us up."

Officers who pushed their men too hard now sometimes did so at their peril. Beginning in the summer of 1969, there began to be reports of "fragging"—the murder or attempted murder by enlisted men of their fellow soldiers, mostly junior officers and noncommissioned officers—usually by way of fragmentation grenades. Most fragging took place behind the lines, among noncombat support units, usually the violent outcome of arguments over race or women or drugs or simple personal dislike rather than the war itself.

But some fraggings were battle related. After Hamburger Hill, parties unknown were said to have advertised a $10,000

bounty in the underground newspaper *GI Says* for the fragging of Blackjack Honeycutt, who had ordered his men up that bloody slope too many times. Colin Powell, then a major in the Twenty-third Infantry Division stationed at Duc Pho, made a point of moving his cot every night, both to thwart enemy informants who might be following him and to "rule out attacks on authority from within the battalion itself."

"It was a totally different army than what we sent to Vietnam in 1965," Vincent Okamoto remembered. "The new lieutenant comes in, all gung-ho for body count. He wants contact. He goes crazy, and says, 'I want a volunteer for this, I'll commit you to this.' That new gung-ho officer is a clear and present danger to the life and limb of the grunts. The men would give subtle hints, like a little note saying, 'We're going to kill your ass if you keep this up.' Or instead of a fragmentation grenade, they might throw a smoke grenade in an officer's hooch or bunker. And if they didn't correct their behavior and outlook, yeah, they would frag them."

ABOVE War and peace: U.S. tankers waiting for ARVN forces to drive the enemy toward them south of the DMZ show sympathy with the antiwar movement back home. Even General Creighton Abrams admitted privately, "I need to get this army home to save it."

I HAVE SEEN THE ENEMY, HE IS ME, JUST LIKE ME

In the spring of 1970, Specialist Stuart Ness from Portland, Oregon, was serving with Company A, First Battalion, Sixty-first Infantry, Fifth Infantry Division, just south of the DMZ. "We would go out for two or three weeks at a time on search-and-destroy missions," he remembered, "always searching during the day, finding nothing, setting up a perimeter at night, waiting for you-know-who." One night he was on guard in his foxhole manning a .50-caliber machine gun when he spotted the silhouette of a North Vietnamese soldier some distance away. He radioed in and was told to take one shot. He switched from automatic to single and squeezed the trigger. The man fell.

As soon as the sun was up, Ness's platoon searched the area and found the dead soldier, shot through the chest. "He was young like us," Ness recalled, "and had a fairly new uniform." It was clear that he had not been in battle long. In his backpack they found a couple of pairs of clean socks, a brand-new 9mm Chinese-made pistol still in its wax wrapping, and a diary in Vietnamese with only a single entry. Army intelligence translated it and gave him a copy. He hopes to someday take a copy of it to the Vietnam memorial in Washington as a tribute to the North Vietnamese soldier. Whenever he reads it, he says, he realizes "I have seen the enemy, he is me, just like me."

Already I've been to the battle-field, however, there is one matter which I find a little strange. Our enemy has already lost many killed in battle, but never have I seen even one [American] body on the battlefield. According to what I have been told by persons in battle, "When the enemy counterattacked, we shot many. With much merit they tried to crawl up and pull back their dead." As for American soldiers, I don't understand what ideals they were equipped with, as they were very loyal to their comrades.

Our comrades were sacrificed, their bodies will arrive today; for seven days already since [they were] killed we have not been able to carry the bodies out. On the weakening battlefield, I sit upon the defensive bunker, my head in my palms, not having a mat to cover my body, while at this time the commanding cadre here still relax, play chess, and laugh. Why do they build fame and position for themselves upon the bones and blood of other people? They look for one more star on their chests and our brothers endure hardships, sacrificing people by the hundreds. They have killed our friends, caring nothing for life.

Our comrades are very young, hungry, beautiful. But look! "They are going the wrong way. Where are they going? In the direction of 100 men, resting 1,000 years.

Where are they going? The green and sad forest. Tell me the location—red earth—B-52? Brothers, as you go, will there be a tomorrow?"

Our Party lacks wisdom. They use the objective of struggling for party membership, certificates of commendation and decorations in order to excite our Party members to go eagerly to dangerous areas, so that in the end they'll receive the certificate of death. Because there is no one to carry them out, our wounded brothers must also be sacrificed.

Our Chairman Ho has said for the soldiers who are still living: "The resistance must be prolonged further, we must sacrifice many more people, much more property." Sacrifice many more people, more property? How many more lives will have to be sacrificed before this country will be liberated? How many young men remain for Vietnam to send to the battlefield to achieve the future victory? The bodies of thousands of young men have already been left lying in the green forests of a strange land, thousands of children have said farewell to their families and now have said goodbye forever to their homeland. Our country is miserable because of this war. And how many more brave men will yet go to quell revolt to make the country peaceful?

LEFT Exhausted North Vietnamese troops pause along a jungle path just below the DMZ. The sight of their obvious weariness was thought likely to damage morale back home, so this photograph was not published during the war.

The problem grew so serious at one point that American military commanders stopped issuing grenades for a week throughout Vietnam and then ordered shakedown inspections to search for unregistered ordnance.

The number of fraggings increased as U.S. forces dwindled between 1969 and 1971. By the time the last U.S. combat troops left Vietnam in 1973 the Army had investigated nearly eight hundred cases.

DON'T CALL US COWARDS

LIEUTENANT COLONEL ELI P. HOWARD JR., commander of the Third Battalion of the 196th Light Infantry Brigade, Americal Division, was a career soldier with a fierce reputation and a forbidding manner, heartily disliked by the draftees he ordered into battle again and again. "He was trying to make a name for himself," Sergeant John Borrelli of A Company recalled. "Body count was his goal. He made us dig up North Vietnamese graves to count bodies. If you didn't get enough body count, you didn't get clean clothes, maybe you didn't get enough rations to eat. If intelligence said there's a buildup of North Vietnamese in a particular area, without checking into it, he'd load you on helicopters and combat-assault you into the middle of it."

Once he'd promised his men hot pizza if they scored any confirmed kills and was furious when he found out that a freshly arrived lieutenant had rounded up several men of military age rather than shoot them. The company's nickname was the "Alpha Annihilators," Howard reminded the men. "Do you know the definition of 'annihilator'? It's not going to do any good to send these people in for interrogation, so they can come right back out here and shoot at you again."

"Howard," Borrelli recalled, "was what we all considered to be the most miserable son-of-a-bitch we ever met. The general consensus was he needs to go." Some of the men in Alpha Company were said to have paid a "Kit Carson"—a South Vietnamese scout—$400 to dress as a guerrilla and shoot Colonel Howard as he stepped off his helicopter. "For a few dollars," Borrelli remembered, "this guy would go kill his mother and father." The would-be assassin opened fire with an AK-47 as Howard stepped off a helicopter. He riddled the chopper but somehow missed the colonel. "After that," the sergeant said, "Howard was not a happy man. He went airborne, and sent a message down to the company commander, 'Your men just tried to kill me. You will pay for that.' He combat-assaulted us into the Song Chang River Valley thirty miles south of Danang

between, I believe it was, two regiments of North Vietnamese. It was a payback mission."

Private Lester Beaupré from Caribou, Maine, and brand-new to Alpha Company arrived just in time to go along. "They gave me an M16, a hundred rounds of ammo, and put me on a helicopter," he recalled. "I see this valley coming up, and I could see tracers coming up. The chopper was coming down backwards and we were probably like sixteen feet off the ground. I'm sitting there, and I heard somebody say—I thought he said, 'Hump!'—but it was 'Jump!' And he took his foot and he stuck it in my back and kicked me off the helicopter. So I landed on the ground on all fours. I fell right next to a foxhole and this big guy reached up, grabbed my leg, and pulled me down in. I stayed there for most of that day. I was looking at the 'old' guys,

ABOVE A soldier holds the hand of a dying member of his squad, mortally wounded during savage fighting in the Hiep Duc Valley in the summer of 1969.

who had been there a while, and I said, 'Wow!' They were dirty, their eyes were set deep in their heads, they were scary looking. Within a month I ended up looking like them. It didn't take too long to get old there."

"For five days," Borrelli recalled, "we had to try to fight our way out. They slaughtered us. It was terrible. Everybody that walked point got killed or wounded. No food, no water, no sleep."

On August 19, a helicopter carrying Commander Howard and seven others dipped down too close to a hidden North Vietnamese position on the terraced slope of a hill labeled 102 on Army maps and was shot from the sky. Howard and everyone else aboard were killed. When the news reached the men of Alpha Company, they cheered, Borrelli remembered. "Then a message comes in to us, 'Saddle up, move out.'" They were to go and find Howard's body. "Well, we'd just given a big 'Hurrah.' We didn't care if they ate him. We didn't want to go looking for him."

They went anyway. One hundred and nine of them—nearly

ABOVE AND OPPOSITE LEFT Three members of A Company (left to right) Sergeant John Borrelli (smoking a cigarette), Private Lester Beaupré (facing the camera), and Private James Bryant. The men of A Company remembered they'd burned one village so often that when one elderly woman saw them coming she would torch her home herself.

half of whom were "green seeds," new to combat—were choppered into the valley where hundreds of soldiers belonging to the Third North Vietnamese regiment were waiting for them, hidden in spider holes and deep bunkers reinforced with logs and skillfully masked by brush and banana leaves. Two men were killed and ten were wounded the first day. At midday, the heat rose to 110 degrees. Enemy ground fire was so thick at first that helicopters were unable to reach them with food or water. "We had one and a half cans of C rations in three days," one man recalled.

Enemy fire seemed to come from everywhere and nowhere. "You just couldn't see them," a medic remembered. "I saw two guys die right there in front of me and I couldn't get to them. I was pinned down. I said I couldn't get to them, so my buddy moved out toward them maybe three yards and he got a bullet in the head. . . . Those guys—the North Vietnamese—were right beside us and we couldn't shoot back." At night, mortar shells fell among the men.

On the third day, helicopters flying low and racing over the terrain to elude enemy fire managed to drop ammunition, water, and crates of rations. Most of the water containers burst. Ammunition and ration cases broke open and scattered between Company A and the enemy bunkers. "The dinks got some of that stuff," a private remembered, "but at least we each had one whole can of Cs that night."

On the fourth afternoon they finally fought their way up Hill 102 through a labyrinth of bunkers. When they reached the top, there were just forty-six of them. Eight had been killed. Fifty-five had been wounded or had collapsed from heatstroke. The exhausted survivors weren't sure they'd killed a single enemy soldier. No one claimed even to have seen one.

From his headquarters on a hilltop across the valley, the battalion's new commander, Lieutenant Colonel Robert C. Bacon, radioed fresh orders: as soon as it was light, he said, Alpha Company was to head down the hillside again to gather up the bodies of the last two men killed.

Kept from sleep by still another mortar attack, the men talked among themselves all night. Sergeant Borrelli remembered how the men felt: "We follow orders all the time. We go out in small numbers, in platoon-size elements of under thirty guys looking for trouble. It's stupid. But we do it. Now it was time an outfit stood up and said, 'You're killing men for no good reason. And that's it. If you want to put us in jail, put us in jail. I'll go. I'll have a place to lay down every night, three meals a day. It's got to be better than being shot at every day and watching my friends die.'"

By the time morning came, five men—all of them short-timers—had been designated to speak for the whole company. They told Lieutenant Eugene Schurtz Jr.—a recent ROTC graduate, just three weeks in country—that it would be suicidal to

fight their way back down that hill again. Instead, they wanted a helicopter so they could explain their need for reinforcements to the Army inspector general.

Schurtz radioed to Lieutenant Colonel Bacon, now at the helicopter crash site helping to gather up what was left of Colonel Howard and his companions. "I'm sorry, sir," Schurtz said, "but my men refused to go."

"Repeat that, please," Bacon said. "Have you told them what it means to disobey orders under fire?"

He had, and they understood it, Schurtz said, but "some of them have simply had enough—they are broken. These are boys who have only ninety days left. They want to go home in one piece."

Bacon wanted to know if only enlisted men were involved. What about the squad and platoon leaders?

"That's the difficulty we have," Schurtz answered. "We've got a leadership problem. Most of our squad and platoon leaders have been killed or wounded."

Bacon told Schurtz to talk to his men again. "Tell them that to the best of our knowledge the bunkers are now empty. The enemy has withdrawn. The mission of A Company today is to

ABOVE Robert Bacon, who ordered A Company back into the valley, photographed earlier in the war

recover their dead. They have no reason to be afraid." Schurtz was to ask for a show of hands to see if the five designated soldiers really spoke for the whole company.

Schurz conferred again with his men, then got back on the radio with Bacon. "They won't go, Colonel," he said. He hadn't dared ask for a show of hands for fear they'd all stick together, "even though some might prefer to go."

Bacon sent a helicopter to the ridgeline carrying three emissaries with orders to "give them a pep talk and kick them in the ass." Sergeant Okey Blankenship, a combat veteran from Panther, Virginia, got there first.

"One of them was crying," Blankenship recalled. They were exhausted, they said, couldn't take more nighttime mortar attacks or daytime firefights with an invisible enemy. They needed rest and food and reinforcements and mail from home. "One of them yelled at me that his company had suffered too much and that it should not have to go on," Blackenship said. "I answered him that another company was down to fifteen men [and] was still on the move . . . I lied to him, and he asked me, 'Why did they do it?'"

"Maybe they've got something a little more than what you've got."

"Don't call us cowards," the soldier said, running toward Blankenship, fist cocked. "We are not cowards."

Memories differ as to what happened next. One member of the company remembers the overwrought soldier striking Blankenship. Others recall that the sergeant simply turned his back and walked away. Whatever happened, in the end the weary men gathered up their weapons and staggered back down the hill to bring their friends' bodies back for burial. The enemy had slipped away. Sergeant Borrelli and some of the other men resented the way their actions were portrayed in some later accounts. "There wasn't a coward standing there," Borrelli recalled. "And it just aggravates me to listen to the stories, over the years, that have called us cowards. It's absolutely not the case. We just were beat. We never should have had to go back down. But we did go back down."

No one in A Company was charged with mutiny. No direct order had actually been disobeyed. The whole business was over in less than an hour. Lieutenant Schurtz was given a desk job but not reduced in rank. There would be clearer cases of combat refusal in the months to come. The Department of the Army would cite more than 380 court-martial cases involving "acts of insubordination, mutiny and willful disobedience" in 1970 alone. And in April of that year, John Laurence and a CBS camera crew would be on hand when the men of Charlie Company, Second Battalion, Seventh Cavalry, First Air Cavalry Division, returning from a patrol, refused a direct order to return to a landing zone by the same jungle path they'd followed after land-

ing on it, for fear of being ambushed. "I'm not going to walk there," one GI said on camera. "Nothing doing. . . . It's a suicide walk. We've had too many companies, too many battalions want to walk the road. They get blown away." By then such events were so common that *Stars and Stripes* could run a front-page headline, "TROOPS PRAISED FOR BALKING AT CO'S ORDER," along with an interview with the deputy commander of the brigade that praised the men's "common sense." "Thank God," he said, "we've got young men who question. The young men in the Army today aren't dummies, they are not automatons. They think."

But because the story of Company A took place relatively early in the game and because the journalists Peter Arnett and Horst Faas had been with Colonel Bacon and overheard the early-morning radio exchange, it became headline news—the first hint that GIs in Vietnam were growing increasingly reluctant to follow orders without question.

James Reston of *The New York Times* saw in the story of A Company a metaphor for what was becoming of the war:

The President is no longer saying that military victory in Vietnam is "vital" to the national interest. He is not claiming that a compromise or even a defeat in Vietnam would result in the loss of Southeast Asia. . . . Accordingly, battle for bunkers in the Songchang Valley are tactical moves in the President's strategy of retreat. He is asking Company A to fight for time to negotiate a settlement with Hanoi that will save his face but may very well lose their lives. He is also carrying on the battle in the belief, or pretense, that the South Vietnamese will really be able to defend their country and our democratic objectives when we withdraw, and even his own generals don't believe the South Vietnamese will do it. It is a typical strategy and the really surprising thing is that there have been so few men, like the tattered remnants of Company A, who have refused to die for it. . . .

The more the President says he's for peace, the more troops he withdraws from Vietnam, the more he concedes that Southeast Asia is not really vital to the security of the United States, the harder it is to ask for the lives of the men of Company A. They may not be typical, but they are a symbol of his coming dilemma. He wants out on the installment plan, but the weekly installments are the lives of one or two hundred American soldiers, and he cannot get away from the insistent question: Why? To what purposes? The breaking point comes in politics as it came to Company A, and it is not far off. What will now be gained by this incessant killing? And how will the President or anybody else explain or excuse it?

VIETNAMIZATION

THE DOUBTS James Reston expressed about South Vietnam's ability to survive on its own were widely shared in Washington and Saigon.

"I don't think any of us thought of Vietnamization as a winning strategy," Leslie Gelb, then at the Pentagon, remembered. "I think we thought of it as the way to extricate ourselves from the war. And if we could help the South Vietnamese in the process, that would be a damn good bonus."

A good many U.S. servicemen felt the same way. "The reason I was ordered home early," Merrill McPeak remembered, "was because President Nixon announced the policy of Vietnamization. Now, Vietnamization was a lie, but it had an element of truth in it. We were leaving, and that sealed the South's fate. I knew it. And I think anybody who was conscious, who could see what was going on, knew it."

In Saigon, Duong Van Mai Elliott recalled, "when Nixon announced the phased withdrawal, turning over the fighting to the Vietnamese, which was something the French had tried before—they called it '*jaunissement*,' 'yellowizing' the war—we knew the Vietnamese army was not up to fighting this war. If they couldn't do it with the Americans, how were they going to do it without the Americans?"

Vietnamization was little more than a gamble, as Henry Kissinger wrote: "Henceforth, we [the United States] would be in a race between the decline of our combat capabilities and the improvement of South Vietnamese forces, a race whose outcome was at best uncertain."

The word "Vietnamization" itself angered many South Vietnamese. Who, they asked, did the Americans think had been fighting the communists all these years? "It was the Vietnamese who had sacrificed and suffered most," a former ARVN general wrote. "Vietnamization was not a proper term to be used, . . . especially when propaganda was an important weapon." Another commander remembered that "we officers felt [it] was just a way for the U.S. to get out . . . and [leave] the South Vietnamese armed forces to take the responsibility for defeat." Some dismissed the program as the "U.S. Dollar and Vietnamese Blood-Sharing Plan."

But as U.S. soldiers began to leave South Vietnam in ever-greater numbers—Nixon would announce the redeployment of 35,000 more men in September, an additional 50,000 in December, with more announcements expected to follow—American weaponry and materiel poured in: 855,000 individual and crew-served weapons, 1,880 tanks and armored vehicles,

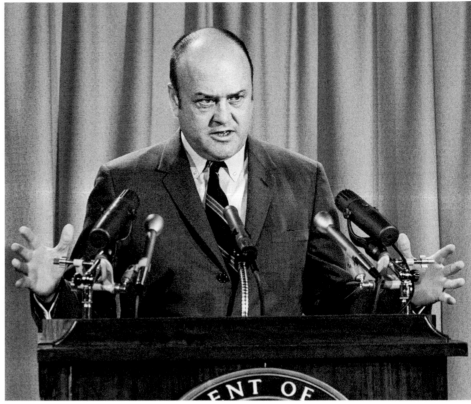

44,000 radio sets, 1,000 helicopters and fixed-wing aircraft, and so many thousands of jeeps and trucks that one congressman complained that U.S. taxpayers were being asked to "put every South Vietnamese soldier behind the wheel." American taxpayers would also ensure that South Vietnam's defense forces—the Regional and Popular Forces as well as the ARVN—expanded to more than a million men by 1973, that the South Vietnamese air force grew six times in size from its 1964 figure, and that the South Vietnamese navy came to command a fleet of 1,700 vessels, large and small. Washington also funded the construction of 200,000 homes for military dependents in an effort to reduce the startling number of annual desertions—125,000 in 1969, 150,000 the following year—and raised soldiers' pay 19 percent in a losing effort to outstrip the rampant inflation fueled by the infusion of millions of GI dollars into the economy.

Hanoi professed to be unimpressed by what it called "puppetization." "It is nothing but hackneyed juggling," said the North Vietnamese premier, Pham Van Dong. "To use Vietnamese to fight Vietnamese is indeed an attractive policy for the United States. When one has money and guns, can there be a better way to reach one's aims than simply to distribute money and guns? Unfortunately, in the present epoch, such a paradoxical move is

ABOVE Secretary of Defense Melvin Laird, the Nixon administration's most consistent advocate of Vietnamization

ABOVE South Vietnamese officers in training to take over from the Americans

flatly impossible. . . . Certainly there is no means, no magic way, to 'ize' the war into something other than the most atrocious and most abominable war in history."

Skeptics on the allied side remained dubious, too. "It didn't make any sense," Neil Sheehan remembered, "because we tried that in 1962 and '63. We were just giving them more furniture. The people in charge hadn't changed." Fifteen years after the French war ended, and despite elections and the adoption of a constitution that had seemed to promise a larger role for civilians in South Vietnam's political life, the country was still run by a military clique whose members perpetually jockeyed for power, and its armed forces were still led by forty-odd generals, most of whom had fought for France and none of whom was interested in expanding their ranks, for fear of losing their share of the profits and power.

General Abrams labored mightily to improve training. Instructors who had never been in battle were slowly replaced by

ABOVE South Vietnamese officers in training to take over from the Americans

combat veterans. Efforts were made to bridge the gulf between the poor peasant draftees who made up the bulk of the enlisted men and the upper-class officers who too often scorned them.

American and South Vietnamese units had undertaken joint operations in the past, but U.S. forces had almost invariably played the lead role. Now Abrams ordered much closer integration, convinced that the only way to increase South Vietnamese combat readiness was to provide what one grateful South Vietnamese commander called "on-the-job or in-action training in which U.S. units performed the role of instructor by giving real-life positive examples of combat actions and counteractions." ARVN commanders had to unlearn some American lessons, too. Easy access to U.S. air and artillery power had shaped the way the South Vietnamese had come to wage the ground war. "It had become common practice for infantry units to hold back," Major General Nguyen Van Hinh remembered, "wait for the target to be torn apart by fire, and then just move in to count the bodies." That access would gradually disappear, and South Vietnamese forces would have to learn to make do without it. "Damnit," General Abrams told members of his staff, "they've

got to learn they can't do it all with air [power]. They've got to do it on the ground, with infantry. If they don't, it's all in vain."

South Vietnamese were still too often commanded by officers who owed their position to family or political connections rather than military skill and who prized personal wealth above patriotism. Some commanders kept the names of hundreds of "ghost" soldiers on their rosters—dead men or deserters or people who had never existed—so that they could pocket their salaries every month. Others happily accepted bribes from other men who also remained on the rosters but were not required actually to serve. One U.S. adviser denounced the "incompetence, corruption, timidity, and ... Mandarin attitude of ... officers who have absolutely no concern for the welfare of their men." But there were also ARVN officers, like a regimental commander with whom adviser James Willbanks worked in the Eighteenth ARVN Division, who paid the living expenses of his men's widows out of his own pocket.

Some commanders still remained unwilling to risk their reputations by aggressively moving against the enemy: the Twenty-second ARVN Division claimed to have set up eighteen

hundred ambushes in three months—and to have killed just six enemy soldiers.

There were other problems. The military was riddled with enemy agents; the CIA estimated in 1970 that there could be as many as thirty thousand of them. The language barrier often distorted communication between South Vietnamese commanders and the U.S. advisers assigned to them. Those advisers were rapidly rotated in and out; one veteran ARVN officer remembered having had to get to know forty-seven of them over the course of the war. The shiny new military equipment looked impressive when it arrived on the loading docks but quickly came up against the lack of replacement parts and a country-wide dearth of mechanics trained to maintain it; by late 1971, six thousand pages of instruction manuals for helicopter repair would remain untranslated and half of South Vietnam's choppers could not safely leave the ground.

ABOVE A squadron of U.S. helicopters, newly given to the South Vietnamese, approaches an airstrip near Vi Thanh in the Mekong Delta, prepared to pick up ARVN troops and ferry them into action.

Despite the skepticism of many within MACV, and in the face of continuing corruption and often weak leadership, some ARVN units proved outstanding in combat, among them the First Division that General Abrams would choose to take over from the Americans below the DMZ because, he said, they were "the strongest and best."

U.S. troops may have been showing ever-increasing signs of demoralization—no GI wanted to be the last to die in a losing cause—but the danger to them was always finite; they knew when they were going home. ARVN troops had no such luxury. Drafted at eighteen, they were to serve until their thirty-eighth birthday and had little choice except to persevere in what seemed to be an endless war. At least one U.S. adviser to an ARVN unit, secure in the likelihood that he'd be safely out of the war within twelve months, felt himself "not fit to polish their boots."

ABOVE Men of the Eleventh Armored Cavalry Regiment fold the U.S. flag before turning over Black Horse Base Camp, forty miles east of Saigon, to the South Vietnamese.

GO FOR BROKE

SHORTLY AFTER Nixon returned from his meeting with President Thieu at Midway in June, he had declared the door to peace open and invited "the leaders of North Vietnam to walk with us through that door." They had not done so. There was a relative lull in the fighting in South Vietnam as the communists rebuilt and reconfigured their forces, but their posture in Paris remained unchanged.

Nixon feared that if real progress toward a settlement was not made soon, "Johnson's war" would become his. To move things along—and to do so before antiwar students returned to school and antiwar congressmen and senators got back to Capitol Hill—the president "resolved to 'go for broke,'" he wrote, "in the sense that I would attempt to end the war one way or the other—either by negotiated agreement or by an increased use of force. . . . I decided to set November 1, 1969—the first anniversary of Johnson's bombing halt—as the deadline for what would in effect be an ultimatum to North Vietnam."

On July 15, Nixon sent a carefully worded letter to Ho Chi Minh. "I realize that it is difficult to communicate meaningfully across the gulf of four years of war," he said. "But precisely because of this gulf, I wanted to take this opportunity to reaffirm in all solemnity my desire to work for a just peace. . . . As I have said repeatedly, there is nothing to be gained by waiting. . . . You will find us forthcoming and open-minded in a common effort to bring the blessings of peace to the brave people of Vietnam. Let history record that at this critical juncture, both sides turned their face toward peace." But, he warned, American patience was running out. Unless there was a breakthrough in the negotiations by November, he would have no choice but to take "measures of great consequence and force."

On August 4, in an apartment building on the Rue de Rivoli in Paris, Henry Kissinger held a secret talk with two North Vietnamese negotiators—the first in a series of clandestine meetings that would continue off and on for three frustrating years. The North Vietnamese remained immovable. Kissinger repeated the warning already conveyed to Ho Chi Minh; if there was no change in their position by the deadline he'd set, President Nixon would be forced to "consider steps of grave consequence."

A few days later, the fighting in South Vietnam flared up again. Mortar and sapper attacks hit more than one hundred American and South Vietnamese installations. "The most generous interpretation of these attacks," Kissinger remembered, "could not avoid the conclusion that Hanoi did not believe in gestures, negotiation, goodwill or reciprocity."

On August 30, Nixon received a response to his earlier letter, signed by Ho Chi Minh. It was courteous. He acknowledged that the United States needed to emerge from the conflict with "honor," and said he was "deeply touched at the rising toll of death of young Americans"—though he also said that U.S. "governing circles," not the Vietnamese, were responsible for them. But there was not a hint of compromise. The Vietnamese people were "determined to fight to the end." To achieve what Nixon had called "a just peace . . . the United States must cease the war of aggression, withdraw their troops from South Vietnam, and respect the right of the population of the South and of

ABOVE Ho Chi Minh (left) and North Vietnamese prime minister Pham Van Dong confer in Ho's garden, not long before his death.

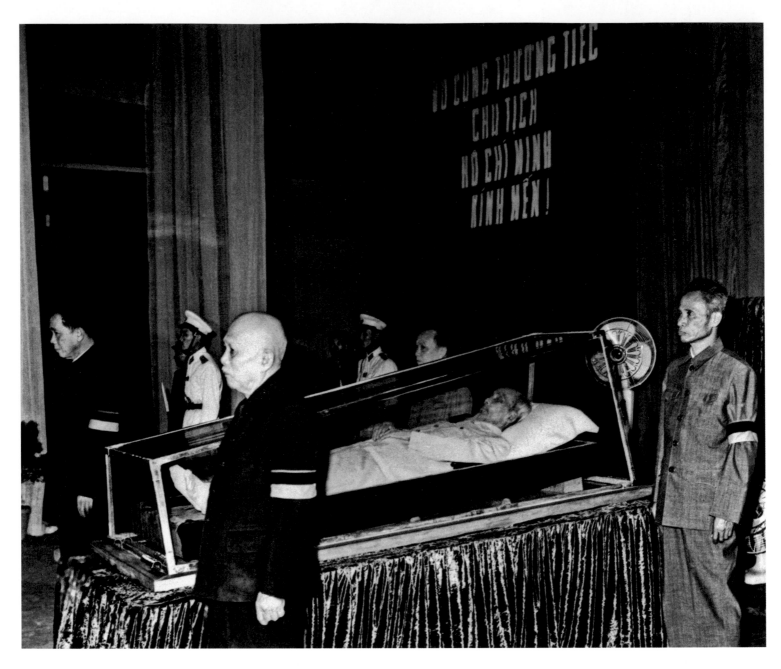

the Vietnamese nation to dispose of themselves without foreign influence." Nothing less would do. No mention was made of the deadline Nixon had set and Kissinger had reiterated.

It is not clear whether or not Ho Chi Minh personally wrote the letter Nixon received—though there is no reason to suppose he did not share its defiant spirit. But he was said to be seventy-nine now—like so much about him, the precise date of his birth was shrouded in mystery—and other leaders had long since assumed the day-to-day power he once had wielded. His lungs were congested. He had developed an irregular heartbeat. At 9:45 in the morning on September 2—the twenty-fourth anniversary of the declaration of Vietnamese independence he had read out in Hanoi's Ba Dinh Square—he died.

One hundred and twenty-one countries sent official condo-

lences. Washington said nothing but did call a one-day bombing halt in the South. North Vietnam went into mourning. Ho Chi Minh had been "Uncle Ho" for decades, after all, the living embodiment of the struggle against the French, the Saigon government, and then the Americans. More than 100,000 people attended his funeral. "I was so emotional when I went past Uncle Ho's coffin," General Dong Sy Nguyen recalled. "I couldn't

ABOVE At Ho Chi Minh's state funeral, his preserved corpse is flanked by four of his most important colleagues (left to right), Party First Secretary Le Duan, Vice President Ton Duc Thang, chairman of the National Assembly's Standing Committee Truong Chinh, and Prime Minister Pham Van Dong, September 12, 1969.

GO PUBLIC

On September 2, 1969, the same day Ho Chi Minh died, an unusual press conference was held at the National Naval Medical Center in Bethesda, Maryland. Two ailing ex-prisoners of war, Robert Frishman and Douglas Hegdahl, who had recently been escorted home by the antiwar activist Rennie Davis, spoke in public for the first time about the treatment they and their fellow prisoners had received at the hands of the North Vietnamese. Hanoi continued to insist that although they still considered American prisoners war criminals, they were invariably treated "humanely." Navy Lieutenant Frishman did most of the talking, refuting that claim by listing the abuse he and others had endured: the withholding of mail and lack of medical care, long periods of solitary confinement, torture, and forced "confessions."

Petty Officer Second Class Douglas Hegdahl was quiet and self-effacing. Unlike most American prisoners, who had been shot from the sky, he had been rescued from the sea. Serving aboard the USS *Canberra,* he'd disobeyed orders and crept up on deck to watch a night bombardment. As he stepped past a five-inch gun, it discharged. He lost his footing and fell into the Gulf of Tonkin. The warship steamed away into the darkness. Vietnamese fishermen picked him up and turned him over to the authorities, who thought him so clueless that his North Vietnamese guards called him "the incredibly stupid one." But once released, he turned out to be a gold mine of information. To the tune of "Old McDonald Had a Farm," he had memorized the names of more than two hundred prisoners. Thanks to him, scores of American families would find out for the first time that their sons and husbands and fathers were still alive. Within a few days of the press conference, Hanoi's

treatment of the prisoners began to improve—"a lot less brutality," one captive remembered, "and larger bowls of rice."

The Johnson administration had generally downplayed the prisoner issue, hoping quiet diplomacy might bring the men home. Beginning earlier in the year, the Nixon administration had begun a "go public campaign," meant to put the plight of American prisoners and those unaccounted for at the center of things—and to provide a continuing rebuke to those in the antiwar movement who seemed more sympathetic to North Vietnamese civilians than they were to U.S. servicemen.

Nixon vowed that there could be no peace until all U.S. prisoners had come home and Hanoi had provided a strict accounting of those missing in action. No one knew how many there were. Most prisoners were held in or around Hanoi, but other American captives, like Hal Kushner, were struggling to survive in makeshift jungle camps in South Vietnam.

The administration worked closely with groups of POW wives, including the largest, the National League of Families of American Prisoners and Missing in Southeast Asia, headed by Sybil Stockdale, the wife of the senior-most POW, Navy Commander Jim Stockdale. More than fifty million POW/MIA bumper stickers would be sold during the war. Five million Americans began wearing tin or copper bracelets engraved with a missing man's name and date of loss.

"As long as the North Vietnamese have any Americans," Nixon said, "there will be Americans in South Vietnam and enough Americans to give them an incentive to release the prisoners." Eventually, the journalist Jonathan Schell

wrote, "many people . . . following the president's lead, . . . began to speak as though the North Vietnamese had kidnapped four hundred Americans and the United States had gone to war to retrieve them."

"At the outset," Henry Kissinger wrote, the go public campaign "rallied support at home, though in later years it was turned against us, as the prisoners became an added argument for unilateral withdrawal." There was a flaw built into the administration's relentless emphasis on POWs: Nixon could end the draft and withdraw every single U.S. soldier on his own, but he would never be able to solve the problem of the prisoners and the missing without the cooperation of Hanoi.

"If it is true that [the POWs] will not be released until the U.S. gets out," one prisoner's wife would ask, "then why don't they set a date and get out now?"

ABOVE Douglas Hegdahl sweeps his Hanoi prison courtyard.

ONLY A STONE WOULDN'T BE TERRIFIED

"I was seventeen years old and living in Hanoi when Ho Chi Minh died," recalled the former North Vietnamese infantryman and postwar novelist known as Bao Ninh. (His real name is Hoang Phuong.) "To us he was the father of the Vietnamese nation." The city was "a sea of mourning people. I had never seen my father crying, but he cried that day. My mother and our neighbors also cried."

Bao Ninh had been born in a bomb shelter in Nghe An Province during the French war in 1952. His mother was a schoolteacher, his father a soldier in the Viet Minh. Both were communists, and in 1954 they'd settled in Hanoi, moving to the countryside from time to time when it seemed likely that U.S. bombers were on the way. At fifteen, Bao Ninh saw an American pilot shot down over a nearby lake and joined the crowd that surrounded him when he was brought to shore; later, he learned from Radio Hanoi that the captured pilot was Naval Commander John S. McCain III, son of the Commander-in-Chief, U.S. Naval Forces, Europe, Admiral John S. McCain Jr.

On September 6, 1969—just four days after Ho's death—Bao Ninh joined the army. "At the recruiting station they had singers and poets, working up the spirit of those signing up," he remembered. "There were two types of people—those full of anti-American spirit, signing their forms in their own blood. And those like me. We were told to go and went." Political ideology had little to do with his decision to sign up. He just thought he should do his duty to the country, just as his father had—and he hoped wearing a uniform would impress girls. He and his fellow soldiers would go into battle dutifully shouting, "For socialism, we should advance!" because the political officers insisted that they do so. But his

notion of what life would be like under socialism was fuzzy: there would be no rich and poor, he guessed; everyone would be equal. "The Americans thought we were followers of Marxism," he recalled. "They were wrong. We fought for our country, so that there would be no more bombing, no more wars, so that parents wouldn't have to leave their homes, there would be no more people killed, there would be no more of the fire and smoke of war."

After three months of combat training—half as much as earlier soldiers had received—he and his comrades in the Twenty-seventh Glorious Youth Brigade boarded a train for the city of Vinh, north of the DMZ. From there they set out for the South along the Ho Chi Minh Trail, keeping to narrow forest footpaths rather than following the wider truck routes subject to frequent bombing. He traveled light: Bao Ninh recalled carrying only three sets of Chinese-made uniforms and a soft hat, five stolen U.S. grenades, rubber sandals, ammunition, and his AK-47.

The brigade's destination was the province of Kon Tum in the heart of the Central Highlands. It took nearly four months to reach it. There, and in adjacent jungle-covered provinces, Bao Ninh would find himself fighting the enemy for six years—first the Americans and South Vietnamese combined, and then the South Vietnamese alone. For six months he was a stretcher bearer. Then he became a rifleman.

It was a war of logistics: "The Americans dropped bombs so that we would have nothing to eat. Their hope was that we would starve and have to surrender. Not a kilogram of rice reached the Central Highlands. But they didn't understand Vietnamese soldiers. We produced the rice ourselves. I'd been a high school student in the city but now I became a farmer. It wasn't enough. We were in a constant state of hunger. All the army gave us was salt.

"I'm sure being an American

ABOVE Bao Ninh, photographed after the war

soldier wasn't enjoyable. Life could be miserable. But they never starved. When they were wounded, they got first aid. If they caught malaria, they got medicine. If a soldier was killed, his body was not left in the jungles. It was picked up by a helicopter. When we seized the position of an American unit, we looked for their food first of all. It was called 'C rations,' in a small bag. A regular soldier's bag was like the food you carried for a picnic. It contained everything you could enjoy."

His first contact with the enemy was farcical. He and a friend blundered into a clearing just as three equally startled Americans emerged from the jungle on the other side. Everyone opened fire—and then ran. "We shot at one another only to escape," he recalled. "There was no hero in that clash."

There were few heroes in those that followed, either, and the sheer scale of American destructiveness was daunting. "If they noticed a movement in the forest," Bao Ninh remembered, "the Americans would fire hundreds of shells to eliminate the forest. It was American wealth. In the dry season if a cluster of napalm bombs were dropped, the jungle would turn into what we called a 'sea of fire.' Can you imagine a sea of fire? It's impossible to describe the horror." When bombing or shelling began, the men split into three-man groups so that only so many, huddled in trenches and bomb shelters, might be killed at once. But when the bombs started falling, Bao Ninh remembered, "only a stone wouldn't be terrified."

"From 1970 on," he recalled, "our enemy on the battlefield was the army of South Vietnam. The tragedy of the war was the Vietnamese killing each other. The firepower was still American, but the flesh and blood was Vietnamese. A South Vietnamese soldier was not different from me in any way. He had the same good and bad points as mine. We ate the same rice, drank the same water. We shared the same culture, listened to the same music. We read the same books, used the same alphabet. I was cowardly in one way, and he was cowardly in the same way. I was brave in one way, and he was brave in the same way. No difference. We called them 'puppets.' They called us 'Viet Cong.' They were just labels. It was a civil war."

believe that he was gone. I myself, and the entire nation, had put all of our hopes and our trust in him. This was a deeply painful moment for me, and for the country." Plans for a mausoleum were quickly drawn up, and specially trained embalmers from the Mausoleum Group, the same Moscow laboratory that had worked on the corpses of Nikolai Lenin and Josef Stalin, were flown in to prepare his body for perpetual viewing.

Some in Washington hoped a struggle for power within the politburo might now weaken Hanoi's willingness to resist, but it was quickly clear from a memorial speech Le Duan made before the National Assembly that nothing had changed. North Vietnam, he promised, would dedicate itself unwaveringly to Ho's final wishes—to defeat the American aggressors, liberate the South, and unify the country.

Meanwhile, Kissinger—refusing to believe that "a fourth-rate power like North Vietnam doesn't have a breaking point," and convinced that the United States needed to make good on Nixon's threat by striking a "savage, punishing blow" to Hanoi—had secretly put his staff to work drawing up a plan calculated to do as much damage as possible to North Vietnam in just four days. Code-named "Duck Hook"—for reasons no one could later quite remember—the plan included massive B-52 attacks on Hanoi and twenty-eight other sites, the mining of Haiphong and other ports, and the bombing of the railroad lines that led to China. According to some Kissinger aides—though not Kissinger himself—a tactical "nuclear device" was to block passes between North Vietnam and China.

If Hanoi failed to make serious diplomatic concessions after this four-day assault, it was to be followed by another and another until they did. Contingency plans called for these later attacks to include destruction of the Red River dikes, sure to flood vast areas and drown countless civilians, and a full-scale invasion of the North.

Nixon seemed to like the plan at first. He dropped hints that something big was going to happen on November 1 in talks with foreign leaders and with Republican leaders on Capitol Hill. William Rogers and Melvin Laird first learned of it from reading a newspaper column and were appalled. They pleaded with the president not to undertake it. There was no assurance it would work—there were few industrial targets left to bomb, blockades were never complete, no one could predict how Moscow or Beijing would react—but it was certain to inflame the antiwar movement, further divide the country, and endanger the Nixon presidency. Far better to reemphasize the importance of Vietnamization, they urged.

Nixon took their views under advisement. On September 16

DAYS OF RAGE

As organizers worked out the last details for the peaceful nationwide Moratorium, members of a radical breakaway faction of the Students for a Democratic Society—the "Weathermen," so called from a line in a Bob Dylan song, "You don't need a weatherman to know the way the wind blows"—called for more violent action. It was now a real revolutionary's duty to shed his or her "white-skin privilege," they argued, join a global Third World revolution, and violently overthrow "the AmeriKKKan empire." "Kill all the rich people," said Bill Ayers, one of their leaders. "Break up their cars and apartments. Bring the revolution home. Kill your parents, that's really where it's at."

Less interested in ending the war than in sparking a violent revolution, they called for four "Days of Rage" in Chicago. Their leaders assumed that thousands would rally to their cause. Only a few hundred did. On Monday, October 6, they blew up a statue in Haymarket Square that honored seven policemen killed by an anarchist's bomb in 1884. (It would be reconstructed—and blown up again by the Weathermen the following year.) Two nights later, wearing gas masks, motorcycle helmets, and goggles, and armed with chains, brass knuckles, and lead pipes, they gathered in Lincoln Park, where the police had waded into demonstrators during the Democratic convention the year before. "If you have anything short of a mortal wound," one of their leaders shouted, "you are expected to fight on," then sent them out into the streets of the wealthy nearby neighborhood called the Gold Coast, breaking shop windows and car windshields, assaulting passersby, and charging police barriers. Three nights later, they did it again, breaking their way through the Loop this time. Before it was all over, 6 had been shot and

287 had been arrested, some more than once. Seventy-five policemen had been injured, and a city attorney had been paralyzed for life. "I don't know what your cause is," a Chicago citizen told one would-be revolutionary as he was shoved into a paddy wagon, "but you have just set it back a hundred years." Fred Hampton, Chicago chairman of the Black Panthers—himself soon to be murdered in his bed by local police—denounced the Weathermen as "anarchistic, opportunistic . . . *Custeristic*."

In March 1970, in a town house in Greenwich Village, three members of what was now called the Weather Underground inadvertently blew themselves up while making pipe bombs with which they had planned either to kill people at Columbia University or slaughter everyone attending an Army noncommissioned officers' dance at Fort Dix. "The best to be said for the Weathermen," Todd Gitlin wrote, "is that for all their rant and bombs, in eleven years underground they killed nobody but themselves." (Eight years after the war had ended, four ex-members did kill a guard and two police officers while robbing a Brinks truck.)

During the 1969–70 academic year, there would be some 250 major bombings and attempted bombings in

the United States, most of them the work of lone wolves. Courthouses, induction centers, and ROTC buildings were favorite targets. So were Manhattan corporate headquarters—IBM, Safeway, Socony-Mobil. University libraries were hit, too, and at Stanford University an anti-ROTC crowd set a fire that destroyed the life's work of a visiting Indian anthropologist.

Bill Zimmerman deplored what the members of the Weather Underground and their mimics were doing to the reputation of the peace movement, but he understood the atmosphere that had helped produce it: "Nineteen sixty-nine was the year in which most of us were most alienated and felt most like revolutionaries, and it led to a lot of crazy responses. I wanted the country to undergo a radical transformation, a redistribution of wealth and power. But to try to bring that about through armed struggle in the United States was insane. These were all infantile fantasies that people came to out of the frustration of not having a workable strategy for ending the war."

ABOVE Weathermen, helmeted and ready to wreak havoc in Chicago's Haymarket Square. Behind them is the pedestal of the statue honoring the Chicago police, which they'd already destroyed.

he announced that another 40,500 troops would be on their way home by December 15. Three days later, in hopes of calming the campuses and undercutting the upcoming Moratorium protests scheduled for October 15, he announced that he was canceling the draft calls for November and December, lifting the threat of conscription from anyone older than twenty, and planning to implement a simple lottery system; those who drew high numbers would no longer have a personal stake in the debate over the war.

As October 15 drew closer, the president grew more and more concerned about the Moratorium's potential impact. It was, after all, to be the first national demonstration directed at him personally. A column by David Broder was anxiously passed around the White House: "It is becoming more obvious every passing day that the men and the movement that broke Lyndon B. Johnson's authority in 1968 are out to break Richard M. Nixon in 1969. The likelihood is great that they will succeed again, for breaking a President is, like most feats, easier to accomplish the second time around." Nixon considered holding a press conference during the evening news hour on the day of the demonstration to deflect attention from the marchers, and he had his aides talk with Reverend Billy Graham about declaring a National Day of Prayer "to show our sympathy with peace."

Some advisers warned him to be respectful of those preparing to march. Instead, asked for his opinion about them at a televised press conference, he was dismissive. "I understand that there has been and continues to be opposition to the war in Vietnam on the campuses, and also in the nation," he said. "As far as this kind of thing, we expect it. However, under no circumstances will I be affected whatever by it." "Nixon goofed," one Moratorium organizer said. "It sounded like he didn't care what the American people thought."

On the eve of the Moratorium, North Vietnamese premier Pham Van Dong sent a message applauding "peace- and justice-loving American personages" for their efforts to end the U.S. "aggressive war," and ending, "May your fall offensive succeed splendidly." Nixon sent Spiro Agnew out to demand that the Moratorium's organizers "repudiate the support of the totalitarian government which has on its hands the blood of forty thousand Americans."

But nothing the Nixon administration could do dampened the enthusiasm of those participating in the Moratorium. It was the largest outpouring of public dissent in American history up to that time. More than two million people are thought to have taken part in cities and towns all across the country. Church bells tolled. The names of the dead were read aloud. Organized and orchestrated by believers in the two-party system, it was peaceful, middle-class, carefully focused on ending the war. "It's

nice," one marcher said, "to go to a demonstration without having to swear allegiance to Chairman Mao."

Colleges canceled classes. More than a thousand high schools took part. Two hundred thousand people marched in Manhattan. The college-age children of Nixon's two closest aides, H. R. Haldeman and John Ehrlichman, marched on their campuses. So did Melvin Laird's son. Spiro Agnew's fourteen-year-old daughter wanted to join the crowd but was forbidden to do so by her father. Carol Crocker, whose views on Vietnam had steadily shifted since her brother Mogie had been killed there, marched with friends from Goucher College in Baltimore. "I'd never been with that many people at one time, just the energy of the crowd itself was tremendous," she remembered. "I wondered if everybody was in it for the right reasons. I wasn't there to drink or smoke pot. Not in those situations. This to me was serious business. This was the business of living life. This was not a party. I didn't just want to be with the crowd. I didn't just want to make noise. I wanted to make a difference. And I, in no way, wanted to dishonor my brother."

In Washington, D.C., one thousand House and Senate staffers stood on the Capitol steps in silent protest of the war. Coretta Scott King, the widow of Dr. Martin Luther King Jr., spoke before a crowd of fifty thousand at the Washington Monument and then led thousands of silent marchers holding candles streaming past the White House, where Nixon sat alone, writing notes to himself on a yellow pad: "Don't get rattled—don't waver—don't react."

That evening all three networks offered ninety-minute reports on events around the country. On CBS, Walter Cronkite declared the Moratorium "historic in its scope. Never before had so many demonstrated their hope for peace."

Organizers were already planning a second Washington demonstration in mid-November. It was meant to last two days, and they hoped for still bigger crowds.

In the face of that kind of opposition, Duck Hook was shelved. "The Moratorium had undercut the credibility of the ultimatum," Nixon recalled; a dramatic escalation of the war would "risk a major American and worldwide furor and still not address the central problem of whether the South Vietnamese were sufficiently confident and prepared to defend themselves against a renewed communist offensive at some time in the future."

Instead, Nixon asked for television time on the evening of November 3 for a major address on Vietnam. Rumors spread that he was going to announce a breakthrough in Paris, a mas-

OVER The Moratorium crowd blankets the Washington Mall, October 15, 1969.

ABOVE Men of the 198th Light Infantry Brigade on combat patrol near Chu Lai wear black armbands in support of the demonstrations back home.

sive troop withdrawal, perhaps even an agreement on a ceasefire. The president spent several days at Camp David, working and reworking what he wanted to say, but when the time came to deliver the speech there was little in it that was new. He said again that ending the war at once would be "the easy and popular course to follow," but that to do so would "result in a collapse of confidence in American leadership, not only in Asia but throughout the world." Therefore, the United States planned to fight on until either the communists agreed to negotiate a fair and honorable peace or South Vietnam proved capable of defending itself on its own—whichever came first. The rate at which Americans would continue to come home would be dictated by the pace of Vietnamization, the level of enemy activity, and progress at the negotiating table. American casualties and enemy infiltration were down. South Vietnam's armed forces were bigger, better armed, better trained. Sixty thousand U.S. troops were already home or on their way. More were going to

follow. All that was needed was patience on the part of the American people. "And so tonight, to you, the great silent majority of my fellow Americans—I ask for your support," Nixon said. "I pledged in my campaign for the presidency to end the war in a way that we could win the peace. I have initiated a plan of action which will enable me to keep that pledge. The more support I can have from the American people, the sooner that pledge can be redeemed; for the more divided we are at home, the less likely the enemy is to negotiate at Paris. Let us be united for peace. Let us also be united against defeat. Because let us understand: North Vietnam cannot defeat or humiliate the United States. Only Americans can do that."

By and large, the press was unenthusiastic. "It was a speech that seemed designed not to persuade the opposition, but to overwhelm it," wrote James Reston, "and the chances are that this will merely divide and polarize the debaters in the United States, without bringing the enemy into serious negotiation." The president would dispatch his vice president to attack his critics: they were "an effete corps of impudent snobs," Agnew said, "nattering nabobs of negativism," "rotten apples."

The general public's support for the speech was overwhelming. A Gallup telephone poll taken immediately afterward showed that 77 percent of those called approved of the president's message. A more sophisticated survey taken by the Gallup organization a few days later found that Nixon's overall approval rating had jumped from 52 to 68 percent. Most Americans still wanted to get out of Vietnam, but they wanted to do so as a matter of policy rather than collapse. Three hundred House members cosponsored a resolution of bipartisan support for the president's stand and more than half the members of the Senate signed a letter saying more or less the same thing. The White House orchestrated an elaborate behind-the-scenes campaign to rally public support, but even when those efforts were discounted, the outpouring was remarkable: fifty thousand telegrams and thirty thousand letters overwhelmingly backing the president. "We've got the liberal bastards on the run now," Nixon told his aides, "and we're going to keep them on the run."

A SYSTEMATIC HOMICIDE

NO PROVINCE had suffered more during the American war than the coastal province of Quang Ngai. More than 70 percent of its villages had been shelled by Navy ships, bombed, bulldozed, or burned to the ground, and more than 40 percent of its people had been forced into refugee camps before Private Tim O'Brien from Worthington, Minnesota, got there in 1969. "It was a province that was viewed much as, I guess, many Americans might view redneck America," he remembered. "Sort of country bumpkins. They may have been country bumpkins, but they were fiercely independent."

O'Brien served in Alpha Company, Third Platoon, Fifth Battalion, Twenty-third Americal Division, headquartered at a landing zone called Gator—"thirty or forty acres of almost-America," he remembered, with hot showers and cold beer. "There was no sense of mission. There was no sense of daily purpose. We didn't know why we were in a village, what we were supposed to accomplish. So we'd kick around jugs of rice and search houses and frisk people, not knowing what we were looking for and rarely finding anything. And somebody might die, one of our guys, and somebody might not. Then we'd come back to the same village a week later or two weeks later and do it all over again. It was like chasing ghosts."

An American APC accidentally crushed one man from O'Brien's company. An enemy grenade skittered off O'Brien's helmet and exploded, wounding a GI standing a few feet away. But mines and booby traps were the greatest menace, he remem-

bered. "Somewhere around 80 percent of our casualties came from land mines of all sorts. I'd always thought of courage as charging enemy bunkers or standing up under fire. For me, just to get up in the morning in Vietnam and look out at the land and think, 'In a few minutes I'll be walking out there and will my corpse be there? Or there? Will I lose a leg out there?' Just to walk through Quang Ngai day after day from village to village and through the paddies and up into the mountains, just to make your legs move, was an act of courage that if, say, you were living in Sioux City, it wouldn't be courageous to walk to the grocery store or down Main Street and just have your legs go back and forth. But in Vietnam, for me, just to walk felt incredibly brave. I would sometimes look at my legs as I walked, thinking, 'How am I doing this?'"

Back in the spring, Tim O'Brien's outfit had been sent into an area of operations the Americans called "Pinkville"—so called because it was colored pink on Army maps—clusters of villages that included a hamlet they called My Lai 4. "We hated going there," he recalled. "When we'd get the word, 'You're headed for "Pinkville,"' one guy would say to another, 'Somebody's going to die' or 'Somebody's going to lose a leg.' We were terrified of the place. It was littered with land mines. The expressions on the villagers' faces, including children of, say, five or six years old, had a mixture of hostility and terror. I can't say many villagers anywhere received us with open arms. But this place was special. And I remember talking to fellow soldiers thinking, 'What is it with this place?' And then about three-quarters of the way through my tour in Vietnam the story of the My Lai massacre broke."

On November 12, 1969—nine days after Nixon urged his fellow countrymen to be patient and three days before the second Moratorium was slated to begin—the Dispatch News Service in Washington moved a story by the investigative journalist Seymour Hersh. Thirty-five newspapers across the country picked it up. Twenty months earlier, on the morning of March 16, 1968, as the American public was focused on Khe Sanh and the aftermath of the Tet Offensive, 105 men from a rifle company belonging to the Americal Division, and led by Lieutenant William Calley, had been ordered to helicopter into the hamlet of My Lai 4. Since arriving in Vietnam, Calley's company had lost twenty-eight men to mines and booby traps and unseen snipers. Two days earlier, a popular squad leader had been killed. They had been told that a unit of Main Force Viet Cong—perhaps two hundred men—was waiting for them, and they were eager for revenge.

The company commander, Captain Ernest Medina, gave his men a pep talk the evening before they boarded their choppers. The men later failed to agree on his exact wording, but most remembered it this way:

"Our job is to go in rapidly and to neutralize everything. To kill everything."

"Even women and children?"

"I mean everything."

When they landed in the hamlet, they received no hostile fire—though in the confusion of their landing, accompanied by U.S. artillery and helicopter fire, some of them may have thought they did—and they certainly encountered no enemy soldiers. Instead, over the next four hours, Medina, Calley, and their men rounded up and systematically murdered more than four hundred defenseless old men, women, children, and infants. Many of the women and girls were raped or sodomized before they were shot. Eighteen of the dead were pregnant. Fifty of them were three years old or younger.

An Army photographer named Ronald Haeberle, assigned to provide morale-boosting images for Army publications, wandered through the scene photographing the dead as well as those

about to die. His images, published later in the *Cleveland Plain Dealer* and then in *Life,* did more than any written words could to bring home to the American public the horror of what had happened.

There would have been still more slaughter had a helicopter pilot named Hugh Thompson Jr. not landed between the men and some of their intended targets and ordered his crew to open fire on their fellow Americans if they did not stop shooting civilians.

At the same time, just a mile or so away, the second platoon from the same task force murdered nearly one hundred more villagers.

ABOVE Charlie Company begins its combat assault on My Lai. **OPPOSITE TOP** Huddled together, women and children watch their killers approach. **OPPOSITE BOTTOM** A small boy tries to shield his still smaller sibling from American fire.

Tim O'Brien read Seymour Hersh's article at LZ Gator. "Suddenly," he remembered, "it was like a window shade going up and there's light, and we understood what had engendered this horror in these kids' faces and the fear and the hatred. A hundred and some American soldiers in four hours or so, butchering innocent people in all kinds of ways—machine-gunning them and throwing them in wells and scalping them and killing them in ditches and taking a lunch break and then doing it some more. A systematic homicide."

Mike Wallace of CBS tracked down and interviewed former Private First Class Paul Meadlo, who had taken part in the killing and had had his foot blown off the next day—a sign, he had come to believe, of God's unhappiness with him for what he'd helped to do.

MIKE WALLACE: How many people did you round up?
PAUL MEADLO: Well, there was about forty to forty-five people that we gathered in the center of the village. And we placed them in there, and it was like a little island, right there in the center of the village, I'd say.
WALLACE: What kind of people—men, women, children?

MEADLO: Men, women, children.

WALLACE: Babies?

MEADLO: Babies. And we all huddled them up. We made them squat down and Lieutenant Calley came over and said, "You know what to do with them, don't you?" And I said, "Yes." So l took it for granted that he just wanted us to watch them. And he left, and came back about ten or fifteen minutes later and said, "How come you ain't killed them yet?" And I told him that "I didn't think you wanted us to kill them, that you just wanted us to guard them." He said, "No, I want them dead."

WALLACE: He told this to you, or to you particularly?

MEADLO: Well, I was facing him. So, but the other three, four guys heard it and so he stepped back about ten, fifteen feet, and he started shooting them. And he told me to start shooting. So I started shooting, I poured about four clips into the group. . . .

WALLACE: And you killed how many at that time?

MEADLO: Well, I fired my automatic. So . . . you just spray the area on them and so you can't know how many you killed because it comes out so doggone fast. So I might've killed ten or fifteen of them.

WALLACE: Men, women, and children?

MEADLO: Men, women, and children.

WALLACE: And babies?

MEADLO: And babies. Why did I do it? Because I felt like I was ordered to do it. And it seemed like— Well, at the time I—felt like I was doing the right thing. I really did. Because, like I said, I lost buddies, I lost a good—damn good—buddy—Bobby Wilson—and it was on my conscience. . . . So after I done it, I felt good. But later on that day it was getting to me. . . .

WALLACE: It's so hard, I think, for a good many Americans to understand that young, capable, brave American boys could line up old men, women, children, and babies and shoot them down in cold blood. How do you explain that?

MEADLO: I wouldn't know.

COUNTERCLOCKWISE FROM OPPOSITE TOP An old man hauled from his home waits to be killed; some of the dead clustered where they fell, and scattered along a path; and Charlie Company taking a lunch break, just a few yards from a heap of corpses. There would be more murders after lunch.

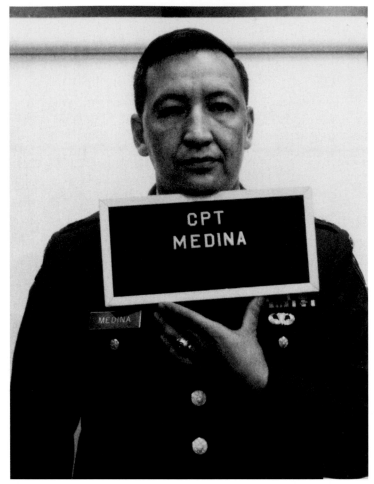

The killing of civilians has happened in every war. In Vietnam, it was not policy or routine, but it was not an aberration, either. Still, the scale and deliberateness and intimacy of what happened at My Lai was different. "They were killing Vietnamese point-blank with rifles and grenades," Neil Sheehan recalled. "They were murdering them directly. They weren't doing it with bombs and artillery. If they'd been doing it with bombs and artillery, nobody would have said a word, because that was going on all the time."

Not every soldier participated in the killings that day. Some led villagers to safety. But a failure of military leadership at nearly every level had created the conditions that made the massacre possible.

What had happened at My Lai may have shocked the American public. But it was not news to the Army. Hugh Thompson, the helicopter pilot who had tried to stop the massacre, reported what he had seen. So did at least five other pilots. The word went steadily up the chain of command—all the way to the division

ABOVE LEFT AND RIGHT Lieutenant William Calley and Captain Ernest Medina being booked for war crimes

commander, Major General Samuel W. Koster. No one took any action. Instead, the brigade log was falsified to say that 128 Viet Cong had been killed by U.S. artillery. The slaughter was covered up. The Army Public Information Office released a widely disseminated story that described an operation that "went like clockwork" in which the "jungle warriors" of the Eleventh Brigade had killed 128 Viet Cong in a running "day-long battle," chalking up the largest body count in the brigade's history. On the strength of reports like these, General Westmoreland had sent his official congratulations.

Later, back in the States, a former Army corporal named Ronald Ridenhour, who had heard about what had happened from several men who had been there, wrote letters describing the killings to the president, the secretary of defense, and more than two dozen other high-ranking officials. Later, a reporter would ask him why he'd done so. "I guess I just wrestled with my own conscience to try to decide what action to take," he said. "I had to do something. I couldn't just rest with this knowledge for the rest of my life. . . . I couldn't live with myself if I did."

President Nixon's first reaction when he heard the story was to investigate those who reported the killing. He demanded to

know who was backing them: "It's those dirty rotten Jews from New York who are behind it," he was sure of it. He instructed his aides to "discredit witnesses," investigate Seymour Hersh and Mike Wallace, "get ring-wingers with us," and "get out the facts about [communist] atrocities at Hue." Defense Secretary Laird said he wished he could "sweep the whole thing under the rug," but knew he couldn't. Eventually, General Westmoreland assigned Lieutenant General William R. Peers, a veteran of thirty months as a troop commander in Vietnam with a reputation for fairness and objectivity, to head a panel to look into the matter. He was told to confine his probe to questions of a cover-up, not to delve into the event itself. He ignored those instructions and eventually found that thirty persons, including the division commander, Major General Koster, had either conspired to conceal atrocities or had committed them. In announcing his findings, General Peers had wanted to call what had happened at My Lai what it clearly had been—a "massacre." His superiors made him use the phrase "a tragedy of major proportions." In the end, the Army would indict twenty-five officers and men, including the leader of the first platoon, Lieutenant William Calley.

My Lai: **TOP LEFT** Ronald Ridenhour, whose conscience did not allow him to remain silent about what he'd heard had happened in the hamlet **TOP RIGHT** Pilot Hugh Thompson Jr., who saved some civilians by putting his helicopter down between them and U.S. troops **ABOVE** Lieutenant General William R. Peers, who led the Army investigation

A WHOLE NEW LEVEL

ON THURSDAY EVENING, November 13, the day after the My Lai story ran in newspapers across the country, more than forty thousand people began gathering at Arlington National Cemetery for what was called a "March of Death." For thirty-eight straight hours and in the face of biting cold and gusts of driving rain, they streamed in single file across the Arlington Bridge and on into the heart of the nation's capital. A placard hung from each marcher's neck bearing the name of someone who had been killed in the war, and when they passed the White House they shouted it out. Most marchers were young, but here and there were older people—parents or family members, presumably—who had asked for particular names. (Thirty-odd names had tactfully been withdrawn when families objected to their being displayed.) The long procession ended at the Capitol, where each placard was slipped into a wooden coffin.

On Saturday, the 15th, the second Moratorium began. It would be different from the first. The organizers of the first Moratorium—Sam Brown and other veterans of the McCarthy campaign—had succeeded in attracting to the antiwar movement people made uneasy by the radical voices and street violence that had been so prominent at the Pentagon march in 1967 and in the streets of Chicago in 1968. But this occasion would be less predictable. They had formed a wary alliance with the New Mobilization Committee (the MOBE), itself a loose and fractious coalition of sixty-odd antiwar organizations, ranging all the way from the Episcopal Peace Fellowship to the Social-

ist Workers Party. Its leaders, some belonging to the Old Left, some to the New, were pledged to nonviolence, but some of their members were not.

On the eve of the demonstration four Weathermen turned up at the Moratorium office to suggest that a contribution of $20,000 for legal fees incurred following the recent Days of Rage they'd staged in Chicago might prevent violence the next day in Washington. Unwilling to accede to what they saw as blackmail, the Moratorium leaders sent them away.

The crowd that gathered on the Mall the next morning was enormous—estimated at 800,000 by its organizers and by the White House at 250,000—and overwhelmingly peaceful. Democratic senator George McGovern and Republican senator Charles Goodell of New York spoke. Pete Seeger led the crowd in chorus after chorus of John Lennon's "Give Peace a Chance." Hawkers sold out their stock of buttons reading "Effete Snobs for Peace." Buses parked bumper to bumper formed an impenetrable wall around the White House, and three hundred airborne troops were quietly stationed in the adjacent Executive Office Building just in case there was trouble. President Nixon

ABOVE Participants in the antiwar "March of Death" pass the White House, each pausing to speak the name of someone who had died in Vietnam. "No problems at the White House," H. R. Haldeman noted in his diary that night. "Just single file of candle carriers with name placards of war dead. . . . Mostly solemn and quiet. P[resident] not interested, spent two hours at the bowling alley." **OPPOSITE** The second Moratorium Against the War, November 15, 1969, drew the largest crowd ever seen in Washington up to that time.

claimed that he was too busy watching football on television to pay attention.

This time there was trouble on the periphery. Helmeted militants tried to get into the South Vietnamese embassy and, when tear gas drove them back, ran up and down Connecticut Avenue smashing windows. As the speeches ended, Jerry Rubin and Abbie Hoffman began leading several thousand people toward the Justice Department.

Jeremy Larner, a speechwriter for Senator McCarthy in 1968, now returned to freelance writing, caught up with Hoffman as they marched.

"What do you think of all this, Abbie?"

"This is more moral," he says, surveying the sea of heads and hair, "but Woodstock had more dope."

Abbie is more impressed, he tells me, with the people who, it is alleged, have decided to protest the war by setting off bombs in New York business buildings. "They're heroes," he grins at me. "Kids will see that and get more committed—on a whole new level."

I guess we get to some new level right after the assembly, when a battalion of militants—the "Mad Dogs," they call themselves—marches across the Mall to the Justice Department wearing helmets and carrying knapsacks full of rocks and bottles. These are the mixed media with which they will try to make the march their own.

At the Department building the cops hold back while MOBE marshals try to call off the Mad Dogs. This gives the Dogs a chance to incite the spectators: "Who're you with, the people or the pigs?" (That's "people" as in "the streets belong to the people," "people" meaning "us.") While the marshals argue, the militants break windows, plant Vietcong flags, explode paint bombs and perform various other death-defying stunts bringing us nearer each day to the brave new world. Then it's tear gas time again, and cops in gas masks march in solid rows down one block at a time, once more avoiding contact except where absolutely forced upon them.

There is one more thing left to prove. As demonstrators and bystanders run in panic, Mad Dogs loft bottles which fall among the crowd. That will show them what the cops are like! A screaming girl beats girlishly on the face of a bottle-thrower, collapses sobbing in the street. Mad Dogs pull out phony bandages, wrap their heads and yell for the crowd to "make a stand" as it retreats block by block from Constitution Avenue. They leave some windows broken in the shopping district: one belongs to a black-owned baby-clothes store. What are the political reactions, I wonder, of the shoppers who are gassed? Are they "people," as in "power to the people"?

The Dogs move on to Union Station, where they throw bottles at trainloads of marchers who will not "stay and fight."

Despite the violent actions of a few, the next morning's *New York Times* story about the demonstrations read "Generally Peaceful." "The October Moratorium proved that the peace movement was respectable," Jeremy Larner concluded. "The November Moratorium proved the movement could survive the threat of violence."

Nonetheless, plans for a December Moratorium were scrapped. "October was too big for our own good," Sam Brown said. "It would have been healthier and simpler for us to start slowly and grow month by month." The president's November 3 speech had done its work, another organizer admitted: "It was a moral disaster, but it was very brilliant and it will make us lie low for a few months"—until people began to see that it was just "a public relations cover-up for a continued war." The organizers of the Moratorium worked to keep the movement alive on a local level. The MOBE broke into its constituent parts.

Meanwhile, the Washington demonstration had struck a chord among some U.S. troops in Vietnam. Fifteen marines patrolled near Danang with black armbands as a sign of solidarity. Captain Alan Goldstein, an Army dentist at Long Binh, collected 136 names on a petition in support of the Moratorium. "I said I believed that everybody should take a stand on this," he recalled. " 'If you want the war to end, sign this.' All of a sudden, I'm getting letters from Army people stateside asking to be put on the list. One West Point guy went back to his commander and the guy says, 'This is pretty close to treason. Sign this and you can kiss your career goodbye.' I mean, these guys have a lot at stake and they're signing it."

And on Thanksgiving Day, there was a demonstration at the 71st Evacuation Hospital at Pleiku, as well, where medical personnel and a handful of patients had resolved to fast rather than enjoy the traditional holiday dinner as if all were right with the world. "On Thanksgiving," Joan Furey recalled, "the Army did what the Army does—they're going to bring in turkey; they're going to bring in mashed potatoes and apple pie, and whatever. By this point, a lot of us were very, very cynical about the war and what was going on. 'Don't give me this Thanksgiving nonsense, you know. This is all crazy.' And so we decided that we would have a fast for peace. They actually called it 'John Turkey Day.' But we weren't going to make a big deal about it. We knew there were going to be TV people there. A couple of the organizers were looking for people to talk on camera. They came to me.

ABOVE Joan Furey at work

ARE WE BOUND TO FIGHT FOREVER?

When Nurse Joan Furey took part in a Thanksgiving Day fast at the 71st Evacuation Hospital at Pleiku in 1969, her parents back on Long Island were startled—neither she nor they had had much sympathy with antiwar protestors before she'd gone to Vietnam. Their daughter wrote home to explain what she'd done. Her mother thought the letter was so eloquent and she was so proud of her daugher, that she saw that it was published in the local paper, *The Port Jefferson-North Shore Record*.

Dear Mom & Dad,
    By now I'm sure you've heard of our Thanksgiving Day fast, and my part in it. The information that has flowed back to us from the States leads me to believe that much was left out. Knowing how people react to it, I'm going to try & explain to you the motives behind it and the part I played. I do not wish for you to think of me as an extremist, and I believe you have the right to know exactly what happened and why.
    One year ago I volunteered to come to Vietnam because I knew that my skills as a nurse were needed and I strongly believed I had an obligation to my country and to the young men who are fighting over here. During the ten months I have been here those beliefs have been fortified rather

than destroyed. But Vietnam has opened my eyes to the destruction of war. I have lived with it, worked with it, and viewed it all too often. Due to my profession I get a very narrow look at the glory of war. After the battle, after the heroics, when the fight is finished—that is when I and the other medical people work. We are the clean-up committee.

Day after day, week after week, 10, 11, 14, 16 hours a day, 6 or 7 days a week, we work with the injured & maimed. We see our country's young men come through the doors of this hospital—many that do will never be quite the same again, for the loss of a limb or two & sometimes three, the destruction of a face or the ruination of a mind, will hinder their growth in our society. Right alongside of them come the women and children & young men of this country we are in, in the same condition only with nothing to return to—no home or family or modern medical facility to rehabilitate them. Destroyed not by the U.S. forces but by the enemy we are fighting. Many of them may have helped the "G.I." in the next bed to safety or saved him from an ambush, or maybe the "G.I." did the same for him. And, all you can think to yourself is, Why? For what purpose is man so bent on destroying himself?

Can I ever explain the feeling one has after taking care of a young 19-year-old fellow for 20, 25 days, progressing toward health only to have him relapse. To work with a group of people to bring him back from the edge, so he can go home to his 18-year-old wife, and then to stand by helpless & watch him die—knowing that nothing in this world can save him—no

prayers, no tears, & no medicine. To stand in the emergency room & maybe lend a hand if needed & see five men 21 to 39 years of age brought in, burned beyond recognition so that even their dog tags can't be read. Injuries, that in the U.S. would be considered priority cases & here they must wait for five other patients because "they are not that bad." To look up as the doors open and another patient is wheeled in from surgery & wonder if it will ever end? And then go home at the end of a long day & read about our home, that we all want to go back to, and what do we read? Riots, killing, theft, etc. After a while there is only one question to ask—Why?

This question is being asked more and more as my year comes to an end. For destruction is the rule, not the exception in war.

Why is it necessary for man to constantly be at war? Why can't we live together peacefully? Today is the anniversary of Pearl Harbor—how far have we come? Are we bound to fight forever?

Will my children be destined to fight and die in another land, at another time, for another reason? Or if things continue as is—will they die in America, in our own country? Will they hate and be hated so much that they must fight for the right to live? Will there be no place on this earth that man can live without battle? What is the misery gene in our makeup? Is there nothing we can do? Are we destined to destroy ourselves, the way other worlds have before us?

That is why I fasted— peacefully—There were no demonstrations here—it was an individual thing and yes I took part

in it. I took part because I am a concerned American, because I love my country and I love people and I don't wish to spend the rest of my life watching us destroy each other—in Vietnam, in Africa, in Egypt, Israel, Nigeria, Europe and the United States. I took part in it because it was a sacrifice— a very small one—granted but it was presented as an offering for something better. A belief that the God I have believed in since childhood is not dead, but as alive as the people in this world make Him.

We are about to celebrate His birth, and people will join together in groups to sing carols, "Peace on Earth Good Will to Men." How easy it is to sing, how hard it is to practice.

Yes, I fasted for an end to war, for the end of destruction, needless death and bitter hate. Yes I fasted for Peace on Earth and Good Will to all Men. There is nothing left to do!

Love, Joan

I said, 'No. Look, I'm going to fast and do my thing.' I said, 'But I really don't want to be involved with any media.' "

That morning, Furey was on duty in the ICU when one of her patients took a sudden turn for the worse. "Some patients, they just get into your heart," she remembered. "His name was Timmy. I think he was eighteen. I had been taking care of him for a couple of days. He had a gunshot wound to the chest. It was really touch and go with him, but he had seemed to be stabilizing. Then, he started to get shocky, had trouble breathing. So I called the doc. They rushed him into the operating room. I had a rule, I didn't go into the OR. I went to triage in the ER. I did the ICU. But you're not going to get me inside the OR. But for some reason I wanted to go in with this patient. The surgeon cut into his chest. And put a tube in there. And what came out of his chest . . . he had a massive infection in his chest and around his thoracic cavity and his lung. I knew it was unlikely he was going to survive an infection like that. And I just lost it. I just got so angry at all of it—at the uselessness of it all. I remember walking out of the OR, ripping off my gown, ripping off my mask. I walked outside and asked, 'Where are those reporters?' "

An ABC camera crew was waiting. "I'm just fasting against any type of war or hostility that brings needless injury to innocent people all over the world," she said into the camera, "not just Vietnam but everywhere, including the United States of America." Later, Furey made a holiday call to her parents back home on Long Island. They hadn't seen her on television, her mother said, "but one of the neighbors had called and said she saw you on the evening news and that you were demonstrating against the war. What was that about?" "These were my World War II patriotic parents, who were not going to understand," Furey recalled. "I mean, 'You don't demonstrate against the war in a war zone.' But by that time, of course, I had the attitude, 'What are they going to do? Send me to Vietnam?' "

THE BRAVEST THING

MARINE CORPORAL JOHN MUSGRAVE had very nearly died in combat below the DMZ in the autumn of 1967. Wounded in the jaw and shoulder, his ribs shattered, lung pierced, nerves cut, he had spent seventeen months in Navy hospitals. He was now enrolled at Baker University in Baldwin City, Kansas. But wherever he went, the war was never far away. "Let's just say that being a Marine combat veteran on a college campus in 1969 and 1970 wasn't a real good thing to be if you wanted to get dates and be popular," he recalled. "When I came home, it seemed like I didn't have anything to give to anybody

else. And the peace movement for a while got real nasty calling veterans 'babykillers.' It did more than piss us off. It broke our hearts. What were they thinking? You don't turn your backs on your warriors. I didn't trust anybody anymore. Just my family."

Musgrave was so hurt by the way some people treated him that he volunteered to return to Vietnam. The Marines turned him down because of his injuries, and asked him to help recruit men, instead. He did for a time, but when students asked him questions about the war he couldn't answer, he also began to read about how and why it was being fought. "I had friends in country on a second tour, and I still considered myself a Marine. But the more I read the less I found myself able to defend our presence there. So then I just stopped talking to everybody."

He gradually came to feel as if he were being torn in two, and was still haunted by the memory of those Marines who had died while he had lived.

"I was dating my .45 in those years," he remembered. "Coming home at night after drinking and pressing it up against my temple or putting it under my chin, wondering if this was going to be the night I was going to have the guts to do it.

"One night I had a round chambered and I'd taken the safety off. And I thought, I'm really going do it tonight, you know. Like, whew, I'm really going to do it. I had two dogs and I'd let my dogs out. And they jumped on the front door and scratched. They wanted in. And I put the safety back on the pistol and set it down and went and let them in. And they were so open in their love for me that I literally said out loud, 'Whoa, if I really want to do this I can do it tomorrow.' And I put the pistol in the drawer, and I think that was the closest I came. I think maybe I would have killed myself that night. But something as simple as my dogs wanting back in stopped that thought. I'm really glad that it didn't happen. But at the time it just made so much sense."

It was Richard Nixon's troop withdrawals that finally turned Musgrave against the war. "If it ain't worth winning," he thought

ABOVE John Musgrave and a girlfriend at Baker University

to himself, "it ain't worth dying for." His loyalty to the Marines would not yet let him express his opposition in public, but he did tell a campus antiwar meeting that they should stop acting as if they didn't give a damn about the men who had been asked to fight—and received a standing ovation.

Jack Todd's shift in attitude took time as well. While attending the University of Nebraska, he had undergone Marine officer training and hoped to become a platoon leader in Vietnam, but he'd damaged his knees while running track in high school and in the end the Marines processed him out as "NPQ"—Not Physically Qualified. He believed that that exempted him from having to take part in a war he was coming to see as immoral. That had not been an easy conclusion for him to reach: his uncle had been fired on at Pearl Harbor; a cousin had parachuted into Normandy on D-Day; another had fought his way ashore on Guadalcanal; and still another had been killed during a kamikaze attack. But he denounced the war as editor of *The Daily Nebraskan,* and took part in antiwar demonstrations on and off campus. After he was graduated, he began work as a reporter on *The Miami Herald.*

Then, in the autumn of 1969, two full years after the Marines had let him go, he was stunned to receive a draft notice from the Army. He considered going to Canada then; he had

the romantic notion that he might land a job on the *Toronto Star,* the newspaper that had first hired Ernest Hemingway. But his Cuban-born girlfriend was not willing to go with him. So he quit his job and drove to his parents' home in Scottsbluff, Nebraska. "I reported for my physical and showed them my discharge from the Marine Corps," he recalled, "and I remember a sergeant saying, 'But you were discharged from an officer program. We're drafting you as a private.'"

One evening while he was home he visited a high school friend named Sonny Walter, who had just been discharged from the Army after a year in Vietnam. That was "the turning point for me," he recalled. "He took me down to his basement and showed me some horrible pictures of Vietnam from his service there." Three dead GIs zipped into body bags. Grinning soldiers with what Todd remembered as "dead eyes," wearing necklaces of severed ears. Enemy sappers—or what was left of them—hanging from the perimeter wire. Another GI holding up a severed head for the camera. "His portrayal of the war was as a complete unbridled nightmare," Todd remembered. "He had tears in his eyes, pleading with me not to go. He even offered to drive me to Canada. All wars are horrifying, but Vietnam had very unique ways of being horrifying. And he really brought it home for me. I think everything that happened after that had its seeds in that evening."

Todd reluctantly reported for basic training at Fort Lewis, Washington, in November. "Morale just could not have been worse. It seemed to include even the sergeants and the officers. Nobody wanted to go to Vietnam. America just seemed to have

ABOVE LEFT AND RIGHT Jack Todd and the sort of picture that finally turned him against the war: a dead sapper hung on the barbed wire at a firebase below the DMZ, with a sign addressed to the enemy reading, "SURRENDER QUICKLY TO AVOID SUCH A TRAGIC DEATH."

shifted from the Woodstock high of the summer to this sort of bitter Nixonian low." Todd and another member of his unit began to talk at night about what it meant to be true to one's conscience. They read Henry David Thoreau, Leo Tolstoy, and Mahatma Gandhi. Those opposed to war on religious grounds could apply for conscientious objector status. But because Jack Todd also questioned the existence of God, that avenue was closed to him. "There were really two choices. It was go to jail or go to Canada. And, for me, going to jail—that one, I couldn't face." His mother was frail with periodic heart trouble; he believed seeing her son led off to prison might kill her. "So I went to Canada," he recalled. "I remember that last beautiful drive, from Seattle to Vancouver, all the towering Douglas firs along the road. It was January 4, 1970. After we crossed the border, it was a breeze, they just sort of waved us through and I remember just looking in the rearview mirror, thinking, 'Man, there goes my country. I'll never see it again.' I get called a coward all the time. It took me a long time not to feel that what I had done was cowardly, because I still had that ingrained military feeling inside. Now I think that was the bravest thing I ever did."

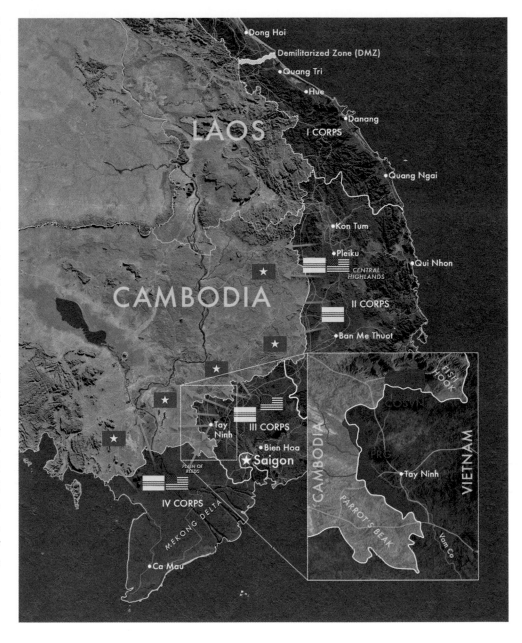

INCURSION

ON FEBRUARY 21, 1970, in a modest workman's house in an industrial suburb of Paris, Henry Kissinger began a new series of secret negotiations—talks so secret neither the secretary of state nor the secretary of defense nor the head of the CIA nor the Joint Chiefs of Staff was told about them. His negotiating partner from now on would be Le Duan's close political ally, Le Duc Tho. He was a white-thatched veteran of the nationalist struggle—he'd joined the revolution at sixteen and endured ten years in a French prison—and was invariably courteous but also doctrinaire and uncompromising. Kissinger and Nixon had hoped that the uptick in the polls that followed the president's November speech might have nudged the North

closer to compromise. It had not. The sole "reasonable" solution to the war, Le Duc Tho reiterated, was total American acquiescence in Hanoi's terms—unconditional withdrawal of U.S. forces on a fixed deadline and the dissolution of the "warlike" Saigon regime. He dismissed as "dribbles" the fact that more than 100,000 Americans had now gone home, and was openly scornful of the whole concept of Vietnamization. "Before there were over a million U.S. and puppet troops, and you failed," he

ABOVE The Cambodian incursion: Targets of U.S. and ARVN troops would include communist supply bases just inside Cambodia as well as the supposed locations of the Central Office for South Vietnam (COSVN), the headquarters from which the war in the South was directed, and the jungle-built capital of the newly created Provisional Revolutionary Government (PRG).

said. "How can you succeed when you let the puppet troops do the fighting . . . how can you win?"

Kissinger admitted that he had no answer.

Twenty months had now gone by since Nixon's inauguration, and peace seemed no nearer. Thwarted in his desire to strike a bold blow against the North, frustrated at the continuing impasse in Paris, and angered by the antiwar demonstrations that had undermined his ultimatum, the president searched for another opportunity to make the kind of dramatic show of force he thought would force Hanoi to make the concessions that would lead to peace.

Cambodia would provide it. Its politics were intricate and little understood in Washington, but for years, Prince Sihanouk had struggled to keep his country out of the war that had torn Vietnam apart. It was a delicate, demanding business. Officially neutral, he permitted North Vietnam and the NLF to establish

military bases in his country so long as they did not venture too far into its interior and provided only limited support for the Khmer Rouge, the native communist movement that threatened his regime, but he also had raised no objection to Nixon's decision to bomb those same bases so long as he could claim to know nothing about it.

Then, in March 1970, while Sihanouk was overseas on a diplomatic mission, the right-wing prime minister, General Lon Nol, and a coterie of like-minded generals seized power and promptly ordered all NLF and North Vietnamese forces out of Cambodian territory. Nixon, caught by surprise but eager to take advantage of the new situation, immediately dispatched arms to the undermanned, underequipped Cambodian army.

For years, the American military had wanted permission to cross the Cambodian border and clean out the enemy sanctuaries there. Now, Nixon would give them their chance. It would

withdrawal was a boy's job. Cambodia is a man's job." Since he knew the secretaries of defense and state would oppose his decision, they were not to be consulted.

As the planning went forward, Nixon became tense and agitated, had trouble sleeping, drank heavily in the evenings, and wrote himself notes to keep his courage up—"Need for Self-Discipline in all areas. Polls v. right decision. Dare to do it right—alone." He repeatedly watched the film *Patton,* in which George C. Scott, playing the World War II hero and standing before a giant American flag, intoned lines he especially liked: "Americans love a winner and will not tolerate a loser. Americans play to win all the time. I wouldn't give a hoot in hell for a man who lost and laughed. That's why Americans have never lost and will never lose a war . . . because the very thought of losing is hateful to Americans."

It was hateful to Nixon, too. Twice in recent months, the Democratic-controlled Senate had rejected his nominees for the Supreme Court. Sending troops into Cambodia would be a chance, he said, to show "those Senators . . . who's really tough." He knew that what he was about to do would reawaken the

help a friendly government survive and, more important from the administration's point of view, it would buy more time for Vietnamization. "This," Nixon told Kissinger, "is what I've been waiting for."

On April 19, he announced the largest troop withdrawal yet—150,000 Americans would be returning home over the next twelve months. The message seemed to be that Vietnamization was proceeding on schedule, that the president's plan was working. But shortly afterward he told H. R. Haldeman, "Cut the crap out of my schedule, I'm taking over here. Troop

ABOVE AND RIGHT South Vietnamese troops move into Cambodia. They had been told to expect fierce opposition. Instead, for the most part, the enemy simply slipped deeper into the interior, where neither U.S. nor ARVN troops could follow, and then returned to reclaim their bases when the Americans and South Vietnamese withdrew.

relatively dormant antiwar movement but professed not to care: since he knew he was "going to get unshirted hell for doing this at all," he said, he might as well "go for all the marbles."

And so, on the evening of April 30, just eleven days after his withdrawal announcement had seemed to imply that the war really was winding down, he told a vast television audience that he was widening it. Using a pointer, he showed his audience the main targets of the joint American and South Vietnamese operations already under way—two jagged salients that jutted out into South Vietnam—the Parrot's Beak and the Fishhook—just thirty-three and fifty miles from Saigon, respectively. Fifty thousand American troops were to clean out the Fishhook sanctuaries and seize the COSVN headquarters located there, while thirty thousand ARVN troops with U.S. air support would storm into the Parrot's Beak.

"This is not an invasion of Cambodia," he said—the White House had already told the press it preferred the word "incursion." American and South Vietnamese troops would not push farther than thirty-five miles into Cambodian territory and

would pull back once their goals had been accomplished. He would rather be a "one-term president," he said, "than see this Nation accept the first defeat in its proud 190-year history." He made it appear that the survival of American civilization itself somehow hinged on the success of this operation.

My fellow Americans, we live in an age of anarchy, both abroad and at home. We see mindless attacks on all the great institutions, which have been created by free civilizations in the last 500 years. Even here in the United States, great universities are being systematically destroyed. . . . If, when the chips are down, the world's most powerful nation, the United States of America, acts like a pitiful, helpless giant, the forces of totalitarianism and anarchy will threaten free nations and free institutions throughout the world.

The morning after the speech, the president visited the Pentagon for a briefing. He was still keyed up. "Let's blow the hell out of them," he said. Afterward, a reporter recorded his exchange in the corridor with a young secretary whose husband was serving in Vietnam and who wept as she told him, "I loved your speech, Mr. President. It made me proud to be an American."

"I wrote that [speech] for those kids out there," he told her.

ABOVE U.S. troops on their way out of the Memot Rubber Plantation in the Fishhook region of Cambodia, where COSVN was believed to have been hiding. Although the communist headquarters was targeted many times during the war, it was never found, let alone destroyed.

"I have seen them. They're the greatest. You see these bums, you know, blowing up the campuses. Listen, the boys that are on college campuses today are the luckiest people in the world, going to the greatest universities, and here they are, burning up the books, storming around about this issue . . . you name it. Get rid of the war and there will be another one. Then out there [in Vietnam], we have kids who are just doing their duty. And I have seen them. They stand tall, and they are proud."

Overnight, the antiwar movement came to life again. How could sending troops into another country in Southeast Asia help bring peace to the region? Three of Henry Kissinger's closest aides had resigned in protest before the mission began, warning that there would be "blood in the streets" if it went forward. Fifty junior State Department employees signed a letter of protest. The presidents of thirty-seven universities warned the White House of trouble to come. Student strikes were scheduled at more than one hundred schools. Nixon was unmoved: "Don't worry about divisiveness," he wrote in a note to himself. "Having drawn the sword don't take it out—stick it in hard. Hit them in the gut."

On the afternoon of May 4, Nixon was sitting alone in his hideaway office in the Executive Office Building adjacent to the White House when H. R. Haldeman stepped in. He looked "agitated," Nixon recalled. Haldeman said he had just read over the wires that the National Guard had opened fire on student protestors at Kent State University in Ohio.

The president paled. "Are they dead?" he asked.

Haldeman said he was afraid so. Nixon was "very disturbed," Haldeman noted in his diary. "Afraid his decision set it off, and that it is the ostensible cause of the demonstrations there. . . . [He] kept after me all the rest of the day for more facts. Hoping rioters had provoked the shooting, but no real evidence they did, except throwing rocks at the National Guard. Talked a lot about how we can get through to the students, turn this stuff off."

In his memoirs, Nixon would write that "those few days after Kent State were amongst the darkest of my presidency." He couldn't stop thinking about his own daughters and the dead students' grieving parents, he wrote. But at the time he issued an official statement startling in its coldness: "This should remind us all once again that when dissent turns to violence it invites tragedy."

The facts of what had happened emerged slowly. Two evenings earlier in Kent, Ohio, a large throng of young people—

ABOVE National Guardsmen with bayoneted rifles stand by as the ROTC building in Kent, Ohio, goes up in flames, May 2, 1970. A small group of militants had set the blaze, but thousands of students turned out to watch the fire, and some hurled rocks at the guardsmen.

most of them Kent State students, some motivated by anger at the president's speech, many simply full of beer and irate when local police closed all the downtown bars early—ran through the downtown streets breaking forty-seven store windows and injuring a policeman. The mayor, alarmed at what was happening and persuaded that the SDS was somehow behind the disturbance, called the Republican governor, Jim Rhodes, and asked him to send in the National Guard.

Guardsmen arrived the next evening—too late to stop a crowd from setting the ROTC building on fire—and moved onto the campus, where they forbade any "gathering"—by

ABOVE A student throws back a tear gas grenade on the Kent State University campus on the morning of May 4. The National Guard commander had urged them, "For your own safety, go to your homes and dorms." The students felt they *were* home, that it was the guardsmen who were out of place. "Pigs off campus!" they shouted.

which, one officer said, they meant any group larger than three persons. Governor Rhodes came to Kent, too. Locked in a close senatorial primary race, he saw in the town's troubles an opportunity to out-tough-talk his opponent. Radical outside agitators were to blame, he said. They were "worse than the Brown Shirts and the Communist elements . . . we are going to eradicate the problem. We are not going to treat the symptoms."

On Monday morning, some three thousand students were gathered on the Commons. Some were simply moving from class to class. Others planned to attend a rally called to protest Nixon's widening of the war and the presence of the National Guard on campus. The guardsmen's weapons were loaded with live ammunition, though no one in the crowd knew it. The students were ordered to disperse. They stood their ground. Tear gas scattered some of them. Others gave the troops the finger. One waved a black anarchist flag.

The guardsmen seemed to fall back. But then, members of

Troop G wheeled around and opened fire on students gathered in and around a parking lot. Sixty-seven rounds in thirteen seconds killed two young women and two young men, one of whom had been an ROTC scholarship student and had simply been an onlooker. Nine more students were wounded; one was permanently paralyzed.

Several hundred angry, grieving students sat down and demanded to know why the guardsmen had fired on their friends. An officer ordered them to "disperse or we will shoot again." Only the anguished pleas of geology professor Glenn Frank averted further tragedy. "I am begging you right now," he told the students, his voice breaking. "If you don't disperse right now, they're going to move in, and it can only be a slaughter. Would you please listen to me? Jesus Christ. I don't want to be a part of this." The crowd melted away.

The father of one dead girl was quoted as saying, "my child is not a bum." During the days that followed, more than four mil-

lion college students all across the country would demonstrate against the war. Four hundred and forty-eight campuses closed down.

Tim O'Brien had served his time in Vietnam, come home, and was living in St. Paul, Minnesota. "There was a huge march after the Kent State shootings," he recalled, "and I joined the march, just as a body, not a leader. I wasn't vocal at all. But I just wanted to put my body amidst these hundred thousand. That same march I was doing in Vietnam—that had seemed senseless and purposeless and without direction—here it felt sensible and purposeful and with direction, heading for that state capitol to say 'No.'"

ABOVE G Troop opens fire. The mystery of who ordered them to do so has never been solved. "Everything happened so fast," one of the guardsmen remembered. "It was like a car wreck."

"I was so angered by what had happened, I felt so alienated from my own government," Bill Zimmerman recalled. He was then between jobs and living in Boston. "In retrospect I know the government didn't order the execution . . . but at the time it certainly looked as though we had evolved to a point where the government was ready to kill protesting students. And that so outraged me I joined another antiwar demonstration, in Cambridge this time. Several people threw Molotov cocktails into the ROTC building, and I was a member of the crowd holding the cops and the firemen off so the building would burn. We failed. Eventually, they were able to save the building. Obviously, burning down a building wasn't going to stop the war and it wasn't going to gum up the war machine. But having just seen those kids killed at Kent State, we felt we had to do something to respond and the ROTC building was a target of opportunity. That's how we reacted. It wasn't strategic, it was emotional."

The ROTC offices at Northwestern might have burned, too, but for the intervention of a student leader. Professor Sam Hynes remembering stepping out of the library a day or two after Kent State and "looking across a meadow that lay in front of the library called Deering Meadow. There was this little bump on Deering Meadow. You wouldn't call it a hill anywhere except in Cook County. But we called it a hill. And on top of the hill students and faculty members had set up a microphone

and loudspeakers. And there was a professor, a young professor of mathematics, as I remember, who was haranguing the audience in a speech full of obscenities to show how passionate he was about this issue. And suddenly along the back of the crowd opposite where I was, a line of people appeared. They were all carrying flaming torches and chanting, 'Burn the ROTC. Burn the ROTC.'"

Eva Jefferson saw them, too. The African American Air Force officer's daughter who had entered college uninterested in the Vietnam War, and convinced her government would never lie, was now the student body president. "There were never mass demonstrations at Northwestern," she remembered. "That just never happened. I really think it was because kids had been murdered. We wanted to be peaceful; we wanted to be very militant about thinking the war was wrong; we wanted to say killing kids was bad. But we also didn't want the buildings burned down."

OPPOSITE Mary Ann Vecchio, a fourteen-year-old runaway from Florida who happened to be visiting the campus, screams in horror as Kent State student Jeffrey Miller lies dying on the ground. "His life was running down the sidewalk—running, just kept flowing," another student remembered. "And there was nothing to be done." **ABOVE** Students at Louisiana State University in Baton Rouge protest the killings. More than one-third of the nation's college students boycotted classes that spring.

"Eva Jefferson was up there on the mound in charge of this whole thing," Sam Hynes remembered, "and she simply took the microphone away from the professor and said calmly, 'Proctors, would you go out and put those torches out?'" Jefferson herself remembered things slightly differently, but the impact of her words was the same. "Now I can hardly believe that I did this," she recalled, "but I said something to the effect of, 'These torches remind me of other times and other places. Please do not burn the building down.' And they stopped."

For some veterans home from the war, the Kent State killings awakened memories they'd tried to forget. Former Marine Corporal Bill Ehrhart was now a student at Swarthmore College, near his hometown in eastern Pennsylvania, when he saw the Pulitzer Prize–winning photograph that showed a girl howling in anguish as a student bled to death in the Kent State parking lot. "I just looked at this thing," he recalled. "And I came unglued. I don't know how long I sat down on the curb. I don't know if I was there for fifteen minutes or an hour and a half. Just had a breakdown. Just crying, sobbing uncontrollably. All I could think was it's not enough to send us halfway around the world to die, now they're killing us in the streets of our own country. I have to do something. And finally, when I finally cried myself out, I got up and I joined the antiwar movement."

John Musgrave was still attending Baker University when he heard what had happened "I thought, my God, we're killing our

ABOVE Eva Jefferson, student body president at Northwestern University, pleads for calm in the aftermath of Kent State.

own children now," he recalled. "We've really gone mad. That's when I was hiding from things. I wasn't in anybody's movement then. I was just drinking. But that was one of the things that told me America needed a wake-up call."

The administration braced for trouble. The New MOBE, a hastily thrown together coalition of antiwar groups, called for a mass protest in Washington on Saturday May 9. Tens of thousands of demonstrators were expected. Truckloads of National Guardsmen were spirited into the basements of government buildings in case there was violence. Buses again encircled the White House; security officials feared that demonstrators were planning to jump the fence so they could be martyred on the lawn.

On Friday evening, the president sought to defuse things by holding a press conference in the East Room. Twenty-four of the twenty-six questions he answered had to do with Cambodia and the student protests. He was sweating and visibly unsettled. He claimed that the incursion had bought six or eight months for the South Vietnamese to further strengthen their forces, pledged that all U.S. troops would be pulled out before long, and said that he shared the demonstrators' desire for peace—but that if he were to do what they wanted and withdraw from Vietnam, the communists would "massacre the civilians there by the millions."

Then he retired to the residence, where, "agitated and uneasy," as he said himself, and fortified by Scotch, he made forty-seven telephone calls, including seven to H. R. Haldeman and eleven to Henry Kissinger. He went to bed, couldn't sleep, and suddenly announced at 4:22 a.m. that he wanted to show the Lincoln Memorial to his valet, Manolo Sanchez. The Secret Service scrambled to organize a limousine. Aides rushed to catch up with it. So did the president's physician.

Students in sleeping bags around the memorial woke to find the thirty-seventh president of the United States among them. He told them he could understand their hatred of the war—he had himself once been "as close to being a pacifist as anybody could be"—but that he hoped that hatred "would not turn into a bitter hatred of our whole system, our country, and everything it stood for."

"I hope you realize we are willing to die for what we believe in," one student said. He did, Nixon answered, but "we [are] trying to [build] a world in which you will not have to die for what you believe in, in which you are able to *live* for it."

Then, leaving the startled demonstrators behind, Nixon and Sanchez drove to the Capitol building, where the president led his valet onto the House floor, then moved on again to have breakfast at the Mayflower Hotel before reluctantly heading back to the besieged White House.

"Very weird," Haldeman wrote that night. "P. completely

FEARMONGERS

In the aftermath of Kent State, President Nixon appointed William Scranton, the former Republican governor of Pennsylvania, to head the presidential Commission on Campus Unrest. "Don't let higher education off with a pat on the ass," Nixon told Scranton; instead of giving in to student protestors, he said, "faculties should toss them out." Nixon saw the commission primarily as a public relations ploy: he wanted open hearings, he told Haldeman, "because it keeps the student unrest issue alive through the summer and works to our advantage." And he wanted to be sure "some really horrible types testify."

But Scranton took the job seriously. Among the witnesses he called was Eva Jefferson, the president of the Northwestern student body who, during the strike on her campus after Kent State, had kept other students from setting fire to the ROTC building. Radical friends had told her not to bother testifying; they said it would simply legitimize a government inquiry. But she had come anyway, she said, because she felt "that we have to keep trying to get our voices heard." If change didn't come, if the commission made solid recommendations and the administration did not act on them, she warned, "you are going to radicalize people. . . . People are going to see more and more that they can't get anything done through the system . . . and the only way the system is going to move . . . is to blow up buildings."

Her earnest eloquence caught the public's attention, and in September, David Frost invited Eva Jefferson and Vice President Agnew to appear together on his television program.

Agnew, in the midst of a countrywide congressional campaign in which he sought to paint the antiwar movement as dangerously radical, saw an opportunity

to accuse Jefferson of having encouraged violence.

She would have none of it. "What I attempted to do before the Scranton Committee," she said, "was to explain what could motivate someone to blow up a building. I did not say I endorse this, and if you read my testimony quite carefully, you'll know that I didn't. And it's this type of just picking up on what allegedly I said instead of really studying what I said, that really disturbs me. . . . You're making people afraid of their own children. Yet they're your children, they're my parents' children, they're the children of this country. . . . There's an honest difference of agreement on issues, but when you make people afraid of each other, you isolate people. Maybe this is your goal. But I think this can only have a disastrous effect on the country."

"Let me say first that isolating people is not my goal," Agnew responded. "If that were true, I wouldn't be here tonight. . . . Let me take exception to that oft-repeated rationale that violence is the only way to get results."

Jefferson did not back down: "I was trying to explain to you the rationale

of some students who are openly revolutionary," she answered. "You're not listening to what I'm saying."

Agnew wasn't interested in listening. "Dividing the American people has been my main contribution to the national political scene," he once boasted. "I not only plead guilty to this charge, but I am somewhat flattered."

"Nixon and Agnew hoped to politically benefit from making us out to be these scary, horrible, violent people," Jefferson remembered many years later. "We weren't. We were against the war. We thought the war was wrong. We thought we were lied to. And we were in the streets. America has always had a rich tradition of protests. We were founded by protesting England. So to make people afraid of their kids I think was wrong. But that's what they were about. They were fearmongers."

ABOVE Spiro Agnew. Antiwar leaders, he said, were "political hustlers . . . who would tell us our values are lies" and "If, in challenging them we polarize the American people, I say it is time for a *positive polarization*. . . . It is time to rip away the rhetoric and divide on authentic lines."

beat and just rambling on. I'm concerned about his condition. The decision, the speech, the aftermath, killings, riots, press, etc., the press conference, the student confrontation have all taken their toll, and he has had very little sleep for a long time and his judgment, temper and mood suffer badly."

THE TIME HAS COME
TO DRAW THE LINE

ON MAY 6, three days before the president's early-morning visit to the Lincoln Memorial, a small group of medical students had gathered in Battery Park at Manhattan's southern tip to protest the war and the Kent State shootings. One of them entered a nearby construction site and tore down an American flag the steelworkers had set up there to express their solidarity with the administration. "The steelworkers piled out . . . and pitched into [the students]," one eyewitness remembered. "Several were beaten up, though nothing much about it got into the papers."

That same afternoon, another group of students marched up Broadway toward city hall, chanting as they walked: "One, two, three, four, we don't want your fucking war."

Pete Hamill, a columnist for the *New York Post,* reported what some onlookers had to say: "'Listen to their language,' said a 40-ish man in a wrinkled suit standing next to me. 'Those goddam bums *should* be shot, I wish to Christ I was in the National Guard.' 'What would you do?' I asked him. 'Shoot them, mow them down. If they don't like this country let them go back to goddamned Russia.'"

From a building at the corner of Maiden Lane, steelworkers rained beer cans and clumps of asphalt down on the marchers. Hamill asked the police officer in charge of the parade's escort why he wasn't sending his men up to make arrests. "Don't worry about it," the officer answered, indicating the marchers, "these bums don't respect anything."

The angry onlookers and the hostile policeman were not alone. Despite the invasion of Cambodia, despite the killings at Kent State and the countrywide student demonstrations that had followed them, the president's approval rating had actually risen, and fully half the country approved of the Cambodian operation. A Gallup poll showed that 58 percent of those responding blamed the students for what had happened at Kent State; only 11 percent blamed the guardsmen. Residents of Kent filled the local newspaper with letters commending the National Guard and condemning the students: they were "surly, foul-mouthed, know-nothing punks," one letter writer said. "Live ammuni-

tion!" another wrote. "Well, really, what did they expect, spitballs?" The parents of the dead ROTC student received a flood of mail from strangers suggesting that "the police and army [should] kill a lot *more* students," that they should be grateful their boy was dead since he'd been "just another communist." Eventually, an Ohio grand jury would hand down twenty-five indictments, mostly Kent State students and not a single guardsman.

On May 8, demonstrators had returned to Lower Manhattan. Perhaps one thousand young people, mostly from New York University and Hunter College, gathered in the morning at Broad and Wall Streets to hear speakers call for an immediate withdrawal of American troops from Vietnam and Cambodia. Around noon, some two hundred construction workers wearing hard hats and carrying wrenches and steel bars, some wrapped in American flags, suddenly appeared and closed in from four sides, chanting, "All the way, USA," and "Love it or leave it!"

Some steelworkers later said they'd been offered a bonus by their bosses if they would "break some heads"; Mayor John Lindsay would blame Peter J. Brennan, the president of the New York Building and Construction Trades Council, for the violence that followed, and there were hints that White House aides may have been involved behind the scenes as well. But the men needed little urging. "A lot of these guys feel they have legitimate grievances," one witness explained. "They are almost the only segment of the population government hasn't paid much attention to. People whom they feel beneath them, the blacks and Puerto Ricans, for instance, demonstrate and get attention. The college kids, the more violent of them, spit on the flag and burn buildings; others demonstrate and cause upheavals and they, too, get attention. These construction men got the feeling they were in a kind of limbo, with nobody paying much attention to them. Obviously, there is a lot of frustration here."

"Don't try and fight them," one protestor said when he realized the rally was surrounded by hard hats. "The police are here to protect us."

But they didn't protect them. Instead, most stood back and watched while the workers charged into the crowd, beating men and women alike. Watching from the windows above, office workers cheered and threw streams of ticker tape and data-processing punch cards.

More hard hats poured into the area, many from the site of the new Twin Towers. They ripped down the Red Cross flag from historic Trinity Church, where injured students were being treated at an impromptu first-aid station, invaded two dormitories at Pace University, beating students and smashing windows, and stormed into city hall demanding that the American flag, flying at half-staff by order of Mayor Lindsay as part of a "Day of Reflection," be hauled back up again.

When an assistant to the mayor tried to stop a steelworker from attacking a student who was already being beaten by three other workers, she remembered, "He yelled at me, 'Let go of my jacket, bitch'; and then he said, 'If you want to be treated like an equal, we'll treat you like one.' Three of them began to punch me in the body. My glasses were broken. I had trouble breathing, and I thought my ribs were cracked." Some seventy demonstrators were treated for injuries, some of them serious.

A few days later, Peter Brennan called for a mass rally to "show our support for our country and our boys in Asia," meant to "let anti-Americans know where the construction workers stand." Almost every construction site in the city closed down so that more than 100,000 hard hats, along with longshoremen, tradesmen, and office workers, could march up Broadway beneath a forest of American flags.

"Thank God for the hard hats," Nixon said, and invited the rally's leaders to the White House, where they presented him with a flag pin and a hard hat. Later, he would make Peter Brennan his secretary of labor.

The antiwar demonstration in Washington on May 9 had drawn somewhere between fifty thousand and seventy-five thousand people, mostly young, mostly peaceful. Peaceful demonstrations took place in other cities, too. But there was arson at campuses all across the country that day—Colorado State and Long Island University, the University of Iowa and the University of Michigan, East Carolina University and Concordia Teachers College in River Forest, Illinois.

Two hundred and eighty-one ROTC buildings had been attacked during the first six months of the year; an average of four had been set ablaze every day since the Cambodian incursion began. According to the Treasury Department, between January 1, 1969, and mid-April 1970, there had been 4,330 bombings in the United States and another 1,475 attempted bombings, most employing Molotov cocktail–style incendiaries as well as explosives. Perpetrators ranged from gangsters

ABOVE Manhattan construction workers rush antiwar demonstrators on Wall Street, May 8, 1970. Peter Brennan, the head of their union, praised his men. "They did it because they were fed up with violence by antiwar demonstrators, by those who spat on the American flag."

ABOVE Tens of thousands of building trades workers march on New York's city hall to show their support for the war, and call for the impeachment of Mayor John Lindsay because he had lowered the flag to half-staff after the killings at Kent State, May 20, 1970.

and Klansmen to African American extremists and right-wing Minutemen, but more than half of the bombings that had been solved stemmed from campus disorders.

Like his predecessor in the White House, Richard Nixon was convinced that foreign agents—Russian, Cuban, North Vietnamese, he wasn't sure which—were behind much of the American opposition to the war. And, like Johnson, he was furious when no American intelligence agency seemed able to come up with the evidence to prove him right. On June 5, he called in the heads of all the U.S. spy agencies—the FBI, CIA, NSA, and military intelligence—and, as one of them recalled, "chewed our butts." Then he presented a plan, drawn up by a zealous young aide named Tom Charles Huston, that would give the White House control over all intelligence gathering and officially sanction all manner of illicit activity, including warrantless wiretaps, the opening of private mail, and "black bag jobs"—surreptitious break-ins to install taps and bugs on people the White House deemed dangerous. The FBI was already doing most of those unlawful things—and more—under a draconain program called COINTELPRO, while the CIA was illegally opening mail under its own Operation Chaos.

J. Edgar Hoover, the longtime head of the FBI, pronounced the plan unworkable—largely because it would have undermined his own authority. Attorney General John Mitchell thought it was unnecessary. The president reluctantly withdrew it. But his frustration with antiwar demonstrators did not subside. "We have to find out who controls them," he told an aide. "Get our guys to rough them up at demonstrations."

On June 30, the president announced that the last American soldiers had pulled out of Cambodia; South Vietnamese troops would remain there for another three weeks. He assured the country that it had been "the most successful operation of this long and difficult war," but its results were actually mixed. Sixteen million rounds of ammunition had been seized; so had 45,000 rockets, 62,000 grenades, 3,000 individual weapons, and 14 million pounds of rice. Almost 12,000 bunkers were destroyed and 16,000 acres of jungle cleared. The important port of Sihanoukville was closed; the North would now have to move its heavy weapons down the Ho Chi Minh Trail instead of trucking them overland to communist base camps. Because it would force North Vietnam to take months to rebuild its Cambodian bases, the operation also secured precious time for Saigon to strengthen its forces, but it did not secure South Vietnam's western border and enemy forces were soon slipping back and forth across it just as they always had. Communist agents had forewarned the enemy. Both COSVN and the jungle capital of the new Provisional Government managed to slip away northward while communist troops fled eastward and Hanoi resolved to provide far greater support for the Khmer Rouge, expanding a civil war that would eventually lead to one of the worst genocides of the twentieth century.

The incursion had alarmed America's allies abroad: a secret poll taken by the U.S. Information Service in four European and four Asian countries showed that American prestige had fallen alarmingly in recent weeks. And it had galvanized the growing opposition on Capitol Hill. On June 30, the Senate had voted 58–37 to bar further funding for Americans fighting in Cambodia without congressional approval. It was a largely symbolic gesture—the last U.S. troops had already withdrawn across the border back into South Vietnam, and the House would vote the measure down a few days later—but it represented the first time either chamber had voted to limit a commander in chief's war-making power.

On August 24, four antiwar protestors set off a bomb intended to destroy the Army Math Research Center at the University of Wisconsin. It killed a postdoctoral student named Robert Fassnacht and injured four other people, none of whom had anything to do with that institution. Eight days later, Senator George McGovern made an impassioned speech on the Senate floor in favor of an amendment to an appropriations bill he and Republican Senator Mark Hatfield of Oregon had introduced, setting December 31, 1971, as the final date for U.S. withdrawal from Vietnam. "Every senator in this chamber is partly responsible for sending fifty thousand Americans to an early grave," he said. "This chamber reeks of blood. . . . Do not talk about bugging out, or national honor, or courage. It does not take any courage at all for a congressman, or a senator, or a president to wrap himself in the flag and say we are staying in Vietnam because it is not our blood that is being shed. . . . So before we vote, let us ponder the admonition of Edmund Burke, the great parliamentarian of an earlier day: 'A conscientious man would be cautious how he dealt in blood.'"

Nixon warned the senators that if they tied his hands the responsibility for "an ignominious American defeat" would be theirs, and the amendment was defeated 55–39—but a Gallup poll taken three weeks later showed that well over half the American people had supported it. It was clear that the president had begun to run out of support on Capitol Hill—just "one step ahead of the sheriff," he said.

Nixon had hoped that his apparent willingness to widen the war and the damage the Cambodian incursion would do to the enemy's logistical base would force concessions from Hanoi. They did not. Instead, facing congressional elections that fall, Nixon would feel the need to make an important concession of his own. He had already begun to withdraw thousands of U.S. troops without the reciprocal North Vietnamese withdrawal upon which he'd once insisted. Now he called for a ceasefire in place and a total halt on U.S. bombing throughout all of Indochina as a first step toward peace. The Senate adopted a resolution that called the president's new initiative "fair and equitable." President Thieu was alarmed; he thought his steadily strengthening forces would eventually be able to eliminate the NLF but doubted they could ever defeat the combined communist forces. It didn't matter: Hanoi rejected the proposal the next day.

Meanwhile, Nixon was preoccupied by the upcoming congressional elections. The president who had urged Americans to "lower our voices" was now determined to do all he could to raise them. He wanted both to add to Republican numbers in Congress and to defeat candidates in both parties who criticized his conduct of the war.

The vice president was to be the tip of the spear. Agnew was "the perfect spokesman to reach the silent majority," Nixon said, and advance men were instructed to make sure demonstrators—

preferably waving NLF flags—could get close enough to him to anger the "disaffected Democrats, . . . blue-collar workers . . . and working-class white ethnics" Nixon hoped to win over. "If an egg is thrown and hits the vice president—all the better," the president said. "If the vice president were slightly roughed up by those thugs, nothing better could happen for our cause." And "if anybody so much as brushes against Mrs. Agnew, tell her to fall down."

Nixon himself campaigned in ten states and in San Jose, California, on October 29, seemed to take his own advice. A big hostile crowd gathered outside the municipal auditorium in which he was speaking and began banging on the closed doors. "We wanted some confrontation and there were no hecklers in the hall," Haldeman wrote in his diary that evening, "so we stalled the departure a little so they could zero in outside and they sure did." Leaving the auditorium, the president stepped up onto the hood of his limousine and raised his arms in the "V" sign he'd learned from President Eisenhower and had made his own. "That's what they hate to see!" he told an aide. It "made them mad," Haldeman continued. "They threw rocks, flags, candles, etc., as we drove out, after a terrifying flying wedge of cops opened up the road." Nixon seemed delighted. "So far as I know," he wrote, "this was the first time in our history

that a mob had physically attacked the President of the United States."

Nixon ended the campaign with a harsh assault on the anti-war movement: "Let's recognize these people for what they are. They are not romantic revolutionaries. They are the same thugs and hoodlums that have always plagued the good people. . . . For too long, and this needs to be said and said now and here, the strength of freedom in our society has been eroded by a creeping permissiveness in our legislatures, in our courts, in our family life, and in our colleges and universities. For too long, we have appeased aggression here at home, and, as with all appease-ment, the result has been more aggression and more violence. The time has come to draw the line."

In the end, drawing the line did not work. The Republicans picked up two seats in the Senate but lost nine in the House. Nixon's reaction was to double down. "Politics over the next two years is not a question of bringing in the blacks and liberal sena-tors and make them feel they are 'wanted,'" he told Haldeman. "It's going to be cold steel."

ABOVE Outside an auditorium in San Jose, California, President Nixon climbs onto his limousine and dares antiwar demonstrators to do their worst.

SEEING AMERICANS AGAIN

BY BAO NINH

FIRST VISITED the United States in the summer of 1998, when I was invited to attend a literary conference in Montana with four other Vietnamese writers. We flew from Hanoi to Taiwan to Los Angeles. As we crossed the Pacific Ocean, passing through many time zones, I buried myself in sleep and woke up only when the plane hit the tarmac. At passport control, we found ourselves in a huge hall, and I was abruptly taken aback: there were Americans all around us, lots of them! I will never forget that strange feeling. It was bizarre, unbelievable, surreal, that I, a veteran of the Vietnam People's Army, was in the United States, surrounded by Americans.

The first time I ever saw Americans was when I was twelve years old. It wasn't actually blond-haired, blue-eyed Americans that I was seeing up close. The Americans I saw that day were F-4 Phantom bombers, brutally attacking small towns on the shore of Ha Long Bay. It was August 5, 1964, and I was at the beach on a school trip, swimming with my classmates. That was right after the Tonkin Gulf incident, the day American President Lyndon B. Johnson announced his decision to expand the war throughout Vietnam.

After that day my life, the lives of my parents, brothers and sisters, the lives of all Vietnamese, were completely turned upside down. From then on, we lived under a sky that was almost always ablaze with the roar of jets, bomb blasts, and sirens. Bomb shelters were dug along all the streets and beneath every house in Hanoi. Electricity and running water were in short supply. We dimmed the lights at night. Food, clothing and fuel, paper, books, and other necessities of life were rationed, but there wasn't enough of anything to meet the needs of the people. There were long lines outside stores. Children sixteen and younger were evacuated to the countryside, separated from their parents. It was not so different from the experiences of British children in London in 1940, but the children of Hanoi endured all of this much longer—from 1964 to 1973—and our life during wartime was tougher.

My family was originally from Dong Hoi, a small town in central Vietnam so flower-filled it was called "the Town of Roses." In 1946, most of my extended family moved to Nghe An, in North Vietnam, where I was born in 1952. In 1954, after the Geneva Accords, my parents moved to Hanoi. In the early days of the bombing, our village of Dong Hoi was almost completely leveled; all that remained was the charred wall of our church and the tower of a water reservoir. Bombs and artillery from the American Seventh Fleet killed thirty-two people in my extended family in 1965 alone.

Still, as far as I can remember, in spite of the death and destruction, people did not seem demoralized. Contrary to what the Pentagon expected, the relentless bombing motivated many of us to join the military. I wanted to sign up in September 1969, a few months before my eighteenth birthday. Why? I wanted to fight foreign aggression, to be an honorable man, and to be a good citizen. My parents urged me to go to college and refused to sign the form to permit me to enlist at seventeen. But I was determined, and in the end, they gave in. My mother cried when she signed the papers.

By then the war had already been going on for five years, and the level of violence was at its peak. In 1969, no one in Hanoi really believed what the official government propaganda had been telling us about the war. When I volunteered, I had no illusions about my fate. I was not brave or fast or especially creative. I was not a warrior. I knew I had little chance of surviving. Nevertheless, regardless of whatever happened to me, I was sure that the Vietnamese people would defeat any aggressor, and that we would reunify the country. I didn't think we would win a victory like my father's generation had at Dien Bien Phu, and I also understood that the Americans were many times stronger than the French. But I strongly believed, as did most of my comrades, what President Ho had told us many times—that eventually the United States would give up and go home.

In January 1970, after three months of boot camp, where we were taught to use AK-47s, RPGs, and hand grenades, our unit set off on the long march down the Ho Chi Minh Trail to the Central Highlands. We arrived in Kon Tum in May and were dispersed to different combat units. I was assigned to the Tenth Division, Battalion Two, directly under the Board of Commanders of B3 Front. (In 1973, I was transferred to Battalion Five, Regiment Twenty-four, and served there until the end of the war.) The enemies we faced in the Central Highlands when I was there were the Twenty-second and Twenty-third South Vietnamese Divisions and the American Fourth Infantry and First Air Cavalry Divisions.

In 1970, when Richard Nixon began Vietnamization, which many mockingly said would change only "the skin color of the corpses," the United States gradually reduced the number of their troops in our country. But the fierceness of the war did not diminish in the slightest, nor did the American presence on the battlefield. Every minute, every hour, it seemed, they were there, flying ten thousand meters above the earth in B-52s and pouring bombs down on us, raining 105mm, 155mm, and 175mm artillery shells on us from miles away. A single B-52 attack or artillery barrage could level a mountain, fill a river with mud, turn a rain forest to ash. I was a scout and rarely had the chance to exchange fire directly with American soldiers. Instead, I mostly observed them from afar through my binoculars. But I did regularly see some Americans at close range—the crews of armed helicopters. Our troops exchanged fire with them daily as they clung to the doors of their Cobras and Hueys and fired machine guns at us. The OH-6 scout helicopters were easiest to spot. They flew just over the tops of trees and hovered a couple of meters above our hiding places. The crews fired their M16s or threw grenades at us, taking the chance that we might shoot them down with our AK-47s or submachine guns. Those adept and courageous fighters sometimes flew so low we could see their faces and make out the color of their hair, sometimes even their eyes.

The last time I caught sight of American combat troops close up, on the ground, was late one morning in April 1971, near An Khe Pass. I saw a platoon of airborne troops on patrol on Highway 19. They seemed relaxed, not particularly cautious, walking down the road in single file, skirting the edge of their base. They didn't know there were three of us scouts silently following their every move, monitoring them from behind thick camouflage on a hill about one hundred meters off the road, and they had absolutely no idea that a strongly armed NVA unit was waiting for them at the bend of the road half a kilometer ahead. To this day, I see them clearly in my mind, as if they were right in front of me. I especially remember a radio operator carrying a PRC-25 backpack radio. I can't understand why as radio operator he wasn't beside the company commander, but instead was pulling up the rear, trailing behind the group. He seemed nonchalant, with no bulletproof vest, no helmet, no M16 or grenade launcher, just the radio on his back. He had short brown hair, no beard or moustache. Through my binoculars I saw that he was chewing something, probably gum. He was just ambling along, kicking an empty Coke can as he walked. Fifteen minutes later the sound of gunfire told me his platoon had walked into our ambush.

I never found out what happened to that radio man, have no idea whether he made it or not. In 1998, during my first trip to the United States, whenever I was visiting a university or high school and saw young boys and girls in auditoriums and hanging out on the lawns, I would see again the face of that young soldier, hear the clatter of that empty Coke can on the road. He was just like a kid on the way home to his mother after school, playing with whatever he happened to come across.

It's been a long time, but I still have nightmares from the war. I still hear the hiss of hundreds of bombs being dropped from B-52s, the roar of artillery barrages and the thrum of the helicop-

ters' rotors. I still see platoons of American Marines in bulletproof vests and helmets jumping out of Chinooks, brandishing their M16s. Worst of all, I can't forget the dreadful nightmare of dioxin. In the spring of 1971, when we were stationed west of Kon Tum, we were sprayed repeatedly with Agent Orange. I didn't know if the Americans on those C-123 Caribous knew anything about the terrible toxicity of the liquid they sprayed, or if only the chemical companies that manufactured it knew. We understood all too well its horrible destructive force. As soon as the Caribous passed over us, the sky would turn dark with a strange, thick, milky rain. The jungle canopy broke apart, ulcerated, and fell to the ground. Leaves, flowers, fruits, even twigs, all silently dropped. Green leaves turned black, crumpled. Grass withered and died. I witnessed many cruel scenes in the war, but that brutal massacre of nature is what comes back to me most often and disturbs my sleep.

The last time I saw Americans was in the final days of the war. We had advanced deep into Saigon and made it almost all the way to Tan Son Nhut airport. The Americans I saw in April 1975, like the ones I first saw in August 1964, were in the air, flying above us in F-4 Phantoms. But this time, they were covering the retreat of all remaining American military, civilian, and diplomatic personnel from South Vietnam. The last American was evacuated from Saigon in the early morning of April 30, 1975, and by noon the Saigon regime announced its surrender. The brutal war that had seemed for so long as if it would never end was finally over.

My unit stayed in Saigon for a few weeks, until mid-May 1975, and then we were sent back to the Central Highlands, given the task of searching for the bodies of our comrades who had been killed, and collecting their remains. At the end of that year, after six years in the South, I went home. I don't know the overall survival statistics, but out of the twenty-five boys from my high school who went to war, eleven were killed. Of the three young men from my apartment building in Hanoi who enlisted with me, I was the only one to return.

Now, twenty-three years after I made it back home, I was seeing Americans. I will never forget the days we spent in the large university auditorium at the conference in Missoula, Vietnamese and American veteran writers sitting side by side, discussing our countries' literatures, sharing our work. Literature really does have its own magic. In Missoula I heard for the first time the famous verses of Henry Wadsworth Longfellow's "The Arrow and the Song," translated into Vietnamese and read for us by the poet Nguyen Duc Mau. Longfellow's words resonated beautifully with the conference's atmosphere: friendship, love of life, and peace. In the same spirit, Professor Philip West, the director of the Mansfield Center, read an English translation of "Visit to Khan Xuan Temple" by the

Vietnamese poet Ho Xuan Huong. *Tranquil afternoon of spring on pavilion site. Light in heart and clear in mind.* The verses of the Vietnamese poet, a nineteenth-century contemporary of Longfellow's, sounded to me like music, soaring into the peaceful Missoula air. Although I did not speak English, I could still feel the spirit of the poems the Americans had written and were reading to us. When I met those writers, I tried my best to keep my astonishment to myself. Was Kevin Bower, this quiet man with a warm friendly smile who's squeezing my hand, really a machine gunner in the First Air Cavalry Division in An Khe? What could novelist Larry Heinemann have in common with a combat soldier in the Twenty-fifth Tropical Lightning Division who fought in the bloody battles in Tay Ninh? How could Bruce Weigl, the author of such romantic verse, be a soldier who had helped relieve the horrific siege of Khe Sanh?

The conference also included veterans who came from all over Montana to witness the exchange of American and Vietnamese writers, and to see us, their former enemies. Marmon Momaday, a Native American Cheyenne, told me so when we shook hands. He'd been in the 173rd Airborne Brigade, and fought near Dak To. The sheriff of Missoula, Peter Lawrenson, served in Vietnam from 1970 to 1972 as an adviser to the ARVN in Kon Tum. When he found out I was a veteran of the Tenth NVA Division, which he had fought, he greeted me as a long-lost friend. During our time in Montana, Sheriff Lawrenson drove us around the state to Helena, Great Falls, Billings. In Missoula, we were taken to the memorial to soldiers who had been killed in Vietnam. It was a week after Memorial Day, and lots of people were still visiting the site. At the foot of the large stone slab engraved with names of the fallen, people had left some flowers, a postcard, a class picture, an old notebook or diary, a military compass, a 1966 issue of *Stars and Stripes,* a flask with two tiny glass cups, and a vintage Zippo lighter. There was also a birthday cake with candles on top. The Missoula memorial was much smaller than the Wall in Washington, D.C., but the sorrow and compassion it evoked in visitors was no different. Most, I assumed, probably knew the men whose names were carved into the stone, but there were also visitors from other places. I met a retired teacher and mistook her for the mother of a fallen soldier. My interpreter explained that she came from San Francisco, and had taught high school in Missoula for years. Whenever she returned, she would visit her "Tommy" at the memorial. He was one of her students, had graduated in 1970, and was immediately drafted. The next summer, his family received a death notice. He was killed less than a year after graduation. Why was his life so short? At eighteen, he had finished high school, become a soldier, and after six months of hard training, had boarded a plane with his friends, flown halfway around the world, landed somewhere in Vietnam, maybe Danang, put on a bulletproof vest and helmet, and taken a rifle to the battlefield. An inexperienced soldier, maybe he was killed in the first few minutes of his first battle. I wondered if that unfortunate student had been able to celebrate his nineteenth birthday, whether he had been in Vietnam long enough even to see the sun rise?

On that trip, we spent more than a month in America, traveling from Montana to Massachusetts, Rhode Island, New York City, and Washington, D.C. Everywhere we went, from the conference to meetings with publishers, bookstores, and readers, we were welcomed with open arms. The warmth and friendship of Americans toward us Vietnamese writers evoked my sympathy for the people and the country today, and made me think about the unjustness and cruelty of the war the United States had prosecuted in Vietnam twenty-five years earlier.

I was forty-six, and I understood very well the inexorable passage of time. As months and years passed, the war had steadily receded. It didn't seem to cast much of a shadow on daily life in America, or in Vietnam. The wounds it inflicted seemed mostly to have scarred over. But throughout my visit to America, the memories of the war that I had buried for so long came back, clearer and sharper than before. Even today, the war still comes back to me, spreads its wings over my daily life and my writing. Like anyone who has lived through war, I dream that future generations will one day be at peace, will abandon the weapons of war. But I know my dream is impossible. As a writer and especially as a veteran, I know that underneath the beautiful green meadows of peace are mountains of bones and ashes from previous wars, and, most awful to contemplate, the seeds of future wars.

My generation, the people who lived through the Vietnam War, learned a great deal from our miserable and tragic experience. I wonder whether the lessons we absorbed at such tremendous cost are being passed on to future generations? If they are not understood, or if they are forgotten, are we doomed to repeat the same mistakes, commit the same crimes, repeat the same disasters, spread the same sorrows?

CHAPTER NINE

A DISRESPECTFUL LOYALTY

JANUARY 1971–MARCH 1973

ARVN troops atop an armored personnel carrier, on their way into Laos on the first day of the second phase of Operation Lam Son 719, February 8, 1971

IT'S A WIN, SEE?

B Y EARLY 1971, Richard Nixon had been president for two years. The war he had promised to end quickly seemed no nearer to that goal. The Paris negotiations—both secret and public—remained deadlocked. The National Security Council reported that the United States could neither force North Vietnamese troops to leave South Vietnam nor persuade Hanoi to withdraw them at the negotiating table. The president's war-making powers were coming under attack on Capitol Hill. Antiwar sentiment was growing, and the presidential election was less than two years away.

Something new was needed, Nixon told an aide, "something dramatic in North Vietnam that will make the other side negotiate." He hoped that Laos would provide it. Despite the turmoil the Cambodian incursion had caused at home and the anxiety it had inspired among America's allies abroad, it had seriously weakened the enemy's ability to mount an offensive from within that country. But to compensate for the losses suffered there, the North Vietnamese had feverishly expanded and improved the Ho Chi Minh Trail, which threaded its way down through Laos to a series of base areas along the South Vietnamese border. It protected them with some twenty-two thousand ground troops and twenty antiaircraft battalions. Soon, six thousand combat troops were filing south each month.

To cut the trail at least for a time in order to stop them and to preempt the possibility of an offensive being launched from Laos—an offensive that might include an assault on Hue and would surely disrupt Vietnamization—Nixon ordered up another "incursion."

This time, South Vietnamese troops would have to do the fighting on their own. Over the strenuous objection of the administration, an amendment to the 1971 foreign aid authorization bill sponsored by Republican senator John Sherman Cooper of Kentucky and Frank Church, Democrat of Idaho, had become law the previous December. It barred the use of American ground troops in Laos or Cambodia. Not even the American advisers with whom ARVN units had fought could accompany them into combat in Laos. The U.S. could provide only air and artillery support.

The plan General Creighton Abrams drew up in consultation with General Cao Van Vien, chief of the Joint General Staff, was to be called Lam Son 719, after the site of a long-ago battle in which the Vietnamese defeated a Chinese army.

In late January, in an operation called Dewey Canyon II, a U.S. brigade would secure and repair Highway 9 up to the Lao-

tian border, reopen Khe Sanh as a forward operating base, and position artillery where it could best support South Vietnamese forces as they pushed into Laos.

In early February, after the Americans had prepared the way, Phase II would begin: South Vietnamese forces were to follow Highway 9 across the border, accompanied by B-52 strikes meant to safeguard their passage, and airborne troops, helicoptered in to establish firebases north and south of the road to protect their flanks. Their target was an enemy base area near a strategic junction of supply routes called Tchepone, some thirty-one miles inside Laos. When they reached the midpoint, helicopter-borne forces were to rush ahead to seize Tchepone and be waiting to link up with them as they advanced along the highway. Planners thought it would take no more than four or five days for everything to fall into place.

In Phase III, the ARVN were to spend nearly two months conducting operations near Tchepone and the area immediately south of it, seeking out and destroying massive stores of weapons and supplies said to be hidden there.

Finally, in mid-April—just before monsoon rains made movement down the Ho Chi Minh Trail virtually impossible— Phase IV would begin: a well-planned and orderly withdrawal that would leave elite commando units behind to harass the enemy.

Richard Helms, director of the CIA, favored the operation but warned that South Vietnamese troops were likely to "run into a very tough fight." Admiral Thomas Moorer, now chairman of the Joint Chiefs, agreed, but promised that it would be "the enemy's last gasp." Henry Kissinger told H. R. Haldeman that the incursion could "in effect end the war." Only Secretary of State William Rogers raised serious objections: the North Vietnamese had learned of the plan in advance; there was sure to be a serious battle; South Vietnamese forces had never faced such a severe test on their own; a defeat would do immeasurable harm to Vietnamization.

The president overruled him. "It was a splendid project on paper," Kissinger would later write. "We allowed ourselves to be carried away by the daring conception, by the unanimity of the responsible planners in both Saigon and Washington, by the memory of the success in Cambodia, and by the prospect of a decisive turn. . . . Its chief drawback, as events showed, was that it in no way accorded with Vietnamese realities."

OPPOSITE South Vietnamese infantry and tanks proceed warily along the grandly named Highway 9 into Laos. It was "a long, narrow, roller coaster of a road," one reporter wrote, "whose rising dust is white, then orange, sometimes dark brown; it cuts through elephant grass, bamboo trees, and nine-foot stalks topped by ostrich-like plumes, and is just wide enough for one truck to squeeze by another."

Phase I—the American portion—went smoothly, and on February 8, Phase II began as the head of a seemingly endless column of infantry, tanks, APCs, and other vehicles rumbled across the border, past a sign that read, "WARNING, NO U.S. PERSONNEL BEYOND THIS POINT."

Things almost immediately began to go wrong. Rain turned the dusty road into a slough and grounded the helicopters on which the ARVN depended for supplies. The enemy pounded the column from the hills on either side of the highway. Expected to pull back as they had in Cambodia, they stood and fought, instead. Three days in, the advance reached the midpoint to Tchepone and came to a halt. President Thieu had privately urged the overall commander, Lieutenant General Hoang Xuan Lam, to proceed with great caution; if he took three thousand casualties, he was to cancel the operation altogether. (Thieu was standing for reelection in the fall and may not have wanted high casualty figures to cut into his victory margin.)

The column proceeded no farther. Meanwhile, North Vietnamese reinforcements flooded into the area until seventeen thousand ARVN found themselves facing some sixty thousand enemy troops. The South Vietnamese lines of command remained unclear; some commanders refused to follow orders given by their superiors. One by one, the North Vietnamese attacked the isolated firebases north of the highway that were supposed to have shielded the now-stalled column. Their tactics were the same each time: they surrounded the ARVN positions, pounded them day and night with mortar, rockets, and artillery, and reduced aerial supply with antiaircraft fire. Poor communications compounded the problems the ARVN faced; until now, American air controllers had always communicated with American pilots in the air. But there were no Americans on the ground in Laos. South Vietnamese air controllers spoke little English. U.S. pilots spoke no Vietnamese. The result was often confusion and misdirected strikes.

For the most part, ARVN forces fought well, and they took a fearful toll of the enemy. But they were outnumbered and outgunned, and as the North Vietnamese advanced on their positions, often employing tanks as well as infantry, some men panicked.

Nixon was exasperated. "If the South Vietnamese could just win one cheap one," he complained to Kissinger on February 27. "Take a stinking hill . . . bring back a prisoner or two. Anything!"

Initially, the Laos incursion sparked less domestic dissent than its Cambodian predecessor had because no U.S. ground troops were involved, but it had an impact nonetheless. At 1:32 a.m. on March 1, an anonymous caller reached a Capitol Hill operator to warn her that the building would be blown up in thirty minutes: "Evacuate the building," the voice said. "This is in protest of the Nixon involvement in Laos." Half an hour later, a bomb went off in a men's room in the Senate wing. No one was injured. The Weather Underground claimed credit: "Our plans can be as creative and ingenious as the bamboo booby traps of the Vietnamese," their handout said.

That same day in Saigon, without warning, President Thieu informed General Abrams and Ambassador Ellsworth Bunker that he was changing the mission for his forces in Laos: instead of destroying the enemy's base, he now wanted simply to send an airborne force in to capture Tchepone, declare victory, and then pull out as fast as possible. "You go in there just long enough to take a piss and then leave quickly," he told General Lam. Although privately disappointed in the South Vietnamese performance on the battlefield, Nixon could understand the political value in Thieu's sudden change of plan: "It would be a great public relations coup if the ARVN actually reached Tchepone," he said, even if the abandoned village had no military significance.

Tran Ngoc Hue—"Harry Hue," to the Americans—who had led the elite Hac Bao company of the First ARVN Division during the battle for Hue, was now a major in command of the Second Battalion, Second ARVN Regiment, which, with the Third Battalion, was to lead the way to Tchepone. The night before the air assault was to begin, he had dinner with his U.S. adviser, Lieutenant Colonel David Wiseman. He had heard how badly things were going in Laos, he remembered, felt that he was unlikely to come back, and asked his American friend whether, if something happened to him, he could take care of his wife and children. Wiseman—who felt terrible that he was not able to go into combat with the men alongside whom he had been fighting—said he would.

The next morning, March 6, 120 helicopters assembled at Khe Sanh and took off in what was said to be the largest airmobile operation of the war. There was nothing left of Tchepone when they reached their target but ruined buildings and the corpses of enemy soldiers killed by U.S. bombs, but President Thieu called its capture "the biggest victory ever . . . a moral, political, and psychological Dien Bien Phu" for the enemy. Hue was promoted to lieutenant colonel on the spot for having helped to capture the campaign's new objective. He and his men spent three days searching for enemy supplies and were then ordered to join forces with ARVN troops at a fire support base south of Highway 9 and await orders to withdraw.

Thieu was calling an early end to Operation Lam Son 719.

Abrams was furious. He urged Thieu to send in another whole division. "The NVA must be stopped," he said, "and a major battle, which might even be the decisive battle of the war, must be won." Thieu wasn't interested.

Kissinger talked it over with President Nixon.

HENRY KISSINGER: My view is that politically . . . the North Vietnamese will flag this into a big victory if [the ARVN] leave, no matter how they leave, if they leave this quickly. And militarily we won't get everything [we'd hoped for] out of this operation. We'll get the caches, which are important, and the [enemy] casualties, but . . . if they could hang in there another three or four weeks, they're not under bad attack right now. What I think it is . . . is that Thieu wants to have a victory parade in Saigon and use it that way. Well, I don't think we should do anything. I don't think we should force them to stay. If they could stay, say, another month, . . . and then start slowly to withdraw, then . . . the rainy season will prevent any shipments. As it is now, they could probably make up in April what they lost in March. I think the strategic gain for us next year is worth some casualties this year. But we can't insist on it. We can't. . . .

RICHARD NIXON: No, no, we can't insist on it, particularly, Henry, because if we insist and they take a bang, they'll squeal.

KISSINGER: That's right. Absolutely. . . .

NIXON: Well, what is the situation? How bad is the [enemy] buildup? Is it . . . really hairy?

KISSINGER: That isn't the reason [they want to withdraw]. I think it's electoral politics. . . . I must tell you honestly, now that I've seen the operation, this South Vietnamese army is not as good as we all thought.

NIXON: Oh, I know that. . . . They're just fooling around. . . . We knew they weren't that good. . . . I would prefer they stay. I'm with you. But, Henry, I have become completely fatalistic about the goddamn thing. I don't think they're up to a real bang. I don't think they're up to it.

KISSINGER: That's what worries me.

NIXON: And if they're not up to it, I don't want them to

ABOVE North Vietnamese troops race past South Vietnamese dead to plant their flag on an ARVN firebase in Laos. Moments later, they would abandon it out of fear of U.S. bombers.

take a hell of a bang. I'd rather have them get out, and then we're going to get the hell out and hope and pray that nothing happens before 1972. Let's face it . . . if my reelection is important, let's remember, I've got to get this off our plate.

The South Vietnamese withdrawal will "kill us domestically," Kissinger had complained to Admiral Moorer. "If they had told us a week ago they were [going to begin pulling out] we could have said we have our victory."

The president planned to say that anyway. "The main thing, Henry, on Laos," he told Kissinger, "I can't emphasize too strongly: I don't care what happens there, it's a win. See? And everybody should talk about that."

DIGNITY

Army Doctor Hal Kushner had been a prisoner of the Viet Cong in South Vietnam for more than three years. He had survived ill-treatment and a host of illnesses, and had buried thirteen of his fellow captives who had died of starvation and sickness and despair.

Conditions within the camp had improved slightly in recent months. "We had finally become accustomed to the jungle," another prisoner remembered. "Canned goods had been added to our food ration. . . . Color was returning to our anemic-dull eyes." But then "with all this, it looked as though we were to be killed by our own bombs"—errant bombs from periodic U.S. air raids on a nearby North Vietnamese base camp. "We worried ourselves to sleep at night," another prisoner remembered, "contracting involuntarily like worms when a jet flew over."

On February 2, a flight of U.S. helicopters had suddenly filled the sky above the camp—six troop-carrying ships, several Cobra gunships, a medevac chopper painted white and marked with a red cross, and a light bubble-top observation helicopter that dipped so low, Kushner recalled, that "we could see the rank on the aviator's collars."

For a moment, the prisoners thought they were about to be liberated, but the helicopters flew on to engage the enemy elsewhere. Still, it was clear that the camp's security had been compromised, and its commander decided it should be abandoned and its prisoners marched the 560 miles to North Vietnam. "American prisoners were becoming more important politically," Kushner remembered. "We knew that. And I think as a result of that they decided they were going to move us to North

Vietnam for two reasons—one, security, and two, they could take better care of us and could use us as bargaining chips."

Life in the North would be far better, their guards assured them, and Kushner wanted to believe them. "There was no trepidation. I felt it would be better. I know they told Jews getting on the train that it was going to be better at Auschwitz. But I really wanted to believe. I knew they weren't going to kill me, because they could already have killed me easily."

He and five others began their trek two days later, accompanied by six armed guards; it would go on for fifty-seven days. The six remaining American prisoners would follow ten days later. Four ARVN prisoners were left behind.

Each man was issued a plastic ground sheet; a hammock, which seemed luxurious after sleeping on a bamboo pallet for so long; a can of condensed milk and another of mackerel; and a ten-day supply of rice. Water was carried in a two-gallon oilcan; one man hefted it in the morning, a second in the afternoon.

They walked across the rugged Central Highlands. "I thought I was going to die because my knees swelled up like volleyballs," Kushner remembered. To keep him from giving up, another prisoner reminded him of how much he wanted to see his family again. There were stopping places every ten miles or so, "liberation camps" operated by the NLF that were little more than lean-tos, and more substantial "socialist camps" established and run by the North Vietnamese. One day they were given a ride in a Russian truck and were so happy not to be walking that they sang "Where Have All the Flowers Gone?" until their guards made them stop.

Two weeks into their journey they crossed a little stream and joined the Ho Chi Minh Trail in Laos. They passed through an area that had been hit by American B-52s the night before: "Trees were twisted and uprooted, craters covered every square inch, bomb holes on top of bomb holes," a member of Kushner's party remembered. Yet crews of young men and women, hundreds of them, were already at work repairing the road. "They were just like little ants," Kushner remembered. "That was very impressive to me, gave me a sense of their determination."

As they kept walking, one prisoner recalled, they encountered hundreds of other travelers moving up and down the trail: "young and old, men and women, kids and babies, civilians and wounded soldiers. Some civilians said they were going to North Vietnam to escape life under the Saigon government. . . . We saw an eight-year-old boy with one eye, a pretty eighteen-year-old girl with an arm missing, and others with a gruesome assortment of war wounds. They had been hit, they said, during bombing raids on their villages."

They also encountered fresh troops heading south. Some struck out at them as they passed with rifle butts or hiking

sticks; others offered candy and cigarettes. They passed a unit of three hundred uniformed women, led by female officers armed with machine pistols. At the waystations at which they stopped for the night they fielded questions from curious civilians who wanted to know their names and where they were from.

"I got stronger on the way," Kushner remembered. "And our guards would tell people that I was a doctor and refugees would come up to me and they would show me their lesions or their wounds. And I would give advice. And actually, it was not a bad experience after the initial fatigue wore off. In a village I stole a uniform. I saw it hanging on a clothesline. It was kind of nondescript, didn't have any rank or anything on it. Just khaki pants and a khaki shirt. I stole it and folded it up and put it in my pack."

They somehow passed safely through the area of Route 9 where the ARVN invasion of Laos was still under way, and eventually reached North Vietnam, where they and a group of just-captured ARVN prisoners were loaded onto a truck and driven north to the coastal city of Vinh, where they were to board a train for Hanoi.

The railway platform was crowded with hundreds of ARVN prisoners captured during the Laos invasion. Kushner was

shoved into a boxcar along with scores of South Vietnamese. "I was a little frightened that these prisoners I was with were going to hurt me because there were hundreds of them," he recalled. "So I just kind of stayed by myself. I had a little canteen with water, and I slept on my pack. It took about twelve or thirteen hours to go one hundred and eighty miles because the train went very slowly. When we were pulling into Hanoi I took my little khaki uniform—which was all pressed because I had slept on it—and I took the canteen and I poured it on my hands and I slicked my hair back. And I put on this fresh uniform. And when I got off the train I was met by an officer in a jeep. And he just looked at me and he said, 'You're an officer, aren't you? You come here.' I just felt very proud that I looked good when I came off that train. And those South Vietnamese, they looked like they'd been on a train for eighteen hours, and I looked better than that. So I felt like I had some dignity. It was important to have that. So he put me in a jeep and they took me to a prison in Hanoi that we called the 'Plantation.'"

ABOVE North Vietnamese troops escort ARVN prisoners, captured in Laos, toward the North. The slogan their officers had taught them said, "Let them come to us, but do not let them return home."

WHO'S RESPONSIBLE?

O FF AND ON for sixteen months, the horrors of My Lai had
continued to make headlines. Finally, on March 29, 1971,
at Fort Benning, Georgia, after thirteen days of deliberation,
a jury of six officers found Lieutenant William Calley guilty
of murdering twenty-two Vietnamese civilians and assault with
intent to murder a Vietnamese child.

The other twenty-three officers and men who had been
indicted were either acquitted or would have their cases dismissed. The commander of the Americal Division, General
Samuel Koster, who had flown over the slaughter in a helicopter but professed to know nothing about it, resigned from his
post as superintendent of the U.S. Military Academy at West
Point and was demoted and stripped of a Distinguished Service
Medal.

Two days after the verdict in his case, Calley was sentenced
to life imprisonment at hard labor. A crowd was waiting outside
the courtroom. A woman from New Orleans shrieked, "He's
been crucified! Lieutenant Calley killed one hundred communists singlehanded. He should get a medal."

The verdict and the sentence would prove as controversial
as the war itself. According to Gallup, nearly 79 percent of
the American public disagreed with the verdict. Some people

believed that everyone involved should have gone to jail; others argued that Calley had been made a scapegoat for the criminal misdeeds of his superiors. Still others felt a systemic failure of leadership had occurred in a chain of command that stretched all the way up to the commander in chief. And there were many who believed that the lieutenant had done nothing wrong; that he'd just been doing his duty.

Within 24 hours, the White House received more than five thousand telegrams and nearly three thousand telephone calls protesting the verdict.

Nixon, who told an aide that it was "an obsolete idea that war is a game with rules," saw political advantage to be gained from the public outcry. John Dean, his White House counsel, urged him not to intervene until the appeals process was over, but the president saw "no political gain for us in that." He wanted to be "on the side of the people for a change, instead of always doing what's cautious, proper, and efficient." He ordered Calley freed from the stockade and placed under house arrest while he reviewed the verdict. Gallup found that 83 percent of respondents favored the president's action. So did Governors George Wallace of Alabama and Jimmy Carter of Georgia. A song called "The Battle Hymn of Lieutenant Calley" sold a million copies within a week.

"To think that out of all those men, only one . . . was brought to justice," said Lieutenant General Samuel Peers, who had headed the Army panel that investigated the incident. "And now

he's practically a hero. It's a tragedy." Captain Aubrey Daniel, who had successfully prosecuted Calley, wrote the president an open letter, accusing him of compromising "such a fundamental moral principle as the inherent unlawfulness of the murder of innocent persons"; the president's "political expediency," he wrote, had left the impression that Americans were "no better than our enemies." A military appeals court would eventually reduce Calley's term to twenty years, the secretary of the Army would cut it to ten, and after just three and a half years under house arrest, he would be paroled by Nixon's successor as president, Gerald Ford.

More than forty years after the verdict, Tim O'Brien, who had witnessed the silent anger and resentment of those residents of Pinkville who had survived the massacre, asked, "Who's responsible? The human beings who did this. These are war crimes. The individual human beings who put a rifle muzzle up against a baby's head and shot the brains out of that baby, nothing happened to them. Nothing!"

OPPOSITE TOP Lieutenant William Calley is escorted from the court building at Fort Benning, Georgia, after he is found guilty of murdering civilians at My Lai. **BOTTOM** *Newsweek* asks the question that consumed the country following the verdict. **ABOVE** Alabama governor George Wallace, considering a run for president, visits Calley in hopes of cementing the votes of those who thought him a scapegoat.

ONLY THE MADMEN WOULD STAY

IN LAOS, things had gone from bad to worse for the South Vietnamese. Harry Hue and his battalion wound up on a hilltop south of Tchepone, encircled by vastly superior enemy forces. They did their best to hold on. Hue called in B-52s so close to his position that shrapnel fell among his men. When water ran out, they drank their own urine. The enemy kept coming. Finally, with annihilation certain, he reluctantly radioed for extraction. Twenty-eight of the forty helicopters sent for that purpose were hit and taken out of action. Hue was on the radio, calling for more fire to protect his men until choppers could reach them, when a mortar shell hit nearby, knocking him unconscious. Shrapnel lodged in his face, arm, and leg. His men believed him doomed and affixed an identity tag to his foot. Darkness had fallen on March 19 by the time he regained consciousness. His men had received orders to attempt to break out before they were overrun. They planned somehow to carry him with them. He ordered them to leave him and save themselves. Fifty-six men managed to make it out from a battalion that had numbered six hundred.

The next morning, North Vietnamese troops found Hue slumped against a tree trunk, unable to stand. He asked his captors to shoot him. They refused. He was interrogated by a North Vietnamese colonel who turned out to come from his family's home village near Hue and recognized him as the ARVN hero of the battle that had retaken that city from the communists during the Tet Offensive. Hue was carried north along the Ho Chi Minh Trail to Hanoi, where he spent the next thirteen years in prison. Lieutenant Colonel Wiseman, who had promised to care for his family, would eventually keep that pledge and sponsor Hue and his family's emigration to the United States.

The South Vietnamese retreat had quickly become a rout. "[The enemy] were everywhere, and they were so daring," one ARVN soldier who made it to safety recalled. "Their firepower was so enormous, and their shelling was so accurate, that what could we do except run for our lives?"

"The most heartbreaking thing," another said, "was that we left behind our wounded friends. They lay there, crying, knowing the B-52 bombs would fall on them. They asked buddies to shoot them, but none of us could bring himself to do that. So the wounded men cried out for grenades, first one man, then

Wounded South Vietnamese return to Khe Sanh toward the end of Operation Lam Son 719. "The papers and radio in Saigon kept saying there was a Laos victory," a corporal said. "What a joke. We ran out like wounded dogs."

another, then more. I could not bear it. We ran out about midnight, we heard the bombs explode behind us. No more bodies! They all became dust. Some men who were wounded in the legs or arms tried to run out with us, but they could not make it."

American chopper pilots risked their lives again and again trying to lift the South Vietnamese out to safety. Lieutenant Colonel William N. Preachey, commander of an aviation battalion that flew helicopter support missions during the operation, never forgot their desperation.

ABOVE An unhurt ARVN soldier flees the Laotian battlefield. Photographs like this were remembered when the courage and resolve that other South Vietnamese soldiers showed in the face of overwhelming odds were largely overlooked.

"They would do absolutely anything to get out of Laos. . . . The healthy would run over the dead and wounded. We would hover at six or seven feet and the crew chief and gunner would lay on their bellies and pull people up. If you got on the ground they would turn the helicopter over. A later tactic was to run and jump on the shoulders of people and grab onto the skids. The helicopters would get up to three thousand or four thousand feet, and after five or ten minutes, they'd get tired and turn loose. I can still see the bodies coming through the sky."

One South Vietnamese Marine who made it out clinging to a helicopter's skids was unrepentant: "Each helicopter could have been the last one, so what choice was there for me? Only the madmen would stay and politely wait for the next helicopter."

"The [South Vietnamese] Marines were brave men, well led,

well supplied, who had a certain élan and a certain confidence in themselves when they went in," a U.S. adviser recalled. "When they came out, they'd been whipped. They knew they'd been whipped and they acted like they had been whipped." "I am afraid that we will have a lot of deserters," one veteran ARVN sergeant said. "When many of the men get back to the rear, and think back on what they have been through, and hear the other soldiers talk, then their fear will get worse."

Saigon lost some nine thousand men—killed, wounded, or missing—roughly half the number it had sent across the border. Waiting at Khe Sanh and watching the helicopters drop down one after another filled with dead and wounded ARVN, sometimes with able-bodied soldiers dangling below them, journalists and photographers found it hard to believe the Nixon administration's assurances that "the operation has gone according to plan," that the withdrawal was merely "mobile maneuvering."

As ARVN forces staggered back into South Vietnam and moved east along Route 9, crowds of weeping women, children, and old men—dressed in white, the color of mourning—appeared along the road, begging for news of the men who were missing. In Vietnam, the dead must receive proper burial so their restless souls can have peace, and their families need to know the time of their deaths so they can honor them each year.

Each side publicly claimed victory. Hanoi declared the incursion "the heaviest defeat ever" for "Nixon and Company." President Thieu staged a victory parade in Saigon, but kept the battered Airborne and Marine divisions in the far north so that demoralized men could not tell their stories in Saigon, and when reporters for *Time* and *Newsweek* and several opposition papers disagreed with his claims of triumph, he banned those issues of the magazines and confiscated the newspapers.

Privately, Thieu blamed the United States for failing to provide his men an adequate air umbrella—though more than 10,000 airstrikes had been made and 160,000 helicopter sorties had been flown, seeking to supply, defend, and rescue his forces. It was clear to most observers that without U.S. air and artillery support a defeat for the South Vietnamese forces would have been a disaster. Nixon and Kissinger blamed General Abrams for having "misled" them as to "what might be accomplished." The president wondered if the general's heavy drinking had impaired his judgment and came close to replacing him in the field.

"The polls show us the lowest we've been," Haldeman wrote at the end of March. "The credibility figure is way down, the rating on handling the Vietnam War is the lowest it's been. . . . The Laos withdrawal effect is at [the decline's] . . . bottom." George Gallup found Nixon's job approval had fallen to 50 percent, the lowest of his presidency so far; the Harris poll pegged it at 41 percent.

Nixon was determined to turn things around, to make the Laos adventure into a triumph. On April 7—the day after the operation officially ended—he claimed in a televised address that it had proved that "Vietnamization has succeeded" and enabled him to bring home an additional 100,000 Americans by December 1.

The president concluded the broadcast by laying his speech aside and recalling a recent White House ceremony during which he'd presented the Medal of Honor to the widow of Marine Sergeant Karl Taylor, killed charging an enemy machine gun in an effort to shield his men. The Marine's two sons, Karl and Kevin, had been present. Kevin was four years old, Nixon said, and "as I was about to move to the next recipient, Kevin suddenly stood at attention and saluted. I found it rather difficult to get my thoughts together for the next presentation. My fellow Americans, I want to end this war in a way that is worthy of the sacrifice of Karl Taylor, and I think he would want me to end it in a way that would increase the chances that Kevin and Karl, and all those children like them here and around the world, could grow up in a world where none of them would have to die in war; that would increase the chance for America to have what it has not had in this century—a full generation of peace."

Earlier in the year, Nixon had ordered the Secret Service to install a secret voice-activated recording system in the Oval Office. His motive, he would later claim, was simply to have a complete record of his conversations without the need for anyone to sit in and take notes, but his "primary intent," according to Haldeman, was actually to "protect himself from the convenient lapses of memory of his associates." In any case, he liked the system so much he expanded it to include his hideaway office in the Executive Office Building, the Cabinet Room, Aspen Cottage at Camp David, and a number of White House telephones.

The tape recorder was running that evening, when Kissinger called to congratulate him on his speech.

OPERATOR: Dr. Kissinger, sir.
RICHARD NIXON: Yeah.
HENRY KISSINGER: Mr. President?
NIXON: Yeah. Hi, Henry.
KISSINGER: This was the best speech you've delivered since you've been in office.
NIXON: Well, I don't know. I think November 3 was better but . . . we'll never have a moment like that again. . . .
KISSINGER: . . . I don't know whether you saw the commentary afterwards.
NIXON: Of course, I don't look at the commentary. I don't care what the bastards say.

Kissinger told him John Chancellor of NBC and Dan Rather and Marvin Kalb of CBS had all been "very positive." Nixon laughed: "They're probably afraid Agnew will jump on them."

NIXON: Yeah. I'll tell you one thing. This . . . little speech was a work of art. I mean, . . . I know a little something about speechwriting. And . . . that little conclusion . . . it was no act because no actor could do it.

KISSINGER: No.

NIXON: No actor in Hollywood could have done that that well.

KISSINGER: It's the best—

NIXON: I thought that was done well. Didn't you think?

KISSINGER: First of all, no actor could have written it, to begin with.

NIXON: Yeah.

KISSINGER: You couldn't have done it unless you had meant it. . . . I had a lump in my throat when I heard it.

The president and his adviser again hoped that the Soviets would persuade Hanoi to make concessions in Paris. "And if it doesn't work," Nixon said, "I don't care. I mean, right now if it doesn't work—[and] I'm going to find out soon—. . . then I'm going to turn right so goddamn hard it'll make your head spin. We'll bomb those bastards right . . . off the earth. I really mean it."

WE *ARE* THE TROOPS

THE LAOS INVASION eventually stirred the antiwar movement into renewed action, though differences over tactics and rivalries between peace factions and their leaders now made united action almost impossible. Everyone agreed that there should be another mass demonstration in Washington that spring, but they couldn't even settle on a date. Rennie Davis and David Dellinger called for massive direct action during the first days of May, promising to "stop the government," create "the spectre of social chaos," and "raise the cost of the war to a level unacceptable to America's rulers." No one would be in overall charge. Groups were free to follow their own dictates. "We just agreed not to get in each other's way," one organizer remembered.

One peace organization worried the Nixon White House more than any other that spring. Some 2,300 war veterans,

members of a five-year-old organization called Vietnam Veterans Against the War (VVAW), were coming to town on April 18, planning to camp on the Mall between the Lincoln and Washington monuments for a week of lobbying and demonstrating. They called their plan Operation Dewey Canyon III.

"It was the first time in history that veterans came home from a war and said—while the war was still going on—'This war's got to stop,'" John Musgrave recalled. "The American people might not listen to a bunch of long-haired hippie kids—what do they know? But the working class, the great Silent Majority Richard Nixon always talked about—his Silent Majority that would back him by being silent—we were *their* kids."

To undercut them, Charles Colson, a self-described "hatchet man" for Nixon, planted derogatory stories about the VVAW's leaders with friendly reporters and helped set up a rival group

called Vietnam Veterans for a Just Peace, pledged to support the president's policies. Nixon himself suggested falsely that only 30 percent of the organization's members were real veterans. (That was all right, one veteran said. "Only 30 percent of us believe Nixon is president.")

The Justice Department went to court to deny them a permit to camp on the Mall, but they set up their tents anyway. District police—some of whom had been in Vietnam themselves—were reluctant to try to dislodge them. "We are not going out there at one in the morning and pick up some wounded veteran and throw him into the street," one lieutenant said. "We don't treat people like that."

Pat Buchanan, then a White House aide, warned the president that the veterans were "being received in a far more sympathetic fashion than other demonstrators. The 'crazies' will be in

town soon enough," he continued, "and if we want a confrontation, let's have it with them." The administration backed down. "Don't bust the Vietnam vets on the Mall," Nixon ordered. "Avoid confrontation."

Led by a group of Gold Star mothers, some one thousand veterans—most wearing jungle fatigues, some in wheelchairs, others on crutches—began their week by marching to Arlington National Cemetery, where they asked to lay two wreaths

ABOVE Vietnam Veterans Against the War move onto the Mall. John Kerry is the tallest man in the second row to the left of the banner. It was unseasonably chilly in Washington, and at night a stranger turned up at the VVAW encampment with a car full of blankets for the shivering protestors. "I don't agree with what you guys are doing," he said, "but it's cold tonight."

and were turned away. Over the next few days they seemed to be everywhere, staging guerrilla theater, lobbying congressional offices, at the Pentagon seeking to turn themselves in for war crimes, at the Supreme Court demanding a ruling on the constitutionality of the war.

The Daughters of the American Revolution happened to be holding their annual congress in Washington that week, and as a group of chanting veterans passed, one woman stepped out into the street and approached a marcher. "Son," she said, "I don't think what you're doing is good for the troops."

"Lady," he answered, "we *are* the troops."

John Musgrave was among the marchers. So was former helicopter crew chief Ron Ferrizzi. "It was great therapy," Ferrizzi remembered. "We were working it out ourselves. Vets taking care of vets. We were generals in our own right. And we didn't join anything. We *became* something."

John Musgrave's opposition to the war had grown slowly but steadily since his return from Vietnam. "It finally dawned on me," he remembered, "and this was a long painful process, that I wasn't helping anybody by keeping my mouth shut." His loyalty to the Marine Corps never wavered, even as his faith in its mission in Vietnam dwindled. "Yes, I was a Marine, but I was first and foremost a citizen of the United States of America," he explained. "And being a citizen, I had certain responsibilities. And the largest of those responsibilities is standing up to your government and saying no when it's doing something that you think is not in this nation's best interest. That is the most important job that every citizen has. I served my country as honorably when I was in Vietnam Veterans Against the War as I did as a United States Marine, and in fact I conducted myself as a Marine the whole time I was in VVAW—my whole life I've conducted myself as a Marine."

On April 22, John Kerry, a Yale-educated former Navy lieutenant who had commanded a swift boat in the Mekong Delta and was one of the organization's leaders, was invited to address the Senate Foreign Relations Committee, still chaired by J. William Fulbright. "It was standing room only in the committee room," John Musgrave recalled. "I was crammed up against the wall in the very back, and when John gave that presentation I felt like he was speaking for all of us."

"I am not here as John Kerry," he began. "I am here as one member of the group of one thousand which is a small representation of a very much larger group of veterans in this country, and were it possible for a lot of them to sit at this table they would be here and have the same kind of testimony."

Kerry offered a litany of cruelties committed by Americans, culled from the testimony of some 150 veterans, delivered earlier that year at a Detroit conclave organized by the VVAW and called the "Winter Soldier Investigation": "They told the stories of times that they had personally raped, cut off ears, cut off heads, taped wires from portable telephones to human genitals and turned up the power, cut off limbs, blown up bodies, randomly shot at civilians, razed villages in a fashion reminiscent of Genghis Khan, shot cattle and dogs for fun, poisoned food stocks, and generally ravaged the countryside of South Vietnam in addition to the normal ravages of war and the normal and very particular ravaging which is done by the applied bombing power of this country."

Despite Kerry's testimony, only some Winter Soldier witnesses claimed to have actually done these things themselves; many had merely heard about them, and almost none had ever reported them to their superiors. Still, the cumulative impact of their testimony was powerful. Not only had Americans done all these things, Kerry continued, but they had done them on "a day-to-day basis with the full awareness of officers at all levels of command." The United States had unwittingly "created a monster, a monster in the form of millions of men who have been taught to deal and to trade in violence, and who are given the chance to die for the biggest nothing in history; men who have returned with a sense of anger and a sense of betrayal which no one has ever grasped."

Nothing that could possibly happen in Southeast Asia could threaten the United States, he said; the people whose freedom Americans were supposed to be defending were not free, but subject to a corrupt dictatorial regime. "We rationalize destroying villages in order to save them . . . learned the meaning of free-fire zones, shoot anything that moves, . . . watched the . . . glorification of body counts. . . . Now, we are told that the men who fought there must watch quietly as American lives are lost so that we can exercise the incredible arrogance of Vietnamizing the Vietnamese . . . and [because] we can't say that we have made a mistake. Someone has to die so that President Nixon won't be—and these are his words—'the first president to lose a war.' How do you ask a man to be the last man to die in Vietnam? How do you ask a man to be the last man to die for a mistake? Finally, this administration has done us the ultimate dishonor. They have attempted to disown us and the sacrifice we made for this country. In their blindness and fear they have tried to deny that we are veterans or that we served in 'Nam. We do not need their testimony. Our own scars and stumps of limbs are witnesses enough for others and for ourselves.

"We wish that a merciful God could wipe away our own memories of that service as easily as this administration has wiped their memories of us. But all that they have done and all that they can do by this denial is to make more clear than ever our own determination to undertake one last mission to search out and destroy the last vestige of this barbaric war, to pacify our own hearts, to conquer the hate and the fear that have driven

this country these last ten years and more, and so, when, in thirty years from now, our brothers go down the street without a leg, without an arm, or a face, and small boys ask why, we will be able to say 'Vietnam,' and not mean a filthy obscene memory but mean instead the place where America finally turned, and where soldiers like us helped it in the turning."

The committee room erupted in applause. "I thought, I have never heard such an incredible speech that says exactly what I'm feeling," Musgrave recalled. "It was extraordinary. Extraordinary." Many Americans watching on television felt the same way.

But many of the more than three million service members who had also served in Southeast Asia felt that Kerry's testimony had personally defamed them. Former First Lieutenant Phil Gioia, who had served one tour with the Eighty-second Airborne, helped uncover communist atrocities in Hue, and then returned for a second tour with the First Cavalry, spoke for many: "What I saw in Vietnam was not the soldier that Mr. Kerry or his colleagues were describing at that time. There was no widespread atrocity. There were a couple of units that went right off the rails and we can talk about that. But . . . they were not out-of-control animals, which was the way they were portrayed. . . . I'm still very angry about that."

The next day, seven hundred VVAW members gathered at the U.S. Capitol. "We'd originally intended to put our medals in a body bag and have them delivered to Congress," Musgrave recalled. "But the Nixon administration erected this big wire and wood fence on the steps of our Capitol to keep *us* out—keep out the young men and women who were fighting that war. And all that did was piss us off and give us the greatest photo opportunity that we could ever have had."

One by one, the veterans stepped up to a microphone to identify themselves and speak out against the war if they liked, then hurled their medals onto the Capitol steps—Silver Stars, Purple Hearts, Bronze Stars, Distinguished Flying Crosses.

"I don't want these fucking medals, man!" Ron Ferrizzi said into the mic. "The Silver Star—the third highest medal in the country—it doesn't mean anything! Bob Smeal died for these medals; Lieutenant Panamaroff died so I got a medal; Sergeant Johns died so I got a medal; I got a Silver Star, a Purple Heart, Army Commendation medal, eight air medals, national defense, and the rest of this garbage—it doesn't mean a thing!" Ferrizzi remembered years later that "throwing my medals back was probably harder than going to the war." His family in Philadelphia had warned that if he did that they wanted nothing more to do with him. "But I figured if this medal is so important let's *make* it important. Here it is. You can have it back. End the

ABOVE Civilians and veterans alike applaud John Kerry at the end of his testimony before the Senate Foreign Relations Committee, April 22, 1971.

war in Vietnam. What else is there? There was nothing else. I wouldn't put them on my wall for my son. That was the last thing in the world I would ever want my son to revere."

"It was a difficult decision for me," Tom Vallely remembered. "I did it out of a disrespectful loyalty. I was proud of my military service. But I wanted to say, 'I don't think you guys know that much, the American military. I think you should think again about this enterprise. And here you go, pal.'"

"When we threw our medals away," Musgrave remembered, "that got people's attention because America values those things. So do we. That's why it was so important."

In the days immediately following the veterans' protest, other groups of antiwar activists moved into the capital, somewhere between 250,000 and 500,000 of them. The most radical, a consortium of fringe groups who called themselves the May Day Tribe, threatened to close the city down. For three days, they staged hit-and-run raids throughout Washington—blocking bridges and traffic circles, smashing windows, hurling rocks, burning cars. Some twelve thousand were arrested—seven thousand on a single day, the largest number of arrests in twenty-four hours in United States history.

"If Richard Nixon thought *this* week was something," Rennie Davis told the press as the demonstrations finally came to an end, "wait until the next round. This is only a warm-up of what is going to come. This is going to continue until the war ends."

But other protestors drew other lessons. "I realized coming away from Washington that our whole strategy was wrong," Bill Zimmerman remembered, "and that we were becoming more and more militant at a time when more and more Americans were opposing the war but were turned off by our militancy. So we were doing exactly the wrong thing."

The White House was initially pleased at the public's reaction. Sympathy for the veterans was largely forgotten in the face of three days of street fighting. Polls showed that 76 percent of Americans approved of the arrests. But the same polls showed that by almost the same percentage Americans no longer believed they were being told the whole truth about Vietnam.

John Musgrave returned to his parents' home in Missouri, not sure how he would be received. "I got home. My dad's a true believer, you know. But he was already receiving threats because I'd thrown away [my] medals. And that pissed my dad off. And

OPPOSITE Former helicopter crew chief Ron Ferrizzi hurls his medals. By the time the demonstration ended there would be fourteen Navy and Distinguished Service Crosses, one hundred Silver Stars, and more than one thousand Purple Hearts on the Capitol steps. President Nixon was alarmed at the respectful television coverage the veterans received. "They're really killing us," H. R. Haldeman noted in his diary, "and we have no way to fight back."

you would've thought I hadn't done anything wrong. Somebody outside the family was messing with me. He said, 'Son, don't worry. Those were your medals. You paid for them. You can do anything you want with them. They want to jack with us, they'll face us both. We'll take them on in the driveway.' You know, 'Yo, Dad!'"

ON A THIEVERY BASIS!

ON JUNE 12, 1971, Richard Nixon's daughter, Tricia, married Edward Cox in the White House Rose Garden. The wedding was still news the next day. But another story on the front page of *The New York Times* caught the president's attention.

The article, by Neil Sheehan, was the first installment of what came to be called the "Pentagon Papers"—seven thousand pages of highly classified documents and historical narrative, compiled secretly at the orders of former Secretary of Defense Robert McNamara, who had hoped that a study of the decision-making process that had led the United States to become so deeply involved in Vietnam would help future policymakers avoid similar errors.

Two copies of the report had been stored at the Washington headquarters of the RAND Corporation, for which Daniel Ellsberg, one of the study's thirty-six authors, worked as an analyst. Ellsberg had once supported the war; he'd served in the Pentagon and spent two years working for the State Department in Vietnam. But he had come to see it as profoundly immoral and hoped that if Americans understood how administration after administration had misled them about what was being done in their name, they might help bring it to an end.

He and Anthony Russo, another RAND employee, secretly copied most of the report. Ellsberg offered it to three leading antiwar senators—William Fulbright, George McGovern, and Charles Mathias of Maryland—hoping they would be willing to reveal its contents. None dared do it.

Meanwhile, Neil Sheehan, who had been reporting on Vietnam since 1962 and had already secretly seen some of the documents, asked Ellsberg to show him the whole report. "I thought I knew most of what was worth knowing about the war," Sheehan recalled, "and suddenly I didn't. This wasn't a reporter's version of an event, it was *their* version of an event. It was their telegrams, their orders, their memoranda, et cetera."

The documents showed that American presidents and their closest advisers had steered the United States toward deeper and deeper involvement in Vietnam, despite their own grave doubts

about the chances for victory. They had known from the first that the Saigon government was weak and incompetent, that the enemy was disciplined and resilient, and that the bombing of the North wasn't working. Yet they had routinely lied about all of these things to Congress and the American people.

"At that point I was very passionate about the war," Sheehan remembered. "I felt that it was really wrong because we were getting a lot of Americans and a lot of Vietnamese killed for no purpose. We were going to lose this war. And so I vowed to myself when I saw this material that this is never going to go back into a government safe again. The American public had paid for it with the lives of their sons and with their treasure, and it was going be published."

On the morning of June 13 the president was still euphoric about Tricia's wedding and the breathless television coverage of

ABOVE *The New York Times* resumes publication of the Pentagon Papers, July 1, 1971. Its editors had initially decided to publish them, they wrote, "because the documents, all dating from 1968 or earlier, belonged to the American people, were now part of history, could in no sense damage current military operations or threaten a single life, and formed an essential element in an understanding by the American people of the event that has affected them more deeply than any other in this generation, the Vietnam war."

it and also pleased to learn that for the second week in a row the U.S. Vietnam casualty figure was down to fewer than twenty. William Rogers reported that in the last twenty-four hours there'd been no combat activity involving American troops anywhere in Vietnam.

The newspaper story about the Pentagon Papers initially didn't disturb Nixon. After all, the documents reflected badly on his Democratic predecessors, not on him.

RICHARD NIXON: That piece in the *Times* is, of course, a massive security leak from the Pentagon. . . .

WILLIAM ROGERS: Is that—

NIXON: It all relates . . . of course, to everything up until we came in.

ROGERS: Yeah.

NIXON: And it's hard on Johnson, it's hard on Kennedy, it's hard on Lodge. . . . McNamara had the study made—started—and then it was continued by Clifford. But it's really something. They said, according to [White House aide General] Al Haig, four thousand secure documents were apparently just leaked to the *Times*.

ROGERS: Isn't that awful?

NIXON: Goddamn.

ROGERS: Of course, McNamara looks lousy too. He comes out looking—

NIXON: Yeah, I didn't read the piece—but he looks, apparently—

ROGERS: He looks bad.

NIXON: . . . McNamara started [it]. Then Clifford got in, he makes McNamara look bad.

ROGERS: Yeah.

NIXON: And trying to make him[self] look good.

ROGERS: God, they're a bunch of scoundrels, aren't they?

At a staff meeting the next day Henry Kissinger took a very different view. Publication of such top-secret material "will totally destroy American credibility forever," he said. "It will destroy our ability to conduct foreign policy in confidence. No foreign government will ever trust us again. We might just as well turn it all over to the Soviets and get it over with." If the *Times* were permitted to reveal the classified secrets of earlier presidents, he told Nixon, it was only a matter of time until someone leaked his own.

And there was another problem, well summarized by Haldeman: the Pentagon Papers might hurt the Democrats in the short run, he told his boss, but they would eventually undercut the reputation of the presidency itself: "To the ordinary guy, all this is a bunch of gobbledygook. But out of the gobbledygook comes a very clear thing, which is: you can't trust the government, you can't believe what they say, and you can't rely on their judgment. And that the infallibility of presidents, which has been an accepted thing in America, is badly hurt by this, because it shows that people do things the president wants to do even when it's wrong. And the president can be wrong."

That was precisely the impact the Pentagon Papers would have on Marine First Lieutenant Karl Marlantes, recovered from his wounds and back in the States, when the first newspaper story appeared: "That changed our whole attitude toward government," he said. "Up until then, the president wouldn't lie. After then, they always lie."

The Justice Department obtained a temporary court order forbidding the *Times* from publishing further installments, on the grounds of national security. But soon, both *The Boston Globe* and *The Washington Post* were also printing excerpts.

Then, on June 30, 1971, the U. S. Supreme Court, citing the First Amendment, ruled 6–3 that the *Times* had the right to publish the stolen documents. "I went down into the basement to wait for the presses to start to roll," Neil Sheehan recalled. "It was just an exquisite moment of vindication of the freedom of the press in this country and how important it is."

That same day, Nixon ordered Attorney General John Mitch-

ell to try to discredit Daniel Ellsberg, who had just been indicted by a federal grand jury for theft and conspiracy under the Espionage Act of 1917.

RICHARD NIXON: Don't you agree that we have to pursue the Ellsberg case?

JOHN MITCHELL: No question about it. No question about it. This is the one sanction we have, is to get at the individuals. . . .

NIXON: Let's get the son of a bitch into jail.

KISSINGER: We've got to get him, we've got to get him. . . .

NIXON: Don't worry about his trial. Just get everything out. Try him in the press. Try him in the press. Everything, John, that there is on the investigation, get it out, leak it out. We want to destroy him in the press. Is that clear?

MITCHELL: Yes.

Nixon feared that Ellsberg possessed more classified documents that would show that the president himself had lied about the secret bombing of Cambodia and Laos, and he believed that Ellsberg had had help and wanted to know the names of his co-conspirators. He created a private, clandestine investigative unit within the White House that came to be called "the plumbers." John Ehrlichman eventually ordered them to burglarize the office of Ellsberg's Los Angeles psychiatrist in search of material with which to smear him.

Nixon privately feared something else, as well: exposure of the secret role his campaign had played in torpedoing the Vietnam peace talks on the eve of his election three years earlier—a role that President Johnson had then privately called "treason." Nixon was told that the safe at another Washington think tank, the Brookings Institution, contained a report on the events leading up to LBJ's decision to halt the American bombing of North Vietnam. Concerned that the FBI might have bugged his campaign plane and that there might be records of incriminating conversations, Nixon wanted his "plumbers" to break into Brookings, crack the safe, and remove the file.

"I want it implemented on a thievery basis," he told Kissinger and Haldeman. "Goddamn it, get in and get those files. Blow the safe and get it."

None of it was legal. Nixon evidently did not care.

The Brookings break-in would never take place; the FBI had not bugged Nixon's plane, so there were no transcripts, in any case. The burglars did break into Ellsberg's doctor's office but failed to find his file. But Nixon's continuing obsession with those he considered his enemies would be the eventual undoing of his presidency.

THE ONE-MAN ELECTION

BETWEEN January 1 and July 1, twenty-two different resolutions seeking to curtail the president's power to wage war or to set a firm target date for total withdrawal of American forces had been offered in Congress. They had either failed to pass or had not been legally binding, but they were unmistakable evidence that the public's patience was growing thin. The Cambodian invasion had bought some precious time for Vietnamization—Washington believed that the enemy could not mount another major offensive until early in 1972—but Henry Kissinger worried that the administration might not be able to get through the current year without Congress "giving the farm away."

Eager to move forward, he persuaded Hanoi to restart the

ABOVE Vice President Ky and President Thieu preside together over a Saigon parade celebrating South Vietnam's supposed triumph in Laos, May 1971.

secret talks, suspended while South Vietnamese troops were in Laos, and offered the most comprehensive proposal Washington had yet put on the table. The United States promised to set a date for a total U.S. withdrawal under international supervision and for the first time did not insist that Hanoi also pull out its troops (provided they stopped infiltrating into South Vietnam or its neighbors). Washington also called again for a cease-fire in place, in Laos and Cambodia as well as Vietnam this time, and suggested that all prisoners of war held by both sides be released as part of an agreed-upon timetable for withdrawal.

Kissinger and his counterparts met twice more in secret that summer. The atmosphere seemed more cordial than it had been before. Elements of Hanoi's counterproposals seemed to mesh with the American offer. The two sides seemed to be inching toward one another at last.

Just two major issues remained. One seemed potentially resolvable, more a matter of semantics than substance. Hanoi wanted "reparations" for "the damage caused by the U.S. in the war zones of Vietnam"; both Lyndon Johnson and Richard Nixon had pledged that the United States would help rehabilitate all of Indochina, including North Vietnam, once the war

had ended. "But we would do it of our own accord," Kissinger said, "not as an obligation."

The real sticking point remained the fate of Nguyen Van Thieu. Hanoi continued to insist that before there could be any possibility of peace the South Vietnamese president had to be swept from power, along with the other "warlike and fascist" members of his regime—Vice President Nguyen Cao Ky and Prime Minister and Minister of Defense General Tran Thien Khiem. Le Duc Tho suggested to Kissinger that Thieu's removal could be effected quietly, without public comment, to avoid embarrassment. The South Vietnamese constitution, drafted at American insistence and with considerable American input, provided for a four-year presidential term. Thieu was up for reelection on October 3. Surely the United States could arrange things so that he lost, Le Duc Tho suggested, and if that weren't feasible there was always assassination. The talks broke up.

"It is obvious that we cannot do [Hanoi's] political work for them," Kissinger told Nixon. "For all his faults, Thieu has been a loyal ally. Moreover, the recent publication of the Pentagon Papers with their revelations about American complicity in the coup against Diem would make our involvement in Thieu's

removal even more unpalatable. Last but not least, I am not even sure we could remove Thieu if we wanted to, unless we were prepared to engage in a major confrontation whose only certain result would be the destruction of South Vietnam's political fabric and everybody's self-respect."

President Thieu was sometimes called *le grand louvoyeur*—"the grand maneuverer"—and now, faced with an election he had not wanted but also did not wish to lose, he would live up to his reputation. He was perpetually fearful of a coup and quick to undercut anyone he saw as a potential rival: when his one-time friend the much-admired former province chief Tran Ngoc Chau entered politics, denounced corruption, and championed a negotiated peace, Thieu had him dragged from the National Assembly, tried for treason, and imprisoned.

When Thieu was elected president in 1967 he had defeated a field of seven opponents with just 34.8 percent of the vote. This time, he was determined to win big, and he hoped that a

ABOVE NLF prisoners at the Bien Hoa prison camp swear allegiance to the South Vietnamese government in order to win their release—a goodwill election-year gesture by President Thieu.

program called Land-to-the-Tiller, which distributed landlords' holdings among their tenants, would help increase peasant support for his candidacy.

He had just two likely challengers. General Duong Van "Big" Minh worried Thieu most. He was warmly remembered by many in South Vietnam for having led the junta that overthrew Diem eight years earlier, but he was no favorite of Washington. He was thought "lackadaisical," according to Henry Kissinger; a CIA officer who was fond of him said he had "the body of an elephant and the brain of a mouse." But he had the support of the "Third Force"—the loose coalition of Buddhists, Catholics, intellectuals, students, and politicians who favored the creation of a ruling coalition that would include the Provisional Revolutionary Government.

Thieu's other serious challenger was his gaudy perennial rival, Vice President Ky. Once a champion of invading the North, Ky now declared military victory impossible and argued instead that the PRG be recognized as a political party and that Saigon negotiate directly with Hanoi in search of a settlement.

The president set out to eliminate Ky from the race so he

ABOVE After winning his one-man race for president, President Thieu swears himself in for a second term. "It is obvious," one veteran Saigon journalist wrote, "the whole ludicrous performance has left his government in a more precarious political position than ever, both internally and with the Communists. It is equally obvious that United States policy-makers are largely devoid of ideas about how to cope with the situation."

could take on Minh alone. He announced that he was "streamlining" his cabinet and jettisoned several ministers whose first loyalty was to his rival, then pushed a bill through the National Assembly requiring anyone wishing to challenge him for the presidency to obtain the written endorsements of 40 assembly members or 100 members of the 550-person provincial councils, appointed to advise the government. (Before promulgating his law, he had safely amassed for himself 452 council votes and those of 102 legislators.)

Ky crisscrossed the country lobbying provincial councilors and managed to collect 102 signatures, only to have the Supreme Court reject his candidacy on the dubious grounds that 40 of his endorsers had previously pledged themselves to Thieu. General Minh, who had himself collected more than the requisite one hundred legislator signatures, accused Thieu of "dishonest tricks," and said he was thinking of withdrawing from the race himself.

Minh went to the Americans with evidence of Thieu's trickery—instructions from the president to his handpicked province chiefs, ordering them to buy off or lock up opposition leaders and urging them to issue duplicate registration cards to supporters so they could vote more than once. The deputy U.S. ambassador wired the White House that if Thieu "decided to go through with a one-man sham election. . . . The outlook would be growing political instability."

"The U.S. government," Henry Kissinger wrote, then "wound up in the curious position of searching for opponents to a president who was conducting a war as our ally." Ambassador

Bunker called first on General Minh. He was thought unlikely to win more than 30 percent of the vote and constituted no real threat to Thieu, but a respectable showing by him would lend at least a little legitimacy to the president's inevitable victory. Bunker offered to provide campaign funds if he would stay in the race. Minh angrily turned him down and withdrew the following morning: "I cannot put up with a disgusting farce that strips away all the people's hope of a democratic regime and bars reconciliation of the Vietnamese people," he said.

The Supreme Court then suddenly reversed itself and ruled that Ky could contest the election after all. "It was a political decision," one justice later admitted. "[I]t was clear that we had to do something to give the president a legal opponent." Bunker offered money to Ky, too, but he refused to run.

The result, a referendum on Thieu's performance as president, not an election, seemed to make a mockery of Nixon's solemn assurance that the seventeen and a half million people of South Vietnam "must have the freedom to choose" their government. Two South Vietnamese veterans burned themselves alive in protest. Students, shouting anti-Thieu and anti-American slogans, burned vehicles and battled riot police in the Saigon streets. Tear gas broke up protests organized by Buddhists and members of the opposition in the National Assembly. Ky formed a coalition called the Citizen's Coordinating Committee to Oppose Dictatorship and urged a boycott of the polls.

Nonetheless, according to official figures, 87.9 percent of the more than 6.3 million eligible voters went to the polls on October 3—and Thieu claimed to have won 94.3 percent of their votes.

"We have accepted the man sent to us by the American gods," one bitter Saigon resident said. Almost no one in the city, American or South Vietnamese, believed the vote totals, according to *The New Yorker*'s Robert Shaplen. The best estimates were that only about half the eligible voters in the countryside actually bothered to go to the polls; in the cities, the total was thought to have been as low as 30 percent. "There is some evidence that a number of officials," he reported, "including province chiefs appointed by Thieu, gave out obviously inflated figures to embarrass him, because they felt that the whole exercise was ridiculous and unnecessary. . . . American officials here are no longer trying to hide their disappointment over Thieu's performance but are simply gritting their teeth; barring an unlikely signal from the White House they will continue to give [him] their full support."

The same day the South Vietnamese president was reelected, Henry Kissinger made still another secret offer to Hanoi—six months after the signing of a final agreement a new presidential election, conducted under international supervision, would be held, and President Thieu would resign his office a month

before the vote so he could run without being able to call on the powers of the government to boost his candidacy. A month after that, U.S. forces would be gone but for a small residual force. Hanoi did not respond. It had other plans.

NOT TOO HAPPY

ARMY CAPTAIN JAMES H. WILLBANKS arrived in Vietnam in December 1971. Like tens of thousands of Americans before him, he flew into Tan Son Nhut airport and when the door opened was staggered by the humidity and heat—stepping off the plane, he remembered, was "like putting on a wet, hot coat." The bus waiting at the bottom of the stairs had wire mesh over the windows to thwart anyone who might want to lob a grenade inside. There was the usual Army bureaucracy to contend with, filling out forms, dragging his duffel bag from one line to the next, waiting to find out what unit he'd been assigned to—all experiences his predecessors had gone through.

But things were different now. America's combat role had virtually ended. Willbanks had volunteered to become an adviser to the South Vietnamese. He remembered an NCO at Camp Alpha, the holding area for U.S. military personnel coming and going, telling him and some other new arrivals "that the war was

ABOVE Captain James H. Willbanks, newly arrived in South Vietnam and about forty-five minutes from being wounded

basically over, that we wouldn't even get a Combat Infantry-man's Badge. As it turned out he was wrong on both counts."

Born in Hot Springs, Arkansas, the son of a career Army NCO whose assignments forced his family to move often, Will-banks felt closest to the place where he spent the most time as a boy, Copperas Cove, just outside Fort Hood, Texas. He emerged as a lieutenant from the Texas A&M University Corps of Cadets in 1969 and was sent to Germany to serve as a platoon leader with the Second Battalion, Thirtieth Infantry, Third Infantry Division, stationed at Schweinfurt.

It was not a reassuring experience. "It was very difficult to think that the U.S. Army in Europe at that time could have defeated a determined Girl Scout troop," he remembered. "It was in desperate trouble."

Willbanks was not alone in that opinion. "The morale, discipline and battleworthiness of the U.S. Armed Forces are, with a few salient exceptions, lower and worse than at any time in this century and possibly in the history of the United States," a retired Marine colonel wrote. In Vietnam, "the rearguard of a 500,000 man army, in its day . . . the best army the United States ever put in the field, is numbly extricating itself from a nightmare war the Armed Forces feel they had foisted on them by bright civilians who are now back on campus writing books about the folly of it all." And as that withdrawal accelerated all the problems that plagued that fast-dwindling force—alcohol, drugs, indiscipline, fragging, racial conflict, plunging morale—spread to infect U.S. armed forces everywhere, including Germany.

"The Army did some really stupid things," Willbanks explained, "and one of them was sending to Germany troops from Vietnam with less than six months to go in the Army. You can imagine what kind of morale and motivation problems we had." His platoon was half the size it was authorized to be. Six of his men were in prison when he got there, all for violent crimes, including murder. The use of heroin and other hard drugs was rampant. So was crime—extortion, thievery, armed robbery. White and black soldiers battled one another on and off the base. Weapons disappeared. Duty officers conducting inspection sometimes carried locked and loaded .45s. "There were places in the barracks where you took your life in your hands," Willbanks remembered.

After more than a year of it he'd had enough. "I figured it was safer in Vietnam than Germany," he said. He volunteered to serve as an adviser and attended an eleven-week course at Fort Bragg, followed by several more weeks of language study at Briggs Field. "Only the U.S. Army would send you to El Paso, Texas, to learn Vietnamese," he remembered. "Vietnamese is a very difficult tonal language. I'm a Texan who is tone deaf,

apparently. It was very difficult, but the idea that we were there and trying the language went a long way with the South Vietnamese I worked with."

In Vietnam, he served first with a unit of the Royal Thai Army that was packing up to head home, and then became an adviser to the Forty-eighth Regiment of the Eighteenth ARVN Division stationed near Xuan Loc, twenty-two miles east of Saigon. Adviser ranks were thinning, too; when he arrived there were somewhere between sixty and seventy Americans on his Division Combat Assistance Team; by the time he left a year later there would be only twenty.

Willbanks was modest about the adviser's role: "Let's be honest. What I had was a U.S. Army name tag that made me the embodiment of the U.S. commitment to support the South. I was usually working with a battalion commander. I wasn't advising him. He'd been fighting for twenty years. I was a twenty-three-year-old captain who'd been in the Army for two and a half years. But I had a radio and was able to tap into the U.S. air support remaining in country—helicopters, tactical helicopters, tactical air, medevacs. I was the phone booth on the ground."

His outfit took some fire during his first ten-day search-and-clear mission. "A little frightening, a little exhilarating," he remembered. "Once it was over it felt like, 'Wow, I'm glad that's done, let's move on to the next thing.'" The second operation was uneventful, he recalled, just another long walk in the jungle trying to fit himself through the Vietnamese-sized openings the ARVN cut for themselves through the undergrowth. The area was quiet, for the most part. "I never saw Viet Cong," he recalled, "not in a year," and the North Vietnamese seemed at first to be lying low.

"The first time I was wounded was in an area that had been deemed 'green'—free of the enemy," he recalled, "but someone forgot to tell the North Vietnamese." On his third mission, moving through a vast rubber planation, his battalion inadvertently came too close to an enemy base camp and was ambushed—"a classic Fort Benning ambush," Willbanks called it, regimental sized with automatic weapon fire to the front and mortars in the rear to keep the men pinned down. Willbanks slipped behind a tree to return fire. An RPG hit the trunk and detonated, sending a piece of shrapnel into his right knee.

Within moments, the battalion and its commander had fled the field, taking Willbanks's radio with them and leaving him and several other wounded men unable to call for help and on their own. They struggled for twelve hours to fight their way out of the kill zone. "There were other guys who were hurt worse than I was and we were kind of dragging them," Willbanks recalled. Long after dark, they reached an ARVN outpost. "They didn't want to send a helicopter out to get us because no one was in danger of dying during the night. So they sent ground vehicles and picked us up the next day."

Recuperating in a military hospital at Long Binh, Willbanks was interviewed about what had happened by a member of the advisory team. He said he "was not too happy" that "these guys had run off and left me. . . . Shortly thereafter, I got word through another captain that my senior adviser said I was to keep my mouth shut about the incident. . . . It was kind of a political thing: 'These guys are going to do better because we say they're going to do better.' Interestingly enough, the ARVN division commander was later awarded a U.S. Bronze Star for having landed his helicopter in a hot zone to rescue me—which was kind of interesting, because when he came and picked me up he looked an awful lot like a Vietnamese private in a jeep. But that's just one of those things."

Willbanks was back at the ARVN base, on crutches, within a week. Years later, asked for his assessment of the South Vietnamese forces with whom he served, he was careful in his response. "I think the ARVN get a bad rap," he remembered, "but I'll also tell you it's a very complex issue. I worked with all three regiments of my division for over eight months, and the combat performance was uneven. One regiment was very good, one was average, and one was not very good at all." All three characteristics would be put on display during the North Vietnamese offensive that was soon to begin.

STOP THIS OFFENSIVE

BACK IN JULY of the previous year, Richard Nixon, who had once been celebrated for the ferocity of his anticommunism, had astonished the world by announcing that before May 1, 1972, he planned to visit China, restoring diplomatic relations that had been severed when the communists seized power there more than two decades earlier. The United States had gone to war in Vietnam in part to block supposed Chinese expansionism. What would Nixon's visit mean for President Thieu's future—or for that of his country? Thieu was afraid he knew. "America has been looking for a better mistress," he would tell an aide, "and now Nixon has discovered China. He does not want to have the old mistress around. Vietnam has become old and ugly."

Hanoi was alarmed by Nixon's announcement, too, and was already troubled that the American president was seeking détente—an easing of tensions—with the Soviet Union. The North Vietnamese remembered how Moscow and Beijing had advised Ho Chi Minh to accept the Geneva partition of

BELOW Soviet leader Nikolai Podgorny embraces Le Duan in Hanoi, demonstrating that while the USSR was moving toward détente with the United States, it was not abandoning North Vietnam.

Vietnam—a decision they soon came to regret. Concerned that warmer relations between the United States and China might mean less support from Beijing, they accused the United States of "perfidious maneuvers" aimed at trying to divide and conquer the communist world.

North Vietnam's patrons—now increasingly hostile rivals—rushed to reaffirm their backing for Hanoi. The deputy premier of China flew in to pledge that Beijing's economic and military aid would not only continue but increase in 1972. Not to be outdone, Moscow dispatched President Nikolai Podgorny to Hanoi, promising to provide plentiful "additional aid without reimbursement."

Over the months that followed, military supplies of a different kind and in unprecedented quantities streamed into North Vietnam, overland by railroad from China and by sea from the Soviet Union: more than one thousand Soviet tanks, hundreds of antiaircraft and antitank missiles, long-range artillery that fired seven rounds per minute and was accurate up to seven-

teen miles. The new weaponry demanded new kinds of technical skills, as well. Twenty-five thousand North Vietnamese were sent to Soviet-bloc countries for training; more than three thousand tank crews attended Soviet armory school in Odessa.

Ever since the Laotian incursion, Le Duan and his allies in Hanoi had planned to launch yet another offensive as soon as the rains stopped in early 1972. They had deliberately stalled the Paris talks for months. "They were diddling Henry along," Nixon said, while pouring men and supplies into the South so that when a ceasefire in place was finally negotiated they and not Saigon would have the upper hand.

The ARVN's poor performance in Laos encouraged them. So did the steadily shrinking size of the U.S. military presence in the South—there were under 100,000 U.S. soldiers in country now, only a fraction of whom were combat troops. President Nixon's political predicament reassured them, too. Facing reelection in the fall, he seemed unlikely to recommit U.S. forces to save the Saigon regime—especially when that recommitment might offend the Chinese, whom he was about to visit, or the Soviets, with whom he planned important talks later in the year. Finally, the growing cordiality between the U.S. president and its political benefactors continued to worry Hanoi, and a major assault seemed the best way to remind both Beijing and Moscow that North Vietnam's revolutionary fervor remained as fierce as ever.

OPPOSITE A South Vietnamese Marine carries the corpse of a comrade killed trying to slow the North Vietnamese advance down Route 1 from Quang Tri toward Hue, April 30, 1972. **ABOVE** The 1972 North Vietnamese Offensive was to proceed on three widely separated fronts, but the fiercest fighting would take place in and around the provincial capitol of An Loc.

This offensive would be different from those that had preceded it. There was little talk of a popular uprising this time; this was to be a full-scale conventional military assault on three different fronts in South Vietnam, spearheaded by tanks and artillery.

First, three divisions were to pour across the DMZ, take Quang Tri and Hue, and capture South Vietnam's two northernmost provinces.

Three more divisions based in Cambodia and Laos were then to drive eastward, take An Loc, the capital of Binh Long Province, and move south along Highway 13 toward Saigon, just sixty-five miles away.

Finally, two more divisions would capture Pleiku and Kon Tum in the Central Highlands while a third took the coastal province of Binh Dinh, effectively cutting the country in half.

U.S. intelligence knew something was about to happen, but where and when the attacks would come and how large they

ABOVE An ARVN soldier pauses for prayer in what remains of a cathedral in the city of La Vang after the South Vietnamese reoccupied Quang Tri Province in June.

would be remained unclear. January passed with no attack. So did Tet in February. "On again, off again, gonna come, didn't come," one rumor-weary U.S. civilian adviser wrote in early March. "It has been a virtual merry-go-round this month of pending action that never materialized."

Both General Adams and Ambassador Bunker were out of the country when it finally did materialize, at precisely noon on Thursday, March 30, with a thunderous artillery barrage all along the DMZ. It was the day before Good Friday, so the Americans would remember the battles that followed as the "Easter Offensive"; the South Vietnamese would call it "the Summer of the Flames." North Vietnamese troops poured into the northern provinces. ARVN commanders did not distinguish themselves. General Hoang Xuan Lam, the overcautious commander of Lam Son 917, now corps commander in the North, was caught completely by surprise. His men fell back. Over the protests of its American advisers an entire regiment—fifteen hundred troops with all their heavy weapons—surrendered at Camp Carroll. Quang Tri Province passed into enemy hands.

If the ARVN crumbled, as it seemed to be doing, everything Nixon and Kissinger had worked for was imperiled. Vietnamization would be exposed as a myth. The American bargaining position at the upcoming Strategic Arms Limitation Talks (SALT) with the Soviet Union would be weakened. The president's reelection would be jeopardized. Nixon, Haldeman noted, "feels very strongly that we've got to make an all-out effort and that it's really a do or die proposition. . . . Both he and Henry agree that no matter what happens now, we'll be finished with the war by August. Either we will have broken them or they will have broken us."

Nixon refused to stop or even slow the pace of troop withdrawals. He announced that twenty thousand more men would start for home by July 1, bringing the total left behind to just under fifty thousand. Instead, he would employ American airpower.

"I think we shouldn't panic now," Kissinger told the president five days after the offensive began. "In a way it's a godsend. We should give them a tremendous punishment."

RICHARD NIXON: We lose if the ARVN collapses. . . . That's a question we can't even think about. If the ARVN collapses a lot of other things will collapse around here. If they were going to collapse they had to do it a year ago. We can't do it this year, Henry.

HENRY KISSINGER: Right. They're not going to collapse, I know—

NIXON: You see what I mean. We can't take it.

KISSINGER: I agree, that's why we've got to blast—

NIXON: That's right.

KISSINGER:—the living bejeesus out of them. . . .

NIXON: Let's don't talk about 'If the ARVN collapses.' . . . We're playing a bigger game. We're playing a Russian game, a Chinese game, an election game—

KISSINGER: That's right.

NIXON:—and we're not going to have the ARVN collapse.

The next day, the president ordered massive bombing of North Vietnamese forces in the South as well as targets in North Vietnam as far north as Vinh, the first U.S. bombing of that country in four years. "I want you to go down there," Nixon told U.S. Air Force General John W. Vogt, who was about to take command of the Seventh Air Force, "and use whatever air you need to turn this thing around. . . . Stop this offensive."

THE KIND OF WAR WE CAME TO FIGHT

AS AMERICAN BOMBS began to fall, the North Vietnamese launched the second phase of their offensive, an all-out assault on An Loc, the capital of Binh Long Province. A prosperous but unprepossessing town—just six blocks long and eleven blocks wide—and surrounded by 100,000 acres of rubber plantations, it was home to just fifteen thousand Vietnamese with another five thousand hill people living in villages nearby. Its importance lay in its location—it stood astride Highway 13, a paved all-weather road that led south to Saigon—and in its status as a provincial capital whose loss to the enemy would be a psychological blow to the South Vietnamese regime.

By April 12, North Vietnamese forces had captured Loc Ninh, the nearest town to the north, and had surrounded An Loc with some thirty-six thousand troops. Hunkered down inside the town were just seven thousand South Vietnamese belonging to the Fifth ARVN Division, Rangers, and Binh Long provincial forces.

That afternoon, as enemy artillery shells and rockets rained on the town, Captain James Willbanks and Major Raymond M. Haney, both advisers to the Eighteenth ARVN Division, were deposited on a soccer field in its center, by a chopper pilot who didn't dare land. A two-battalion task force from their division had fought its way there from Loc Ninh to join the defenders. Three American advisers had been wounded in that struggle, and Willbanks and Haney had volunteered to replace them on the battlefield. They made their way to a building that served as task force headquarters.

The next morning, Willbanks remembered, he was installing a radio antenna on the roof when he heard "a tremendous explosion." He ran downstairs and into the street. "Panic-stricken South Vietnamese ran by, shouting, 'Thiet giap!'—a phrase he had not been taught in the El Paso language school. "However, as I ran around the corner of the building, it became all too apparent that the ARVN were yelling, 'Tanks!' Rumbling down the street toward us from the north was a column of North Vietnamese T-54s. So began the battle of An Loc."

The sight of the North Vietnamese tanks moving toward them terrified the ARVN at first. But the officers commanding the enemy's armor proved inept. Their tanks moved slowly, kept to the streets instead of moving cross-country, and were not accompanied by infantry—all basic errors in tank warfare. And South Vietnamese soldiers soon found that they were not as invulnerable as they looked. Captain Harold Moffett, an adviser with the Rangers, never forgot the impact on him of seeing a tank being taken out by a single soldier: "This little guy goes out to hunt a forty-ton piece of metal with a light antitank weapon on his back weighing two to three pounds. That's beyond belief, and it inspired me. How do you describe a little ARVN soldier fighting tanks? I was pretty well frightened like everyone else till it was determined we could knock them out with the weapons we had."

ABOVE James Willbanks at the entrance to the six-by-four-foot bunker in which he lived during the siege of An Loc, alongside what he remembered as "a million rats"

Those tanks not taken care of on the ground were destroyed from the air by Cobra attack helicopters firing armor-piercing rockets.

The colonel commanding the North Vietnamese forces had assured his superiors that he would take the town in less than ten days, but the battle would go on for the better part of three months, the longest siege of the Vietnam War. It was "more like World War One than anything else," Willbanks remembered. "We were in bunkers. They were attacking almost constantly—four thousand to ten thousand rounds a day."

Most important to the survival of the town's defenders was the amplitude of air support brought to bear by Major General James F. Hollingsworth, commander of the Third Regional Assistance Command. He was a sinewy, tough-talking veteran who had been wounded five times while serving in Patton's Army. "Once the communists decided to take An Loc," he said, "and I could get a handful of soldiers to hold and a lot of American advisers to keep them from running off, that's all I needed. Hold them and I'll kill them with airpower, give me something to bomb and I'll win."

"Hollingsworth rounded up anything that could fly and that could carry anything that would blow up," Willbanks remembered, "and he sent it in our direction on a daily basis as fast as he could send it." U.S. Air Force, Navy, and Marine Corps aircraft bombed enemy positions around the city while gunships of all kinds attacked the advancing tanks. So many planes flew in and out of the airspace above the town each day that directing air traffic became a major challenge. But the damage done to enemy troops massed in the open was devastating. "This," one American adviser said, "was the kind of war we came to fight."

Still, it was a close thing. Three times—twice in April and once in mid-May—the enemy came close to overwhelming the town. At one point its defenders were clinging to just half a square kilometer of ruined houses and cratered streets.

No supplies could reach them by road, and enemy antiaircraft fire forced flights to stay above eight thousand feet, making accurate drops difficult. At one point, Willbanks remembered, "we were in pretty bad straits because we were running out of food and ammo. We captured this young North Vietnamese lad and we asked him, 'What are you subsisting on?' He said, 'Fruit cocktail. Your Air Force gives us more than we can eat.'"

"For the first couple of weeks," Willbanks recalled, "no wounded could be lifted out. Then we were able to get some out south of town. That's where we had the infamous 'Olym-

Carrying two rocket-propelled grenades, a South Vietnamese soldier, his uniform showing the wear of unbroken weeks of battle, surveys the ruins of An Loc after relentless enemy shelling and U.S. bombing.

By mid-June, the wounded could be airlifted out at last and South Vietnam began replacing the exhausted men of the Fifth ARVN Division. "Some of the South Vietnamese flown out were barefoot," one U.S. pilot said; "some were too exhausted to do more than shuffle."

In the end, the South Vietnamese military sustained 5,400 casualties at An Loc, including 2,300 killed or missing. Perhaps 10,000 North Vietnamese died, their bodies often left unburied amid the wreckage of eighty-odd burned-out tanks and other vehicles.

Rudolph Rauch, a *Time* correspondent, was one of the first reporters to helicopter into what was left of the town. "There are perhaps six buildings left . . . , none with a solid roof," he wrote. "There is no running water or electricity. Every street is shattered by artillery craters and littered with the detritus of a battle that saw every kind of war. Everywhere you walk you hear the crackle of shifting shell fragments when you put your foot down."

The record of An Loc's defenders had been mixed. The commander of the Fifth ARVN Division rarely left his bunker. Some of his men used idle moments to loot homes and fire on Rangers trying to retrieve air-dropped supplies. But other South Vietnamese soldiers, notably the Rangers and the Territorial Force, Willbanks remembered, fought with "almost superhuman valor and skill."

"The important fact," Rauch wrote, "is that the city held. 'The only way to approach the battle of An Loc is to remember that the ARVN are there and the North Vietnamese aren't,' says an American adviser. 'To view it any other way is to do an injustice to the Vietnamese people.' But for the foreseeable future, An Loc is dead—as dead as the hundreds of North Vietnamese who were caught in the city's northern edge by U.S. bombing and whose putrefaction makes breathing in An Loc so difficult when the afternoon breeze comes up. Perhaps the best that can be said is that the city died bravely, and that—in a year that [includes] the fall of Quang Tri—that is no small achievement."

Sporadic shells were still falling on An Loc in early July. On the 9th, Brigadier General Richard J. Tallman landed in the ruined town with several of his staff officers to coordinate the continuing reinforcement effort. James Willbanks was among the advisers who went out to greet him. An artillery shell hit nearby. Everyone ran for cover. A second shell fell among the running men. The general was mortally wounded. Three officers and a South Vietnamese interpreter died instantly. Willbanks was wounded and momentarily knocked unconscious. When he came to, he recalled, "I could touch the guys that were killed. So why it didn't get me and got those guys I'll never know," he recalled. "It's something I've wrestled with for years."

pic wounded' incident, where stretcher bearers dropped the wounded guys and jumped on the helicopters. . . . But I will also tell you that for every guy that did that there were five guys who stayed and fought until they were killed, wounded, or relieved."

One day a North Vietnamese tank rolled into a Catholic church and killed some one hundred civilians cowering there; then, having expended their ammunition, the crew hung a white flag from the radio antenna, expecting to surrender. The pilot of a gunship overhead asked what he was to do about the tank. "Blow it away," was the answer.

Residents of the town spent weeks huddled underground. "We lived with the soldiers," one recalled. "We cooked and slept in our bunkers and relieved ourselves in tins and threw them out of the bunkers. No one worried about burying the dead, and the wounded were often left to die." A shell hit the morgue, hurling corpses into the air. Others virtually destroyed the hospital, though its roof was clearly marked with a red cross; afterward, an ARVN surgeon remembered, it housed "one thousand dead and wounded jumbled together."

When civilians did try to flee, the North Vietnamese drove them back into the encircled city with rockets and artillery. Asked after the war why this had been done, a political officer was unrepentant: "The revolution shelled this civilian crowd because this was a crowd of puppet civilians filled with reactionaries and counterrevolutionaries. We could not exempt them, and we had to teach them a lesson."

ABOVE Stretcher bearers carry a wounded South Vietnamese soldier past all that's left of a Soviet-made T-54, its deck decorated with an enemy skull, An Loc.

I HAVE THE *WILL* IN SPADES

IN EARLY MAY, with Quang Tri occupied by the enemy, An Loc still under siege, and North Vietnamese forces surrounding Kon Tum and moving on Hue, the Easter Offensive had seemed to be succeeding. General Abrams cabled the White House that "the senior [South Vietnamese] leadership has begun to bend and in some cases break . . . and cannot be depended on to take the measures necessary to stand and fight."

ABOVE RIGHT Navy crews load five-hundred-pound bombs aboard the Seventh Fleet's USS *Constellation,* part of the accelerated bombing of North Vietnam ordered by President Nixon.

ABOVE Demonstrators opposed to the renewed bombing of North Vietnam move down Central Park West in Manhattan, April 28, 1972.

Nixon sent Kissinger to Paris with a blunt message: "Settle or else!" He proposed a halt to the bombing provided both sides return to the status quo on the day the offensive began, followed by serious negotiations. Le Duc Tho dismissed the offer out of hand. North Vietnamese forces were carrying the day; there was no need to call a halt unless Washington were willing to abandon both Thieu and Vietnamization. "That was Hanoi's last chance," Nixon noted in his diary. "I decided now it was essential to defeat North Vietnam's invasion."

Le Duan's latest offensive was another great gamble.

So was Nixon's next move to defeat it. He was scheduled later that month to travel to Moscow, where he and Soviet leader Leonid Brezhnev were to sign an arms control treaty, the first agreement to limit nuclear armaments since the Cold War began. When Brezhnev warned him not to take any action in Vietnam that might imperil the upcoming summit, Nixon responded that since the North Vietnamese offensive would not be sustainable without weapons and supplies provided by the Soviet Union and China, he had no alternative but to act forcibly. "We can lose the summit and still not lose the country," he told Kissinger. "But we cannot lose this war without losing the country."

On May 8, he told the country he was extending air and naval assaults on North Vietnam indefinitely. But then he went further: "There is only one way to stop the killing," he said. "That is to take the weapons of war out of the hands of the international outlaws of Vietnam." Accordingly, eleven thousand mines were to be laid in North Vietnamese waters to block further access to Haiphong Harbor, where Soviet supply ships regularly docked.

He made a direct appeal to Moscow not to see this action as anything other than an attempt to end a war that had gone on far too long: "Let us not slide back toward the dark shadows of a previous age. We do not ask you to sacrifice your principles or your friends, but neither should you permit Hanoi's intransigence to blot out the prospects we together have so patiently prepared."

Antiwar critics were quick to denounce the president. Senator George McGovern called "this new escalation reckless, unnecessary and unworkable . . . a flirtation with World War III." Senator Edmund Muskie of Maine accused the president of "risking a major confrontation with the Soviet Union and with China and . . . jeopardizing the major security interests of the United States." But a Lou Harris poll found that 59 percent of those polled supported the president's decision and only 24 percent disapproved.

In any case, Nixon's gamble paid off. The Soviets and the Chinese both formally denounced the American bombing, but neither took any action of their own. Nixon traveled to Moscow, and on May 26, the United States and the Soviet Union signed the Anti-Ballistic Missile Treaty.

Meanwhile, the greatly expanded bombing campaign in North Vietnam—code-named Operation Linebacker because of the president's fondness for football—got under way. "Those bastards are going to be bombed like they've never been bombed before," he said. "What I am directing is bombing, all out," Nixon told Admiral Moorer. "You are to hit . . . North Vietnam. . . . You are to aim for military targets. You are not to be too concerned about whether it slops over [into civilian areas]. . . . If it slops over, that's too bad. . . . We must punish the enemy in ways that he will really hurt this time." Lyndon Johnson hadn't had the will to do that, he said, but "I have the *will* in spades."

The bombing campaign had three objectives: to destroy military supplies wherever they could be found in North Vietnam; to cut off any possibility of replenishing those supplies; and to interdict any shipments intended for the battlefield in the South. Targets were selected by military commanders rather than civilians in the White House. More than four hundred bridges between Hanoi and China were destroyed, many of them high in the Annamite Mountains where rapid repair was impossible. Highways were hit. Rail lines were disrupted and railyards

destroyed. Petroleum storage facilities, power-generating plants, military barracks and training camps and air defenses were all bombed.

The Linebacker bombing, Leslie Gelb recalled, "was much more extensive than the bombing campaign under Lyndon Johnson. And from a standpoint of pressuring them to make concessions at the negotiating table, historically that's how you did it. Only it didn't work with these guys. They took the pounding."

Somehow, as the journalist Joseph Kraft reported in *The New Yorker*, North Vietnam was "not paralyzed. Large quantities of

ABOVE Luong Toan, eighty-four years old, makes his way through the ruins of the town of Thong Nat; a few days earlier, he had narrowly escaped bombing at Thanh Hoa, several miles to the south. Both towns were hit by U.S. bombs because a highway and a railroad line ran through them.

OUR FANTASY

"Jane Fonda was one of our major fantasies," John Musgrave remembered. "I mean *major* fantasies. And we couldn't believe it when that fantasy went to North Vietnam. She was held to a different standard of conduct by being our fantasy, our dream girl. It was like our dream girl betrayed us."

Throughout the war, a steady stream of Americans opposed to the war had visited Hanoi, including the folk singer Joan Baez, Lyndon Johnson's attorney general, Ramsey Clark, David Dellinger of the War Resisters League, Tom Hayden of the Indochina Peace Campaign, the writer Susan Sontag, and Cora Weiss of Women Strike for Peace. They carried mail to and from POWs and sometimes helped arrange for their return home.

But no visitor made more headlines than the actress Jane Fonda. During two weeks in the summer of 1972, with Operation Linebacker under way, she broadcast at least ten times over Radio Hanoi, denouncing American bombing of civilians as a war crime, accusing POWs of being war criminals, and urging the North Vietnamese to hold out against American imperialism.

"I don't know what your officers tell you [about what you] are loading," she broadcast to U.S. air crews, "those of you who load the bombs on these planes. But one thing you should know is that these weapons are illegal, and that's not just rhetoric. They were outlawed, these kinds of weapons, by several conventions of which the United States was a signatory. . . . And the use of these bombs or condoning the use of these bombs makes one a war criminal."

"We have understood that we have a common enemy—U.S. imperialism," she told North Vietnamese students. "We have understood that we have a common struggle and that your victory will be the victory of the American and all peace-loving people around the world."

"She's taken a lot of heat," Musgrave recalled, "and deservedly so. Yes, we have a right to be pissed off at her. But, you know, she wasn't the only one. She's just the only one we fantasized about."

LEFT Jane Fonda visits an antiaircraft emplacement near Hanoi, 1972.

goods move at a fairly rapid clip all the time." So many trucks came and went in Hanoi while he was there, he said, that the downtown had become "a kind of national parking lot."

In the city, air raids had become almost routine, Kraft wrote. They were invariably preceded by a pilotless reconnaissance plane that flew too fast to be hit by antiaircraft guns or the new surface-to-air (SAM) missiles supplied by the Soviets.

Only the noise of the drone's breaking through the sound barrier announces its advent. It is a startling noise—like a sudden clap of thunder—but after almost four months of bombing hardly anybody in Hanoi bothers to look up. The drone is dismissed with a shrug as "the noon plane." . . .

Danger is first signaled by a pre-alert broadcast through loudspeakers all over town which announces that American planes have been sighted . . . at a distance of about thirty miles. A second pre-alert soon afterward announces that the planes are within the fifty-kilometer radius. Then, within a few minutes the alert itself sounds—a long, wailing siren note that rises, dips, and then rises again. Minutes later, the planes come into sight—fighter-bombers, floating lazily, and then diving on targets to drop bombs which can be heard though not seen as they fall. As soon as the planes are visible, the racket of the anti-aircraft guns begins. Almost simultaneously the SAMs can be seen, powered upward by rocket engines that give off a faint red glow. During the raid of July 4th, it was possible to follow the glow of a missile until a plane was struck and sent spinning to earth, trailing a cloud of black smoke.

Each evening at 11:30 the North Vietnamese government radio signed off with an announcement of the number of planes shot down that day—and a running tally of hits on B-52s since the war began.

Laser-guided and electro-optical guided munitions were employed by U.S. forces for the first time during Operation Linebacker, greatly improving the accuracy of targeting, according to the military. But the improvement was only relative and, to those unfortunate enough to be the victims of even the slightest inaccuracy, irrelevant.

Kraft was taken into the countryside to see the bombing's impact there. The day before he reached a trading town called Hung Yen, thirty-six miles from the capital, its center had been hit by eighteen blast bombs and four antipersonnel bombs, each containing almost two thousand steel pellets. Seventeen people died, twenty-five more were wounded, and forty-five homes were destroyed. In one, he found a woman trying to reassemble members of her family—"a charred jawbone, a hank of hair, what looked like a leg"—while muttering to herself, "My brother and sister were innocent." In another ruined home he met a seventy-two-year-old man, a Catholic, who had lost his wife, his only son, and his grandson while they were saying their prayers: "He stood in the rubble, a toothless old man, and raised his fists to the heavens. 'I feel deep hatred against the Americans,' he shouted. 'As long as I live, I will have hatred in my heart!' "

The mother of Le Minh Kue, the girl who went to work on the Ho Chi Minh Trail at sixteen with a Hemingway novel in her backpack, went into labor in a bomb shelter during one air raid. "The whole village was burning," her daughter remembered, "so there was no one there to help her except my ten-year-old brother." He ran out to a well for water, cut the umbilical cord, and bandaged his mother's wounds. Somehow all three survived.

When the Easter Offensive finally ended in October, Hanoi would be able to point to some concrete gains. It held roughly half of the four northernmost provinces of South Vietnam as well as several largely unpopulated patches along the borders of Cambodia and Laos, and, because South Vietnamese forces in relatively pacified areas had been required to move elsewhere to meet the enemy threat, fresh opportunities had opened up for the NLF to rebuild the infrastructure the pacification program had tried to eradicate. But the ARVN, supported by American advisers and augmented by American airpower, had recaptured most of the territory the North had tried to seize. The three massive assaults on widely separated targets with which the offensive had begun had proved far too ambitious, Operation Linebacker had reduced Hanoi's ability to resupply its forces remaining in the South, and of the roughly 200,000 soldiers who had taken part, more than half were estimated to have been killed, while nearly all of the armor the North Vietnamese had recently received had been destroyed. The North Vietnamese chief of staff warned the senior cadre of COSVN that losses had been so great it was unlikely the North could mount another offensive for at least three years—and it might take as long as five.

South Vietnam had suffered terrible losses, too. Some 25,000 civilians had died in the fighting and nearly a million more had been driven from their homes. The ARVN had lost 45,000 men. But they had halted the enemy onslaught and then pushed it back—proof positive, Nixon said, that Vietnamization was working, that South Vietnam would soon be able to defend itself. Still, American airpower had been central to that victory. It was thought to have accounted for at least half the enemy dead. Many, both in Saigon and Washington, feared that without it the outcome would have been very different. But President Thieu drew a different lesson from the same set of facts: so long as he could call upon the Americans when his forces got into trouble, he could continue to believe that South Vietnam might yet survive and eventually win the war.

ABOVE AND TOP Photographer Nick Ut and the village of Trang Bang as napalm engulfed it **OPPOSITE TOP** Ut's Pulitzer Prize–winning photograph of Kim Phuc pleading for help **BOTTOM LEFT** Journalists try to help the badly burned girl. **BOTTOM RIGHT** Kim Phuc, now a Canadian, with her own child

PLEASE HELP ME!

On the morning of June 8, 1972, Nick Ut, a twenty-one-year-old South Vietnamese photographer working for the Associated Press, was accompanying ARVN troops on Highway 1, moving toward a village called Trang Bang, to dislodge North Vietnamese forces that had occupied it during the Easter Offensive.

Ut was beginning to put his cameras away, ready to return to Saigon, when he saw a South Vietnamese fighter suddenly dip down toward the fleeing refugees, whom the pilot mistook for the enemy.

As napalm engulfed the village Ut began clicking. "Oh, my God, it's a good picture," he said to himself. Then, emerging from the black smoke, several children were seen running toward him, including one girl whose clothing had been burned off completely. He kept shooting.

When the girl reached Ut and several other reporters standing with him she stopped running and kept saying in Vietnamese, "Too hot, too hot," and "Please help me, please help me!" Her skin was peeling off her back. Ut borrowed a raincoat from a South Vietnamese soldier to cover her. A BBC reporter helped find water. "Without help, I knew she would die," Ut recalled. He drove the badly burned girl, whose name was Kim Phuc, and several other injured children to a hospital in Saigon. She had burns over 30 percent of her body.

Then he raced to the AP darkroom to find out what he had caught on film. He was pretty sure he had good pictures, but when his photo editor saw them he said he couldn't send them out on the wire: the girl was naked. Ut's boss, the legendary combat photographer Horst Faas, took one look and overruled the editor. They were to be captioned and sent immediately to AP headquarters in New York.

Nick Ut's photograph appeared on front pages around the world the next day and won him the Pulitzer Prize. For many Americans—even many of those who had supported the war—the image seemed to signal that it had to be brought to an end.

LET'S BE PERFECTLY COLD-BLOODED

RICHARD NIXON sometimes liked to muse about the role chance had played in his remarkable career. Few people were shrewder about politics than he, but he was too stiff and self-conscious to be a natural politician and he had been thought finished until John Kennedy's death in Dallas allowed him to return unexpectedly to center stage. On May 15, 1972, something like that had happened again. Former Alabama governor George Wallace—who had run up an impressive string of Democratic primaries and whose appeal to white working-class voters threatened to disassemble Nixon's Silent Majority—was shot and permanently paralyzed by a demented would-be assassin. Had Wallace won the Democratic nomination or—more likely—had he lost it and then run as a third-party candidate siphoning off Republican votes, Nixon's reelection chances would have been anything but certain.

To enhance those chances and find material that might be used to smear the opposition, Nixon aides working for the Committee for the Re-Election of the President authorized another break-in, this time at Democratic National Headquarters in the Washington, D.C., apartment complex called the Watergate. All five burglars had been caught, and some in the White House had already begun to worry about what they might be persuaded to reveal to the authorities.

Meanwhile, in July, Nixon's luck seemed to hold when the Democrats gathered in Miami to choose their presidential nominee. George McGovern was a decorated bomber pilot in World War II and an early and ardent critic of the Vietnam War. His message was uncompromising: he called for an end to the bombing of the North, a halt to congressional funding for the war, and immediate withdrawal from Vietnam once the POWs were released. Buoyed by a youthful and unpaid legion of supporters, many of whom had worked for Robert Kennedy and Eugene McCarthy four years earlier, he had defeated two more middle-of-the-road contenders in the primaries, Hubert Humphrey and Edmund Muskie.

Among those who seconded his nomination at the convention was Valerie Kushner, the wife of Hal Kushner, who had recently made his painful way from a jungle camp in South Vietnam to a prison in Hanoi. At first, the families of prisoners and those missing in action had overwhelmingly supported the Nixon administration because of its stated commitment to the return of their husbands and fathers and sons as a condition for peace. But as the months dragged on with little apparent progress, some began to disbelieve their promises. Valerie Kushner was among them. She had campaigned in the primaries

for McGovern, she told the delegates, because "I knew that he would bring my husband home."

Party reformers, determined to get away from boss rule and the "smoke-filled room" style of politics they blamed for what had happened in Chicago four years earlier, had rewritten the rules in 1972 to provide opportunities for groups that had felt themselves underrepresented—women, minorities, young people.

The goal was worthy. The result was chaos. On the final night of the convention, after the name of Senator Thomas Eagleton of Missouri, McGovern's choice for vice president, was placed in nomination, delegates ate up precious television time nominating thirty-nine other candidates, including Dr. Spock, Mao Tse-tung, and Archie Bunker. "Speakers were indulged and self-indulgent," Nixon thought, watching from his summer home in San Clemente, California. "There was no semblance of orderly procedure. . . . The scene had the air of a college skit that had gotten carried away with itself and didn't know how to stop."

By the time the presidential nominee began his acceptance speech, intended to introduce him to the American electorate, it was 2:48 in the morning. By then, a television audience of more than 17 million had shrunk to 3.6 million. Even in California most people had gone to bed; only in Hawaii, where it was 8:48 in the evening, could American voters watch the candidate in prime time.

McGovern was the son of a Methodist minister and his words that morning had something of the pulpit about them: "In Scripture and in the music of our children we are told: 'To everything there is a season, and a time to every purpose under heaven.' . . . This is the time for truth, not falsehood. . . .

"During four administrations of both parties, a terrible war has been charted behind closed doors. I want those doors opened, and I want that war closed. . . . Within ninety days of my inauguration, every American soldier and every American prisoner will be . . . back home in America where they belong. . . .

"Together we will call America home to the founding ideals that nourished us in the beginning. From secrecy and deception in high places, come home, America. . . . From the waste of idle hands to the joy of useful labor, come home, America. From the prejudice of race and sex, come home, America. . . . Come home to the affirmation that we have a dream. Come home to the conviction that we can move our country forward. Come home to the belief that we can seek a newer world. And let us be joyful in that homecoming. . . . May God grant us the wisdom to cherish this good land and to meet the great challenge that beckons us home."

The delegates linked arms and broke into spontaneous song:

"Glory, Glory, Hallelujah," "Battle Hymn of the Republic," and "We Shall Overcome."

That early-morning singalong turned out to be the high point of the Democratic campaign. When McGovern, who barely knew his running mate, discovered that Eagleton had failed to tell him he'd twice undergone electroshock treatments for depression, he told the press he was behind Eagleton one thousand percent anyway, then five days later dropped him from the ticket. Six other potential vice presidential nominees then turned him down before Sargent Shriver, a Kennedy in-law and the former head of the Peace Corps, agreed to make the race with him. Then, at the urging of the antiwar activist David Dellinger, he sent an emissary to Paris to speak in secret with the North Vietnamese delegation to the peace talks, hoping to arrange for the release of forty POWs. The discussion came to nothing, and when reporters got wind of it, McGovern denied he'd had anything to do with it.

Democrats were fatally divided. Many who were fed up with the war were also uncomfortable with the notion of accepting

ABOVE George McGovern and his first vice presidential pick, Thomas Eagleton, meet the press. McGovern "is beginning to remind us of those schoolteachers who couldn't keep the class," Jimmy Breslin wrote as the campaign began. "Nice people," but "the erasers flew when they turned their backs."

defeat and offended by the excesses of the antiwar movement. The AFL-CIO, Democratic to the core, refused to endorse the party's candidate. So did Chicago mayor Richard Daley. In early August, a Harris poll showed McGovern 23 percentage points behind Richard Nixon, the largest gap between Democratic and Republican presidential candidates since scientific polling began.

The Republican gathering in the same city later in the month was less convention than coronation. The delegates, the journalist Theodore White wrote, were "clean, neat people. This correspondent counted only three bearded delegates . . . two of them from New York. And no long-hairs. . . . The California delegation at the Republican convention . . . was so different from the California delegation to the Democratic convention that it might have come not from a different state, but from a different country or a different era—no cowboy boots, no open collars, no Indians, few blacks, no blue-jeaned girls." Governor Ronald Reagan of California warned that "our traditional two-party system has become a three-party system—Republican, McGovern, and Democrat." Barry Goldwater denounced McGovern for having "already surrendered to the enemy before the election has even been held." New York governor Nelson Rockefeller nominated Nixon as the president "who has brought us to the threshold of peace."

Nixon was an old hand at acceptance speeches. This was to be his fifth.

"Standing in this convention hall four years ago," he told the delegates and a vast prime-time TV audience, "I pledged to seek an honorable end to the war in Vietnam. We have made great progress toward that end. We have brought over half a million men home, and more will be coming home. We have ended America's ground combat role. No draftees are being sent to Vietnam. We have reduced our casualties by 98 percent. We have gone the extra mile, in fact we have gone tens of thousands of miles trying to seek a negotiated settlement of the war. We have offered a ceasefire, a total withdrawal of all American forces, an exchange of all prisoners of war, internationally supervised free elections with the communists participating in the elections and in the supervision. There are three things, however, that we have not and that we will not offer. We will never abandon our prisoners of war. Second, we will not join our enemies in imposing a communist government on our allies—the 17 million people of South Vietnam. And we will never stain the honor of the United States of America."

A week after the Republican convention, Nixon was leading McGovern in the polls by thirty-four points.

That same month, when Nixon and Henry Kissinger had discussed the prospects for peace and the likely future of South Vietnam, their tone was considerably less elevated.

RICHARD NIXON: Let's be perfectly cold-blooded about it. If you look at it from the standpoint of our game with the Soviets and the Chinese, from the standpoint of running this country, I think we could take, in my view, almost anything, frankly, that we can force on Thieu. Almost anything. I just come down to that. You know what I mean? . . . Because I look at the tide of history out there, South Vietnam probably can never even survive anyway. I'm just being perfectly candid—I—

HENRY KISSINGER: In the pull-out area—

NIXON: We also have to realize, Henry, that winning an election is terribly important. It's terribly important this year—but can we have a viable foreign policy if a year from now or two years from now, if North Vietnam gobbles up South Vietnam? That's the real question.

KISSINGER: If a year or two years from now North Vietnam gobbles up South Vietnam, we can have a viable foreign policy if it looks as if it's the result of South Vietnamese incompetence. If we now sell out in such a way that, say, within a three- to four-month period, we have pushed President Thieu over the brink . . . domestically in the long run it won't help us all that much because our opponents will say we should've done it three years ago.

NIXON: I know.

KISSINGER: So we've got to find some formula that holds the thing together a year or two, after which—after a year, Mr. President, Vietnam will be a backwater. If we settle it, say, this October, by January '74 no one will give a damn.

THIS IS IT

IN OCTOBER, Hanoi agreed to return to Paris. With its latest offensive blunted, its harbors mined, still suffering from intensive bombing, now under pressure to be more flexible from both China and the Soviet Union, and resigned to Nixon's almost certain re-election, it was time to talk. "The situation is now ripe," said Le Duc Tho.

Nixon had set September as the last possible moment for an agreement. He was determined to win a historic election victory in November. When voters went to the polls on Election Day he wanted to be close enough to a peace treaty to reassure mod-

THE PRIDE OF A REVOLUTIONARY

In October 1972, a CIA case officer named Frank Snepp was given an unusual assignment: he was to see if he could obtain useful intelligence from a mysterious North Vietnamese prisoner who had managed to withstand twenty-two months of torture and interrogation without breaking. Years later, Snepp would remember him as "the most extraordinary man I met in Vietnam."

Nguyen Tai, the son of a prominent Vietnamese novelist, joined the revolution at eighteen in 1944. By the time he was twenty-one he was directing covert warfare in French-occupied Hanoi— organizing assassination teams to kill Frenchmen and those who collaborated with them, sending a woman with a valise full of explosives to board a French navy vessel and sink it, making her perhaps history's first female suicide bomber. After the French departed, he denounced his own father for daring to criticize the communist regime, and was made head of Hanoi's version of the Soviet KGB. Under his direction, every one of the U.S. spies and saboteurs who parachuted into North Vietnam in 1963 was captured or killed, and those senior party members who dissented from Le Duan's plans for a General Offensive, General Uprising were methodically purged.

In 1964, adopting an assumed name and leaving his wife and three young children behind, he was sent to the South and, as the clandestine chief of security for Saigon and the surrounding Gia Dinh Province, strictly followed the orders he'd been given to recruit spies and "to exploit every opportunity to kill enemy leaders and vicious thugs." Hundreds of South Vietnamese and scores of Americans were killed by his assassins—shot, stabbed, blown up.

South Vietnamese forces captured him in 1970. Although he was the highest-ranking North Vietnamese intelligence agent ever to fall into South Vietnamese hands, he claimed at first to be a lowly captain, freshly arrived from the North. His captors did not believe him. CIA interrogators were brought in. He shifted to a second cover story: he was a North Vietnamese agent, intending to move on to France. They didn't believe that, either.

He was turned over to the South Vietnamese. Weeks of torture followed. He was beaten while hanging from the ceiling, forced to sit on a stool around the clock for days, denied food and water, subjected to electric shocks and the Vietnamese version of waterboarding. He did his best to tell his torturers only things that they already knew or that could not be checked.

"I had the pride of a revolutionary," he remembered, "so I was determined to defeat my enemies. I was never going to lose to that gang. But then I was betrayed, identified by a traitor who pointed me out and said, 'That's Mr. Duc Ong'—that was my code name. I stared at him and later he committed suicide out of guilt."

The torture resumed. The South Vietnamese now tried to get him to reveal the identities of his agents and the whereabouts of NLF bases. "I thought that if I didn't die," he remembered, "they might get the information out of me and then I would have betrayed my organization." Fearing that he might eventually be made to give in, he tried to slash his wrists with fragments of a metal mirror but failed to cut himself deeply enough.

When he still maintained his silence, he was blindfolded, moved to a white, windowless room, and turned over

to a series of CIA interrogators. They engaged him in a game of wits in which he more than held his own.

One of his interrogators was Frank Snepp. "When I walked into that interrogation room this was one of the most disciplined men I had ever seen," Snepp recalled. "He had learned to tell time by the chemistry of his body. He was in a snow-white room. No windows. No way of knowing whether it was day or night. And yet he knew he had to get up at six o'clock and go through calisthenics."

There was more to his routine than that; each day, he saluted a star he had scratched on the wall, representing the North Vietnamese flag, then silently recited, in turn, the North Vietnamese national anthem, the South Vietnamese liberation anthem, and "The Internationale."

Once, Snepp asked him about his family. "I cannot think about my wife and children," he said. "The only way I can survive this is by putting all such hopes aside. Then there are no disillusions or disappointments."

It was Snepp who brought the news of the Paris Accords to the prisoner in early February 1973. "If what you tell me is true," Nguyen Tai said, "then this is the happiest day of my life." American interrogation ended that day. "I was led to believe Tai had been exchanged in the prisoner exchange that followed the ceasefire," Snepp recalled. "But he hadn't. He was left in the snow-white room for another two years."

OPPOSTE AND ABOVE The North Vietnamese spy Nguyen Tai, before his ordeal began and long afterward

erates but to have signed nothing that might cause hawks and conservatives to accuse him of selling out South Vietnam. "Let's try our best not to have it before the election," he told Kissinger. "The more that we can stagger past the election, the better." But Kissinger was determined to hammer out an agreement before Election Day. His motives seem to have been mixed. To the president's frequent consternation, his role in organizing Nixon's visits to China and Moscow had made him an international celebrity in his own right. A successful negotiation with Hanoi would only add to his luster. But more than that, he thought he could use election day as a sort of deadline, implying to his negotiating partners that there was no telling what Nixon might do to end the war once he'd safely been returned to office. "There was somehow this compulsion to come to some kind of an agreement quickly," recalled John Negroponte, then a young Foreign Service officer serving on the U.S. peace delegation. "I remember Le Duc Tho when he produced the draft agreement, saying to Kissinger, 'You're in a hurry, aren't you? You want to do this quickly.' The response was 'Yes.'"

In any case, each side had moved toward the other. Under the new plan, Kissinger and Le Duc Tho worked out a ceasefire to be followed within sixty days by the withdrawal of all U.S. forces and the release of all American POWs. Washington, which had already dropped any objection to North Vietnamese troops remaining in the South, was now willing to accept the creation of a tripartite electoral commission to be composed of the Saigon regime, the Provisional Revolutionary Government, and a neutralist faction that was to arrive at a long-term settlement once the ceasefire went into effect. Meanwhile, Hanoi no longer insisted that Thieu be removed before the shooting stopped, provided that the PRG was permitted fully to participate in political life.

On October 12, an ebullient Kissinger returned from Paris and reported to his chief. "Well, you got three out of three, Mr. President [the visit to China, the Moscow summit, and now a Vietnam peace agreement]. It's well on the way."

"You got an agreement?" Nixon asked. "Are you kidding?"

"No, I'm not kidding."

The president and Al Haig listened as Kissinger outlined the plan. Nixon was pleased but wary. "Let me come down to the nut cutting, looking at Thieu. What Henry has read to me, Thieu cannot turn down. If he does, our problem will be that we have to flush him and that will have flushed South Vietnam. Now, how the hell are we going to come up on that?"

Although Nixon had promised Thieu during their 1969 Midway meeting that he would be consulted every step of the way as Kissinger's talks with Hanoi proceeded, he had in fact rarely been kept fully informed. Nixon sought, with vague guarantees and calls for unity, to ease his anxiety about plans for his

country's future being cobbled together by the United States and his sworn enemies: "I give you my firm assurance that there will be no settlement arrived at, the provisions of which have not been discussed personally with you beforehand. . . . The American people know that the United States cannot purchase peace or honor or redeem its sacrifices at the price of deserting a brave ally. This I will not and will never do . . . but for us to succeed on this last leg of a journey, we must trust each other fully." Thieu was not comforted.

"Both the P[resident] and Henry are realizing in the cold light of dawn . . . that they still have a plan that can fall apart," H. R. Haldeman noted in his diary, "mainly the problem of getting Thieu aboard. . . . The settlement he's got is the best [he] is ever going to get and unlike '68 when Thieu screwed Johnson [and] he had Nixon as an alternative, now he has McGovern . . . which would be a disaster for him, even worse than the worst possible thing Nixon could do to him."

Kissinger was scheduled to arrive in Saigon on October 18, bringing with him the Paris agreement for Thieu's last-minute approval. He hoped for a signing ceremony on the 31st, one week before election day. But the night before he arrived, a document found in an underground NLF bunker in Quang Tri Province was placed on the South Vietnamese president's desk. It was entitled "General Instruction for Cease-Fire." To him, it suggested that communist cadres in an isolated province of his own country already knew more than he did about what Kissinger and Le Duc Tho had agreed to in Paris.

Thieu was furious. "I wanted to punch Kissinger in the mouth," he told an aide. John Negroponte thought his anger was wholly justified: "Imagine being given an agreement concerning the fate of your own country and being told that you really don't have any input in the matter. And, oh by the way, we didn't even yet have the Vietnamese translation because that hadn't been completed. So we gave him the English version of the agreement. As a professional diplomat, somebody who's been in this business all my life, I've got to tell you an awful lot of diplomatic rules were broken there."

Thieu refused to approve the agreement. "If we accept the document as it stands," he told Kissinger, "we will commit suicide—and I will be committing suicide." He then took his objections public. Allowing North Vietnamese troops to remain in the South would be the death of his country, he told the South Vietnamese people. The proposed tripartite commission was simply a variation on the coalition the communists had always demanded; if he were to agree to it, and the communists took over, perhaps five million of his countrymen would lose their lives.

Kissinger returned to Washington and, despite the awkward impasse in Saigon, held a press conference at which he declared, "We believe peace is at hand." His intention was evidently to keep the North Vietnamese on board while he renewed efforts to bring Thieu along, but critics saw such a strong hint of imminent peace given only a little over a week before Election Day as political gimmickry.

Nonetheless, on November 7, Richard Nixon won the stunning reelection victory he'd hoped for—521 electoral votes to McGovern's 17, more than 60 percent of the popular vote, every single state except Massachusetts, and the District of Columbia.

Now, the president set out to complete the peace agreement negotiated before the election. The last remaining obstacle was Thieu. To convince him that he was not being abandoned, Nixon ordered a massive new airlift of military equipment to South Vietnam. The United States had already just completed a program called Enhance, meant to replace all the weapons and equipment the ARVN had lost during the Easter Offensive. Now, Enhance Plus would provide an additional 266 aircraft, from fighter bombers to helicopters, 72 tanks, nearly 300 armored vehicles, 56 howitzers, and 1,726 trucks. "If we had [given] this aid to the *North* Vietnamese," one American general said, "they could have fought us for the rest of the century."

Nixon privately assured Thieu that he stood ready to intervene with airpower when the North Vietnamese violated the agreement—which both he and Thieu were sure they'd do—but warned that he would be unable to do so if the American public and the U.S. Congress came to see Thieu as an obstacle to peace. If Saigon balked, he was confident, Congress would simply pass a resolution offering to withdraw all U.S. troops in exchange for the U.S. POWs and leave South Vietnam to the tender mercies of Hanoi.

Thieu was pleased with the new weaponry and tucked the president's letters away, but he was still unwilling to approve the agreement. Instead, he came up with sixty-nine objections to it: he remained opposed to any form of coalition government, wanted the North Vietnamese army to go home, insisted the DMZ be made permanent. Kissinger thought many of his objections "preposterous," but dutifully raised them when the talks resumed on November 20. It was now Le Duc Tho's turn to be angry. "We have been deceived by the French, the Japanese, and the Americans," he told Kissinger, "but the deception has never been so flagrant as now. . . . You told us this was a fait accompli and you swallowed your words. What kind of person must we think you to be?"

The haggling continued. Then, on December 13, Le Duc Tho said he needed to return to Hanoi for several days for "consultations." "We could only conclude," John Negroponte remembered, "that maybe they were having some doubts about whether they wanted to go through with the agreement because we had sent so many supplies to Saigon in the intervening weeks." That was not the problem. There was dissension on the communist side, as well. Hanoi, like Washington, had not bothered to consult with its southern allies when it dropped the two demands that meant the most to the NLF and the PRG—the removal of Thieu and the release of some thirty thousand of their prisoners languishing in his jails. "Hanoi's message was clear," one bitter PRG official remembered. "It cared more about . . . American prisoners of war . . . than it did" about them.

Kissinger, frustrated and out of favor with his chief, cabled Nixon that the agreement seemed to be falling apart: "Hanoi is almost disdainful of us because we have no effective leverage left, while Saigon in its short-sighted devices to sabotage the agreement knocks out from under us the few remaining props." The only way out, he thought, was to "turn hard on Hanoi"—by which he meant resumption of massive bombing—while keeping pressure on Thieu.

Nixon needed little urging. He had never shared Kissinger's full faith in negotiations, had never entirely abandoned the fantasy of somehow *winning* the war as opposed to simply ending it. He ordered Kissinger to suspend the talks, falsely accused Hanoi of having abandoned the negotiations when they had asked for only a few days' delay, and then, on December 18, unleashed Linebacker II, a round-the-clock bombing of North Vietnam on an unprecedented scale. "I don't want any more crap about the fact that we couldn't hit this target or that one," he told Admiral Moorer. "This is your chance to use military power to win this war and if you don't I'll consider you responsible."

The president seems to have had two simultaneous objectives in mind: to make a show of forcing North Vietnam back to the negotiating table, and to demonstrate to Thieu and Thieu's admirers in the United States the near-limitless American air power he would be willing to wield against the North should it violate the letter or the spirit of the document he was insisting the South Vietnamese president sign.

The bombing went on for twelve days—eleven days, a break for Christmas, and a final day of bombing. During that time, U.S. warplanes dropped 36,000 tons of bombs on North Vietnam—more than had fallen between 1969 and 1971. It would be remembered as the "Christmas Bombing."

Around the world, antiwar demonstrators returned to the streets. The prime minister of Sweden compared the United States to Nazi Germany. The pope called the bombing—which flattened whole neighborhoods in Hanoi, Haiphong, and elsewhere and killed more than 1,600 civilians—"the object of daily grief." James Reston of *The New York Times* pronounced the raids "war by tantrum"; Tom Wicker called them "shame on earth." Republican senator William Saxbe of Ohio suggested that the president had taken leave of his senses.

North Vietnam shot down fifteen B-52s along with eleven other aircraft. Ninety-three crewmen were reported missing.

Forty-five new prisoners of war were locked up in Hanoi, one of whom died in captivity. The North Vietnamese boasted that it was "Dien Bien Phu in the air."

On December 26, the Americans mounted the most intense B-52 attack in history—120 bombers, each carrying an assortment of 108 500- and 750-pound bombs, hit 10 targets in Hanoi and Haiphong in just 15 minutes,

"And all of a sudden," Hal Kushner remembered, in his Hanoi prison cell he heard "an Arc Light operation, B-52s—*bom-bom-bom-bom-bom*—and it's all around. It's just exploding. Everyone knew they were B-52s. And the two years that I was there that was the first time I ever heard a bomb. And it was close. It was really close. It was frightening but we were still cheering, cheering because something was finally happening."

In his village, Huy Duc heard and saw the bombing, too. "I witnessed all of it," he recalled. "I was ten years old. My village was shattered. No trees were left. Fish in the river were killed. Water buffaloes and people died. Six of my neighbors were killed, including a woman who was pregnant."

A nephew of Duong Van Mai Elliot also died. The son of a sibling who had stayed in the North, he was killed by a bomb that destroyed a nearby power plant. "It didn't hit him or his house but his family found him dead standing under the stairwell, still holding onto his bicycle. He had been asphyxiated by the force of the explosion. In Hanoi in those days a bicycle was your most precious possession, so he had taken this bike in, hiding it with him in order to save it."

The B-52s destroyed what little was left of the North Vietnamese air defense system. The country was now virtually defenseless against further air attacks. Meanwhile, both the Chinese and the Soviets pressed Hanoi to resume negotiations rather than absorb more punishment. "The most important [thing] is to let the Americans *leave*," Zhou Enlai told a North Vietnamese official. "The situation will change in six months or a year."

Hanoi signaled its willingness to return to Paris. Nixon gave Kissinger grim instructions: the United States should either agree to an immediate settlement on the best terms he could negotiate or "we would break with Thieu and continue the bombing until the North agreed to return our POWs" and U.S. forces could all come home. "Well," Nixon told Kissinger as he left for Paris, "one way or another, this is it."

In the end, it took just six days to draft an agreement different only in the most minor details from the one that had been worked out in November. "We bombed the North Vietnamese into accepting our concessions," John Negroponte recalled.

President Thieu still had to be convinced. Nixon was adamant that he now give in. "Brutality is nothing," Nixon told Al Haig. "You have never seen it if this son of a bitch doesn't

go along, believe me." He wrote Thieu three personal letters, containing both threats and promises. He was determined that the agreement be initialed on January 23 and signed in Paris four days later, he said in his first letter. If necessary he would act alone, though if that happened he said he would have to "explain publicly that your government obstructs peace. The result will be an inevitable and immediate termination of U.S. military and economic assistance which cannot be forestalled by a change of personnel in your government." (Thieu seems to have taken this talk of "a change of personnel" as a threat, a not-so-subtle echo of language used by John F. Kennedy in a conversation with Walter Cronkite in 1963, just before the Diem regime was overturned.)

Thieu continued to resist.

In his second letter, Nixon reiterated his insistence that if Thieu failed to sign he faced "a total cutoff of funds to assist your country." But he also pledged that "the freedom and independence of the Republic of Vietnam remains a paramount objective of American foreign policy," that Washington would continue to recognize Thieu's government as the "sole legitimate government of South Vietnam, and would not recognize the right of foreign troops to remain on South Vietnamese soil," and—most important from Thieu's point of view—"the U.S. will react vigorously to violations of the Agreement."

A third Nixon letter set a deadline: if Thieu didn't agree to sign by 1200 Washington time on the 21st, the president would have no choice but to announce that Kissinger was authorized to initial the agreement "without the concurrence of your government."

The South Vietnamese president finally gave in.

"The Americans really leave me no choice," Thieu told an aide, "either sign or they will cut off aid. On the other hand, we have an absolute guarantee from Nixon to defend the country. I am going to agree to sign and hold him to his word."

"Can you really trust Nixon?"

"He is an honest man and I am going to trust him."

Two days later, on January 22, 1973, at his ranch in the Hill Country of Texas, Lyndon Baines Johnson, the president who had committed the United States to a ground war in Vietnam and then had seen that war undercut his domestic social programs and end his political career, died of congestive heart failure.

The following evening, Richard Nixon spoke to the nation. Twenty-eight years after the United States first became involved in Vietnam, it was finally getting out. "I have asked for this radio and television time tonight for the purpose of announcing that we today have concluded an agreement to end the war and bring peace with honor in Vietnam and in Southeast Asia. . . . The ceasefire, internationally supervised, will begin at 7 p.m.

this Saturday, January 27, Washington time. . . . Within sixty days from this Saturday, all Americans held as prisoners of war throughout Indochina will be released.

"During the same sixty-day period, all American forces will be withdrawn from South Vietnam. . . .

"Throughout these negotiations we have been in the closest consultation with President Thieu and other representatives of the Republic of Vietnam. This settlement meets the goals and has the full support of President Thieu and the government of the Republic of Vietnam, as well as that of our other allies who are affected."

American prisoners of war—591 of them—were to be released in batches of 40. Those who had been in captivity the longest were to come home first. Everett Alvarez—who had been shot down eight and a half years earlier, just after the Tonkin Gulf incident in 1964—was among them. "For years and years we've dreamed of this day," he said, "and we kept faith—faith in God, in our president, and in our country."

Hal Kushner's turn came in mid-March. "They called our names," he remembered, "and I walked out in the sunlight. The first thing I saw was a girl in a miniskirt. She was a reporter for one of the news organizations. I'd never seen a real live miniskirt. And there was a table with the Vietnamese and American authorities on one side, and there was an Air Force brigadier general in Class A uniform. He looked magnificent. I looked at him and he had breadth, he had thickness that we didn't have. He had on a garrison cap and his hair was plump and moist and

our hair was like straw. It was dry and we were skinny. And I went out and I saluted him, which was a courtesy that had been denied us for so many years. And he saluted me and I shook hands with him and he hugged me—he actually hugged me. And he said, "Welcome home, Major. We're glad to see you, Doctor." The tears were streaming down his cheeks. It was just a powerful moment. And then this liaison officer came out and got me and escorted me onto this C-141, this beautiful white airplane with an American flag and 'USAF' on the tail. And they had these real cute flight nurses on there. They were all tall and blond and they were just gorgeous. And we got on this thing and we sat in these seats and one nurse said, 'We have anything you want.' You know. 'What do you want?' And I wanted a Coke with crushed ice and some chewing gum."

ABOVE In Hanoi, as North Vietnamese officials and soldiers look on, Hal Kushner is greeted by Air Force Brigadier General Russell Ogan, director of the military's Prisoners of War/Missing in Action Task Force, which supervised the POWs' journey home. **OVER, LEFT** Freedom: At a prisoner exchange in Quang Tri Province on the south bank of the Thac Han River on March 17, 1975, soldiers, family members, and a thicket of South Vietnamese flags greet a boatload of ARVN prisoners **RIGHT BOTTOM** Just across the river, North Vietnamese prisoners splash toward their comrades on shore. **RIGHT TOP** Meanwhile, on the same day, at Travis Air Force Base in California, Lieutenant Colonel Robert L. Stirm is welcomed home by the family he hasn't seen in more than six years.

VIETNAM AND THE MOVEMENT

TODD GITLIN

H OW IS IT that, after eight years of pulverizing warfare, the wealthiest and most powerful nation on earth failed to conquer what the exasperated president Lyndon Johnson called "this damn little piss-ant country"?

All these years later, this unsettling question deserves to unsettle. During the prewar years, and on into the war, America thought of itself as a nonstop winner. (Never mind that the Korean War had ended in stalemate.) Was the United States not the very incarnation of worthy and nonstop triumph? A question premised on American defeat was out of bounds because American defeat itself was unthinkable. Yet it deserved, and deserves, to be asked.

Any serious answer must feature, first of all, the fortitude, discipline, and brilliance of Vietnamese troops led by a communist regime that, before the American disaster, had won the mantle of nationalist leadership and driven out the French colonialists. But any account that omits the American antiwar movement is seriously incomplete. The movement helped bring down two war presidents, divide the political class, demoralize its leadership, shatter its families, and upend public opinion. This polymorphous movement began on the fringes of American society, widened and deepened, and for all its frailties, contentions, and absurdities grew into a veto force that dampened the war and helped avert even more death and destruction. Such an achievement deserves not only understanding but awe.

1

In 1983, I was invited to speak at a conference on the Vietnam War at the University of Southern California, along with former government civilian and military officials, journalists, veterans, historians, and anti-warriors like myself. In my talk, I called the American movement "the largest and most effective antiwar movement in history."

Milling around in the lobby afterward, I was approached by a man who looked vaguely familiar. "You're mistaken about the most effective antiwar movement," he said bluntly. I looked at his badge and recognized his name: Roger Hilsman Jr. We in the movement followed the comings and goings of higher-ups with keen attention. Hilsman had been closely involved with making Vietnam policy under John F. Kennedy; he had risen to the position of assistant secretary of state for Far Eastern affairs; after Kennedy was assassinated, Lyndon Johnson fired him, though Hilsman's exit statement said he was resigning. Evidently Johnson found him too willing and eager to criticize the military.

I asked Hilsman what more effective antiwar movement he had in mind. "The Bolshevik revolution!" he said, grinning puckishly.

I had to laugh—appreciatively. "Peace, Bread, and Land" was, indeed, a popular Bolshevik slogan in 1917. Very likely, Lenin's campaign against the war was decisive in the uprising that installed the Bolsheviks in the Kremlin. So in a way Hilsman had a point. By the summer of 1917, the Russians had suffered over eight million dead and wounded (about forty for every one the U.S. suffered in Vietnam). Some two million soldiers had deserted. The Russian economy was wrecked. There were food riots. Russia was desperate for peace. Meanwhile, the anti-monarchists who took power in February persisted in pursuing the war. That was a grand, epoch-making mistake.

The Bolsheviks knew a ripe political issue when they saw one. Within three months they were in power. Three months later, they signed a treaty with Germany and pulled out of the war.

But face-to-face with Roger Hilsman, I didn't have the quickness of mind to say that his clever riposte was more than a little unfair, since the Bolsheviks were not, strictly speaking, an antiwar movement. They were more than that, in a way—they certainly changed history, though not for the good—but in another way they were less. Campaigning for peace was, for them, a means to a grander and far more dangerous end. Before they were peace campaigners, they were Bolsheviks—autocratic Communists. In America, the sequence was the opposite—and even then the analogy is deceiving. Our antiwar movement spawned, among other things, a mélange of revolutionary Communists, whose arcane delusions and flamboyant actions made them useful bogeymen for the government though they numbered hundreds or thousands in a movement of millions. The movement was the big story, and the Communists were parasitic on it.

So I stand by my original claim. The American antiwar movement was an unprecedented force. It helped contain the war, helped prevent several catastrophic escalations, and contributed to extricating American troops and stopping the bombers. This took eight years. Had the movement been more clearheaded and less desperate, it might well have achieved the same mission more quickly. No one will ever know, although we can make educated guesses.

2

But what *was* this movement? It eludes simple definition. Movements, like clouds, don't have sharp edges—this is one reason why journalists have a hard time getting a grip on them. The antiwar movement was far more than the alphabet soup of organizations that tried to lead or at least influence it, that won esteem or notoriety depending on who was doing the estimating. It did not have a headquarters or officers. It was not a network of celebrities. It was a *movement*—a social force, a work in progress, an ensemble, confusing, contentious, irregular, raucous, immense. The millions who passed through it—and they were many millions—were as various as America itself. They were young and old, drawn from all classes (contrary to stereotypes, there were plenty of white working-class people who identified), a churning amalgam of the angry and ashamed who disagreed about many things but shared a conviction that a misbegotten and gravely misguided war in the three nations of the former French Indochina—Vietnam, Laos, and Cambodia—had to be stopped.

The movement was polymorphous and it showed up everywhere in American life—a target, a spectacle, a joy, a curiosity, a donnybrook, a bogeyman; a sort of world of its own. It had its magazines and newspapers, its documentary films, its songs, its poems; its celebrities, heroes, and villains; its symbols, slogans, gestures, and insignias. It had its images, for better and worse, on the TV news, although it failed to make any more than a passing imprint during the prime time hours. Like the war itself, Hollywood feared to divide or upset its audience. Blood and failure had to stay off the screen until the war was well over. (Astoundingly, the only big-screen movie to come out of the war while it was still raging was John Wayne's *Green Berets*, which he financed himself because he believed so devoutly in the war, at a time when the studios and the bankers fled the subject.)

The movement had its own coast-to-coast culture. In 1968, my girlfriend, Honey Williams, and I were driving cross-country from New York to our home in San Francisco in a "driveaway" car, a favored means of ground transportation for the impecunious. You answered an ad in the paper, picked up the owner's car, delivered it on the other side of the country, and the owner might even pay all your expenses. This particular car, a boxy little Simca, was a lemon. It broke down in Iowa. We called the owner and explained the situation. The repair would be expensive. He said he would foot the bill. We made the repair and kept driving west. Past Lincoln, Nebraska, near the town of York, the car broke down again. This time the owner said to sell the pathetic thing and then take the train west; graciously, he would reimburse our fare. It was a Saturday, and the only Simca dealer in Lincoln was a Seventh-day Adventist, which meant he wouldn't open till Sunday. We arranged with AAA to tow us there, but after buying tickets on the next transcontinental train we had run out of money and had none left for an overnight stay.

We were near the campus of the University of Nebraska, so we walked over to the student union. Spotting a student wearing a button sporting an omega symbol—the symbol of draft resistance, having first become the standard symbol of *electrical* resistance—we approached him and explained our situation. He readily agreed to put us up overnight. We were members of the same lodge, or fraternity, or sub-society of the saved.

The omega was only one movement symbol. There was also, on bumper stickers and jackets and on chains around the neck, the peace symbol. There was the two-finger V sign—adapted from World War II's V-for-victory. The movement also had its stereotypes, its gags, its folk heroes ("General Waste More Land" was a favorite at California demonstrations). It had its virtual uniforms (used army jackets); its rituals; its surprises; its winters, springs, summers, and autumns of discontent. It had its own calendar, its revered battles, its biannual mobilizations, April 15 and October 15, starting in 1965, on both coasts—in New York or Washington, and also San Francisco.

During these turnouts en masse, despite the stereotype that this was a movement of "baby boomers," it was not at all strictly a youth movement, though surely most of the time its most visible participants were young, most of them college and high school students—many of them radical, many not so radical but mainly spurred by fear of the draft. Within a few years, the movement encompassed members of the armed forces and the clergy, women's groups, trade unionists, African Americans, Hispanics, Asian Americans, doctors, lawyers, businessmen, nurses, teachers, social workers, scientists, architects, and city planners. There was no profession that lacked an antiwar caucus. There was no region where the movement did not emerge. This was not only a morally necessary life-saving mission but a sort of nation within the nation.

The movement evolved a whole repertory of tactics and targets. Researchers identified purveyors of war research; university class ranks were opposed when they were used to select draftees; military recruiters were resisted, as were recruiters from corporations like Dow Chemical, which manufactured napalm, the jellied gasoline that horrifically burned human flesh; troop trains were blocked; so were draft headquarters; eventually, draft records were stolen, or set afire, sometimes with home-made napalm. Antiwar candidates ran for office. Red paint was thrown, and rocks. Buildings were occupied.

Millions took part, mostly in low-cost, low-risk ways that comported with their personal styles and their commitments to normal life. They signed petitions. They wrote letters to Congress. They wrote checks. They wrote poems, they wrote essays, they wrote letters to the editor. They attended antiwar poetry readings. They marched now and again, especially if a friend, someone respected, invited them along. They caused unpleasantness—or screaming fights—at family dinners. Families ruptured. In officialdom, minds changed—though not all minds, not by any means. But as reported by Tom Wells in his magisterial history, *The War Within: America's Battle over Vietnam,* many government officials, at all but the highest level, had to contend with dissidents at home. On October 15, 1969, National Security Advisor Kissinger's aide William Watts was working on a presidential speech announcing a major escalation of the war. Vietnam Moratorium marchers were just the other side of the White House fence. Watts took a break from his writing, went out for a stroll, and saw his wife and children walking by, holding candles. "I felt like throwing up," he told Wells many years later. After the Cambodia invasion six months later, he resigned.

Most activists, most of the time, risked little for most of what they did, but many risked a great deal. Significant numbers of active-duty service men and women wore their uniforms in antiwar parades; they attended "pray-ins" on Army bases; they published scores of antiwar newspapers with titles like "Fed Up" and "Up Against the Bulkhead." Many were court-martialed. Encouraged by antiwar coffee houses in base towns, they helped conscientious objectors and deserters, circulated underground papers, supported each other.

The movement undermined authorities and decorum. Rock musicians taunted high officials, and high school students defied teachers and principals. The movement disrupted ceremonies not only by the usual means—picketing officials, booing them, caricaturing them—but by unusual means from unusual suspects. Most of the 1969 graduating class of Brown University stood and turned their backs when Henry Kissinger got an honorary degree. The self-described "oobie-doobie girl" Carole Feraci, a singer with the couldn't-be-more-mainstream Ray Conniff singers, at a Nixon White House celebration of the fiftieth anniversary of the vehemently pro-war *Reader's Digest,* held up a banner that read "Stop the Killing," and, as Conniff tried to yank her banner away, coolly addressed the president: "President Nixon, stop bombing

human beings, animals and vegetation. You go to church on Sundays and pray to Jesus Christ. If Jesus Christ were here tonight, you would not dare to drop another bomb. Bless the Berrigans and bless Daniel Ellsberg."

Nixon stared at her with a frozen smile. Feraci later told reporters that she did not belong to any antiwar group, adding, "If an oobie-doobie girl like me has courage, [perhaps] the rest of the people will, too."

At the core of the movement were probably tens of thousands, possibly hundreds of thousands, for whom the war was not an "issue" or a "problem" or a "mistake," not even intellectually containable as a shame or tragedy or crime, but an ongoing personal trauma, a badge of identity—as if to say, "I am not that kind of American"—and a life challenge. It may seem presumptuous to strike an analogy with the experiences of American military men in and above Vietnam—certainly a soldier's fear and courage were not so often required of anti-warriors, though an activist who moved to Canada to avoid the draft and had to miss weddings and funerals was no slouch in sacrifice—but there was this in common: The war was shattering and visceral—an experience, even if a vicarious one. It could be interrupted but never relieved for long. It was a tireless incubus.

The war, and the movement against it, and the anti-authoritarian culture that grew up around them—it is impossible to separate out the strands of change—wreaked havoc with life plans. Sometimes dramatically: the Justice Department referred 207,000 names to U.S. attorneys for prosecution for draft resistance; of those, 25,000 were indicted, 9,000 were convicted, and some 3,250 were sent to prison. Some 30,000 fled to Canada or elsewhere. Estimates of military deserters run from 80,000 to 200,000, though not all of these were self-conscious political resisters. In a much-publicized 1967 case, the Brooklyn dermatologist Howard B. Levy was court-martialed and convicted at Fort Jackson, South Carolina, for refusing to train Green Berets in medical skills that would be used as "another tool of political persuasion" in Vietnam. If that wasn't enough, he was charged with "making public statements with design to promote disloyalty and disaffection among the troops." He was the first American to argue a so-called Nuremberg defense in court, arguing that such medical training would entail a breach of medical ethics and complicity in war crimes. Sentenced to three years in prison, Captain Levy was released after twenty-six months.

The war was an incitement to conscience, and a dismantler of authority, but also a great demoralizer in the armed forces, leading not only to absences without leave but desertions and rampant drug use. Armed attacks by troops on their officers were common enough to warrant a colloquialism: "fragging," short for the hand grenades frequently used in order to destroy not only the body of the victim but evidence of the crime. And, of course, wherever individuals undertook radical life-changing action, the lives of loved ones were also derailed.

As long as draft exemptions remained for married men, teachers, and members of other professions, the war changed careers, too, at least long enough for the purpose of evading the draft. It also changed ideas of how professionals ought to conduct themselves. Professors, realizing that neither they nor their students knew very much about Vietnam, invented a new educational format, an extracurricular one—the teach-in. At first, the State Department sent its own debaters to university campuses, but they did not win the arguments, and the teach-ins went on without them.

The teach-ins were only the most visible sign of enormous questions coming to the surface. What did it mean that the United States was bombing to smithereens a country understood in the public mind as a "domino" that needed shoring up so that other nations, also called "dominoes," would not also "fall"? How did it come to pass that the U.S. dropped a greater tonnage (twice as great? four times as great?) on Vietnam, Cambodia, and Laos than the total tonnage the U.S. dropped in all theaters of war—on three continents—during the entirety of World War II? Imagination was beggared.

And so the war challenged professors to consider their public obligations as bringers of reason, and to consider whether they had properly done their duty to convey knowledge if they confined their teaching to classrooms. They were also pressed to consider whether to make their values and analyses of current events more explicit than before. So were many other professionals. Eventually, university presidents were lobbying Washington, along with college newspaper editors and members of student councils.

When the authorities defied reason, they lost credibility with citizens who cared about reason—in particular, the campus world. Lyndon Johnson was accused of opening up a "credibility gap" because he was lying about the war, but Richard Nixon deepened the gap to crater proportions, and increasingly the unreasoning mobs that trusted in Nixon turned bitterly against the campuses, which they saw, not without reason, as allied with defiant Negroes and disrespectful of law and order. By his last year of office, President Johnson was avoiding college campuses. Richard Nixon avoided all but the obscure ones and military academies. In June 1969, his first year in office, at a speech at General Beadle State College, in Madison, South Dakota, he spoke bluntly: "Our fundamental values [are] under bitter and even violent attack. . . . We live in a deeply troubled and pro-

foundly unsettled time. Drugs, crime, campus revolts, racial discord, draft resistance—on every hand we find old standards violated, old values discarded."

He assured his audience that the government would repel attacks by force if necessary: "We have the power to strike back if need be, and to prevail. . . . It has not been a lack of civil power, but the reluctance of a free people to employ it that so often has stayed the hand of authorities faced with confrontation."

President Johnson had prosecuted antiwar activists, but Nixon did so all the more, directing his security apparatus to work to smoke out enemy agents they imagined were pulling the strings of the antiwar movement. Although the CIA found no significant foreign influences, the FBI established counterintelligence programs (COINTELPRO, for short) targeting antiwar and black militant groups. Toward that end, they hired informers (in 1969, 120 of them in Students for a Democratic Society and other New Left groups) and passed along destructive political directives. They tapped phones, opened mail, inflamed dissension, spread nasty rumors about leaders, and maintained a list of thousands (the "Security Index") to be interned in case of national emergency. A 1971 burglary by antiwar activists at the FBI office of Media, Pennsylvania, showed just how obsessed the federal agents were with surveilling, containing, and aborting largely lawful protests. Meanwhile, local police departments conducted their own infiltrations and planted agents provocateurs to justify police assaults. So did military intelligence, which, contrary to law, directed 1,500 officers to report on domestic dissent. Even as activists won many acquittals at trial, vast resources had to be drained into defense.

3

Still, for all its burdens, the movement did restrain the war. It moved policy, though never as much as it wanted. How much it did accomplish was obscured, often deliberately. The executive branch was opaque and Congress was slow-moving. Inside the movement, many activists felt that however it grew in size and reach, it was ineffectual. Perhaps ending the war was no more than an earnest but idle dream? The spectacle of large numbers of the like-minded congregating in public places was cheering, but it was hard to be convinced that the movement was saving lives. At the movement's core, fright fed desperation. Clear thinking suffered. Revolutionary fantasies flourished—all the more so because the Nixon administration kept insisting that the movement was getting nowhere. On November 3, 1969, just before the November 15 Moratorium march, Nixon delivered a handwritten speech declaring that he would be "untrue" to his "oath of office" to let national policy be "dictated" by a "vocal minority" trying to "impose" its views "by mounting demonstrations in the street." Posing before stacks of congratulatory telegrams, Nixon put his feet up on his desk and told staffers, "We've got those liberal bastards on the run now."

November 15 came, and a barricade made of fifty-seven city buses reinforced the White House fence as a festive crowd gathered. Eventually, half a million citizens gathered on Pennsylvania Avenue and nearby streets. The president let it be known that he would be spending part of the afternoon watching the Ohio State–Purdue game on television. *The Washington Post* reported that "the White House was about as normal . . . as it would be any time that there is an all-day air raid alert limited to the area immediately surround[ing] the Executive Mansion." By now, this acerbic tone was no longer unusual in the establishment press.

Demonstrations so imposing did register with Congress, and pushed it gradually to limit war spending. As early as 1966, and even more in 1968, opposition to the war was making itself felt in Democratic primaries, and there were antiwar Republicans as well. American casualties mounted, as did the war's financial costs. All these forces converged to put a lid on the war. Now, when earnest, well-prepared students lectured senators and congressmen, they sometimes changed minds. Most consequential were the October and November 1969 Moratorium actions. Nixon had delivered an ultimatum to Hanoi. While announcing plans to withdraw some troops, he was also contemplating what he called "Operation Duck Hook," which would consist of (1) additional airstrikes against North Vietnam, including passes and bridges at the Chinese border; (2) intensified air and ground attacks; (3) the mining of Haiphong and other ports; and (4) the possible use of nuclear bombs on North Vietnam's border with China or perhaps elsewhere in the north. Nixon reconsidered. The movement's pressure was surely a factor.

Nixon was a shrewd politician. He was as adroit at co-optation as he was clumsy at repression. He phased out the draft. He withdrew some troops, "Vietnamizing" the ground war as he converted much of the American effort into an air war. With his support, Congress voted to lower the voting age to eighteen, and the states ratified the Twenty-sixth Amendment, to this effect, in record time. In the eyes of a population that did not pay close attention, Nixon gave an impression of "ending the war." Meanwhile, as many activists burned out, others courted confrontations with the police, destroyed property, and, eventually, planned violent attacks against persons. (Because their bombs malfunctioned, most of the victims were the terrorists themselves.) Despair fueled panic and delusion. Perhaps one or two hundred would-be revolutionaries, clueless about how morally and intellectually lost they were, turned to terror attacks.

Some activists recovered from desperate militancy to lobby against war measures. As others burned out, the activists who remained were, on balance, more practical. They turned toward direct results. They benefited from the 1971 publication of the Pentagon Papers. Published widely in major newspapers, these documents made it plain, even to doubters, that the government had been concealing and lying about war plans for many years, and (as Daniel Ellsberg wrote later) that the prime motive of American presidents from Kennedy onward was to punt—to avoid being blamed for losing the war. Whatever veneer of respectability the war had enjoyed was stripped away.

Despite his landslide reelection in 1972, Nixon's political base was narrowing. Congress passed an amendment calling for an immediate cutoff of war spending. In 1973, Congress passed a War Powers Act and rejected a Nixon request for military aid. By then, Nixon was writhing in the grip of the Watergate scandals. In 1971, he had established a clandestine goon squad in the White House, known as the "Plumbers"—they were supposed to fix leaks. Their first mission was a burglary of Ellsberg's psychiatrist, in search of material for discrediting him. Then, operating under the Committee for the Re-Election of the President, they tried to bug the headquarters of the Democratic National Committee. The Plumbers were arrested. An honest judge forced revelations. The reporting of Bob Woodward and Carl Bernstein, among others, kept the heat on. Nixon's efforts at covering up unraveled. One devastating revelation followed another. Nixon's intense paranoia about the Pentagon Papers release had boomeranged.

Nixon was not impeached for his war activities. One war-related charge was proposed—falsification of records pertaining to the secret bombing of Cambodia—but the House Judiciary Committee voted it down. But although Congress was not disposed to reckon with the war as such—and arguably the public at large had no interest in that either—the awfulness of the war lay just underneath the surface. To wage that war, Nixon had turned the White House into a nest of criminal conspiracy. The war was the precondition and the unacknowledged spur for his ignominious resignation. The war was good for tyrannical tendencies, which, in the end, were rolled back because Nixon overreached. Legal and political institutions were resilient enough to stop him. The reckless pursuit of war undid the pursuers.

And then what? The antiwar insurgency that brought America to the boiling point was so sweeping a challenge to authority and customary order as to reverberate for decades. It was a life changer. It was also, not coincidentally, an extraordinary episode in the history of democracy. A war that had been so popular at first—however ignorantly, however undeclared and thinly grounded in law—was brought to an end with an impressive boost from popular action.

There is a lesson here about the actual life of a democracy. Democracy is not a synonym for a periodic majority vote. In 1964, Lyndon Johnson was elected president on a platform of "seeking no wider war," running against Barry Goldwater, who sought exactly that. Vital democracy requires an ongoing two-way or multi-way process of responsiveness. Living democracy depends not just on the rules for choosing rulers but on the quality and resolve of the populace—on what they *do*. It requires opportunities to change the popular will. It requires that minorities have a chance to become majorities by resorting to popular action—assemblies, mobilizations, and counter-mobilizations. In a constitutional democracy, it requires respect for the Constitution.

The antiwar movement, in my view, would have been more effective, and sooner, if it had worked harder to bid for the soul of America and not renounce it. It would have done better not carrying the flags of the National Liberation Front and Hanoi and carrying more of the Stars and Stripes. It would have been more effective if it had been smarter, more strategic, if it had won over more people with arguments rather than bluster.

The odds were always against a sustained movement. Its strength lay in its unity, but that was a sometime thing. Internecine fights and revolutionary delusions got the better of it. By the time the war ended, the movement was not there to celebrate what was, after all, an extraordinary victory. It did not so much end as peter out in fragments, fatigue, and disillusion. It failed to create a continuing force—indeed, the Weathermen faction of Students for a Democratic Society destroyed the largest left-wing organization in the country. So the antiwar movement, qua movement, did not survive to play a part in postwar politics. Whether, in any case, as diffuse and divided as it was, it could have adapted to a much different world—to the economic disruptions of the 1970s and the Reaganite sequel—may be doubted.

The movement receded in memory—more a long moment than a movement. But in the lives of millions, what a moment it was.

CHAPTER TEN

THE WEIGHT OF MEMORY

MARCH 1973–APRIL 1975

A motorcyclist weaves his way among abandoned military boots left behind by ARVN forces as they fled toward Saigon in April 1975.

A HISTORIC DAY

AT TAN SON NHUT AIR BASE on Thursday afternoon, March 29, 1973—the same day the final batch of American POWs flew home from Hanoi—a ceremony was held to bid an official farewell to the last American troops left in South Vietnam—sixty-eight Army, Navy, and Air Force personnel who had been in charge of processing the day's withdrawal. They were not actually the last U.S. uniformed service personnel on their way home. More than 800 American truce observers were to leave in the next few days, and 159 embassy Marine guards and 50 military attachés and a 14-man graves commission were to stay on, alongside several thousand civilians—diplomats, contractors, and CIA operatives as well as a host of former military personnel who, to get around the provisions of the treaty,

ABOVE A North Vietnamese observer working for the Four-Party Joint Military Commission, set up under the Paris agreement, counts U.S. soldiers as they board a jet at Saigon's Tan Son Nhut airport, March 29, 1973.

were now wearing civvies and working for the Saigon government. But both that government and the departing MACV commanders saw the symbolic importance of an airport ceremony to mark the formal end of American participation in the war.

General Frederick C. Weyand, whose foresight about the enemy's intentions had helped defend Saigon during the Tet Offensive and who now found himself the last commander of U.S. forces in Vietnam, supervised the official closing of MACV headquarters and presided over the furling of the colors. He told the departing men to "hold their heads up high for having been a part of this selfless effort." Since all the Army band musicians had long since gone home, the American National Anthem had to be played on a phonograph.

As the Americans filed onto the C-141 Air Force jet that was to take them on the first leg of their journey, Lieutenant Colonel Bui Tin, a North Vietnamese member of the Four-Party Joint Military Commission, created under the agreement to observe the ceasefire, stepped forward with a gift for the man he believed would be the last to board, Master Sergeant Max Beilke, from Alexandria, Minnesota. It was a delicately painted scroll and a pack of postcards of Ho Chi Minh.

"This is a historic day," Tin said. "It is the first time in one hundred years that there are no foreign troops on the soil of Vietnam."

But the absence of foreigners did not mean the end of violence. "There's going to be a full-blown war starting up after we leave," one two-tour U.S. veteran said. "The fighting has never stopped, anyway." As if to prove it, just across the tarmac a woman wept over her husband's coffin, draped in the red and yellow flag of South Vietnam, one of twenty-one coffins fresh from the battlefield.

Over the next two years, the forces of North and South Vietnam would continue to savage one another. And the Vietnamese people would find themselves back where they had been before the Americans came—engulfed in an apparently endless civil war. The South's future still hung in the balance—would it survive intact and on its own, or would it be subsumed by the North? Between these two positions there continued to be no possibility of compromise.

President Thieu still stood by his "four nos"—no negotiation with the communists, no role for them in South Vietnamese politics, no surrender of territory, and no coalition government.

Hanoi was no less adamant that Thieu's regime was illegitimate and doomed.

Neither North nor South Vietnam had ever had any intention of observing the ceasefire for which the agreement called. Within three weeks there had already been some three thousand violations by both sides.

Thieu, in command of a million-man army, the fifth largest on earth, and confident that Washington would come to his aid with massive airpower should his forces get into serious trouble ("You can count on us," Nixon would tell him face-to-face that spring), set out to take back areas the NLF had seized in the weeks leading up to the signing of the peace agreement. It was a costly campaign—six thousand dead within three months—but largely successful. "The flag of South Vietnam should be everywhere," one of his closest advisers said, "even over the remotest outpost of the country." Every inch of South Vietnam was to be defended—something Thieu had been unable to achieve previ-

ABOVE ARVN soldiers fight for a road near Tay Ninh the day after the signing of the Paris agreement and despite the ceasefire it was supposed to usher in.

ously even with the help of more than half a million Americans. The unintended result was that his forces were stretched too thin; every hamlet his men recaptured increased their vulnerability to attack.

The Nixon administration did what it could to bolster him. "The only way we will keep North Vietnam under control is not to say we are out forever," Kissinger told a White House speechwriter. "We don't want to dissipate the reputation for fierceness that the president has earned." Nixon went on bombing Cambodia, in part to remind Hanoi of his willingness to employ American power, turned U.S. bases over to the South Vietnamese rather than dismantle them, and continued, in violation of the treaty, to dispatch military hardware to Saigon labeled "nonmilitary."

Meanwhile, Hanoi and the NLF bided their time. They continued to send men and supplies into South Vietnam as well as Laos and Cambodia despite their pledge not to do so, and remained determined eventually to destroy the Saigon regime. But they were battered and battle weary after the fierce fighting and still fiercer bombing that had preceded the peace agreement and needed time to rebuild. They also wanted to do nothing so precipitous as to cause U.S. B-52s to return to the sky.

Then, things began to change. The Watergate scandal grew steadily that spring. Blackmail. Enemies lists. Dirty tricks. The vice president forced to resign. Cover-up. Abuse of power. Secret tapes. As the president's secrets tumbled out, his influence on

Capitol Hill steadily dwindled, and with it the likelihood of ever resuming the conflict that had once been Lyndon Johnson's war but was now intimately identified with Nixon. In May, the House ended air operations over Cambodia. In June, it voted to halt all military operations on or over all of Indochina by August 15—and forbade their resumption without congressional approval. In July, over Nixon's veto, it passed the War Powers Act, requiring the president to notify Congress within forty-eight hours that U.S. forces were being sent into harm's way and then to obtain congressional approval if they were to remain there more than sixty days.

Thieu continued to act as though massive American airstrikes remained only a radio call away, as if he could forever call on an infinite inflow of up-to-date American weaponry. In late 1973, he declared the start of "the Third Indochina War" and ordered his forces to attack territories held by the Provisional Revolutionary Government. The ARVN were badly mauled this time, and, instead of gaining ground against the enemy, lost it.

Meanwhile, Hanoi had begun to build a new paved highway within South Vietnam itself, down which convoys of two hundred to three hundred vehicles would soon begin streaming—trucks, tanks, and heavy guns—moving in broad daylight, safe from American air attack. The North Vietnamese also began laying down a giant oil pipeline to fuel their vehicles in the South. Another great offensive was clearly in the cards, but no one, not even in Hanoi, yet knew when it might begin.

INCREDIBLE

THERE WAS NOW a new U.S. ambassador in Saigon, Graham Martin, a convinced cold warrior whose loathing for the enemy had been deepened by the death of a son in Vietnam. Since the ceasefire, he assured Congress, the ARVN had shown "increasingly self-evident self-confidence and up-beat morale. . . . If we remain constant in our support," the United States has "every right to confidently expect the [Saigon government] can hold on without the necessity of U.S. armed intervention."

The South Vietnam he described was unrecognizable to many South Vietnamese. The economy was collapsing. With the American military presence gone, one out of five Vietnamese was without work—roughly the same ratio that had defined the Great Depression in the United States. GIs had poured some $400 million into the local economy every year; that was gone now too. "There were many mistakes made by the Americans," Duong Van Mai Elliott recalled, "but the biggest mistake was

creating the sense of dependency." Prices soared. Wages plummeted. The South Vietnamese piaster would be devalued twelve times in eighteen months.

Corruption, always present, became omnipresent. According to a postwar RAND study of twenty-seven former senior officers and civil servants, every single high-ranking member of the Saigon regime had been on the take. A syndicate with connections that reached into the prime minister's office somehow smuggled out of the country sixteen thousand tons of brass shell casings worth $17.3 million. Province chiefs sold rice to the enemy, levied personal taxes on vehicles passing through their territories, and siphoned off funds meant for refugee resettlement.

Ambassador Martin made light of the problem: "A little corruption . . . oils the machinery," he told Congress, and compared Saigon to turn-of-the-twentieth-century Boston. But corruption was no laughing matter to the poor, who suffered most from its ubiquity. Policemen preyed on them; so did the clerks who issued licenses and identity cards and local officials who connived with wealthy landlords to twist the "Land-to-the-Tiller" law and deprive them of their new holdings.

Corruption continued to undercut the military, as well. Only one of the four corps commanders was said to be clean. In addition to keeping rosters of "ghost soldiers," some commanders sponsored "ornament soldiers," men who paid them for safe assignments, and "flower soldiers," who paid still more not to show up at all. Everything seemed to be for sale—weapons, ammunition, ponchos, tents.

Navy crews sold to local fishermen precious fuel meant for patrolling the Mekong Delta. Artillery support cost between one and two dollars per round. In some areas, medevac helicopters were said to hover above wounded men, bargaining before they would agree to airlift them out. In one area, the going rates were said to be eight dollars for an enlisted man, double that for an NCO, and for an officer, twenty-five dollars and up.

Understandably—and despite Ambassador Martin's assurances—ARVN morale had declined steadily since the Laos incursion. Some of the same problems that had plagued the American Army in its last months in Vietnam also haunted the South Vietnamese—alcohol, thievery, heroin addiction. As many as twenty thousand men deserted each month, most heading home to try to help their families survive in such hard times. The authorized strength of combat battalions fell from eight hundred to five hundred.

"Our leaders continued to believe in U.S. air intervention even after the U.S. Congress had expressly forbidden it," a member of the South Vietnamese Joint General Staff remembered. "They deluded themselves into thinking this perhaps simply meant that U.S. intervention would take a longer time to come." Each corps commander was told that if he got into serious dif-

ABOVE Richard Nixon leaves the White House for the last time, August 9, 1974. With him go the guarantees of U.S. support upon which the Saigon regime's survival depends.

ficulty he should radio the U.S. Seventh Air Force base in Thailand and request air support, then hold his ground for a week or two until Congress got around to authorizing it.

But by the spring of 1974, Congress was in no mood to authorize anything more for South Vietnam. In April, in its foreign aid request for the 1975 fiscal year, the administration asked for $1.45 billion for Saigon. There was intense debate in both houses of Congress. In the end, the United States provided just $700 million.

"This is incredible," Thieu told an adviser. "First the Americans told me at Midway to agree to the withdrawal of a few thousand troops and I would still have half a million Americans left to fight with me. Then, when they withdrew more troops, they said, 'Don't worry, we are strengthening you to make up for the American divisions that are being withdrawn.' When the pace of withdrawal speeded up in 1972, they told me, 'Don't worry, you'll still have residual forces and we are making up for the withdrawals with an increase in air support for your ground troops.' Then after there was a total withdrawal and no more air support, they told me, 'We will give you a substantial increase in military aid to make up for all that. Don't forget the Seventh Fleet and the air bases in Thailand are there to protect you in case of an eventuality.' Now you are telling me American aid is cut by sixty percent. Where does that leave us?"

Far worse, from Thieu's point of view, was to follow. He had largely staked South Vietnam's survival on Richard Nixon's personal pledge that North Vietnamese aggression would be met by renewed American airpower. And when, on August 8, rather than face impeachment by the Senate, Nixon became the first president in American history to resign his office, Thieu closed his office door and refused to see anyone.

His claim to leadership in South Vietnam had been largely built upon his supposed closeness to the Americans. Now that had come under grave question. In early September, a coalition of Catholic lay and religious leaders called the People's Anti-Corruption Movement, led by Father Tran Huu Thanh, published "Indictment No. 1," a manifesto denouncing the president for tolerating corruption that "robs the people down to their bones." It accused members of Thieu's own family, by name, of large-scale profiteering and demanded to know whether he

felt ashamed of his clan's greed and callousness when his soldiers were "lacking rice to eat, clothes to wear and houses to live in—and wives sometimes have to sell their bodies in order to feed their children." In response, Thieu did not deny that members of his family were corrupt, only that no one had ever presented evidence of bribery against him personally. He tried to defuse the opposition by dismissing four cabinet members and three corps commanders and demoting nearly four hundred field-grade officers. But it was not good enough. Thousands of protesters, Catholic and Buddhist alike, took to the streets. "We want a president who serves the people," speakers shouted, "not a president who steals from the people." They were met by riot police and a new set of draconian decrees that centralized still more power in the president's hands. He now claimed the right to close down any newspapers that printed what he considered "groundless news" or "slander" of the government. Reporters and opposition politicians were beaten. News of fresh repression in Saigon further solidified opposition to Thieu's regime on Capitol Hill.

The ARVN, one South Vietnamese officer wrote, like the Americans who had trained and armed it for nearly twenty years, "had acquired the habits of a rich man's army." Now, their commanders complained, they were about to be asked to do far more with much less. Precisely how severe shortages would be in the coming months was difficult to gauge. The administration had sent so much military hardware in the weeks before the settlement that no one was able to keep track of it all. Much of it "sat around rusting," as one U.S. official admitted; still more was reported missing, sold or stolen off the shelves. Maintenance and spare parts were continuing problems, too: at one point, one out of five aircraft, one-third of all medium tanks, and half the armored personnel carriers were out of action.

But fuel really did fall low. So did ammunition. Artillerymen in the Central Highlands who had been required to fire one hundred shells a day would soon be limited to just four. Infantrymen were cut back to eighty-five bullets a month. "With one grenade and eighty-five bullets a month, how can you fight?" asked ARVN General Lam Quang Thi. "After you've shot all eighty-five bullets, you can't fight anymore. Defeat was inevitable."

ABOVE Opposition members of the South Vietnamese National Assembly set fire to photographs of President Thieu. In the months following Nixon's departure, Thieu's grip on power weakened steadily.

THE CONVOY OF TEARS

IN NOVEMBER 1974, the politburo and Central Military Commission met in Hanoi to discuss strategy. Some members urged continued caution. They worried that if they tried to push Saigon to the point of collapse too quickly, the Americans might yet return. Final victory, they calculated, would come in 1976.

Ever impatient, Party First Secretary Le Duan did not want to wait that long. "Now that the United States has pulled out," he said, "it will be hard for them to jump back in. And no matter how they may intervene they cannot rescue the Saigon administration from its disastrous collapse." But all the previous offensives he had set in motion—in 1964, in 1968, in 1972—had

ABOVE At a high pass on the Ho Chi Minh Trail, General Vo Nguyen Giap (center, with helmet) congratulates General Dong Sy Nguyen, commander of the Ho Chi Minh Trail. By 1975, Nguyen recalled, with nine divisions of engineers and 120,000 laborers at work along the trail, it took less than a week to move a whole infantry division from Quang Binh, well above the DMZ, to Loc Ninh, just seventy-six miles northwest of Saigon.

ended in failure. This time, he turned to General Vo Nguyen Giap, the architect of the great victory over the French at Dien Bien Phu, who had been sidelined during the Tet Offensive.

Giap ordered a "test" attack to see if the Americans would bring airpower back to bear as they had during the Easter Offensive two and a half years earlier. In December, North Vietnamese forces attacked Phuoc Long, northeast of Saigon. Within three weeks they had overrun the entire province and had killed or captured thousands of ARVN defenders. General Van Tien Dung, the North Vietnamese chief of staff, expressed his surprise and delight at the ease with which victory had been achieved; the ARVN, he said, now found themselves forced to fight a "poor man's war."

The United States did nothing in response. The new president, former Michigan congressman Gerald Ford, was preoccupied with other problems—inflation, unemployment, tensions in the Middle East—and unaware of the secret pledges Nixon had made to Thieu. He held a press conference that offered the South Vietnamese no comfort. He had asked for additional aid for Vietnam shortly after taking office and quickly learned that there was little lingering enthusiasm for it in Congress. A good

many legislators now shared Majority Leader Mike Mansfield's weariness at seeing "pictures of Indochinese men, women, and children being slaughtered by American guns with American ammunition in countries in which we have no vital interests." Now, asked whether he was considering any additional measures to aid the Saigon government, Ford said he was not. During his first State of the Union address he did not utter the word "Vietnam."

"To me, with the communist flag planted in a provincial capital just to the north of Saigon, the handwriting was on the wall," remembered Captain Stuart Herrington, now working for the Defense Attaché Office. "I then communicated with my family and told them that even though my tour was supposed to take me till August I would be home sooner. And then I began quietly—one little box at a time—to mail my possessions out of Vietnam."

On March 13, General Dung's forces attacked Ban Me Thuot, in the heart of the Central Highlands, where his forces outnumbered the overextended ARVN nearly six to one. They took it within two days, and then turned toward two other cities, Pleiku and Kon Tum.

For weeks, the ARVN top command had warned Thieu that his already weakened forces were spread too thin, that it was no longer possible to defend the entire country. He had angrily differed with them. But now, suddenly, he changed his mind. He ordered his troops to abandon the Central Highlands, withdraw under fire, and then regroup and retake Ban Me Thuot. It would have been a near-impossible task even with a carefully worked-out plan. Thieu had none. The North Vietnamese had cut the main road leading down to the coastal plain, so the retreating ARVN had no choice but to follow an unpaved disused logging road. Territorial Forces encamped alongside them were meant to provide a screen for the retreating ARVN and their families but were unaccountably never told what was happening. "When everyone saw our troops withdrawing, and heard the communists were coming," remembered General Pham Duy Tat, a seasoned Ranger commander, "they panicked and ran. Many had their families with them. They had to get out, too. How could we abandon them? How could they leave

ABOVE North Vietnamese troops ford a river on the way to attack Ban Me Thuot, in the heart of the Central Highlands, in March 1975.

their families to the communists? So our soldiers, their families, the civilians, everybody ran."

The result was a catastrophe. As the ARVN and Territorial Forces fled south, 400,000 terrified civilians fled with them. The soldiers cursed Thieu, one officer remembered: "Some reached the limit of their despair and killed the officers. An artillery battalion commander who was marching in the retreating column was shot to death by soldiers who wanted his beautiful watch. The despair was so great that at one point two or three guerrillas arriving at the scene could make prisoners of a hundred Rangers." Thousands died, killed by North Vietnamese shells and machine gun fire, trampled by fellow refugees, run over by retreating tanks, blown apart by South Vietnamese bombs dropped by pilots who mistook them for the enemy. Reporters called it the "Convoy of Tears."

Meanwhile, Pleiku and Kon Tum fell to the North Vietnamese as well. In just ten days, six entire provinces, a full infantry division, the equivalent of another division of Rangers, and tens of thousands of territorial and support troops with all their weapons and equipment had fallen to the communists. Bao Ninh, then still serving in the Central Highlands, understood what was happening: "After thirty years of inconclusive war, suddenly we realized, Saigon was going to lose. Even a regular soldier like me could see that."

Bao Ninh's prediction of that long-awaited victory would look better, day by day.

ABOVE North Vietnamese tank crews get a last-minute briefing before moving on Kon Tum. **LEFT** At the end of their headlong flight, survivors of the exodus from the Central Highlands crowd along the bank of the Da Rang River near the city of Tuy Hoa, March 23, 1975.

regime got into serious trouble. He would say nothing about bombing in his reply, pledged only his "continuing support" and dispatched General Weyand to survey the situation firsthand. "Ford doesn't seem to care," Thieu told an aide. "He is going off on vacation at Palm Springs while we are dying."

MARCH 27

GENERAL WEYAND arrived in Saigon, called on President Thieu, and assured him again of President Ford's "steadfast support," then set off on a six-day tour of the embattled country to see what, if anything, could be done to save it.

MARCH 25

WITH THE SOUTH VIETNAMESE on the run and losing the equivalent of more than a battalion a day and with no sign the Americans would come to their aid, the Politburo cabled new orders to General Dung in the South. He was now to "make a big leap forward" and seize a "once-in-a-thousand-years opportunity to liberate Saigon before the rainy season" that would begin at April's end. While communist forces moved toward Saigon from the west and south, Dung was to drive his columns south a thousand miles along the coast, rolling up one city after another as he went, and to do it all in less than two months. He would name his operation the "Ho Chi Minh Campaign."

On the same day, Thieu broadcast a new "order of the day," exhorting his forces to halt the communist advance "at all costs." "All of you," he said, "must be determined and strong like a fortress, which the aggressors, no matter how brutal and fanatical they may be, will be unable to shake. . . . I have led you through many dangerous circumstances in the past. This time, I am again by your side." He was, in fact, safely ensconced in his palace from where he asked President Ford for what he called "a brief but intensive B-52 strike" to halt the enemy advance. Ford's hands were tied, and he had never been shown the letters from Nixon pledging to intervene militarily if the Thieu

ABOVE U.S. army chief of staff General Frederick Weyand and U.S. ambassador Graham Martin meet with President Thieu at the Presidential Palace in Saigon. "We will get you the assistance you need," Weyand told Thieu at the end of his visit, "and will explain your needs to Congress."

MARCH 29

THE NORTH VIETNAMESE entered Danang, South Vietnam's second largest city. It "was not captured," an American reporter remembered, "it disintegrated in its own terror. Of the 50,000 South Vietnamese soldiers stationed in and around the city, hardly any raised a rifle in its defense." People came out of their homes to wave and cheer as the North Vietnamese marched past. Le Minh Khue, who had survived years as a volunteer working on the Ho Chi Minh Trail, was now a war correspondent, riding in a truck in the midst of the advancing North Vietnamese army. The road was littered with boots and uniforms stripped off by retreating ARVN troops. She remembered seeing young men in ill-fitting civilian clothes who had clearly served in the South Vietnamese army. "I saw the fear on their faces," she remembered. "I just felt badly for them. A defeat like that was terrible. I didn't feel that this was something that we should rub in anyone's face." She was assigned to stay in an ARVN officer's abandoned home, where she found the family's belongings still packed in suitcases piled in the front room. They'd clearly fled in a hurry. "I went into a small room, the room of a little girl," she recalled. "On the ironing board there was still material to make an *ao dai*. It hadn't been sewn yet. I was afraid. I didn't understand what happened to that family. Where were they? The neighbors told me the family had tried to flee by barge. But the barge sank and all of them drowned, an entire family. I felt that the souls of that family would probably come back to their house. I was afraid. I had to ask friends to spend the night with me. After that, I went into some other houses of people who fled and I saw everything from their every-

day lives was still there—all of their most precious possessions, albums, pictures of their children, papers, deeds, titles—just scattered around. This was the collapse of a whole system."

Paul Vogle, a UPI reporter, was aboard the last American plane to leave Danang. It almost didn't make it. The moment the Boeing 727—flying in from Saigon—touched down, hundreds of desperate people charged across the tarmac toward it, some in jeeps, some on scooters, most simply running for their lives. The moment the tail ramp came down, members of the First ARVN Division's crack unit, the Hac Boa, or Black Panthers, began clawing their way on board. When an old woman tried to get on with them, a soldier kicked her in the face. As the plane began taxiing for takeoff, ARVN troops who'd been left behind opened fire. Someone threw a grenade, which jammed the wing flaps open. As the plane lumbered into the air, the ramp was still down, and the legs of seven soldiers clinging to the landing gear could be seen dangling in the air. On the way to Saigon at least one soldier fell into the South China Sea. Two hundred and sixty-eight people had crowded into the cabin, which was meant to hold 189. Perhaps 60 more squeezed into the cargo hold. "Only two women and one baby among them," Vogle wrote. "The rest were soldiers, toughest of the tough, meanest of the mean. They were out. They said nothing. They didn't talk to each other or to us. They looked at the floor." Vogle walked up the aisle gathering up their weapons and ammunition. "They

didn't need them anymore. . . . They had gone from humans to animals and now they were vegetables."

Meanwhile, on the same Danang beach where U.S. Marines had landed nearly ten years earlier, beginning America's combat involvement in Vietnam, 16,000 South Vietnamese soldiers fought with one another and with 75,000 terrified civilians for space aboard an improvised fleet of freighters, tugs, and fishing boats headed southward for Cam Ranh Bay, Vung Tau, Saigon—anywhere they hoped the northern troops might somehow not follow. Hundreds drowned struggling to reach the boats. Hundreds more were killed by enemy shells raining down on the beach.

The rout continued. "After Danang," one reporter wrote, "provinces stretching along three hundred miles of coastline fell like a row of porcelain vases sliding off a shelf."

North Vietnamese colonel Ho Huu Lan, who had survived day after day of battle around Con Thien, in Hue, and on Hamburger Hill, remembered how different this headlong pursuit

ABOVE From an LST anchored offshore, South Vietnamese Marines watch fellow Marines struggle to escape from China Beach at Danang, the same beach on which U.S. Marines had first landed ten years earlier. As enemy shells explode behind them, Marines unable to swim take their chances with a chain of inner tubes. Hundreds drowned.

was, how happy it made him. "We would look at the map every day and see how far the ARVN had retreated. It was amazing. We were making more progress in a day than we made in years. One day was like twenty-five years of progress. There was panic. I felt that I could chase away a company all on my own. Clearly, they had given up. They didn't have any will to fight. Our slogan was move as fast as possible—and then move faster!"

"Who would have believed the northern part of the country would be lost by the end of March?" the CIA analyst Frank Snepp remembered. "Eighteen North Vietnamese divisions, with five in reserve, were now arrayed against basically six South Vietnamese divisions. The manpower imbalance was about three or four to one in favor of the communists. This was breathtaking. The refugee problem was overwhelming." "Eight provinces have been lost in the past three weeks," he cabled Washington that day, "four more are in imminent danger, and over a million people have been left homeless, placing incalculable strains on the economy. . . . Huge stocks of ammunition and hardware have been abandoned. The entire complexion of the Vietnam war has altered and the government is in imminent danger of decisive military defeat."

It seemed clear to Snepp and to many others that the time had come to begin serious preparations for the evacuation of

ABOVE AND RIGHT Panic in Danang: A cargo net lifts a refugee family onto a freighter, while South Vietnamese Marines fight for places aboard another ship bound for a port further south.

all the Americans still in Saigon and as many as possible of the 200,000 South Vietnamese and their families who had cooperated with them in one capacity or another. Thomas Polgar, the CIA station chief, sent Snepp to make that case to the ambassador. Martin was not impressed.

"Basically, Martin said to me, 'You're wrong, Mr. Snepp. I have better intelligence.' And I said, 'Sir, six divisions have been destroyed in less than a month.' He said, 'We will save this situation. You're being overly alarmist.' And that moment was terrifying because I knew if Martin failed to realize how serious the military situation was he would never authorize our planning for a rational evacuation of our Vietnamese friends."

Graham Martin had not been appointed ambassador, he said, to "give Vietnam away to the communists." He had convinced himself that, rather than face a bloody climactic battle, the South Vietnamese could somehow still create a redoubt around Saigon strong enough to persuade the enemy to agree to a peaceful transfer of power to a coalition government. He was sure that so much as a hint of American flight would panic the population and undercut the possibility of that peaceful solution. Accordingly, that same day, Martin instructed his deputy, Gerhard Lehmann, to assure a group of disbelieving U.S. officers and newspaper reporters that "militarily, the North Vietnamese do not have the capability to launch an offensive against Saigon. No evacuation is under way."

Philip Caputo had been among the first Marines to land in Vietnam. Now, he was back as a reporter for the *Chicago Tribune*, assigned to cover what looked to be the final days of the republic he'd been sent to help save from communism. "The ambassador couldn't believe this was all ending the way it was ending," he remembered. "They would come out with these statements to the effect that the South Vietnamese are going to pull back and turn Saigon into another Stalingrad or that the North Vietnamese were going to negotiate. I called it the 'Great American Delusion Machine.' This was DENIAL in capital letters, in neon."

Cam Ranh Bay had been a special point of pride for U.S. military engineers, a vast modern deepwater port conjured up in a matter of months on the site of an old fishing village. It had been headquarters for Operation Market Time, the U.S. Navy's ambitious effort to deny the enemy resupply by sea. Tens of thousands of fresh U.S. troops had first landed there at the sprawling Air Force base from which countless tactical air sorties had been flown when called for from the battlefield.

There were no Americans left there now. Instead, the city was filled with tens of thousands of desperate refugees from Danang and beyond, "starving and gasping from thirst," according to Le Kim Dinh, reporting for *The New York Times*. "Money does not matter," he wrote. "Fortunes are stolen from some, and these are robbed by others. Piasters, gold, diamonds, bits of priceless family treasure—none of it means anything in comparison with the need to survive. At Cam Ranh, the suffering of the civilians was far and away the worst, with babies dying on ships or ashore, with the body of an old man lying ignored all day on the pier." The retreating ARVN suffered, too. Most of their commanders had already abandoned them and flown to Saigon. Shock troops dispatched from the capital to defend military installations found themselves shooting it out with soldiers who were systematically looting homes and shops. Eleven ships crowded with still more soldiers and civilians from Danang waited offshore. Some passengers had paid as much $1,200 each, hoping to be carried all the way to Saigon, only to be forcibly offloaded here. "It was said that Saigon authorities were not willing to permit a flood of refugees into the capital," Kim wrote. "But some said it was just a question of money. 'When they are willing to pay another one million piasters per person, then those ships will set sail for Saigon,' a military man said. No one has any clear idea how many have died. Bodies eventually just disappear. One wealthy man is said to have been murdered shipboard in front of his wife, and his body was thrown overboard. Four babies were reported trampled to death on another ship. . . . For nearly everyone who traveled so far to get here, this appeared to be the end of the line—waiting and listening for the approaching rumble of North Vietnamese tanks."

APRIL 2

TAM KY, QUANG NGAI, Qui Nhon, Nha Trang, Cam Ranh Bay—the North Vietnamese kept moving closer and closer to Saigon. Joe Galloway was there, covering the retreat. "It was stunning to sit there writing the daily leads on the fall of all these places we'd come to know," he recalled. "I would look and say, 'Oh that province. Wait a minute, that's where My Lai is.' You just were overwhelmed with ten years' worth of history and seeing all of it come unglued."

Thomas Polgar sent a cable to CIA headquarters recommending that President Thieu be removed and replaced by General Duong Van Minh, who might then be able to form a coalition government that could satisfy the North Vietnamese and forestall further bloodshed.

OPPOSITE Two members of a U.S. civilian crew struggle to maintain order among people desperate to climb aboard a transport plane at Nha Trang, April 1, 1975.

AT A LITTLE AFTER FOUR in the afternoon, a C-5A Galaxy transport plane took off from Tan Son Nhut bound for the United States. Aboard were 243 infants and children, all said to be orphans or the unwanted offspring of American servicemen. Rumors had spread that Eurasian children would somehow be in special danger from the advancing communists. Ambassador Martin had persuaded President Ford to provide $2 million for an emergency program called Operation Babylift to get as many of the children out of the country as fast as possible. It would, the ambassador told South Vietnam's deputy prime minister for social welfare, "help reverse the current trend of American public opinion to the advantage of the Republic of Vietnam. Especially when these children land in the United States, they will be subject to television, radio, and press coverage and the effect will be tremendous." Also aboard were a number of women who worked for the embassy and the CIA who were slipped on in order to get out of Saigon without raising an alarm. Twelve minutes into the flight, the locks of the rear loading ramp failed, the door separated from the plane and sliced through the tail. The plane broke into four parts. Some parts burst into flame. One hundred and thirty-eight passengers were killed, including seventy-eight children. When word of the crash began to spread, Joe Galloway was assigned to go out to the Air Force 7th Field Hospital near Tan Son Nhut and stand by. "I had just gotten there," he recalled. "And I was back around at the emergency entrance when an ambulance pulled in and backed up. The back doors opened and they brought out a stretcher with the bodies of babies piled on it. I don't know how many—a dozen, fifteen, eighteen. First, it broke my heart. And second, I thought, even when we try to do something right in this place it goes so horribly wrong. I just couldn't take it anymore. I turned around and I walked back to the bureau. It took me hours. And I just left. I went home to Singapore. I couldn't do it anymore."

Back in Washington that same day, General Weyand reported to the president on what he'd seen in Vietnam. "The current military situation is critical," he said. "The probability of the survival of South Vietnam as a truncated nation in the southern provinces is marginal at best." There was no way for the ARVN to recapture all the land they'd had to abandon, but there was a slim chance that with an immediate outlay of $722 million to replace all the weaponry that had been lost during the headlong ARVN flight—744 artillery pieces, 446 tanks and armored personnel carriers, 12,000 trucks, and much more—enough regiments might be armed to mount a defense of Saigon itself. But even if that didn't work, he continued, the appropriation

would help fortify the people's plunging morale. Many of Ford's aides thought that requesting such a sum this late in the game was pointless: opposition to further aid was strong on Capitol Hill and growing stronger; it was unlikely that the weaponry could reach the city's defenders before they were overwhelmed; and if it did reach them, it would merely prolong the inevitable. But Henry Kissinger, now Ford's secretary of state, favored the request: while "on one level it was preposterous," he recalled, since "Vietnam was likely to collapse before any equipment could get there," he argued that it should be honored because it might gain a little time for evacuation and "we would at least have discharged our moral obligation."

General Weyand made one additional recommendation: "For reasons of prudence, the United States should plan now for a mass evacuation of some six thousand U.S. citizens and tens of thousands of South Vietnamese . . . Nationals to whom we have incurred an obligation and owe protection." It should also be made plain to the North Vietnamese that if they tried to interfere with the evacuation once it was under way, the United States would respond with force.

APRIL 5

WHEN THERE WAS no second C-5A transport immediately available to fly the surviving children out of Saigon, an American businessman named Robert Macauley mortgaged his home to charter a Boeing 747 from Pan American Airlines. The uninjured survivors from the crashed plane were carried aboard and flown to San Francisco International Airport. The president and first lady were there to receive them. In the end, some three thousand infants would be lifted out of Saigon before enemy shelling of Tan Son Nhut made further flights impossible. Most were adopted by Americans, some by Canadians and Australians. Later, it would develop that many of the children had not been orphans at all, merely the children of parents so poor they'd had no choice but to leave their offspring temporarily in orphanages, always assuming they would one day return for them. Because everything happened so fast and so little paperwork was completed, subsequent reunions between adopted children and their birth parents would prove virtually impossible.

Philip Caputo now found himself attending daily briefings held by both sides in the struggle. Each struck him as delusional. At five each afternoon, he wrote, ARVN officers held forth in front of a big lighted map. "'The North Vietnamese have been

stopped,' said the briefers, who had been through the Looking Glass so long they couldn't remember what it looked like on the other side. . . . But when it came to creativity, the North Vietnamese proved themselves as superior to the Southerners as they had on the battlefield." The 1973 treaty permitted the North to keep a detachment of "ceasefire observers" in a small compound near Tan Son Nhut airport, and so each day a communist colonel offered reporters Hanoi's version of what was happening. South Vietnam was not witnessing a North Vietnamese offensive, he always insisted; this was a "people's uprising." How did "the people" obtain the tanks that were rumbling down Route 1? Where did the heavy guns that rained shells on the retreating ARVN come from? They'd all been commandeered from the puppet army, he said.

Nearly two-thirds of South Vietnamese territory had now been lost to the communists. "The one ending no one could have imagined in Vietnam, an outright battlefield victory for one side or the other," Arnold R. Isaacs, a reporter for the *Baltimore Sun*, wrote after Danang's fall, "now seems not only possible but perhaps inevitable."

TOP President Gerald Ford feeds one of the infants aboard the first successful Babylift flight at San Francisco International Airport. **ABOVE** Hanoi citizens pause to mark the steady progress of the North Vietnamese advance toward Saigon.

APRIL 8

JUST BEFORE eight thirty in the morning, a South Vietnamese fighter bomber swooped low over the Presidential Palace and dropped four bombs, roared on to strafe a fuel storage dump on the far side of the Saigon River, and then landed at a communist-held airport at Phuoc Long. Hearing the bombs, Frank Snepp's boss ordered him to climb up onto the roof to find out what was happening. "I saw the Presidential Palace down the street with trails of smoke coming from the corners," he recalled. "It was a shock. It meant that Saigon itself was vulnerable." That same day, Snepp remembered, the CIA's best intelligence source supplied what he called "a crucial update of the intelligence already in hand. [COSVN] had just issued a new 'resolution' calling for . . . a move against the capital . . . with no allowance whatsoever of a negotiated settlement. All the 'talk'

of negotiations and a possible coalition government was merely a ruse to confuse the South Vietnamese and to sow suspicion between them and the Americans." The ambassador's reaction to this news was to reaffirm his faith that an international settlement was still possible. "He was picking up these noises from the French and others," Snepp recalled. "He desperately wanted to believe there was a chance for South Vietnam to survive."

Meanwhile, thirty-seven miles northeast of the city, General Dung's forces were preparing to attack the town of Xuan Loc. If it fell, Highway 1 would be open all the way to Saigon. The Eighteenth ARVN Division, which was defending the town, was outnumbered and outgunned, but its commander, General Le Minh Dao, was determined to resist. "I vow to hold Xuan Loc," he said. "I don't care how many divisions the other side sends against me. I will knock them down." The next day the North Vietnamese would hit Xuan Loc with three thousand artillery and rocket rounds. The ARVN resolved to hold on.

APRIL 10

IN THE INTERNAL DEBATE over the request for additional funds, President Ford sided with Kissinger and appealed before a joint session of Congress for emergency aid to Saigon. "A vast human tragedy has befallen our friends in Vietnam and Cambodia . . . ," he began. "The situation has reached a critical phase requiring immediate and positive decisions by the government." The North Vietnamese had consistently violated the 1973 peace agreement, he charged, sending into South Vietnam tens of thousands of fresh troops and tons of modern weapons. "In the face of this situation, the United States—torn as it was by the emotions of a decade of war—was unable to respond. We deprived ourselves by law of the ability to enforce the agreement, thus giving North Vietnamese assurance that it could violate that agreement with impunity. Next we reduced our eco-

nomic and arms aid to South Vietnam. Finally, we signaled our increasing reluctance to give any support to that nation struggling for its survival." The military crisis was now acute, and time was very short, he continued; General Weyand had assured him that if there were any chance at all to "stem the onrushing aggression, . . . stabilize the military situation, and permit the chance of a negotiated settlement," $722 million "in very specific military supplies" was needed "without delay." There was no applause. Most legislators—and their constituents—thought military aid at this stage could not possibly make any difference to Saigon's survival.

OPPOSITE AND ABOVE Chinook helicopters fill the sky above Highway 1 with red dust as they lift civilians out of the Xuan Loc area, while refugees race for another helicopter as the climactic battle there is about to begin.

There was another crisis as well, Ford told his silent listeners: "I must, of course, as I think each of you would, consider the safety of nearly six thousand Americans who remain in South Vietnam and tens of thousands of South Vietnamese employees of the United States government, of news agencies, of contractors and businesses for many years whose lives, with their dependents, are in very grave peril. If the very worst were to happen, at least allow the orderly evacuation of Americans and endangered South Vietnamese to places of safety." Accordingly, he asked for an additional sum of $250 million for "economic and humanitarian aid" to cover the cost of rescuing Americans and endangered Vietnamese. Both sums were needed immediately.

A reporter asked Henry Kissinger if requesting all that money wasn't really just an attempt to lay the blame on Congress for what was about to happen to South Vietnam.

"We are not trying to saddle Congress with anything," he answered. "We aren't after a negative vote just to get it over with."

Another newsman asked if there was to be an "evacuation" of all the Vietnamese who had worked with the Americans.

No, Kissinger answered, "just a thinning out."

APRIL 12

AT ABOUT NINE O'CLOCK in the morning, a hulking transport helicopter eased down onto a football field not far from the American embassy in Phnom Penh, Cambodia. Three hundred and sixty-five Marines with M16 rifles and grenade launchers leaped out and formed a perimeter. The communist Khmer Rouge were poised to seize the city they had besieged for nearly a year now, and American officials and some of the Cambodians who had worked closest with them were fleeing to safety. Within a little over an hour, 82 Americans, 159 Cambodians, and 35 "third-country nationals" had climbed aboard relays of helicopters and lifted off, headed for the USS *Okinawa* in the Gulf of Thailand. The U.S. ambassador to Cambodia, John Gunther Dean, carried with him a letter from one of the pro-American generals who had helped topple Prince Sihanouk in 1970. At the last minute, Dean had offered him a place on his helicopter. "I cannot, alas, leave in such a cowardly fashion," the general wrote. "I never believed for a moment that you [Americans] would have this sentiment of abandoning a people which has chosen liberty." Word that the Americans had fled Phnom Penh did not inspire confidence or calm growing fears in Saigon.

APRIL 13

BRIGADIER GENERAL RICHARD E. CAREY, commander of the Ninth Marine Amphibious Brigade, called on Ambassador Martin to discuss an evacuation plan. It provided four options: airlift by commercial airliner; a military airlift; a sealift by cargo ships anchored in the port of Saigon; and, as a last resort, Operation Frequent Wind, evacuation by flights of helicopters to a flotilla of U.S. Navy ships in the South China Sea. General Carey's Marines were to supply both the security force and the fleet of helicopters, should they be needed. Martin professed little interest. He would still tolerate no outward sign that the United States intended to abandon South Vietnam, he said. "The visit was cold [and] nonproductive," Carey remembered, "and appeared to be an irritant to the ambassador." Martin somehow still clung to the hope that a negotiated settlement could save Saigon.

APRIL 14

FOR THE FIRST TIME since World War I, the entire Senate Foreign Relations Committee called on the president at the White House. There would be no further military funds for Vietnam, they said. "I will give you large sums for evacuation," New York's Jacob Javits told the president, "but not one nickel for military aid." Frank Church feared that the United States risked involvement in a "very large war" if it attempted to evacuate all the South Vietnamese who had been loyal to the United States. Joseph Biden of Delaware went further. "I will vote for any amount for getting the Americans out. I don't want it mixed with getting the Vietnamese out."

Bui Diem, South Vietnam's ambassador to the United States who had helped draft the communiqué welcoming the first American Marines to Danang in 1965, spoke for many South Vietnamese. "The U.S. spent billions and billions in Vietnam. But at the last minute the Congress washed their hands. I didn't think that was good for a big nation like the U.S. to behave like that. Because by that time we weren't asking for the blood of American soldiers. It was a kind of supplementary aid that we asked for. I'm very sorry about it. It is not up to a diplomat to use strong words against the Americans, but I felt deeply sorry about it."

APRIL 16

PANIC SPREAD FURTHER in Saigon as newspapers reported that Defense Secretary James Schlesinger—hoping to win support for the Thieu regime in Congress—had publicly predicted that perhaps 200,000 South Vietnamese would be butchered if the communists took over.

APRIL 17

BECAUSE FRANK SNEPP was determined to persuade both his station chief, Thomas Polgar, and Ambassador Martin that time really was running out, that defeat was very near, he called in the man he believed to be the best-informed agent working for the CIA: "He'd always been right. Everyone believed what he said." His message was clear: "They're going to strike Saigon in time for Ho Chi Minh's birthday on May 19, which is just a month away." "One of the most terrifying things he told us," Snepp recalled, "was that the North Vietnamese were going to shell Tan Son Nhut airfield. I briefed American civilians, I briefed American journalists and businessmen, and I briefed Marines who were showing up to assist with the evolving evacuation planning. They were astounded because Ambassador Martin had convinced [many of] them and convinced himself that the communists would allow for a ceasefire, a coalition government, and a peaceful transition. Our intelligence didn't support that at all. This had reached such a point that Martin's deputy was editing broadcasts on American radio in Saigon to suppress bad news."

One of those with whom Snepp spoke was Master Sergeant Juan Valdez, in charge of Marine Corps security guards at the Saigon embassy. He had been one of the first Marines to land in Vietnam in 1965, and, ten years later, it seemed clear that he would be among the last to leave. "The situation didn't sound good," Valdez remembered. "We started doing more training, going out to the rifle range and doing more firing. But when

you're on embassy duty you really don't have much of any support weapons. You have shotguns, revolvers, and tear gas. That's about the extent of it. You can't face a big force coming at you with that type of weapons."

That evening, Henry Kissinger cabled Ambassador Martin. "We have just completed an interagency review of the state of play in South Vietnam. You should know . . . there was almost no support for the evacuation of Vietnamese and for the use of American force to help protect any evacuation. The sentiment of our military and CIA colleagues was to get out fast and now." He had already asked the ambassador to see to it that he reduce the U.S. presence to roughly two thousand people by the end of the following week. He now wanted that effort accelerated.

APRIL 17

PHNOM PENH FELL to the Khmer Rouge. Armed revolutionaries stormed into the city and would drive every single citizen into the countryside at gunpoint, the beginning of a four-year orgy of killing that would account for the loss of some two million lives.

ABOVE A Khmer Rouge soldier brandishes a pistol and orders Phnom Penh storekeepers to abandon their shops and leave the city.

PRESIDENT THIEU learned that near the town of Phan Rang his own retreating troops, angered at his policies, had bull-dozed and defaced his family's ancestral tomb—an insult with special meaning for any Vietnamese. He had become, one officer remembered, "the most hated man in Vietnam." Thieu claimed to be unshaken: the ARVN must fight on, he said, "to the last bullet and the last grain of rice."

Radio Hanoi promised that those South Vietnamese who had cooperated with the Americans would be "kindly treated in the spirit of national reconciliation and concord, free from all hostilities and suspicions." But tens of thousands of South Vietnamese refused to believe them. Panic continued to spread.

In the evening, speaking into a dictaphone, Stuart Herrington summarized the dilemma Ambassador Martin continued to face: "If he orders evacuation and we commence the operation because we are afraid that further delay may make evacuation impossible, the very order itself and the initiation of even a limited evacuation risks triggering the conditions we are afraid of in the first place. But if we wait until things have gotten to where it is essential to evacuate, we may not be able to get away—as Danang and Nha Trang [where South Vietnamese employees of the consulate had been left behind to face the communists] dramatically illustrated."

FRIGHTENED DEPOSITORS crowded Saigon banks as people withdrew their savings. The black market rate for dollars jumped from 750 to 3,000 piasters as would-be evacuees accumulated hard cash with which they hoped to bribe their way onto a ship or airplane.

In the evening—and at Henry Kissinger's personal prompting—Ambassador Martin asked to see President Thieu, "as a friend," he said. His generals were likely soon to ask him to resign, he told the president, and the North would never negotiate so long as he remained in office. Thieu asked if his resignation would help persuade Congress to provide the assistance South Vietnam needed. Maybe, Martin said, but he suspected that was "a bargain whose day has passed." Thieu said only that he would do what was best for his country.

THE SIEGE OF XUAN LOC finally ended just before dawn. The ARVN had held on for twelve days and killed hundreds of enemy troops before being overwhelmed. But Highway 1 was now open all the way to Saigon.

That evening, Thieu addressed the nation on television. He spoke for ninety minutes, by turns angry and tearful. He excoriated the United States: "You Americans with your 500,000 soldiers . . . were not defeated," he said, "you ran away." Americans "have let our combatants die under the hail of shells. This is an inhumane act by an inhumane ally." To defeat the North without U.S. help was an impossible task—"like filling the ocean with stones." He continued: "I ask my countrymen . . . to forgive me my past mistakes. . . . I am resigning, but I am not deserting."

Thieu's successor, Vice President Tran Van Huong, was elderly, ailing, nearly blind. He asked that his predecessor be exiled from Vietnam. Otherwise, he said, "I will be accused of running a Thieu government without Thieu." Meanwhile, he urged the shattered army to fight on. Hanoi professed to see no difference between the new president and the old. The change was just "a puppet show. . . . Now that the U.S. imperialists' reactionary lackey regime . . . is moving toward complete collapse, the Ford administration's attempts to breathe life into this clique are futile and useless."

NEWS OF THIEU'S RESIGNATION led Vietnamese to begin gathering in ever-greater numbers at the DAO—the sprawling Defense Attaché's Office compound, adjacent to Tan Son Nhut airport, that had once been "Pentagon East," the MACV headquarters from which American commanders had directed their war. Now it served as a collection point, first for hundreds and then for thousands of South Vietnamese, desperate to find a place on one of the steady stream of C-130 and C-141 transports now taking off for Guam and the Philippines.

There was still no coherent plan for evacuating the large number of ordinary Vietnamese who had worked for the Americans. "It looks like if we don't take care of our people, nothing will be done," the head of one Defense Department unit said. Individuals and organizations scrambled to get friends onto outbound flights, with or without the necessary papers. "We began

going to Vietnamese friends," Frank Snepp remembered, "and smuggling them out on cargo aircraft that were leaving with their cargo bays empty. We began mounting basically a black airlift around the ambassador's orders without his knowing it. And these people were showing up at Clark Air Base in the Philippines without any papers. I was very concerned that our best agent be looked after, the one who had reported so often so accurately on communist plans. And we didn't look after him. He was left behind." Employees of military agencies fared best because their bosses had access to the airport; those who had worked for civilian outfits like the United States Information Agency would mostly find themselves stranded.

Better-connected Vietnamese did not have to suffer such indignities. Bui Diem flew back from Washington to get his wife and mother out before it was too late. "I knew already that America will do nothing because the war was over from the American point of view. The last day I was in Saigon I got the good luck of having the help of Ambassador Martin to help my mother and my sister out. But I felt deeply, deeply sorrowful about my life."

"I knew that the end was approaching and I had to get out," the sometime politician Phan Quang Tue recalled. "When I and my immediate family and my father and his immediate family went to the airport and we were getting into the C-40, I said to myself, 'This is crazy. Why do we have to leave under these con-

CLOCKWISE FROM TOP LEFT Waving their credentials, Vietnamese clamor to board a U.S. embassy bus bound for Tan Son Nhut airport; families file onto a C-141 transport plane; and weaponless ARVN troops file down Highway 1 toward Saigon, trying to stay ahead of the enemy.

ditions?' It was so humiliating. I carried that humiliation with me to the United States. When I got in line to sign up for a job, I reminded Americans of Vietnam, which they hated. You have to lose a nation and a dream to feel that humiliation."

APRIL 23

STUART HERRINGTON managed to evacuate some two hundred Vietnamese—employees of his department as well as their closest relatives. (Their families averaged ten members each, but there was room for only seven.) They had no passports or visas and had to be smuggled, fifty at a time, in an unmarked truck past South Vietnamese security police, then spirited onto a plane bound for Guam. With them went twenty-seven friends of Herrington's, intelligence officers from the ARVN Military Security Service. "One officer handed me his pistol as he climbed into the dark recesses of the truck," Herrington recalled, "telling me in a subdued voice that he would not need it in Guam or America." ARVN enlisted hoping to get out were largely out of luck.

Gerald Ford was the convocation speaker at Tulane University that day. Like the war in Vietnam, he said, the War of 1812 had not ended as Americans had wished, but General Andrew Jackson's victory over the British at New Orleans after that war had officially ended soon restored the country's self-esteem. "Today," he said, "America can regain the sense of pride that existed before Vietnam. But it cannot be achieved by refighting a war that is finished as far as America is concerned. As I see it, the time has come to look forward to an agenda for the future, to unify, to bind up the nation's wounds, and to restore its health and its optimistic self-confidence." The students roared their approval. America was moving on.

APRIL 24

THE U.S. NAVAL ATTACHÉ proposed to Ambassador Martin that some thirty thousand evacuees be allowed to board U.S. Sealift Command ships docked on the Saigon River. He refused and insisted that the vessels sail away empty. Later, asked about his decision at a congressional hearing, he offered "no apology whatsoever. Had we attempted to load those ships there was universal agreement, from those who understand Saigon, that we should have had an immediate panic situation." Agreement

had not, in fact, been universal: one captain had defied orders and loaded seven hundred Vietnamese associates and their families aboard his ship before steaming out to sea.

APRIL 25

THE TIME HAD COME for Thieu to leave the country. After dark, Thomas Polgar, the CIA station chief, arranged for three black sedans to ferry him, the former prime minister General Tran Thien Khiem, and a handful of his closest aides, to the airport, where an American DC-6, with its lights off, was waiting on the tarmac.

Frank Snepp drove one of the cars: "We showed up at Prime Minister's Khiem's house. Everybody was drinking. Then, suddenly, Nguyen Van Thieu drives up in his limousine. His hair was slicked back and he was very well dressed, looked like he'd stepped out of an Asian edition of *Gentleman's Quarterly*. He went in the house. A few minutes later Thieu came out and got in. General [Charles J.] Timmes, who was a CIA operative, got in with him. We started off for Tan Son Nhut, and I could see his face in the mirror. He was sweating slightly. He and Timmes were discussing what it had been like in Military Region I years ago, where they'd served. 'What a great time it was,' Timmes said to Thieu. 'Pacification is one of your greatest accomplishments.' Thieu agreed. Timmes asked, 'Where is your wife?' 'Oh, she's in London buying antiques.' It was a surreal conversation. And there was a stench of Scotch in the car, I'll never forget that. We went out onto the blacked-out tarmac at Tan Son Nhut. I switched off my lights. I couldn't see anything. I nearly ran over my own boss. He was on the tarmac waiting with a blacked-out aircraft to take Thieu out of the country. The door clicked open. Thieu leaned over to me and grasped my hand and said, 'Thank you. Thank you.' Later, a reporter asked an ARVN officer why Thieu had fled the country instead of taking command of a combat division and leading the defense of his embattled capital. 'He would have been killed almost instantly,' the soldier answered, 'and not by a communist bullet.'"

Thieu was flown to Taiwan, where Anna Chennault, the wealthy Chinese American fundraiser who had acted as the go-between between Thieu and Richard Nixon during the 1968 presidential campaign, brought him a private message from President Ford: it was not a good time for him to visit the United States, it said; antiwar feelings were too strong. "It is so easy to be an enemy of the United States," Thieu said, "but so difficult to be a friend."

That same day, in Washington, House and Senate conferees reached formal agreement on legislation authorizing $327 million for evacuating Americans and "friendly Vietnamese"— more than President Ford had asked for. But there were to be no further funds for the military. "The string had run out for the United States," General Jack Cushman recalled. "The public was just not going to support that. You couldn't ask them to do that. By that time they had been convinced they were striking a match on a bar of soap."

APRIL 27

IN THE MORNING, for the first time in five years, rockets landed in the heart of Saigon. Five thousand people lost their homes to the fires they caused. Retreating ARVN troops now filled the streets. It was the signal for the North Vietnamese to begin their main assault on Saigon. They attacked from five sides "like a hurricane," their commander said.

The docks at the U.S.-built Newport Harbor were now within artillery range of the enemy. The White House ordered all American cargo ships to sail out to sea without waiting to take on passengers. There now could be no organized sealift.

The communists began shelling the seaside town of Vung Tau, just south of the city. Thousands of terrified people clambered into any vessels they could find—rowboats, fishing craft, an unseaworthy Saigon ferry— and sailed out to sea in hope of rescue by the Americans. The USNS *Greenville Victory* eventually took aboard more than ten thousand frightened people. Before the exodus ended, over sixty thousand refugees from Vung Tau would be picked up by carrier ships. But thousands more were left behind, floating helplessly at sea.

RIGHT Saigon residents flee the shelling of Saigon's center that began on April 27.

Despite all the evidence, Ambassador Martin cabled Kissinger that "it is the unanimous opinion of the senior personnel here that there will be no direct or serious attack on Saigon." "A lot of us," Frank Snepp recalled, "began to wonder whether the ambassador had lost his grip on reality. He had come down with pneumonia in the final days. He was terribly enfeebled. And it's possible this affected his judgment."

APRIL 28

SHORTLY AFTER DAWN, North Vietnamese commandos cut off the last road out of the city. One hundred and forty thousand enemy troops were now within an hour of downtown Saigon. "I got a call that morning," Frank Snepp recalled, "from a Vietnamese-Chinese woman named Mai Ly with whom I had had a relationship off and on over the years. She said, 'You've got to get me out of the country. You've got to get me and my child out of the country.' I had seen her recently, and she indeed had a child, and I had been led to believe it might be mine. She said, 'You must get us out of the country.' I said, 'I can't. The ambassador has got me slotted in for a briefing. Call me back in an hour.' And she said, 'If you don't get us out I'll kill myself and this child.' I said, 'Just call me back.' I briefed the ambassador.

OPPOSITE TOP AND BOTTOM Refugees crowd aboard a vessel at Vung Tau while Americans hustle toward a helicopter at Tan Son Nhut. **ABOVE** General Duong Van Minh, newly sworn in as South Vietnam's president in the Independence Palace, Saigon. The figure in the mural behind him is Tran Hung Dao, a thirteenth-century ruler whose forces resisted three Mongol invasions.

And I later discovered that she had killed herself and the child. I don't know if it was mine. But something happened to me in that moment. I realized I had done what the Americans had often done in Vietnam. They had forgotten that we were dealing with human beings. My experience in Vietnam had often been like a B-52 strike from on high. I never had to confront the consequences of my action. I could just let the bomb doors open and still remain detached. This experience changed all that. I realized I was no better than many of the other Americans who had been in Vietnam and had not paid attention to the fact that these were people we were working with."

Evacuation planners had quietly designated two spots within the U.S. embassy as potential helicopter landing zones—a courtyard that could accommodate large choppers and the helipad on the embassy roof, meant for smaller ones. A handsome old tamarind tree stood in the center of the courtyard. The Marines had repeatedly asked Martin for permission to cut it down so it wouldn't interfere with the lift-offs and landings they were certain would soon have to begin. He refused. That tree was a symbol of American resolve, he said; cutting it down "would send the wrong message."

A little after five o'clock, General Duong Van "Big" Minh was sworn in as the new president of South Vietnam. Over the years, Minh had boasted of his contacts with the communists, and so after just six days in office, Tran Van Huong had been prevailed upon to resign so the National Assembly could choose Minh, a president better suited to negotiate with the enemy. The new president called for an immediate ceasefire and pledged to assemble a government drawn from all parts of the neutralist "Third Force." He then asked that all American employees of the Military Attaché Office leave Vietnam within twenty-four hours.

Ten minutes later, five American-made A-37 aircraft cap-

tured from the South Vietnamese and piloted by North Vietnamese airmen dropped bombs on South Vietnamese air force
planes parked on a runway at Tan Son Nhut. Seven planes were
destroyed. It was the only North Vietnamese air raid of the war.
Ambassador Martin ordered that the airlift from the airport
should be stepped up to sixty C-130 flights the following day
so nine thousand evacuees could get out before further damage
could be done to the airport.

APRIL 29

AT 3:58 A.M., North Vietnamese rockets began falling on Tan Son Nhut. Two Marine guards, Lance Corporal Darwin Judge of Marshalltown, Iowa, and Corporal
Charles McMahon Jr. of Woburn, Massachusetts, were killed
instantly—the last American servicemen to die from enemy fire
in the Vietnam War. "It was a direct hit," Juan Valdez recalled.
"I was very upset and very mad. I still blame the ambassador
for that. This shouldn't have happened. If the ambassador had

taken action and gotten people out of there instead of trying to
think that he was going to negotiate with the North Vietnamese, this would have never happened."

Rockets and artillery shells tore at parked planes and cratered
the runways. Civilians and airmen and ARVN troops battled
one another to get on any aircraft that still seemed likely to try to
take off. By first light it was clear that it would no longer be safe
to use fixed-wing aircraft. The battered runways were blocked
by wrecked planes and littered with jettisoned bombs and fuel
tanks. General Homer Smith, the defense attaché, told Ambassador Martin that they had run out of evacuation options. It
was time to call in the helicopters from the offshore fleet and
launch Operation Frequent Wind, he said. Martin, exhausted
and ill, still refused to do it. Instead, he ordered the cargo flights
to continue. The White House backed the ambassador—and
issued a statement saying no orders to evacuate had been given.
A Defense Department official then drove the ambassador to
the airport so he could see things for himself: the runways were
clearly unusable, and rioting South Vietnamese soldiers had
overrun one loading area.

Reluctantly, Martin called Henry Kissinger and asked for the
helicopter evacuation to begin. The tamarind tree was hacked

down so choppers could land safely within the compound. "We had to get chain saws," Valdez recalled. "It was Sea Bees, mostly, with a couple of Marines, and they had to chop this big tree down, cut it in pieces, tow it away. And then they had to get the fire department to wash off all the debris and everything so when the choppers landed they wouldn't suck up all that debris into the engines."

At 10:48 that morning, Saigon time, President Ford's order to execute Operation Frequent Wind—rescue by squads of helicopters flying back and forth from a flotilla of thirty American warships forty miles offshore—reached U.S. officials in the South Vietnames capital. Within half an hour, a prearranged signal to evacuate was broadcast over the American radio station in Saigon: it was meant to begin with Bing Crosby singing "White Christmas," but at the last minute a copy of that record could not be found, so Tennessee Ernie Ford's version signaled the exodus. A cryptic message followed: "The temperature in Saigon is one hundred and five degrees and rising."

Americans and "high-risk" Vietnamese gathered at prearranged collection points and boarded convoys of buses to the DAO compound at Tan Son Nhut. As the buses moved through the crowded streets, angry Vietnamese beat on their sides.

Philip Caputo was aboard one of the buses. "The airfield was under rocket and heavy artillery fire. The North Vietnamese were just walking these shells—these big 130mm. artillery shells—all over the airfield, destroying the runway. The building they took us to was shaking from the impact of the shells." The evacuees were divided into helicopter teams of fifty each and led, one group at a time, out of the DAO compound. They moved down one hallway and rounded a corner into another. "Gentlemen!" a reporter said. "We have turned the corner in Vietnam!" "Yeah," another answered, "and if you look down this hall, you'll see"—a dozen voices completed his sentence—"the light at the end of the tunnel!" When the signal was given to run to their helicopter, shells were still exploding, Caputo remembered, "close enough that you could hear the incoming go overhead. There was room for people but not for luggage on the helicopter and some guy yelled, 'Drop everything!

OPPOSITE AND ABOVE The beginning of the end: North Vietnamese rockets make further flights from Tan Son Nhut impossible; and from the White House family quarters, President Ford gives the order to begin the helicopter flights that will end America's adventure in Vietnam. It is 10:33 p.m., Washington time, April 28, 1975.

Drop everything!' And I dropped everything I had except some notes and some maps. All my clothes—everything. There were a lot of Vietnamese on board, Vietnamese who had worked for us. One woman managed, small as she was, to run on there with a good-sized carry bag of gold bars. The chopper took off, and we're flying toward the coast. And you could look down and all you could see all around Saigon, all around the airfield, were plumes of smoke from burning buildings and exploding artillery shells. And then, finally, we crossed over the coastline. And I'll never forget seeing the entire Seventh Fleet and all of these merchant ships that had been press-ganged into naval service, dozens and dozens of them. I said to myself, 'This fourth-rate peasant army has whipped us.' I just remember this sense of disbelief—disbelief and relief at the same time."

Members of Duong Van Mai Elliott's family were among the last Vietnamese to be helicoptered out of Tan Son Nhut. "My mother didn't want to leave," she recalled. "She said she didn't want to be a refugee again. She'd been a refugee too many times." And there was another reason: her daughter Thanh had joined the Viet Minh decades earlier, and with the war's ending there was now a chance that they might be reunited. "She said

she wanted to stay and see Thanh. My father was determined to leave because he was afraid that if he stayed or if we stayed we'd be killed. They argued, but in the end my mother yielded. Commercial flights were very hard to get on. They didn't have the money to buy tickets for all of them. And which country to go to? No country would take them in. By trial and error, by pure chance or by miracle, they somehow ended up on an American list of people who had to be evacuated. And it was so sudden that they couldn't take anything with them. South Vietnamese soldiers guarding the airport let them through, but they said if the Americans don't come and get you we'll come in and kill you, because they were being left behind to face the communists and my family was fleeing."

The situation at Tan Son Nhut was now too dangerous even for helicopters, and buses full of potential evacuees were being turned away and forced to find their way back through the chaotic city streets in search of some other means of escape. Keyes Beech, a veteran war correspondent with *The Chicago Daily News,* was one of a number of newspapermen aboard one of them. Its driver had run away the night before, so an embassy auditor who had never driven a bus found himself behind the

OPPOSITE A U.S. Marine struggles to keep desperate Vietnamese from climbing over the embassy wall. **ABOVE** Duong Van Mai Elliott's father and her niece Jeanette Le aboard the USS *Hancock,* two of twelve members of her family to be airlifted out that day, April 30, 1975

ABOVE Vietnamese line the swimming pool within the embassy compound, hoping to board one of the helicopters that come and go all day.

wheel. "We careened through the streets," Beech recalled, "knocking over sidewalk vendors, sideswiping passing vehicles, and sending Vietnamese scattering like leaves in the wind. . . . [They] beat on the doors, pleading to be let inside." Young men on motorcycles wove through the crowds shouting, "Yankee Go Home" at every foreigner they saw. ARVN wandered aimlessly, sometimes firing their weapons into the air. The bus finally reached the embassy. "Several hundred Vietnamese were pounding on the gate or trying to scale the wall," Beech remembered. "There was only one way inside: through the crowd and over the [fourteen-] foot wall."

Guarding the wall were Juan Valdez and his marines. "We were supposed to get Americans out of there and other nationals like the British and the South Koreans—as well as the South Vietnamese that worked for us in the embassy. But we started getting people who said they were part of the embassy but had different papers altogether. It just went to chaos. It got to a point where we sealed the gates and we could no longer open those gates to let in vehicles or even embassy employees. So a number of Marines stood on the gate. The CIA was behind us, and they were pointing at the people who were supposed to get out. When they found their way to the front, we would reach over with our arms, pull them up, and bring them in."

"Once we moved into that seething mass," Keyes Beech remembered, "we ceased to be correspondents. We were only men fighting for their lives, scratching, clawing, pushing ever closer to that wall. We were like animals. Now, I thought, I know what it's like to be a Vietnamese. I am one of them. But if I could get over that wall I would be an American. My attaché case accidentally struck a baby in its mother's arms and its father beat at me with his fists. I tried to apologize as he kept on beating me while his wife pleaded with me to take the baby.

Somebody grabbed my sleeve and wouldn't let go. I turned my head and looked into the face of a Vietnamese youth. 'You adopt me and take me with you and I'll help you,' he screamed. 'If you don't, you don't go.' I said I'd adopt him. I'd have said anything. . . . There were a pair of Marines on the wall. They were trying to help us kick the Vietnamese down. . . . One of them looked down at me. 'Help me,' I pleaded. 'Please help me.'" The Marine pulled Beech to safety.

Somehow, Frank Snepp had managed to make his way inside. "It was chaos in my operations room. We were getting calls on our radio, the diamond radio network—the exclusive CIA communication system—from agents and from some of our own people, screaming for help. Some Americans had left their billets so rapidly that morning they'd left their radios behind. So their Vietnamese friends were on the radios begging to be rescued. 'I'm Han the driver.' 'I'm Mr. Ngoc, your translator.' And I stood there wondering how in the world we could reach them. It's one of the most horrible memories of that day, because I could hear them on the radio and I knew that we couldn't get to them."

Elsewhere in the embassy, officials dumped bags of currency into an oil drum and set it on fire—millions of dollars in embassy contingency funds went up in smoke—while Marines feverishly shredded armloads of classified files, then stuffed the trash into bags and heaped them in the courtyard. "When the choppers finally began coming in," Snepp remembered, "the downdraft ripped open those bags and there was classified confetti all over the parking lot."

Snepp dropped by the ambassador's office several times that day. Martin hadn't sent any of his own personal classified documents to be destroyed. "Finally," he recalled, "I found him sitting on the floor shredding them by hand. And I said to him, 'Mr. Ambassador, can I help you?' And he said no. He was lost."

"Before too long," the British journalist James Fenton wrote, "the large helicopters, the Jolly Green Giants, began to appear, and as they did so the mood of the city suffered a terrible change." More than fifty U.S. helicopters now crisscrossed the sky over Saigon, picking up evacuees from designated rooftops as well as the embassy and the DAO compound, ferrying them to the fleet far out at sea, then returning for more. "There was no way of disguising this evacuation by sleight-of-hand, or, it appeared, of getting it over quickly," Fenton continued. "The noise of the vast helicopters, as they corkscrewed out of the sky, was a fearful incentive to panic. The weather turned bad. It began to rain. And as the evening grew darker, it seemed as if the helicopters themselves were blotting out the light. It seemed as if the light had gone forever. All the conditions conspired against calm. All over Saigon there were people who had been

promised an escape. . . . Always the beating of the helicopter blades reminded them of what was happening. The accumulated weight of the years of propaganda came crashing down upon a terrified city."

As evening fell, Ambassador Martin feared both that the pace of the helicopters' coming and going was too slow and that the president was now about to call for an end to the evacuation of anyone who was not an American citizen. In a cable to Deputy National Security Advisor General Brent Scowcroft at the White House, his anger and bitterness were undisguised. "Perhaps you can tell me how to make some of these Americans abandon their half-Vietnamese children, or how the president would look if he ordered this. . . . Commander seventh fleet messaged me about hour and half ago, saying he would like to stand down about 2300 hours and resume [helicopter flights] tomorrow morning. I replied that I damn well didn't want to spend another night here. . . . I am well aware of the danger here tomorrow and I want to get out tonight. But I damn well need at least 30 CH-53 [transport helicopters] or the equivalent to do that. . . . I repeat I need 30 CH-53s and I need them now!"

The helicopters continued to come and go. "About nine fifteen that night," Frank Snepp remembered, "Polgar went to the ambassador and told him all CIA personnel had been ordered by their headquarters to leave immediately. He said to us, 'Let's go,' and we walked down the hallway. There were Vietnamese waiting there and the Marine guards pushed them out of the way. I could not bear to look at their faces because we were being saved and they weren't. From the chopper I could see out towards Bien Hoa—the old storage place for materiel—where explosions were going up as the North Vietnamese began to torch the place. And out beyond that on the highway leading into the city North Vietnamese vehicles and tanks with their lights on were moving toward the city from every direction. Finally, we made it out to the South China Sea and the chopper settled onto the deck of the USS *Denver*. And that was the end. I was devastated. I think about that day all the time. It's as vivid now as it was then, and the question that keeps running like a loop is what could we have done differently to forestall that day? And the answer is always the same, we should have remembered we were dealing with these people. This wasn't just about American policy or prestige or anything of the sort. And we forgot that. We forgot it."

That same evening, in the Saigon prison where the North Vietnamese agent Nguyen Tai had been confined in his white, windowless cell for months, no guard appeared after dinner to pick up his dinner plate. The electricity and water had already been cut. Tai could hear rockets exploding in the distance. Clearly, something serious was happening.

THE HELICOPTERS flew in and out of the embassy compound into the early hours of the morning. Ambassador Martin had wanted to be the last man to leave. But at about four o'clock, a C-46 touched down on the roof. The commander—code name "Lady Ace 09"—carried orders from the president himself. Martin was to leave—*now*. "I guess this is it," Martin said. The ambassador and his immediate staff were to be escorted up through the building to the roof so as not to call undue attention to what was taking place: "Do not let (the South Viets) follow too closely. Use Mace if necessary but do not fire on them." As Martin was helped aboard the helicopter, he was handed the furled American flag that had flown from the flagstaff that day. He lifted off at 5:57 and headed out to sea.

As the ambassador had feared he would, the president had also ordered that from then on only Americans were to be evacuated. There were still some 420 South Vietnamese crouched in the courtyard, carefully separated into eight groups so that when the time came to board there would be no pushing and shoving. Time and again they had been assured that helicopters were on the way to pick them up. They watched as two more helicopters came and went, lifting out the last few members of the embassy staff. Stuart Herrington was one of two officers who had been helping to keep the exodus orderly. Now, he recalled, "I was directed to stay with the Vietnamese and keep them 'warm,' meaning don't give them any hint that all these promises we made to them are for naught. I couldn't believe we could be so close—six large helicopters would have cleaned those folks out—and that what was happening was happening. I felt sick at heart. It was dark out so I didn't have to worry about looking these folks in the eye. Instead, I made my excuses and said I had to go to the bathroom. And then I took a circuitous route to the back door of the chancery building and made my way to the roof. I felt awful, naturally. You couldn't possibly be in that set of circumstances and not be just shattered." When the helicopter carrying him and his fellow officer lifted off, Herrington remembered, "We sat silently," and flew out above the upturned faces of the patient Vietnamese, who were still convinced they were to be rescued. "If I had tried to talk, I would have cried. I know of no words in any language that are adequate to describe the sense of shame that swept over me during that flight."

One hundred and twenty-nine Marines remained in the compound. They, too, did their best to pull back into the embassy without alerting the Vietnamese that they were being left behind. They almost made it. "The crowd in the street realized that we were leaving," Juan Valdez recalled. "They started coming over the walls, over the fence. We locked ourselves

inside the embassy and closed the doors. And put the bars down to lock the doors. And then we all found ourselves up on the embassy roof."

The crowd stormed through the now-open gates. Someone commandeered a fire truck and rammed it through the back door of the chancery. When people rushed in behind it, James Fenton followed them. "The typewriters were already on the streets outside, there was a stink of urine from where the crowd had spent the night, and several cars had been ripped apart. . . . The place was packed and in chaos, files, brochures and reports were strewn about." A plaque commemorating the five Americans who died defending the embassy during the Tet Offensive

ABOVE Ambassador Graham Martin meets the press aboard the USS *Blue Ridge*, the fleet's flagship, as the evacuation comes to an end. **OPPOSITE** An evacuation helicopter lands on the deck of a U.S. Navy ship off the Vietnam coast.

had been ripped from the wall. Fenton found a smashed portrait of President Ford and a framed quotation from Lawrence of Arabia: "Better to let them do it imperfectly than to do it perfectly yourself, for it is their country, their way and your time is short."

In Washington, Henry Kissinger was speaking to the press. Reporters asked him if the ignominious retreat from Saigon wasn't evidence that the whole Vietnamese effort had been a colossal error. He refused to take the bait: "I think this is not the occasion, when the last American has barely left Saigon, to make an assessment of a decade and a half of American foreign policy, because it could equally well be argued that if five administrations that were staffed, after all, by serious people dedicated to the welfare of their country, came to certain conclusions, . . . maybe there was something in their assessment, even if for a variety of reasons the effort did not succeed. . . . But I would think that what we need now in this country, for some weeks at

least, and hopefully for some months, is to heal the wounds and to put Vietnam behind us and to concentrate on the problems of the future."

A reporter asked Kissinger if he was confident that all the Americans who wanted to come out of Saigon were now out. Kissinger said he thought so. An aide handed him a note. It said 129 Marines had somehow been left behind on the embassy roof.

Helicopters were dispatched to pick them up.

Eventually, only Sergeant Valdez and his ten-man embassy security unit remained. "Then everything stopped," he recalled. "Until that time [the helicopters] were coming in pretty steady. But then we just found ourselves left there, and we started wondering, 'Why did they stop,' you know? Eventually we got word that it was because the admiral had decided to stop the Marines from flying because they had been flying continuously around the clock. Anyway, we were sitting around in the dark in our own

ABOVE Navy crewmen push a helicopter overboard to make room for others attempting to land. "The image that remains in my mind," former adviser James Willbanks recalled, "is the picture of the helicopters being pushed over the side of the carrier, because the helicopter was everything in Vietnam—it was 'dust off,' it was resupply, it was fire support, it was everything—and all I could think of was what a waste, what a waste." **OPPOSITE TOP** The helicopter carrying the last U.S. Marines lifts off from the embassy roof; Master Sergeant Juan Valdez is in the center, farthest from the camera. Word that they'd made it reached the White House at 8:00 p.m., Washington time, April 29, 1975—and sparked jubilation. **BOTTOM** From the left: White House Chief of Staff Donald Rumsfeld; Henry Kissinger; Richard Smyser, a staffer with the National Security Council; General Brent Scowcroft; and Ron Nessen, the White House press secretary

little thoughts. Not doing too much talking. I started thinking maybe the North Vietnamese would direct those artillery rounds that they had directed the day before at Tan Son Nhut onto the embassy roof and that would have blown us off because there was no way we could escape. The other thought that came to my mind was we only had small arms weapons. Eventually we would run out of ammunition. But we pretty much decided that we were going to fight it out anyway and if we have to get killed, so be it. That was it. We didn't want to surrender."

More than an hour went by. The sun began to rise. Then, Valdez remembered, they saw puffs of smoke "coming from way out at sea." It was a helicopter. "It was a relief because we had already started seeing North Vietnamese tanks coming down the road. The helicopter came in and one of the Marines, I

believe it was Staff Sergeant [Michael] Sullivan, my assistant, grabbed me and started pulling me in as the ramp's going up."

At 7:53 a.m., April 30, 1975, the last helicopter lifted off the embassy roof with Valdez and his men aboard. More than fifty thousand people had been evacuated aboard fixed-wing aircraft, and nearly seven thousand more had been lifted out by helicopter during Operation Frequent Wind, more than one thousand Americans and almost six thousand Vietnamese.

The American war in Vietnam was finally over.

The Republic of Vietnam had just four more hours to live.

A frightened ARVN guard appeared at the door of Nguyen Tai's cell early that morning. The North Vietnamese army was just an hour or so away, he said. A second guard, equally anxious, reported that every one of his superiors had run away. Tai agreed to vouch for all four of the guards who remained if they would help him stay alive in the crossfire that he feared would follow. They agreed and let him out of his cell for the first time in years. He climbed with them to the roof, where he told the guards to hang white flags and to write in chalk, "Don't shoot. There are prisoners here." Then he sat down with them to wait.

As North Vietnamese troops continued to move into the city from all sides, their supporters rose up to join them. "At 8:15 that morning," Nguyen Thanh Tung remembered, "the attack began everywhere in the city. I was excited. Everything was ready, but it was boiling in my mind. I raised the first flag in the government building of District 9." For the past four years, she had pretended to be a simple street seller while secretly organizing NLF sympathizers to be ready for this day. Few can have sacrificed more for her cause. She had lost her parents, eight brothers, and her husband, battling first the French, then the Americans. She herself had fought the Saigon government since the moment it was established in 1955. And just a few weeks earlier, with victory almost in sight, she had had to absorb the news that her two soldier sons, who had been a source of fierce pride to her, had both been killed fighting the South Vietnamese on the same day. "After I raised the flag," she remembered, "the local people brought out their own flags, small and large. Everybody fulfilled their assignments, to take over all the places. The forces of the Saigon regime ran like ducks. I didn't know what to say. I just shouted, 'Oh my God, everybody, my comrades, we have won our independence! Liberty has come!' The local women were surprised to see me, a street vendor, revealed as a leader like this. They grabbed me and tossed me up in the air, like volleyball players with a ball. While I was waiting for the surrender, I was thinking of my family, and so many families. So many people had been killed. In a couple of hours, everybody would rejoice."

President Minh spoke from the Presidential Palace at mid-morning. He urged what was left of the South Vietnamese army to stop fighting. "We are here waiting," he said, "to hand over the authority in order to stop useless bloodshed."

"If Minh hadn't ordered the surrender, it would have been horrific," recalled Bao Ninh, whose unit had now reached the outskirts of Saigon. "We all would have died. My friends who served in the ARVN still curse President Minh. They hate him because he ordered them to surrender, letting the communists win. But they forget if he hadn't given that order, they wouldn't have survived and gone to the USA and become American citizens. They would have died with me in Saigon."

"When President Minh declared the surrender," South Vietnamese General Pham Duy Tat remembered, "I still had my personal command helicopter. I still had a pilot." He had done his best to oversee the hopeless retreat from the Central Highlands, and when things fell apart his American adviser urged him to leave, even pledged to care for his family once it got to the United States. "But finally," he remembered, "I decided to stay, not to flee. I gave the helicopter back to the Air Force. There were two reasons: To be honest with you and with myself, I really disliked the Americans at that point. They came to Vietnam to help us fight the communists, and they abandoned us. Not only did they pull out of Vietnam, they also cut off the aid. Obviously, they wanted South Vietnam to collapse. Secondly, I looked at my Ranger unit. None of my Rangers ran away. How could I, as a Ranger, abandon my post? When I decided to stay, I knew I had to accept what was going to happen to me. Everybody was talking about a bloodbath those days. As a Catholic, I couldn't commit suicide as some other people did. So I accepted my fate."

That morning, Colonel Tran Ngoc Toan still commanded what was left of the Fourth South Vietnamese Marine Battalion near Bien Hoa, just twenty miles east of Saigon. He had been fighting the North Vietnamese for sixteen years and had survived terrible wounds suffered at the battle of Binh Gia. One of his men took him aside. The soldier was carrying a small portable radio under his arm, Toan recalled, "and he said he'd heard 'Big' Minh call on us to lay down our arms and surrender. I got mad at him." But there was nothing he could do. His commanding general had long since bribed his way aboard a ship and fled the country. An American friend had urged Toan to get out, too, he remembered. "But I said no. I can't desert my country." Still, further fighting was pointless. His men saw to it that he traded his camouflage uniform for civilian clothes. "I decided to walk to Saigon, back to my family," he remembered. "Viet Cong were everywhere. I wanted to die. Yeah. By that time I wanted to die right away. I didn't want to live anymore. But I thought about my family, my children. One was nine years old. The other was four. So, I thought about them and kept walking back to my family."

A row of North Vietnamese tanks rumbled past the newly abandoned U.S. embassy toward the Presidential Palace. James Fenton ran out into the street and flagged down the first one. A soldier invited him to jump on. "The tank speeded up and rammed the left side of the palace gate. Wrought iron flew into the air, but the whole structure refused to give. I nearly fell off. The tank backed again, and I observed a man with a nervous smile opening the center portion of the gate. We drove into the grounds of the palace, and fired a salute. . . . Soon the air became full of the sound of saluting guns. Beside the gate, sitting in a row on the lawn, was a group of soldiers, former members of the palace guard. They waved their hands above their heads in terror. An NLF soldier took his flag and, waving it above his head, ran into the palace. A few moments later, he emerged on the terrace, waving the flag round and round. Later still, there he was on the roof. The red and yellow stripes of the Saigon regime were lowered at last."

General Minh offered to hand over power to the first soldiers to enter the red-carpeted reception room. They laughed at him. "All power has passed into the hands of the revolution," one officer said. "You cannot hand over what you do not have." But Colonel Bui Tin, the same soldier who had said farewell to U.S. troops at Tan Son Nhut nearly two years earlier, was more conciliatory toward Minh and his staff. "You have nothing to fear," he said. "Between Vietnamese there are no victors and no vanquished. Only the Americans have been beaten. If you are patriots, consider this a moment of joy. The war for our country is over." Minh was escorted from the palace. Within hours, victorious soldiers were calling Saigon Ho Chi Minh City.

It was noon.

The streets were littered with ARVN boots and uniforms, James Fenton reported, "and . . . in the doorways, one would see young men in shorts, hanging around with an air of studied indifference, as if to say, 'Don't look at me, I always dress like this—it's the heat, you know.' . . . Occasionally, the relinquished jeeps of the former regime came past, full of youths in gear that was intended to look like Viet Cong attire. These new revolutionary enthusiasts were immediately distinguished in appearance and behavior from the real thing. Some of them were disarmed on the spot."

A South Vietnamese police officer walked to a memorial built to honor those who had fallen defending South Vietnam. He saluted it, stood there for a time, and then shot himself in the head.

North Vietnamese troops reached Nguyen Tai's prison around twelve thirty. He ran downstairs and out the door, and embraced the first soldiers he saw, weeping with joy. The battalion commander greeted him and let him ride along so he could see the jubilant crowds for himself.

The North Vietnamese regimental commander, Lo Khac Tam, who had first tasted combat in the first full-scale battle of the American war in the Ia Drang Valley, now found himself watching that war end in Saigon. "It was strange that it had such a quick and rapid, and unexpected end," he remembered. "I couldn't have imagined how happy I would be. All of Saigon lit up like a giant fireworks display. But I didn't want to go out to the streets. I immediately thought of my fallen comrades-in-arms. The war had ended, and I had survived, but I cried tears of deep sorrow over the loss of my comrades."

Back home, Americans who had been involved in Vietnam and watched Saigon's fall on television experienced a host of conflicting emotions, too.

Rufus Phillips, who had been associated in one way or another with Vietnam since the earliest days of America's involvement there, "felt so bad that it's hard to describe. I had tears in my eyes. And it was really hard to watch those films of the helicopters departing. And I knew that a lot of Vietnamese I knew personally had been left behind."

"My first reaction was elation," recalled Bill Zimmerman, who had been working to end the war since 1965. "I felt like applauding. I felt like riding on one of those tanks and waving a North Vietnamese flag along with all the other Vietnamese patriots who were doing that. And then I realized or began thinking about all the sacrifice and all the suffering that had been the center of our attention for the previous eleven years— all the wasted lives, all the lost careers, all the people who had made sacrifices to end the war, all the people who had been injured and killed in the war, the resources no longer available to Americans in poverty. It became a very bittersweet moment. Glad that it was over. Glad that the right people had won in the end. But tremendously sad and mournful about the incredible loss suffered by our country, their country, and all the people in both countries."

"I felt relief that the destruction, the killing, finally came to an end, and I didn't care which side won," Duong Van Mai Elliott remembered. "It was a very messy ending to a very messy war. I felt a sense of relief, but also a sense of sadness. To me,

ABOVE A North Vietnamese tank pushes through the gate of the South Vietnamese presidential palace, April 30, 1975.

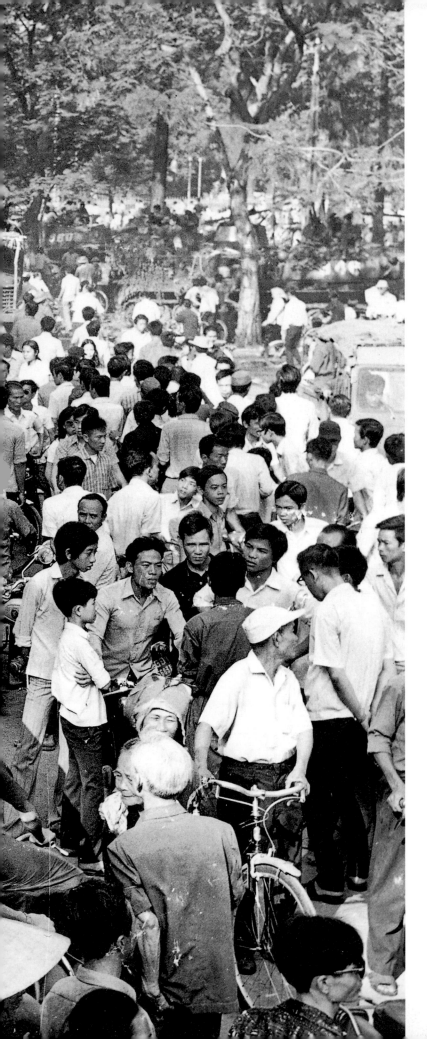

Vietnam won. The Vietnamese people won because they finally could live normally. And I felt sad because I saw that my family was again fleeing—this time from their homeland—and their future was very uncertain. And I knew that with the communists taking over, Vietnamese society would be changed drastically."

"That day I got a call from the VVAW national office from some friends of mine from the old days," John Musgrave recalled. "They were having a big celebration drinking booze and one of them said, 'Oh well, it's a great day, isn't it?' And I said, 'Are you nuts? No, it's not a great day.' I mean, now I know for sure that it was all for nothing. There ain't no doubt in my mind now. To see America leaving like that after we'd given sixty thousand, almost sixty thousand of our sons and daughters. That wasn't something to celebrate. I knew we were abandoning millions of South Vietnamese that had trusted us, thrown in their lot with us, and I knew bad things were going to happen to them. That wasn't anything to celebrate. I thought it was just one of the saddest moments I've ever seen in American history. I could take no pleasure in it."

"I happened to be at a conference at Tufts University," recalled Lewis Sorley, who served as an executive officer with a tank battalion in 1966 and 1967. "The dean there was a former ambassador who spoke to us late on that day—that fateful day, as it turned out. And he said he had just come back from Washington, where the spring weather was beautiful and the daffodils were in bloom, to Boston, where it was as gloomy and gray as it was in his heart. And people hissed at him and booed him. I was there in uniform. One of my great regrets was that I did not get up and start laying waste to those people who disrespected the ambassador and his sorrow at the fall of South Vietnam."

"What I held on to at that time," remembered Mike Heaney, who had been wounded in an ambush in 1966 in which ten men from his platoon were killed, "was that maybe we have learned a lesson that we, as a country, as a young country, needed to learn—that we just can't impose our will on others. So my men didn't die in vain. They died to teach us something valuable. Unfortunately, I don't really know that we have learned that lesson. But that's the way I felt then."

On May Day, the day following the fall of Saigon, crowds turn out to have a look at the men who have captured their city and obliterated their government. A French diplomat thought a third of the city's citizens were frightened, a third were enthusiastic, and another third were indifferent. General Van Tien Dung, who had commanded the Ho Chi Minh campaign and triumphed far faster than he and his superiors had imagined, realized that "the conclusion of this struggle was the opening of another, no less complex and filled with hardship."

DUST OF LIFE, DUST OF WAR

VIET THANH NGUYEN

WHENEVER AMERICAN SOLDIERS spend time in a foreign country, they usually leave behind a legacy of the forgotten children they fathered with local women. In Vietnam, these mixed-race children with American fathers are called *bui doi*, or "the dust of life." The Vietnamese people, victims of French and American racism, look down on these Amerasian children without any sense of hypocrisy. Vietnamese people, so sensitive about how people of other races treat them, mistreat their own in a way that is all too human. Children of mixed blood remind those of pure blood of the violations done to their country and their identity. These children are doomed by the racism of their countrymen to be blown about in the streets and alleys, to fend for themselves.

Their fate reminds me of another kind of dust, the detritus blown into the air when a bomb or shell hits the ground, or when a war shatters a country. Native soil displaced and dispersed, people scattered on the wind and the tide. They, too, are the dust of life, or the dust of war, carried far and wide. After the end of the war that needs no name—if one has lived through a war, it is ever and only the war—hundreds of thousands of Vietnamese people fled their country by air and ocean. They became refugees, the so-called boat people. It is a dehumanizing term, calling forth feelings ranging from pity to revulsion from those who watch their life-and-death struggles on the South China Sea. I prefer to call these people "oceanic refugees." If that term is not appropriate, then I will settle for "heroes," for these people were courageous rather than pitiful, embarking on a journey that perhaps only half survived.

Americans know that over fifty-eight thousand of their soldiers died in the war, but no one knows how many Vietnamese people fled their country, or how many disappeared at sea. Americans have recorded the names of every single one of their dead, but no one has tracked all the names of the missing Vietnamese. Call the difference what you will: power, privilege, inequality, injustice, irony. The difference between a strong country and a weak country, even if the weak country did defeat the stronger one, can be measured by their abilities to remember their dead and their missing.

But what of the dust of life and the dust of war? Who remembers them? The Vietnamese diaspora now number over three million in more than thirty countries, or about the same number as live in Thanh Hoa, the third-largest city in Vietnam after Hanoi and Saigon/Ho Chi Minh City. Three million is a little smaller than the population of the city of Los Angeles, and a little larger than Chicago. The majority, nearly two million, are in the United States, but sizable populations of more than 100,000 live in Cambodia, France, Australia, Taiwan, Canada, Germany, South Korea, and Japan. I wonder about the anomalous thousands who live in New Caledonia, Qatar, or Israel. As strange as it occasionally feels to be a Vietnamese American, at least I have a large community of fellow Vietnamese Americans from which to draw support. But to be one of a handful of Vietnamese in Israel seems to be a lonely existence—nearly as lonely, I imagine, as those Vietnamese political prisoners of the late nineteenth and early twentieth century who were dispatched into exile by their French overlords to Réunion Island in the Indian Ocean.

The significance of the Vietnamese diaspora can be measured not only in numbers but in function. It is the third force between the binary poles of Vietnam and the United States. The diaspora simultaneously belongs to or in both countries and yet at the same time is an occasionally discomfiting, even threatening, presence. For the victorious communists of Vietnam, the overseas Vietnamese who fled in the 1970s and '80s were "puppets" who had been manipulated by the French and then the Americans. The state was happy to see these "traitors" leave, and yet, in a Vietnamese version of catch-22, the state imprisoned them if they were caught leaving. From overseas, the Vietnamese diaspora became even more of a danger to the Communist Party. Freed from the regime's oversight, the diaspora became a refuge for anticommunist feeling, especially in the United States and Australia, both of which had fought against Vietnamese communism.

Despite the fact that the southern Vietnamese were American allies, and indeed were the people in whose name the United States fought its Vietnam War, the initial reception to Vietnamese refugees was lukewarm. Congress, to its credit, opened the doors to refugees, but in the recessionary 1970s, the majority of Americans did not want them. Most of the first wave of 150,000 Vietnamese refugees were rescued from South Vietnam in April, with the final stage of the evacuation signaled by the song "White Christmas" on Armed Forces Radio. They were sent to American bases in the Philippines or Guam, which had stationed many of the planes used to bomb Southeast Asia. Perhaps to erase that memory, the operation was dubbed "New Life." The ironies, or the absurdities, were accentuated by the fact that the admiral in charge was the father of rock star Jim Morrison. Another irony was that many of these Vietnamese refugees felt compelled to express their gratitude at being rescued, even though they thought that the United States had betrayed them. They would save their resentment for their own homes and their own communities, expressed in their own language, spoken out loud with the assurance that Americans neither could listen nor cared to understand.

Once in the United States, most of the refugees would be sent to four camps in Southern California, Arkansas, Florida, or Pennsylvania. I ended up in the latter, at Fort Indiantown Gap, where I personally experienced the logic of dispersal favored by the U.S. government. Fearful of having large concentrations of Vietnamese and other Southeast Asian refugees, the government sent the refugees to all parts of the country. This is why significant populations of Hmong can be found in Montana and Wisconsin, cold and white states which are unlikely places that they would have chosen to live in. The Hmong were residents of the highlands of Laos, and many had fought on the American side during the war, mobilized by the CIA. As the war ended, most were unceremoniously abandoned by the CIA and left to fend for themselves, with disastrous human consequences. As for my family, no one had heard of Pennsylvania, or the city we settled in, Harrisburg. In order to leave the camp, refugees had to have sponsors who would guarantee that we would not be a drain on welfare. No sponsors would take my entire family, however, so my parents went to one sponsor, my ten-year-old brother went to another, and my four-year-old self went to a third. While my separation from my parents only lasted a few months, it was interminable to me. This history—the residue of war, the impersonality of bureaucracy, the randomness of chance—remains imprinted on me.

I experienced my first white Christmas in Harrisburg. Photographs of that time show me, four years old, bundled up in a brown parka, a smile on my face. I enjoyed Harrisburg for the three years that we lived there, a time when I was blissfully unaware of the whiteness of my world or the conditions in which we lived. Only on returning thirty years later and driving the streets of my old neighborhoods did I realize that our first home, so large in my memory, was much reduced in reality, a small box in a lower-middle-class suburb. Our second home, rambling and Gothic in my mind, was in a depressed neighborhood of decaying houses whose only visible residents were African Americans, gathered on the stoops. All over the country, other Vietnamese, Cambodian, and Laotian refugees found themselves in alien and bewildering situations, in cold climates, in all-white provinces, in urban ghettos, in the Midwest and the Deep South. For many, these situations were not the America that they had seen in Hollywood movies or magazine photos. Some stayed; some, hearing of more attractive cities, girded themselves for another move.

My parents heard from a close friend who had been settled in San Jose, California, that the weather and economic opportunities were good. She had opened perhaps the first Vietnamese grocery store in the city. My parents had risked their futures and gambled with their lives twice before. The first time was in 1954, when Vietnam, already divided into three by the French during their period of colonial rule, was divided into two by agreement of the French, the Americans, the Soviets, and the Chinese. The Vietnamese of all sides reluctantly went along. My parents were northern Catholics, and persuaded by their priests and by CIA rumors of anti-Catholic persecution under a northern communist regime, they fled south with 800,000 other Catholics. Then, in 1975, they fled again to the United States, leaving behind an adopted teenage daughter, my sister, whom I would not see for nearly four decades, on my return to Vietnam. The prospect of moving yet once more in 1978 must have been daunting to my parents, but much less so as economic migrants versus refugees fearing bloodbaths.

Thousands of other refugees were likewise moving from their places of initial settlement across the United States to Dallas, Houston, Seattle, New Orleans, Arlington, San Jose, and especially Orange County in Southern California, the places that would become home to the largest concentrations of Vietnamese. They began a process of Americanization that would eventually transform them in the perception of other Americans, from being unwanted refugees to being another manifestation of the Asian American model minority. My brother, for example, was ten years old when he arrived in the United States in 1975. In 1982, he graduated valedictorian of his public high school and went to Harvard. Today he is a doctor and professor and chaired the White House Committee on Asian American and Pacific Islanders.

Rags-to-riches stories like his were far from unusual, and affirmed for other Americans the continuing viability of the American Dream. The educational success of some of these young Vietnamese refugees was compounded by the economic success of the refugee community as a whole. In the cities where they settled in large numbers, Vietnamese refugees took the most common route to establishing their claim to America: they bought property, especially commercial property. In the American capitalist dream world, the commercially successful "ethnic enclave" (versus the not-so-successful and equally visible "ghetto") is a vocal and visible statement that the members of the ethnic group in question have become good, or at least acceptable, neo-Americans.

My parents did their part by opening perhaps the second Vietnamese grocery store in San Jose, a couple of blocks from their friend's store. If this competition caused any tension, I was unaware of it. The friend eventually sold her small store and moved on to open a much bigger furniture store. My parents would also eventually move on from their grocery store to opening a jewelry store and acquiring other business property. But before they did so, they endured a decade of working in the New Saigon Mini Market at least ten hours a day, every day of the year except Easter, Christmas, and New Year. Then they would come home, boil organ meat for dinner, and resume work for another hour or two, a second shift in which I assisted. I rolled coins, counted cash, stamped checks, food stamps, and coupons for Women, Infants, and Children and Aid to Families with Dependent Children. Then I wrote down the tally in the ledger and added up the total on a calculator. Long before I learned how to type, I knew the numbers of the calculator by heart.

Our experiences of hard labor were common among Vietnamese refugees, although my parents were uncommonly talented in making money. As businesspeople in Vietnam, they had not been high on the ladder of prestige, the upper rungs of which were occupied by the political and military elite. But in capitalist America, they had the ability to prosper. This was not the case for many other Vietnamese refugees, either those who came from the working class or those who came from the political and military elite and who discovered that their prestige meant nothing in the United States. Their skills in government, law, and war were usually not transferable. Downward mobility for these elites was the norm, and stories of military officers and judges becoming janitors circulated. For the working class, the grind of survival continued as it did in the old world. A lucky few—some of the bankers and technocrats, for example—resumed their careers with the American companies that had employed them in Vietnam.

Regardless of their level of economic success, almost all the Vietnamese refugees suffered emotionally. They had lost their country, and, in many cases, they had lost their property, their prestige, their identities. Many had lost relatives, either to death or separation. I remember faces in photographs, those of my grandparents, all in Vietnam. Only my father's father would live long enough to see his child return to the North in the early 1990s, forty years after he had left. The other grandparents would die while my parents lived in the United States. I was too young to understand what a parent's death would mean to a child who had not seen them in decades, who could not be by their deathbed. Fear and lack of comprehension struck me at seeing my mother break down crying on receiving news of her mother's death. At twelve years or so of age, I felt only shame and embarrassment at having to wear a white band of mourning around my head as we drove through the city streets to a funeral mass. Wearing that band was Vietnamese tradition, but it was also a sign of our alien stature in the United States.

The suffering endured by these refugees saturated their lives and those of their children, even as their American neighbors remained mostly ignorant. For Americans, "Vietnam" meant the Vietnam War, and the Vietnam War really meant America's war. During the 1980s and '90s, I watched almost every movie made by Hollywood about the war, an exercise I do not recommend. The experience confirmed for me that Americans saw the war as about them, with the Vietnamese people of all sides relegated to the margins, where they were mostly to be silent, saved, raped, or killed. American books about the war, fiction or nonfiction, were not much better. At the same time that Vietnamese refugees knew that other Americans were not interested in them, they also feared that their children, raised on American soil, might be forgetting their language and their history. These refugees also knew that communist Vietnam was erasing the memory of their own existence in Vietnam, and now they could see that the same might be being done in America.

Much of refugee culture was therefore about preserving the history of the South Vietnamese. During gatherings of the refugees, the South Vietnamese anthem would be played, and veterans paraded in military uniforms. Vietnamese language schools tried to teach the language to the younger generation. Lunar New Year celebrations and religious events were occasions to reinforce the customs and culture of the old world, and to renew bonds in the new world, in whatever country the refugees found themselves in. Vietnamese-language newspapers and publishing houses reported on the lives of the Vietnamese and functioned as an oppositional press to the communist Vietnamese media.

Not least, Vietnamese musicians, singers, entertainers, and producers put on shows and acts in nightclubs, which would eventually lead to a few different music labels and televised variety shows. The most famous is *Paris By Night*, a song-and-dance extravaganza filmed in exotic locales from Las Vegas to Paris, and then marketed as videotapes and DVDs to the Vietnamese diaspora. Currently in its 119th episode, *Paris By Night* was also popular in Vietnam in the 1980s and '90s, when its production values exceeded what the Vietnamese entertainment industry could produce. Shut out by Hollywood, Vietnamese refugee entertainers used the song-and-dance platform to tell stories about Vietnamese people and history.

Not everything was a success for Vietnamese refugees, however. Far from it. While some Vietnamese refugees became model minority success stories, many Vietnamese refugees did poorly when it came to education and economics. The first wave of refugees was more adaptable to American culture, given that they came from Westernized political and military elites. Later refugees often came from the working class or the lower ranks of the military. They were not as equipped to succeed in an American environment, and welfare dependency rates were high. War trauma likely played a role in making adjustment difficult. Gang violence in the Vietnamese community was pervasive, as young men, and some women, turned to crime and preyed on their own community, whose vulnerabilities they knew well.

Perhaps that propensity to violence was inherited from soldier fathers, or passed on through being refugees from war violence. In one notorious 1991 incident, four young men seized a Good Guys Electronics store in Sacramento, California, and held dozens hostage, ostensibly in a bid to get passage back to Vietnam. Three of them died in a shootout with police after killing three hostages. The violence of the war seemed to beget more violence even after the war ended. In a now-forgotten atrocity from 1989, a drifter named Mark Purdy armed with an AK-47 opened fire on a Stockton, California, schoolyard full of Southeast Asian children during afternoon recess. He killed five of them, ages six, eight, and nine. Domestic violence within the Vietnamese community was high, but not spoken of in public. This violence was a function not only of possible war trauma, but also of the decline in status of Vietnamese men. Warriors and workers in a Vietnamese patriarchal society, many found themselves grappling with a loss of prestige, authority, and earning power in their new countries. Taking out frustrations on wives and children was not uncommon.

Meanwhile, memories of the past would keep returning to Vietnamese refugee communities through the arrival of new refugees. In the 1980s, Vietnam began to release prisoners from its reeducation camps, and the United States, through its Humanitarian Operations Programme, absorbed many of them. These prisoners were former soldiers, politicians, lawyers, bureaucrats, and intellectuals affiliated with the southern Vietnamese government who had not managed, or who had not wanted, to escape in 1975. Some had been stranded, some had decided to stay and defend their country, and some had gambled on the mercy of the victors. The promises of reunification and reconciliation offered by the communist Vietnamese turned out to be empty. The victorious government sent hundreds of thousands to reeducation camps, although an exact number may never be known, for the same reason as

an exact number of oceanic refugees may never be known. It is not in the interest of the victors to record such figures. Likewise, the numbers of those who died in the camps may remain unknown. But the reports of the survivors are gruesome, testifying to torture, starvation, hard labor, and ideological indoctrination, in addition to deaths by execution, illness, hunger, accidents, and land mines. Those who survived and made it overseas became among the most vociferous anticommunist opponents of the regime.

At least they made it to host countries. For thousands of other refugees, the oceanic ones, the journey led to countries that did not want them. These refugees had been driven to flee because the communist regime had persecuted them, either because they or their family members were affiliated with the southern regime, or because they were ethnic Chinese. In another irony, China, one of communist Vietnam's biggest allies during the war, had turned on Vietnam in the postwar years. The victorious Vietnamese were insufficiently grateful and showed too much allegiance to China's rival, the Soviet Union. Meanwhile, China's other Southeast Asian mentee, the Khmer Rouge, had provoked Vietnam with murderous border assaults (the Khmer Rouge hated the Vietnamese because of the history of Vietnamese colonialism in Cambodia, as well as the fact that much of South Vietnam was formerly Cambodian territory). Vietnam responded by invading Cambodia at the end of 1978, and China responded by invading northern Vietnam in a brief, bloody, and inconclusive war in 1979. The fallout for the ethnic Chinese of Vietnam was to be singled out by the Vietnamese regime, shaken down for their money and gold.

These were the political and economic reasons that drove hundreds of thousands of people to flee the country on overcrowded fishing boats and trawlers, many not made for voyages on the open sea. Their destination was Malaysia, Indonesia, Hong Kong, Singapore, or the Philippines. The boats often broke down, or were capsized and sunk in storms, or were assaulted by Thai pirates. Some boats were rescued by passing cargo ships, but many other cargo ships avoided them. Some boats made it to shore but were towed out to sea by the local navies, for the governments of potential host countries had little desire to take in refugees. The crisis became a global one, and images of the "boat people" made headline news all over the world in the late 1970s and '80s. Under a United Nations agreement brokered in 1979, the host countries of Southeast Asia would permit the refugees to stay in camps until countries of settlement could be found for them. For some of the refugees, the desperate journey was rewarded with salvation. Others died along the way, and thousands of others never made it out of the camps. In the Philippines, some refugees spent more than a decade waiting for settlement, and some never left. In Hong Kong, refugees were kept in what basically amounted to prisons, and many were deported to Vietnam. They responded with hunger strikes, riots, and immolations.

Why were so many countries reluctant to take refugees? Perhaps the answer could be found in the United States' own response to refugees. The U.S. took in hundreds of thousands of Southeast Asian refugees out of a sense of obligation, and also because it was good foreign policy to highlight the abuses of a communist country. At the same time, the United States was rejecting refugees from Haiti. Those refugees were black, and there was no geopolitical benefit for the United States to take them. Refugees are the unwanted, the zombies of foreign policy who threaten to wash over our shores in human waves, take over our homes, and contaminate our minds and bodies. Vietnamese and other Southeast Asian refugees got a pass, but some of them would encounter the American fear of refugees once again. These people had moved to Louisiana and formed one of the largest Vietnamese American settlements there, a thriving community that was hit, along with the rest of New Orleans, by Hurricane Katrina in 2005. Tens of thousands of New Orleans residents were rendered homeless and lived in fraught conditions. Images of their plight were broadcast on television and printed in newspapers, and some of the media called these displaced people "refugees."

The reaction was swift. President George Bush said, "The people we're talking about are not refugees. They're Americans." Jesse Jackson agreed with him for perhaps the first and only time: "It is racist to call American citizens refugees," Jackson said. "To see them as refugees is to see them as other than Americans." The view of Bush and Jackson is that there is something fundamentally un-American about being a refugee, since America could never possibly be such a wreck that its people would have to become refugees. This is the wish fulfillment of the American Dream, and to disturb that dream might be dangerous. The bipartisan reaction only drove home the precarious situation of Vietnamese refugees, who, if they held on to their refugee status, would also be holding on to their non-American status. But being a refugee could be as much a psychic condition as a legal one. Many refugees, me included, have never forgotten what it was like to be a refugee, even if now we might be among the bourgeoisie.

People often call me an immigrant, and describe my novel *The Sympathizer* as an immigrant story. No. I am a refugee, and my novel is a war story. The Vietnamese diaspora is partly an immigrant community but mostly a refugee community, created because of war and the forces of displacement that a war

unleashes. The devastation of war is hard to leave behind for those who have endured it, and if sometimes there are happy endings, sometimes there are not. I think of how the dust of life, the Amerasians, went from being spit on in Vietnam during and after the war to becoming, briefly, prized possessions with the passage of the Amerasian Homecoming Act. Congress recognized that American soldiers had left behind children and that it was the duty of the country to take those children in. Relatives who had wanted nothing to do with these children suddenly came calling, for Amerasian children were now the ticket out of Vietnam. These relatives treated the Amerasians well until they came to the United States, whereon some of these relatives had no more use for them. So the dust of life in Vietnam became the dust of life again in America, unwanted by their Vietnamese relatives and unknown to their American fathers. Their stories are among the saddest of the war and its aftermath.

Over the past few decades, the diversity of the diaspora has grown in complexity. No single story can encompass the diaspora's experiences. Many of the Vietnamese who now live in eastern Europe, for example, came not as refugees but as cheap labor in the postwar years, shuttled between friendly communist countries. While Vietnamese Americans became the model minority, the Vietnamese in eastern Europe were often perceived by their host countries in much more negative terms because of their origins as guest workers and their reputation as petty criminals. Now, many Vietnamese who go overseas from Vietnam do so as international students, because they have either earned scholarships or come from rich families. In the United States, these students are sometimes regarded with suspicion by Vietnamese Americans who fled communism, because the students often have ties to the regime through their parents. The greatest irony of this situation is that Vietnam is communist in name and politics only. In practice it is a capitalist country, and many of the capitalists are communist cadre or their relatives. Not without justification, some American visitors observe that the United States actually won the war in the postwar years, noting the triumph of the dollar in Vietnam and the positive image that many Vietnamese hold of the United States. This only goes to show that the war in Vietnam was not simply a war for freedom or democracy. It was very much a war about communism versus capitalism, in which economic ideology would prevail.

The unevenness of the world, its resistance to a simple binary between a good, capitalist America and a bad, communist Vietnam, is also highlighted by how many young Vietnamese Americans have chosen to return to Vietnam to make their fortunes. Vietnamese American actors and directors, shut out of Hollywood, are now stars in the burgeoning Vietnamese film industry. Entrepreneurs have used their bilingual and bicultural skills to open all manner of small and large enterprises, becoming cultural and economic ambassadors and brokers who work for multinational corporations and banks. Young Vietnamese Americans, and Vietnamese from all over the diaspora, go to Vietnam to study the language and culture in hopes of finding a connection with the country of their parents and grandparents.

The dust continues to settle, slowly, from the war. Sometimes it gets in the eyes and one has to cry. Sometimes it settles on the skin and hair, and we bring it with us wherever we go. And sometimes it simply remains invisible, and forgotten.

EPILOGUE

I N VIETNAM, the Communist Party is triumphant," the former Marine Tom Vallely remembered. "And they have their own sense of exceptionalism, and their exceptionalism gets in their way just like our exceptionalism got in our way. So they unify the country in a military sense and then they don't really unify the country after that. They try, but they fail."

In the end, there was no bloodbath on the scale many had feared, although hundreds of people in the countryside are thought to have been killed in individual acts of revenge or political retaliation.

Those who had served the Thieu regime—from generals to postal clerks—were required to attend "reeducation" camps. "When referring to the camps," the journalist Huy Duc remembered, "the press used the term 'going to study.' No one ever said 'going to prison.'" Enlisted men were assured that they would only have to submit to three days of "study"; officers wouldn't have to attend for more than a month.

"Some believed they were going to the camps for a short time. But not me," ARVN General Pham Duy Tat recalled. "I was detained in a reeducation camp for seventeen and a half years. I was among the last one hundred people to be released."

A million and a half people are believed to have undergone some form of indoctrination.

ARVN cemeteries were bulldozed or padlocked, as if the memory of an independent South Vietnam and those who had died for that cause could be obliterated. "The communists, in their effort to erase vestiges of the former regime," Duong Van Mai Elliott said, "have not allowed the South Vietnamese who lost their sons in the war to mourn, to have their graves, and to honor their memory. That the winners would not accommodate the losers in some way caused a division that lasts to this day."

At a reeducation camp, an instructor exhorts former ARVN officers to memorize communist doctrine so they can be reintegrated into Vietnamese society, 1976.

THE HUGE MISTAKES

AFTER THIRTY YEARS OF WAR, much of Vietnam lay in ruins. Three million people are thought to have died, north and south. Still more were wounded. Thousands of children fathered by American servicemen were left behind.

Villages needed to be rebuilt; land had to be reclaimed. Cities were choked with refugees. Millions were without work. President Ford imposed an economic embargo. Washington refused to recognize the new government of Vietnam.

But Le Duan and his allies on the Politburo remained optimistic. "Nothing more can happen," one committee member said. "The problems we face now are trifles compared to those in the past." Le Duan resolved, with Soviet help, to turn all of Vietnam into what he called an "impregnable outpost of the socialist system." Hanoi forcibly collectivized agriculture in the South, virtually abolished capitalism, nationalized industries, and appointed planners to run it all along strict communist lines.

The result was economic disaster. Inflation rose as high as 700 percent a year. People starved. "Nothing was more terrible than those ten years after the war," Bao Ninh remembered. "Our living standard collapsed completely. It was terrible. During the war, people could accept hardship. But after the war, it was caused by the huge mistakes of the Stalinist economic policies, the economic problems of communism."

LEFT Children at a ruined, shell-pocked school near Quang Tri
BELOW A legless veteran wheels himself between rice paddies.

EXODUS

To compound its problems, Vietnam found itself once again at war—caught between the interests of the two communist powers that had once been its staunchest allies, China and the Soviet Union.

After the brutal Maoist regime of Pol Pot in Cambodia raided border areas, Vietnamese troops—with Soviet arms and encouragement—crossed the frontier in 1978 and overthrew it. A frustrating ten-year counterinsurgency campaign followed, which some called "Vietnam's Vietnam." Before it was over, the Vietnamese would lose some fifty thousand more men, almost as many as the Americans had lost in their war.

Meanwhile, China—determined to punish Vietnam for invading Cambodia and to show Moscow it would not have a free hand in Southeast Asia—sent eighty-five thousand troops storming into northern Vietnam. They devastated areas along the border before the Vietnamese pushed them back.

A million and a half people would eventually flee Vietnam—supporters of the old Saigon regime, refugees from the renewed fighting along the Cambodian border, and ethnic Chinese residents of Vietnam, whom the new government had treated especially harshly. Hundreds of thousands died. Others suffered in refugee camps throughout Southeast Asia.

Some 400,000 eventually reached America, where they settled in nearly every state—industrious, entrepreneurial, more eager to take part in American political life and more likely to become American citizens than other immigrant groups from Asia.

For that first generation of Vietnamese Americans, memories of their homeland could never be erased. Tran Ngoc Chau—who had fought for both the Viet Minh and France, had served the Saigon regime as a soldier and province chief and then been targeted by it—settled in Los Angeles. "I'm very happy now after almost thirty years, that I did make a good choice for me, for my family," he said, "although I wish I could go back to Vietnam to die there. I want to say to my children, 'Well, I want to go back to Vietnam to live out the rest of my life,' but I have no such courage because I would hurt their feelings, and I don't want them to misunderstand me."

Vietnamese refugees come ashore in Malaysia, 1978.

WELCOME BACK

IT IS AS OLD as war itself. The ancient Greeks called it "divine madness." It was "soldier's heart" in the Civil War, "shell shock" during World War I, and "combat fatigue" in World War II. Following Vietnam, it was given a new name, "post-traumatic stress disorder," PTSD. There was no more of it after Vietnam than there had been after earlier conflicts, but more had been learned about it.

"I was with one of my daughters at an intersection," the former Marine Karl Marlantes recalled, "and some guy came up behind me and blasted the horn. When I came to my senses I was on the hood of his car trying to kick his windshield in. And there were people all over looking at me. This is crazy, this is crazy. And I said to myself, 'Well, this is weird.' And I sort of slinked back to my car. My daughter, she was about four, looking at me—'Wow, what's that all about?' And I go, 'What *is* that all about?' I had no idea. I had no idea that it was even related to the war. And what you learn is that PTSD doesn't go away. But now if someone honks the horn, and it startles me, my heart rate's still going to go up and it'll be there for five minutes. But—ten, nine—it's just some asshole, he's had a bad day at work—eight, seven, six—no one's shooting at you, you're safe—it's seven, six, five, four, three, two, one. And I can control it, whereas I couldn't do that before because I didn't understand what was going on."

Adding to the pain many veterans felt was their country's eagerness to forget the war. There were few parades. In many ways, everyone came home from Vietnam alone. "When I got home again," Vincent Okamoto remembered, "my mom and dad were there, my brothers and sisters and my wife were embracing, but I couldn't relate to my wife or my mother what I had seen, what I had done in Vietnam. I could have talked to my brothers about it, but they knew I didn't want to. And so it was just something unsaid, you know, 'Welcome back, Vince, you've been through the ringer but welcome back.'"

Returning home was complicated for the other side, as well. "I was one of very few who experienced the joy of coming home," Bao Ninh recalled. "I showed up at the door after six years of fighting. Six years without a letter. For six years my mother had no idea if I was alive or dead. Can you imagine the happiness of a mother? The war made women most miserable and then most happy. My mother cried, didn't say anything. We didn't make a scene. Vietnamese are like that. My mother right away thought of our neighbors, who had just received a death notice. In our apartment building six young men who served, and I was the only one to return. We didn't dare celebrate, didn't dare express our joy, because our neighbors lost their children."

U.S. soldiers returning from an unpopular conflict faced an uncertain future.

THE WALL

IN APRIL 1981, a panel of eight architects and sculptors gathered in an airplane hangar at Andrews Air Force Base, outside Washington. They were there to choose the winning design for a Vietnam memorial for the nation's capital from more than 1,400 submissions.

The memorial was the brainchild of a single stubborn veteran, a former rifleman named Jan Scruggs who, after suffering a frightening flashback, told his wife he wanted to "build a memorial to all the guys who served in Vietnam. It'll have the name of everyone killed." With other veterans, he established a nonprofit organization, the Vietnam Veterans Memorial Fund, and went to work collecting money and making plans. In the end, some 650,000 Americans would contribute more than $8 million.

The judges chose submission number 1026. The architect was Maya Ying Lin, a twenty-one-year-old student at Yale University. "I had a general idea that I wanted to describe a journey,"

LEFT Friends reunite at the Vietnam Veterans Memorial wall.
ABOVE Jan Scruggs, Maya Lin, and a model of her design

RION CAUSEY   As you get out of the car and you approach the wall, the intensity of it grabs you. You go up, you see the names, you touch the names. It's intense.

she said, "a journey that would make you experience death and where you'd have to be an observer, where you could never really fully be with the dead. It wasn't going to be something that was going to say, 'It's all right, it's all over.' Because it's not."

Differences about the war initially colored people's feelings about the proposed design. Some who believed the war had been unjust and immoral feared that the monument was somehow meant to glorify it. Others feared that its stark design failed to do justice to the cause for which Americans had fought and died. The writer Tom Wolfe dismissed it as "a tribute to Jane Fonda." One veteran denounced it as "a black scar . . . the color of sorrow and shame and degradation . . . in a hole, hidden as if out of shame."

But in an official vote of support for Maya Lin's design, the American Gold Star Mothers spoke for many. "Nowadays," they said, "patriotism is a complicated matter. Ideas about heroism, or art for that matter, are no longer what they were before Vietnam. And there is certainly no consensus yet about what cause might have been served in the Vietnam War. But perhaps that is why the V-shaped, black granite lines merging gently with the sloping earth [convey] the only point about the war on which people may agree: that those who died should be remembered."

The wall was officially completed in the autumn of 1982.

LEWIS SORLEY   I did not like the Vietnam wall. I considered it an ugly black ditch and that it said that the only people to be commemorated are the dead, not because they're heroes but because they're victims. I didn't go. Until one year they were going to put a wreath in front of the name of my roommate. I had to go. And I've gone every year since then to remember those we lost. I walk down to the far left, and I run my fingers over that name.

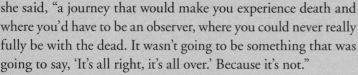

ABOVE Maya Lin's rendering of the Memorial

VINCENT OKAMOTO   You go to that wall—even my son who was nine years old when I first took him—and you see over fifty-eight thousand names and you know that unwritten behind each name there's a mother or a father or a wife or a daughter whose lives were forever shattered by that damn war.

CAROL CROCKER   I didn't want to go. It was a beautiful summer morning. Went to the Lincoln Memorial first, a comforting place to be. And then I crossed the street and walked in toward the entrance. And at first you can't really see the wall and you're coming down into the grassy hill. When I caught sight of it I literally lost my breath. Of course, I wept. I found my brother's name. I had help getting lifted up so I could touch it. I looked at my brother's name in the company of all those other people. There was sadness. But now he wasn't alone either. He was in the company of people. And he was there for people to know and to think about. And he wasn't forgotten. And he wasn't lost. It was incredibly healing and freeing for me.

NANCY BIBERMAN   I've been to the wall more than once. When I look back at the war and think of the horrible things we said to vets who were returning, calling them "baby killers" and worse, I feel very sad about that. I can only say that we were kids too, just like they were. It grieves me, it grieves me today. It pains me to think of the things that I said and that we said. And I'm sorry, I'm sorry.

JOHN MUSGRAVE   As I was walking toward it from the reflecting pool, there were so many names on those walls. And all of a sudden my throat swole up and I thought, "I can't do this. I can't do this right now." And I collapsed. And all the tears I'd been holding back—I didn't cry, I sobbed. I was on my knees, sobbing. I couldn't stop. I couldn't get my breath. And I was so grateful to God that it was there. I thought, This is going to save lives, this is going to save lives.

ALL AT PEACE

TOM VALLELY had served with the Marines in Vietnam. Sixteen years later, the country drew him back. He eventually founded the Vietnam Program of the Kennedy School at Harvard, which helped educate some of the country's future leaders. "I got very involved in the reconnecting between the United States and Vietnam and how that reconnection takes place. I spent a decade of my life helping to put those pieces together."

Although the United States did not have diplomatic relations with Vietnam, veterans had begun going back on their own—revisiting places where they had fought, meeting old foes, planting trees and building schools, trying to put the war behind them.

Vallely worked closely with other veterans, including three U.S. senators, who became among the most influential American advocates for normalizing relations: John McCain from Arizona, who had endured six years as a prisoner of war; John Kerry from Massachusetts, the ex-commander of a swift boat who been a leading spokesman for Vietnam Veterans Against the War; and Bob Kerrey of Nebraska, a former Navy SEAL.

Their task would not be easy.

Hanoi insisted that the United States make good on a promise to provide funds for reconstruction. For its part, the United States demanded a complete accounting of the more than two thousand Americans whose remains had never been recovered. Hanoi—which had more than 300,000 missing of its own—initially refused to cooperate.

But events both within Vietnam and far beyond its borders slowly moved things along. Le Duan died in 1986. His successors adopted what they called *"doi moi,"* a more pragmatic reformist economic policy.

As the Cold War ended, Soviet aid disappeared, and Hanoi finally began to help U.S. military teams search for American remains.

"The architects of normalization are the Vietnamese," Tom Vallely said. "It's not the Americans. The normalization of Vietnam is a strategy of the Vietnamese Communist Party to join the world. And the United States makes it hard for them to join the world. Senator John McCain insists, 'You want to have normalization? All your prisoners need to be out of reeducation camp.' 'You want normalization?' John Kerry asked. 'I need all the information about the missing.'"

In 1994, after the Vietnamese met the Americans' demands, the United States lifted its trade embargo. Full normalization came the following year. The new American ambassador, Pete Peterson, had spent six years in Hanoi as a POW. In November 2000, President Bill Clinton traveled to Vietnam—the first American president to visit that country since Richard Nixon reviewed U.S. troops there thirty-one years earlier.

In subsequent years, hundreds of American veterans would return to Vietnam.

"Some of my comrades who live in cities often meet American veterans," recalled Le Cong Huan, who had fought the ARVN and their American advisers at Ap Bac. "They don't speak each other's language, but they're so happy to meet, and they hug each other. They treat each other as veterans treat veterans. We have put the past behind us. Even though I still have bullets in my body, I want to close the war chapter. Now we should look to the future when our children can go to America to study, to learn the best, most beautiful things from the Americans, and get to know the people there."

Michael Heaney, recovered from his wounds, remembered his return to Vietnam in 2008: "I got in touch with a provincial vets organization, a huge organization of Vietnamese vets. All former enemies but now mellowed quite a bit like me. You know, they're guys my age, grandpas. And after we got past the initial checking each other out and deciding whether this was a political thing or not, they could not have been more gracious and more loving. They took me under their wings like a brother soldier. We exchanged painful memories, stories. I did a little ceremony honoring the guys I'd lost, honoring the Vietnamese enemies that we'd killed. Just telling them they could all be at peace now. It was a wonderful, wonderful trip. You don't get closure, but you get some peace. I got some peace."

OPPOSITE Arizona congressman John McCain returns to Vietnam, 1985. **ABOVE** Michael Heaney returns with a North Vietnamese veteran to the site of the ambush in which ten of Heaney's men died and he was himself wounded.

GHOSTS

IN VIETNAM, the land has largely healed. Old animosities have mostly been buried. But ghosts remain. Americans and Vietnamese work together to clean up places where Agent Orange has poisoned the earth. Unexploded ordnance, half hidden in the ground, still takes lives each year. Aged mothers and fathers from northern Vietnam sometimes still roam the South, seeking to discover what happened to their sons and daughters.

"The parents of the soldiers in my unit trusted me to look after them," remembered General Lo Khac Tam, whose platoon first fought in the Ia Drang Valley. "Some of their bodies have never been found, and I feel guilty day and night. In my dreams, I'm haunted by brutal scenes of war and death. I think it's because I haven't found them for their families. Every day, people call me asking, 'My son served in this company of that regiment. He was killed on the battlefield. Have you found him?' I have to answer that I haven't."

"I think you could say that the Vietnam War was a heroic song, but it was also a great tragedy," the soldier and historian Nguyen Ngoc said. "Now, in Vietnam, we are starting to rethink the war, to ask the questions—Was the war necessary to achieve justice? Was it right? The war is over. Now we need to focus on living. What is most important now is that we find some meaning, some lessons in the war for our lives."

"As we finally came lurching out of Vietnam, we were beginning to doubt ourselves," General Sam Wilson remembered. "That's a foreign feeling for an American. We seldom doubt ourselves. This turned out to be the most bitter, the most divisive—or second most bitter and second most divisive—war in our entire history. And we still hurt because of it. We have feelings of guilt about Vietnam."

More than four decades after the war ended, the divisions it created between Americans have not yet wholly healed. Lessons were learned—and then forgotten. Divides were bridged—and then widened. Old secrets were revealed—and new secrets were locked away.

The Vietnam War was a tragedy, immeasurable and irredeemable. But meaning can be found in the individual stories of those who lived through it, stories of courage and comradeship and perseverance, of understanding and forgiveness and, ultimately, reconciliation.

Children play in an abandoned U.S. helicopter near Danang, where the American war began.

ACKNOWLEDGMENTS

I've been fortunate enough over the past three decades to write about historical subjects ranging back to colonial times. But until beginning this book I'd never tried to tackle events that took place during my lifetime. It has been an instructive experience: things I was certain I knew proved to be untrue; everything was more complicated than I'd thought it was; shades of gray replaced the stark, black-and-white version of events I'd nurtured all these years.

To begin with, I'd like to thank Ken Burns yet again for taking on an intimidating topic and allowing me to help frame and tell the story. It's a privilege every time.

It's been a pleasure, as it always is, to work with Lynn Novick, whose determination to get the story right and to do justice to our witnesses spurred everyone who worked on this extraordinary project to greater effort.

Sarah Botstein has been essential from the beginning, performing superbly too many tasks to list here. I am especially grateful for those times when she stopped what she was doing to help keep the author on a more or less even keel.

A quartet of people on the Florentine Films team helped me in a host of different ways—Mariah Doran, Lucas Frank, Stephen Sowers, and Mike Welt. I'm grateful to each and all of them. I'd also like to thank interns Chau Hoang and Jonah Velasco, and, in Washington D.C., researcher Polly Pettit.

A professional's professional, Salimah El-Amin amassed the remarkable library of more than twenty-four thousand photographs from which we drew for both the book and the series—and was always willing to track down still more when needed. Twenty more volumes this size could be produced from the images she and Lucas Frank lovingly gathered.

I owe a special debt to David Schmidt, who found me materials almost as fast as I could think of them, then scoured the manuscript for errors and helped me correct the ones he found. I've never had that kind of invaluable help before; I hope never to be without it again.

The handsome maps, which were initially created for the series and which make Vietnam seem like a real place in which real things happened, are the creation of Brian Oakes. Megan Ruffe ably oversaw their adaptation from screen to printed page. Erik Villard of the U.S. Army Center of Military History helped check them for accuracy.

Neither this book nor the film series it amplifies could have been completed without Tom Vallely, who has been simultaneously our guru, witness, fixer, contact man, cheerleader, and conscience. I'm grateful, too, to two people without whose help we could never have included so many eloquent Vietnamese voices—Ho Dang Hoa and Ben Wilkinson.

Two historians proved especially helpful in shaping this volume: Colonel Gregory A. Daddis, who cast a seasoned soldier's eye over this civilian's attempt to write military history; and Professor Edward Miller, who read every word of the text and saved me from more bush-league mistakes than I would like to admit. The errors that survive are mine, of course, but I'll always be grateful to both of them for trying to keep me from making them.

I'd also like to thank someone I have never met but to whom I am profoundly grateful—Merle Pribbenow, whose translations of important Vietnamese documents and generosity in sharing them again and again helped make the seemingly inexplicable understandable.

This is the tenth book I've been blessed to publish with Knopf. There is no more skilled or supportive team in the publishing business, and I'd like to thank Peter Andersen, Kevin Bourke, Zakiya Harris, Kathy Hourigan, Andy Hughes, Sonny Mehta, and Andrew Miller, and Amy Stackhouse. But I want to pay special tribute to Maggie Hinders, who designed every page, put up with my all-too-frequent changes of mind, and was never satisfied until she got things right. This is the second book we've done together and she tells me she's sorry to have finally finished laying it out. Me, too.

Finally, I'd like to again thank my wife, Diane, who makes it possible for me to make it through these projects with such patience, love, and grace.

—Geoffrey C. Ward

FUNDING FOR *THE VIETNAM WAR* PROVIDED BY

Bank of America, Corporation for Public Broadcasting, PBS, David H. Koch,
Blavatnik Family Foundation, Park Foundation, The Arthur Vining Davis Foundations,
The John S. and James L. Knight Foundation, The Andrew W. Mellon Foundation,
National Endowment for the Humanities, The Pew Charitable Trusts,
Ford Foundation Just Films, Rockefeller Brothers Fund, and

Members of The Better Angels Society:
Jonathan & Jeannie Lavine, Diane & Hal Brierley, Amy & David Abrams,
John & Catherine Debs, Fullerton Family Charitable Fund, The Montrone Family,
Lynda & Stewart Resnick, The Golkin Family Foundation, The Lynch Foundation,
The Roger & Rosemary Enrico Foundation, Richard S. & Donna L. Strong Foundation,
Bonnie & Tom McCloskey, Barbara K. & Cyrus B. Sweet III, The Lavender Butterfly Fund

WITNESSES

This book is built around the vivid, often harrowing personal memories of the more than one hundred men and women in both the United States and Vietnam whose names follow, survivors of the war who were willing to talk about it. G.C.W.

Everett Alvarez
Le Duc Anh
Bruce Austin
Nguyen Van Bay
Lester Beaupré
Nancy Biberman
Dwight Birdwell
John Borrelli
Anne Harrison Bowman
Philip Brady
William Brogan
Nguyen Thoi Bung
Ken Campbell

Philip Caputo
Rion Causey
Tran Ngoc Chau
Le Van Cho
Max Cleland
Le Quan Cong
Herman Conley
David Countryman
Carol Crocker
Jean-Marie Crocker
Jack Cushman
Cao Xuan Dai
Bui Diem

Huy Duc
Bill Ehrhart
Duong Van Mai Elliott
Ron Ferrizzi
Joan Furey
Joseph Galloway
Robert Gard
Charles Garefin
Leslie Gelb
James Gillam
Phil Gioia
Alan Goldstein
Donald Gregg
Ho Thi Ha
Roger Harris
Matt Harrison
Victoria Harrison
Mike Heaney
Stuart Herrington
Nguyen Thi Hoa

Jan Howard
Le Cong Huan
Harry Hue
Ira Hunt
Samuel Hynes
Jurate Kazickas
Le Minh Khue
Nguyen Quang Khue
Hal Kushner
Ho Huu Lan
John Laurence
Luu Van Loi
Pham Luc
Josh Mantz
Karl Marlantes
Craig McNamara
Merrill McPeak
John Musgrave
John Negroponte
Mme Nghe

Truong Thi Nghe
Nguyen Ngoc
Dong Si Nguyen
Nguyen Nguyet Nguyet
Bao Ninh
Tim O'Brien
Vincent Okamoto
Eva Jefferson Patterson
Rufus Phillips
Gary Powell
Juan Ramirez
Robert Rheault
James Scanlon
Frank Scotton
Neil Sheehan
Gary Skogen
Wayne Smith
Frank Snepp
Nguyen Thanh Son

Lewis Sorley
Nguyen Tai
Lo Khac Tam
Pham Duy Tat
Tran Cong Thang
Lam Quang Thi
Tran Ngoc Toan
Jack Todd
Nguyen Van Tong
Phan Quang Tue
Nguyen Thanh Tung
Nick Ut
Juan Valdez
Thomas Vallely
George Wickes
James Willbanks
Sam Wilson
Bill Zimmerman

SELECT BIBLIOGRAPHY

For reasons of space I have listed here only the books, articles, and websites that yielded the most material in the course of my writing. But I do want to give special thanks to Jean-Marie Crocker for allowing us to use excerpts from her extraordinary unpublished manuscript about her equally extraordinary son. G.C.W.

BOOKS

Ahern, Thomas L., Jr. *Classified: The C.I.A. and the Counter-Insurgency.* Lexington, 2010.

Allen, Michael J. *Until the Last Man Comes Home: POWs, MIAs, and the Unending Vietnam War.* Chapel Hill, 2009.

Alvarez, Everett, Jr., and Anthony S. Pitch. *Chained Eagle: The Heroic Story of the First American Shot Down over North Vietnam.* Washington, DC, 2005.

Andelman, David A. *A Shattered Peace: Versailles 1919 and the Price We Pay Today.* Hoboken, 2014.

Anderson, David L., ed. *The Columbia History of the Vietnam War.* New York, 2011.

Appy, Christian G. *American Reckoning: The Vietnam War and Our National Identity.* New York, 2015.

———. *Working-Class War: American Combat Soldiers and Vietnam.* Chapel Hill, 1993.

Appy, Christian G., ed. *Patriots: The Vietnam War Remembered from All Sides.* New York, 2004.

Arnett, Peter. *Live from the Battlefield.* New York, 1995.

Associated Press. *Vietnam: The Real War.* New York, 2005.

Atkinson, Rick. *The Long Gray Line.* New York, 1989.

Bartholomcw-Fcis, Dixie R. *The OSS and Ho Chi Minh: Unexpected Allies in the War against Japan.* Lawrence, 2006.

Bartimus, Tad, Denby Fawcett, Jurate Kazickas, Edith Lederer, Ann Bryan Mariano, Anne Morrissy Merick, Laura Palmer, Kate Webb, and Tracy Wood. *War Torn.* New York, 2002.

Baskir, Lawrence M., and William A. Strauss. *Chance and Circumstance.* New York, 1978.

Beckwith, Charlie A., and Donald Knox. *Delta Force.* New York, 1983.

Berg, A. Scott. *Wilson.* New York, 2013.

Berman, Larry. *Lyndon Johnson's War.* New York, 1989.

———. *No Peace, No Honor: Nixon, Kissinger, and Betrayal in Vietnam.* New York, 2001.

Beschloss, Michael. *Reaching for Glory.* New York, 2002.

Beschloss, Michael R., ed. *Taking Charge: The Johnson White House Tapes, 1963–1964.* New York, 1998.

Bilton, Michael, and Kevin Sim. *Four Hours in My Lai.* New York, 1993.

Bingham, Clara. *Witness to the Revolution: Radicals, Resisters, Vets, Hippies, and the Year America Lost Its Mind and Found Its Soul.* New York, 2016.

Biondi, Martha. *The Black Revolution on Campus.* Los Angeles, 2012.

Boston Publishing Company, eds. *The American Experience in Vietnam: Reflections of an Era.* Boston, 1988.

Bradley, Mark Philip. *Imagining Vietnam & America: The Making of Postcolonial Vietnam, 1919–1950.* Chapel Hill, 2000.

———. *Vietnam at War.* New York, 2009.

Breslin, Jimmy. *The World of Jimmy Breslin.* New York, 1967.

Brigham, Robert K. *ARVN: Life and Death in the South Vietnamese Army.* Lawrence, 2006.

Brinkley, Douglas. *Cronkite.* New York, 2012.

Brinkley, Douglas, and Luke A. Nichter, eds. *The Nixon Tapes: 1971–1972.* New York, 2014.

———. *The Nixon Tapes: 1973.* New York, 2015.

Brocheux, Pierre, and Claire Duiker, trans. *Ho Chi Minh: A Biography.* New York, 2007.

Brocheux, Pierre, and Daniel Hémery. *IndoChina: An Ambiguous Colonization 1858–1954.* Los Angeles, 2009.

Burrows, Larry. *Larry Burrows: Vietnam.* New York, 2002.

Buzzanco, Robert. *Masters of War.* New York, 1996.

Caputo, Philip. *13 Seconds: A Look Back at the Kent State Shootings.* New York, 2005.

———. *Means of Escape: A War Correspondent's Memoir of Life and Death in Afghanistan, the Middle East, and Vietnam.* New York, 2009.

———. *A Rumor of War.* New York, 1996.

Chafe, William H. *Never Stop Running.* Princeton, 1998.

Chanoff, David, and Doan Van Toai. *Vietnam: A Portrait of Its People at War.* New York, 2009.

Clark, Gregory R., ed. *Quotations on the Vietnam War.* Jefferson, 2001.

Clifford, Clark, and Richard C. Holbrooke. *Counsel to the President: A Memoir*. New York, 1991.

Coan, James P. *Con Thien: The Hill of Angels*. Tuscaloosa, 2004.

Corbett, John. *West Dickens Avenue: A Marine in Khe Sanh*. New York, 2003.

Corn, David. *Blond Ghost: Ted Shackley and the CIA's Crusades*. New York, 1994.

Cortright, David. *Soldiers in Revolt: GI Resistance During the Vietnam War*. Chicago, 2005.

Cosmas, Graham A. *MACV: The Joint Command in the Years of Escalation 1962–1967*. Washington, DC, 2006.

Crocker, Jean-Marie. "Son of the Cold War: A Personal History." 1995. Manuscript.

Cronkite, Walter. *A Reporter's Life*. New York, 1996.

Currey, Cecil B. *Victory at Any Cost: The Genius of Viet Nam's Gen. Vo Nguyen Giap*. Washington, DC, 2005.

Cutler, Thomas J. *Brown Water, Black Berets: Coastal and Riverine Warfare in Vietnam*. Annapolis, 2012.

Daddis, Gregory A. *No Sure Victory*. New York, 2011.

———. *Westmoreland's War: Reassessing American Strategy in Vietnam*. New York, 2014.

———. *Withdrawal: Reassessing America's Final Years in Vietnam*. New York, 2017.

Dallek, Robert. *Flawed Giant: Lyndon Johnson and His Times, 1961–1973*. New York, 1998.

———. *Nixon and Kissinger: Partners in Power*. New York, 2007.

———. *An Unfinished Life*. Boston, 2003.

Davis, Vernon E. *The Long Road Home: U.S. Prisoner of War Policy and Planning in Southeast Asia*. Washington, DC, 2000.

Diem, Bui, with David Chanoff. *In the Jaws of History*. Bloomington, 1999.

Dong Si Nguyen. *The Trans-Truong Son Route: A Memoir*. Hanoi, 2005.

Dougan, Clark, and Samuel Lipsman. *The Vietnam Experience: A Nation Divided*. Boston, 1984.

Doyle, Edward G., and Samuel Lipsman. *The Vietnam Experience: America Takes Over*. Boston, 1985.

———. *The Vietnam Experience: Fighting for Time*. Boston, 1983.

———. *The Vietnam Experience: Setting the Stage*. Boston, 1981.

Doyle, Edward G., et al. *The Vietnam Experience: Passing the Torch*. Boston, 1981.

Doyle, Edward G., and Stephen Weiss. *The Vietnam Experience: A Collision of Cultures*. Boston, 1984.

Doyle, Edward G., Samuel Lipsman, and Terrence Maitland. *The Vietnam Experience: The North*. Boston, 1986.

Drury, Bob, and Tom Clavin. *Last Men Out*. New York, 2011.

Duc, Huy. "The Winning Side: The Liberation." 2012. Manuscript.

Duiker, William J. *Ho Chi Minh*. New York, 2000.

Duncan, David Douglas. *War Without Heroes*. New York, 1970.

Dyson, Michael Eric. *I May Not Get There with You*. New York, 2001.

Ebert, James R. *A Life in a Year*. New York, 1993.

Ehrhart, W. D. *Vietnam-Perkasie: A Combat Marine Memoir*. Jefferson, 1983.

Elliott, David W. P. *The Vietnamese War: Revolution and Social Change in the Mekong Delta 1930–1975*. New York, 2003.

Elliott, Mai. *RAND in Southeast Asia: A History of the Vietnam War Era*. Santa Monica, 2010.

———. *The Sacred Willow: Four Generations in the Life of a Vietnamese Family*. New York, 1999.

Ellsberg, Daniel. *Secrets*. New York, 2002.

Emerson, Gloria. *Winners and Losers: Battles, Retreats, Gains, Losses, and Ruins from the Vietnam War*. New York, 1976.

Fallows, James. *National Defense*. New York, 1981.

Farber, David. *Chicago '68*. Chicago, 1988.

Farrell, John A. *Richard Nixon: The Life*. New York, 2017.

Fawcett, Denby, et al., ed. *War Torn: Stories of War from the Women Reporters Who Covered Vietnam*. New York, 2002.

Franklin, H. Bruce. *M.I.A. or Mythmaking In America*. New Brunswick, 1993.

Fulghum, David, and Terrence Maitland. *The Vietnam Experience: South Vietnam on Trial*. Boston, 1985.

Gaddis, John Lewis. *The Cold War: A New History*. New York, 2007.

———. *George F. Kennan: An American Life*. New York, 2011.

———. *We Know Now: Rethinking Cold War History*. New York, 1997.

Gardner, Lloyd C. *Pay Any Price: Lyndon Johnson and the Wars for Vietnam*. New York, 1995.

Garrow, David J. *Bearing the Cross: Martin Luther King, Jr., and the Southern Christian Leadership Conference*. New York, 1986.

Gilbert, Marc Jason, ed. *Why the North Won the Vietnam War*. New York, 2002.

Gilbert, Marc Jason, and William Head, eds. *The Tet Offensive*. Westport, 1996.

Gitlin, Todd. *The Sixties: Years of Hope, Days of Rage*. New York, 1993.

Goldstein, Gordon M. *Lessons in Disaster: McGeorge Bundy and the Path to War in Vietnam*. New York, 2008.

Goscha, Christopher. *Vietnam: A New History*. New York, 2016.

Grace, Thomas M. *Kent State: Death and Dissent in the Long Sixties*. Amherst, 2016.

Grant, Zalin. *Survivors: Vietnam P.O.W.s Tell Their Stories*. New York, 1994.

Gross, Michael. *My Generation: Fifty Years of Sex, Drugs, Rock, Revolution, Glamour, Greed, Valor, Faith, and Silicon Chips*. New York, 2000.

Haass, Richard N., and Meghan L. O'Sullivan, eds. *Honey and Vinegar: Incentives, Sanctions, and Foreign Policy*. Washington, DC, 2000.

Halberstam, David. *The Making of a Quagmire: America and Vietnam During the Kennedy Era*. Lanham, 2008.

Haldeman, H. R. *The Haldeman Diaries: Inside the Nixon White House*. New York, 1994.

Haldeman, H. R., with Joseph DiMona. *The Ends of Power*. New York, 1978.

Hallin, Daniel C. *The Uncensored War*. New York, 1986.

Hammond, William M. *Public Affairs: The Military and the Media 1968–1973*. Washington, DC, 1996.

———. *Reporting Vietnam: Media and Military at War*. Lawrence, 1998.

Hayslip, Le Ly, with Jay Wurtz. *When Heaven and Earth Changed Places*. New York, 1989.

Herring, George C. *America's Longest War*. 4th ed. New York, 2001.

Herrington, Stuart A. *Peace with Honor? An American Reports on Vietnam 1973–1975*. New York, 1983.

———. *Silence Was a Weapon: The Vietnam War in the Villages*. Novato, 1982.

Hubbell, John G. *P.O.W.* Lincoln, 2000.

Hughes, Ken. *Chasing Shadows*. Charlottesville, 2014.

———. *Fatal Politics: The Nixon Tapes, the Vietnam War, and the Casualties of Reelection*. Charlottesville, 2015.

Hunt, Andrew E. *David Dellinger*. New York, 2006.

———. *The Turning*. New York, 1999.

Hunt, Ira A., Jr. *The 9th Infantry Division in Vietnam*. Lexington, 2010.

Hunt, Michael H., ed. *A Vietnam War Reader*. Chapel Hill, 2010.

Hunt, Richard A. *Pacification: The American Struggle for Vietnam's Hearts and Minds*. Boulder, 1995.

Hunting, Jill. *Finding Pete*. Middletown, 2009.

Isaacs, Arnold R. *Without Honor: Defeat in Vietnam and Cambodia*. Baltimore, 1998.

Isaacson, Walter. *Kissinger: A Biography*. New York, 1992.

Jacobs, Seth. *America's Miracle Man in Vietnam*. London, 2004.

———. *Cold War Mandarin*. Lanham, 2006.

Jones, Howard. *Death of a Generation*. New York, 2003.

———. *My Lai: Vietnam, 1968, and the Descent into Darkness*. New York, 2017.

Kaiser, David. *American Tragedy: Kennedy, Johnson, and the Origins of the Vietnam War*. Cambridge, 2000.

Karnow, Stanley. *Vietnam: A History*. New York, 1997.

Keating, Susan Katz. *Prisoners of Hope: Exploiting the POW/MIA Myth in America*. New York, 1994.

Kimball, Jeffrey. *Nixon's Vietnam War*. Lawrence, 2004.

———. *The Vietnam War Files: Uncovering the Secret History of Nixon-Era Strategy*. Lawrence, 2004.

Kirkpatrick, Rob. *1969: The Year Everything Changed*. New York, 2009.

Kissinger, Henry. *Ending the Vietnam War: A History of America's Involvement in and Extrication from the Vietnam War*. New York, 2003.

———. *White House Years*. New York, 2011.

———. *Years of Renewal*. New York, 2000.

Kulik, Gary. *"War Stories": False Atrocity Tales, Swift Boaters, and Winter Soldiers—What Really Happened in Vietnam*. Dulles, 2009.

Kurlansky, Mark. *1968: The Year that Rocked the World*. New York, 2005.

Kutler, Stanley I., ed. *Encyclopedia of the Vietnam War*. New York, 1996.

Lair, Meredith H. *Armed with Abundance*. Chapel Hill, 2011.

Langguth, A. J. *Our Vietnam*. New York, 2000.

Lanning, Michael Lee, and Dan Cragg. *Inside the VC and the NVA*. College Station, 2008.

Larner, Jeremy. *Nobody Knows*. New York, 1970.

Laurence, John. *The Cat from Hue*. New York, 2002.

Lawrence, Mark Atwood. *The Vietnam War: A Concise International History*. New York, 2008.

Le Minh Khue. "The Merriment Was Short-Lived." In *Patriots: The Vietnam War Remembered from All Sides*. Christian G. Appy, ed. New York, 2004.

Lepre, George. *Fragging: Why U.S. Soldiers Assaulted Their Officers in Vietnam*. Lubbock, 2011.

Leuchtenburg, William. *The American President: From Teddy Roosevelt to Bill Clinton*. New York, 2015.

Lewy, Guenter. *America in Vietnam*. New York, 1978.

Library of America, comps. *Reporting Vietnam, Part One: American Journalism, 1959–1969*. New York, 1998.

———. *Reporting Vietnam, Part Two: American Journalism, 1969–1975*. New York, 1998.

Lien-Hang T. Nguyen. *Hanoi's War*. Chapel Hill, 2012.

Lipsman, Samuel, and Stephen Weiss. *The Vietnam Experience: The False Peace*. Boston, 1986.

Lipsman, Samuel, Stephen Weiss, Clark Dougan, and David Fulghum. *The Vietnam Experience: The Fall of the South*. Boston, 1986.

Logevall, Fredrik. *Choosing War: The Lost Chance for Peace and the Escalation of War in Vietnam*. Los Angeles, 1999.

———. *Embers of War: The Fall of an Empire and the Making of America's Vietnam*. New York, 2012.

MacGarrigle, George L. *Taking the Offensive: October 1966 to October 1967*. Washington, DC, 1998.

Mann, Robert. *A Grand Delusion: America's Descent into Vietnam*. New York, 2002.

Marlantes, Karl. *What It Is Like to Go to War*. New York, 2011.

Marr, David G. *Vietnam 1945: The Quest for Power*. Los Angeles, 1997.

———. *Vietnamese Anticolonialism 1885–1925*. Los Angeles, 1971.

Maslowski, Peter, and Don Winslow. *Looking for a Hero*. Lincoln, 2004.

Maurer, Harry. *Strange Ground: Americans in Vietnam, 1945–1975: An Oral History*. New York, 1989.

McCoy, Alfred. *A Question of Torture: CIA Interrogation, from the Cold War to the War on Terror*. New York, 2006.

McMaster, H. R. *Dereliction of Duty: Lyndon Johnson, Robert McNamara, the Joint Chiefs of Staff, and the Lies That Led to Vietnam*. New York, 1997.

McNamara, Robert S. *In Retrospect: The Tragedy and Lessons of Vietnam*. New York, 1996.

McNamara, Robert S., and James Blight. *Argument Without End: In Search of Answers to the Vietnam Tragedy*. New York, 1999.

McPeak, Merrill A. *Hangar Flying*. Lake Oswego, 2012.

Means, Howard. *67 Shots: Kent State and the End of American Innocence*. Boston, 2016.

Military Region 8: 30 Years of Resistance (1945–1975). Hanoi, 1998.

Miller, Edward. *Misalliance*. Cambridge, 2013.

Miller, Edward, ed. *The Vietnam War: A Documentary Reader*. Malden, 2016.

Millett, Allan R., Peter Maslowski, and William B. Feis. *For the Common Defense*. New York, 1984.

Moise, Edwin E. *Tonkin Gulf and the Escalation of the Vietnam War*. Chapel Hill, 1996.

Moore, Harold G., and Joseph L. Galloway. *We Were Soldiers Once and Young*. New York, 1992.

Morgan, Ted. *Valley of Death*. New York, 2010.

Morris, Roger. *An Uncertain Greatness: Henry Kissinger and American Foreign Policy*. New York, 1977.

Morrocco, John. *The Vietnam Experience: Thunder from Above*. Boston, 1984.

Mott, William H. *Military Assistance: An Operational Perspective*. Westport, 1999.

Moyar, Mark. *Triumph Forsaken: The Vietnam War, 1954–1965*. New York, 2006.

Murphy, Edward F. *Dak To*. New York, 1993.

———. *The Hill Fights: The First Battle of Khe Sanh*. New York, 2003.

———. *Semper Fi Vietnam*. New York, 1997.

Musgrave, John. *Notes to the Man Who Shot Me*. Lawrence, 2009.

Neer, Robert M. *Napalm: An American Biography*. Cambridge, 2013.

Nelson, Deborah. *The War Behind Me: Vietnam Veterans Confront the Truth about U.S. War Crimes*. Philadelphia, 2008.

Newman, Rick, and Don Shepperd. *Bury Us Upside Down*. New York, 2006 .

Nghia M. Vo. *Vietnamese Boat People, 1954 and 1975–1992*. Jefferson, 2006.

Nguyen Tien Hung and Jerrold L. Schecter. *The Palace File*. New York, 1986.

Nicosia, Gerald. *Home to War: A History of the Vietnam Veterans' Movement*. New York 2001.

Nixon, Richard. *The Memoirs of Richard Nixon*. New York, 1990.

Nolan, Keith William. *Death Valley*. Novato, 1999.

———. *Operation Buffalo: USMC Fight for the DMZ*. New York, 1992.

Oberdorfer, Don. *Tet!: The Turning Point in the Vietnam War*. Baltimore, 2001.

Okamoto, Vincent. *Wolfhound Samurai*. Placentia, 2008.

Oliver, Kendrick. *The My Lai Massacre in American History and Memory*. New York, 2006.

Olson, James S., and Randy Roberts. *Where the Domino Fell*. Malden, 2014.

Page, Tim. *Another Vietnam: Pictures of the War from the Other Side*. Washington, DC, 2002.

Perlstein, Rick. *Before the Storm*. New York, 2009.

———. *Nixonland*. New York, 2008.

Phillips, Rufus. *Why Vietnam Matters*. Annapolis, 2008.

Pike, Douglas. *The Viet Cong Strategy of Terror*. Cambridge, 1970.

Pimlott, John. *Vietnam: The Decisive Battles*. New York, 1990.

Powell, Colin L., and Joseph E. Persico. *My American Journey*. New York, 1995.

Powers, Thomas. *The War at Home*. New York, 1973.

Prados, John. *The Blood Road: The Ho Chi Minh Trail and the Vietnam War*. Hoboken, 2000.

———. *The Hidden History of the Vietnam War*. Chicago, 1995.

———. *Vietnam: The History of an Unwinnable War*. Lawrence, 2009.

Prados, John, and Ray W. Stubbe. *Valley of Decision: The Siege of Khe Sanh*. Annapolis, 2004.

Prehmus, Drew. *General Sam*. Sydney, 2011.

Prochnau, William. *Once Upon a Distant War*. New York, 1995.

Quinn-Judge, Sophie. *Ho Chi Minh: The Missing Years*. London, 2003.

Reeves, Richard. *President Kennedy: Profile of Power*. New York, 1994.

———. *President Nixon: Alone in the White House*. New York, 2002.

Remnick, David. *King of the World: Muhammad Ali and the Rise of an American Hero*. New York, 1998.

Richardson, Peter. *A Bomb in Every Issue*. New York, 2009.

Robbins, James S. *This Time We Win: Revisiting the Tet Offensive*. New York, 2010.

Rochester, Stuart I., and Frederick Kiley. *Honor Bound: American Prisoners of War in Southeast Asia, 1961–1973*. Annapolis, 2007.

Rogers, Bernard W. *Cedar Falls Junction City: A Turning Point*. Washington, DC, 1974.

Safer, Morley. *Flashbacks: On Returning to Vietnam*. New York, 1990.

Sallah, Michael, and Mitch Weiss. *Tiger Force: A True Story of Men and War*. New York, 2006.

Sander, Robert D. *Invasion of Laos, 1971*. Norman, 2014.

Savage, Sean J. *JFK, LBJ, and the Democratic Party*. Albany, 2004.

Schlesinger, Arthur M., Jr. *A Thousand Days: John F. Kennedy in the White House*. New York, 2002.

Scranton, William, et. al. *The Report of the President's Commission on Campus Unrest*. 1970.

Shaplen, Robert. *The Road from War: Vietnam 1965–1970*. New York, 1970.

Sheehan, Neil. *After the War Was Over: Hanoi and Saigon*. New York, 1991.

———. *A Bright Shining Lie*. New York, 1989.

Sheehan, Neil, Hedrick Smith, E. W. Kenworthy, and Fox Butterfield. *The Pentagon Papers, as Published by the New York Times*. New York, 1971.

Sherwood, John Darrell. *War in the Shallows*. Washington, DC, 2015.

Sheshol, Jeff. *Mutual Contempt*. New York, 1997.

Skurki, William J. *Soldiering On in a Dying War*. Lawrence, 2011.

Small, Melvin. *At the Water's Edge: American Politics and the Vietnam War*. Chicago, 2005.

Smith, George W. *The Siege at Hue*. Boulder, 1999.

Snepp, Frank. *Decent Interval: An Insider's Account of Saigon's Indecent End Told by the CIA's Chief Strategy Analyst in Vietnam*. Lawrence, 2002.

Sorley, Lewis. *A Better War*. New York, 1999.

———. *Thunderbolt: From the Battle of the Bulge to Vietnam and Beyond: General Creighton Abrams and the Army of His Times*. New York, 1992.

———. *Westmoreland*. New York, 2011.

Sorley, Lewis, ed. *Vietnam Chronicles: The Abrams Tapes 1968–1972*. Lubbock, 2004.

Spector, Ronald H. *Advice and Support: The Early Years: The U.S. Army in Vietnam*. Washington, DC, 1985.

———. *After Tet: The Bloodiest Year in Vietnam*. New York, 1993.

Summers, Anthony. *The Arrogance of Power: The Secret World of Richard Nixon*. New York, 2000.

Thomas, Evan. *Being Nixon: A Man Divided*. New York, 2015.

———. *Robert Kennedy: His Life*. New York, 2000.

Toczek, David M. *The Battle of Ap Bac, Vietnam*. Westport, 2001.

Topmiller, Robert J. *Lotus Unleashed: The Buddhist Peace Movement in South Vietnam*. Lexington, 2002.

Tran Ngoc Chau and Ken Fermoyle. *Vietnam Labyrinth*. Lubbock, 2012.

Tran Van Don. *Our Endless War: Inside Vietnam*. New York, 1987.

Tran Van Quang. *Twenty-five Days and Nights in Hue*. Merle L. Pribbenow, trans.

Trong Nhu Tang, David Chanoff, and Doan Van Toai. *A Vietcong Memoir*. New York, 1986.

Truman, Harry S., and Robert H. Ferrell. *The Autobiography of Harry S. Truman*. Colorado, 1980.

Tucker, Spencer C., ed. *The Encyclopedia of the Vietnam War: A Political, Social, and Military History*. Santa Barbara, 2011.

Turley, William S. *The Second Indochina War*. Lanham, 2009.

Turner, Karen Gottschang, with Phan Thanh Hao. *Even the Women Must Fight: Memories of War from North Vietnam*. New York, 1998.

Turse, Nick. *Kill Anything That Moves*. New York, 2013.

Updegrove, Mark K. *Indomitable Will: LBJ in the Presidency*. New York, 2012.

Vandevanter, Lynda, ed. *Visions of War, Dreams of Peace*. New York, 1991.

Varon, Jeremy. *Bringing the War Home*. Los Angeles, 2004.

Veith, George J. *Black April: The Fall of South Vietnam 1973–1975*. New York, 2012.

Vennema, Alje. *The Viet Cong Massacre at Hue*. New York, 1976.

Walt, Lewis W. *Strange War, Strange Strategy*. New York, 1970.

Wells, Tom. *The War Within: America's Battle Over Vietnam*. Lincoln, 2005.

Westheider, James E. *The African American Experience in Vietnam: Brothers in Arms*. New York, 2008.

———. *The Vietnam War*. Westport, 2007.

White, Theodore H. *The Making of the President 1968*. New York, 1969.

———. *The Making of the President 1972: A Narrative History of American Politics in Action*. New York, 1973.

Whitlow, Robert H. *U.S. Marines in Vietnam: The Advisory & Combat Assistance Era: 1954–1964*. Washington, DC, 1977.

Wiest, Andrew. *Essential Histories: The Vietnam War 1956–1975*. Oxford, 2002.

———. *Vietnam's Forgotten Army: Heroism and Betrayal in the ARVN*. New York, 2008.

Wiest, Andrew, Mary Kathryn Barbier, and Glenn Robins, eds. *America and the Vietnam War*. New York, 2010.

Wiest, Andrew, and Michael J. Dodge, eds. *Triumph Revisited: Historians Battle for the Vietnam War*. New York, 2010.

Willbanks, James H. *Abandoning Vietnam: How America Left and South Vietnam Lost Its War*. Lawrence, 2004.

———. *The Battle of An Loc*. Bloomington, 2005.

———. *A Raid Too Far*. College Station, 2014.

———. *The Tet Offensive: A Concise History*. New York, 2007.

———. *Vietnam War Almanac: An In-Depth Guide to the Most Controversial Conflict in American History*. New York, 2013.

Willkins, Warren. *Grab Their Belts to Fight Them: The Viet Cong's Big-Unit War Against the U.S., 1965–1966*. Annapolis, 2011.

Witcover, Jules. *1968: The Year the Dream Died*. New York, 1998.

Wolff, Tobias. *In Pharaoh's Army: Memories of the Lost War*. New York, 1994.

Yarborough, Thomas Y. *A Shau Valor: American Combat Operations in the Valley of Death, 1963–1971*. Philadelphia, 2016.

Young, Marilyn B. *The Vietnam Wars 1945–1990*. New York, 1991.

Zimmerman, Bill. *Troublemaker: A Memoir from the Front Lines of the Sixties*. New York, 2012.

ARTICLES

"Congress Probes Alleged U.S. Massacre in Vietnam." *CQ Almanac 1969*, 25th ed. http://library.cqpress.com/cqalmanac/cqal69-1246997.

"The Conscientious Objector and the First Amendment." *The University of Chicago Law Review* 34, no. 1 (1966): 89.

"No Ky and a Big Win." *Newsweek*, August 16, 1971.

"Protest: The Banners of Dissent." *Time*, October 27, 1967.

"South Viet Nam: Electing a President." *Time*, September 8, 1967.

"Supreme Court, 6–3, Upholds Newspapers on Publication of Pentagon Report." *The New York Times*, July 1, 1971.

"There IS a New Nixon." *The Boston Globe*, August 10, 1968.

"The War: Drift & Dissent." *Time*, August 11, 1967.

"The War: Joy in Seattle." *Time*, July 18, 1969.

"The War: The Changing of the Guard." *Time*, August 19, 1968.

"U.S. Captain Tells How 76 Men Died in Battle." *Los Angeles Times*, June 25, 1967.

Ahern, Thomas L. "CIA and the Generals: Covert Support to Military Government in South Vietnam." George Washington University. February 2009. http://nsarchive.gwu.edu/NSAEBB/NSAEBB284/1-CIA_AND_THE_GENERALS.pdf

Andrade, Dale. "Westmoreland Was Right." *Small Wars & Insurgencies* 19, no. 2 (2008).

Andrade, Dale, and Lieutenant Colonel James H. Willbanks. "CORDS/Phoenix: Counterinsurgency Lessons from Vietnam for the Future." *Military Review*, March–April 2006.

Apple, R. W. "Ky Denounced by Buddhists." *The New York Times*, May 16, 1966.

———. "Vietnam: The Signs of Stalemate." *The New York Times*, August 7, 1967.

Buckley, Kevin. "The Alpha Incident." *Newsweek*, September 8, 1969.

Buckley, Tom. "The ARVN Is Bigger and Better, But . . ." *The New York Times Magazine*, October 12, 1969.

Chapman, William. "55,000 Rally Against War; GI's Repel Pentagon Charge." *The Washington Post*, October 22, 1967.

Du Plessix Gray, Francine. "The Moratorium and the New Mobe." *The New Yorker*, January 3, 1970.

Fenton, James. "The Fall of Saigon." *Granta* 15 (1985).

Fitzgerald, Frances. "Fire in the Lake." *The New York Times*, May, 27, 1966.

Galloway, Joe. "A Reporter's Journal from Hell." *The Digital Journalist*, 2002.

Gallup. "Do you approve or disapprove of the court martial finding that Lt. Calley is guilty of premeditated murder?" Gallup Survey #7145, April 1971.

Goodwin, Gerald F. "Race in the Crucible of War: African American Soldiers and Race Relations in the 'Nam." PhD thesis, Ohio University, 2014.

Guillermot, François. "Autopsy of a Massacre on a Political Purge in the Early Days of the Indochina War (Nam Bo 1947)." *European Journal of East Asian Studies* 9, no. 2 (2010).

———. "Death and Suffering at First Hand." *Journal of Vietnamese Studies* 4, no. 3 (2009).

Hackworth, David. "About Face." *Newsweek*, May 23, 1966.

———. "The Bloody Checkerboard." *Newsweek*, May 23, 1966.

Heinl, Robert D., Jr. "The Collapse of the Armed Forces." *Armed Forces Journal*, June 7, 1971.

Herbers, John. "Vietnam Moratorium Observed Nationwide by Foes of the War." *The New York Times*, October 16, 1969.

Hersh, Seymour M. "Coverup-I." *The New Yorker*, January 22, 1972.

———. "Kissinger and Nixon in the White House." *The Atlantic*, May 1982.

Jian, Chen. "China's Involvement in the Vietnam War, 1964–1969." *The China Quarterly*, no. 142 (1995).

Keeley, John B. "My Disillusionment Deepened." *The Washington Post*, July 6, 1981.

Kennedy, Robert F. "Things Fall Apart; the Center Cannot Hold . . ." *The New York Times*, February 10, 1968.

Larner, Jeremy. "The Moratorium—A View from the Inside." *Life*, November 28, 1969.

Lien-Hang T. Nguyen. "The War Politburo: Vietnam's Diplomatic and Political Road to the Tet Offensive." *Journal of Vietnamese Studies* 1, nos. 1–2 (2006).

MacAuley, Lacy. "How the Institute for Policy Studies Helped Release the Pentagon Papers." Institute for Policy Studies, June 13, 2011.

Miller, Edward. "Religious Revival and the Politics of Nation Building: Reinterpreting the 1963 'Buddhist Crisis' in South Vietnam." *Modern Asia Studies* 49, no. 2 (2014).

O'Brien, Tim. "The Vietnam in Me." *The New York Times*, October 2, 1994.

Pohle, Victoria. "The Viet Cong in Saigon: Tactics and Objectives During the Tet Offensive." Rand Corporation, January 1969. http://www.rand.org/dam/rand/pubs/research_memoranda/2005/RM5799.pdf.

Pribbenow, Merle L. "General Vo Nguyen Giap and the Mysterious Evolution of the Plan for the 1968 Tet Offensive." *Journal of Vietnamese Studies* 3, no. 2 (2008).

Reilly, Robert. "The Inclination for War Crimes." *Military Review*, May–June 2009.

Reston, James. "A Whiff of Mutiny in Vietnam." *The New York Times*, August 27, 1969.

Robbins, William. "Ex-POWs Charge Hanoi with Torture." *The New York Times*, September 3, 1969.

Roberts, Steven V. "Girls, Bands and Ticker Tape Greet Troops from Vietnam in Seattle." *The New York Times*, July 11, 1969.

Schell, Jonathan. "A Reporter At Large." *The New Yorker*, March 9, 1968.

Shaplen, Robert. "Letter from Vietnam," *The New Yorker*, November 13, 1971.

Sheehan, Neil. "Dissidents' Area in Danang Shrinks." *The New York Times*, May 22, 1966.

———. "'68 Gain Was Seen by Westmoreland." *The New York Times*, March 21, 1968.

———. "Vietnam Archive: Pentagon Study Traces 3 Decades of Growing U.S. Involvement." *The New York Times*, June 13, 1971.

Sterba, James P. "Men of Company A Defend Behavior Under Fire." *The New York Times*, September 1, 1969.

Sullivan, Patricia. "S. Vietnamese Gen. Nguyen Chanh Thi." *The Washington Post*, June 27, 2007.

Sully, François. *Newsweek*.

Tran Do. "Tet 1968: A Strategic Raid." Merle L. Pribbenow, trans. Unpublished document.

Vann, Michael G. "Of Pirates, Postcards, and Public Beheadings: The Pedagogic Execution in French Colonial Indochina." *Historical Reflections/Réflexions Historiques* 36, no. 2 (2010).

Warner, Geoffrey. "The United States and Vietnam 1945–65." *International Affairs* 48, no. 4 (1972).

Webster, Rich. "The Hero of the Battle of Kontum Refutes Neil Sheehan." *Vietnamese & American Veterans of the Vietnam War*, May 2013.

Young, Robert B. "Prisoner of War: 'You Either Had a Sense of Humor or Went Crazy.'" *The Washington Post*, May 14, 1972.

WEBSITES

"America's Wars." Department of Veterans Affairs. 2016. https://www.va.gov/opa/publications/factsheets/fs_americas_wars.pdf.

Defense Casualty Analysis System. "Vietnam Conflict Extract Data File." National Archives and Records Administration. https://aad.archives.gov/aad/fielded-search.jsp?dt=2513&tf=F&cat=all.

Elliott, Steve. "Selective Service Expands Alternatives for Conscientious Objectors." U.S. Army. April 22, 2010. https://www.army.mil/article/37811/selective-service-expands-alternatives-for-conscientious-objectors.

Galloway, Joe. "General Sam, We Hardly Knew Ye." Military.com. January 7, 2004. http://www.military.com/NewContent/0,13190,Galloway_010704,00.html.

Hartzel, Jack T. "Operation Kingfisher, A Show of Force." Third Battalion Fourth Marines. http://thundering-third.org/4members/OpKingfisher29.html.

Palmer, Laura, and Jurate Kazickas. "Foreign Correspondents in Vietnam." Vietnam Womens Memorial. http://www.vietnamwomensmemorial.org/pdf/lpalmer.pdf.

Willbanks, James H. "Hell on Hamburger Hill." HistoryNet.com. May 2009. http://www.historynet.com/hell-on-hamburger-hill.htm.

Zampini, Diego. "North Vietnamese Aces: MiG-17 and MiG-21 Pilots, Phantom and 'Thud' Killers." Ace Pilots. March 2012. http://acepilots.com/vietnam/viet_aces.html.

INDEX

Page numbers in *italics* refer to illustrations.

ABC, *330,* 443
Abrams, Creighton W., Jr., 267, 290, *299,* 318–19, 342, 345, 348, 356, 360, *360,* 369, 389–90, 403, 408, *411,* 420, 467, 468, 477, 499
  appointed MACV commander, 317, *317,* 320–1
  bombing halt favored by, 347
  improved ARVN training as focus of, 418–19
  MACV Objectives Plan of, 387–8
  troop withdrawals and, 397–8
accelerated pacification, 340–2, 365, 386, 388, 398
Acheson, Dean, 126, 299, *299*
Adams, Eddie, 149, *150,* 274–5, *275,* 494
Adams, John Quincy, 148
AFL-CIO, 507
African Americans, 163, *163,* 303, 408
After-Action reports, 68
Agency for International Development, U.S. (USAID), 102, 128, 129, 196, 197, 256, 267, 332, 363
Agent Orange, 58, 158, 406, *406,* 462, 587
Agnew, Spiro, 323, *323,* 347, *347,* 349, 351–2, 427, 430, 455, *455,* 459–60, 478
Agosto-Santos, Jose, 322
Aiken, George, 276
Air Force, U.S., 115, 156, 160, 176, 178, 231, *278,* 327, 369, 496, 524, 538, 562
  Seventh Field Hospital, 540
  377th Combat Security Police, 268, *269*
  Thunderbird aerobatic team, 372
Alabama, 317, 338
Alabama, University of, 81
Algeria, 22, 91
Ali, Muhammad, 163
Alliance of National, Democratic, and Peace Forces, 400
Alvarez, Everett, 105, 178, 179, *182,* 183, 513
Amerasians (Vietnamese children of U.S. soldiers), 566, 575
Americal (23rd Infantry) Division, U.S., *320,* 356, 411, 413, 431–2, 472
  Fifth Battalion, Company A, 431

Eleventh Brigade, Company C, 431–7, *432, 435,* 436
196th Brigade, U.S., 336, 338
  Third Battalion, Company A, 413–16, *414, 415*
198th Brigade, 430
American Gold Star Mothers, 582
American Homecoming Act, 570
American Legion, 157
American Revolution, 123, 160
Anderson Air Force Base, *401*
Andrews Air Force Base, 581
An Khe, 131, 135, 149, *153,* 166, 462
An Loc, battle of, *vii,* 494, 495–6, *495, 496,* 498, *498, 499*
Annam, 6, 7, *8,* 12, 23, 45
Annamite Mountains, 373, 501
Annie's Bar, *408*
An Quan pagoda, 274
Antenna Valley, 370
Anti-American Youth Shock Brigade for National Salvation, 118, 158–9
Anti-Ballistic Missile Treaty, 501
antiwar movement, xii–xiii, *xxi,* 120–1, *120, 121,* 131, 164, 191, *191,* 194, *195,* 230, 247, 369, *383,* 398, 516–21
  active military personnel in, 440–3, 518
  Cambodia invasion in, 449
  "Christmas Bombing" and, 511
  Days of Rage in, 426, 438
  global spread of, 303–4, *303*
  Kent State killings and, 451, 453–4, 456
  Laos invasion and, 478
  Manhattan hard-hat attack and, 456–7, *457*
  "March of Death" in, 438, *438*
  Moratorium protests in, 404, 426–7, *427,* 431, 438, *438,* 440, 518, 519, 520
  in 1968 Democratic convention protests, 329–30, *329, 330,* 332, *332,* 334–6
  Nixon and, 364, 369, 438, 440, 446, 454, 456, 458–9, 460, 518, 519–20
  October 21, 1967, march of, 230, 232–4, *232, 233*
  public opinion on, 336
  returning troops and, 403, *403*

shortcomings of, 521
students in, 304, *304,* 352–3, *353,* 384, 427, 455, 517
tactics of, 517–18
Vietnam veterans in, 478–81, *479, 481,* 482, *482*
violence and bombings by, 426, 457–8, 459, 520
An Truong Thanh, 224
Ap Bac, battle of, 72, *73, 75, 76,* 100, 113, 152, 155, 264, 357, 585
Apple, R. W., 222–4, 301
Arkansas, 567
Arlington, Va., 567
Arlington Memorial Bridge, 232
Arlington National Cemetery, 174, *174,* 438, 479–80, 483
Armed Forces Radio, 566
Army, U.S., xii, 36, 58, *59,* 107, 119, 122, 123, 142, 156, 160, 161, 166, 174, 189, *194,* 198, *199,* 203, *203,* 211, 212, 216, 222, 227, 238, *239,* 257, 260, 299, 307, 317, 327, 336, 353, 354, 356, 360, 372, 384, *384,* 389, 413, *414,* 416, 426, *432,* 436, 437, 440, 444, 489, 490, 518, 524, 527
  one-year Vietnam tours of, 127
  Public Information Office of, 436
  racial incidents in, 409
  Rangers, 175–6
  see also specific regiments and divisions
Army Commendation Medal for Heroism, 160
Army of the Republic of Vietnam (ARVN), *see* South Vietnamese army (ARVN)
Army Reserves, U.S., 222, 292, 293
Arnett, Peter, 62, 77, *142,* 416
"Arrow and the Song, The" (Longfellow), 462
A Shau Valley, 390, 391, 393
Asia, 4, 12, 25, 40, 45, 53, 175
Associated Press (AP), 62, *63,* 81, *142,* 263, 274, 393, 504
Associated State of Vietnam, 48–9
Astoria, Oreg., 319
August offensive (1968), 321
August Revolution, 15, 47, 48, 100
Austin, Bruce, 370, 371
Australia, 147, 251, 281, 335
Ayers, Bill, 426

Bac Lieu Province, 363
Bacon, Robert C., 415–16, *415*
Baez, Joan, *161,* 404, 502
Baez, Pauline, *161*
Baig, Mirza, 259, 263
Baker, Ray Stannard, 3
Baker University, 443, *443,* 454
Ball, George, 56, 84, 125–6, *125,* 294, *299*
Ba Long Valley, 220
Baltimore, Md., 352
Baltimore Sun, 276, 541
Ba Nghe, 74, 75, 76
Ban Me Thuot, 266, 531, *531*
Bao Dai, Emperor, 15, 23, 24, 25, 28, 32, 36, *38,* 46, 47, 48, 49, 70
Bao Ninh, xiii, 185, 424–5, *424,* 461–3, 533, 562, 575, 578
Barrier Island, *189*
Bastogne, 317
Batangan Peninsula, 356, *357*
Baton Rouge, La., *453*
Bay of Pigs invasion, 53, 84, 294
BBC, 314, 504
Beatles, 269
Beaupré, Lester, 413–14, *414*
Beckwith, Charles "Chargin' Charlie," 132, 134, *134,* 175
Bedworth, Gifford, 248–9
Beech, Keyes, 555–7
Beijing, 62
Beilke, Oax, 524
Bellow, Saul, 131
Ben Cat, *xv*
Ben Hai River, 219
Ben Suc, 187, *187*
Ben Tre, *278,* 279
Ben Tuong, 62
Berlin, 24, 95, 290, 292, 299
Berlin Wall, 53
Bernstein, Carl, 520
Biberman, Nancy, 583
Bidault, Georges, *22*
Biden, Joseph, 544
Bien Hoa, 52, 267–8, 305, *307,* 324, 557
Bien Hoa Air Base, 42, 107, 110, 198
Bien Hoa prison camp, *487*
Bien Hoa Province, *222*
Bigart, Homer, 62, 63, 91
Binh Dinh, 149, 494
    Operation Masher/White Wing in, *100, 145,* 149–50, 152–4, *153*
Binh Duong Province, 62
Binh Gia, battle of, *109,* 110–13, *111, 113,* 114, *114,* 119, 197, 292, 562
Binh Long Province, 494, 495
Binh Xuyen, 32, *32, 36, 37,* 85
Black Horse Base Camp, *420*
Black Panthers, 408, 426
Black Power movement, 408, 409, *409*
Blackstone Rangers, 409
Blankenship, Okey, 416
Blue Ridge, USS, *558*
boat people, 566, 569–70, *576*
bodies, identification of, 227, 244
body counts, 239, 324–5, 370, 371, 393, 436
    emphasis on, 356, *357,* 360, 389
    inflation of, 154, 199, 218
Bolshevik revolution, 4, 516

Bong Son, 149, *150*
Bong Son Plain, 247
"Border Battles," 224, 240, 251
Borrelli, John, 413, 414, *414,* 415, 416
Boston, Mass., 4, 40, 90, 156, *218,* 230, 302, *383,* 453, 527
Boston Globe, 324, 485
Bouncing Betty mine, 214
Bower, Kevin, 463
Bradley, Omar, 126, *299*
Brady, Philip, 109–11, 112, *113,* 119, 122, 197, 256, 267–8
Brennan, Peter J., 456, 457, *457*
Breslin, Jimmy, 128, 129, *507*
Brewster, Kingman, 164
Brezhnev, Leonid, 500
Briggs Field, 490
Brinkley, David, 233, 396
Brinks Hotel bombing, 110, *110*
British Indian Army, *20*
Broder, David, 427
Bronze Star, 286, 372, 384, 481, 491
Brookings Institution, 485
Brooklyn College, 230
Browne, Malcolm, 62, *63, 79,* 81, 164
Brown, Sam, 397, 404, 438, 440
Brown University, 518
"Brown Water Navy," 356
Bryant, James, *414*
Buchanan, Pat, 479
Buc Pho, 234
Buddha, 78, *79*
Buddhism, Buddhists, 23, 32, 85, 86, 147, 164, *172,* 206, *206,* 224, 235, 274, 288, 488, 529
    Catholic clashes with, 100, 102
    Diem regime and, 78, *79,* 80–1, 83, *83,* 84, 100
    Ky regime and, 168–72, *169,* 196
    self-immolation by, *79,* 81, 172
    "Struggle Movement" of, 169–70, *169*
Bu Gia Mop, 160
Bui Diem, 13, *13, 22,* 116, 147, 347, 349, 352, 399, 544, 547
Bui Dinh Dam, 72, 73–4
Bui Hong Ha, 268–9
Buis, Dale, 42
Bui Tin, 524–5, 563
Bulge, Battle of the, 256, 290, 317, 319
Bunche, Ralph, 191
Bundy, McGeorge, 53, 93, 98, 101, 103, 104, 114, *115, 125,* 299, *299,* 336
Bundy, William, 93, 104, 106, 125
Bunker, Ellsworth, 194, 246, 247, 267, *271,* 273, *317,* 320, 321, 339, 343, 345, 347, 348, 360, 363, 468, 488–9, 494
Burke, Edmund, 459
Burma, 7, 23, 26, 27, 53, 128
Busby, Horace, 126
Bush, George W., 570

California, 95, 302, 310, 353, 397, 506, 517, 567
California, University of, at Los Angeles (UCLA), 305
Calley, William, 431–2, 434, 437, *473*
    murder conviction of, 472–3
Ca Mau, *51*
Ca Mau Peninsula, 6, 67, *67, 341,* 406
Cambodia, xvii, 7, 24, 28, 32, 54, 103, 114, 132, 139, 160, 176, 188, 211, 224, 244, 257, 292, *315,*

316, 321, 325, *325, 328, 328,* 387, 399, *400,* 401, 406, *445,* 486, 494, 503, 517, 543
    Lon Nol coup in, 446–8
    North Vietnamese arms smuggled through, 155
    U.S. bombing of, 369, 386, 485, 519, 520, 526, 527
    U.S. evacuation of, 544
    U.S. invasion of, 446–9, *447, 448,* 454, 456, 457, 459, 467, 468, 486, 518
    Vietnamese invasion of, 569, 576
Cambridge, Mass., 453
Cam Lo, 212, 221
Cam Ne, *127,* 128
Camp Alpha, 489
Camp Carroll, 212, 218, 265, 494
Camp David, 430, 477
Camp Upshur, 231
Cam Ranh Bay, 131, *131,* 231, 251, *251,* 303, 409, 535, 538
Canada, 31, 147, 288, 355
    draft resisters and deserters in, 318, 319, 355, 444–5, 518
Canal Zone, 175
Canberra, USS, 423
Can Tho, *165,* 224
Cao Dai, 32, 36
Cao Lao Party, 86
Cao Van Vien, 467
Capitol, U.S., 364, 481, *483*
Caputo, Philip, 117, 124, 128, 154, 171, 330, 538, 540–1, 553, 555
Carey, Richard E., 544
Carmichael, Stokely, 191, *302,* 408
Carnegie, Okla., *244*
Carpenter, Terry, 166
Carter, Jimmy, 473
Carver, George, 299
Castro, Fidel, *526*
Catholics, Catholicism, 7, 21, 32, *35,* 43, 44, 46, 48, 49, 78, 81, 83, 86, 110, 147, 168, 169, 186, 216, 288, *307,* 488, 498, 503, 528, 529, 562, 567
    Buddhist clashes with, 100, 102
    in Diem regime, 80
Causey, Rion, 235–7, *237,* 238, 582
CBS, 84, 127, *127,* 128, 148, 149, 150, *150,* 227, 246, 276, 277, 290, *291,* 326, 330, 416, 427, 433, 478
CBS Evening News, 290
Central Highlands, 19, 86, 110, 114, 131, *133,* 135, 149, 173, 198, 211, 235, *236,* 240, 250, 260, 266, 310, 321, 322, 384, 386, 409, 424, 461, 462, 494, 529, 531, *531,* 533, *533,* 562
Central Intelligence Agency (CIA), 15, *35,* 36, 53, 63, 69, 78, 81, 84, 100, 103, 128, 170, 196, 234, 246, 273, 293, 299, 329, 339, 340, *340, 347,* 349, 360, 369, 419, 445, 458, 459, 467, 488, 508, 509, 519, 524, 536, 538, 540, 542, 545, 548, 556, 557, 567
Central Office for South Vietnam (COSVN), 54, 60, 188, 369, 387, 401, *445, 448,* 459, 503, 542
Ceylon, 19
Chamberlain, Neville, 298
Chancellor, John, 478
Charbutt, Jay, 393
Chateauroux-Déals U.S. Air Force base, *231*
Chennault, Anna Chan, 347, *347,* 349, 351–2, *352,* 548

Chennault, Claire, 347
Chiang Kai-shek, 17, 25
Chicago, Ill., 301, 329, 330, *330, 332,* 335, 336, 338,
        426, *426,* 438, 507, 566
    1968 Democratic National Convention in, 328–30,
        329, 332, *332,* 334–6, 426
Chicago, University of, 164
Chicago Amphitheater, *329*
Chicago Daily Defender, 303
Chicago Daily News, 555
Chicago Sun-Times, 330
Chicago Tribune, 301, 330, 538
Chieu Hoi ("open arms") Program, 128, 340
Chi Hoa Prison, 269
"Children of Vietnam, The" (Pepper), 190
China, 6, 7
    Vietnam's border with, 22
    Vietnam's conflicted history with, 6
China, Nationalist, 14, 17, 21, 25
    fall of, 25
    Ho Chi Minh in, 5, 45, 47
    Vietnam's bonds with, 14
China, People's Republic of, 26, 28, 45, 49, 52, 53,
        62, 86, 93, 95, 103, 105, 155, 176, 177, 194,
        209, 224, 255, 281, 300, 347, 349, 364, 401,
        425, 501, 510, 520, 567, 569
    aid to North Vietnam by, 125, 184, 493, 500
    atomic bomb acquired by, 106
    continuation of Vietnam War urged by, 100, 206
    First Indochina War and, 48
    Nixon's opening to, 491, 493
    Soviet rift with, 41
    U.S. relations with, 508
    Vietnam invaded by, 569, 576
    Vietnam negotiations and, 301, 512
China Beach, *535*
China Sea, 67
Cholon, 86, 279, *307*
Christian, George, 291
Christian Science Monitor, 317, 350
"Christmas Bombing," 511–12
Chu Chi, 308
Chu Huy Man, 132, *133,* 134
Chu Lai, 248, 384, 409, *409, 430*
Chu Pong Massif, 132, 135, *135,* 139
Church, Frank, 122, 296, 467, 544
Churchill, Winston, 53, *98,* 298
Chu Y Bridge, *308,* 309
Cincinnati, Ohio, 301
Citizen's Coordinating Committee to Oppose
        Dictatorship, 489
City University of New York, 164
Civil Guards, South Vietnamese, 41, 62, 63, 69, 73,
        74
Civil Rights of 1964, 98, 190, 221
Civil War, U.S., xi, xxi, 160, 189, 310, *310,* 578
"Claims of the Annamite People, The," *3,* 45
Clark, Ramsey, 502
Clark Air Base, 547
Clean Air Act, 126
Cleveland Plain Dealer, 432
Cleveland Press, 276
Clifford, Clark, 245, 273, 292, 293–4, 298–300, *299,*
        305, *310,* 320, 339, 351, 352, 365, 484, 485
    bombing halt favored by, 321, 347, 348
    deescalation urged by, 298–9, 399
    Vietnam policy questioned by, 294, *294,* 296
Clinton, Bill, 585

Coast Guard, U.S., 160
Cochinchina, 7, 8, 10, 12, 17, 19, 21
COINTELPRO, 459, 519
Colbert, Claudette, 384
Colby, William, 339, *340,* 341–2
Cold War, 26, 27, 48, 58, 500, 585
Cole, Thomas, *145*
Collins, J. Lawton "Lightning Joe," 36
Colonial School, 4
Colorado State University, 457
Colson, Charles, 478
Columbia University, 304, *304,* 384, 426
Combat Infantry Badge, 159
Commission on Campus Unrest, 455
Committee for the Re-Election of the President, 506,
        520
Communist International (Comintern), 5, 45
Communist Party, 23, 46, 49, 69, 146, 566, 573
Communist Party, Chinese, 48
Communist Party, French, 4, *5,* 21, 45
Communist Party, Indochinese (ICP), 5, 14, 21, 42,
        45, 48
Communist Party, Vietnamese, 42, 44, 47, 585
Communists, 363, 459, *488,* 516
"Concerned Uprisings," 43
Concordia Teachers College, 457
Confederacy, 303, 409
Confederate flag, 408*n,* 409
Confucianism, 5, 6, 44, 46
Congress, U.S., 27, 48, 58, 104, 126, 147, 194, *195,*
        221, 276, 292, 296, 342, 398, 459, 481, 484,
        486, 511, 518, 528, *534,* 543, 544, 545, 546,
        566, 570
    aid to South Vietnam reduced by, 527, 528, 530–1
    antiwar movement and, 519, 520
Congressional Medal of Honor, 161
Conley, Herman, 370
Conniff, Ray, 518
conscientious objectors, 161, 518
Con Son Island, 38, 40, 70, 308
Constellation, USS, 105, *499*
Constitution, U.S., 521
Con Thien, *201,* 212, 214, 216, *216,* 217, *217,*
        218–19, *218, 220,* 224–5, *229, 238,* 535
    siege of, 225, 227, *227,* 229–30, 238, 240, 265
"Convoy of Tears," 533
Cook County, Ill., 453
Cooper, John Sherman, 467
Corbett, John, 257, 259, 264
CORDS (Civil Operations and Revolutionary
        Development Support), 196–7, *196,* 247,
        267, 339, *340,* 363
Country Joe & the Fish, 404–5
Cox, Edward, 483
Cox, Tricia Nixon, 483, 484
Coy, Gary, 237–8
Crocker, Candy, *123,* 143, 174
Crocker, Carol, 98, 108, 123, 143, 173, 174, 199,
        310, 352–3, *353,* 427, 583
Crocker, Denton, Sr., 98, 108, 122, 131, 143, 159,
        172, 174
Crocker, Denton Winslow, Jr. "Mogie," 98, *98,*
        108–9, 122, 123, *123,* 129, *129,* 143, *143,*
        159, 160, 168, 172, 175, 199, 310, 352, *353,*
        427
    death of, 173–4, *173, 174*
Crocker, Jean-Marie, 98, 108, 109, 122, 123, 129,
        143, 159, 172–4

Crocker, Randy, *123,* 143
Crocker family, 143, *143*
Cronkite, Walter, 84–5, 92, 290–1, *291,* 330, 427,
        512
Crosby, Stills & Nash, 404
Cuba, 71, 94, 123, *526*
    Bay of Pigs invasion of, 53
Cuban Missile Crisis, 71, 94, 95
Cu Chi, 268, 324, *325,* 327
Cushman, John H., 67, *67,* 549
Custer, George Armstrong, 135
Czechoslovakia, 24, 335

Daily Nebraskan, 444
Dai Viet ("Greater Vietnam") Party, 13
Dak To, 198, 211, 216, 240, 246, 463
Dalat Military Academy, 109, 280
Daley, Richard J., 329–30, *329,* 335, 336, 507
Dallas, Tex., 567
Danang, xi, 7, 85, *97,* 122, 124, 128, 146, 154, 160,
        168, 169, *169, 189,* 212, 214, *266,* 267, 303,
        320, 321, *327,* 338, 390, 413, 440, 538, *587*
    ARVN abandonment of, 534–5, *535, 536,* 541,
        546
    Buddhist protests in, 170, 171
    in Tet Offensive, 265–6
Danang Air Base, 127, 189, *408*
    U.S. Marines landed at, 115–17, *116,* 119, 120,
        155, 535, *535,* 544
    Vietnamese reception committee at, 116, *117*
Danang River, *170*
Daniel, Aubrey, 473
Da Rang River, *533*
Daughters of the American Revolution, 480
Davidson, Philip, 264, 266
Davis, Rennie, 330, 423, 478, 483
"Days of Rage," 426, 438
Dean, Arthur, 126
Dean, John, 473
Dean, John Gunther, 544
Declaration of the Rights of Man, French, 16
Defense Attaché's Office (DAO), 546, 553, 557
Defense Department, U.S., 62, 63, 67, 125, 146, 165,
        186, 203, 293, 294, *294,* 406, 409, 448, 483,
        546, 552
    see also Pentagon
de Gaulle, Charles, 17, 101
Dellinger, David, 230, 232, 478, 502, 507
Delta Med, 239
De Mau Mau, 409
Demilitarized Zone (DMZ), *xvii, 31, 155, 182,* 186,
        194, *201,* 209, *211,* 212, 214, 217, *218,* 219,
        224, *227,* 256, 265, 279, 298, 302, 305, 343,
        347, 350, 373, 398, *411,* 412, *412,* 420, 424,
        443, *444,* 494, 511, *530*
Democratic National Committee, break-in at, 506,
        520
Democratic National Convention
    of 1968, 328–30, *329,* 332, *332,* 334–6, 338, 426
    of 1972, 506–7
Democratic Party, Democrats, 40, 93, 94, 126, 234,
        247, 297, 298, 301, 310, *310,* 328, 329, 330,
        335, *335,* 338, 345, 347, 460, 485, 506, 507,
        520
Denton, Jeremiah, Jr., 179
Denver, USS, 557
DePuy, William, 187, 299
deserters, American, 355, 444–5, 518

Dewey, A. Peter, 17–19, *19,* 20
Dien Bien Phu, battle of, *1,* 26–8, *27, 28, 31,* 35, 49,
    113, 246, 257, 461, 468, 512, 530
Dinh Truong Province, 356
Diplomat and the Warrior, The, 234
Dirksen, Everett, 349–50, 352
Dispatch News Service, 431
Distinguished Flying Cross, 481
Distinguished Service Cross, 76, *136,* 328, *483*
Distinguished Service Medal, 251, 472
Dominican Republic, 123, 147
"domino theory," 27, 91, 94, 148, 519
Dong Ap Bia, *see* Hamburger Hill
Dong Ha, *25,* 212, 214, 239, 265
Dong Hoi, 461
Dong Sy Nguyen, *375,* 422, 425, *530*
Dow Chemical, 120, 518
draft, draft resisters, 160–1, *162,* 163–4, *164,* 517,
    518, 520
draft cards, burning of, 120, *121,* 191, 230, 319
Dubček, Alexander, 335
"Duck Hook" plan, 425, 427, 520
Duc Pho, 149, 248, 411
Dulles, John Foster, 28, *32,* 36, *38*
Dump Johnson Movement, 234
Duong Van Mai, 35, *35,* 80, 81, 86, 117
Duong Van Minh "Big Minh," 86, 101, 224, 488,
    489, 538, 551, *551,* 562, 563
Durbrow, Elbridge, 43
Dutch, 7, 12
Dylan, Bob, 426

Eagleton, Thomas, 506, 507, *507*
East Asia, 47
East Carolina University, 457
Easter Offensive (1972), 493–6, *493,* 498–501, 503,
    504, 511, 530
East Germany, 61
Economist, 186
Ehrhart, Bill, 157, *157, 189,* 206, 265, 281, 282, 284,
    454
Ehrlichman, John, 427, 485
Eighty-second Airborne Division, 288, 481
Eisenhower, Dwight D., xii, 36, *38,* 41, 53, *53,* 83,
    91, 93, 126, 234, 322, 364, 398, 460
    "domino theory" of, 27
elections, U.S.
    of 1964, 90, 106, 107, *107,* 157
    of 1968, 263, 296, 301, 322, 328–30, *329,* 332,
        332, 334–6, 338–9, 345, *345,* 347–51, *347,*
        397
    of 1970, 459–60
    of 1972, 506–7, *507,* 508, 510, 511, 520
Eller, Frank P., 109, 111–12
Elliott, David, 164, 271
Elliott, Duong Van Mai, 164–5, *165,* 166, 271, 343,
    363, *363,* 417, 512, 527, 555, *555,* 563, 565,
    573
Ellsberg, Daniel, 483, 485, 518, 520
Emerson, Henry "Hank," 159–60, *159*
"End the Draft" week, 230, 232
England, *see* Great Britain
English, Lowell, 256–7
Enhance program, 511
Episcopal Peace Fellowship, 438
Escoffer, Auguste, 4
Espionage Act (1917), 485
Europe, 17, 25, 47, 49, 178, 365

European colonialism, 4
Evanston, Ill., 336
Ewell, Julian J., 356, 357, *357,* 360, *360,* 389
Executive Office Building, Washington, D.C., 438,
    449, 477

Faas, Horst, 159, 416, 504
Face the Nation, 246
Fallows, James, 163
Farina, Mimi, *161*
Fassnacht, Robert, 459
Federal Bureau of Investigation (FBI), 108, 190, 234,
    329, 349, 355, 369, 458, 459, 485, 519
Felt, Harry D., 77
Fenton, James, 557, 558–9, 562–3
Feraci, Carole, 518
Ferrizzi, Ron, 260, *260,* 335, 480, 481, 483, *483*
Fifth Infantry Division, U.S., Sixty-first Regiment,
    First Battalion, Company A, 412
Fifty-second Aviation Battalion, *115*
First Amendment, 485
First Cavalry Division, U.S., 61, 134, 166–8, 247,
    260, 307, 408, 461, 463
    Third Brigade, 149
    Seventh Cavalry
        First Battalion, 135, *139,* 142, *153*
        Second Battalion, 136, 139–40, *139,* 416
    Ninth Cavalry, First Squadron, 247, 260
    Eleventh Armored Cavalry, *420*
    Seventeenth Armored Cavalry, F Troop, 336, 338,
        369–72
First Indochina War, *24, 25,* 28, 35, 42, 67, 69, 70,
    90, 139, 155, 207, 264, 280, 281, 360, 363,
    418, 424, 508
    atrocities in, 22, 26
    China and, 25
    end of, *1,* 28
    French casualties in, 22, 26
    JFK on, 90–1
    outbreak of, 21–2
    as proxy war, 48
    U.S. and, 22, 24, 26, 27, 190
    see also Dien Bien Phu, battle of
First Infantry Division, U.S., 128, 408
First Marine Division, U.S., 187, 189, 212, 281–2
    First Military Police Battalion, 189
    First Regiment, First Battalion, 281–2, *282,* 284–5,
        284, 285, 291
    Forward Headquarters, 281
    Ninth Regiment, 390
        First Battalion, 214, 217–18, 220–4, 229–30,
            229, 238–40
        Second Battalion, 218–20, 225, 227, 229, *229,*
            339
Fishel, Wesley R., 41
Fishhook region, 369, 448, *448*
Florida, 567
Flynn, John, 116
Fonda, Jane, 502, *502,* 582
Ford, Gerald R., xi, 473, 530–1, 534, 540, *541,* 543,
    544, 548, 549, 553, *553,* 557, 558, 559, 575
Ford, Tennessee Ernie, 553
Ford Foundation, 299
Foreign Affairs, 399
Foreign Intelligence Advisory Board, 294
Forrestal, James V., *53*
Forrestal, Michael V., 78, 92–3
Fort Benning, 61, 75, *129,* 142, 305, 472, *473*

Fort Bragg, 186, *203,* 305, 322, 490
Fort Dix, 122, 123
Fort Hood, 490
Fort Indiantown Gap, 567
Fort Jackson, 518
Fort Leavenworth, 175
Fort Lewis, 318, 444
Fort Sill, *244*
For Whom the Bell Tolls (Hemingway), 118
Four-Party Joint Military Commission, 524, *524*
Fourteen Points, 3
Fourth Infantry Division, U.S., 303, 384, 409, 461
fragging, 411, 413, 518–19
France, *3, 8, 10, 12,* 14, 15, 18, *18,* 19, 20, *20,* 21,
    27, 28, 31, *31,* 32, 36, 38, 40, 41, 49, 56, 74,
    78, 90, 91, 95, 101, 102, 115, 117, 125, 147,
    198, 206, 246, 257, 308, 314, 417, 418, 508,
    509, 511, 530, 576
    Ho Chi Minh in, 3–4, *5,* 44–5
    Ho Chi Minh in negotiations with, 47–8
    Indochina as colony of, xii, 3–4, *6,* 7–12, 16, 17,
        44–5, 46, 73, 164, 248, 315, 361, 363, 517,
        567
    Nazi defeat of, 12, 13, 47
    in reoccupation of Indochina, 17, *17, 22*
    U.S. aid sought by, 22, 24
    see also First Indochina War
Frank, Glenn, 451
Frederickson, Mike, 319
Free France, 19
French Legion of Honor, 18
French Ministry of Colonies, 4
French Revolution, 4
French Riviera, 36, 49
French Union, 21
Friendly, Fred, 148
friendly fire, 150, 151, 198, 230, 391, 393
Frishman, Robert, 423
Frost, David, 455
Fulbright, J. William, 146–7, 148, 149, 182, 183,
    301, 480, 483
Fulbright hearings, 146–7, 148–9, *148*
Furey, Joan, 384–6, *384, 385,* 440–2, *441*

Galbraith, John Kenneth, 170
Galloway, Joseph Lee, 124, *124,* 131, 132, 134, 136,
    137, 139, *139,* 168, 363, 538
Gallup, George, 291–2, 477
Gallup poll, 221–2, 296, 310, 336, 338, 386, 431,
    456, 459, 472, 473
Gandhi, Mohandas K., 445
Gard, Robert, 154, 195, 357, 360
Garefin, Charles, 370
Garvey, Marcus, 4
Gavin, James, 234
Gelb, Leslie, 195, 233, 417, 501, 503
Gellhorn, Martha, 166
General Beadle State College, 519
General Mobilization Law, 321
General Offensive, General Uprising, 100, 206, 209,
    255, 268, 276, 307, 310, 508
    see also Tet Offensive
Geneva, 26, 28, 308
Geneva Accords, 32, 37, 49, 122, 461, 491, 493, 567
Georgetown University, 164
Georgia, 160
Germany, 17, *31,* 126, 256, 317, 490, 516
Germany, Nazi, 12, 13, 47, 131, 178, 511

Gia Dinh Province, 508
Gia Long, 6–7
Gia Long palace, *85*
Gillam, James T., 409–10
Ginsburgh, Robert N., *293*
Gioia, Phil, xi, 288, *289,* 481
Gio Linh, 212, 214
GI Says, 411
Gitlin, Todd, 330, 336, 426, 516–21
Go Cong Province, 356
Goddard, Paulette, 384
Goldberg, Arthur, 299
Goldstein, Alan, 440
Goldwater, Barry F., 90, 104, 106, *107,* 157, 323,
    507, 521
Goodell, Charles, 438
Gore, Albert, Sr., 330
Goucher College, 352–3, *353,* 427
Gracey, Douglas, 18, 19
Graham, Bill, 427
Grateful Dead, 404
Gravel, Marcus J., *291*
Graves Registration, 154
Grayson, Bruns, 203
Great Britain, 3, 4, 5, 7, 12, 16, 17, 18, 19, 27, 28,
    37, 45, 95, 108, 122, 147, 301, 548
Great Depression, 527
Great Society, 94, 98, 115, 126, 397
Great Terror of 1936–38, 45
Greece, 24, 298
Green Berets, *see* Special Forces, U.S.
Green Berets (film), 517
Greenville Victory, USNS, 549
Greenwich Village, N.Y., 426
Gregg, Donald, 63, 196–7
Group 599 (North Vietnamese unit), *375*
Gruening, Ernest, 106
Guam, *401,* 546, 548, 566
Gurkha, 18

Habib, Philip, 299
Haeberle, Ronald, 432
Haig, Al, 484, 510, 512
Haight-Ashbury neighborhood, San Francisco, 230
Haiphong, 7, *13,* 21–2, 35, *35,* 177, 194, 209, *209,*
    511, 520
    U.S. bombing of, 176, *182,* 224, 292, 298, 512
Haiphong Harbor, mining of, 425, 500
Halberstam, David, 62, *63,* 67, 71, 77, 86, *160,* 395
Haldeman, H. R., *347, 347,* 350, 366, 427, *438,* 447,
    449, 454, 455, 456, 460, 467, 477, *483,* 485,
    494, 510
Ha Long Bay, 461
Hamburger Hill, battle for, *390,* 391, 393, *393,*
    394–5, 398, 411, 535
Hamill, Pete, 456
Hamilton, George, 163
Hamlet Evaluation System, 196–7, 340
Hampton, Fred, 426
Hancock, USS, *555*
Haney, Raymond M., 495
Hanoi, xii, *1,* 7, *12,* 13, 14, 15, 21, 22, *22,* 24, *24,*
    25, 35, 41, 46, 47, 62, 67, 85, 106, *114,* 127,
    143, 146, *178, 182,* 206, 221, 223, 233, *271,*
    316, 321, 376, 424, 471, 474, *491,* 502, 506,
    508, 511, *513, 541,* 566
    air defense system of, 125
    Ba Dinh Square in, 16, *16,* 17, 422

bombing of, 176, 185, *185,* 194, 224, 292–3, 298,
    461, 503, 512
Hanoi, University of, 13, *13*
"Hanoi Hilton," 207
Hanoi Radio, *266*
Harkins, Paul D., 58, 62, 63, *63,* 68, 72, 77, 86, 91,
    100, 103
Harlem, N.Y., 4
Harriman, W. Averell, *299,* 304–5, 345
Harris, Lou, 247, 329, 349, 501
Harris, Roger, 156, *157,* 218–20, *218,* 225, 227, 229,
    230, 265–6, 301–3
Harrisburg, Pa., 567
Harris poll, 247, 477, 507
Harrison, Anne, 175, 353, 354, 355
Harrison, Bob "Robin," 353–5, *354*
Harrison, Matthew Clarence, Sr., 175
Harrison, Matthew, Jr. "Chips," 175–6, *176,* 198–9,
    199, 240, 241, 243–5, 353, 354, *354,* 355
Harrison, Victoria, 175, 353, 355
Hartzel, Jack, *227*
Harvard University, 161, 567
    Vietnam Program of the Kennedy School at, 585
Hatfield, Mark, 459
Ha Tinh Province, 209
Havens, Richie, 404
Hawaii, 95, 506
Hayden, Tom, 304, 330, *502.*
Head Start, 98
"Headway Reports," 63, 68
Heaney, Michael, 152–3, 166–8, *167,* 565, 585, *585*
Hegdahl, Douglas, *423*
He Grows Under Fire (Cao), 72
Heinemann, Larry, 463
helicopters, *587*
    impact of, 59, *59,* 260
    NLF downing of, 74, *75,* 111
    in Saigon evacuation, 552–3, 555, *556,* 557, 558,
    558, 559–61, *560*
Helms, Richard, 273, *347,* 467
Hemingway, Ernest, 118, 158, 444, 503
Hendrix, Jimi, 404
herbicides, 58, 406
    see also Agent Orange
"Heroic Soldier from Anti-aircraft Company #5 Loads
    Artillery" (photograph), *316*
heroin, *410*
Herr, Michael, *262,* 279, *282*
Herrington, Stuart, 197, 341, 342, 360, 531, 546,
    548, 558
Hersey, John, 131
Hersh, Seymour, 431, 433, 437
Hiep Duc Valley, *413*
Highway 1, 281, 338, 504, 542, *543,* 546, *547*
Highway 9, 467, *467,* 468
Highway 13, 494
"Hill Fights," 257
Hill 102, 414, 415
Hill 484, battle for, xvii, 367–9, *368*
Hill 861A, 257, *259*
Hill 875, 240, 241, *243,* 245, 246, 353
Hill 937, *see* Hamburger Hill
Hill 1338, 198, 240, 245, 353
Hilsman, Roger, Jr., 83–4, 516
Hiroshima, atomic bombing of, 47
Hitler, Adolf, 25, 304
Hmong, 567
Hoa Hao, 32, 36

Hoa Lo (prison), 207
Hoang Duc Ninh, 363
Hoang Phuong, *see* Bao Ninh
Hoang Xuan Lam, 468, 494
Ho Chi Minh, xii, *3,* 8, 12, 13, *14,* 15, *15,* 17, 20, *21,*
    22, *22,* 23, 24, *24,* 25, 27, 32, 36, 37, 41–2,
    70, 90, *101,* 104, 113, 115, 148, *155,* 158–9,
    158, 177, 183, 234, 255, 277, *314,* 315, 345,
    366–7, 400, 412, 421–2, *421,* 423, 461, 491,
    493, 524, 545
    acceptance of Geneva Accords favored by, 49
    in appeal for Chinese military aid, 60, 62
    in China, 5, 45, 47
    as cofounder of French Communist Party, 4, *5,* 45
    death of, 422, *422,* 424–5
    Diem compared to, 44, 46, 49
    early years of, 4, 44–6
    and end of World War II, 47–8
    in founding of Indochinese Communist Party, 5
    in France, 3–4, *5,* 44–5
    guerilla warfare favored by, 100–1, 206
    Lenin's influence on, 4, 45
    loss of power by, 101, 209
    in negotiations with France, 21, 26, 28, 31, 47–8
    popular image of, 44
    rebuilding of North Vietnam as focus of, 41
    in return to Indochina, 14, 47
    in Soviet Union, 5, 45, 46
    U.S. aid sought by, 47
    Viet Minh founded by, 14, 47
    in Vietnamese Independence Day declaration,
    16, *16*
"Ho Chi Minh Campaign," 534, *565*
Ho Chi Minh City, *see* Saigon
Ho Chi Minh Road, 38, 40
Ho Chi Minh Trail, 42, 106, 118, 122, 131, *155,* 176,
    212, 256, 341, 370, 373, *375, 376, 378, 380,*
    388, 390, 398, 424, 459, 461, 467, 470, 474,
    503, *530,* 534
    U.S. air strikes on, 108, 158–9
    women truck drivers on, *377, 377,* 380–1
Hochmuth, Bruno, *239*
Hoffman, Abbie, 440
Ho Huu Lan, 209, 214, 217–18, 279, 535–6
Hoi An, 189, 224, 265, 266
Holland, 290, 356
Holliday, Dwight, *xxiii*
Hollings, Fritz, 142
Hollingsworth, James F., 496
Holmes, Ben, 174
Holmes, Michael, 336–8, *337,* 369–72, *371, 372*
Holt, Harold, 251
Honey, P. J., 146
Honeycutt, Weldon F. "Blackjack," 391, 393, 411
Hon Gai, 105
Hong Kong, 5, 12, 45, 355, 569
Honolulu, Hawaii, 397
Honolulu Conference (1966), *146,* 147, 148, 149
Hood, Richard, *176,* 198, 199
Hoover, J. Edgar, 191, 234, 369, 459
Hope, Bob, *327*
Horner, Garnett D. "Jack," 276–7
Horse Shoe, 206
Hotel Majestic, Saigon, 26, 58, 304
House of Representatives, U.S., 106, 427, 431, 459,
    527, 548–9
    Armed Services Committee of, 146, 276
    Judiciary Committee of, 520

Houston, Tex., *345,* 567
Houston Astrodome, *348*
Howard, Eli P., Jr., 413, 414, 415
Howard, Jan, 338
Howard, Jimmy, 338
Ho Xuan Huong, 462–3
Hue, 4, 6, 7, 15, 23, 25, 32, 36–7, 44, 46, 69, 78, 80,
    83, 85, 106, 169, 209, 224, *253,* 265, 267,
    282, 390, 437, 481, *493,* 494, 499, 535
  ARVN headquarters in, 280, 281, 285, 286
  Buddhist protests in, 170, 171, *172*
  Citadel (Old City) in, *279,* 280–2, *280,* 284–6,
    284, 285, 286, 287
  Imperial Palace in, 280, 281, 286
  MACV compound in, 280, 281, 282
  New City in, 280, *280*
  NLF mass murders in, 288, *289*
  Tet Offensive in, 279–87, *279,* 290, *291*
Hue, University of, 284
Hughes, John C., *115*
Hughes, Richard J., *222*
Humanitarian Operations Programme, 569
Humanité, L', 3
Humphrey, Hubert, 32, 50
  in 1968 presidential race, 301, 328–9, 330, 335,
    335, 338–9, *339,* 345, *345,* 347, *348,* 349,
    397
  as vice president, *98,* 115, 175, 246, 247
Hungary, 209, 257, 292
Hung Yen, 503
Hunt, Ira, 357
Hunt, Sam, 168
Hunter College, 456
Hunting, Pete, 57, *57*
Huntley-Brinkley Report (TV show), 275
Huong Van Ba, 321
Huran, S.Dak., *339*
Hurricane Katrina, 570
Huston, Tom Charles, 458–9
Huy Duc, 209, 264, 292, 314, 512, 573
Huynh Cong Than, 264–5, 267, 273, 310
Huynh Van Cao, 71–2, 76–7
Hyannis Port, Mass., 84
Hynes, Liz, 336
Hynes, Mandy and Jo, 336
Hynes, Samuel, 161, 274–5, 335–6, 453, 454

Ia Drang Valley campaign, *133,* 134–7, *135, 136,*
    139–40, *142,* 143, 149, 157, 167, 243, 563,
    587
"I-Feel-Like-I'm-Fixin'-to-Die Rag" (song), 404–5
India, 7, 23, 31, 41, 170, 212
Indiana, 301, 310
Indianapolis, Ind., 301
Indian Ocean, 566
"Indictment No. 1" manifesto, 528
Indochina, xi, *8,* 21, 24, 26, 27, 28, *31,* 44, 45, 48,
    64, 90–1, 94, 98, 120, 513
  Catholic missionaries in, 7
  communists in, 12, 14, 23
  as French colony, xii, 3–4, *6,* 7–12, 16, 46, 73, 164,
    248, 315, 361, 363, 517
  French reoccupation of, 17, *17,* 19–21, *22*
  Japanese occupation of, 12, *13,* 15, 25, 47
  Nationalist Chinese troops in, 17, 21
  nationalist movements in, 10–12, 13
  OSS in, *14,* 15, *15,* 16, 17–19, *21*
  partition of, 31–2, 49, 491, 493

  rearming of Japanese soldiers in, 18, *18*
  see also First Indochina War; North Vietnam; South
    Vietnam
Indochina Peace Campaign, 502
Indochina War, 48, 49
Indochinese Union, 7
Indonesia, 7, 27, 53, 304, 569
International Red Cross, 178
International Security Affairs, 195
International Voluntary Service (IVS), 57
Iowa, University of, 457
Iron Triangle, 186–7, *188,* 211
Isaacs, Arnold R., 541
Italy, 147, 303

Jackson, Andrew, 548
Jackson, Jesse, 570
Jakarta, 304
Japan, 4, 14, 17, 18, *18, 20,* 25, 58, 173, 203, 365,
    511
  expansionism of, 47
  Indochina occupied by, 12, *13,* 15, 47
  surrender of, 16
Javits, Jacob, 544
Jefferson, Eva, 231, *231,* 353, 453–4, *454,* 455
Jefferson, Thomas, 16
JFK (film), 92
Johns Hopkins University, 122
Johnson, Harold K., 194, 222, 292
Johnson, Lady Bird, *332*
Johnson, Lucy, 178
Johnson, Lyndon Baines, xii, 53, *53,* 84, 89, 90, 92,
    98, 101, 102, 103–5, 106–8, *107,* 120, *125,*
    128, 146–8, *146,* 149, 153–4, 157, 160,
    170–1, 175, 176, 178, 190, 191, 194, 195,
    195, 196, *222,* 223–4, 232, 245–6, *246,*
    251, 256, 263, 273, 290, 291, 292–4, *293,*
    294, 296–301, 303, 305, 310, 317, 320,
    328–9, *332,* 336, 338, 339, *345, 347, 348,*
    350–2, *351,* 355, 367, 369, 386, 397, 398,
    420, 427, 458, 484, 485, 486, 501, 510,
    516, 521, 527
  additional troops committed by, 293, 300
  antiwar movement and, 234
  bombing resumed by, 146
  in call for negotiations, 122–3
  Christmas bombing pause ordered by, 146
  "credibility gap" of, 123, 186, 519
  death of, 512
  in decision not to run for re-election, 300–1, *300*
  as determined not to "lose" Southeast Asia, 100
  Diem coup opposed by, 98, 100
  escalation of war by, 93, 143, 461
  full bombing halt ordered by, 348–9
  JFK's character compared to, 94–5
  McNamara fired by, 245
  North Vietnam bombing campaign ordered by,
    114–15
  obstinacy of, 95
  Paris negotiations and, 343, 345, 347
  partial bombing halt ordered by, 300, *300,* 304,
    316, 321
  public opinion and, 221–2, 250–1
  Tet Offensive and, 276–7, 292–3
  U.S. advisers increased by, 103
  U.S. ground troops committed by, 115–16
  U.S. troops levels increased by, 126
  Vietnam choices as viewed by, 94–5, 104, 116

"Wise Men" convened by, 126, 299–300, *299,*
    364–5
Johnson, Tom, *332*
Johnson administration, 115, *127,* 195, 222, 234,
    296, 297, 305, 338, 347, 423
  optimism about war expressed by, 245–7
Johnson family, *332*
Joint Chiefs of Staff, U.S., 56, 71, 104, 122, 123, 126,
    172, 176, 245, *246,* 263, 292, 345, 364, 369,
    445, 467
  escalation of war urged by, 103, 107, 224
  troop increases sought by, 194, 222, 293
  U.S. ground troops requested by, 116
Joint General Staff, South Vietnamese, 467, 527–8
Joplin, Janis, 404, 405
journalists
  attempted muzzling and misleading of, 58, 62–3
  increased Vietnam coverage by, 124
  unvarnished reporting by, 62–3, *63,* 67, 77, 127–8,
    222–3, 290, 393, 477
  Vietnam deaths of, 124
  women as, 216
Judd, Donald, *176,* 198, 199
Judge, Darwin, 552
Ju Ju, 409
Justice Department, U.S., 479, 485, 518
Justice Department building, Washington, D.C.,
    440

Kalb, Marvin, 478
Kalischer, Peter, 290
Kansas State University, 297
Karch, Frederick J., 116
Karnow, Stanley, 58
Katzenbach, Nicholas, *246*
Kazickas, Jurate, 216, *216*
Keeley, John B., 154
Kennan, George F., 24, 148–9, *148,* 293
Kennedy, Edward, 329, 393
Kennedy administration, 81, 83, 90, 93
  ambiguous Vietnam record of, 90
Kennedy, John F., xii, 26, 32, 40, 48, 52–4, 58, 71,
    78, 81, 98, 100, 127, 240, 293, 294, 296,
    297, 301, 322, 398, 484, 512, 516
  assassination of, 89, 90, 506
  communist containment as goal of, 91
  complete review of Vietnam policy planned by, 93
  in Cronkite interview, 84–5, 92
  and Diem murder, 86, 89, 92
  election of, 43, 52–3
  on First Indochina War, 90–1
  as fundamentally ambivalent about Vietnam
    situation, 94
  inaugural address of, 52, *53,* 57, 95
  Laos and, 94
  LBJ's character compared to, 94–5
  limits of power understood by, 91, 94
  military aid to South Vietnam approved by, 91
  and possible post-1963 conduct of Vietnam War,
    90–5
  in refusal to send ground troops to Vietnam, 56,
    91, 92, 93
  restraint as preference of, 95
Kennedy, Pat, 26
Kennedy, Robert F., 26, 81, 91, 93, 94, 234, 245,
    296–8, 304, 305, 328, 506
  assassination of, 310, *310*
  in 1968 presidential campaign, 297, *297,* 301, 310

Kent State killings, *383,* 449–51, *449, 450, 451,*
  453–4, *453,* 454, *454,* 455, 456
Kerrey, Bob, 585
Kerry, John, *479,* 480–1, *481,* 585
Khai Dinh, Emperor, *6*
Khe Mon, 25, 149
Khe Sanh Marine Combat Base, 212, 256–7, 260,
  262, 270, 290, *293,* 307, 317, 384, 431, 467,
  468, *474,* 477
  siege of, *225,* 257, 259–60, *259, 262,* 263–4, *263,*
    273, 276, 307, 463
Khmer Rouge, 446, 459, 544, *545,* 569
  genocide by, 545
Khrushchev, Nikita, 52, 53, 71, 94, 106
Kien Hoa Province, 69, *69,* 356
Kilburn, Gerald, *59*
Kim Phuc, 504, *504*
King, Coretta Scott, 427
King, Martin Luther, Jr., 190–1, *191,* 427
  assassination of, 301, *302,* 303, 310, 323, 329,
    408
Kiowa, 244, *244*
Kissinger, Henry, 345, *352,* 364–5, *365, 366,* 369,
    387, 397–8, 417, 422, 423, 447, 449, 454,
    467, 468–70, 477–8, 485, 487, 488–9,
    494–5, 500, 507–8, 512, 518, 526, 540, 543,
    544, 545, 546, 551, 552, 559, *560*
  "Duck Hook" plan of, 425, 427
  in secret negotiations with North Vietnam, 398,
    421, 445–6, 486, 489, 510–11
  U.S. credibility as priority of, 365
Knowlton, William A., 267
Komer, Robert "Blowtorch," 196, 247, 267, 292, 339,
  340
Kon Tum Province, 266, 303, 424, 461, 462, 463,
    494, 499, 531, 533, *533*
Korea, 25–6, 58
Korean War, 25–6, 27, 28, 31, 32, 36, 41, 56, 58,
    91, 103, 104, 109, 117, 126, 135, 156, 189,
    191, 203, 235, 244, *244,* 303, 317, *393,* 398,
    410, 516
Koster, Samuel W., 436, 437, 472
Kosygin, Alexei, 221
Kraft, Joseph, 501
Krulak, Victor, 85, 211
Ku Klux Klan, 303, 409, 458
Kushner, Hal, 247–50, *248, 249,* 260, 310, 321–2,
    355, 423, 470–1, 506, 512, 513, *513*
Kushner, Toni-Jean, 248
Kushner, Valerie, 506

Laird, Melvin, 365, 397, *417,* 425, 427, 437
Lake, Veronica, 384
Lam Quang Thi, 529
Lam Quang Tho, 74, 77
Landing Zone Albany, *135,* 140, *140, 142*
Landing Zone Gator, 431, 433
Landing Zone Two Bits, 247, *249,* 260
Landing Zone X-Ray, 135–7, *135, 137,* 139, 140,
    149
land mines, 431
Land-to-the-Tiller program, 488
Lane, Sharon, 384
Lansdale, Edward, 36, 363
Lansing, Robert J., *3*
Laos, xvii, 7, 24, 28, 42, 53, 56, 91, 94, 95, 103, 155,
    158, 173, 176, 191, 194, 211, 212, 220, 224,
    244, 256, 292, 316, 321, 373, 377, 381, 387,

    390, 393, 406, *469,* 471, *471,* 474, *474,* 476,
    477, 478, 494, 503, 517, 526, 567
  South Vietnamese invasion of, *465,* 467–70, 471,
    486, *486,* 493
  U.S. bombing of, 108, 467, 485, 519
  U.S. invasion of, 467
  see also Ho Chi Minh Trail
Larner, Jeremy, 440
La Thi Tam, *158*
Laurence, John, 149–50, *150,* 152, 225, 227, 284–6,
    290, 292, 416
Lawrenson, Peter, 463
Le, Jeanette, *555*
"Leatherneck Square," *211,* 212, *214,* 218, 265
Leclerc, Jacques-Philippe, 19, *20*
Le Cong Huan, 73, 74, 75, 76, 100, 264, 585
Le Duan, 42, *42,* 60, 78, *101,* 104, 106, 110, 113,
    119, 125, 140, 146, 206–7, 255, 307, 314,
    367, *422,* 425, 445, *491,* 493, 508, 530, 575,
    585
  large-scale actions urged by, 100–1
  moderates purged from party by, 101
  Tet Offensive and, 264, *265*
Le Duc Tho, 445–6, 487, 500, 508, 510, 511
Lee, Bernard, 190
Lehmann, Gerhard, 538
Le Khac Tam, 135
Le Kim Dinh, 538
LeMay, Curtis, 338
Le Minh Dao, 542
Le Minh Khue, 118, *118,* 158–9, 503, 534–5
Lemnitzer, Lyman, 91
Lenin, Vladimir, 4, 5, 14, 45, 516
Leninism, 48
Lennon, John, 438
Le Quan Cong, 357
Le Van Cho, 212
Levine, David, *234*
Levy, Howard B., 518
Liberation Army, 59, 209
Liberation Radio, 265
Lieu An, *152*
Life, 40, 116, 191, 394–6, 432
Lin, Maya Ying, xii, 581–2, *581, 582*
Lincoln, Abraham, 20, 190
Lincoln, Nebr., 517
Lincoln Memorial, Washington, D.C., 454, 456, 583
Lindsay, John, 456
Loc Ninh, 240, 495, *530*
Lodge, Henry Cabot, Jr., 81, 83–4, 85, *85,* 86, 89, 92,
    100, *146,* 169, 170, 484
Logan, John A., *330*
Logan Act (1799), 349
Logevall, Fredrik, 90–5
Lo Khac Tam, xiii, 131–2, 135, 136–7, 139, 563, 587
London, 4, 303
London *Times,* 22
Long An Province, 264, *342, 343*
Long Binh, 267, 326–7, *327,* 409, 440, 491
Longfellow, Henry Wadsworth, 462, 463
Long Island University, 547
Lon Nol, 446
Look, 216
Los Angeles, Calif., 230, 566, 576
Louisiana, 570
Louisiana State University, *453*
Lowenstein, Allard, 234, *234,* 247
Lowry, William, 154

Lozada, Carlos, 241
Luong Toan, *501*
Ly Tong Ba, 74

MacArthur, Douglas, 189, 240
Macauley, Robert, 540
Mad Dogs (antiwar militants), 440
Maddox, USS, 104, *105*
Mailer, Norman, 332
Mai Ly, 551
Main Force (NLF), 54, 56, 77, 100, 127, 132, 142,
    206, 279, *279,* 314, 320, 321, 388, 389–90,
    400, 431
  casualties of, 314
  in combined offensive, 206–7, 240
  in Tet attack on Hue, 279, *279,* 281, *285*
  in Tet attack on Saigon, 292
  in Tet Offensive, 314
  Ninth Division, 111, 188, 292
  271st Regiment, 110
  272nd Regiment, 110
Malaya, 7, 53, 108
Malaysia, 132, 569, *576*
Malcolm X, 408
Manchester, N.H., *247*
Manfull, Melvin, 116
Mansfield, Mike, 32, 71, 122, 182, 296, 531
Mansfield Center, 462
Mao Zedong, 22, 25, 41, 48, 153, 427, 506
"March of Death," 438, *438*
March on the Pentagon, 230, 232–3, *232, 233,* 234,
    336
marijuana, 410, *410*
Marine Amphibious Force, 218
Marine Corps Hymn, The, 257
Marine Reserves, U.S., 319, 353, 354
Marines, U.S., xi, xii, *97,* 107, *119,* 123, 124, 127,
    127, 128, 149, 156–7, 160, *163,* 170, *170,*
    171, 188, *189,* 190, 194, 197, 203, *204,* 206,
    206, 209, *214,* 216, *220, 225,* 231, 245, 256,
    259, 262, 263, *263, 264,* 265, 267, 279, 290,
    303, 307, 319, 330, 354, 356, *357,* 391, *404,*
    443, 444, 480, 496, 524, 538, 553, *569,* 585
  casualties suffered by, 218
  in Con Thien siege, 225, 227, *227*
  Danang landing of, 115–17, *116,* 119, 120, 155,
    535, *535,* 544
  Ninth Amphibious Brigade, 544
  in Saigon evacuation, 545, 551, *555,* 556–7, 558,
    559–61, *560*
  Third Amphibious Force, 168
  Third Regiment, 154
  Twenty-sixth Regiment, 257
  Vietnam buildup of, 122
  see also specific divisions
Marin Junior College, 353
Maritime Zone, 35
Marketplace Massacre, 216, 217, *217*
Marlantes, Karl, xii, 238, 319, *319,* 367–9, *368,* 485,
    578
Marm, Walter, Jr., 135
Marshall, George, 24
Marshall Plan, 298
MARS station, 248
Martin, Graham, 527, *534,* 538, 540, 544, 545, 546,
    547, 548, 551, 552–3, 557, 558, *558*
Marx, Karl, 14
Marxism, 4, 5, 37, 45, 46, 48, 424

Massachusetts, 248, 511
Mathias, Charles, 483
May Day, *565*
May Day Tribe, 483
Mays, Robert, 75
McCain, John S., III, 424, 585, *585*
McCarthy, Eugene, 183, 247, *247*, 248, 296, 297,
298, 301, 310, 328, 330, 334, 338, 339, 404,
438, 440, 506
McCarthyism, 234
McChord Air Force Base, 403
McCloy, John, 126
McCone, John, 84
McGaha, Harold, 236
McGee, Frank, 296
McGovern, George, 115, 122, 183, 234, 328, 438,
459, 483, 501, 510
in 1972 presidential race, 506–7, *507,* 511
McMahon, Charles, Jr., 552
McNamara, Robert S., 53, *53,* 56, 62, 63, 84, 86, 89,
93, 98, 100, 102, 103, *103,* 105, 114, 115,
116, 125, *125,* 143, 146, 154, 163–4, 165,
176, 178, 186, 212, 233, 273, 294
history of Vietnam War (Pentagon Papers) ordered
by, 195, 483, 484, 485
LBJ's firing of, 245
reduction of U.S. war effort urged by, 194–5
Vietnam negotiation urged by, 245
McNaughton, John T., 365
McPeak, Merrill, 372–3, *373,* 380, 381, 405, 408,
417
Meadlo, Paul, 433–5
Medal of Honor, 241, 477
Media, Pa., 519
Medicare, 98, 126
Medina, Ernest, 431–2
Meet the Press, 350
Mekong Delta, *xix,* 7, 19, 32, 54, *54, 56, 58, 59,* 60,
69, 71, 72, *103,* 154, 155, 177, 211, 255,
260, 264, 307, 326, 356, *357,* 360, 363, *389,*
408, *419,* 480
Mekong River, 122, 255
Mellon, Bob, 268
Memot Rubber Plantation, *448*
Mendenhall, Joseph, 85
"Menu" attacks, 369
Merrill's Marauders, 128
Miami Beach, Fla., 322, 328
Miami Herald, 444
Michigan, University of, 120–1, 457
Michigan State University, 41
Midway Island, 397, *397,* 399, 400, 420, 510, 528
Military Assistance and Advisory Group, U.S.
(MAAG), 41, 91
Military Assistance Command, Vietnam (MACV), *56,*
58, 62, *63,* 68, 91, 113, 128, 158, 186, 187,
188, *195, 196,* 197, 211, 235, 238, 240, 246,
255, 264, 267, 268, 280, 281, 282, 299, 356,
360, 388, 389, 398, 406, 420, 524
Abrams appointed commander of, 317, *317,*
320–1
inflated body count and, 154, 176, 199, 218
journalists and, 124, *124*
misleading statements by, 140, 290
Westmoreland appointed commander of, 103
military, U.S.
African Americans in, 163, *163,* 303, 408–9
drug use in, 410, *410,* 490, 518

fragging in, 411, 413, 518–19
indiscriminate killing of Vietnamese by, 356–7,
360
low morale and breakdown of discipline in,
408–11, 413–16, 444–5, 490, 518–19
minorities and working class in, 163
racism in, 408–9, 490
support for antiwar movement in, 440–3
women in, 384–6
see also specific armed services
Military Attaché Office, U.S., 551
Miller, Edward, 44–9
Miller, Jeffrey, *453*
"Mini-Tet," 307, *307, 308,* 309, 310, 321
Minneapolis, Minn., 298
Minutemen, 458
Miremont, James, *xxiii*
Missing in Action (MIA) campaign, 585
Mississippi, 234, 317
Missoula, Mont., 462–3
Missouri, 336, 483
Missouri Ozarks, 336, 337
"Misty" (Project Commando Sabre), 372–3, *373,*
380–1
Mitchell, John, 345, 347, 459, 485
Mobile Riverine Force, 278, 356, *357*
Moffett, Harold, 495
Momaday, Marmon, 463
Montague, USS, 35
Montana, 461, 463, 567
Moore, Harold G. "Hal," 135–7, *136, 137,* 139, 142,
149, 154
Moore, Julia Compton, 142
Moorer, Thomas, 467, 470, 501, 511
Moratorium to End the War in Vietnam, 426, 431,
518
November march of, 438, *438,* 440, 519–20
October march of, 427, *427,* 440, 520
Morel-Fatio, Antoine Léon, *6*
Morrison, Jim, 567
Morse, Gerald "Ghost Rider," 235, *235,* 236, 238
Morse, Wayne, 106, 182
Municipal Theater, *16*
Murphy, Major, 265
Musgrave, John, 156–7, *157,* 203–4, 212, 214, 216,
217, *217,* 218, 220–1, 229–30, 233–4,
238–40, *238, 239,* 443–4, *443,* 454, 478,
480, 481, 483, 502, 565, 583
Muskie, Edmund, 501, 506
My Lai massacre, *383,* 431–7, *432, 437,* 438, 472–3,
473
My Son, *119*
"My Son" (song), 338
My Tho, *61,* 255, 277–9, 388

NAACP, 191
Nagasaki, atomic bombing of, 47
Nakayama, Jim, 139
Nam Dinh, 186
Nam Ho Province, *316*
napalm, 58, *64,* 74, 137, 504, *504,* 518
Nashville, Tenn., 301
National Assembly, South Vietnamese, 3, 21, 70, 387,
422, 425, 487, 488, 489, *529,* 551
National Farmers Union, 298
National Guard, 160, 301, 317, 329, 404, 454, 456
in Kent State killings, 449–51, *449, 450, 451,*
453

nationalist conflicts, JFK on, 90–1
National League of Families of American Prisoners and
Missing in Southeast Asia, 423
National Liberation Front (NLF), xvii, *xix,* 57, 59,
63, 67, 71, *73,* 74, 75, *76, 77,* 78, 85, 86,
91, 92, 103, 110, 117, 119, 123, 124, 134,
140, 143, 147, 148, 154, 159, 163, *165,* 169,
170, 171, 175, 178, 186–7, 191, *196,* 197,
209, 211, 223, 232, 236, 237, 245, 250, 251,
260, 266, *269, 275,* 276, 278, *278,* 284, 286,
296, 308, *315,* 320, 321, 324, 326, 327, 328,
328, 330, 336, *342,* 343, 345, 356, 357, 363,
370, 385, 387, 398, 399–400, *400,* 406, *406,*
425, 436, 459, 460, 470, 490, 509, 510, 511,
521, 563
areas under control of, 194, 224, 255, 293, 342,
360
casualty rates of, 176
in coordinated attacks, 224
defectors from, 62, 69, 342
early defeats of, 60–2
in fighting with ARVN after U.S. withdrawal,
525–7
formation of, 43
growing power of, 100, 114, 125
infrastructure of, 340, 341, 386, 388, 503
Main Force of, *see* Main Force (NLF)
in mass murders of Hue civilians, 288, *289*
in Mini-Tet attacks, *307, 308,* 309–10
North Vietnamese supplying of, 155, 176
Paris negotiations and, 339, 347, 349, 352
part-time militias of, 54, 73, 127
as POWs, *487*
RAND study of, 164–6
Regional Force of, 54, 196, 340, 342, 417
in runup to Tet Offensive, 255, *255, 256,* 264–5,
265
in Tet Offensive, 267–71, *268, 271,* 273, *273,*
274–5, 277, *277,* 279, 290, *313*
Tet Offensive casualties of, 292
villagers' support for, 128–9, *189,* 340, 341
261st Regional Battalion of, 72–3
514th Provincial Battalion of, 72
National Mobilization Committee to End the War in
Vietnam ("the Mobe"), 191, 438, 440, 454
National Naval Medical Center, 423
National Police, South Vietnamese, 267, 274, 291,
360
National Political Congress, South Vietnamese (1966),
170
National Press Club, 246
National Security Action Memorandum (NSAM)
263, 92
National Security Action Memorandum (NSAM)
273, 92
National Security Agency (NSA), 349, 458
National Security Council, 26, 78, 91, 93, 114, 196,
293, 347, 397, 467, *560*
National Urban League, 190
Nation of Islam, 163, 409
Native Americans, 244, *244*
Navy Cross, 368
Navy, U.S., *51,* 108, 115, 156, 160, 176, 178, 182,
211, 212, 221, 238, 285, 287, 318, 329, 356,
364, 443, *473,* 480, 496, *499,* 524, 538, 544,
558, 560
Navy SEALS, U.S., 278, 585
NBC, 148, 233, 274, 275, 296, 478

NBC Nightly News, 396

Nebraska, 310

Nebraska, University of, 231, 444, 517

Negroponte, John, 106, 113–14, 510, 511, 512

Ness, Stuart, 412

Nessen, Ron, *560*

Newark, N.J., 301

Newfield, Jack, 310, 332, 334

New Hampshire Democratic primary, 247, *247,* 296, 297

New Mexico, 349

New Orleans, La., 548, 567, 570

Newport Harbor, 549

New Republic, 26

New Saigon Mini Market, 568

Newsweek, 62, 296, 310, 410, *473,* 477

New York, N.Y., *xxi,* 41, 108–9, 190, 191, *191,* 194, 301, 310, *500,* 517

   antiwar protests in, 120, *121,* 304

   hard-hat attack on antiwar marchers in, 456–7, *457*

New York Building and Construction Trades Council, 456

New Yorker, 223, 360, *399,* 489, 501

New York Herald Tribune, 83, 123, 128

New York Post, 456

New York Times, 42, 58, 62, *63,* 86, 91, 171, 185, 186, 222, 232, 263, 296, 301, 304, 321, 323, *334,* 369, 393, 405, 416, 440, 483, 484, *484,* 485, 511, 538

New York University, 456

New Zealand, 147

Nghe An Province, 4, 44, 424, 461

Ngo Dinh Can, 37

Ngo Dinh Diem, xii, *32, 37, 40,* 47, 54, 58, 60, *62,* 69, 70, 72, 74, *85,* 101, 102, 109, 168, 171, 224, 308, 356, 360, 363, 487, 488, 512

   assassination attempts against, 68

   brutal regime of, 38, 40, 41, 43, 73, 81

   Buddhists and, 78, *79,* 80–1, 83, *83,* 84

   Catholicism of, 32, 46

   coup plots against, 43, 81, 85–6, 90, 92, 93, 94, 102, 147

   in departure from Indochina, 48–9

   early years of, 32, 44–6

   growing U.S. disenchantment with, 81, 83–5

   Ho Chi Minh compared to, 44, 46, 49

   Japanese aid sought by, 47

   Mansfield's report on, 71

   murder of, 86, *86,* 89, *89,* 92, 100

   1963 coup of, 109

   popular image of, 44

   proclaimed president of South Vietnam, 37, 49

   in referendum victory over Bao Dai, 36–7, *38*

   reunification vote rejected by, 41, 49

   student protests against, 83

   U.S. ambivalence toward, 32, 36, 56

   U.S. press and, 62–3

   U.S. support of, 40–1, 42, 49, 53, 91

Ngo Dinh Diem Road, 38

Ngo Dinh Kha, 46, 48

Ngo Dinh Luyen, 37

Ngo Dinh Nhu, 37–8, 43, 49, 53, 60, 62–3, 71, 78, 83, *83,* 84, 85, *86,* 363

   murder of, 86, *86,* 89, *89,* 93

Ngo Dinh Thuc, 37, 46, 78, 80, 85

Ngo family, 74

Ngo Quang Truong, 280

Nguyen Cao Ky, xiii, 86, 125, *146,* 147, 149, 168, 169, 170–2, *172,* 196, *221, 251,* 268, 273, 274, 363, 387, *486,* 487

   in 1967 presidential election, *223,* 224

   in 1971 presidential election, 488, 489

Nguyen Chanh Thi, 168–9, 170

Nguyen Duc Mau, 462

Nguyen dynasty, 6, 7, 10, 13, 32, 44, 46, 280

Nguyen Hoang Bridge, 281

Nguyen Khanh, 86, 101–2, *103,* 110, 116, 147

Nguyen Ngoc, xiii, 42, 206–7, 288, 587

Nguyen Ngoc Loan, 171, 274

Nguyen Nguyet Anh, 376–8, *377, 378,* 380–1

Nguyen Quang Khue, 380

Nguyen Tai, 273, 508–9, *509,* 557, 562, 563

Nguyen Thanh Son, 240, *241,* 243

Nguyen Thanh Tung, 308–9, *308,* 562

Nguyen Thi Hoa, 286–7

Nguyen Thi Hoa, Mrs., 209, *209,* 279

Nguyen Van Bay, 177, *177*

Nguyen Van Hinh, 36, 418

Nguyen Van Hoang, 209

Nguyen Van Hung, 314–15

Nguyen Van Lem, 274

Nguyen Van Mo, 185

Nguyen Van Nho, 111–12

Nguyen Van Thieu, xiii, 86, 125, *146,* 147, 149, 168, 169, 170, *221,* 251, 266, 267, 270, 273, 339, 340, 343, *347,* 363, 366, 386, 400, 403, 459, *486, 487,* 491, 500, 503, 508, 512, 513, 530, 534, *534,* 538, 545, 573

   after U.S. withdrawal, 525–6, 527, 528

   and ARVN collapse, 531

   elected South Vietnamese president, *223,* 224

   growing opposition to, 528–9, *529*

   and Laos invasion, 468, 477

   Nixon's meeting with, 397–9, *397*

   North Vietnam's insistence on removal of, 487

   Paris negotiations and, 345, 347–8, 349, 350, 351–2, 360, 387, 510–11

   resignation and flight of, 546, 548

   in rigged presidential election, 487–9, *488*

   South Vietnamese army expanded by, 321

Nguyen Van Tong, 111, 112, 113, 292

Nguyen, Viet Thanh, 566–71

Nha Trang, 266, 538, *538,* 546

Nhu, Madame, 63

Nicolson, Harold, 3

Night Hunter program, 356–7

19th parallel, 347

Ninh Tuan Province, *57*

Ninth Infantry Division, 267, 292, 356, *357,* 360, 389, *389,* 408

   Sixtieth Infantry Regiment, Third Battalion, 403

Ninth NLF Division, 188

Nixon, Pat, 364

Nixon, Richard M., xii, 43, *53,* 83, 328, *351,* 352, *352,* 356, 360, 364–7, 386, 393, 396, 403, 408, 416, 421–2, 423, 443, 445, 455, 457, *460,* 461, *473,* 477–8, 479, 483, *483,* 484–7, 489, 494–5, *499,* 506, 525, 526–7, *528, 529,* 534, 548, 585

   antiwar movement and, 364, 369, 438, 440, 446, 454, 456, 458–9, 460, 518, 519–20

   bombing halt and ceasefire ordered by, 459

   Cambodia bombing ordered by, 369

   Cambodia invasion ordered by, 446–9, 454, 467

   elected president, 351

   "enemies" obsession of, 485

   expanded bombing campaign and, 500–1, 503

   inauguration of, 364

   Laos invasion and, 467, 468–70, 477

   LBJ peace efforts thwarted by, 345, *345,* 347–51, *347,* 485

   My Lai Massacre and, 436–7

   in 1968 presidential race, 301, 322–4, *323,* 329, 336, 338, 345, *345,* 347–51, *347,* 349, 397

   1970 election and, 459–60

   in 1972 presidential race, 507–8, 510, 511, 520

   opening to China of, 491, 493

   Paris negotiations and, 420–1, 512

   peace agreement announced by, 512–13

   public opinion and, 430–1, 456, 477, 501

   resignation of, 528, *529*

   secret taping system installed by, 477

   Thieu's meeting with, 397–9, *397*

   troop withdrawals ordered by, 397–9, *399,* 417, 425, 427, 430, 447, 494, 520

   U.S. credibility as priority of, 365, 430

   Vietnam herbicide operations canceled by, 406

   Watergate scandal and, 526

   withdrawal proposal of, 387

Nixon administration, 427, 481, 506, 519, 526

   POWs and, 423

   "Vietnamization" policy of, 365, 398, *399,* 404, 417, 425, 430, 445, 447, 461, 467, 477, 486, 500, 503, 520

Nolting, Fredrick, 53, 71, 83, 84

North Africa, 18, *31,* 91, 290

North Atlantic Treaty Organization (NATO), 24–5

North Carolina, *203,* 305

Northern Highlands, 47

North Korea, 25, 26, 276, 277

North Vietnam, 47, 48

   August offensive of, 321

   "Big Battles" strategy of, 100, 125, 140, 206

   big offensives strategy abandoned by, 387

   in Binh Dinh campaign, 149–50

   Catholic exodus from, 32, *35*

   "Christmas Bombing" (1972) of, 511–12

   clandestine sabotage raids in, 100, 103

   combined offensives ordered by, 206–7

   draft in, 314–15

   Easter Offensive (1972) of, 493–6, *493,* 498–501, 503, 511, 530

   first U.S. air strike on, 105–6

   French withdrawal from, 32

   "General Offensive, General Uprising" strategy of, 100, 206, 209, 255, 268, 276, 307, 310, 508

   Geneva Accords and, 49

   land-reform policies of, 41, 118

   negotiations rejected by, 146, 221

   Ninth Party Plenum in, 100–1

   NLF controlled by, 43

   NLF supported by, 155

   and Paris peace negotiations, *see* Paris peace negotiations

   political dynamic of, xii

   in preliminary negotiations with U.S., 304–5, 321

   purges in, 207

   rebuilding efforts in, 41

   soldiers' return to, 578

   Soviet and Chinese aid to, *62,* 125, 184, 214, 493, 500, 503

   strategy debate in, 100–1

   Tet Offensive of, *see* Tet Offensive

North Vietnam (continued)
   U.S. bombing of, 115, 118, 122, 124, 125, 142,
      143, 146, 176–8, *182,* 184–6, 206, 297, 495,
      499, 500–1, 503, 519
   U.S. ground troop commitment as inspiration to,
      119
   U.S. POWs in, 178–9, 182–3, *182, 183*
   U.S. retaliatory airstrikes on, 108, 114–15
   U.S. withdrawal demanded by, 123
North Vietnamese army (NVA, PAVN), xiii, 150, 167,
     201, 214, 217, 227, 236, 238, 239, 310, *313,*
     321, *325,* 328, 367, 370–1, 398, 462, 490
   in advance on Saigon, 534–6, 538, 541–2, *541*
   casualty rates of, 176
   in combined offensives, 206–7, 224, 240
   disease in, *314,* 316
   in fighting after U.S. withdrawal, 525–7, *525, 526*
   in final assault on Saigon, 549, *549,* 562, *565*
   in final offensive, 530, 531, *531,* 533–6, *533*
   in I Corps zone, 214
   Group 599 of, *375*
   Ia Drang campaign of, 132, 134–7, *135,* 139–40,
     142, 157
   in Laos, *469, 471*
   resupply of, 155, 176, 503
   South infiltrated by, 101, 106, 110, 114, 125, 131,
     142, 166, 209, 255, 314–16, 341, 461, 467,
     470–1, 493
   in Tet attack on Hue, 279, 280–1
   Tet Offensive casualties of, 292
   weariness and low morale in, 412, *412*
   Third Regiment, 414
   Tenth Division, 461, 463
   Twenty-fourth Regiment, 461
   Twenty-ninth Regiment, 390
   Twenty-seventh Glorious Youth Brigade, 424
   Sixty-sixth Regiment, 131
   174th Regiment, 240
   559th Transportation Group, 155
Northwestern University, 231, 336, 353, 453–4, *454,*
    455
Nugent, Luci Johnson, *332*
Nung people, 14
nurses, 384–6
Nyuyen Thi Binh, Madame, 400

Oakland, Calif., 301
O'Brien, Greg, *319*
O'Brien, Kathy, *319*
O'Brien, Tim, 318–19, *319,* 431, 433, 451, 473
Ochs, Phil, 232
Office of Strategic Services (OSS), *14,* 15, *15,* 16,
    17–19, *20, 21*
Ogan, Russell, *513*
Oglesby, Carl, 121
Ohio, 449, 456
Okamoto, Vincent, xii, 305, *305,* 307, 324–5, *325,*
    326, 327, 328, *328,* 340–1, 408, 411, 578,
    583
Okinawa, battle of, 203
Okinawa, USS, 544
101st Airborne Division, U.S., 109, 235, 390, *390,*
    393
   First Brigade, 131, *131, 236*
   187th Infantry Regiment, Third Battalion, 391,
     393
   327th Infantry Regiment, First Battalion, 234,
     235–8, *235, 236, 237*

173rd Airborne Brigade Combat Team, U.S., *xv,* 123,
    129, *188,* 199, 216, 240–1, *241,* 244, 245,
    303, 463
   Second Battalion, *xv,* 198, 240–1, *241,* 243–5, *243*
    Company A, 159–60, 173, 198–9, 240, 241,
     243
    Company C, 198–9
199th Light Infantry Brigade, U.S., *260*
Operation Babylift, 540, *541*
Operation Bald Mariner, *357*
Operation Beefup, 58, 60, 68
Operation Buffalo, 217, 218, 230
Operation Cedar Falls, 186–7, *187,* 188
Operation Chaos, 459
Operation Delaware Valley, 391
Operation Dewey Canyon, 391
Operation Dewey Canyon II, 467
Operation Dewey Canyon III, 478
Operation Duc Than 1 (Operation Victory 1), 72–8
Operation Frequent Wind, 544, 552, 553, 561
Operation Game Warden, 155
Operation Hawthorne, 173, *236*
Operation Kingfisher, *218,* 219–20, *220,* 225
Operation Lam Son 719, *465,* 467–70, *467, 469,*
    471, *471,* 474, *474,* 476–8, *476*
Operation Lam Son 917, 494
Operation Linebacker, 501, 502, 503
Operation Linebacker II, 511–12
Operation MacArthur, 240
Operation Market Time, 155, 538
Operation Masher/White Wing, *145,* 149–50, *150,*
    152–4, *153,* 166, 175
Operation Neutralize, 227
Operation Niagara, 257, 263–4
Operation Passage to Freedom, 32, *35*
Operation Prairie, 214, *214*
Operation Rolling Thunder, 115, 118, 186
Operations Mission, U.S., 69
Operation Speedy Express, 356, *357, 360,* 389
Operation Sunrise, 62
Operation Wheeler, 235, *237*
Orange County, Calif., 567
Oregon, 310
Ortiz-Rivera, Luis, 322
Ovnand, Charles, 42
Oxford University, 319, *319,* 367

Pac Bo, 14, *15*
Pace University, 456
pacification, 128–9, 147, 196–7, *196,* 247, 293, 320,
    340–2, 356, 365, 386, 388, 389, 398, 408,
    548
Pakistan, 23
Panama Canal Zone, 353
Panamaroff, Lieutenant, 481
Pan American Airlines, 540
Panmunjom, 276
Paris, 3–4, *3,* 10, 13, 19, 21, 24, *35,* 36, 45, 70, 91,
    303–4, *303*
Paris Accords (1973), 509, *524, 525,* 543
Paris By Night (variety show), 568
Paris Peace Conference (1919), *3,* 330
Paris peace negotiations, 304, 321, 338, 339, 343,
    345, 347, 349, 350, 352, 360, 366, 387, 397,
    399, 400, 420–1, 430, 467, 478, 493, 500,
    507, 508, 512
   Kissinger's secret talks in, 398, 421, 445–6, 486,
     489, 510–11

Parris Island, S.C., 157, *163*
Parrot's Beak, 448
Password (TV show), 216
Pather Lao, 91
Patton (film), 447
Patton, General, 496
Peace Corps, 57, 507
Pearl Harbor, Japanese attack on, 442, 444
Pearson, Drew, 277
Peers, Samuel, 473
Peers, William R., 437, *437*
Pennsylvania, 567
Pentagon, 230, 336, 438, 480
   October 21, 1967, march on, 232–4, *232, 233*
   see also Defense Department, U.S.
Pentagon Papers, 195, 483–5, *484,* 487, 520
People's Anti-Corruption Movement, 528
People's Army of Vietnam (PAVN), *see* North
    Vietnamese Army
Pepper, William, 190
Perfume River, 279, 281, *282,* 288
Perkins, Jack, *330*
Peter, Paul, and Mary, 232
Peterson, Pete, 585
Pham Duy Tat, 531, 533, 562, 573
Pham Quoc Nam, 308
Pham Quoc Trung, 308
Pham Van, *342*
Pham Van Dong, 400, 417–18, *421, 422,* 427
Pham Van Tam, 308
Phan Boi Chau, 10
Phan Chu Trinh, 44, 45
Phan Huy Quat, 116
Phan Quang Dan, 70, *70,* 83, 86, 275
Phan Quang Tue, xiii, 70, *70,* 83, 86, 275, 363,
    547–8
Phan Rang, 57, 546
Philadelphia, Pa., *310*
Philippines, 16, 53, 147, 288, 546, 547, 566, 569,
    570
Phillips, Kevin, 338
Phillips, Rufus, 69, 563
Phnom Penh, 544
   Khmer Rouge capture of, 545, *545*
Phoenix Program, 340–2, *343,* 363, 386, 388
Phu Bai, *239,* 265, 281, 290
Phu Loi, 187
Phuoc Long, 530, 542
Phuoc Tuy, 110
Pilgrim State Hospital, 384
"Pinkville," 431, 473
Pittsburgh Courier, 191
Plain of Reeds, 72, 77
Playboy, 230, 265
Pleiku, *115,* 266, 384, *384,* 386, 494, 531, 533
   NLF attack on, 114
Plei Mei, *135*
   siege of, 132–3, *133,* 134, *134,* 175
"Plumbers," 485, 520
Pocket Guide to Vietnam, A, 203
Podgorny, Nikolai, *491,* 493
Polgar, Thomas, 538, 545, 548, 557
Politiburo, North Vietnamese, 534, 575
Pol Pot, 576
Poolaw, Pascal Cleatus, Sr., 244, *244*
Popular Forces, South Vietnamese, 196, 211, 340,
    342, 370, 417
Porcella, Steve, 248

Port Jefferson–North Shore Record, 441
Powell, Colin, 411
Powell, Gary, 369, 370, 371, *371*
Preachey, William N., 476
Presidential Palace, Saigon, xi, 43, 83, *89,* 271, 276, *534,* 542, *551,* 562, *563*
    Tet attack on, 269
Presidential Unit Citation, *236*
Prison Camp One, 250
prisoners of war, NLF, *487*
prisoners of war, U.S., 178–9, 182–3, *182, 183,* 310, 321–2, 355–6, 512
    malnourishment and disease of, 470
    moved to Hanoi, 470–1
    Nixon administration and, 423
    return of, 513, *513,* 524
Prisoners of War/Missing in Action Task Force, *513*
"Project 100,000," 163–4
Project Commando Sabre ("Misty"), 372–3, *373,* 380–1
provincial forces, South Vietnamese, 495
Provisional Revolutionary Government (PRG), 400–1, *400, 445,* 459, 488, 510, 511, 527
public opinion
    on antiwar movement, 336
    Calley verdict and, 472–3
    Nixon and, 430–1, 456, 477, 501
    Tet Offensive and, 291–2
    Vietnam War and, 146–7, 149, 172, 194, 221, 247, 296, 310, 321, 386, 393, 395, 459, 477, 483
Pueblo, USS, North Korean seizure of, 276
Pulitzer Prize, *275,* 504
Purdy, Mark, 569
Purple Heart, *239,* 481, *483*

Quakers, 161, *366*
Quang Binh Province, *313,* 530
Quang Duc, Thich, self-immolation by, *79,* 81
Quang Duc Province, 160
Quang Nai Province, 206
Quang Nam Province, 235, 404
Quang Ngai Province, 356, 431, 538
Quang Tri Province, 219, 390, *493,* 494, 498, 499, 510, *513, 575*
Quantico Marine Corps Base, 231, 302
Quick Kill Reaction Course, *203*
Qui Nhon, 114, 149, *150,* 256, 266, 538
Quint, Bert, 246

race riots, 221, 301–2, *302, 303*
racism, 163
    in U.S. military, 408–9
Radboon, Vallop, *150*
Radio Hanoi, 178, 255, 301, 314, 355, 424, 502, 546
Radio Saigon, 265, 308, 314
Ramparts, 190, *191*
RAND Corporation, 164–6, 271, 406, 483, 527
Rather, Dan, 478
Rauch, Rudolph, 498
Reader's Digest, 40, 518
Reagan, Ronald, 323, 507
rear-echelon support (REMFs), 326–7, *327*
Red Cross, 250, 334, 456
Red River, 425
Red River Delta, 6, 7, 14, 15
REMFs, 326–7, *327*

Remington, Tom, 243
"Report from Vietnam" (CBS report), 290–1
Republican National Committee, 58
Republican National Convention, of 1972, 507
Republican Party, Republicans, 40, 93, 126, 301, 322, 323, *323,* 329, *335,* 338, 347–8, *347,* 349, 459, 460, 506, 507, 520
Resolution 15, 42
Resor, Stanley R., 403
Reston, James, 58, 323, 416, 417, 430, 511
Réunion Island, 566
Reuters, *76, 78*
"Revisionist Anti-Party Affair," 207
Revolutionary Youth League of Vietnam, 5
Revolution Path, The (Ho Chi Minh), 5
Rhodes, Jim, 450
Ridenhour, Ronald, 436, *437*
Ridgeway, Matthew, *299*
Risner, Robert, *182*
Rivers, L. Mendel, 276
Rivers, Mendel, 146
Riverside Church (Manhattan), 190
Robb, Charles, 338
Robb, Linda Johnson, *332*
Robinson, Jackie, 191
Rockefeller, Nelson, 323, 345, 507
Rockefeller Foundation, 53
Rockpile, 212
Rogers, William, 364, 425, 467, 484–5
Rome, University of, 303
Romney, George, 323
Roosevelt, Franklin Delano, 16, 98
Rostow, Walt Whitman, 53, 56, *246, 273,* 276, *293, 299,* 351
ROTC, 353
Route 1, *493,* 541
Route 9, 307, 477
Route 559, *see* Ho Chi Minh Trail
Route 606, *218,* 219
Roxbury, Mass., 156, 218, *218,* 302
Royal Thai Army, 490
Royko, Mike, 330
Rubin, Jerry, 230, 232, 440
Rudd, Mark, *304*
Rumsfeld, Donald, *560*
Rusk, Dean, 53, 56, 81, 94–5, 98, 120, *125,* 126, *127,* 171, 234, *246, 273,* 275, 276, *293, 294,* 296, 298, *299,* 321, 345, 350, 351
Russell, Bertrand, 178
Russell, Richard, 115–16, 183
Russia, 516
Russo, Anthony, 483

Sacramento, Calif., 569
Safer, Morley, 127–8, *127,* 290, 326
Safire, William, 351
Saigon (Ho Chi Minh City), 4, 7, *8, 10,* 15, 17, *17, 18,* 20, *20,* 26, *32,* 35, *35, 37, 38,* 44, 54, 56, 59, 60, *62, 63,* 69, 70, *79,* 84, 92, 106, 109, 113–14, 119, 142, 164, *169, 196,* 206, 218, *221,* 224, *265,* 281, 321, 410, *410, 474, 488,* 510, *523,* 527, 543
    bank run in, 546
    bar girls and prostitutes in, 361, *361*
    black market in, 361–2, *363*
    Brinks Hotel bombing in, 110, *110*
    Buddhist protests in, 80, 81, *83,* 170
    Caravelle Hotel in, 290

    Cercle Sportif in, 267
    Citadel of, *6*
    criminal cartel in, 32, 36
    evacuation of "high-risk" South Vietnamese allies from, 546–9, *547,* 553, 555–6, 561, 566–7
    fall of, xi, 462, 549, *549,* 551–3, 555–61, 562, *565*
    final NVA advance on, 534–6, 538, 541–2, *541, 565*
    French-Vietnamese conflict in, 18–19
    Mini-Tet attacks in, *307, 308,* 309–10
    1963 coup in, 86
    political corruption in, 37
    population explosion in, 361
    Presidential Palace in, xi, 43, 83, *89,* 269, 271, 276, *534,* 542, *551,* 562, *563*
    refugees in, *307,* 310, 361, *361*
    renamed Ho Chi Minh City, 563
    rioting in, 122
    Tan Son Nhut airport of, *see* Tan Son Nhut Airport
    Tet Offensive in, 257, 264, 267–71, *268, 270, 271,* 273, *273,* 274–5, 276, *277,* 279, 290, 292, 308, 524
    U.S. embassy in, 36, 58, 80, 113, 245–6, 269–70, *270, 271*
    U.S. evacuation of, 536, 538, 540, 544, 545, 548–9, 551–3, *551, 553,* 555–63, *558*
Saigon Mission Council, 119
Saigon River, 26, 58, 155, 542, 548
Saigon Times, 399
Saigon University, 116
St. Patrick's Cathedral, 310
St. Paul, Minn., 451
Salisbury, Harrison, *185,* 186
Salt Lake City, Utah, 338
Sam Son, 118
San Antonio, Tex., 298
Sanchez, Mando, 454
Sanders, Robert, 303
San Francisco, Calif., *230, 345,* 517, 540, *541*
San Jose, Calif., 460, *460,* 567, 568
Santana, 404
Saratoga Springs, N.Y., 98, 109, *123,* 173, 174, 199
Saratogian, 173
Sarraut, Albert, 4, *6,* 45
Savage, Ernie, 135
Saxbe, William, 511
Scanlon, James, 60, 61, *61,* 68, 74, 75–6, *76,* 77
Schakne, Robert, 290
Schell, Jonathan, 423
Schlesinger, James, 545
School of the Colonies, 45
Schurtz, Eugene, Jr., 415–16
Scott, George C., 447
Scowcroft, Brent, 557, *560*
Scranton, William, 455
Scranton Commission, 455
Scruggs, Jan, 581, *581*
Sealift Command, U.S., 548
Seattle, Wash., 403, *403,* 567
Second Armored Regiment, U.S., 60, *61*
II Field Force, U.S., 360, *360,* 389
Secret Service, U.S., 329, 454, 477
Security Index, 519
Seeger, Pete, 438
Selective Service, 160
Self-Defense Corps, South Vietnamese, 41

Senate, U.S., 26, 91, 106, 115, 245, 296, 349, 427, 431, 447, 459, 460, 468, 528, 548–9
    Armed Services Committee of, 183
    Foreign Relations Committee of, 146, *148,* 296, 480, *481,* 544
Seoul, 276
17th parallel, 31, 32, 42, 49, 95
Seventh Air Force, U.S., 268, 495, 528
Seventh Fleet, U.S., 149, 155, 186, 285, 461, *499,* 528, 555
71st Evacuation Hospital, U.S., 384, *384,* 440–2
Shade, George, 221, 230
Shaplen, Robert, *223,* 360, 363, *399,* 489
Sharp, Ulysses S. Grant, 104
Sheehan, Neil, 58–9, 62, 63, *63,* 68, 71, 77, 81, 84, 100, 137, 139, 153, 171–2, 296, 300, 361, 363, 418, 436, 483, 484, 485
Shriver, Sargent, 507
Sihanouk, Norodom, 155
Sihanouk, Prince, 446, 544
Sihanouk Trail, 155
Sihanoukville, 155
Silverman, Burton, *334*
Silver Star, 244, 260, 282, 286, 335, 404, 481, *483*
Singapore, 540, 569
Sixth Fleet, 24
Sly and the Family Stone, 404
Smeal, Bob, 481
Smith, George W., 285
Smith, Hedrick, 296
Smith, Homer, 552
Smith, Jack, 139–40
Smith, Wayne, 408–9
Smyser, Richard, *560*
Snepp, Frank, 508, 509, 536, 538, 542, 545, 546–7, 548, 551, 557
Socialist Party, French, 4, *5*
Socialist Workers Party, 438
Song Be, 240
Song Chang River Valley, 413
Songchang Valley, 416
Song Ve Valley, 235
Sontag, Susan, 502
So Proudly We Hail! (film), 384
Sorensen, Carl, *150*
Sorley, Lewis, 565, 582
South Carolina, *163,* 518
South China Sea, 38, 115, 155, 178, 211, 373, 401, 535, 544, 557, 566
South Dakota, 310
Southeast Asia, xi, 26, 40, 43, 47, 58, 68, 71, 84, 90, 106, 108, 122, 124, 147, 175, 176, 194, 240, 245, 365, 408, 416, 449, 480, 481, 566, 567, 570, 576
    "domino theory" and, 27, 91, 94, 148, 519
Southern California, University of, 516
South Korea, 25, 154, 276
South Korean army, in Vietnam War, 147, 149
South Vietnam, 569
    additional U.S. aid to, 511
    anti-Diem assassinations in, 43
    assassination of officials in, 43
    communist "regroupees" in return tp, *40,* 42–3
    communist victories in, 54–5
    corruption in, 360, 361, 527
    deteriorating situation in, 90, 95, 100, 101, 125, 168
    Diem proclaimed president of, 37, 49

economic collapse of, 527
French in, 32
French withdrawal from, 36
Geneva Accords and, 49
government instability in, 360
Kennedy's refusal to send ground troops to, 56
Khanh regime in, 101–3
lack of stable government in, 321
political corruption in, 36–7, 43, 68
presidential election in, *221, 222,* 223–4, *223*
prisoner exchanges in, *513*
refugees flight from, 546, *554*
refugees in, 32, 187, *187,* 356, 431, 503, 536, *536,* 538
succession of coups in, 116, 125, 147
tactical zones in, 211, *211*
U.S. advisers to, 103
U.S. aid to, 36, 40, 49
U.S. anticommunist policy toward, 32, 40, 43
U.S. civilian advisers in, 41
U.S. civilian volunteers in, 57
U.S. military aid to, 56, 417
U.S. support of, 92
I Corps tactical zone of, 168–9, 171, 194, 211, *211,* 212, 214, 257, 267, 548
II Corps tactical zone of, 132–3, 211
III Corps tactical zone of, 211, 279
IV Corps tactical zone of, 211, 363
South Vietnamese air force, 417
South Vietnamese army (ARVN), *25,* 49, *51, 54, 56, 57, 60, 62, 63, 64,* 73, *73, 75, 76, 76,* 77, 78, 80, 84, 86, 100, 101–2, 127, *134,* 147, 149, 150, 154, 169, *169, 170,* 171, 172, 173, 186, 187, 188, 197, *197,* 206, 209, 223, 237, 240, 246, 255, *260,* 265, 279, 285, 296, 300, 307, 308, 310, 329, 341, 363, 388, 393, 410, *411, 437, 445,* 463, 494–5, 504, 511, *513, 523,* 548, 552, *573,* 585
    Abrams's focus on improved training for, 418–19
    in battle with Binh Xuyen, 36, *37*
    in Cambodia invasion, *447,* 459
    collapse of, 530, 531, 533, 534–6, 538, 540–1, *547,* 549, 556, 562–3
    in continued fighting after U.S. withdrawal, 525–7, *525, 526*
    corruption in, 419, 527
    in defense of Xuan Loc, 542, 546
    desertions from, 125, 292
    early victories of, 59–62, 68
    expansion of, 321, 361, 417, 430
    guerilla attacks on, 43
    lack of fuel and ammunition in, 529
    in Laos invasion, *465,* 467–70, *467, 469,* 471, *471, 474, 474,* 476–8, *476,* 486, *486,* 493
    low morale in, 527
    in 1963 coup, 86, *89,* 109
    as reluctant to engage enemy, 71, 72, 122, 419
    surrender of, 562
    Tet Offensive and, 264, 266, 267, 269, 273, 277–8, *277,* 280–2, *284,* 287
    U.S. advisers to, 56, 58, 67–8, 89, 91, 109, 114, 489–91, 495, 503
    U.S. military aid to, 71, *419*
    U.S. training of, 41
South Vietnamese Army (ARVN), units
    Airborne Brigade, 43
    Armored Command, 269
    Military Security Service of, 548

Provincial Reconnaissance Units, 341, *343*
Rangers, 58, 110, 132, *134,* 257, 495, 498, 531, 533, 562
Special Forces, 38, 83, 132
First Division, 168, 280, 390, 420, 468
    Hac Bao (Black Panther) Company, 280–1, 286, 468, 535
Second Armored Cavalry Regiment, 74
    Fourth Mechanized Rifle Squadron, 74
Second Regiment, 468
    Second Battalion, 468
Fourth Corps, 72
Fifth Division, 495, 498
Seventh Division, 60, 61, 71, 72, 74, 255, 277
Eleventh Division, *239*
Eighteenth Division, 419, 495, 542
    Forty-eighth Regiment, 490
Twenty-first Division, 67
Twenty-second Division, 419, 461
Twenty-third Division, 461
South Vietnamese Marines, *89,* 119, 171, *493, 535, 536*
    Fourth Battalion ("Killer Sharks") of, 109, 110–13, *111, 113,* 562
South Vietnamese militias, 132
South Vietnamese navy, 417
Soviet Union, 16–17, 21, *27,* 28, 45, 46, 47, 49, 52, 53, 84, 94, 106, 115, 143, 148, 155, 177, 178, 194, 207, 216, 221, 224, 255, 276, 293, 300, 314, 335, 364, 369, 399, 401, 478, 485, 501, 503, 510, 567, 569, 575, 576, 585
    aid to North Vietnam by, 125, *493,* 500, 503
    China's rift with, 41
    containment of, as U.S. policy, 24–5
    expansionism of, 17
    First Indochina War and, 48
    military aid to North Vietnam by, 214
    negotiations urged by, 512
    North Vietnam and, *491*
    North Vietnam supplied by, 184
    North Vietnam urged to adopt cautious approach by, 100
    Paris negotiations and, 352
    U.S. relations with, 71, 366, 491, *491,* 493, 508
    Vietnam negotiations urged by, 206, 301
    World War II deaths in, 17
Spanish Civil War, 118
Special Forces, U.S. (Green Berets), 58, 122, 132, *133, 135,* 186, 198, 220, 240, 372, 518
Spellman, Francis, 32
Spock, Benjamin, 190, 191, 232, 506
Stalin, Joseph, 17, 28, 45
Stanford University, 426
Stanton, Frank, 128
Stars and Stripes, 218, 233, 236, 416
State Department, U.S., 17, 53, 58, 62, 80, 85, 124, 146, 196, 224, 299, 449, 483, 519
State of the Union address, 98
Stills, Stephen, *405*
Stirm, Robert L., *513*
Stockdale, Jim, 423
Stockdale, Sybil, 423
Stockton, Calif., 569
Stone, Dick, 174
Stone, Oliver, 91, 92
Stonewall, Tex., *332*
Stout, Dennis, 234–5
Strategic Arms Limitation Talks (SALT), 366, 494

Strategic Hamlet Program, 60, 62, 63, *66*, 67, 78, 100, 101
"Struggle Movement," 169, *169*
Student Nonviolent Coordination Committee (SNCC), 80, 191
Students for a Democratic Society (SDS), *120*, 121, 304, 426, 450, 519, 521
Sully, François, 62–3
"Summer of Love," 230
Sun Tzu, 14
Supreme Court, South Vietnamese, 488, 489
Supreme Court, U.S., *121*, 163, 447, 480, 485
Swarthmore College, 454
Sympathizer, The (Nguyen), 570

Taiwan, 548
Tallman, Richard J., 498
Tam An, *62*
Tam Ky, 538
Tan Lap, 43
Tan Son Nhut airport, 19, *19*, 231, 267, 268, *269*, 327, 403, 462, 489, 524, *524*, 541, 540, 545, *547*, 548, *551*, 552, 553, *553*, 555, 560, 563
Tan Thanh Tay hamlet, *89*
Tan Thoi, 72, 73, 74
Tan Thoi hamlet, 72
Taylor, Karl, 477
Taylor, Karl, Jr., *477*
Taylor, Kevin, 477
Taylor, Maxwell, 56, 58, 84, 86, 89, 91, 102, 103, 106, 109, 110, 115, *299*
Tay Ninh Province, 54, 463, *525*
Tchepone, 467, 468, 474
teach-ins, 519
television
    Fulbright hearings and, 147, 148–9, *148*
    Vietnam War and, 127–8, *127*, 290–1
    Vietnam War coverage on, 275
Tenth Division, Battalion Two, 461
Tenth NVA Division, 463
Territorial Forces, South Vietnamese, 498, 531, 533
Tet (Lunar New Year celebration), 255, 256, 264, 265, 266, *266*, 267, 269, 360, 369, 494
Tet Offensive, 257, 266–73, 293, *293*, 296, 297, 298, 299, 301, 305, 307, 310, *313*, 319, 320, 364, 367, 387, 388, 431, 474, 530, 558
    as costly failure for North, 292, 314, 321
    in Hue, 279–87, *279*, 290, *291*
    in My Tho, 277–9
    NVA and NLF in runup to, 255, *255*, *256*, 264–5, *265*
    in Saigon, 257, 264, 267–71, *268*, *270*, *271*, 273, *273*, 274–5, 276, *277*, 279, 290, 292, 308, *524*
    U.S. public opinion and, 291–2
Texas A&M University Corps of Cadets, 490
Thac Han River, *513*
Thailand, 26, 27, 115, 147, *150*, 178, 528
Thailand, Gulf of, 6, 544
Thanh Hoa, *501*, 566
Thanh Liem, *207*
Thanksgiving Day fast, 440–2
Theses on the National and Colonial Question (Lenin), 45
Third Force, 100, 166
Third Indochina War, 527
Third Infantry Division, U.S., Thirtieth Regiment, 490

Third Marine Amphibious Force, U.S., 168
Third Marine Division, U.S., 117, *201*, 212, 214, *239*, 257, 463
    Third Regiment, U.S., 154
    Fourth Regiment, U.S., First Battalion, 367–9
    Ninth Regiment, U.S.
        First Battalion, 189, 217–18, *217*, 220–1, 229–30, *229*
        Second Battalion, 189, 218–20, 225, 227, 229, *229*
        Third Battalion, *201*
Third Regional Assistance Command, U.S., 496
Thomas, Allen, Jr., 303, 408
Thomas, Allison, *15*
Thomas, Duff, 173
Thompson, Hugh, Jr., 432, 436, *437*
Thong Nat, *501*
Thoreau, Henry David, 445
"Three Readiness Campaign," 119
"Tiger Force," 234, 235–8, *236*, 237
Time, 58, 109, 317, 386, 477, 498
Timmes, Charles J., 548
Tinh, Captain, *61*
Tobacco Road, 305
Today (TV show), 246
Todd, Jack, 231, *231*, 444–5, *444*
Toilers of the East, University of, 5
Tokyo, 304
Ton Duc Thang, *422*
Tonkin, 7, 12, 14, 17, 21
Tonkin, Gulf of, *105*, *107*, 108, 319, 423
    U.S.-North Vietnamese clashes in, 104–6, 120, 461, 513
    U.S. patrols in, 100
Tonkin Gulf Resolution, 106
Topping, Seymour, 26
Toronto Star, 444
Torres, Reuben, 288
Tou Mong, *236*
Tou Morong, 173
Tran Cong Thang, 376–8, *377*, *378*
Trang Bang, 504, *504*
Tran Hung Dao, *551*
Tran Huu Thanh, 528
Tran Le Xuan "Madame Nhu," 38, 81, 83, *83*, 85, 286
Tran Ngoc Chau, *23*, *25*, 68–9, *69*, 487, 576
Tran Ngoc Hue "Harry Hue," 25, 280–1, 468, 474
Tran Ngoc Toan, 109–10, *109*, 112–13, 119, 562
Tran Thien Khiem, 487, 548
Tran Van Hai, 360
Tran Van Huong, 224, 546, 551
Tran Van Tra, 59
Travis Air Force Base, *513*
Trinh Thi Ngo "Hanoi Hannah," 321
Trinity Church (New York), 456
Tri Quang, Thich, 168, 169–70, *169*, 171, 172
Truman, Harry, xii, 16, 25, 26, 27, *53*, 104, 126, 293, 298
Truman administration, 25, 26, 195
Truong Chinh, 48
Truong Dinh Dzu, 224
Truong Nhu Tang, 400, 401
Truong Son Mountains, 214, *313*, 316, *375*
Truong Thi Nghe, 73
Tru Vuong, *239*
Tufts University, 565
Tulane University, xi, 548

Tully, Lester A., 282
Turkey, 17, 24, 71, 298
Turner, Nick, *76*, *78*
Turner Joy, USS, 104
Tuy Hoa, *533*
Twain, Mark, 347
20th parallel, 298
Twenty-fifth Infantry Division, U.S., 463
    Fourteenth Regiment, Second Battalion, Company A, 354
    Twenty-Seventh Regiment, Second Battalion, 324–5, *325*, 328, *328*
Twenty-sixth Amendment, 520

unexploded ordnance, deaths from, 587
Union Station (Philadelphia), *310*
United Nations, 16, 83, 122, *191*, 194, 569
United Press International (UPI), 58, *63*, 124, 535
United States
    anticommunist policy of, 53, 126
    anticommunist Vietnamese policy of, 32, 40
    containment policy of, 24–5, 148, 293, 300
    and First Indochina War, 22, 24, 26, 27, 48
    Soviet relations with, 71
    Vietnamese refugees in, 566–9, 570
    Vietnam veterans in, 403, *403*, 578, *578*
United States Information Agency, 81, 128, 172, 459, 547
U.S. News & World Report, 233
USO, *327*
U.S. War Crimes in North Vietnam, 178
Ut, Nick, 504, *504*
U Thant, 122

Valdez, Juan, 545, 552, 553, 556, 558, 559–61, *560*
Valenti, Jack, 170–1
Vallely, Thomas John, 404, *404*, 483, 585, 473
Valluy, Jean, 21
Vam Co River, 268, 401
Vance, Cyrus, 246, *299*
Vann, John Paul, 71–2, 73–4, *73*, 76–7, *279*, 363
Van Tien Dung, 530, 531, 534, 542, *565*
Vecchio, Mary Ann, *453*
Vichy France, 12
Viet Cong, *see* National Liberation Front (NLF)
Viet Minh, 13, *14*, 15, 16, *16*, 17, 18, 19, 20, 31, *31*, 32, 35, *42*, *43*, 67, 69, 73, 129, 149, 155, 177, 206, 257, 280, 555, 576
    Chinese aid to, 25, 48, 49
    Diem's campaign against, 38, 41
    in First Indochina War, 21–2, 23, *24*, 25–8, *28*, 48, 49, 424
    founding of, 14, 47
    Soviet aid to, 48, 49
    Soviet recognition of, 25
Vietnam, China's conflicted history with, 6
Vietnam (unified), 568
    Cambodia invaded by, 569, 576
    Chinese invasion of, 569, 576
    collectivization in, 575
    as communist in name only, 570
    economic problems in, 575
    normalization of U.S. relations with, 585
    oceanic refugees (boat people) from, 566, 569–70, *576*
    reeducation camps in, 569, 573, *573*
    release of prisoners from, 569
    U.S. veterans in return to, 585, *585*

Vietnam, Democratic Republic of (DRV), 47, 48, 49
Vietnamese Americans, xiii, 566–9, 570–1, 576
Vietnamese Courier, 271
Vietnamese diaspora, 566–71, 576
Vietnamese Independence Day, 16, 17
Vietnamese National Army (VNA), 25, 35, 36
Vietnamese people
　disparaging names for, 203, 214
　U.S. troops' indiscriminate killing of, 356–7, 360
　U.S. troops' relations with, 203–4, 206, *206*
Vietnamization, 365, 404, 408, 417–18, *417*, 425,
　　430, 445, 447, 461, 467, 477, 486, 500, 503,
　　520
Vietnam Moratorium Committee, 404
Vietnam Veterans Against the War (VVAW), 478–80,
　　479, 565, 585
Vietnam Veterans for Just Peace, 478–9
Vietnam Veterans Memorial Fund, 581
Vietnam Veterans Memorial Wall, xii, *xxiii*, 463,
　　581–3, *581, 582*
Vietnam War
　African Americans in, 163, *163*, 303, 408–9
　civilian deaths in, xvii, 498, 503, 511
　as civil war, 35, 525
　cost of, 372
　cultural and political divisiveness of, xii–xiii, xxi,
　　587
　end of, xi, 524
　North Vietnamese and NLF troop deaths in, xvii,
　　503
　public opinion and, 146–7, 149, 172, 194, 221,
　　247, 296, 310, 321, 386, 393, 395, 459, 477,
　　483
　refugees in, 153, 154
　South Vietnamese deaths in, xvii, 503
　total Vietnamese deaths in, 575
　U.S.-allied troops in, 147
　U.S. casualties in, 142
　U.S. deaths in, xi, xvii, 143, 251, 310, 372, 394–6,
　　566
　U.S. military's optimism and false reports on, 62–3,
　　68, 71, 77, 199, 222, 223, 245, 246, 251,
　　255–6, 257, 270, 274, 290
　U.S. troop withdrawals in, 397–9, 403–4, 417,
　　425, 427, 443–4, 447, 493, 494, 513
Vietnam Worker's Party, 48
Viet Thanh Nguyen, xiii
Village Voice, 332
Vinh Long Province, 37
"Visit to Khan Xuan Temple" (Ho Xuan Huong),
　　462–3
Vi Thanh, *419*
Vogle, Paul, 535
Vogt, John W., 495
Vong Tang, 209
Vo Nguyen Giap, 13, 14, *14, 15,* 16, 21, 22, 25, 26,
　　27, 28, *28,* 49, 206, 209, 257, 292, 530,
　　530
Voting Rights Act of 1965, 98, 126, 190, 221
Vung Ro Bay, 155
Vung Tau, 535, 549, *551*

Wallace, George, 81, 338, 349, 473, *473,* 506
Wallace, Mike, 433–5, 437
Wall Street, *xxi*
Wall Street Journal, 393
Walt, Lewis W., 168, 170, 171, 256
Walter, Sonny, 444
War of 1812, xi, 189, 548
War on Poverty, 221
War Powers Act (1973), 520, 527
Warren, Earl, *53*
War Resisters League, 502
War Within: The: America's Battle over Vietnam (Wells),
　　518
Washington, D.C., *xxiii,* 404, 427, 457, 480, 511,
　　517
　antiwar protests in, *120,* 121, 478–81, *479,* 483,
　　483, 520
　October 21, 1967, antiwar rally in, 230, 232
　post-King assassination riots in, 301, *302,* 303
Washington Mall, *427*
Washington Monument, 427
Washington Post, 95, 191, 233, 485, 520
Washington Star, 276
Watergate scandal, 506, 520, 526
Watts, William, 518
Wayne, John, 517
Weathermen (Weather Underground), 426, 438, 468,
　　521
Weigl, Bruce, 463
Weiss, Cora, 502
Welch, Raquel, *327*
Wells, Tom, 518
Wesak Day, 80
West, Philip, 462
West Berlin, 98
West Germany, 61, 304
Westmoreland, William, 109, *115,* 122, 146, 149,
　　153, 154, 172, 176, 186, 188, 189, 196, 204,
　　211–12, 216, 235, 240, *246,* 247, 263, 264,
　　266, 271, 273, 276, 277, 294, 300, 317, 403,
　　436, 437
　additional troops requested by, 125–6, *125,* 142–3,
　　194, 296
　appointed MACV commander, 103
　congressional speech of, 194, *195*
　Khe Sanh as focus of, *293*
　optimistic statements by, 199, 222, 223, 245, 246,
　　251, 255–6, 257, 270, 274, 290
　pacification program and, 128, 147
　in recall from Vietnam, 299
　Tet Offensive and, 267, 270, 274, 292–3, 299
　three-phase strategy of, 127, 147
　U.S. troops requested by, 115, 116
West Point, U.S. Military Academy at, 109, 175, *176,*
　　198, 275, 353, 355, 472
Weyand, Frederick C., 257, 267, 268, 524, 534, *534,*
　　540, 543
Wheeler, Earle G., 172, *246,* 256, 263, 273, 276,
　　292 3
White, Theodore H., 54, 349, 507
"White Christmas" (song), 553

White House, *351,* 352, *366,* 427, 438, *438,* 449,
　　454, 477, 518, 520, *553*
　Oval Office in, *294,* 300, *352,* 477
　Rose Garden at, 483
　Situation Room in, *293,* 301
White House Committee on Asian American and
　　Pacific Islanders, 567
Whitworth, Robert, *320*
Who, 404
Wicker, Tom, 511
Wickes, George, 18, 19, 20, *20*
Willbanks, James H., xii–xiii, 207, 238, 275, 419,
　　489–91, *489,* 495, *495,* 496, 498, *560*
Williams, Honey, 517
Williams, Samuel "Hanging Sam," 41
Williamsville, Mo., 336, 337
Wilson, Bobby, 435
Wilson, Charles, 32
Wilson, Samuel, 102, 115, 119, 128–9, 186, 587
Wilson, Woodrow, 3, 4, 45
"Winter Soldier Investigation," 480
Wisconsin, 567
Wisconsin, University of, 164, 304
　Army Math Research Center at, 459
Wiseman, David, 468, 474
Wise Men, 299–300, *299,* 364–5
Wolfe, Tom, 582
Wolff, Tobias, 255, 278–9
Women's International League for Peace and Freedom,
　　120
Women's Solidarity Movement, 81
Women Strike for Peace, 120, 502
Woodstock festival, 404–5, *405,* 440, 445
Woodward, Bob, 520
World Bank, 245
World Trade Center (Twin Towers), 456
World War I, 3, 240, 516, 578
World War II, 13, 17, 27, 47, 53, 56, 103, 109, 117,
　　124, 127, 139, 149, 156, 157, 160, 161, 172,
　　178, 191, *199,* 203, 216, 230, 234, 240, 244,
　　256, 282, 290, 305, 318, 322, 356, 363, 384,
　　390, 397, 404, 443, 506, 517, 519, 578
Worthington, Minn., 318, 319, *319*
WTEN (television station), 143

Xa Loi pagoda, 81
Xuan Loc, 490
　siege of, 542, *543,* 546
Xuan Thuy, 304, 305

Yale University, 164, 319, 581
York, Robert, 77
Young, Whitney, 190
Youth for McCarthy, 397
Youth Volunteers, 376

Zais, Melvin, 390, 393
Zhou Enlai, 28, 31, 512
Zimmerman, Bill, xii, 23, 80, *80,* 120, 121, 164, 194,
　　230, 232, 233, 329, 405, 426, 453, 483, 563
Zorthian, Barry, 223

ILLUSTRATION CREDITS

When there is more than one credit for a page the images will be listed clockwise from top left.

ABBREVIATIONS
AP Associated Press
Getty Getty Images
LOC Library of Congress
Magnum Magnum Photos
NARA National Archives and Records
   Administration
VNA Vietnam News Agency

ENDPAPERS
Front: © Philip Jones Griffiths/Magnum
Back: Doan Cong Tinh/Another Vietnam

FRONTMATTER
ii: Le Minh Truong/VNA
vi-vii: Bettmann/Getty
viii: © Bruno Barbey/Magnum
xiv-xv: Henri Huet/AP
xvi-xvii: Larry Burrows/The LIFE Picture Collection/Getty
xviii-xix: Larry Burrows/The LIFE Picture Collection/Getty
xx-xxi: Benedict J. Fernandez
xxii-xxiii: The Washington Post/Getty

CHAPTER 1
0-1: © Robert Capa/International Center of Photography/Magnum Photos
2: La Bibliothèque Nationale de France
3: NARA
5: Keystone-France/Gamma-Keystone/Getty
6: © RMN-Grand Palais / Art Resource, NY; Branger/Roger Viollet/Getty
8: © Neurdein / Roger-Viollet
9: LL/Roger Viollet/Getty
10-11: Alinari Archives/Getty
12: © Ministère de la Culture / Médiathèque du Patrimonie, Dist. RMN-Grand Palais / Art Resource, NY
13: Bui Diem; Keystone-France/Gamma-Keystone/Getty
14: NARA
15: Alex K. Thomas Papers, Bentley Historical Library, University of Michigan
16: Archimedes L.A. Patti Collection, Special Collections and University Archives Department, University of Central Florida Libraries, Orlando Florida (both)
17: Keystone-France/Gamma-Keystone/Getty
18: Bettmann/Getty
19: Nancy D. Hoppin; Francois Sully/Black Star, The Black Star Collection, Ryerson Image Centre, Toronto, Canada
20: George Wickes (all)
21: Archimedes L.A. Patti Collection, Special Collections and University Archives Department, University of Central Florida Libraries, Orlando Florida

22: © Claude Le Ray/SCA/ECPAD/Defense (left); AP (right)
23: Tran Ngoc Chau
24: VNA; VNA; AP
25: Tran Ngoc Hue
27: Apic/Moviepix/Getty; Bettmann/Getty
28: Jean-Claude LABBE/Gamma-Rapho/Getty
29: NARA
30: Keystone-France/Gamma-Keystone/Getty
31: Jean-Claude LABBE/Gamma-Rapho/Getty
33: Howard Sochurek/The LIFE Picture Collection/Getty
34: NARA
35: Duong Van Mai Elliott; Howard Sochurek/The LIFE Picture Collection/Getty
37: Bettmann/Getty
38: AP
39: Bettmann/Getty
40: VNA
42: VNA

CHAPTER 2
50-51: Horst Faas/AP
52: George Silk/The LIFE Images Collection/Getty
53: © Philippe Halsman/Magnum
54-55: Hoang Mai/VNA/Another Vietnam
56: Joe Caneva/AP; The Vietnam Center and Archive, Texas Tech University
57: Jill Hunting (both)
59: James Scanlon; Larry Burrows/The LIFE Picture Collection/Getty
60: Larry Burrows/The LIFE Picture Collection/Getty
61: James Scanlon
62: FOW/AP
63: Larry Burrows/The LIFE Picture Collection/Getty; Neil Sheehan
64: Larry Burrows/The LIFE Picture Collection/Getty
64-65: Larry Burrows/The LIFE Picture Collection/Getty
66: VNA; Larry Burrows/The LIFE Picture Collection/Getty; Rufus Phillips Collection, The Vietnam Center and Archive, Texas Tech University
67: Jack Cushman
69: Ogden Williams Collection, The Vietnam Center and Archive, Texas Tech University
70: Phan Quang Tue (both)
72: LOC (both)
73: LOC
75: Bettmann/Getty
76: LOC; LOC; Nicholas Turner (bottom)
77: Hal Wert/Color Splash
78: Nicholas Turner
79: Malcolm Browne/AP (all)
80: Bill Zimmerman
82: Horst Faas/AP
83: Larry Burrows/The LIFE Picture Collection/Getty; John Loengard/The LIFE Picture Collection/Getty
85: Larry Burrows/The LIFE Picture Collection/Getty

87: Bettmann/Getty
88: Steve Stibbens
89: Steve Stibbens; Douglas Pike Collection, The Vietnam Center and Archive, Texas Tech University

CHAPTER 3
96-97: Bettmann/Getty
98. The Crocker Family
99: Lyndon B. Johnson Presidential Library, Audiovisual Archives
101: VNA
102: Horst Faas/AP
103: Larry Burrows/The LIFE Picture Collection/Getty
105: Naval Historical Center; NARA
106: Sovfoto
107: Lyndon B. Johnson Presidential Library, Audiovisual Archives; SLADE Paul/Paris Match Archive/Getty
109: Tran Ngoc Toan
110: AP
111: AP (both)
113: AP
114: NDN
115: Bettmann/Getty
116: Larry Burrows © Larry Burrows Collection
117: Larry Burrows © Larry Burrows Collection
118: Le Minh Khue
119: Eddie Adams/AP
120: Charles Harbutt [SDS demonstration, D.C., April 17, 1965], Posthumous reproduction from original negative, Courtesy Center for Creative Photography, University of Arizona, © Estate of Charles Harbutt
121: © Hiroji Kubota/Magnum
123: The Crocker Family
124: Joe Galloway (both)
125: Lyndon B. Johnson Presidential Library, Audiovisual Archives
126: AP
127: CBS Photo Archive/Getty
129: The Crocker Family
130: AP
132: Vietnam Military History Museum, Hanoi
133: Bettmann/Getty; Eddie Adams/AP
134: Eddie Adams Photographic Archive, di_10390, The Dolph Briscoe Center for American History, The University of Texas at Austin; Bettmann/Getty
136: Mike Guardia/The Hal Moore Collection
137: Rick Merron/AP
138: Neil Sheehan/The New York Times/Redux
140-141: Rick Merron/AP
142: Rick Merron/AP
143: The Crocker Family

CHAPTER 4
144-145: Henri Huet/AP
146: Lyndon B. Johnson Presidential Library, Audiovisual Archives

148: LOC
150: Eddie Adams/AP
151: Eddie Adams Photographic Archive, di_10848, The Dolph Briscoe Center for American History, The University of Texas at Austin
152: Robert Hodierne
153: Ronnie Guyer
155: The Ho Chi Minh Trail Museum, Hanoi
156: Roger Harris; John Musgrave
157: Bill Ehrhart
158: Van Bao/Another Vietnam; Le Minh Truong/Another Vietnam
159: XVIII Airborne Corps and Fort Bragg
161: Division of Political History, National Museum of American History, Smithsonian Institution
162: © Burk Uzzle
163: © Constantine Manos/Magnum
164: Duong Van Mai Elliott
165: Van Phuong/VNA/Another Vietnam
167: Mike Heaney
168: Christian SIMONPIÉTRI/Sygma Premium/Getty
169: AP
170: AP
172: Bettmann/Getty
173: The Saratogian Newspaper
174: The Crocker Family
176: United States Military Academy (all)
177: © Marc Riboud/Magnum
179: Hulton Deutsch/Corbis Historical/Getty
180: Corbis Historical/Getty
181: Le Quang/VNA/Another Vietnam
182: VNA
183: VNA
184-185: Lee Lockwood/The LIFE Images Collection/Getty
185: The New York Times/Redux
187: © Philip Jones Griffiths/Magnum
188: Bettmann/Getty
189: Bill Ehrhart
191: Ramparts Magazine
192-193: AP
195: Francis Miller/The LIFE Picture Collection/Getty
196: © Philip Jones Griffiths/Magnum
197: Larry Burrows © Larry Burrows Collection
199: Matt Harrison

CHAPTER 5
200-201: David Douglas Duncan, Photography Collection, Harry Ransom Center, The University of Texas at Austin
202: NARA
204-205: © Philip Jones Griffiths/Magnum
206: Bill Ehrhart
207: Mai Nam
208: Bao Hanh/Another Vietnam
209: Nguyen Thi Hoa
212: John Musgrave
213: AP
215: John Schneider/AP
216: Henri Huet/AP
217: Bettmann/Getty
218: Roger Harris
219: NARA
220: Dang Van Phuoc/AP
221: LNC/AP

222: Charles Bonnay/The LIFE Images Collection/Getty
223: AP
225: David Douglas Duncan, Photography Collection, Harry Ransom Center, The University of Texas at Austin
226: David Douglas Duncan, Photography Collection, Harry Ransom Center, The University of Texas at Austin
227: David Douglas Duncan, Photography Collection, Harry Ransom Center, The University of Texas at Austin
228-229: David Douglas Duncan, Photography Collection, Harry Ransom Center, The University of Texas at Austin
231: Eva Jefferson Paterson; Jack Todd
232: © Leonard Freed/Magnum
233: Bettmann/Getty
234: © Matthew and Eve Levine
235: NARA
236: Bettmann/Getty
237: Rion Causey
238: John Musgrave
239: John Musgrave
241: © Fondation Gilles Caron (Contact Press Images)
242-243: Bettmann/Getty
244: The Horace Poolaw Family; Fort Sill National Historic Landmark and Museum
246: Lyndon B. Johnson Presidential Library, Audiovisual Archives
247: Andrew Ward
248: Hal Kushner
249: Hal Kushner
251: Lyndon B. Johnson Presidential Library, Audiovisual Archives

CHAPTER 6
252-253: AP
254: Vo Anh Khanh/VNA/Another Vietnam
256: Vietnam Military History Museum, Hanoi
258-259: David Douglas Duncan, Photography Collection, Harry Ransom Center, The University of Texas at Austin
259: David Douglas Duncan, Photography Collection, Harry Ransom Center, The University of Texas at Austin
260: Ron Ferrizzi
261: AP
262: Bettmann/Getty; David Douglas Duncan, Photography Collection, Harry Ransom Center, The University of Texas at Austin; David Douglas Duncan, Photography Collection, Harry Ransom Center, The University of Texas at Austin
263: John T. Wheeler/AP
265: NDN
266: NARA
268: VNA
269: NARA
270: Hong Seong Chan/AP
271: Dick Swanson/The LIFE Images Collection/Getty
272: VNA; AP
274: Eddie Adams/AP
275: Eddie Adams Photographic Archive, e_ea_0339, The Dolph Briscoe Center for American History, The University of Texas at Austin
277: Nick Ut/AP

278: © Philip Jones Griffiths/Magnum
279: Vietnam Military History Museum, Hanoi
282: Bettmann/Getty
283: Bettmann/Getty
284: AP
285: Bettmann/Getty
286: AP
287: Dang Van Phuoc/AP
288: Phil Gioia
289: Bettmann/Getty; Larry Burrows/The LIFE Picture Collection/Getty
291: NARA
293: Lyndon B. Johnson Presidential Library, Audiovisual Archives
294-295: Lyndon B. Johnson Presidential Library, Audiovisual Archives
297: Lawrence Schiller/Premium Archive/Getty
299: Lyndon B. Johnson Presidential Library, Audiovisual Archives
300: Lyndon B. Johnson Presidential Library, Audiovisual Archives
302: Steve Northup Photographic Archive, di_10847, The Dolph Briscoe Center for American History, The University of Texas at Austin
303: © Bruno Barbey/Magnum
304: Bettmann/Getty
305: Vincent Okamoto
306: Bunyo Ishikawa
307: Bettmann/Getty
308: Florentine Films
309: VNA
311: © Paul Fusco/Magnum

CHAPTER 7
312-313: Le Minh Truong/Another Vietnam
314: The Ho Chi Minh Trail Museum, Hanoi
315: Unknown Photographer/Another Vietnam
316: Nguyen Dinh Uu/Another Vietnam; Mai Nam
317: Horst Faas/AP
318: Harry Ransom Center, The University of Texas at Austin
319: Karl Marlantes
320: Dana Stone/AP
323: New York Daily News Archive/Getty
326: William Foulke Collection, The Vietnam Center and Archive, Texas Tech University
327: © Mark Jury; Bettmann/Getty; © Mark Jury
328: Vincent Okamoto
329: Wally McNamee/Corbis Historical/Getty
331: Julian Wasser/The LIFE Images Collection/Getty
332: Lyndon B. Johnson Presidential Library, Audiovisual Archives
333: Paul Sequeira/Premium Archive/Getty; Agence France Presse/Hulton Archive/Getty; Bettmann/Getty
334: Fred W. McDarrah/Premium Archive/Getty
335: Walter Bennett/The LIFE Picture Collection/Getty
337: Bob and Chuck Riddle (both)
339: SLADE Paul/Paris Match Archive/Getty
340: Horst Faas/AP (both)
341: Vo Anh Khanh/VNA/Another Vietnam
342: Unknown Photographer/Another Vietnam
343: Australian War Memorial (all)
344-345: © Raymond Depardon/Magnum
346: The Richard Nixon Presidential Library and Museum (all)
348: Wally McNamee/Corbis Historical/Getty

351: Lyndon B. Johnson Presidential Library, Audiovisual Archives
352: The Richard Nixon Presidential Library and Museum
353: The Crocker Family
354: Victoria Harrison
357: Bettmann/Getty
358: Henri Huet/AP
359: AP; Henri Huet/AP
360: NARA
361: Koichiro Morita/AP
362: AP
365: The Richard Nixon Presidential Library and Museum
366: Bettmann/Getty
368: John E. Kennedy; Karl Marlantes
371: Bob and Chuck Riddle
372: Bob and Chuck Riddle
373: Merrill McPeak
374-375: VNA
376: Nguyen Thi Nguyet Anh and Tran Cong Thang
377: Nguyen Thi Nguyet Anh and Tran Cong Thang
378: Nguyen Thi Nguyet Anh and Tran Cong Thang
379: U.S. Air Force
380-381: Van Sac/VNA/Another Vietnam
381: Van Sac/VNA/Another Vietnam

CHAPTER 8
382-383: Spencer Grant/Archive Photos/Getty
384: Joan Furey
385: Joan Furey (both)
388: The Ho Chi Minh Trail Museum, Hanoi
389: AP
390: Bettmann/Getty (both)
391: Hugh Van Es/AP
392: Bettmann/Getty
394: The LIFE Picture Collection/Getty (all)
395: The LIFE Picture Collection/Getty (both)
396: The LIFE Picture Collection/Getty (both)
397: Bettmann/Getty
399: Rick Merron/AP
400: VNA
401: Bettmann/Getty
402: State Library Photograph Collection, Washington State Archives
403: Barry Sweet/AP
404: Thomas Vallely
405: Bill Eppridge/The LIFE Picture Collection/Getty
406: Le Minh Truong/Another Vietnam
407: Dick Swanson/The LIFE Images Collection/Getty
408: Keystone-France/Gamma-Keystone/Getty
409: The Wallace Terry Archive/New York Public Library
410: © David Burnett (Contact Press Images)
411: AP
412: Doan Cong Tinh
413: Robert Hodierne
414: John Borrelli; James Bryant
415: James Bryant; Larry Burrows/The LIFE Picture Collection/Getty
417: AP
418: LOC
419: Henri Huet/AP
420: Nick Ut/AP
421: © Marc Riboud/Magnum
422: AFP/Getty

423: © Thomas Billhardt/Camera Work
424: © Catherine Karnow
426: © Bruno Barbey/Magnum
428-429: AP
430: Charles J. Ryan/AP
432: Ronald L. Haeberle/The LIFE Images Collection/Getty
433: Ronald L. Haeberle/The LIFE Images Collection/Getty (both)
434: Ronald L. Haeberle/The LIFE Images Collection/Getty (both)
435: NARA; Ronald L. Haeberle/The LIFE Images Collection/Getty
436: NARA (both)
437: AP (all)
438: Charles Phillips/The LIFE Picture Collection/Getty
439: AP
441: Joan Furey
443: John Musgrave
444: Jack Todd; AP
446-447: Robert Whitaker/Premium Archive/Getty
447: Robert Whitaker/Premium Archive/Getty
448: AP
449: Akron Beacon Journal
450: Popperfoto/Getty
451: Universal History Archive/Getty
452: John Filo/Premium Archive/Getty
453: Louisiana State University Office of Public Affairs Records, Jack Fiser Collection, A0020.01, Louisiana State University Archives, LSU Libraries
454: Northwestern University Archives, James S. Roberts Papers
455: AP
457: Bettmann/Getty
458: Bettmann/Getty
460: © San Jose Mercury News

CHAPTER 9
464-465: Henri Huet/AP
466: Jacques Tonnaire/AP
469: Doan Cong Tinh/Another Vietnam
471: © Bruno Barbey/Magnum
472: Joe Holloway, Jr./AP; From Newsweek, April 12 1971 © 1971 Newsweek Media Group. All rights reserved.
473: Toby Massey/AP
474-475: The Estate of Akihiko Okamura
476: Holger Jensen/AP
478-479: Steven Clevenger/Corbis News/Getty
481: Henry Griffin/AP
482: © Leonard Freed/Magnum
484: Jim Wells/AP
486: © David Burnett (Contact Press Images)
487: AP
488: Bettmann/Getty
489: James Willbanks
491: Sovfoto
492: Koichiro Morita/AP
494: Nick Ut/AP
495: James Willbanks
496-497: © Bruno Barbey/Magnum
498: © Bruno Barbey/Magnum
499: Bettmann/Getty (both)
500: Peter Keegan/Hulton Archive/Getty
501: Lam Hong/VNA/Another Vietnam
502: Nihon Denpa News/AP
504: Nick Ut/AP; Neal Ulevich

505: AP; Joe McNally/The LIFE Picture Collection/Getty; Nick Ut/AP
507: SLADE Paul/Paris Match Archive/Getty
508: Frank Snepp
509: Florentine Films
513: Hal Kushner
514: Tran Khiem/AP
515: Sal Veder/AP; VNA

CHAPTER 10
522-523: Duong Thanh Phong/Another Vietnam
524: Neal Ulevich/AP
525: Barr G. Ashcraft Photograph Collection (PH 007). Special Collections and University Archives, UMass Amherst Libraries
526: E.W. Pfeiffer; VNA
528: Chick Harrity/AP
529: AP
530: The Ho Chi Minh Trail Museum, Hanoi
531: VNA
532-533: Nick Ut/AP
533: VNA
534: David Hume Kennerly/Premium Archive/Getty
535: AP
536: Peter O'Loughlin/AP
536-537: AP
539: AP
541: Gerald R. Ford Presidential Library; Huu Cay
542: Dirck Halstead/The LIFE Images Collection/Getty
543: Nik Wheeler/Corbis Historical/Getty
545: Christoph Froehder/AP
547: Bettmann/Getty; Jacques Pavlovsky/Sygma/Getty; Franjola/AP
549: Jacques Pavlovsky/Sygma/Getty
550: Kim Ki Sam/AP; Dirck Halstead/Hulton Archive/Getty
551: Frances Starner/AP
552: Dinh Quang Thanh/VNA/Another Vietnam
553: David Hume Kennerly/Premium Archive/Getty
554: Nik Wheeler/Corbis Historical/Getty
555: NARA
556: Nik Wheeler/Corbis Historical/Getty
558: Dirck Halstead/The LIFE Images Collection/Getty
559: Dirck Halstead/Hulton Archive/Getty
560: AP
561: Juan Valdez; David Hume Kennerly/Premium Archive/Getty
563: AP
564-565: Lam Hong/VNA/Another Vietnam

BACKMATTER
572-573: © Marc Riboud/Magnum
574-575: Dirck Halstead/The LIFE Images Collection/Getty
575: © Philip Jones Griffiths/Magnum
576-577: K. GAUGLER/AFP/Getty
578-579: John Olson/The LIFE Picture Collection/Getty
580-581: © Peter Marlow/Magnum
581: The Washington Post /Getty
582: LOC; Florentine Films; Florentine Films
583: Florentine Films (all)
584: CBS Photo Archive/Getty
585: Mike Heaney
586-587: Derek Hudson/Premium Archive/Getty

PERMISSIONS ACKNOWLEDGMENTS

Grateful acknowledgment is made to the following for permission to reprint previously published or broadcasted material:

Excerpt from: "The Moratorium—a View from the Inside" by Jeremy Larner. Reprinted by permission of Jeremy Larner.

Excerpts from "Beyond Vietnam: A Time to Break Silence" by Dr. Martin Luther King Jr. Reprinted by arrangement with The Heirs to the Estate of Martin Luther King Jr., c/o Writers House as agent for the proprietor. © 1967 Dr. Martin Luther King Jr. © renewed 1995 by Coretta Scott King.

Excerpts from "Vietnam: The Signs of Stalemate" by R. W. Apple. From *The New York Times* [August 7, 1967]. © 1967 The New York Times. All rights reserved. Used by permission and protected by the Copyright Laws of the United States. Reprinted by permission of PARS International Corp.

Excerpts from *West Dickens Avenue* by John Corbett. Reprinted by permission of Penguin Random House.

Excerpt from "Report from Vietnam" by Walter Cronkite. Reprinted by permission of CBS News Archive.

Excerpt from Mike Wallace interview with Paul Meadlo. Reprinted by permission of CBS News Archive.

Excerpts from "A Whiff of Mutiny in Vietnam" by James Reston. From *The New York Times* [August 27, 1969] © 1969 The New York Times. All rights reserved. Used by permission and protected by the Copyright Laws of the United States. Reprinted by permission of PARS International Corp.

A NOTE ABOUT THE AUTHORS

Geoffrey C. Ward, historian and screenwriter, wrote the script for *The Vietnam War* series and is the author of nineteen books, including *A First-Class Temperament: The Emergence of Franklin Roosevelt,* which won the National Book Critics Circle Award and the Francis Parkman Prize, and was a finalist for the Pulitzer Prize. He has written or cowritten many documentary films, including *The War, The Civil War, Baseball, The West, Mark Twain, Not for Ourselves Alone,* and *Jazz.*

Ken Burns, the producer and director of numerous film series, including *The War,* founded his own documentary film company, Florentine Films, in 1976. His landmark film *The Civil War* was the highest-rated series in the history of American public television, and his work has won numerous prizes, including the Emmy and Peabody Awards, and two nominations for the Academy Award. He lives in Walpole, New Hampshire.

Lynn Novick has been producing and directing acclaimed documentary films about American history and culture for nearly thirty years, including *Prohibition, Baseball, Jazz, Frank Lloyd Wright,* and *The War.* A recipient of the Emmy and Peabody Awards, she conducted most of the interviews that are at the heart of this book.

A NOTE ON THE TYPE

This book was set in Adobe Garamond. Designed for the Adobe Corporation by Robert Slimbach, the fonts are based on types first cut by Claude Garamond (c. 1480–1561). Garamond was a pupil of Geoffroy Tory and is believed to have followed the Venetian models, although he introduced a number of important differences, and it is to him that we owe the letter we now know as "old style." He gave to his letters a certain elegance and feeling of movement that won their creator an immediate reputation and the patronage of Francis I of France.

Composed by North Market Street Graphics, Lancaster, Pennsylvania

Printed and bound by LSC Communications, Kendallville, Indiana